350
S0-BND-703

# OCEANOGRAPHY

CONTEMPORARY READINGS IN OCEAN SCIENCES

# OCEANOGRAPHY
## CONTEMPORARY READINGS IN OCEAN SCIENCES
Second Edition

Edited by R. GORDON PIRIE
UNIVERSITY OF WISCONSIN-MILWAUKEE

New York · Oxford University Press · 1977

Copyright © 1973, 1977 by Oxford University Press, Inc.
Library of Congress Catalogue Card Number: 76-42663
Printed in the United States of America

*To Everyone*
*Interested in Exploring*
*and Understanding Our World's Oceans*

# Preface

## TO THE FIRST EDITION

In collecting these readings, I have emphasized the wide range of topics and the interrelationships of the many disciplines commonly gathered under the term oceanography. These include biology, chemistry, geology, physics, meteorology, navigation, economics, law, conservation, engineering, and aeronautics. Both overview-type articles, which survey some of the generalities of an ocean-science discipline, and in-depth articles, which present a more detailed study within a discipline, are represented. These readings are directed toward two audiences: readers who have a general interest in science and the environment and specialists who wish to broaden their understanding of oceanography outside their own area.

An explanation of why this collection was prepared is in order. In teaching oceanography to science and non-science majors, I discovered that my students frequently wanted additional reading to supplement the typically brief explanations provided in the lectures and by the textbooks; I also discovered that no up-to-date collection of readings was available. There were several solutions, the most obvious being to prepare a book myself.

I have selected nearly 50 introductory and intermediate level articles, most of them published within the past five years; any major changes in the articles were made by the author, or with the author's approval, as indicated at the beginning of each article. In keeping with the international character of oceanography, a number of articles by ocean scientists from other nations have been included to remind the reader to guard against attitudes that engender the parochialism sometimes found in oceanographic research.

Necessarily, some duplications between the articles and oceanography textbooks were unavoidable, but some were intentional—so that the collected readings would also be useful in the absence of an introductory text. Level and depth of coverage, length of article, availability, and the length of the collection itself have all influenced the selection process. Unfortunately, no article on oceanographic engineering could be found to represent this diversified field; those available were either too specific or too general. Also, a note to the non-oceanographer is in order here:

archeological findings are considered resources, and thus the article on such findings appears under ocean resources.

In selecting and editing a collection of readings, there are numerous articles from which to choose. For this reason, it is unlikely that any two editors' selections would be similar. I accept full responsibility for any omissions or failings in this collection.

Sincere thanks are extended to the authors of the articles selected, edited, and republished in this collection. Their full cooperation, willing advice, and friendly encouragement are most appreciated. Obviously, no collection would have existed without the authors' unselfish assistance. The original publishers also cooperated fully in communicating with the author and editor and in obtaining copyright permissions and cost estimates. In many cases, these were tedious tasks.

I should also like to thank my friends and colleagues at universities and oceanographic institutions who aided me in my selection and editing and provided stimulating discussion, advice, and encouragement in many ways and under many circumstances. It is not possible to name all those who helped, but I want specifically to thank M. Grant Gross, Marine Sciences Research Center, State University of New York, Stony Brook, New York; Walter H. Munk, Institute of Geophysics and Planetary Physics, Scripps Institute of Oceanography, University of California, San Diego, California; and David A. Ross, Woods Hole Oceanographic Institution, Woods Hole, Massachusetts, for their assistance. Dr. Ross critically reviewed the manuscript at various stages; Judy Mortonson and Ann Reed critically reviewed the final manuscript and made many helpful suggestions.

I should like to extend special thanks to Ellis H. Rosenberg and Carol Miller of Oxford University Press for their assistance on some special organizational problems. Maureen Ballsieper, Diane Kotsubka, and Mary Polzin typed and proofread the manuscript and ably handled volumes of correspondence.

*University of Wisconsin–Milwaukee*
*Milwaukee, Wisconsin*

R. G. Pirie

# Preface
## TO THE SECOND EDITION

During the preparation of the second edition, I noticed two definite trends in the field of oceanography: (i) The divisions among the classical fields of oceanography (biological, chemical, geological, physical) have become less distinct over the past four years. Published research in the interdisciplinary fields (geochemistry, geophysics, biochemistry, etc.) is more common than ever before; and (ii) There has been a significant increase in the work effort directed towards the ocean environment. This effort is clearly not exclusively an applied scientific approach but often includes a social/political emphasis.

It is hoped that this edition properly reflects these trends. Again, the selection of the articles is mine, as are any oversights and omissions.

The preparation of an anthology requires the cooperation of many professional people: authors, editors, publishers, draftsmen, photographers, etc. My sincere thanks to all of them. I would particularly like to thank Ellis H. Rosenberg, Martha Browne, and Jean Shapiro of Oxford University Press for following this project from beginning to end. Special thanks must also go to Mary Polzin and Amy Saculla for typing and to Deborah Pirie for editorial assistance.

*University of Wisconsin–Milwaukee* R. Gordon Pirie
*Milwaukee, Wisconsin*
*August 1976*

# Foreword

The world of oceanography has experienced several changes since the first edition of this book. In particular, there have been three significant events: the Law of the Sea Conference; the energy crisis; and the increasing awareness of the environmental damage to the ocean and especially to the coastal zone area. The Law of the Sea Conference will most likely lead to each coastal country's gaining a 200-nautical-mile economic resource zone. Within this zone will fall most of the marine deposits of oil and gas as well as most important lanes of marine commerce. How the control (local, regional, or international) of this resource zone by the various coastal countries will affect pollution, exploration of mineral resources, and the freedom of scientific research is almost anybody's guess—the next few years will be interesting. Dr. Pirie has anticipated these situations and has incorporated several new articles that bear on these subjects.

The science of oceanography is historically thought to have begun with the *Challenger* expedition (1872–76); thus, it is just over 100 years old. In the early years of oceanography, the limited technology only allowed descriptions of the physical and chemical characteristics of the ocean and some of the different forms of life it contained. By the late 1920s, echo-sounders had been developed and were being used to determine the shape of the ocean bottom. Later, in the 1950s and 1960s, more sophisticated geophysical devices made the study of the structure below the ocean floor possible. As oceanography evolved, four main disciplines emerged: Biological Oceanography; Chemical Oceanography; Marine Geology and Geophysics; and Physical Oceanography. These divisions are for convenience only, since the ocean is highly complex. For example, sediments in the deep ocean basins are generally composed of the shells of organisms that previously floated in the surface and near-surface waters. These organisms flourished in response to a favorable physical and chemical environment. Thus, a study of their shells can yield information concerning past biological, chemical, and physical conditions in the oceans.

Within the last decade or so, Man's interest in and dependence on the ocean environment have increased manyfold, due in part to a desire to exploit the mineral and food resources of the sea, to solve the problems of chemical and physical marine pollution, and to protect the ocean from dangerous exploitation. Rarely does a week go by without expressions of concern in the press or on television about overfishing, the threatened extinction of some marine species, or a new source of marine pollution. There are also constant reminders that the oceans hold great mineral resources (gas and oil, especially) and food resources, which are needed for our ultimate survival. The energy crisis has dramatically shown the importance of ocean resources to the survival of modern civilization.

What should be done to ensure safe and wise use of the oceans? Laws and regulations are presently being formulated that will affect their future use. Unfortunately, many critical decisions are being made by people who have vested interests in uncontrolled exploitations, little or no understanding of oceanography, or both. Many of the articles in this book have been selected to provide basic information to help the reader develop a better understanding of the oceans and their effective management.

Other articles discuss food chains, ocean currents and waves, plate tectonics, and other more exotic aspects of marine science.

This book of readings, like all others, cannot be comprehensive without extending into many volumes. However, Dr. Pirie has gathered together many solid articles that cover most aspects of oceanography. The significance and the usefulness of oceans—subjects vital to everyone—are well represented.

*Woods Hole Oceanographic Institution* David A. Ross
*Woods Hole, Massachusetts*
*June 1976*

# Contents



*New articles in this edition

## 3 *SEA LIFE*



## 4 *MARINE GEOLOGY*



## 5 *OCEAN RESOURCES*



## 6 *MARINE POLLUTION*

# OCEANOGRAPHY

CONTEMPORARY READINGS IN OCEAN SCIENCES

# 1

# *EXPLORING THE SEA AND SEA FLOOR*

# 1. The Early History of Diving

ROBERT E. MARX 1971

Sitting before my typewriter only ten miles from where the Apollo 14 rocket was successfully launched this morning, I find it all too easy to forget that there are regions of the earth that have not been fully explored. Man has learned a great deal about his natural environment, but much remains to be learned, particularly about the waters that cover more than two-thirds of the earth's surface. In spite of important advances in science and technology, there are many regions of the sea that are still a mystery. For centuries men have struggled to penetrate these regions, struggled against difficulties as formidable as those the astronauts face today.

No one knows who were the first men to penetrate the depths of the sea, nor can anyone be sure why they dived, though it is fairly safe to assume that the pursuit of fish, mollusks, crustaceans and other food was an important reason. Archeologists have established that men were diving as early as 4500 B.C.; Mesopotamian excavations have yielded shells that could only have been recovered from the sea floor by divers. Then there is a gap in diving history of more than a thousand years, until the era of the Sixth Dynasty Thebes in Egypt, around 3200 B.C. The vast number of carved mother-of-pearl ornaments discovered on many archeological sites indicates that diving was widespread.

The Cretans, who flourished around 2500-1400 B.C., worshipped a diving god named Glaucus; he remained the patron god of Greek divers, fishermen and sailors until modern times. A mortal before being exalted to divinity, Glaucus was a fisherman in Anthedon, a village famed for its inhabitants' love of diving. The legendary cause of his immortalization was his discovery of a plant that possessed magical properties. Though there is no evidence that anyone else had his good luck, the early Greek free divers found their work extremely profitable, for they provided the ancient world with most of its sponges and their descendants have done the same to this day. At that time sponges were used for a variety of purposes: soaked in water, they served as canteens for soldiers and travelers; saturated with honey, they were given to infants to

Robert F. Marx is an explorer-archeologist specializing in marine archeology. He is currently with Seafinders, Inc., California, locating and salvaging shipwrecks in deep ocean water. He has written over one hundred scientific reports and popular articles.

From *Oceans Magazine*, Vol. 4, Nos. 4 and 5, pp. 66-74 and pp. 24-34, 1971. Reprinted with light editing and by permission of the author and *Oceans Magazine*.

stop their crying; soldiers used them as padding under their heavy armor; as coverings for wounds, they became makeshift bandages; and, of course, women found many uses for sponges in the home, just as they do today.

Besides sponges, the early free divers of the Mediterranean brought up valuable shells from the sea bottom. Among them were mother-of-pearl shells, oyster shells containing pearls, and murex shells, the source of Tyrian purple, a popular dye. More highly prized than any of the shells was the red coral used for jewelry and ornaments. Red coral was largely responsible for the establishment of trade between the Mediterranean cultures and China: it was the main item desired by the Chinese, who were well aware of treasures from the sea—as early as 2200 B.C. the Emperor Yü was receiving pearls acquired by divers as tribute from the coastal regions of his realm.

The divers of the ancient world must have been remarkably skillful, for red coral is seldom found in water shallower than 100 feet and diving to such a depth without any breathing apparatus is no mean feat. Gulping air into their lungs, they jumped into the sea with no aids other than a stone weight grasped in their arms to carry them down and guide ropes from the boat tied to their waists to bring them up again. Once on the bottom, they jettisoned the weights; when they ran out of air, they either tugged at the ropes and were pulled up to the surface, or ascended hand over hand by themselves. How deep these divers were able to go and how long they were able to remain submerged is not known, but a dive of 100 feet for red coral must have taken at least two or three minutes, and it is very likely that the ancient divers were able to go deeper and remain under longer.

Today the women pearl divers of Japan are able to make continuous dives to depths of 150 feet and remain below as long as five minutes. Several years ago on the island of Tobago, in the Caribbean, I met a 58-year-old Negro diver named Big Anthony, who could free dive as well, or better, than the Japanese divers. Although he was only diving for sport and to break records, his deepest free dive was 190 feet, and the longest I clocked him staying underwater on his own breath was six minutes and ten seconds. To accomplish these fantastic feats he wore nothing more than a face mask—he did not even use any weights. In recent years world records have been established in deep free diving and breath holding in swimming pools, but when these feats are compared with the capabilities of the ancient free divers, the Japanese women pearl divers, or Big Anthony, they do not really amount to much, considering the preparations made and the methods used.

The accomplishments of the ancient free divers are especially remarkable because they usually worked without any protection for their eyes, and anyone who has ever attempted to open his eyes in salt water knows how difficult it is to see underwater. There is evidence that these divers used some curious aids, curious because modern science has shown they were no use at all: for example, oil poured into the ears was supposed to protect the eardrums from water pressure, and a sponge held in the mouth supposedly enabled the diver to remain submerged longer.

The divers' work did not stop with acquiring valuables from the bottom of the sea. They dived for other reasons as well: construction work in rivers and harbors, to recover sunken treasure, and for military purposes. Divers were occasionally assigned bizarre tasks, as an amusing story of the Greek historian Plutarch reveals. Cleopatra persuaded her lover, the Roman general Mark Antony, to participate in a fishing contest. Knowing himself to be a poor fisherman and not wanting to lose face before a lady he was most eager to impress, he hired a diver to keep his hook well supplied with fish. Unfortunately for him, Cleopatra's spies discovered the trick, and Antony's face must have been very red indeed when his first catch on the second day of the contest turned out to be a large dead fish–dried, salted and ready for the frying pan.

So many divers were engaged in the underwater construction business and so keen was the competition among them that they began to form corporations to obtain contracts for jobs. During the second century B.C., the Emperor of Rome granted a concession for conducting all diving operations along the Tiber River to one of these corporations.

The earliest account of divers in quest of sunken treasure is mentioned by Herodotus, a Greek historian who wrote around the middle of the fifth century B.C. According to one legend, about thirty years earlier Xerxes, the King of Persia, had employed a Greek diver named Scyllias and his daughter Cyane to recover an immense treasure from several Persian galleys sunk during a battle with a Greek fleet. After they had brought up the treasure, Xerxes refused to give them the reward he had promised and instead detained them aboard his galley, doubtless for other diving jobs he had in mind. Seething at this treachery, Scyllias and Cyane jumped overboard in the midst of a storm and gained revenge by cutting the anchor cables of the Persian ships, which caused many of them to collide. Angered in their turn, the Persians pursued the culprits as soon as order had been restored, but Scyllias and Cyane managed to escape by swimming to Artemisium, a distance of nine miles, completely underwater. Herodotus expressed some doubt about the last part of the story, since swimming such a distance underwater was a feat unheard of at the time. However, later historians were not so skeptical, believing that the swimmers might have held hollow reeds in their mouths to breathe air from the surface–an early version of the snorkel that millions of divers use today. In fact, it was Pliny the Elder, the Roman scholar and naturalist of the first century A.D., who first mentioned any such breathing device, but it could well have been used earlier.

By the third century B.C., diving for sunken treasure was so common among the Greeks that they passed special laws regarding the division of the finds. Treasure recovered in two cubits of water or less (a cubit was equal to 1½ feet) entitled the diver to a tenth of its value; treasure recovered from between two and eight cubits gave the diver a third of its value; and treasure recovered in depths in excess of eight cubits provided a reward equal to half its value. The part of the treasure not given to the diver was the property of the original owner or, in the event of his death it became the property of the ruler from whose waters it was recovered.

The earliest record of divers engaged in military operations was Homer's mention in the *Iliad* of their use during the Trojan War (1194-1184 B.C. is the traditional date). What their tasks were Homer did not say, but they probably included sabotage of enemy vessels–boring holes in their bottoms or cutting their anchor cables. As in the case of Scyllias and his daughter, these divers may have used snorkels: concealment underwater would have helped them surprise their quarry.

The Greek historian Thucydides gave a contemporary account of divers in warfare in the late fifth century B.C. A band of Spartans on the island of Sphacteria off the southwestern shores of Greece, found themselves besieged by their enemies, the Athenians. Cut off from the outside on which their survival depended, the Spartans used divers who, under cover of darkness, swam underwater past the besiegers' vessels; they returned the same way, carrying animal skins full of victuals that their allies had sent to them. The Athenians, expecting starvation to force the Spartans into quick surrender, were bewildered at first, but soon caught on and stationed sentinels to capture the divers.

About a decade later, when the Athenians tried to attack the harbor of Syracuse in Sicily, they discovered that the Syracusans had constructed underwater barriers to prevent the besiegers' ships from approaching the shore. The Athenians sent divers armed with saws and axes to cut down the obstructions and tie the fragments to towlines so they could be pulled out of the way. Yet as fast as the Athenians removed the obstructions, the Syracusan divers replaced them. In the end the Athenians, who had come as attackers, were attacked themselves when allies of the Syracusans arrived; they lost many ships and more than 40,000 men.

There are many other historical accounts of free divers engaged in military operations. Many concern sabotage of enemy vessels and others recount the reconnaissance work of divers who swam into enemy ports to ascertain naval strength or to eavesdrop on the conversations of enemy leaders aboard their vessels. Divers undoubtedly turned the tide of many a sea battle, and by the fifth century B.C., they were considered so important in warfare that the Romans, ever a war-minded people, took precautions against them: all anchor cables of Roman vessels were made of iron chain to prevent their being cut, and special guards of the fleet, who were divers armed with trident spears, were on duty round the clock to stop enemy divers from infiltrating the defenses underwater.

In 332 B.C., shortly after Alexander the Great had begun his conquest of the world, the island stronghold of Tyre offered such a long and fierce resistance that both attackers and defenders had frequent recourse to divers. On one occasion the defenders used them to destroy a dike of timber that the Macedonians had erected as a blockade. The Macedonians, after reducing the fighting spirit of the defenders, gave their divers the task of destroying the boom defenses of the port.

The most interesting feature of this battle to students of diving history is a legend that Alexander himself descended into the sea in some sort of a container to watch the destruction of the boom defenses. Unfortunately, no further details of this notable event have been preserved. A thirteenth-century French manuscript contains an illustration showing Alexander inside a glass barrel brilliantly lit by two candles. Numerous species of marine life surround him and a large whale dominates the scene, but the painting is an imaginary reconstruction, as are all later illustrations, and no one knows what the container really looked like.

Scanty as the details are, Alexander's descent is historically important as a milestone in man's struggle to master the sea. However, it was not the first such technical advancement. Three decades earlier, in 360 B.C., Aristotle's *Problemata* mentioned a device to aid divers:

> . . . in order that these fishers of sponges may be supplied with a facility of respiration, a kettle is let down to them, not filled with water, but with air, which constantly assists the submerged man; it is forcibly kept upright in its descent, in order that it may be sent down at an equal level all around, to prevent the air from escaping and the water from entering. . . .

It is not known how long such devices had been in existence before Aristotle described them or how widespread was their use. Such diving devices disappear from recorded history until the year 1250 A.D., when Roger Bacon's *Novum Organum* mentioned Alexander's container, but no others. It is the consensus of opinion that few diving aids were in general use before the sixteenth century, which began the age of invention in diving.

Only one other aid to divers discovered during the age of free diving is worthy of note—goggles. Who first invented them and when they were first used is unknown. A ceramic Peruvian vase of the second century A.D., now on exhibit in the American Museum of Natural History in New York City, depicts a diver wearing goggles and grasping two fish in his hands (Figure 1-1). The first historical reference to diving goggles occurs in the reports of fourteenth-century travelers returning to Europe from the Persian Gulf, where pearl divers used goggles with lenses of ground tortoiseshell. The Polynesians, whose underwater exploits are legendary, also used them for several centuries before European ships first visited their waters. Yet

Figure 1-1. Peruvian vase from the second or third century A.D. depicts a diver wearing goggles and holding two fish. (Courtesy of American Museum of National History.)

the free divers of the past never made extensive use of goggles, probably for the same reason divers do not often use them today. Although goggles provide much better underwater vision, the deeper a diver descends, the harder the water pressure forces them against his eyes: his eyesight could suffer severe permanent damage.

Nearly as famous as the brilliant diving exploits of the early free divers of the Old World were those of the Indian and Negro pearl divers of the Caribbean, who remained free divers long after various types of diving equipment were invented and brought into widespread use. Though advanced diving technology has put these divers more or less out of business in recent years, as late as the 1940's they were vigorously plying the trade their ancestors had been engaged in for centuries.

Even before Columbus' discovery of the New World in 1492, many of its aborigines practiced diving, primarily because, like the Mediterranean divers, they found the sea floor a valuable source of food. North American Indians used diving as a basic hunting technique: swimming underwater and breathing through reeds, they were able to approach unwarry fowl and game and capture or kill them with nets, spears or their bare hands. The Mayans of Mexico like the ancient Greeks, venerated a diving god, and a fresco of this deity may be seen today in a temple known as the Temple of the Diving God at the archeological site of Tulum on the eastern coast of Yucatán.

The Lucayan, Carib and Arawak tribes of the Caribbean dove for pearls on a small scale but it did not become a major occupation until the coming of the white man. One

Figure 1-2. Sponge divers, such as these depicted in the Mediterranean about 1200-1400 A.D., wore no breathing devices. Rigorous training developed their lungs to enable them to work underwater for long periods. (Courtesy of the Library of Congress.)

day in 1498, during Columbus' third voyage of exploration, his fleet anchored at the island of Cubagua, near the coast of Venezuela, to obtain a supply of fresh water and fruit. While some of his men were ashore, they noticed a Carib Indian woman wearing a pearl necklace. They made inquiries and informed Columbus that the natives of the island possessed great quantities of valuable and exquisite pearls, which they had found in the adjacent waters. Columbus sent Indian divers in search of oysters, and the result confirmed the story of his men. Immediately after his return to Spain, Columbus reported his find to the king, who ordered that a pearl fishery be established on Cubagua at once. Other large oyster beds were found during the next few years in areas near Cubagua, including Margarita Island, which eventually became the center of the pearl industry, a position it maintains today. Thus Columbus, already assured of his place in history, has another discovery to his credit; over the centuries the Caribbean pearl fisheries furnished Spain with a source of wealth surpassed only by the gold and silver it took from the New World.

Soon after the opening of the pearl fish eries around Cubagua and Margarita, the local supply of divers was exhausted. Many died from diseases that the Spaniards had brought from Europe: others died from overwork at the hands of their greedy employers, who forced them to dive as many as 16 hours a day. The next source of divers tapped by the Spaniards was the Lucayan Indians of the Bahamas, who were then considered the best divers in the New World. The Spanish historian Oviedo, writing in 1535, gave an account of a visit to the pearl fisheries of Margarita where he watched the Lucayan divers in action. He marveled at their fantastic abilities, stating that they were able to descend to depths of 100 feet, remain submerged as long as 15 minutes, and unlike the Carib Indians, who had less stamina, could dive from sunrise to sunset seven days a week without appearing to tire. As the divers of the Old World (Figure 1-2) had done for thousands of years, they descended by grasping stone weights in their arms and dove completely naked except for a net bag around their necks, in which they would deposit the oysters they found on the bottom. So great was the demand for the Lucayan divers in the pearl fisheries, that in only a few decades all of their people were enslaved and the Bahamas were bereft of their former inhabitants, the first natives seen by Columbus on his epic voyage of discovery.

Like the Carib Indians before them, the supply of Lucayans was soon exhausted, and by the middle of the sixteen century the Spaniards were hard pressed for divers. They solved the problem by importing Negro slaves from Africa, most of whom had never dived and in many cases had never seen the sea until their enforced voyage. Amazingly, they adapted at once and became as good divers as their predecessors had been. Women slaves were preferred to men, probably because the extra layers of body fat in their tissues prevented chilling and enabled them to work longer hours. Yet, regardless of sex, the average length of time these divers could work with efficiency was seldom more than a few years. Like the Indians, they suffered much from overwork, fell prey to disease and, as though they did not have enough troubles already, cannibalistic Carib Indians made frequent raids on the pearl fisheries and carried off great numbers of the divers for meals.

The most interesting fact about these early Caribbean divers was their ability to remain submerged for long periods of time. Oviedo's mention of 15 minutes sounds greatly exaggerated, but there are at least six later accounts of travelers in the Caribbean who witnessed the Margarita pearl divers in action during the sixteenth, seventeenth and eighteenth centuries, and all of them made the same statement. Did these travelers merely echo Oviedo, or did the Caribbean divers possess some long-lost secret that enabled them to stay underwater for so long?

Several contemporary accounts mention that the divers themselves claimed they owed their remarkable endurance to (of all things) tobacco. Both the Indian and Negro pearl divers were very heavy smokers, and a letter written by the governor of Margarita in 1617 informed the King of Spain that when the island recently ran out of tobacco the divers went on strike. The governor first resorted to punishment to induce them to go back to work, but finally gave up and sent a ship to Cuba for a new supply.

Though it seems difficult to believe in the tobacco legend, the divers of the Caribbean were said to possess a secret that is less of a strain on our credulity. In 1712 another governor of Margarita wrote that during his fifty years of residence on the island sharks and other monsters had devoured many of the divers, but that only a few years earlier the men had discovered a certain mineral that, when rubbed over their bodies before diving, would repel sharks. Unfortunately for modern man, who is still trying to discover a satisfactory shark repellent, the governor did not identify the mineral.

The Spaniards, who knew when they were on to a good thing, soon found a use for their divers' talents as important as pearl diving—salvage work. Every year from 1503 on, ships from Spain carried supplies across the Atlantic to sustain its new settlements in the New World. On the return voyages these ships carried the treasures and products of the colonies back to the mother country. Because of frequent storms or careless navigation, a great many of them were lost at sea. In major colonial ports like Havana, Veracruz, Cartagena and Panama, teams of native divers were kept aboard salvage vessels, which were ready to depart on short notice to attempt the recovery of sunken treasure. From the sixteenth century to the end of the eighteenth, these divers recovered from Spanish wrecks more than 100,000,000 ducats ($1,250,000,000 in modern currency); they saved the monarchs of Spain from bankruptcy on more than one occasion.

Ironically, when other European nations began colonizing the West Indies, these same divers were instrumental in depleting the Spanish exchequer: their new employers made use of them in salvaging Spanish wrecks, but this time the profits went into English, French and Dutch treasuries.

By the middle of the sixteenth century, when the Spaniards were forced to send their ships across the Atlantic in organized convoys called *flotas* because of increasing attacks by pirates and enemy naval fleets, each vessel carried Indian or Negro divers, who proved invaluable throughout the voyage. Before the *flota* left port, the divers inspected the ships and made necessary repairs underwater. So highly regarded was their opinion that an adverse report from them on a ship's condition was enough to prevent her from sailing, and there is no doubt that they were responsible for saving many a ship and her cargo. Once the *flota* was under way, the divers were in constant demand: since the ships habitually sailed dangerously overloaded, their seams would open in any kind of heavy weather, causing them to leak badly. Once the location of the leak was ascertained, the divers were lowered over the side, where they would seal the leak with wedges of lead or nail large planks over it. Neither method was easy, for the ships had to keep moving so they would not fall behind the protection of the convoy. In 1578 an admiral of a *flota* wrote to the king recommending that a noble title be conferred on one of his divers who, through diligent efforts to keep a number of vessels from sinking, deserved much of the credit for the successful arrival of 12,000,000 ducats in Spain that year.

Another task assigned to the divers, and a profitable one, was a kind of underwater customs inspection. When the *flotas* reached Spain laden with treasures from the New World, a great deal of smuggling went on because of high import taxes; these smugglers developed devious methods to outwit the customs officers of the king. One of the most common was to have dishonest divers attach contraband to the underwater parts of the ship's hull. Another was to throw the smuggled valuables overboard before the customs officers arrived and have divers recover them later. On one occasion a diver found that an enterprising captain had replaced the lower part of the rudder with one he had had made of solid silver while he was in one of the New World ports: the fraud was detected because the paint concealing the silver had worn off during the voyage. Presumably the diver was richly rewarded. Divers engaged in this kind of work generally were well paid, sometimes enough to buy their way out of slavery.

Due to the fact that virtually all of the ships lost in the New World were in relatively shallow water, diving bells were not widely used over the centuries. Their earliest appearance in the New World was in 1612, when an Englishman named Richard Norwood used a primitive type of "diving bell" to hunt for sunken treasure: his device was nothing more than an inverted wine barrel with weights attached to carry him to the bottom. Having decided there was not enough money in his regular line of work—piracy—to suit him, he went in search of some treasure-laden wrecks that reputedly lay in the vicinity of Bermuda. Failing to locate them, he left for the West Indies to look for wrecks there, but history does not say if he met with any success. He probably didn't: a man who could not make a go of it as a pirate in an age when piracy flourished, would hardly have been likely to succeed in a newer, more challenging profession.

Actually it was an American from Boston named William Phips, who made the greatest single treasure recovery. In 1641 a Spanish treasure *flota* totaling over thirty ships was struck by a hurricane in the Florida Straits and nine of them were dashed to pieces on the coast of Florida. The *almiranta,* or vice-admiral's galleon, had lost all of her masts and was full of water. For a week the galleon was carried along at the mercy of the wind and currents. She was finally wrecked on a reef, now known as Silver Shoals, about ninety miles north of the coast of Hispaniola. Only a few of the 600 persons aboard ever reached land–the others perished from thirst and hunger on a small sandpit nearby or in makeshift rafts at sea. The Spaniards searched unsuccessfully for this wreck for years before they finally gave up hope of locating it.

Phips had been bitten by the treasure bug when he listened to sailors' tales as a child. In 1681 he took the savings he had earned as a shipwright and later in his own shipping business and made his first treasure hunt in the Caribbean. Although he did not recover the vast treasure of his dreams, he did locate several wrecks in the Bahamas which more than covered his expenses–a promising beginning for any treasure hunter. Sure that he was destined to hit a real jackpot soon, he decided to go after a Spanish galleon, reputedly laden with gold, that had been lost near Nassau. Phips wanted the best ship, men and equipment possible for the venture. Failing to raise the money in Boston, he went to London in the spring of 1682, hoping to enlist the aid of King Charles II. It was 18 months before he was granted a royal audience, but Phips, a determined man, waited it out, talked to Charles and persuaded him to back the expedition in return for a large share of the profits.

Phips wasted a month on the wreck near Nassau, which turned out to be barren of treasure. He was determined to find another wreck. His crew, however, had other ideas: irate at not having received the expected shares of treasure, they rebelled and attempted to take over the ship and get rich as pirates. With only a handful of loyal men, Phips managed to quell the mutiny and bring the ship into Port Royal, where he was able to sign on a new crew. It was there he first learned of the lost *almiranta* on Silver Shoals.

In 1685, after an unsuccessful search for the *almiranta* in the waters north of Hispaniola, Phips reluctantly returned to England–empty-handed–only to find that the king had died during his absence. The new monarch was not as interested in tales of sunken Spanish treasure and apparently Phips even spent some time in jail. Other eager backers, however, soon persuaded the king to grant permission for the expedition. In 1686 Phips sailed from England with *two* ships.

After arriving in the Caribbean, he detoured to Jamaica and picked up about two dozen Negro pearl divers, refugees from the pearl fisheries of Margarita. Phips sent out one of his ships to search Silver Shoals; he drove himself and his men almost to the breaking point, particularly the divers, who scoured the miles of reef from dawn to dusk. Perseverance was at last rewarded when the wreck was found. One of the divers, sighting a large sea fan, dove down to retrieve it for a souvenir; upon surfacing, he reported sighting traces of a sunken galleon. Phips burst into tears of joy when he heard the news. The next weeks were a constant struggle to bring up the treasure while fighting off pirates who had received news of the windfall. More than 32 tons of silver, vast numbers of coins, gold, chests of pearls, and leather bags containing precious gems were recovered before bad weather and exhausted provisions put an end to the salvage operations. The total value of Phips' recovery in today's currency was over $3,000,000. He received a share large enough to make him one of the richest men in America. After he returned to England, the king knighted Phips and later made him governor of the Massachusetts colony.

Pearl diving, making repairs, detective work, treasure hunting–there seems to be no limit to the jobs entrusted to the Caribbean divers of the past. The memoirs of a French missionary, Père Labat, contains an account of a diver who performed an unusual task that ranks, for sheer excitement, with any adventure tale:

While visiting the Island of St. Kitts, I learned from some people, whom I trust to tell the truth, that in 1676 a large hammerhead shark bit off the leg of a young boy who was swimming in the harbor and this resulted in the death of the boy. A Carib Indian, who was a local diver very skilled in spearing fish underwater, volunteered to kill the shark. To understand the danger of this undertaking, one must first realize that the hammerhead shark is one of the most voracious, powerful, and dangerous fish in the sea. The father of the child who had been killed by the shark was glad of the opportunity of having the monster killed and thus offered the diver a good reward to obtain this poor consolation.

The diver armed himself with two good well-sharpened bayonets and, after raising his courage by drinking two glasses of rum, he dived into the sea. The shark, which had acquired a taste for human flesh, attacked the diver as soon as he saw him. The diver allowed it to approach without doing anything until the moment it was on the verge of making its rush. But at the instant it charged he dived underneath it and stabbed it in the belly with both bayonets. The result of this was at once made apparent by the blood which tinged the sea all red around the shark. Each time the shark rushed the diver, he repeated this same tactic and repeatedly stabbed the shark. This scene was enacted seven or eight times, and then at the end of half an hour the shark turned belly up and died.

After the diver had come ashore, some people went out in a canoe and tied a rope to the shark's tail, and then the shark was towed to the beach. It proved to be twenty feet long and its girth was as large as a horse. The child's leg was found whole in its stomach.

When the age of invention in diving began early in the sixteenth century, its herald was Leonardo da Vinci, the Italian artist famous for his inventions even in his own day. When the Venetians asked him for a device that would aid the divers they were using in their war against the Turks, he designed a snorkel breathing tube more advanced than anything the world had ever seen. It was attached to a leather helmet fitting over the diver's head: the helmet even had glass windows so the diver could see underwater. Leonardo also designed swim fins for the diver's hands and feet to enable him to swim faster and cover longer distances. This gear was the forerunner of the basic skin diving equipment millions of divers use today.

The Venetian Senate, however, rejected his snorkel on the grounds that the Turks would be able to see the end of the tube above the water—the divers would lose the element of surprise. They asked him to design a breathing device which would allow the divers to approach the enemy totally concealed. Leonardo responded to the challenge and designed the first scuba. It resembled his first design, but differed in one important respect: the end of the tube, instead of protruding above the water, was attached to a leather bag containing air. To enable the diver to walk on the sea floor, Leonardo discarded fins in favor of a complete diving suit. The diver, encased in leather from head to toe, with a bag of air on his chest, was supposed to descend carrying a heavy weight, which he would abandon when he wished to come up again.

The idea never got past the drawing board. Though Leonardo was sure it would work—he claimed the diver could remain submerged for four hours—he never tested his invention and refused to divulge it to the Venetians. In his memoirs, written years later, he explained his change of heart:

> How and why I do not describe my method of remaining under water for as long a time as I can stay without eating: and I do not publish or divulge these by reasons of the evil nature of man, who would use these as a means of murder at the bottom of the sea, by breaking the bottom of ships and sinking them altogether with the men in them.

Leonardo's humanitarian scruples merit respect, but they were unnecessary, for experts today know that his invention could never have worked. Far from the four hours that Leonardo envisioned, the diver could not have lasted more than a few minutes, and only then in shallow water.

A few years later, in 1511, several illustrations which appeared in a popular book on warfare revealed two breathing devices by an anonymous inventor. One picture that depicted a diver wearing a scuba very much like Leonardo's device, attracted widespread attention. The helmet had no windows, however, and was therefore useless for anything but an underwater game of blindman's buff; in addition, the air bag was much smaller and would have given the diver even less breathing time. Testing probably revealed the worthlessness of the invention. In any case, no more was heard of it for a long time.

The second invention was just as unworkable as the first. The diver wore the same outfit except for the air bag. Instead, a long tube protruded from the top of the helmet, its open end kept afloat by two small air bags on the surface. Water pressure would only have permitted this device to work in less than two feet of water. Amazingly, the busy inventors of the sixteenth and seventeenth centuries never seem to have realized the importance of water pressure. Designs similar to those followed thick and fast, all showing fantastically long tubes or snorkels, most accompanied by claims stating the great depths that divers could reach with them.

The devices featuring snorkels and breathing tubes belonged to the realm of science fiction, but inventors did achieve a measure of practical success with another device—a diving bell which functioned on a principle described by Aristotle over 1,800 years before. He described a kettle or barrel that was inverted to imprison air and then held level as it descended to keep the air from escaping. It enclosed either a diver's head or his entire body—and it often worked.

The first appearance of a bell in more modern times was in 1531, when divers used one in Lake Nemi, near Rome, to locate two of Emperor Caligula's pleasure galleys, which reputedly had carried treasure when they sank. The barrel-shaped bell, the invention of an Italian physicist, Guglielmo de Lorena, covered the diver's head and torso and was raised and lowered by ropes. The diver within was able to walk upon the lake bed and stay below for nearly an hour at a time before surfacing for fresh air. Within a few weeks he found both wrecks, for which free divers had searched in vain for many years. Unfortunately, locating them was only half the battle: for the next three centuries many unsuccessful attempts were made to raise them. The Italian government finally succeeded, in the late 1920's, only by draining the lake dry.

In 1538 two Greeks designed and built a diving bell, then demonstrated its use in Toledo, Spain, before the king, Emperor Charles V, and more than ten thousand spectators. Unlike de Lorena's bell, it was large enough to hold both inventors, who sat inside with a burning candle. Much to the astonishment of the audience, the flame was still burning when they returned to the surface.

News of the Toledo bell spread like wildfire all over Europe, and many similar bells were built. Their practical use sometimes differed from the Spanish demonstration in one important respect: divers, discovering that remaining inside the bell prevented them from working efficiently, relied on it as a kind of air bank. They swam outside to get the job done and returned to the bell at intervals to gulp air into their lungs. Many bells seem to have served their purpose, no matter how they were employed. Some, on the other hand, were useless, like two diving devices invented by an Italian, Niccolò Tartaglia, in 1551. One consisted of a wooden frame shaped like an hourglass on which the diver stood. The glass bowl enclosing his head assured him of good vision but not much breathing time, since it could not have provided him with more than a few minutes of air. The second invention featured the same hourglass frame, but this time the bowl, which seemed to have no opening, enclosed the diver's whole body. There is no indication that either device was ever built.

In 1616, a German, Franz Kessler, produced a bell that was not attached by ropes to anything on the surface: the diver descended with weights and released them when he wished to ascend. The bell consisted of a wooden barrel-shaped chamber, long enough to reach the diver's ankles. It was covered with leather to keep it watertight and possessed several glass windows at eye level (Figure 1-3). Though tests proved

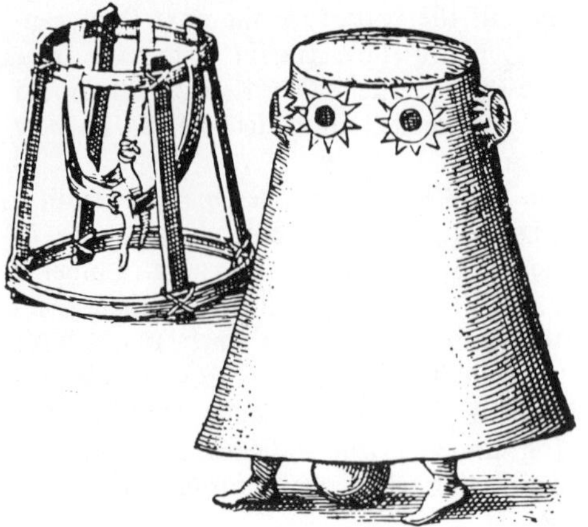

Figure 1-3. A German, Franz Kessler, invented this diving bell in 1616; unlike many earlier designs, it had no connection with the surface.

that Kessler's invention worked, it was clearly ahead of its time and was not widely used.

In 1677 an enormous wooden bell, thirteen feet high and nine feet wide across the rim, was built in Spain and used in the port of Cadaqués to salvage two shipwrecks containing a vast sum of money. The two Moorish divers stayed down for more than an hour at a time. They claimed they could have stayed even longer, but the terrific heat created in the bell by their own breathing forced them to surface to permit the heat to dissipate. They did their work inside the bell and managed to recover several million Spanish pieces of eight. The divers were paid in a novel way: each time they surfaced with treasure, they were permitted to keep as much of it as they could hold in their mouths and hands.

A French physicist, Denis Papin, made a significant improvement in the diving bell in 1689. He devised a way to use a pump or large bellows to supply diving bells with fresh air from the surface. His invention had four great virtues: it permitted divers to remain below for any period of time they chose; it eliminated the danger of carbon dioxide in the air supply which could kill the divers; it made working conditions more comfortable inside the bell, since the fresh air forced out the heat; and, most important of all, it enabled the divers to reach depths of up to seventy feet, since pumping air into the bell under presssure kept the water out. It was not until almost one hundred years later that better pumps were invented and divers could go deeper in the bells.

At about the same time that Dr. Papin came up with his device and even before he tested it, Edmund Halley, the famous English astronomer for whom Halley's comet was named, built a diving bell that used a different method to provide the diver with a continuous air supply. He had the air lowered in leaden casks with valves and tubes attached to them; the divers inside the bell could pull in the end of the tube, open the valve and get as much air as they needed (Figure 1-4). This method was more primitive than Papin's device but it worked better, since the pumps of the period, besides being unable to exert much force, were constantly breaking down.

Halley's bell had several important advantages. More than sixty cubic feet in volume, it was larger than the bell used for salvage in Spain in 1677. It was made of wood with a lead covering that kept it watertight and prevented it from overturning because of unevenly distributed weights. There were glass viewing ports on the sides and an exhaust system on the top to release the hot air produced by the diver's breathing as it rose upward. Halley also provided a way to extend the radius of maneuverability underwater. The diver wore a full diving suit with a helmet to which a flexible tube was attached; another diver inside the bell held the other end of the tube and kept his partner supplied with air. As long as there was enough air lowered in the casks to keep water from filling the bell, Halley's invention could reach depths beyond the capabilities of any other bells in existence. Casks became the principal means of providing fresh air for diving bells until 1788, when an English engineer, John Smeaton, constructed a truly reliable pump that made Dr. Papin's inven-

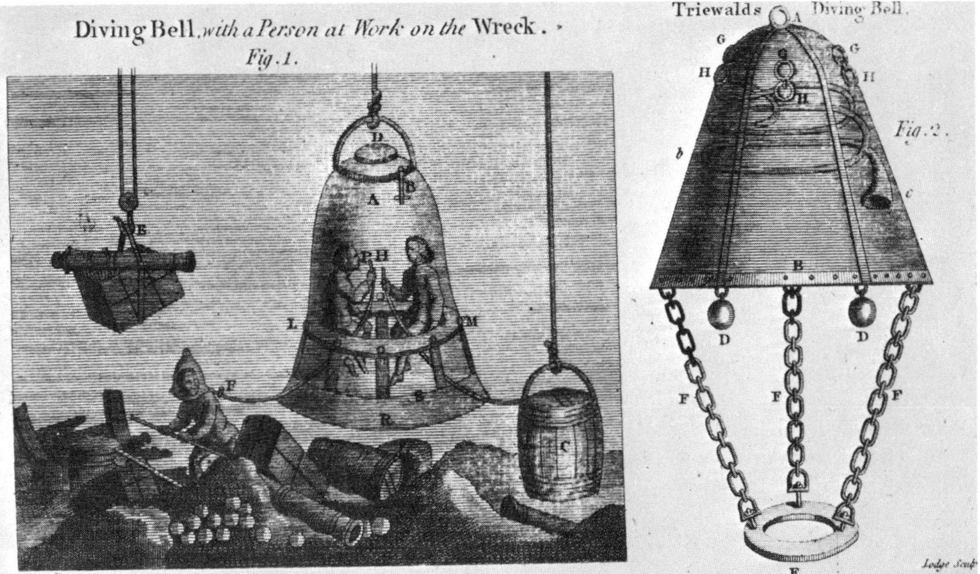


Figure 1-4. The noted English astronomer Edmund Halley invented this diving bell in 1720. Divers received a continuous air supply through tubes attached to a cask lowered from the surface. (Courtesy of National Maritime Museum, Great Britain.)

tion a reality. By the end of the eighteenth century diving bells were so commonplace all over Europe that few large ports were without them. Not only were they used for many different types of underwater tasks, but also to take tourists on sightseeing trips. During a state visit to England in 1818, Archduke Maximilian went down in a bell in Plymouth Harbor and picked up a stone from the bottom as a souvenir.

The earliest design for a diving chamber appeared in 1578 in a book written by an Englishman, William Bourne. It consisted of a wooden chamber, supposedly watertight, made from the hull of a small vessel; in reality, it appears to be the forerunner of the submarine. It was never constructed and very little interest was shown in it.

In 1715 another Englishman, John Lethbridge, obtained a patent for what he called a "diving machine." It resembled a cross between a diving chamber and an armored suit, consisting of an irregular metal cylinder six feet long and 2½ feet in diameter at the head and 1½ feet at the foot. Armholes in the sides allowed the diver to work with his hands and a glass port enabled him to see. The device had no air supply other than what was trapped inside the chamber before it was closed. It was raised and lowered by cables, but could not work deeper than fifty feet, because the increased water pressure caused leaks in the sealings around the armholes, viewing port and entrance hatch. Because Lethbridge's invention failed to extend the limit of the depth divers could reach at that time, it did not attract much attention.

In 1772 yet another Englishman, John Day, built a diving chamber that had no connection with the surface; he asserted that on his first test in a pond he had reached a depth of thirty feet and remained submerged for 24 hours. His story was believed, despite the fact that the chamber could not have provided him with sufficient air for more than five or ten minutes, and he found backers to support another test. This time he planned to go to 130 feet and remain below for twelve hours. With several thousand spectators on hand, the chamber descended in Plymouth Harbor on June 29, 1774, and neither it nor its inventor was ever seen again.

The next attempt to reach great depths occurred in 1831, when a Spaniard named Cervo constructed a small wooden chamber and claimed he could reach a depth of 600 feet with it. On the first trial, to 200 feet, he failed to come up again. Pieces of the chamber floated to the surface, indicating that water pressure had crushed it. This was the last recorded attempt to reach great depths in wooden diving chambers.

In 1849 two Americans, Richards and Wolcott, designed a sphere-shaped metal diving chamber that was meant to be lowered and raised by chains connected to the surface. However, they failed to provide a means of supplying it with air. Their invention was never constructed because of lack of funds, but news of the idea circulated around the world and inventors everywhere turned their efforts to the construction of metal diving chambers.

The first to come up with a workable device was a French engineer named Ernest Bazin. In 1865 he built a chamber to search for treasure in Vigo Bay, Spain. Like the Richards-Wolcott chamber, it did not have a supply of fresh air other than what was trapped before it submerged. This lack did not prevent it from reaching the amazing depth of 245 feet, almost three times the depth any other device had reached, and remaining submerged for a hour and a half. A Venetian named Toselli solved the air supply problem in 1875 by improving Bazin's chamber. He provided it with a huge cylinder of compressed air capable of sustaining the diver inside the chamber for fifty hours underwater.

The way had been cleared: inventors continued to labor, constructing chambers of thicker and stronger metals, making them safe and more comfortable for the men within. In 1934 two Americans, Beebe and Barton, descended in a diving chamber called a bathysphere, which functioned on the same principle as Bazin's chamber but was more highly evolved (Figure 1-5). They reached the fantastic depth of 3,028 feet, a record broken over and over again in the following decades.

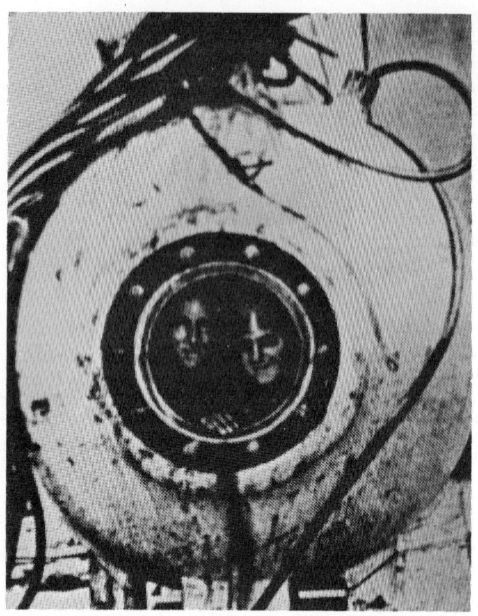

Figure 1-5. Dr. William Beebe and Otis Barton pioneered deep diving in their bathysphere, when they descended 3,028 feet in 1934.

The possibility of a man being able to walk freely on the sea floor dressed in a diving suit and breathing air from the surface through tubes, for centuries as fantastic an idea as walking on the moon, became a reality in 1715, when an English inventor named Becker gave a demonstration of his new invention in London. It consisted of a full leather diving suit and a large globular metal helmet with a window. Three tubes led from the helmet to the surface—one for the diver's expended air and the others for the fresh air that several large bellows pumped down. During the demonstration the diver was able to stay submerged for an hour, but the depth he reached was not recorded. That the invention was put to practical use is known from an account written by a traveler visiting England in 1745. He witnessed divers clad in the Becker gear trying to salvage a recently lost warship; a pump supplied air to them rather than the more primitive and unreliable bellows.

During the eighteenth century the system of pumping air down to divers from the surface seems to have been in use only in England. In fact, while the English had taken this great step forward in diving technology, inventors on the Continent were still turning out drawings and designs that showed divers trying to suck air down through long tubes. Since the pumps used by the English until the beginning of the nineteenth century could only provide air to divers working no deeper than twenty feet, it is not too surprising perhaps that the rest of the world failed to take much notice. It was only with the invention of powerful pumps called air compressors, which could force air down to greater depths, that the kind of diving known as helmet diving became popular.

Augustus Siebe, a German who lived in England, is sometimes called the father of helmet diving. In 1819 he invented the diving suit and helmet that evolved into the standard helmet diving rig now in use all over the world. His invention consisted of a brass helmet, into which air was pumped from the surface by hand-driven air compressors, and a suit made of leather with a canvas overlay to prevent it being cut underwater. The excess air, as well as the diver's expelled breath, was forced out of the suit through vents near the waist. These vents were a great disadvantage because they compelled the diver to remain upright constantly, just like a diving bell, or else all the air pumped into his helmet would rush out through the waist vents.

In 1834, an American named Norcross improved the Siebe diving suit by eliminating the waist vents and placing an exhaust vent for the excess and stale air on top of the helmet. The diver could now bend over or even lie down on the bottom without endangering his air supply. Augustus Siebe, probably not wanting to be outdone by an American, modified his own diving suit in 1837, making it completely watertight and adding Norcross' exhaust vent (Figure 1-6). He went one step further: the diver could now control the vent and expel air only when he thought it necessary. This improvement had two great advantages. First, when the diver wished to reach great depths, he could build up air pressure inside the suit to resist the increasing water pressure outside; otherwise, it would press the suit tightly against his body, thus stopping his circulation and causing temporary paralysis. Second, in case the diver could not communicate with the surface and get pulled up, he could inflate his suit with air until it filled

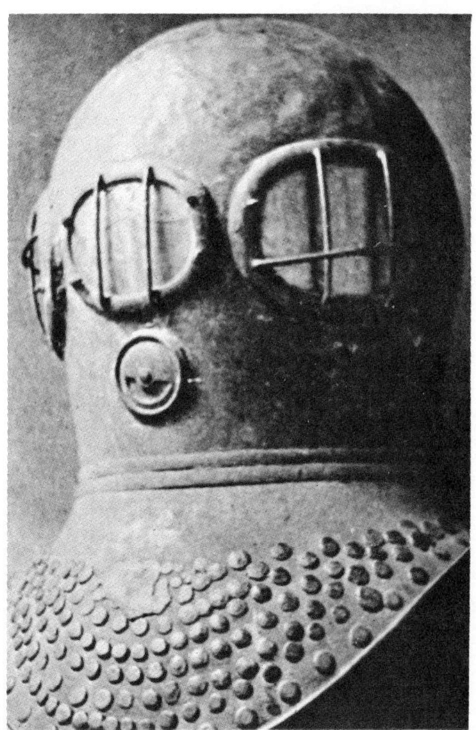

Figure 1-6. Today's "hard hat" diving helmet evolved from an 1819 invention of a German, Augustus Siebe, which consisted of a brass helmet fitted on to a canvas suit. Excess air in the rig escaped through waist vents.

up like a balloon, then surface by himself. This safety factor has saved the lives of many divers over the years.

The first opportunity for the Siebe diving suit to prove its worth came very soon after its inventor had tested it and put it on the market. Half a century before, the 108-gun *Royal George,* the largest and most important ship in the British Navy, had sunk at Portsmouth with the loss of almost a thousand lives. Although the wreck lay in only 65 feet of water, all previous attempts to raise it or destroy it had failed. It was a great hazard to navigation in this busy port, so in 1834 the Admiralty enlisted the services of a civilian diver named Deane to see what he could do about it. Using the Siebe open diving suit, he spent three years surveying the wreck, raised many items, including thirty cannon, and finally came to the conclusion that it could not be raised, since marine worms had eaten through much of the wood. Army engineers later used the Siebe closed diving suit with even greater success to plant explosives that finally demolished the wreck.

When the Siebe rig was first put into general use, nothing was known of the bends or other dangers a diver faced in deeper water. Miraculously, there were no fatalities among the divers working on the wreck of the *Royal George*. There were, however, quite a few accidents, the most serious occurring when a diver's hose broke and all the air rushed out of his helmet. Luckily for him, his plight was noticed on the surface and he was pulled up immediately, his face and neck swollen and bleeding from the ears, eyes and mouth. He spent more than a month in the hospital and was never able to dive again.

The United States Navy did not begin to use helmet diving rigs until late in the 1870's. It inaugurated the first helmet diving school at Newport, Rhode Island, in 1882. For many years official interest in this new branch of naval operations was lukewarm. Divers were given an inadequate two weeks of training, hampered by regulations that limited the depth they could penetrate to sixty feet; they spent most of their time recovering spent torpedoes. Meanwhile, British divers were working in depths of 130 feet, and it was due to their pioneering efforts that so much was learned about the perils besetting divers in deep water. In 1898, when the USS *Maine* was blown up and sunk in Havana Harbor, American divers had their first chance to show what they could do and they came through with flying colors: by recovering the ship's cipher code and the keys to the munitions magazine, they prevented them from falling into enemy hands. In 1914 a naval enlisted man, Chief Gunner George Stillson, established a depth record by diving to 274 feet.

An Englishman named W. H. Taylor invented the first armored diving suit with articulated arms and legs in 1838, the year following the appearance of Siebe's closed diving suit (Figure 1-7). At that time English helmet divers had been working at depths less than 100 feet; Taylor's suit was built to reach 150 feet. Within a decade, others were being made to reach depths of 200 to 300 feet, and by the turn of the century 600 feet. The bends and nitrogen narcosis had finally been recognized as dangers to helmet divers, and interest in these suits grew. However, they never came into widespread use because they have several drawbacks. The most important is that their weight and bulk made underwater mobility impossible: they must depend on surface attendants to move them around on the sea floor. Another is the expense involved in their construction and maintenance. Still another is that if they should develop leaks, the diver within, whose air is at atmospheric pressure, would be drowned instantly as water rushed in.

The desire for total concealment underwater, which had prompted the Venetians to reject Leonardo da Vinci's snorkel, motivated many later inventors to devise versions of scuba that would allow divers to approach enemy ships without any telltale tubes or

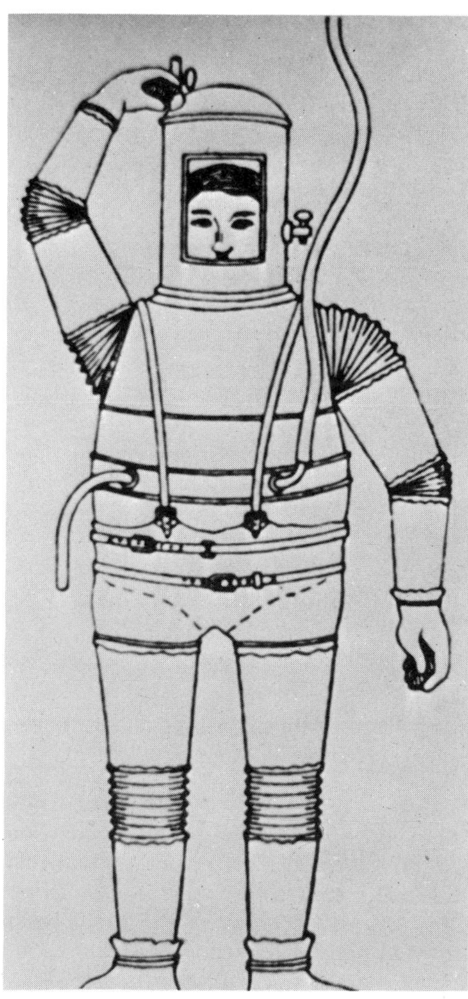

Figure 1-7. In 1838 W. H. Taylor invented the first armored diving suit. It had articulated arms and legs and allowed divers to descend to 150 feet—more than 50 feet deeper than Siebe's suit.

reeds. These inventors were no more successful than Leonardo had been, but they continued to labor, undoubtedly because they knew that a workable device would make its inventor rich.

In Spain, the most war-minded nation in Europe in the sixteenth and early seventeenth centuries, inventors were particularly busy; Spanish archives are full of early scuba designs, some with possibilities, some ludicrous. In 1631, when Dutch supremacy on the high seas was driving Spain to bankruptcy, a desperate King Philip IV offered 10,000 ducats to anyone who could invent a usable scuba. Spies had advised him that the leading Dutch ports of Amsterdam and Rotterdam sometimes harbored as many as 500 ships at a time; he planned to send divers into both ports during a storm to cut anchor cables, thus causing the ships to collide. Since the Dutch had sentinels stationed on all their ships, the scheme could only work if the divers were totally concealed. A special committee was appointed to consider the designs that came in from every corner of the Spanish Empire. Not one of them was found feasible, and the plan to deal a deathblow to the Dutch had to be abandoned.

Although none of the inventions were suitable, several were very interesting, among them three submitted by a Fleming, Florencio Valangren. Two were not scuba at all. The first was a long breathing tube, similar to those that so many inventors were turning out regularly—they didn't work unless they were used close to the surface. This design had an original touch, however: an exhaust valve on the bottom of the tube for the exhalation of foul air. The second design also featured a tube, with the end above the surface connected to a bellows. This was the first known instance of air pumped down to a diver, predating Dr. Papin by many years. The device could have worked in shallow water and, according to the letter Valangren sent along with his designs, similar devices were then in use in Flanders and Holland, mainly for repair work on ships' bottoms. The third design, a very primitive scuba, consisted of a large animal hide pumped full of air by a bellows and dropped by weights to the sea floor. Connected to the hide was a tube with a mouthpiece; the diver, swimming freely in the water, could open it when he needed to take a breath. Valangren's letter stated that this device was also in current use, and there is no reason to doubt him: an air bag made from a large cowhide and lowered in about twenty feet of water would have supplied the diver with at least 15 minutes of air.

Another invention sent to Philip, this one anonymous, is even more interesting, for it took a further step toward the development of practical scuba. It consisted of a tubular air reservoir worn like a belt and probably made of an animal's intestines. At one end was a mouthpiece, and at the other a bellows which would allow the diver to obtain air from the surface without assistance.

In 1679 an Italian, Giovanni Borelli, made the next important attempt at developing a workable scuba. His invention was based on the principle of air regeneration: the diver using it could supposedly breathe the same air over and over again after his spent air was passed through a filter and made fresh. The diver in Borelli's drawing wore a goatskin suit, swim fins and a metal helmet with a window. The air reservoir was the helmet itself, and a copper tube (the filter system) led from the front to the back. Borelli claimed that condensation would collect in the tube and, when the diver exhaled, this condensation would filter out the carbon dioxide from the spent air. His invention probably never got past the drawing board. Almost a hundred years later, in 1776, a Frenchman named Sieur actually built an air-regeneration system that was virtually a duplicate of Borelli's device, and discovered that the filter did not purify the air.

In 1808 a German, Friedrich von Drieberg, invented an apparatus he called the "Triton," which somewhat resembles the scuba of today. It consisted of a metal cylinder filled with air and worn on the diver's back, with a breathing tube leading to his mouthpiece. Most of the time the Triton was not self-contained, because tubes led from it to a pump on the surface. However, if the pump broke down or some other emergency arose, the diver would have sufficient air to stay below for quite some time (Figure 1-8).

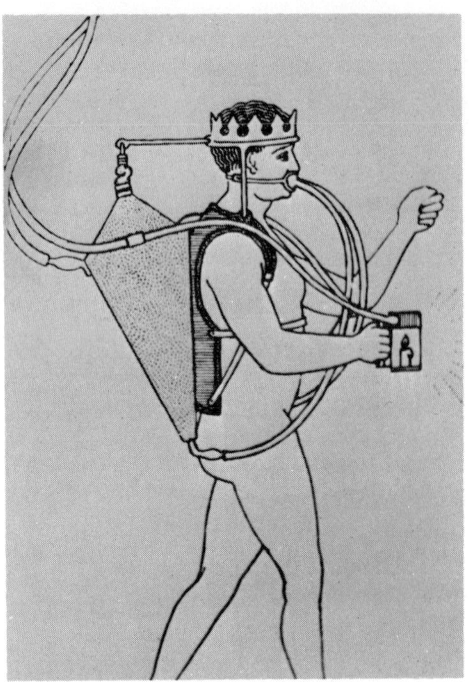

Figure 1-8. An even earlier scuba rig, the Triton, designed by Friedrich von Drieberg in 1808.

An Englishman, William James, devised the first workable and practical scuba in 1825. The air reservoir was an iron cylindrical belt extending from the diver's waist to his armpits. It contained compressed air at a pressure of thirty atmospheres, or about 450 PSI, and the diver breathed through a hose connected to his helmet. He wore a full suit, carried weights, and wore boots instead of fins, so the rig was obviously designed for walking on the sea bottom rather than for swimming (Figure 1-9).

Around the same time, a Brooklyn factory worker, Charles Condert, also developed a workable scuba, which differed considerably from James' in appearance. It consisted of a full diving suit and attached hood, both made of heavy cloth overlaid with gum rubber. At the top of the hood was a hole the size of a pinhead to release spent air. The air reservoir—a four-foot length of copper

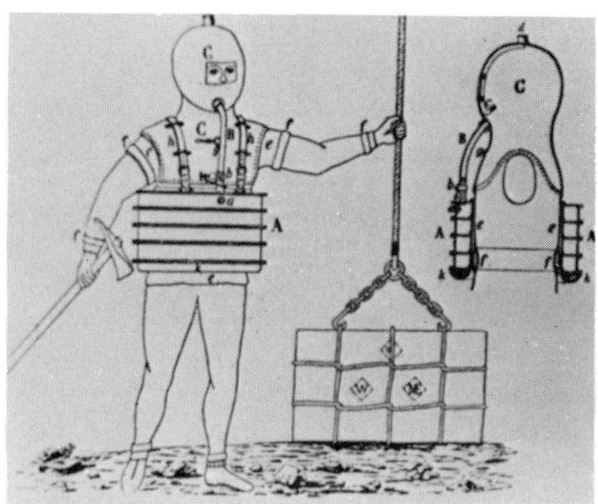

Figure 1-9. The first practical self-contained underwater breathing apparatus (scuba), invented by William James, an Englishman, in 1825.

tubing, six inches in diameter, bent like a horseshoe around the diver's body—had a safety feature that the James gear lacked: a valve to emit air directly into the diver's suit at his discretion, thus preventing water pressure from forcing the suit against his body. Condert successfully used his apparatus to depths of twenty feet in various jobs around the Brooklyn docks until his death in August 1832, when the valve cock between his air reservoir and his suit broke down as he was trying to surface and he became entangled in some underwater obstruction.

The next major advance came in 1865, when two Frenchmen, Benoit Rouquayrol, a mining engineer, and Lieutenant Auguste Denayrouze, a naval officer, designed an apparatus that they called a "self-contained diving suit." In actuality it was not completely self-contained, since it depended on an air supply pumped down from the surface to the metal cylinder on the diver's back; as in the case of Drieberg's Triton, however, it could be disconnected from the surface and function for short periods of time on the air in the cylinder which was constantly maintained at a pressure of forty atmospheres.

The most important feature of the Rouquayrol-Denayrouze invention was an attachment to the air reservoir that regulated the amount of air passing through the tube leading to the diver's mouthpiece. Inside the regulator was a membrane subjected to the outside water pressure; the membrane controlled a valve permitting air at equal or greater pressure to pass into the body of the diver's suit as water pressure increased. Because the regulator sent air into the diver's mouthpiece only when he took a breath rather than constantly, he wasted none of the precious air. This rig could be used in greater depths than the helmet diving rigs of the period, because it required less air and had the safety factor of the reserve air supply in the cylinder. The regulator, a very precise mechanism, played a more important part than any other device in the development of the modern scuba.

Originally the Rouquayrol-Denayrouze apparatus was designed to supply air to a naked diver wearing goggles, but the inventors soon recognized the danger to the diver if his goggles became flattened against his eyes. They replaced them with a face mask, which was attached to the hose leading to the cylinder. The invention was found so satisfactory that many helmet divers began to wear air reservoirs on their backs to free themselves from any connection to the surface. The apparatus was manufactured commercially in 1867 and most of the world's navies soon adopted it officially. Just five years after its invention, Jules Verne immortalized it in his prophetic *Twenty Thousand Leagues Under the Sea.*

In 1876 an English merchant marine officer, Henry Fleuss, invented a simple, compact and lightweight self-contained diving rig, which used pure compressed oxygen rather than compressed air and functioned on an air-regeneration system that worked. Because of the danger of oxygen poisoning below 33 feet, divers using it could not descend to even half the depth they could reach with the Rouquayrol-Denayrouze apparatus; it did make divers totally independent of any surface air supply, however, just as the inventions of James and Condert had. Its main advantage lay in the three-hour breathing supply it provided. The Fleuss apparatus (generally referred to as a closed-circuit oxygen rebreather) closely resembled the Rouquayrol-Denayrouze rig. The components were an air reservoir, regulator, air hose and the filter system that was the heart of the invention: the caustic soda in the filter system absorbed all the carbon dioxide and the diver was able to breathe the same oxygen over and over again. The diver could use it whether he wore a suit or swam naked, whether he chose goggles and mouthpiece, a mask, or even a helmet–versatility was one of its virtues (Figure 1-10).

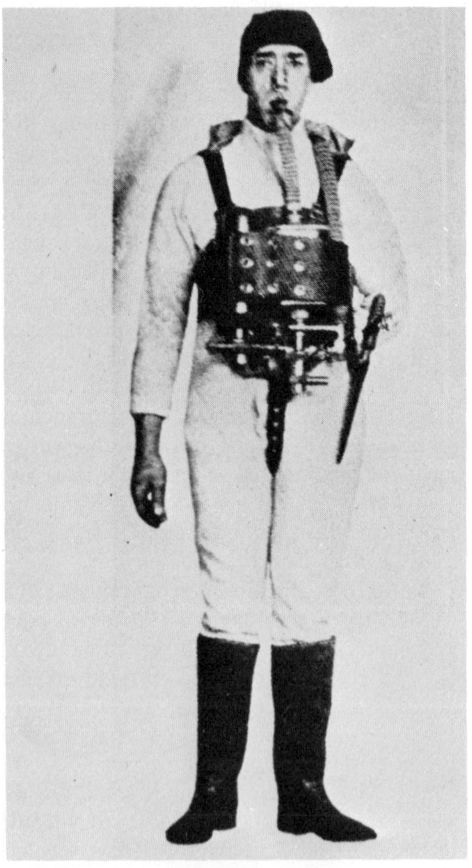

Figure 1-10. A three-hour air supply was the main advantage of this versatile closed-circuit oxygen rebreather invented by an Englishman, Henry Fleuss, in 1876.

Four years after its invention, the Fleuss rebreather proved its value in a crisis caused by the flooding of a tunnel under construction beneath the Severn River near Bristol, England. Before the tunnel could be pumped dry, a large iron door had to be closed. Divers wearing the standard helmet gear were unable to do the job because of obstacles in the tunnel which would have snagged or cut their air hoses. The Rouquayrol-Denayrouze apparatus was unworkable too: disconnected from the surface, it would not have supplied enough air for the duration of the job. Fleuss hired a well-known diver, Alexander Lambert, and taught him how to use the rebreather. Lambert succeeded in closing the door, accomplishing what the builders of the tunnel had almost given up as a lost cause. Three years later, when the same tunnel flooded a second time, Lambert was again successful, but this time nearly lost his life due to the oxygen poisoning that resulted from his extreme physical exertion.

In 1900, Louis Boutan, a French professor of biology and underwater photography pioneer, finding no type of diving equipment to his liking, devised his own scuba. Along with the standard helmet diving suit, he wore a huge cylinder of compressed air on his back, capable of sustaining him for three hours at a depth of seventy feet. As far as anyone knows, no one else ever used his invention.

In 1925, a French naval officer, Yves Le Prieur, invented a scuba unit which was widely used until the development of the Cousteau-Gagnan unit. His unit consisted of a steel cylinder of compressed air worn on the diver's back. An air hose from a regulator at the top of the cylinder connected to a mouthpiece which the diver held in his mouth. He controlled a valve which regulated the amount of air he required; goggles and nose clips completed the unit. The cylinder was quite small and only provided enough air for the diver to remain below for twenty minutes at 25 feet.

After several years of testing the unit, Le Prieur found that the goggles hurt the diver's eyes too much and he replaced them and the nose clips with a full face mask. This wasted more air, but he overcame the problem by using large air clyinders. In 1933, when the new sport of spear fishing or skin diving was becoming popular in the Mediterranean, he obtained a patent and began manufacturing the unit commercially for the growing band of enthusiasts. That same year he invented the first underwater spear gun, propelled by compressed air, and in 1935 the first wet suit.

One of the most puzzling facts in the history of scuba design is the complete neglect of the Rouquayrol-Denayrouze demand regulator for so many years. Both Boutan and Le Prieur made use of a simple regulator that provided the diver with a pressure equal or greater than the ambient water pressure, but both failed to use a demand regulator which would only deliver air when the diver breathed. A great volume of air was being wasted and the diver's bottom time was decreased considerably. Not until 1942 was it brought back into use by the two Frenchmen–Jacques-Yves Cousteau, a close friend of Le Prieur, and Emile Gagnan, an engineer–who created the celebrated aqualung, which millions of people are using around the world today.

# 2. H. M. S. *Challenger* and the Development of Marine Science

HENRY CHARNOCK 1973

The existence of marine science is commonly believed to date from the great *Challenger* Expedition which sailed in 1872. (Figure 2-1) Indeed John Young Buchanan, the Expedition's chemist, held that oceanography started on one particular day in 1873, the day of *Challenger*'s Station I when she first dredged in the depths of the North Atlantic south of Tenerife. In fact, as anyone who has read Margaret Deacon's *Scientists and the Sea*[1] knows very well, marine science has grown gradually over the centuries, at rates depending on individuals and the environment in which they found themselves.

So far as the United Kingdom is concerned the development of the subject since 1800 has been closely linked with that of the Hydrographic Department of what used to be called the Admiralty. In this lecture I shall refer mainly to three Hydrographers in particular, but it will become clear that we oceanographers are well aware of the debt we owe to our friends the naval surveyors.

It is a pity, in some ways, that *Challenger* is not one of the traditional survey ship names. The first of the six H.M.S. *Challengers* (not counting one that was begun in 1844 but not completed) was a brig sloop, launched in 1806 and captured by the French in 1811. The second, also a brig sloop, was launched in 1813 and within three months was helping the Duke of Wellington reduce San Sebastian. She was dismantled in Trincomalee in 1819. The third H.M.S. *Challenger* was a rather larger vessel, a sixth rate of 603 tons launched in 1826. She went aground and was lost on the coast of Chile on the nineteenth of May 1835. As a result she provides a somewhat tenuous link with the Hydrographic Department; her captain was a friend of Robert Fitzroy who was then surveying in H.M.S. *Beagle* and visiting Valparaiso. Fitzroy immediately started a great overland rescue party, saving all but three of the crew of about 175. Charles Darwin, who was sharing Fitzroy's cabin, tells how Fitzroy had to deal very sharply with his senior officer to get things going.

The connection with the *Beagle*, slight

1. Deacon, M. (1971). *Scientists and the Sea 1650–1900.* Academic Press, London and New York, pp. 445.

Dr. Henry Charnock is the Director of the National Institute of Oceanography in Great Britain.

From *Journal of Navigation*, Vol. 26, No. 1, pp. 1–12, 1973. Reprinted with light editing and with permission of the author and the Royal Institute of Navigation, London.



On the Cruise: What did they do, and why?

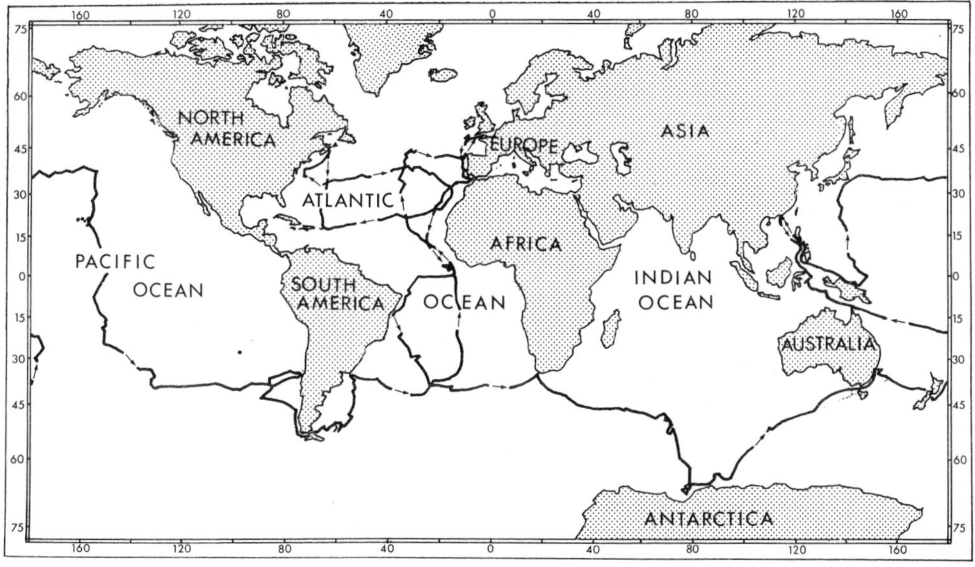


Figure 2-1. The voyage of H.M.S. *Challenger* 1872–6.

though it is, gives me a chance to say something of the Hydrographer at that time, Sir Francis Beaufort, to me a critical figure in the development of marine science. Beaufort was born in 1774 and first went to sea as a 'guinea pig'—that is by paying a hundred guineas—in an East Indiaman. The ship (*Vansittart*) went aground and he spent five days in a boat before being rescued. He was lucky to survive the action off Brest (1 June 1794) and later received serious wounds in action off Malaga.

It was while he was in command of H.M.S. *Woolwich* in 1805 that he made up his famous scale of Beaufort numbers for wind strength and Beaufort letters for weather. Kinsman[2] has discussed the origin of the wind scale; he explains how, after the years of blockade, seagoing officers could estimate exactly how much sail a frigate could carry 'in chase, full and by'. To use the ship itself as a wind instrument thus led to reasonably constant results—it is amusing to note that at the time H.M.S. *Woolwich* was 'en flute', with her guns removed and her gunports vacant holes.

Beaufort was appointed Hydrographer in 1829 and by 1831 was recommending his scales to Fitzroy; they were made mandatory in 1838. His interest in meteorology was of great benefit to international co-operation, then growing quickly due to Fitzroy, Maury and others. He co-operated with other countries in tidal studies too. He was much respected, as a scientist, by scientists, and soon had a good working relationship with Lubbock and Whewell. He was able to organize a period of tidal observations by Preventive Officers all round the English coast and then in 1835 to propose an international scheme:

'If their Lordships should approve of the proposition and will move H.M. Government to invite the co-operation of Denmark, Hamburg, Holland, Belgium, France, Spain, Portugal, and the United States of America, to partake in this useful work, I will lose no

2. Kinsman, B. (1969). Historical notes on the original Beaufort Scale. *Marine Observer,* **39**, 116–124.

time in preparing detailed instructions and printed forms for the uniform entry of the observations.'

The other nations were glad to co-operate and a mass of data was obtained. One result was the prediction of an amphidromic point in the North Sea; confirmation was sought by special observations in H.M.S. *Fairy*.

The Hydrographic Department needed somebody like Beaufort badly. In 1868 Richards was to write[3]:

'it cannot be questioned that on the accession of Captain Beaufort to office and even for some time afterwards both [the Hydrographic Department and the surveying service afloat] were in their infancy, or had but just passed through a most unsatisfactory and turbulent childhood; the tree had been planted, but not matured; the department had not been encouraged or protected by those who saw the necessity of creating it; it was a plant necessarily of a slow growth, and long in yielding fruit; it had been difficult to find a chief thoroughly competent to guide it through its early troubles on shore, and more difficult still to find men competent to carry out his behests afloat; it was a kind of hybrid institution, the one branch of it inviting as it were the opposition of the civil element at Whitehall, the other calculated to encounter the ill-will of the authorities afloat, from the circumstance that it was necessary the officers composing it should be in a measure independent of their authority; and yet this state of things is quite comprehensible without imputing blame anywhere; the chief had to learn his own duty, his colleagues afloat had to learn theirs; marine surveying, both in science and practice, as has been before observed, was but in its infancy: there were, moreover, the means wanting, involving no inconsiderable outlay, and it is scarcely surprising that rulers who could not have seen their way to the great results which have since been attained, should have been chary of providing them. The originators of the department, as will have been seen, contemplated but a very narrow sphere of action for it, and did not foresee the calls which the vast requirements of commerce and navigation would make upon the nation at no distant time; or that it would be the special mission of this country, foremost among the maritime states of the world, principally to provide for these wants.' [. . . AND . . .] 'From the day of his [Beaufort's] appointment, the Hydrographic Department may be said to have assumed a scientific character; and from first to last he was the link which connected the British Admiralty with the scientific bodies of their own country, Europe and America, to the undoubted advantage of either; and by all of which his great abilities and rare talents were fully appreciated and acknowledged, by the only rewards science can bestow.'

To these scientific gifts were added 'singular punctuality and great assiduity' as well as, one suspects, a sense of humor. Certainly some of his correspondence with the almost universally hated Captain Belcher shows high irony. I like to think that it was Beaufort who contrived to have the dragon Belcher appointed to command of H.M.S. *Sulphur*.

But I need not stress Beaufort's virtues; Admiral Collins has already written of them in the Institute's *Journal* and since 1860 the Beaufort Testimonial has been awarded as a prize at the Navigation School at Portsmouth. Suffice it to say that the Hydrographers have been more or less sympathetic to scientists ever since.

Beaufort was ill from 1855 until he died in December 1857, and probably took little interest in the H.M.S. *Challenger* then being built at Woolwich. She was launched on 13 February 1858, a screw steam corvette of 1462 tons, 400 horsepower, 21 guns, 290 men. After an unsuccessful intervention in Mexico in 1860 and the punitive shelling of Rewa in the Fiji Islands in the same year she was at Sheerness, in reserve, when, in 1872, she was commissioned as a survey ship to go round the world exploring the deep ocean.

The resulting *Challenger* Expedition was a huge undertaking, one that was perhaps pos-

3. Richards, G. A. (1868). *A Memoir of the Hydrographic Department of the Admiralty*. Hydrographic Department, London.

sible only in the prosperity of Victorian England. All seagoing science needs teams of workers and expensive facilities; Burstyn[4] has studied the organization of the Expedition as an early example of what we now call 'big science', seeing in it clues to the relationship between individuals and the institutions they create. Then, as now, big scientific projects required skilled political promotion; then, as now, a marine scientist who wanted major facilities did well to call upon the Hydrographer.

The Hydrographer of the time was George Henry Richards who had been appointed in 1863 when returning in *Hecate* from his third circumnavigation of the globe. A tactful man, he had served twice with the irascible Belcher and had even been praised by him:

> 'He has at all times borne the character of an exemplary and steady officer, and is one of the few officers of the *Sulphur* of whom I can speak with unqualified praise, not only for his assiduity in surveying, but for his gallantry during the operation at Canton, and for his exemplary conduct when the other officers of the *Sulphur* were in a state of insubordinate alienation from their Captain.'

It was a time when telegraphic communication was developing rapidly. British cables were soon being laid in many areas of the ocean and in many cases Richards' survey ships were sent to sound the route and get sea-floor samples. There was what now seems ample evidence that marine life could exist at all depths but scientific opinion was divided, mainly owing to Edward Forbes' tentative suggestion that nothing could live below 300 fathoms. Bad theories are well known to be good for science–it is bad observations that do the harm–and Forbes' azoic zone theory was no exception.

Richards agreed that scientists could go to sea in his ships to attempt to dredge animals from the bottom of the deep ocean. This was a bigger concession than it seems; naturalists had been allowed on board, even encouraged, since Beaufort's time, but they did not stop the ship and put things over the side and generally interfere with the routine. Hooker, who sailed to the Antarctic with Sir James Clark Ross from 1839 to 1843 wrote of a requirement:

> 'which no foresight could provide for and no forethought guarantee; and that is, concord! The trials of social life on shipboard are proverbial; and, according to the early traditions of the naval service, a philosopher afloat used to be considered as unlucky a shipmate as a cat or a corpse.'

Successful cruises were made by Wyville Thomson and W. B. Carpenter in H.M.S. *Lightning* in 1868 and, together with Jeffreys, in H.M.S. *Porcupine* in 1869 but both vessels had hired crews who were perhaps less troubled by the early traditions of the naval service. In 1871 Carpenter sailed in *Shearwater* under Captain Nares, primarily to study the circulation at the Strait of Gibraltar. He had excellent co-operation from Nares, and from T. H. Tizard, the Navigating Lieutenant.

Carpenter had been discreetly promoting the idea of a circumnavigation since the 1869 *Porcupine* cruise. He had had some encouragement from Lowe, the Chancellor of the Exchequer, and from H.C.E. Childers, First Lord of the Admiralty, and one can be sure that the Hydrographer would be in favor of a circumnavigation which would prepare for cable laying to all the outposts of Empire. Scientific interest, military advantage, commercial application, national pride; everything needed for a successful grant application was in Carpenter's skilled hands. In May 1871 the Chancellor of the Exchequer was elected to the Royal Society and in June Carpenter asked the Royal Society to appoint a Committee to plan a voyage of marine exploration. By August the British Association had committed itself to

4. Burstyn, H. L. (1972). Pioneering in large-scale scientific organization: The *Challenger* Expedition and its Report. Launching the Expedition. *Proc. Roy. Soc. Edin.*, Section B 72, 47–61.

support a Circumnavigation Expedition, and by October Carpenter had extracted from the First Lord of the Admiralty (now George J. Goschen) a letter promising government support for such an expedition if the Royal Society asked for it. There was a formal exchange of correspondence, the Cabinet gave approval of what they thought a minor matter, and by 2 March 1872 the Expedition was officially on.

It was a considerable achievement, for the government of the day was as keen on accountability as our present one, yet less willing to support science for its own sake. In the Presidential Address to the Royal Society for 1875, for example:

'We must remember that it is not the policy of the Government of this country in its view of the present state of public feeling, . . . to give direct assistance to the study of any science except with a view to the more immediate application of scientific theories to practical purposes, in which the public rather than individuals have a direct interest. Whatever may be thought of the wisdom or soundness of this policy (and in the opinion of some eminent scientific men it is wise and sound), we must shape our course accordingly, doing our endeavour never to allow scientific investigation to be subordinated to practical results; but keeping it ever in advance, remembering too that the Government estimation of the value of scientific investigation is measured more by the amount of interest which it excites than by any standard of its own; whence it follows that the Government is not slow in encouraging researches that interest and instruct the public, whether or not they may be seen to lead to direct practical results.'

Throughout all the delicate negotiations the Hydrographer, like Hydrographers before and since, played a variety of roles. Advising their Lordships, serving on the Royal Society Council and the relevant Committees, keeping in touch with the cable-laying companies, choosing a ship and starting on the alterations and additions she would need. One imagines that Admiral Richards' was the hand on the controls, sometimes perhaps restraining the prickly egotistical Carpenter from going too fast too soon. It must have taken all the Hydrographer's tact to make Carpenter realize that he was not to sail as leader of the Expedition.

The leadership was offered to Wyville Thomson, an enthusiastic pioneer of deep-sea dredging, and the Hydrographer lost no time in appointing Nares to command and Tizard to navigate. There seems to have been little friction and Wyville Thomson was later to write:

'The somewhat critical experiment of associating a party of civilians, holding to a certain extent an independent position, with the naval staff of a man-of-war, has for once been successful'

and he notes that the officers called the scientists philosophers:

'not I fear from the proper feeling of respect, but rather with good-natured indulgence—because we are fond of talking about "evolution", and otherwise holding on to loose ropes; and because our education has been sadly neglected in the matter of cringles and toggles and grummets, and other implements by means of which England holds her place among the nations.'

The Royal Society drew up plans for the scientific side of the expedition and the Hydrographer coped with the logistics and issued sailing orders. *Challenger* commissioned on 15 November and on 7 December sailed from Sheerness for Portsmouth. She left Portsmouth, outward bound and to great public acclaim, on 21 December 1872.

Admiral Richards remarked that such an expedition had been the hope and dream of his life. Both in the organization of the *Challenger* Expedition and of the earlier cruises he had done great service to marine science but in 1874, long before the Expedition was over, he felt obliged to resign as Hydrographer because the post had been made a civilian appointment and he felt an active service officer was needed. He was immediately appointed Managing Director of the Telegraph Construction and Maintenance Company, which laid 76,000 miles of submarine cable under his direction (and later under his Chairmanship). After the Expedition he was thus able to provide ship time for J. Y. Buchanan, the *Challenger* chemist who could not get on with the Establishment of the time. After Richards died in 1896 W. J. L. W[harton] wrote . . .

'He was a man of great ability, of sound commonsense, and of untiring activity, and his unfailing good humour, general shrewdness and kindness to younger members of his profession caused him to be universally beloved and respected'.

Of the Expedition itself there are many accounts, several written by those who took part. From one of them[5] we take the following account of a typical station:

'From the hour of four o'clock in the morning, as soon as the watch has been mustered, the bustle and activity begin, lasting throughout the day and even to the hour when night reminds one of sleep. Pumps are manned, and water is splashed over decks in all directions; and, although apparently unnecessary at times, yet it is absolutely essential to the preservation of the health and comfort of those on board. By six o'clock the washing is nearly finished, when all hammocks are piped up and stowed; it is now time for breakfast consisting of cocoa and biscuit. The hands dress in the rig of the day, and all preparations are made for sounding and dredging. Sails are furled, and steam is ready, for it is essential to keep the vessel's head on to the sea during these operations.

'During the time of sounding and dredging, the ship's company not specially employed on these operations have been mustered at division, attended prayers, and engaged during the forenoon in their various and requisite duties. At noon, dinner is piped, and although consisting, as it usually does, of either salt junk and duff, or fat, greasy salt pork and pea soup, there are few men healthier than the sailor. Grog-time comes next (when half a gill of rum with two parts of water is supplied to each man), and, with the hour for smoking, constitutes a pleasant break in the day. Duty is resumed again at 1.30, and various drills occupy the afternoon until 4.30, when all hands assemble at their station, with rifle, cutlass and pistol, for inspection by their divisional officer.

'The inspection over (we will presume the dredge to be up, and the excitement of the haul subsided), 'Hands! make sail,' is the pipe. Steam is dispensed with, in a short time the sail is all spread, and with a favouring breeze we are running on our course at an eight-knot speed. Supper is now prepared, consisting of tea and biscuit, after which, until 9, smoking is permitted, hammocks having been piped down at 7.30. The commanding officer usually goes the round of the decks, to ascertain that all is correct, when those off duty are expected to turn-in their hammocks, and so ends the day and its duties.

'At 6 p.m. the officers usually dine together, when the incidents of the day, the results of the dredging, the prospect of the morrow, and other affairs which are sure to turn up, form a lively conversational hour. After dinner the assembly of smokers usually muster on the half-deck, where all sorts of yarns and topics engross the attention till bed-time.

'Sunday alone seems to break the monotony and routine of everyday life at sea, when, after divisions and prayers, the remainder of the day is usually spent in reading or sleeping.

'In this manner, and notwithstanding the continued sameness, days and months slip by, until we reach port and again anchor; and only when we look back over the work accomplished can we realize the length of time passed at sea.'

During this time the dredging and sounding party had made the following observations:

1. The exact depth was determined.
2. A sample of the bottom, averaging

5. Spry, W. J. J. (1884). *The Cruise of H.M.S. Challenger,* 10th edn. Sampson Low, Marston Searle & Rivington, London, pp. 319.

from one oz. to 1 lb. in weight, was recovered by means of the sounding instrument which was provided with a tube and disengaging weights.

3. A sample of the bottom water was procured for physical and chemical examination.
4. The bottom temperature was determined by a registering thermometer.
5. At most stations a fair sample of the bottom fauna was procured by means of the dredge or trawl.
6. At most stations the fauna of the surface and of intermediate depths was examined by the use of the townet variously adjusted.
7. At most stations a series of temperature observations were made at different depths from the surface to the bottom.
8. At many stations samples of sea water were obtained from different depths.
9. In all cases atmospheric and other meteorological conditions were carefully observed and noted.
10. The direction and rate of the surface current was determined.
11. At a few stations an attempt was made to ascertain the direction and rate of movement of the water at different depths.

Rope was used for the sounding (*Challenger* started with 20,000 fathoms of 1 inch line on board and had to send for 20,000 fathoms more). She carried wire too but didn't use it–probably Nares did not care to change a technique he knew to be satisfactory from his *Shearwater* days.

One would have to admit they were a bit conservative, but successful the methods certainly were; as station succeeded station both officers and scientists became somewhat bored by the constant repetition. Lord George Campbell, one of the deck officers, wrote in his *Log Letters:*

'Dredging, I may say without fear of contradiction, was our–the naval officers'–bête noire. The romance of deep-water trawling or dredging in the *Challenger,* when repeated several hundred times, was regarded from two points of view; the one was the naval officer's, who had to stand for ten to twelve hours at a stretch carrying on the work, and who, always excepting that he did not like his day's work to have been done in vain, did not know much about, or scientifically appreciate, the minute differences between one starfish, one shrimp, one sea-cucumber, one sea-urchin, and another. The other point of view was the naturalist's, to whom the whole cruise was a yachting expedition, who had not to carry on the practical working of the dredge, to whom some new worm, coral, or echinoderm is a joy forever, who retires to a comfortable cabin to describe with enthusiasm this new animal, which we, without much enthusiasm, and with much weariness of spirit, to the rumbling tune of the donkey-engine only, had dragged up for him from the bottom of the sea.'

But Lord George enjoyed going ashore and he seems to have taken every opportunity of doing so. Over a third of the time was spent in port (which the naturalists used to good purposes). But there was plenty of time for reading, sketching, painting, training a parrot, hunting cockroaches; even gambling for gin and bitters on whether a visible shore was 4 miles away or 6, and whether a new species would be taken in the dredge. One wonders about the odds given, for on average about 15 were taken per station.

The more successful the cruise the more uneventful and the more tedious. Everyone on board *Challenger* must have been glad, happy and justifiably proud when the ship anchored at Spithead on the Queen's Birthday, 24 May 1876. As with many oceanographic expeditions, the real work was just beginning.

There are many who find it difficult to support an enterprise but few who are not happy to share the proceeds; Wyville Thomson had to struggle against the British Museum, who wanted the whole collection rather than just the terrestrial items. And against many British scientists who resented specimens being given to those foreign scientists Wyville Thomson considered best qualified to study them.

He succeeded however and the *Challenger* office he created in Edinburgh can now be seen to be one of the most significant products of the Expedition. For there, in simply furnished rooms (more like a scullery than a laboratory, says Herdman[6]) Thomson created the first invisible college of marine science, a communications centre for marine scientists from all over the world. Notable among the visitors were the Scandinavian oceanographers who were to take up the *Challenger* gauntlet and become the leading marine scientists of the next few decades. Unfortunately Thomson did not live to appreciate the importance of the milieu he had created. Perhaps the circumnavigation had sapped his strength, certainly the administrative wrangles had not helped: he died in 1882, just before Tizard and John Murray in H.M.S. *Triton* verified his predictions about what is now called the Wyville Thomson Ridge. John Murray took over the direction of the work and the long task of supervising the preparation of the fifty large volumes which make up the *Challenger* Reports. It was to take him another thirteen years.

Anybody who has lived with the *Challenger* legend, with the fifty massive green volumes as a background in an often-used library, finds it hard to form a dispassionate view of what the voyage achieved. The biological objects of the cruise were certainly met. That there was life at all depths was fully confirmed; *Challenger* had scooped the pool so far as oceanic–mainly bottom living–organisms were concerned and there were vast numbers of new species to be described, named and classified. By 1890 all 32 of the Zoological Reports were out. The next year saw the publication of the Report on Deep Sea Deposits; Murray and Renard had founded the study of submarine geology. The distribution of oozes and clays, the way in which they were formed, the coral reef problem, all were authoritatively treated in studies that continue to be relevant today. Buchanan had been expelled from the *Challenger* circle by the Treasury, but superb work was done by Dittmar on salinity, on the minor constituents of sea water and on dissolved gases.

By 1895 all fifty Reports were out; it had taken much longer than the financial authorities thought reasonable but the amount of work was immense and there were few previous studies to guide it. A scientific administrator less able and energetic than Murray might well have lost control of such a huge project. In the event the *Challenger* Expedition had magnificently justified the faith that many had put in it. There was only one serious gap–the physics of the sea had been relatively neglected. None of the scientific staff was a physicist and the observations had been left to the ship's officers, to whom they were an extra obligation. Perhaps the technology of the day was not quite ready, perhaps the problem was just too complicated. Whatever the reason, it was left to German scientists, decades later, to make good use of the temperature and density observations. The last *Challenger* Report contains a sad woodcut of the ship, then a coaling hulk at Sheerness. She was finally sold for scrap in 1921.

British marine science proved relatively static after the *Challenger* Expedition. The public had lost interest during the voyage, presumably finding it a bit slow. Murray himself urged Antarctic exploration and it was the heroes of the polar expeditions who made the headlines in the early decades of the twentieth century. The biologists turned to studying live animals in near-shore institutes like the Marine Biological Association at Plymouth and the Scottish Marine Biological Association at Millport. The few physicists there employed their time trying to help fisheries research. The catastrophe of the *Titanic* almost led to a new start when D. J. Matthews and G. I. Taylor went out in the *Scotia* to study the formation of ice and

6. Herdman, W. A. (1923). *Founders of Oceanography.* Arnold & Co., London, pp. 340.

fog, but the war intervened. The 1914-18 war was not such as to need much knowledge of the ocean; there was a submarine menace but the purely defensive convoy system was adequate to cope with it.

So the next H.M.S. *Challenger,* a cruiser of 5880 tons launched in 1902, was in commission at a time when the United Kingdom was relatively inactive in deep-sea science. She gained battle honors in the Cameroons and Zanzibar before she was sold in 1920.

It was during the life of the most recent H.M.S. *Challenger* (launched at Chatham in 1931) that Marine Science, both in the United Kingdom and abroad, became reactivated. She was originally intended as a fishery research vessel but funds ran out. She was commissioned as a survey ship; she saw service during the time when oceanography developed at a fantastic rate. During the Second World War the importance of what is now called military oceanography rapidly became apparent. There was a need to detect submarines but insufficient knowledge of underwater sound; there was a need to land men on beaches but not much known about ocean waves; there was a need to deal with magnetic mines but little information about the magnetic fields of ships. Useful advances were stimulated in all these subjects.

It was a rapidly changing situation: one of this *Challenger*'s captains has recently remarked that when he started in the Hydrographic Service in 1936 there was little connection between science and hydrology, and that we had lost something that we had in the nineteenth century. Fortunately he found himself in command of *Challenger* on a world voyage with scientists on board, and since that time has almost always contrived to have scientists in ships under his command. Nowadays, I am happy to say, there are many captains of survey ships who are ready and willing to take the modern philosophers to study the sea.

It is just twenty years since that H.M.S. *Challenger* reached Portsmouth from her circumnavigation. During her time at sea there were several Hydrographers of the Navy, but I have time to refer to only one of them, Admiral J. A. Edgell, K.B.E., C.B., F.R.S., who served from 1932 to 1945. A man whose first survey ship was *Triton* could hardly be disinterested in marine science and Admiral Edgell did much to encourage it, not only as Hydrographer of the Navy but as Chairman of a Royal Society Committee on Oceanography and in many other groups. He it was who brought to the Scientific Advisory Council of the War Cabinet in 1944 the proposal that plans be made for the post-war formation of a National Institute of Oceanography, with its own deep-sea research vessel. He became chairman of a small group who planned for peace-time marine science while the V bombs were still falling.

To him and to his equally farsighted contemporaries we owe much of the post-war resurgence in this country's physical oceanography. Edgell himself served on the National Oceanographic Council until he died and he helped Sir George Deacon build an international reputation for the Institute and its ships, the Royal Research Ships *Discovery II* and *Discovery.* Many of us remember kindly the personal interest he took, his efficiency with an ear trumpet and his fund of sea stories. We had a lot of time for a man who was willing to go to sea in the North Atlantic on board *Discovery II* at the age of 72.

Since H.M.S. *Challenger* paid off in 1954, progress has been even faster. Nowadays oceanographers have much improved equipment; computers, satellite navigators and temperature-salinity-depth recorders are the sort of gear that is taken for granted. The way in which the research is done has changed too. Long expeditions are rare; the work is intensive rather than extensive, with short cruises designed to check a particular hypothesis or test a promising theory. But in spite of the increased effort we are still very ignorant of the way in which the ocean works and how its biological populations are maintained. We still need enthusiastic scientists and well found ships with co-operative officers and crew. The *Challenger* legend certainly helps and I am glad I can end by paying a brief compliment to two closely-related vessels. One is our rich American cousin *Glomar Challenger,* the deep-drilling ship which is providing new knowledge about the Earth's crust under the ocean.

The second is more one of the family—the Royal Research Ship *Challenger* which is now fitting out on the Clyde. She will be mainly used by scientists of the Scottish Marine Biological Association, whose origins are closely connected with John Murray of *Challenger* Expedition fame. I am confident she will be worthy of her famous name.

# 3. Hydrographic Surveying

ANTHONY G. STEPHENSON 1970

Hydrography encompasses the detailed examination and recording of every body of water–its depth and movement, bottom and sub-bottom, shoreline configuration, and navigational hazards–for reproduction on charts and in tables.

The original hydrographic surveyors were the navigators who discovered new lands, for, wherever they went, they recorded depths, channels, dangers, and coastline details to help assure that future passages would be safer. Each successive ship's captain entering an area added to the information on his chart and wrote a narrative known as the "Pilot." Since that time charts have been updated continually and the Pilot is amended by a periodic circular known as the "Notice to Mariners," which is in part based on the reports of modern navigators.

Government hydrographic departments date back to the early 19th Century and have developed most of the world charts in use today. In the last fifteen years, however, as industry and commerce moved rapidly into the marine environment, there has been a strong call for contract hydrographic surveys to undertake detailed work at specific developing locations.

The hydrographer's expertise encompasses an almost confounding breadth, requiring him to change roles from surveyor to mathematician, from navigator to electronic technician, and at times, from workhorse to diplomat. The fundamental requirement is a thorough grounding in land survey techniques. In land surveying, the problems vary with the terrain (submerged or exposed), but a hydrographic surveyor, whose work may take him to any part of the world, has to be prepared to combat differing environmental difficulties in a variety that his shorebound counterpart rarely encounters. Hydrographic surveying lays heavy stress on versatility, requiring a man to be as adept at mountain climbing as at navigation and drafting.

The first requirement on any hydrographic survey is to locate the vessel accurately (and continuously); it is equally important to be able to relocate an exact position where there are no buoys or beacons to mark the point. There are a variety of methods of "fixing" (locating) a survey boat–

Anthony G. Stephenson, a hydrographer with Decca Survey Systems, Inc., Houston, Texas, emigrated to the United States from Great Britain in 1963. He has conducted hydrographic surveys for port and harbor development, pipeline location, and water pollution studies throughout the world.

From *Oceanology International,* Vol. 5, No. 6, pp. 35-37, 1970. Reprinted with light editing and by permission of the author and *Oceanology International*.

some recent, some traditional. In all cases the designed precision of instrumentation dictates the accuracy obtainable.

Visual methods have their restrictions, but in many instances prove the most effective for economic reasons and, sometimes, even more accurate than more sophisticated alternatives (dependent on location). Triangulation is one method of visual fixing. It calls for setting up two theodolites on shore with the azimuth and distance between them known, and sighting out to the boat's mast. Both instrument operators, at a signal from the boat, observe the angles. Knowing the baseline distance and measuring the two included angles, they can calculate the boat's position. This method is seldom satisfactory, however; in most cases it covers a limited area, and the fact that the fixing team is separated, requiring long-range coordination, contributes to delays and inaccuracies.

A more satisfactory visual method is to use hydrographic sextants. Sextants for hydrographic work are specially designed, can measure larger angles, are lighter, and have a larger field of view than the navigational type. The method involves the observation from the boat of three well-defined marks on shore whose coordinates are known. Two sextant operators simultaneously observe the two angles between the left and center, center and right marks.

The resultant fix is in the form of a three-point problem, mathematically tedious to solve but graphically simple and quick with the aid of an instrument called a station pointer. It is a precise three-arm protractor that reads to a minute of arc. The two observed angles are applied to the station pointer and the arms moved to intersect the three coordinate points on the sounding chart. The intersection of the three arms is the boat's position. Experienced men can take the fix and plot position in only 10 to 15 seconds. The fact that all people concerned with obtaining the fix are in the boat permits excellent coordination, enabling the survey boat to operate without a shore party.

In areas of considerable habitation, conspicuous marks on shore have usually been surveyed previously. This land survey work frees the hydrographer to change marks frequently and still obtain good fixes without the tedium of onshore control surveying.

There are other variations in the use of a sextant; one important one is steering along an arc of a sextant angle, using the geometric principle that the angle subtended by a chord at the circumference of the circle remains constant. The survey party draws up a plotting sheet with the known marks located and swings arcs from two of the marks across the survey area at the required spacing, and notes the subtended angle. Because the line is an arc, it is preferable to keep the subtended angle as large as possible. (Fitting a 90-deg prism to the hydrographic sextant enables reading angles of up to 210 deg.) The sextant is set to the predetermined angle and the boat conned along the arc; another observer sights a second angle to locate the boat's position on the arc.

Visual methods, though sound, are restricted to near shore, under good visibility in daylight hours. In recent years the demand has been great for accurate fixes far offshore, not limited by visibility or darkness. To accommodate these requirements, electronic positioning systems were introduced into hydrography. These enable not only positions to be located accurately well out of sight of land, but in some cases can be used also to guide a vessel along predetermined lines in any direction and at any required spacing and also to return the vessel to spot or rerun a line in the future. The accuracy of these systems is dependent on range, baseline locations, survey accuracy of the onshore transmitting stations, unobstructed paths between shore stations and the ship, and weather conditions. The trained surveyor knows these factors well and either eliminates them or takes them into careful account by adjusting accordingly.

Not all systems on the market are the same, and what is advantageous for some surveys can be disadvantageous for others. There are a variety of systems, some accurate but limited to line-of-sight work and others less accurate but usable over much greater distances.

The modes in which one can use some of the systems create different lane patterns, known as hyperbolic and range-range. The hyperbolic mode requires three onshore stations and creates a hyperbolic pattern radiating from them. In this mode more than one vessel may use the system, but the area of high accuracy coverage is limited by the expansion of the reference lanes. The same instrumentation may be used in the range-range mode for good accuracy over a larger area because there is no lane expansion, but is limited to the use of one vessel. It takes a trained hydrographic surveyor to evaluate all systems and modes to ensure the most accurate and economic results for the survey in question.

Deriving a fix for a vessel at sea, important as it is to the hydrographic survey, is only a locational tool. To help the hydrographer collect other desired data, instrumentation has been modernized and developed. The echo sounder gives precise depths acoustically and has been developed in several variations, all aiming at different requirements. Some, for example, plumb great depths but forfeit accuracy in shallow water. Thought has to be given to the type of vessel to be used, results required, portability, and so on. Many modern depth recorders use a linear scale giving a true graphic "picture" of the seabed. Earlier models used a rotating arm that swung across the paper in an arc that distorted the record. Nonetheless, some models of this kind are more accurate than the newer, straight-line recorders whose manufacturers apparently have not understood the real requirements of the hydrographer.

Echo sounder record paper that has a scale preprinted on it illustrates this lack of understanding of hydrographic work. The hydrographer has to make a tidal reduction on the record to reduce soundings to datum, hence, the printed scale is much less useful than might be thought. Also some echo sounders show little thought to ease of calibration to allow for variation in salinity and temperature. To eliminate a man standing by the instrument to record each fix, a remote event marker switch is a very good feature. Time interval marks, available on some machines, help to correlate tidal information from one or more tidal gauges located close to the area of sounding.

With the rapid increase in ship sizes and drafts, navigational surveys have assumed great importance. With many ports unable to accomodate the huge new ships, new deep water terminals have to be found. Offshore loading and unloading in some areas are essential but expensive. Such facilities require very careful surveys to bring the ship terminal as close to shore as safety permits (perhaps leaving barely a foot beneath the keel of the largest ship at the low-water spring tides) and ensure an area swept of all obstructions.

Instruments such as the side-scanning sonar help locate obstructions between the actual lines of soundings. This instrument sends a narrow horizontal but broad vertical acoustical beam that scans the seabed at right angles to the vessel's track. Undulations, outcrops, or other hazards appear in the record; the strong signal return off the vertical face of an object shows as a black mark on the record, and the total loss of the returning sound on the far side of the object shows as a white shadow.

With the simultaneous use of the echo sounder, side-scanning sonar, and accurate fixing, it is feasible to sweep for obstructions acoustically, but there are other methods. Two boats linked by a thin wire that passes through two streamlined sinkers and attaches to both boats can sweep to a required depth if handled properly. One end of the fine wire is secured to one boat and the other to a winch in the control boat. By the two boats keeping some 200 to 300 feet apart with a winch operator keeping tension on the wire, they can clear the area between them. To ensure complete coverage of the area, it is usual to run a 50 per cent overlap to each side of the swept path, in effect, sweeping the area twice. Attaching a depth meter to each weight provides a method for monitoring the exact depth of the wire.

The oil industry and engineers involved in offshore construction have an ever-increasing need for knowledge of shallow sub-bottom geologic variations. There are instruments that record shallow sub-seabed stratification with high definition, graphically displaying a continuous profile of the geologic stratification. Typical projects requiring this type of survey are offshore drilling platform footings, underwater tunnels, placing piles for a pier, and pipeline routes.

To obtain absolute knowledge of the variation of the strata, it has been essential to drill core holes. Coring gives discontinuous (spot) indications of changes—comparable to taking lead line soundings—not a continuous record such as a precision depth recorder obtains. With the sub-bottom profiler a few reference core holes suffice to identify the changes in strata evident on the profiler record; beyond these baseline samples, changes in the geologic structure can then be charted on the recorder's continuous profile. For surveying pipeline and tunnel routes, this instrumentation is invaluable, virtually eliminating needless encounters with underlying rock and inadequately consolidated sedimentation.

Another use for the sub-bottom profiler is offshore exploration for minerals. Irregularities in the bedrock can create traps that may hold, in highly mineralized areas, many precious metals. Large enough deposits may be minable at a profit.

Extensive sub-bottom surveying can locate these traps, and core samples can determine their probable values. A mineral survey is conducted in much the same manner as a navigational survey, but here bedrock and overburden as well as the seabed are mapped. The likely extent and volume of mineralization can accurately be determined by this method. In contrast, this type of work, done by arbitrary core sampling, is not only extremely expensive but inconclusive.

In these applications the surveyor must choose the correct acoustic transmission frequency, since penetration varies inversely with frequency but definition varies directly with it and both factors depend on the type of sedimentation to be penetrated. The hydrographer must weigh all the requirements before selecting which type of system to use.

Dredging is another industry that has always required hydrographic surveys, and, as ship size increases, exact determination of channel depth becomes more essential. A survey is undertaken before dredging, to determine the volume of excavation. This estimate must be reasonably accurate because a dredging contractor usually bids on the total volume to be removed, and incorrect estimates lead to contractual difficulties. Simultaneous sub-bottom and echo-sounding profiles can locate underlying rock or something that could damage the dredge or affect the dredging time. A post-dredging survey ensures that the area has been completely dredged and protects the client from needless costs of overdredging. The side-scanning sonar finds a role in post-dredging operations to reveal undredged peaks and locate any slumping of channel walls into the navigable water lane. It is an advantage to know how often a channel need be dredged and what area can best receive the spoil. Hydrographic studies using silt samples and current measurements can reveal the likely effects. These same methods are useful in the study of coastal erosion and accretion, important factors in the preservation of coastlines.

Movements of currents and tidal streams have been measured for many years, but the increasing problem of water pollution has imparted a new emphasis. Few studies to determine the effects of the effluent on marine life and human recreation have preceded the installations of outfalls. The assumption that dispersion of an effluent in a much larger body of water will be adequate may or may not prove out. A hydrographic survey can spell the difference, but surveys have usually followed installation, after the damage has been done.

The approach to this type of survey is largely dependent on the type of effluent and the area of discharge. Generally two methods are used. Variations of the water movement can be determined with a current meter by measuring flow velocity and direction at different depths. Such studies can reveal the optimum elevation for an outfall pipe to ensure placement in the maximum current to carry the effluent away with the minimum period of slack water. The next step is to find where and how far the water carries the effluent and whether it carries ashore, concentrates, or disperses. This is achieved by tidal stream studies, usually performed with floats having large vanes extending down to the depth of the discharge. The stream carries the floats away until the tide changes, then carries them back. By observing the direction and velocity of float movements through all states of the tide, it is possible to obtain a very good idea of the dispersal rates over the area.

For thermal discharge studies, similar methods apply, supplemented by temperature surveying. Reasonable results have been obtained with dye discharged into the water at the outfall, which remains visible for one tidal cycle. These studies can also determine if hot water outfall is likely to return to a cooling water intake—of help to power station design.

The types of hydrographic surveys described in this article fulfill basic requirements using fundamental methods. The rapid advancement in computer technology and growth of solid state electronics continue to shrink time requirements and increase accuracies. There are now such innovations as digital echo sounders that can read depths into a shipboard computer for printout onto a chart at the correct location—all while surveying at 30 knots. Or automatic pilots that accept radio fix signals and maintain a vessel along an exact preplotted track. Satellite positioning (in conjunction with other systems) makes possible hydrographic surveys in the deep ocean to an accuracy previously only obtainable no more than 300 miles from land. Although still not as precise as using shore-based stations, the method has opened up the avenues to more accurate knowledge of the oceans.

Pollution studies are also advancing, thanks to digitized computer inputs from continuous reading sensors that monitor dissolved oxygen, salinity, turbidity, temperature, and current velocity and direction. All of these steps help the hydrographer to obtain greater amounts of data in a shorter time and in some cases at a lower cost than do the conventional methods.

Though the instrumental advances in data collection are many, only the correct selection of instrument and procedure can create a meaningful result. Basic data usually require correction, editing, and analysis before presentation in cartographic or tabular format for the client. Throughout these stages the hydrographer ensures that the required accuracy is achieved and that this accuracy is achieved at minimum cost to the client. The client, who is interested in minimum overall cost rather than the minimum daily rate, is coming to realize that, in the oceanographic field as in many others, professional advice pays.

# 4. Aerospace Remote Sensing Oceanography

JOHN W. SHERMAN III 1973

## INTRODUCTION

The use of aircraft and spacecraft instruments to observe the atmosphere and the earth's surface has become known as remote sensing. The best example of this technique relates to meteorology, although current research is directed toward applying remote sensing techniques to agriculture and forestry, hydrology, geology, pollution, cartography, land use, geography, and oceanography. Next to meteorology, oceanography potentially stands to realize the greatest benefit from satellite observation systems, because of the immense extent of the ocean's surface.

The purpose of this paper is to provide a status report on the application of remote sensing techniques to oceanography. There are four basic ocean parameters that can be measured from space: surface wind and topography, surface temperature, sea ice, and ocean color. These space measured ocean parameters can be related to ocean dynamics, biological activity, sea ice, and coastal processes, four general discipline areas that form the basis for the outline of this paper. Each discipline area may have several components. For example, ocean dynamics includes the measurement of phenomena related to surface roughness, winds, temperature, and topography, as well as circulation and water-mass identification. Environmental assessments made for the benefit of fisheries may require combinations of discipline areas, in particular those of ocean dynamics and biological activity.

An abbreviated overview of space-measured ocean features may be found in Sherman (1972), and a more detailed summary in Hanson (1972). The most current compilation of many specific areas of remote sensing ocean research is contained in NASA (1972). The use of buoys with telemetry to satellites can provide detailed surface and subsurface data beyond the capabilities of remote sensors. Such buoy systems will not be addressed in this review, but these systems could become an integral part of a total ocean monitoring system.

John W. Sherman III is with the Spacecraft Oceanography Group of the National Environmental Satellite Service, NOAA, Rockville, Maryland.

From *Environmental Data Service*, September, 1973, pp. 3-12. Reprinted with light editing and with permission of the author and *Environmental Data Service*. A longer version of this article was presented as a paper at the Seventh Session of the Working Group on International Oceanographic Data Exchange of the Intergovernmental Oceanographic Commission, July 9-13, 1973, United Nations Headquarters, New York, New York.

## CONSIDERATIONS IN REMOTE SENSING OCEANOGRAPHY

The detail of data collected by aircraft is not as precise as that collected by a surface vessel. Similarly, spacecraft collect data that are restricted to surface and near-surface features; fortunately, this surface region is the most dynamic portion of the ocean and requires the most frequent observation.

The "freezing" of the ocean surface in near real-time on synoptic scales may be accomplished by remote sensors so that temporal coverage appropriate for the dynamic feature under observation may be accomplished. This aspect is not always possible in the conventional surface approach unless a large array of vessels or buoys is deployed. However, aerospace technology does not replace conventional data collection techniques, which are continually being improved. The ideal is a systems approach combining and coordinating the virtues of surface and aerospace data-collection platforms.

An important consideration in the use of remote sensors in oceanography is that the single parameter which might be sought generally cannot be isolated from other environmental features. As an example, measuring chlorophyll concentration *in situ* is a relatively straightforward procedure. To determine the chlorophyll concentration with a remote sensor requires the analysis and interpretation of surface roughness, sun angle, cloud cover and atmospheric conditions, bottom type in shallow water, and other water components such as suspended sediments.

There are two properties of the interaction of electromagnetic energy with the ocean surface that must be considered in the application of remote sensors to the oceans. These are the roughness features of the ocean surface and the penetration of electromagnetic energy into water.

The surface of the ocean is highly variable. It can be mirror-smooth, acting as a specular reflector under very calm conditions or, when driven by high surface winds for extended periods, it can be an extremely dangerous mass of white water, diffusely scattering electromagnetic energy. These features may be used to advantage in developing remote sensing techniques for the measurement of sea state and surface windfields. On the other hand, this variation and complexity complicates the measurement of ocean color or the determination of sea-surface temperature by a microwave sensor.

Microwave sensors are important in aerospace remote sensing because microwave energy is less attenuated (absorbed and scattered) by clouds than electromagnetic energy in the visible or thermal regions of the spectrum. Such instruments are generally regarded as having "all-weather" capability, that is, they can observe the surface both at night and through cloud cover. The all-weather feature is important because turbulent surface conditions are often accompanied by storm and cloud systems that must be penetrated for surface measurements. Thus, analysis of glitter pattern from visible-region remote sensors permits measurement of surface roughness in cloud-free areas, but either active or passive microwave sensors are needed to make meaningful operational measurements in cloudy weather. The sea-surface temperature can be determined by microwave sensors only after roughness is measured.

The penetration of electromagnetic energy into seawater itself affects the choice of remote sensors for specific applications. In pure seawater, the skin depth (the distance through which the incoming energy is attenuated by $1/\epsilon$ from its original value) at a wavelength of 10cm (3GHz frequency) is about 1 cm; at 10$\mu$m (millionth of a meter) wavelength the skin depth is about 10$\mu$m, and in the blue-green portion of the visible spectrum (0.4 to 0.6 $\mu$m) the skin depth is about 10 to 30 meters. Thus, remote sensing observations from aircraft and spacecraft view either surface or near-surface features.

Within the blue-green portion of the spectrum, the attenuation of light changes as the type of seawater changes. Mean oceanic water and distilled water are optically similar. Changing from mean oceanic water to coastal water increases the optical attenuation, and the region of maximum energy penetration shifts from the blue to the green. Scattering and absorption by matter in the water is primarily responsible for the color of ocean water. Appropriate spectral analysis of the light coming from the ocean can indicate the water's near-surface properties (to depths of no more than 100 meters). All other remote sensor observations, which utilize a portion of electromagnetic spectrum different from the visible region, are constrained to the surface itself.

## STATUS OF REMOTE SENSING IN OCEANOGRAPHY

To date no spacecraft remote sensors have been designed specifically to acquire oceanographic data. However, several sensors on space platforms continue to provide valuable information about the ocean and its interaction with the atmosphere. There are also a number of instruments designed to improve the observation of ocean features currently operational in aircraft. This section will describe some of the capabilities of remote sensors in monitoring ocean dynamics, biological activity, sea ice, and coastal processes.

### Ocean Dynamics

The ocean surface exhibits topographic and thermal features that extend over a wide range of horizontal and vertical scales and vary in both time and space. Topographic changes arise chiefly from geoidal features, seismic events, geostrophic currents, and atmospheric forcing. Thermal features are closely associated with differing water masses whose origin, under certain conditions, may be related to those mechanisms responsible for the surface undulations.

#### 1. Sea-Surface Temperature

Knowledge of the sea-surface temperature distribution over large areas is important in the detection and monitoring of ocean currents, upwelling zones, sea-air interactions, and in water mass identification. Since 1970, operational meteorological satellites have been carrying high-resolution, infrared-imaging radiometers. These imagers are used primarily to map night-time cloud cover and to estimate cloud heights. Where there are no clouds in the field-of-view of the satellite, these instruments effectively sense the temperature of the earth's surface. A number of studies (Curtis and Rao 1969; Rao, Smith, and Koffler 1972; and Rao, Strong and Koffler 1971) have been published showing that horizontal sea-surface temperature distributions can be obtained from these infrared measurements. The Very High Resolution Radiometer (VHRR) of the NOAA-2 operational meteorological satellite represents an increase in capability, and this instrument provides a 1-km spatial resolution and thermal sensitivity of ±1.0°C. Complete global distribution of sea-surface temperature has been achieved using the ITOS-1 satellite thermal scanner (Rao, Smith, and Koffler 1972). This instrument is similar to the NOAA-2 VHRR, but has less spatial resolution (7 km). A comparison between the satellite-derived temperature and ship measurements gives a difference of 1.8°C.

#### 2. Ocean Currents

Ocean currents can also be mapped using the temperature differences between currents and surrounding waters (Curtis and Rao 1969; Maul and Hansen 1972; and Rao, Strong and Koffler 1971), as well as other differences in the environment of the current system. While the improved thermal sensors on the Nimbus-5 and NOAA-2 satellites are providing ever-increasing detail for currents such as the Gulf Stream, including its meanders and cyclonic eddies, the two channels of the NOAA-2 instrument permit contiguous data recording in both the thermal region (10.5 to 12.5 μm) and visible region (0.6 to 0.7 μm) of the spectrum.

In principle, when a surface wind moves differentially with respect to the ocean current direction, the capillary wave structure should be different than if the current were static. As an example, an opposite movement of wind velocity with respect to current velocity would increase the capillary structure. This is shown on the left side of Figure 4-1. The visible channel of the NOAA-2 VHRR was able to map the boundary of the Gulf Stream because of the increased capillary waves on the moving Gulf Stream that counter a surface wind from the northeast. The sun angle was such that the

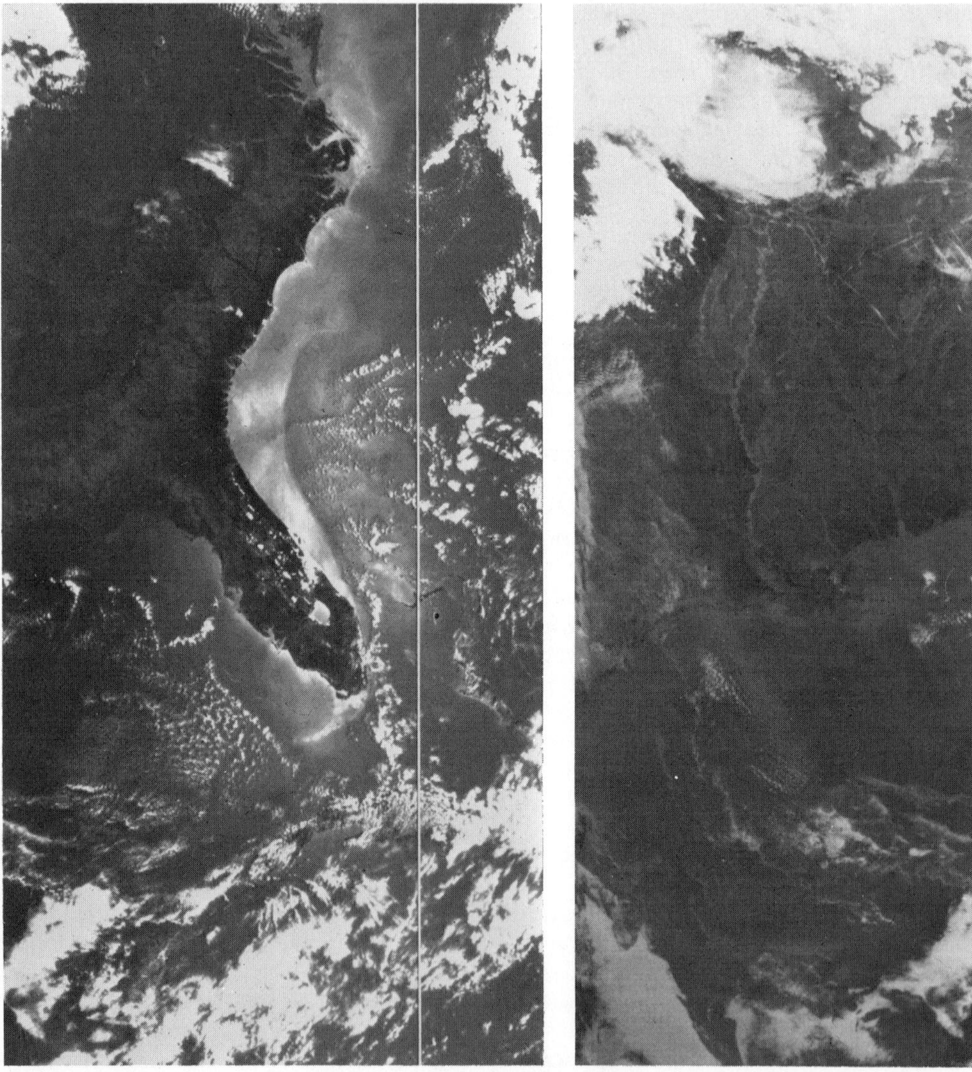

Figure 4-1. NOAA-2 very high resolution radiometer (VHRR) image of the Gulf Stream using the visible (left) and infrared channels. Note Stream directional changes off the Carolinas. Photograph courtesy of Alan Strong, NESS.

coastal waters more specularly reflected the sun into the radiometer, giving these waters increased brightness. The increased capillary structure on the Gulf Stream produced a more diffuse scatter, hence the stream appeared darker. It is postulated that radar imaging systems in space could also detect and map currents based on this same principle, without requiring the critical coupling between satellite orbit and sun angle.

### 3. Sea-Surface Topography

The identifiable causes of changes in ocean surface topography are (in approximate order of decreasing horizontal dimension, with their typical vertical scales): departures of the marine geoid from the reference ellipsoid (50m); earth and ocean tides (1m); wind setups against shorelines (1m); inverse barometric effects (25cm); tsunamis (50cm); storm surges (4m); slopes due to geostrophic currents (50cm); wind-generated gravity waves (1m, but quite variable); and wind-generated capillary waves (1cm).

A system for measuring the horizontal and vertical topographic components of the sea surface would allow observations of important physical characteristics of the ocean. At least five instruments appear capable of making certain of these measurements, and, as a sensor ensemble, potentially all necessary observations. The five instruments are all microwave devices and include multifrequency radiometers, scatterometers, short-pulse, high-precision altimeters, bistatic transmitter/receiver systems, and imaging radars. The latter four are considered active, in that energy is transmitted by the devices. All five instruments are considered to be all-weather. Apel (1972) describes the potential of these microwave instruments.

As an example, the scatterometers considered for space are low-resolution radar systems without ranging capability. The energy transmitted by the scatterometer is reflected by the ocean surface in a manner dependent on the angle of incidence, but most importantly, on the sea-state and surface wind conditions. Generally, the backscattered energy increases as sea-state and surface wind values increase. There have been difficulties in interpreting radar-type data at higher values, however, with evidence that the radar backscatter does not continue to increase indefinitely with wind and sea state. The SKYLAB spacecraft with its cameras, radiometers, scatterometer, and altimeter made a pass over Hurricane Ava in early June. Windfield measurements within this hurricane ranged from about 8 meters per second (15 knots) to about 60 meters per second (133 knots). Significant wave height observations ranged to values as large as 15 meters. This particular SKYLAB pass may be one of the most important missions yet conducted to study the interaction of electromagnetic energy with the sea surface.

### 4. Internal Waves

Of unique interest are internal waves that are detectable by remote sensors because of convergence of natural slicks at the surface or material trapped between layers of different density. The slicks suppress capillary wave action, hence they may be detected in the same manner as the observation of the Gulf Stream discussed earlier. Internal waves have been detected from aircraft and it appears that the Earth Resources Technology Satellite (ERTS-1) is imaging internal waves.

## Biological Activity

The only known means by which remote sensors can obtain data on biological activity is through the observation of ocean color. The color of sea water is determined primarily by nutrients, plankton, suspended sediment, pollutants, and often by bottom type and water depth in shallow areas. Other environmental factors such as atmospheric conditions, surface winds, and sun angle also influence the measurements of color. While many color observations have been made using photography and ERTS-1 scanners, the instruments needed to make color measurements suited for ocean applications are only now being deployed on aircraft. These ocean color scanners are multiple channel, high-spectral resolution (7 to 15 nm), and operate in the 400- to 700-nm region (the visible spectrum).

Once the immediate coastal vicinity is excluded, the major component of ocean color is the chlorophyll contained in all forms of phytoplankton, with chlorophyll-a being the dominant component (Duntley 1972). The ability to detect and quantitatively measure chlorophyll is believed to be essential to understanding the cycle of life in the world's oceans. Such measurements on a global basis eventually could provide estimates of the productivity of the oceans and aid in preservation of "livestock" in the seas.

Remote sensors to study chlorophyll in the oceans will be of a different character than those developed to measure the chlorophyll content of land plants. Chlorophyll has a very high reflectance in the near-infrared region (about 0.72 to 1.0 $\mu$m), hence healthy chlorophyll shows a brilliant red color in infrared terrain photography. The same technique applied to the ocean will detect only surface chlorophyll (in the upper tens of centimeters). The detection of kelp beds and surface algae is an application of such photography. Many ocean plants, however, grow at depths on the order of tens of meters, where near-infrared energy is readily absorbed by water, thus masking the high chlorophyll reflectance.

The detection of chlorophyll beneath the ocean surface is accomplished by using the strong absorption band in the blue region from about 0.42 to 0.46 $\mu$m. As the chlorophyll concentration increases, the upwelled energy in the blue decreases, while a slight increase in relative reflectance occurs in the green portion of the spectrum, with a "hinge point" at about 0.52 $\mu$m that is insensitive to chlorophyll concentration. Absorption in the blue rather than reflectance in the red is being utilized to develop an ocean color system to measure ocean plant resources (Figure 4-2).

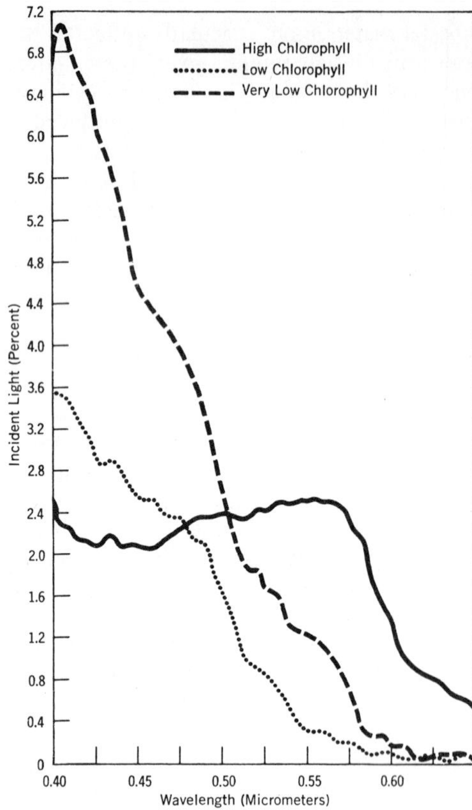


Figure 4-2. Relative energy reflected from sea indicates amount of chlorophyll.

Other forms of biological activity may also be monitored, at least from aircraft, and used for immediate application. The development of night vision devices has made possible the observation of bioluminescent features in the ocean not detectable by the unaided human eye. Many organisms in the ocean will emit light when mechanically, electrically, or acoustically excited, with peak intensity usually around 480 $\mu$m. Low-light-level image intensification devices have been used to locate fish and fish schools at night with very successful results (Stevenson 1972). The fish themselves are not the source of light energy, but rather excite organisms in the water to radiate. Controlled experiments from aircraft have shown that anchovies, euphausid shrimp, menhaden, and

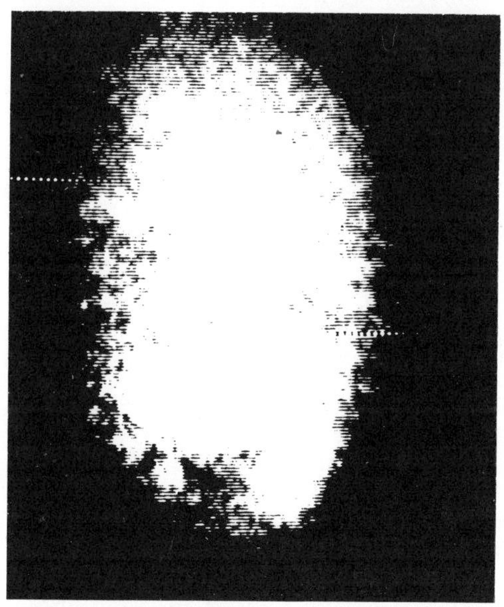

Figure 4-3. Low light level television image of bioluminescence induced by schooling fish. Photograph courtesy of NASA.

sauries can be detected and imaged in a system using a video recorder and display. The commercial potential of this technique may be developed by the fishing industry, utilizing a direct view system to assist in the location and concentration of fish from both ships and aircraft (Figure 4-3).

## Sea Ice

The Arctic and Antarctica are covered with ice, the former with a dynamic ice canopy that reaches thicknesses on the order of 3 to 5 meters, and the latter with a relatively static ice crust covering the continent with ice up to hundreds of meters thick. Ice in the dynamic North Pole region may move as much as 75 km a day, whereas only in the seas which surround Antarctica is there major ice movement at the South Pole. All such ice movement threatens transportation and also affects the atmospheric heat exchange in these regions.

Because of the dynamic nature of the Polar Regions, the lack of year-round illumination, and the prevalence of clouds and fog, microwave sensors are under development to permit the continuous, all-weather observation of ice conditions. These sensors include both active and passive imagers on both aircraft and spacecraft. The latter type was most successful on the Nimbus-5 spacecraft, which carried an electronically scanned microwave radiometer operating at 19.4 GHz (1.55 cm wavelength). The instantaneous field of view of this device is about 22 km, sufficient to see long linear features of ice/water boundaries of about 2 to 5 km width.

Such boundaries are readily determined by microwave sensors because ice has a much higher emissivity than water, although the exact value of this and other properties vary with age and past history. At microwave frequencies the emissivity of ice is about 0.8 to 0.95, and that of water about 0.3 to 0.4. Contrast between ice and water is therefore very high, and passive radiometry can easily be applied to all-weather ice surveillance, though with low spatial resolution (Alishouse, Baker, McClain, and Yates 1971).

Aircraft observations of sea ice at both 10.69 GHz (2.8 cm wavelength) and 19.4 GHz (1.55 cm wavelength) were acquired by NASA during the 1971 and 1972 initial and pilot study phases of the Arctic Ice Dynamics Joint Experiment (AIDJEX) (Campbell and Wilheit, in press). These studies demonstrated that the relative age of ice may be observed and mapped adequately by microwave sensing, regardless of cloud cover. Further improvement in contrast and spatial resolution of images is anticipated for the Nimbus-F spacecraft.

As noted, microwave sensors overcome both cloud conditions and lack of illumination. Thermal infrared sensors are handicapped by clouds, but not by illumination, since these sensors detect the heat radiated by the earth. Water is distinguished from ice primarily because of thermal difference. Hence, ice conditions may be monitored during the polar regions' dark winters and on the Great Lakes using such imagers as the thermal scanner on Nimbus-5 and the Very High Resolution Radiometer (VHRR) on NOAA-2, thus bringing the ocean community one step closer to an operational ice monitoring system.

### Coastal Processes

The general study of coastal marine processes includes: shoal and coastal mapping; large-lake phenomena; physical interaction between ocean, coastal, and river-induced current systems; prevailing climatological conditions; rotation of the Earth about its axis; gravitational effects of the moon and sun; and the effects of man's activities. In addition, coastal marine processes may also be extended to include the relationship between the physical and biological environments (particularly in regions of coastal upwelling and ecologically threatened coastal areas) and the influence of man on this relationship.

Unlike the other major areas of ocean study, investigations in the coastal zone may require greater temporal coverage than is obtainable from polar-orbiting satellites. It now appears that most coastal applications—which involve the circulation system of the coastal region—are best observed from either aircraft or geostationary satellites, so that repeated coverage during specific tidal stages can be obtained. The combination of tidal effects, cloud cover, and sun angle limit the opportunities for quantitative measurements to only a few opportunities each month. Static features such as bottom topography and major divergent and convergent boundaries may well be monitored from polar-orbiting satellites, but assessment of current movement and other dynamic features requires intense coverage during the two major components of the tidal cycle (Mairs and Clark 1972).

In many instances natural colorants may define water masses and permit them to be tracked on a sampled basis during the tidal cycle (Mairs 1970). It appears, however, that the use of tracer dyes gives more experimental control in circulation studies. Other types of additives that might be used are materials employed in ocean dumping that can be monitored to show net changes in water movement through several tidal cycles, as well as the dispersion rates within the water mass.

Coastal mapping uses essentially the same techniques as terrestrial mapping, the major difference being that in many locations land/water interfaces change more rapidly. The bathymetry of coastlines may change on a permanent as well as seasonal basis, because sand shifts with the seasonal environment. In relatively shallow water (to a depth of 20 to 30 meters) remote sensors of several types may be used for such measurement. Present techniques include the use of visible-region photographs or images. In the future laser systems may directly measure the depth from aircraft platforms (Sherman 1972), while in regions where water opacity limits light penetration, wave refraction may be used (Polcyn 1970).

## CURRENT AND PLANNED SATELLITE SYSTEMS

An exhaustive discussion of all space instrument systems applied to ocean observation is beyond the scope of this paper. An abbreviated description of representative space sensors is useful, however, to indicate the range of space platforms that do or will contribute to understanding and monitoring the ocean environment.

### The Nimbus Series

This series of satellites has served in the past as a research and development platform for the meteorological community and operates in a sun-synchronous orbit at about 1,100 km altitude. Historically, the platform has carried infrared images (Nimbus 1, 2, and 3: 3.4 to 4.2 $\mu$m wavelength; 7.5 km spatial resolution at nadir; daily coverage) for the mapping of cloud cover at night. The Nimbus series gave the first look at surface thermal properties of the ocean, and its Automatic Picture Transmission (APT) capability has made it possible for anyone with an appropriate ground receiver to obtain satellite images. Nimbus-5, launched in 1973, has provided data in the thermal infrared (10.5 to 12.5 μm) at resolutions on the order of 0.8 km. Nimbus-5 also carried the first imaging microwave system operating at 19.4 GHz (1.55 cm wavelength) for the prime purpose of mapping water content in the atmosphere. This system has provided the first space microwave images of sea ice, with an instantaneous field-of-view of about 25 km.

Nimbus-F (to become Nimbus-6 after its launch in mid-1974) will carry the first space instrument designed specifically to accomplish an oceanographic objective—the mapping of sea ice. The instantaneous field-of-view is about 25 km, and the frequency of operation is 37 GHz (0.81 cm). Nimbus-G (anticipated mid-1977 launch) will be designed to serve a larger community of users, including those interested in air pollution and oceanography. The payload is not yet defined for the Nimbus-G, but an ocean-color imager and a four-frequency passive microwave scanner for sea state/surface wind measurement research are candidates for the Nimbus-F platform.

## The NOAA (ITOS) Series

The NOAA (ITOS) family of satellites is the operational series that provides daily environmental data, primarily meteorological, on a global basis. The first Improved Tiros Operational Satellite (ITOS) was launched before the formation of NOAA. The series was renamed when NOAA was created in 1970. The satellites operate in a sun-synchronous circular orbit at about 1,460 km altitude.

The current operational satellite is the NOAA-2 platform, launched in the fall of 1972. A significant change in sensor complement took place with NOAA-2; no vidicon cameras were included; instead, their global and local readout functions were assumed by a dual channel Scanning Radiometer (0.5-0.7 μm and 10.5-12.5 μm; 3.5 km and 8.0 km spatial resolution, respectively).

The dual-channel Very High Resolution Radiometer (VHRR) on NOAA-2 has been most impressive for oceanographic purposes. Unlike the Scanning Radiometer, VHRR does not collect global data but, rather, data from selected regions of the globe (direct readout and up to 9 minutes recording time each orbit) with a spatial resolution of 1 km. The two channels are 0.6 to 0.7 μm and 10.5 to 12.5 μm (Figure 4-1).

## The ERTS Series

The first Earth Resources Technology Satellite (ERTS-1) was launched in mid-1972, carrying a payload comprised of two types of imagers and a surface-data collection system. The imagers are a three-channel Return Beam Vidicon (RBV) system and a four channel Multispectral Scanner (MSS) system. Only the latter is currently in use. The satellite's orbit is near polar and sun-synchronous at an altitude of just over 900 km and repeats itself every 18 days. A second satellite, ERTS-B, may be launched at a future date.

The images in the four channels of the MSS cover the spectral intervals of 0.5 to 0.6, 0.6 to 0.7, 0.7 to 0.8, and 0.8 to 1.1 μm with a spatial resolution approaching 100 m, depending on scene contrast. The width of the scene is about 180 km. The choice of channels and the discrimination of features between channels has made this a useful oceanographic research instrument.

## Other Satellites

A number of research and development spacecraft have contributed or will contribute to oceanographic remote sensing. Most noteworthy is SKYLAB, which carries an Earth Resources Experiment Package (EREP) comprised of five basic remote sensors including a camera system, multiple-channel scanner, profiling spectrometer unit, altimeter-scatterometer-radiometer system, and a 20-cm wavelength radiometer. (SKYLAB utilizes a 50° inclination orbit at an altitude of about 430 km.) The Package was not designed specifically for oceanography, but ocean requirements were incorporated into the sensors' design. The basic generic types of ocean instruments that might be deployed on space platforms during the next decade are contained in the EREP system.

A Geodetic Satellite (GEOS-C) is planned to demonstrate and calibrate a satellite microwave altimeter to an absolute accuracy of 5 meters and relative accuracy on the order of 1 meter. The launch of the first Synchronous Meteorological Satellite (SMS-C) that will be validated and made operational is anticipated by mid-1974. Once operational, the satellite will become the first Geostationary Operational Environmental Satellite (GOES-A). Most significant for ocean applications will be the opportunity for multiple, daily looks at the surface thermal features with spatial resolution approaching 1 kilometer.

## CONCLUSION

Remote sensors on satellites, even if not designed primarily for oceanographic observations, have shown that the oceans have dynamic properties whose surface manifestations are measurable from space. In certain cases, the synoptic view is practically obtainable only from space platforms. To quantify the remotely acquired data from aerospace platforms, remote sensors in laboratories and on towers and ships are being employed to provide the link between oceanographic *in situ* techniques and those using aircraft and spacecraft.

The ability to acquire a synoptic view of its surface features in a repeatable manner suitable to the time scale of the feature being observed is critical to understanding the dynamic nature of the ocean. In the coastal environment repeated coverage for circulation studies may be needed in a manner commensurate with the tidal cycle. In the open ocean, the time scale may be on the order of 1 day for surface dynamic features, and 3 to 7 days for mapping and tracking of water masses. For purposes of coastal mapping and bathymetry, the coverage may be increased to seasonal or annual, depending on the region. There is no one fixed orbit or platform that will satisfy all ocean parameter measurements that can be accomplished by aerospace techniques.

The benefits to be derived from aerospace remote sensing are as many-faceted as the impact of the ocean on the affairs of man. Some benefits may be established on a monetary basis, some may serve to improve the general welfare, and others may be restricted at this time to increased scientific understanding of the oceans. The benefits fall generally into the areas of improved weather prediction, hazard warnings, ship route forecasts, fisheries studies to gain understanding of life in the sea, and ecosystems analysis—in particular the problems associated with environmental protection and pollution abatement.

The synoptic view of the oceans provided by remote sensors allows what seem to be very slight changes at a specific point and time to be placed in the context of similar changes in other regions at the same time. The optimum intermix between surface, aircraft, and satellite platforms cannot be operationally determined at this time. It does appear, however, that an efficient system will incorporate each type of platform for environmental monitoring of the oceans. The research that is to be performed with the Nimbus, NOAA, COSMOS, and ERTS series, as well as with SKYLAB, GEOS-C, and SMS/GOES, will help define the role of satellites in this operational system.

## REFERENCES

Alishouse, J. C., Baker, D. R., McClain, E. J., and Yates, H. W. Potential of satellite microwave sensing for hydrology and oceanography measurements. NOAA Technical memorandum NESS 26, 1971.

Apel, John R., Editor. Sea Surface topography from space. NOAA Technical Report ERL 228-AOML 7, 1972.

Campbell, W. J. (in press). NASA remote sensing of sea ice in AIDJEX. WMO Symposium, Technical Conference on the Means of Acquisition and Communication of Ocean Data, Tokyo, Japan, 1972.

Clarke, G. L., Ewing, G. C., and Lorenzen, C. J. Spectral of backscattered light from the sea obtained from aircraft as a measure of chlorophyll concentration. Science, Vol 167, No. 3921, p. 1119. 1970.

Curtis, W. R., and Rao, P. K. Gulf Stream thermal gradients from satellite, ship and aircraft observations. Journal of Geophysical Research, Oceans and Atmospheres, Vol. 74, No. 28, pp. 6984-6990. 1969.

Duntley, S. Q. Detection of ocean chlorophyll from earth orbit. Proceedings 4th Annual Earth Resources Program Review, NASA Manned Spacecraft Center, MSC-05937, Vol. 4, p. 102-1. 1972.

Fritz, S., Wark, D. Q., Fleming, H. E., Smith, W. L., Jacobwitz, H., Hilleary, D. T., and Alishouse, J. C. Temperature sounding from satellites. NOAA Technical Report NESS 59. 1972.

Hanson, K. J. Remote sensing of the ocean. NOAA and the University of Colorado, Wave Propagation Laboratory, Environmental Research Laboratory, Electrical Engineering Department, Boulder, Colo., p. 22-1. 1972.

Mairs, R. L. Oceanographic and sedimentological interpretation of Apollo space photographs, Journal of Photogrammetric Engineering, Vol. 36, No. 1, 1970.

Mairs, R. L., and Clark, D. K. A study of temporal estuarine flow dynamics. Proceedings 4th Annual Earth Resources Program Review. NASA Manned Spacecraft Center, MSC-05937, Vol. 4, p. 112-1. 1972.

Maul, G. A., and Hansen, D. V. An observation of the Gulf Stream surface front structure by ship, aircraft and satellite. Remote Sensing of the Environment, Vol. 2, No. 2, pp. 109-116. 1972.

National Aeronautics and Space Administration. Proceedings 4th Annual Earth Resources Program Review. NASA Manned Spacecraft Center, MSC-05937, Vol. 4, 1972.

Polcyn, F. C., Brown, W. L., and Sattinger, I. J. The measurement of water depth by remote sensing techniques. Rep. No. 8973-26-F, Contract No. N62306-67-C-0243, University of Michigan, Willow Run Laboratories, Ann Arbor, Mich., 1970.

Rao, P. K., Smith, W. L., and Koffler, R. Global sea surface temperature distribution determined from an environmental satellite. Monthly Weather Review, Vol. 100, No. 1, pp. 10-14, 1972.

Rao, P. K., Strong, A. E., and Koffler, R. Gulf Stream meanders and eddies as seen in satellite infrared imagery. Journal of Physical Oceanography, Vol. 1, pp. 237-239. 1971.

Sherman, III, J. W. Remote sensing oceanography. International Workshop on Earth Resource Survey Systems, May 3-14, 1971, NASA SP-283, Vol. 1, pp. 91-105. 1972.

Stevenson, W. H. Fisheries resource identification and assessment studies. Proceedings 4th Annual Earth Resources Program Review, NASA Manned Spacecraft Center, MSC-05937, Vol. IV, p. 91-1, Houston, Tex. 1972.

Strong, A. E., DeRycke, R. J. (in press). Ocean current monitoring employing a new satellite sensing technique. (Science)

Wilheit, T., Nordburg, W., Blinn, J., Campbell, W., and Edgerton, A. Aircraft measurements of microwave emission from Arctic sea ice. Remote Sensing of the Environment, Vol. 2, No. 3, pp. 129-139. 1972.

# 5. The Deep Sea Drilling Project –A Hallmark in Ocean Research

ANONYMOUS 1974

Now in its sixth year of operation, the Deep Sea Drilling Project (DSDP) is certainly one of the most outstanding projects in the world history of oceanography. DSDP has made a remarkable and unique contribution to the field of ocean research, and a better understanding of the age of the earth.

DSDP is a unique effort to increase our knowledge of the earth, the age and history and processes of development of the ocean basins and the structure and composition of the oceanic crust. Equally important is the increase in the information DSDP has made available to the world's scientific community–and, ultimately, to the public at large–concerning the resource potential of vast areas of the surface of the earth beneath the oceans.

Another milestone was achieved in June, 1973, when President Nixon and Premier Brezhnev agreed to a series of accords, prominent among which was a combined effort by the two nations in the field of oceanography.

In February, 1974, U.S. and Soviet scientists signed agreements covering cooperative ocean studies and USSR participation in DSDP. The Soviets will contribute \$1 million each year for five years toward DSDP.

The National Science Foundation (NSF) funds the DSDP as part of the Foundation's Ocean Sediment Coring Program. The prime contract for management of DSDP is with the University of California, with Scripps Institution of Oceanography of the University delegated the management responsibility. The University subcontracts with Global Marine Inc. to accomplish the actual drilling and coring operations with the GMI ship, *D/V Glomar Challenger.*

The 400-ft. vessel is a scientific tool created especially for DSDP. She bears a 142-foot-high drilling tower slightly aft of midships. Among the special capabilities of the ship is dynamic positioning, which through a series of thrusters linked to onboard computers, maintains the vessel in a stationary position in the ocean for the extended periods of time necessary to carry out a drilling operation. She is designed so that the main deck can be awash during a storm without disrupting drilling activities in the elevated superstructures.

In a manner similar to land-based oil drilling, the drill string is made up of a series of 90-foot 5½″ pipe sections. The derrick hook load capacity is one million pounds. Core samples are recovered from preselected drill-

From *Sea Technology*, Vol. 15, No. 3, pp. 31-34, 1974. Reprinted with light editing and with permission of Compass Publications, Inc.

ing sites. The deepest penetration thus far has been 4,265 ft. into the ocean bed.

Scientific planning for the DSDP is provided by advisory panels organized by and operated under the aegis of the Joint Oceanographic Institutions for Deep Earth Sampling (JOIDES). This is a consortium consisting of the Lamont-Doherty Geological Observatory of Columbia University; Rosenstiel School of Marine and Atmospheric Science of the University of Miami, Florida; Scripps Institution of Oceanography of the University of California at San Diego; University of Washington (Seattle); Woods Hole (Massachusetts) Oceanographic Institution; and the Institute of Oceanology of the USSR Academy of Sciences.

The Bundesanstalt fur Bodenforschung of the Federal Republic of Germany is in the process of becoming a member of JOIDES.

Among the technical achievements are these:

–431 holes drilled at 289 different sites for a total of 420,457 ft. drilled below the sea floor.

–165,728 ft. of sediment cored with 5,778 cores recovered and a total of 94,159 ft. of core stored in oceanographic repositories.

–longest drill string suspended from the *Glomar Challenger* was 22,192 ft. long in a water depth of 20,483 ft. at Site 212 in the Eastern Indian Ocean.

–4,265 ft. is deepest penetration beneath the sea floor at Site 222 in the Eastern Indian Ocean.

–of the 42,031.5 hours recorded by the drilling vessel, 51% or 21,224.5 hours were spent drilling and coring—only 2.86% hours were recorded for equipment breakdown and bad weather.

–re-entry of the drill string into a previously drilled hole was made in 13,000 ft. of water on December 25, 1970, in the Caribbean Sea.

Among the major scientific achievements are these:

### Youth Of The Major Ocean Basins.

After five years of drilling in the Atlantic, Pacific, Indian and Antarctic Oceans, the oldest dated rock recovered is about 160 million years old. Compared to the age of the oldest dated continental rock—3.6 billion years—the ocean basins are young features. This is attributed to a process of crustal renewal and destruction called sea-floor spreading. The earth, itself, is probably about 4.5 billion years old.

### Sea-floor Spreading And Continental Drift.

Apart from determining the youth of the ocean basins, drilling results have confirmed a general increase of age of the oceanic floor at increasing distances from the area of crustal generation at the mid-ocean ridges toward the zone destruction in the deep-sea trenches. This strongly supports for the first time, by direct sampling, other geophysical data interpreted in terms of sea-floor spreading and continental drift. Horizontal motions of the crust (continental drift) determined from drilling data, closely support the rates of movement of 1-13 cm/yr (0.4-5 inches per year) estimated from geophysical data.

### Vertical Motions Of The Earth's Crust.

Continental drift theory holds that a single super-continent broke up about 200 million years ago. When this occurred, fragments of continental materials that were in the actual zone of breaking of the continent very slowly sank beneath the sea. Drilling has revealed shallow-water-deposited sediments and even indications of dry land conditions that are overlain by typical deep-sea sediments. Scientists have determined that the average rate of subsidence of such fragments was about 5-10 cm/1000 yr (2-4 inches per thousand years).

Some seamounts have also been found, by comparing sediment types, to have sunk thousands of feet below the ocean surface.

In the Indian Ocean, a major submarine ridge (Ninetyeast Ridge) over 2,800 kilometers long and now 1850 meters (about one mile) below the surface of the sea was shown to have been an island chain with swamps and lagoons. Low-grade coal and peats were recovered, as well as lagoonal sediments and oyster shells.

### Discovery Of Oil In The Gulf Of Mexico.

The Sigsbee Knolls are domelike structures on the smooth floor of the Gulf of Mexico. One of these was drilled and found to contain oil in a "cap rock" that characteristically overlies salt domes. It is hard to estimate the extent of the oil accumulations or the commercial possibilities of the future, but the presence of oil at these depths may encourage future exploration into deep water. The hole drilled by the *Glomar Challenger* was filled with cement to ensure that no oil could escape.

Salt is classically considered a shallow-water deposit and its discovery in the deepest part of the Gulf of Mexico has stimulated considerable discussion and controversy over its emplacement and even over the origin of the Gulf of Mexico.

### Mediterranean Sea Dried Up.

The mass of salt deposits and related sediments, and the environmental interpretation placed on the presence of various species of marine animals and plants that were recovered from the Mediterranean indicate that the Mediterranean Sea dried up about 12 million years ago. Scientists aboard the vessel envisioned the Mediterranean Sea as a deep-water body, much as it is today, when the desiccation occurred, but others have postulated that it was a shallow sea that subsided to its present depths after it dried up. The controversy remains unresolved.

The Mediterranean results rank among the most surprising discoveries made by the *Glomar Challenger* and they have rejuvenated geologic thinking and concepts in that area.

### Paleo-Oceanography.

The types of sediments recovered and the nature of the fossils recovered are indicators of climatic and oceanographic conditions in the past. Through the examination of cores from many locations, scientists can begin to understand the oceanic circulation pattern and climatic changes that have taken place through time. The story is complicated by the fact that the ocean floor is moving relative to the rotational coordinates of the Earth (relative to the Equator or poles), and the continents have also been moving, thus changing the shapes and outlines of the ocean basins. Particularly interesting data have been recovered relative to the ancient climatic variations associated with the onset of glacial conditions.

### Refinement Of Fossil Dating Systems.

The nearly continuous sequence of ancient sediments that have been recovered from the deep sea at many localities provides an unequalled opportunity to observe the details of evolutionary development of the small organisms that lived in the oceans. A better description of the evolutionary trends can be utilized in the refinement of the age-dating system. These fossils are well preserved in the soft sediments of the ocean floor, and the sequence is less likely to be interrupted by erosional processes that are so effective on continental rocks.

### Discovery Of Mineral-Rich Layers.

Minerals such as zinc and native copper have been found in deep-sea sediments. Metal-rich layers, found by earlier sampling techniques, exist in the Pacific Ocean. It now appears that mineral enrichment of the basal sediment layers is not uncommon in the oceans.

### Glaciation In The Antarctic.

By dating and reading the layers of sediments and ice-rafted debris, scientists discovered that the Antarctic has been glaciated—or covered with ice—for at least 20 million years. The finding is in sharp contrast to estimates of five to seven million years which most scientists had previously believed to be the case. It appears that a major and abrupt change in the extent of glaciation took place about five million years ago inasmuch as the ice cover seems to have extended as much as 200 or 300 miles farther than it does now.

The melting process which resulted in the present configuration could have created a world wide rise in sea level on the order of several tens of feet. Indeed, the waxing and waning of the ice sheet continues to affect sea levels worldwide.

Both the early glaciation and the melting may have been related to the circulation of polar waters caused by the separation and movement of Australia from Antarctica. On the same cruise, the first DSDP venture to the Antarctic, it was discovered that Australia did, in fact, break away from the polar continent some 50 million years ago and has been drifting northward at the rate of a few inches a year, confirming an earlier theory.

# 6. Living under the Sea

JOHN E. HUGUENIN RICHARD A. FRALICK 1975

The ability to work effectively in the sea has improved rapidly in the past ten years. In general, advances have come through adapting and modifying approaches, techniques, materials, and subsystems developed mainly in aerospace and military programs. The increased effort has been spurred by at least two motivations: the growing strategic importance of the undersea domain and the resource potential of the world's oceans and seabeds. This focus of attention on the problems and potential of working in the sea has stimulated diving science and technology. Progress in terms of the depth reached by divers and the time spent there has been spectacular.

A great step forward has been the development of saturation-diving techniques (Table 6-1). During the traditional dive, lasting a few hours at most, the blood's dissolved inert-gas content steadily increases, and the time required for subsequent decompression thus increases not only with depth but also with bottom time. After about 24 hours at a given depth, however, the tissues become essentially saturated with inert gas at the pressure equivalent to that depth. The tissues do not absorb significantly more gas no matter how long the diver stays at that level. This condition is known as saturation, and this type of dive is known as a saturation dive. Once a diver is saturated, the decompression period becomes independent of the time under pressure.

Saturation diving has dramatically increased the bottom time available, an advantage that becomes greater with increased depth, since daily decompression is eliminated from the work procedure. Since a short 15-minute dive to 650 feet (198 meters) requires about 5 hours of decompression, the time saving alone can be substantial.

John E. Huguenin is an Assistant Professor in the Department of Mechanical and Aerospace Engineering at the University of Massachusetts, Boston. He is currently involved with aquacultural engineering advisory services, applied research, and education under Sea Grant sponsorship at the Aquacultural Engineering Laboratory, Wareham, Massachusetts.

Dr. Richard A. Fralick is an Assistant Professor of Natural Science at Plymouth State College, University of New Hampshire. His research involves the development of techniques for culturing commercially-valuable seaweeds. He has authored and co-authored many papers on aquatic plants.

From *Sea Frontiers,* Vol. 21, No. 2, pp. 95-103, 1975. Reprinted with light editing and with permission of the authors and *Sea Frontiers,* © 1975 by the International Oceanographic Foundations, 3979 Rickenbacker Causeway, Virginia Key, Miami, Florida 33149.

Table 6-1. Saturation Diving Habitat Experiments in the Sea

| *Project* | *Date* | *Number of divers* | *Diving time* | *Saturation depth (ft)* | *Saturation gas mixture* |
|---|---|---|---|---|---|
| MAN-IN-SEA | Sept. 1962 | 1 | 24 hours | 200 | 97% helium, 3% oxygen |
| CONSHELF 1 | Sept. 1962 | 2 | 7 days | 34 | air |
| CONSHELF 2 | June- | 5 | 1 month | 31 | air |
| | July 1963 | 2 | 7 days | 85 | 75% helium, 25% air |
| MAN-IN-SEA | June 1964 | 2 | 49 hours | 432 | 96.4% helium, 3.6% oxygen |
| SEALAB I | July 1964 | 4 | 11 days | 192 | helium, oxygen |
| SEALAB II | Aug.-Sept. 1965 | 3-ten-man teams | 15 days per team | 204 | 75% helium, 20% nitrogen, 4% oxygen |
| CONSHELF 3 | Aug. 1965 | 6 | 4 days | 82 | helium, 6.5% oxygen |
| | Sept.-Oct. 1965 | 6 | 22 days | 328 | helium, 2.1% oxygen |
| JANUS I | 1968 | 2 | 6 days | 300 | helium, 3% oxygen |
| | | 2 | 6 days | 500 | helium, 2% oxygen |
| TEKTITE I | Feb.-April 1969 | 4 | 60 days | 43 | 92% nitrogen, 8% oxygen |
| HELGOLAND | July 1969 | 4 | 10 days | 64 | air |
| HABITAT II | Nov. 1969 | 5 | 60 hours | 200 | helium, air |
| AEGIR | June 1970 | 6 | 5 days | 520 | 91% helium, 7.2% nitrogen, 1.8% oxygen |
| TEKTITE II | April-Nov. 1970 | 11-five-man teams | 7-30 days per team; total of 915 man-days | 40 | 91% nitrogen, 9% oxygen |
| JANUS II | Sept. 1970 | 6 | 5 days | 660 | 98% helium, 2% oxygen |
| EDALHAB | April 1971 | 3 | 4 days | 33 | air |
| FLARE | Jan.-May 1972 | 10 two- or three-man teams | total of 68 man-days | 45 | air |

Reprinted with permission from Technology Review

## EVER DEEPER AND LONGER

The duration of deeper dives has quickly jumped from minutes to days and weeks, while the depth attainable has also greatly increased. Limits on diving time are now imposed by support facilities, equipment reliability, and psychological factors. Divers have gone below 1,000 feet (300 meters) in the open sea and, though still experimental and risky, it is now possible for men to work for several days at such pressures. Two divers of COMEX (Centre National Pour L'Exploration des Oceans) of Marseilles, France have attained a simulated depth of 2,001 feet (608 meters) in a hyperbaric chamber. This record was achieved as part of the saturation-diving research project Physalie VI (May 24-June 2, 1972).

In similar experiments various mammals have returned in good health from pressure equivalents of over 3,000 feet (912 meters). It is anticipated that in the next few years, men will be able to work effectively in the sea at depths of 1,500 feet (456 meters). While still not proven to be viable, a few contracts have already been signed by diving companies to provide diving services to this depth.

## SURFACE SUPPORT—A VITAL LINK

An additional advantage of the saturation technique is that the diver is physiologically able to make appreciable excursions downward from his saturation depth without requiring decompression to return. The deeper the saturation depth, the farther the diver can go in time and distance. The downward excursion capability is due to the increase in the saturation pressure and the linearity of the pressure increase with depth. If a person saturated to 1 atmosphere of pressure (sea level) descends 100 feet (30 meters), the pressure increases by 300 percent to 4 atmospheres. On the other hand, a diver who is saturated at 300 feet (91 meters) at about 10 atmospheres and who descends an additional 100 feet (30 meters) to 13 atmospheres experiences a smaller relative pressure change of 30 percent and consequently a smaller relative increase in dissolved gases in his blood. Upward excursions, however, remain limited and very dangerous, for at any depth above saturation, the blood becomes supersaturated and the dissolved gases can easily form bubbles.

Most commercial firms using saturation techniques house their divers under pressure in a deck decompression chamber (D.D.C.) aboard a surface vessel and ferry them under pressure to and from the work site by personnel transfer capsules (P.T.C.), also called diving bells. The divers may be saturated to depths above the working depth or to full depth. This approach still requires extensive operations across the air-sea interface and is critically dependent on surface support and surface weather conditions. Compared with the alternative of providing an underwater habitat adequate for extended undersea living, however, this pressurized commuting is still the more flexible, more mobile, cheaper, and safer approach. Except for specialized movable shelters for the underwater welding of pipelines and the occasional use of small diver havens, habitats have not yet proven practical as part of the undersea work systems.

Commercial and military operations have not generally used the habitat approach for several reasons. State-of-the-art habitats still require the use of D.D.C.s and surface vessels for support services and emergencies. To date, they have generally also depended on electric power, communications, piped supplies of premixed breathing gas and fresh water from land or sea surface. In addition, the commercial applications of saturation diving have so far not required the extended diving time in fixed locations that could help justify the use of large habitats. Thus, state-of-the-art habitat projects have generally been saddled not only with the problems and substantial costs of the D.D.C./P.T.C. surface-vessel complex and associated personnel but also those associated with launching, monitoring, and retrieving the habitats at sea.

## ARE SUBMERSIBLES THE ANSWER?

One encouraging trend is that small habitats (Figure 6-1) in shallow depths (less than 100 feet or 30 meters), using air as a breathing mixture (Hydro-Lab, PRINUL, and Helgoland habitats), have successfully used unmanned automated buoys moored to them or have run lines from a nearby shore facility (Sublimnos habitat) to provide the required services. This has tremendously reduced the operating costs of these projects. It is not clear at this time whether this technique can be safely applied to more complex breathing mixtures and greater depths. An additional advantage to shallow habitats and short stay times is that the decompression requirements are cut down or eliminated thus reducing the risks and the requirements for expensive support equipment.

While the D.D.C./P.T.C. approach is seriously constrained by surface and sea conditions, habitats are further hampered by their bulk and immobility. Submersibles

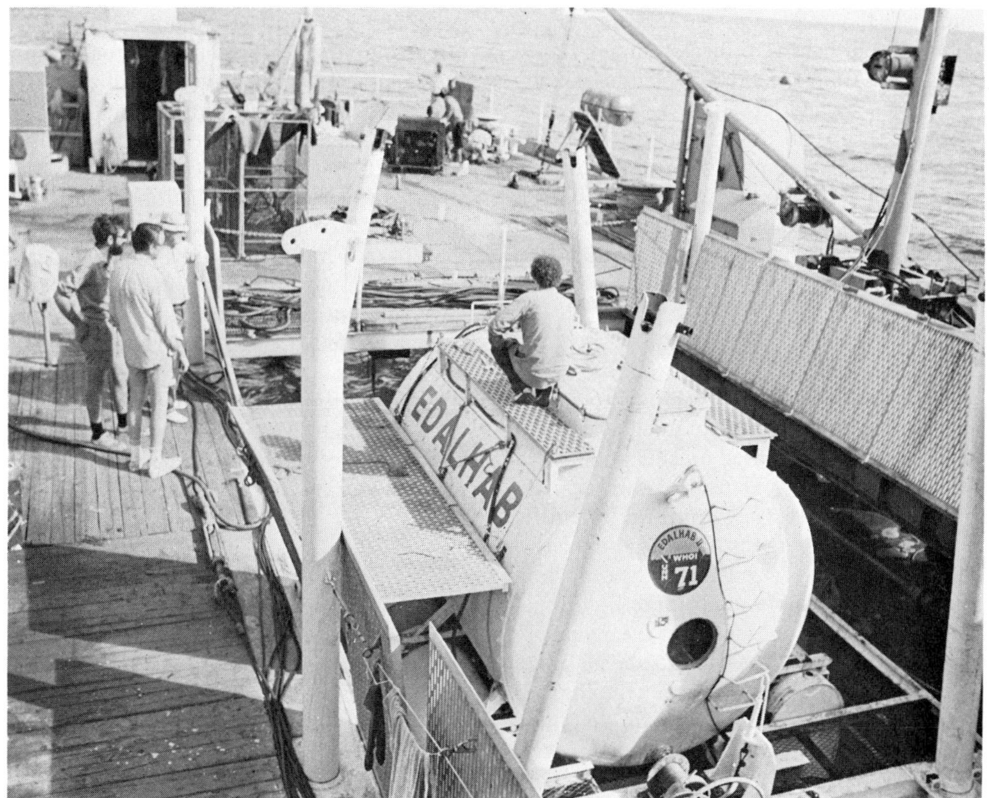


Figure 6-1. Off the Florida coast, Edelhab II was successfully used in project FLARE for more than two months in 1972 by teams of scientists, divers, and engineers to study living reef systems.

with diver lock-out capabilities, built-in decompression chambers, and the capability of deploying themselves directly from ports without assistance may well be the long-term answer. They would combine the advantage of independence from surface support with those of flexibility and mobility. Unfortunately, they would be very expensive to build and operate, and there is not enough current demand to keep even one such large vessel busy enough to justify its design and construction.

## THE CHANGING EMPHASIS

The increase in habitat capabilities was particularly rapid prior to the death of a Sealab III diver in early 1969 and the subsequent cancellation of this ambitious project. Since that time, the interest in habitats has switched from demonstrations of maximum capabilities to the exploitation of proven technology at relatively shallow depths. The motivations have also changed from military and commercial applications to scientific uses. The shallower depths have the advantage of providing a reduction in costs, complexity, and risks, and they permit nonprofessional divers to participate.

Most of the emphasis in past habitat projects has been in developing engineering capabilities, researching human hyperbaric physiology, and in evaluating human behavior in a stressed environment. The interest and perceived need for additional research along these lines appears to be waning. United States government agencies, like the Navy and NASA, which had been active and had the resources, no longer seem as interested in habitat projects. Support must now come from the MUST (Manned Undersea Science and Technology) office of NOAA, from educational institutions, and from regional and private organizations. It appears that substantial funding, such as is necessary for Sealab- and Tektite-type projects, will not be available for at least the next few years.

## TOOLS FOR MARINE SCIENTISTS

Current justifications for habitat projects in the United States, mostly small efforts in shallow depths, are based on educational and research objectives. There is, however, considerable controversy within the scientific and academic communities as to the relative value of placing scientists-in-the-sea compared to alternative and more-traditional methods, even when involving the relatively simpler and lower-cost habitats. While there is disagreement about the cost effectiveness of habitats, there is little doubt that they can be useful scientific tools. Unfortunately, both the proponents and opponents are using relatively subjective arguments.

In spite of the problems associated with habitats, there is nevertheless considerable current interest, as they seem best suited to repetitive or long-term localized observations or measurements. The maximum useful range from a fixed habitat site, even with powered propulsion devices, is on the order of ½ mile (0.8 kilometer). There are a great many small low-cost projects going on in the United States today, most of them associated with universities. The people trained in these projects and the accumulated experiences will probably have a noticeable effect on the future of man's progress into the sea. A recent survey of the United States's need for habitats in undersea research indicates that there exists an identifiable requirement for 400 mission days/year from currently active and qualified scientists. Many of the requirements fall within the 80- to 120-foot (24- to 36-meter) depth range with most of the remainder in shallower depths. Mission durations of about a week are needed. With the growing number of scientists trained in diving techniques along with the continual improvements in these methods, both the acceptability and importance of diving as a scientific research tool can be expected to increase.

## DREAMS FOR THE FUTURE

There are other potential uses for undersea habitats that could develop. An obvious use is in undersea archaeology, due to the extensive diving time in a fixed location required to excavate an ancient sunken vessel. While the costs would be high, a habitat approach could very well be justifiable for this application. Related activities with similar requirements that might also be viable include some types of marine salvage operations. Another use, which is not as farfetched as it may seem, is to provide an unusual vacation experience for those who can afford it. The recreational advantages and tourist appeal are considerable. Finally, there is a dream that undersea habitats may serve as operating bases for future sea farmers and sea ranchers to harvest the seas' bounty. We shall see.

# 2

# *OCEAN CURRENTS AND WAVES*

# 7. Oceanic Surface Currents

JEROME WILLIAMS JOHN J. HIGGINSON JOHN D. ROHRBOUGH 1968

## INTRODUCTION

Anyone having even an elementary acquaintance with the ocean knows of the great currents which exist at its surface. Some of these, such as the Gulf Stream in the North Atlantic and its counterpart in the North Pacific, the Kuroshio, have a profound effect on continental climate. This is usually considered to be beneficial since Great Britain and southwestern Alaska are both warmer than would be expected from latitudinal considerations alone. There are surface currents, however, which may produce harmful effects on the total environment.

One example of this is the Humboldt (Peru) Current which flows northward along the western coast of South America. Under normal circumstances there is a large amount of upwelling associated with the edge of this current providing nutrients for enough phytoplankton to support the largest anchovy population in the world. These fish make up one of the largest single industries in the Peruvian economy and account for the fact that Peru has led the world in fish catch for the last few years. Occasionally, however, the Humboldt Current changes its position enough to cause a cessation of the all important upwelling. Not only do the anchovies disappear, causing the loss of untold millions of dollars to the Peruvian economy, but large numbers of other marine organisms die and decay resulting in hydrogen sulfide being released into the atmosphere.

This change in position of the Humboldt Current is called *El Niño* (after the Christ child because of its usual occurrence during the Christmas season), or sometimes *Callao*

Jerome Williams is associate chairman of the Environmental Sciences Department at the United States Naval Academy. He has also been associated with the Chesapeake Bay Institute of Johns Hopkins University, Maryland. His major research interests are underwater optics, instrumentation, and physical oceanography.

Commander John J. Higginson has been an instructor of oceanography at the United States Naval Academy. He has also been associated with the Apollo Recovery Program as operations officer in Helicopter ASW Squadron Four. He is presently in receipt of orders to Helicopter ASW Squadron Two at Naval Air Station, Imperial Beach, California.

Commander John D. Rohrbough is with the United States Navy and is on the staff of the Studies, Analysis and Gaming Agency of the Office of the Joint Chiefs of Staff, the Pentagon, Washington. He has served as an instructor of oceanography and a member of the staff of the superintendent at the Naval Academy.

From *Sea and Air: The Naval Environment* by Jerome Williams, Lieutenant Commander John Higginson, U.S. Navy, and Lieutenant Commander John Rohrbough, U.S. Navy. Copyright © 1968 by the United States Naval Institute, Annapolis, Maryland. Reprinted by permission.

*Painter*, after the discoloring effects which are caused by the gases of decaying organisms.

Of course not all surface current systems are capable of producing a cataclysm of the order of magnitude of El Niño, but this does not make the knowledge of all surface currents any less important. Benjamin Franklin was aware of this when he produced the first chart of the Gulf Stream to aid American ships make faster crossings of the North Atlantic. But it remained for Matthew Fontaine Maury to initiate the scientific study of ocean currents about three-quarters of a century later.

Maury not only gathered together enough data to generate dependable charts, but he also tried to correlate these data in an attempt to ascertain the causes and variability of ocean currents. This work has continued to the present and is not complete, even today. However, enough information has become available to piece together a reasonably logical description of oceanic surface currents.

## BASIC CAUSES

As in the case of atmospheric motion, one of the major causes of motion in the sea is uneven heating. However, the atmospheric flow pattern discussed previously is somewhat different than that in the ocean, because in addition to the direct effects of uneven heating, there are two other important factors which must be taken into account. These are (1) wind (itself produced by uneven heating) acting on the water surface and (2) the containment of the oceans within the boundaries set by land masses. Due to the interference of land masses, no currents run all the way around the world except in the Antarctic region.

In actuality there are two basic systems which must be superimposed, one upon the other. The first of these is the system produced directly by uneven heating wherein the waters at lower latitudes are heated, become less dense, and spread out over the surface toward the poles (Figure 7-1). As they drift toward the poles these waters are cooled and finally sink. In this manner a giant convection cell is set up similar to the single cell atmospheric model, wherein surface water sinking at the poles flows toward the equator, rises in the equatorial regions, and flows away from the equator along the surface.

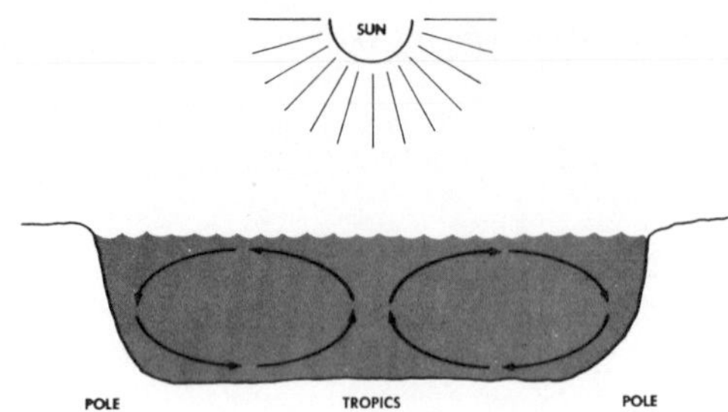


Figure 7-1. Idealized thermohaline flow in the ocean.

In addition to this basic flow poleward, the surface winds, combined with land mass placement, produce a different system. The resulting surface currents are a combination of these two flows. Since by far the greatest effect is due to winds, an attempt will be made to develop a model of ocean currents produced by wind forces and land placement alone. This will then be compared with what actually exists in nature.

## AN OCEANIC CURRENT MODEL

As a start, the model assumes that the winds

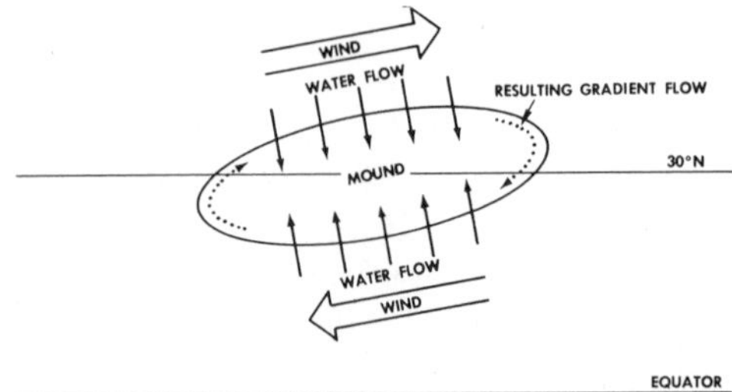


Figure 7-2. Production of an oceanic high pressure area at 30° by prevailing winds.

in existence are those in the three celled theory. This is a reasonable assumption since the tricellular model describes the *surface* winds quite well. As may be recalled, winds in the Northern Hemisphere are northeast in the latitude belt from 0° to 30°, southwest in the belt from 30° to 60°, and northeast again in the belt from 60° to the pole, with a mirror image of this system in the Southern Hemisphere.

When a wind blows there is a transport of the upper layers (about 100 meters thick) at 90° to the right of the wind in the Northern Hemisphere. The result is that with a wind blowing from the northeast, the oceanic surface layers will be caused to move toward the northwest, which is the case between the latitudes of 0° to 30° in the Northern Hemisphere.

Similarly, with a southwest wind the upper hundred meters or so of surface waters are transported to the right and a southeast* flow develops. The effect of these two currents is to pile up water within a region centered somewhere around 30° latitude, as seen in Figure 7-2.

This mound of water piled up by these two wind driven transports creates a high pressure ridge at about 30° latitude. The water, under the influence of this pressure distribution and coriolis force, will produce geostrophic flow toward the southwest between 0° and 30° and toward the northeast between 30° and 60°. Since there are land masses on each side of the ocean, the water must go somewhere. As it completes its path, it tends to produce a current gyre in a clockwise direction about this high pressure cell. Just as in the atmosphere, a clockwise rotation is found about a high.

A little farther north there is a northeast wind between the latitude of 60° and 90° which would cause the surface layer to move toward the northwest. Consequently at 60 degrees latitude water is directed toward the

*Keep in mind that winds are named by where they have been, while currents are described in terms of where they are going.

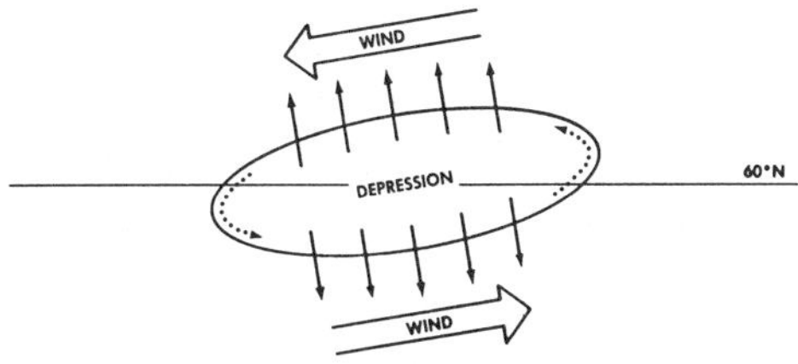


Figure 7-3. Production of an oceanic low pressure area at 60° by prevailing winds.

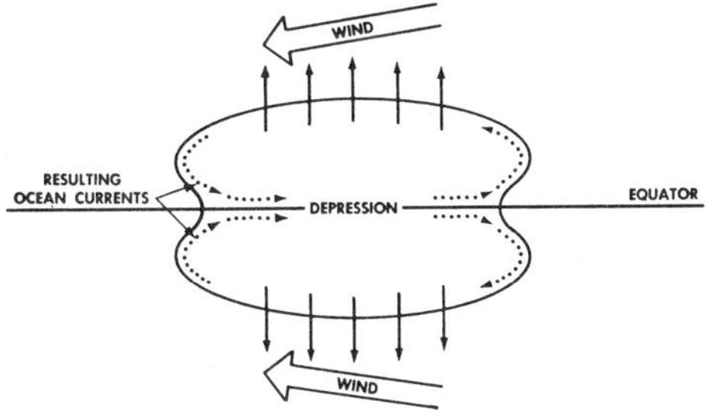


Figure 7-4. Production of an oceanic low pressure area at the equator by prevailing winds. (Note the two gyres produced from this single depression.)

southeast by lower latitude winds and at the same time toward the northwest by winds at higher latitudes (Figure 7-3). This results in a low pressure trough at a latitude of about 60 degrees. Considering both the placement of the continents on each side of the ocean and what has been learned about low pressure regions, the circulation around this low pressure area will result in a current having a counterclockwise direction.

In equatorial regions, the situation may be treated similarly. The winds north and south of the doldrums produce surface layer motion such that in both cases the water motion is away from the equator (Figure 7-4). In other words, close to the equator a low pressure system is developed in the hydrosphere. Once again, counterclockwise rotation would be expected around a low pressure system in the Northern Hemisphere, while clockwise flow would be expected in the Southern Hemisphere. Thus two gyres

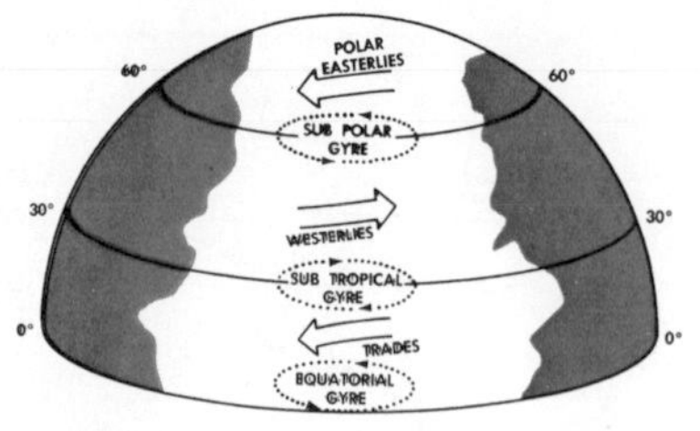


Figure 7-5. The complete model for the northern hemisphere wind driven currents.

result since flow direction about a low is opposite in the different hemispheres.

The model is now complete. Using the tricellular wind theory, it has been shown that the resulting currents in the Northern Hemisphere should consist of a counterclockwise gyre close to the equator (*equatorial gyre*), a clockwise gyre north of that (*sub-tropical gyre*), and a counterclockwise one north of that (*sub-polar gyre*) (Figure 7-5).

Similarly, about the same condition exists in the Southern Hemisphere, except that the gyres rotate oppositely, producing a mirror image. The *equatorial gyre* is clockwise in its rotation, the *sub-tropical gyre* counterclockwise, and the *sub-polar gyre* clockwise, due to the opposite direction of the coriolis force in the southern hemisphere.

## THE MODEL VS. THE TRUE PICTURE

It is now appropriate to compare a simple model with the actual currents existing in the world's oceans. In all of the world's oceans there is a *sub-tropical gyre;* both north and south of the equator this portion of the model appears to hold fairly well. In the Pacific Ocean the *north equatorial gyre* is well established, composed of an equatorial current and an oppositely moving equatorial counter current north of the equator. There is also a *south equatorial gyre,* displaced somewhat north of the geographical equator. This is not surprising from the position of the *intertropical convergence zone* and the *oceanographic thermal equator,* both of which are displaced north of the geographical equator.

In the northern oceans the sub-tropical gyre composed of the *Kuroshio system* in the Pacific and the *Gulf Stream system* in the Atlantic is also very well developed. In addition, the *Irminger current,* an offshoot of the Gulf Stream system,* combines with the *East Greenland current* to produce the sub-polar gyre. However, the sub-polar gyre in the Pacific is not so well developed, although the Alaska current tends to produce a flow of this type.

In both the North and South Pacific there is some evidence of the existence of the sub-polar gyre. In the South Pacific, a polar current running from east to west close to the Antarctic Continent and the West Wind Drift (Antarctic Circumpolar Current) somewhat north of this in the opposite direction, make up the larger portion of the sub-polar gyre. The southern South Atlantic also exhibits very similar properties so that it appears the model fits the southern oceans quite well.

From an unrefined point of view this crude model fits the real ocean quite well, much better than expected from the simplicity of the initial assumptions. It appears that some of the differences between the model and actual current patterns may be explained on the basis of well developed sub-surface currents. Two examples of these are the Pacific Undercurrent (Cromwell current) and the Atlantic Undercurrent, both of which flow from east to west within 1° of the equator. These are both well-developed currents involving transports on the order of thirty million cubic meters per second between 100 and 300 meters below the surface.

In addition the thermohaline effects have not been considered. Changes in density of surface waters produced by warming and evaporation at the lower latitudes cause a

* The *Gulf Stream* system is composed of the *Florida Current, Gulf Stream,* and *North Atlantic current.* See Figure 7-6.

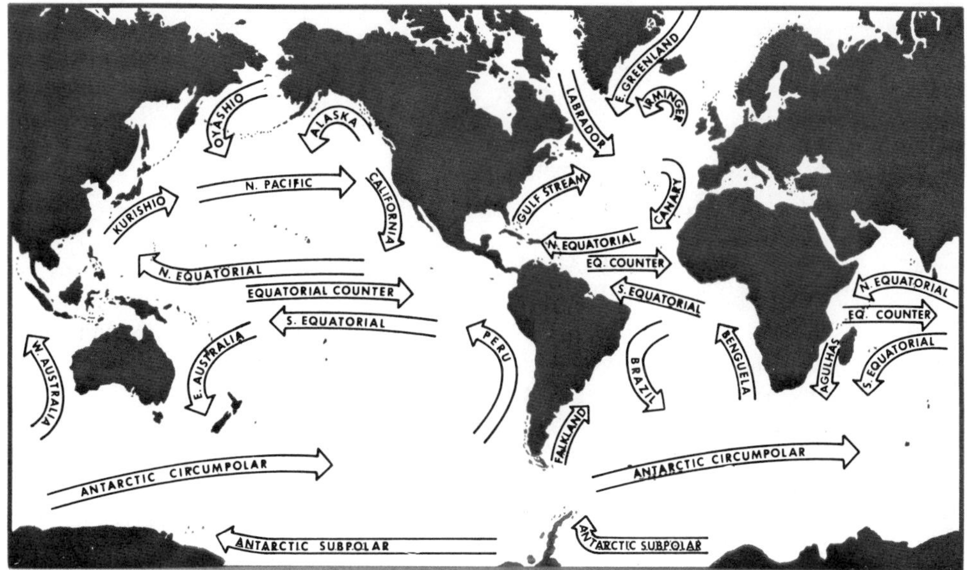


Figure 7-6. Surface currents of the world during the northern hemisphere winter.

general poleward drift at the surface. This would have the effect of strengthening such currents as the Gulf Stream while weakening those tending to oppose the drift such as the Canary current in the North Atlantic. There are, of course, a number of discrepancies in the simple model. One of these is the region of the equatorial Atlantic. Here is found a large transfer of water from the South Atlantic Ocean to the North Atlantic Ocean without the separation of the equatorial gyres that appear in the Pacific. One possible explanation for this breakdown of the equatorial gyres in the Atlantic Ocean is the closeness of the African and South American land masses. Perhaps there just is not enough expanse of water to allow the gyres to develop.

Another unusual aspect of the current systems is found in the Indian Ocean. The Indian Ocean is affected by the winds resulting from the atmospheric pressure systems present over the large Eurasian continent. These monsoon winds seasonally change direction, as do the currents associated with them. Consequently, since the Indian Ocean current systems are very deeply influenced by the winds, the currents north of the equator will be toward the east in the summertime and toward the west during the wintertime (Figure 7-6).

## SOME REPRESENTATIVE NUMBERS

It might be interesting at this point to reflect on the magnitude of some of these current systems. The *Gulf Stream* is probably the most famous of all world surface currents having speeds varying from about half a knot to in excess of three knots. The amount of water transported is somewhere around 113 sverdrups* (about 30 billion gallons per second), which is more than 65 times the amount of water moved by all the rivers of the world combined. Of course all ocean currents are not of this magnitude, but even the smaller ocean currents are involved with water transports many times larger than most rivers.

* A sverdrup (sv) is defined as a transport of one million cubic meters per second.

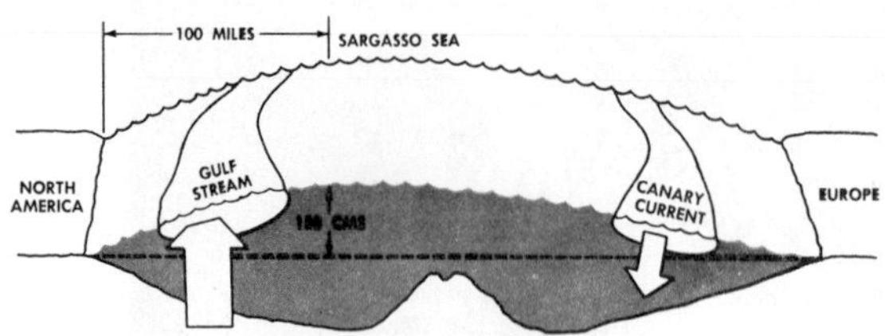


Figure 7-7. The mound in the North Atlantic Ocean associated with the Gulf Stream system.

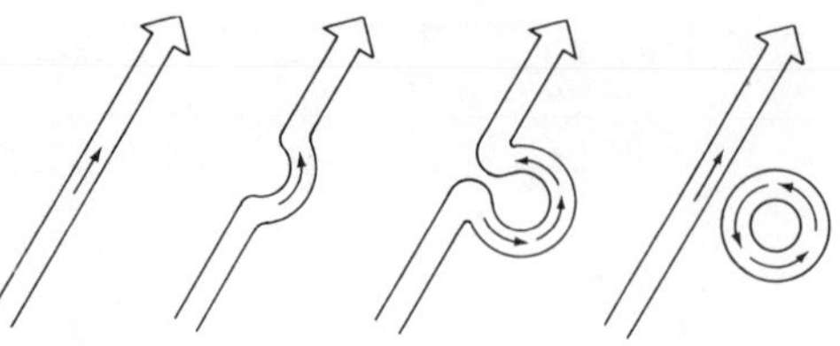

Figure 7-8. Four stages in the formation of an eddy.

Because currents necessarily involve motion, they have the associated surface slopes. This is certainly true for the permanent currents. In the Gulf Stream system for example, the Sargasso Sea, which is the high pressure center of the sub-tropical gyre, is about 150 centimeters higher than the outside edge of the Gulf Stream itself (Figure 7-7). In other words, there is a mound of water in the center of the Atlantic Ocean corresponding to the sub-tropical gyre as there is in the center of all the high pressure gyres in the world's oceans. Similarly, there are depressions in the ocean surface on the order of magnitude of 50 centimeters, corresponding to the centers of the sub-polar and equatorial gyres which are both low pressure systems.

## MATTHEW FONTAINE MAURY

As indicated previously, the first man to use large amounts of ocean data in a systematic study of surface currents, from 1841 to 1853, was Matthew Fontaine Maury, a lieutenant in the U. S. Navy. Using the data accumulated from thousands of old log books, he published the first pilot charts and sailing directions for all the world oceans. As a matter of fact, pilot charts obtained today will bear the inscription, "Founded upon researches made and data collected by Lieutenant M. F. Maury, U. S. Navy."

In addition he laid the foundation for the establishment of the U. S. Weather Bureau, did most of the work in determining the location for the first transatlantic cable, and was instrumental in the establishment of the U. S. Naval Academy. He is also said to have urged the teaching of oceanography at the new institution, a piece of advice which was finally followed over one hundred years later.

## APPLICATIONS

Ocean currents have been discussed as if they were indeed "rivers in the ocean," as Maury described them over 130 years ago. In point of fact, they may be so conceived, but if so, the bed of the river must be considered to change quite rapidly. In the Gulf Stream, for example, the path of the stream varies quite markedly from week to week. Figure 7-8 pictures schematically the Gulf Stream on four different occasions. Note that loops form in the Gulf Stream which break off after a period of time and become eddies having associated currents which may move in a direction opposite to the stream itself.

Of course it is desirable to be able to predict the formation of these eddies, since most well developed current systems appear to have eddies associated with them. However, at this time it is not possible to do this with the desired accuracy; about all that can be done in describing ocean currents is to indicate the average magnitude and direction of the motion at a particular location.

When one refers to a current atlas to determine average currents typically the information is presented in the form of a *current rose* (Figure 7-9). Probabilities of current directions are shown by indicating what percentage of the time currents have been reported in what direction, and what speed

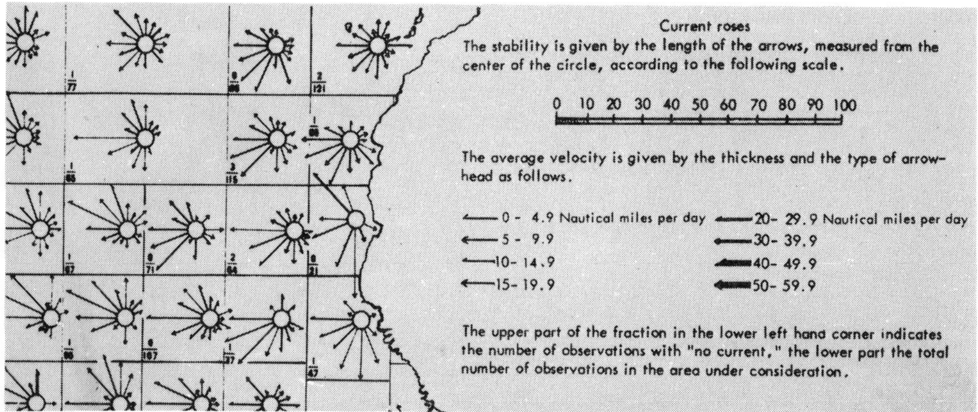


Figure 7-9. Typical current roses.

they had at the time. This allows the mariner to make a good estimate of the way the water will be moving. However, it is important to realize the surface current speed and direction cannot be predicted with absolute certainty.

Aside from the obvious effects of set and drift* on surface ships and other floating material, ocean surface currents occasionally have a fairly large effect on climate. In the main, most of the heat which is exchanged from the lower latitudes poleward is done by means of the moving atmosphere. The major exceptions to this rule are the well developed current systems such as the *Gulf Stream* in the Atlantic and the *Kuroshio*† in the Pacific. These currents involve great volumes of water capable of carrying large amounts of heat. If these current systems pass close to land areas, and if the prevailing winds are such that warmed air is carried over these land areas, the current systems will have an effect on the climate of the adjacent land areas. An example of this is the North Atlantic Current portion of the Gulf Stream system in its passage close to the European continent. The fact that the Gulf Stream is warm and is moving into a relatively cold area, coupled with prevailing westerly winds, makes for a somewhat warmer climate in the British Isles and western Europe than normally would be expected for this latitude. This same effect occurs on the southern coast of Alaska where the effect of the Kuroshio extension (North Pacific Current) is such that this coast has a somewhat more temperate climate than would be expected.

* In navigational parlance set and drift are the direction and magnitude respectively of the current velocity vector.

† So called because the *water is very clear;* Kuroshio means *Black Current* in Japanese.

## CURRENT MEASUREMENTS

Surface currents may be measured in many different ways and they have been measured for many years. Probably the easiest and most obvious way of measuring a surface current is to put a floating object in the water and observe how far and how fast it drifts. This may be a bottle, some sort of a floating drogue, a specially designed float with a radio transmitter or radar reflector for easy tracking, or even a ship itself. In actuality most current measurements which appear on pilot charts are the result of many measured ship drifts from calculated courses. If somewhat more accurate measurements are desired, various devices may be used. One of the most esoteric is the GEK (Geomagnetic electrokinetograph). The GEK consists essentially of two large electrodes which are placed in the surface water to measure the electric potential developed by a moving conductor (sea water) within the earth's magnetic field. This is basically the same principle by which a common electrical generator works, but the output is very much smaller.

One of the big problems in measuring surface currents is obtaining a measurement of water motion with respect to the earth's surface. In the deep ocean it is impossible to anchor in a manner such that a vessel does not drift, so that surface currents are not accurately measured in the deep ocean, due to lack of positioning accuracy. With the advent of better navigational systems, current measurements at sea will become more feasible.

However, if there is some method of fixing a current meter's position with respect to the earth, or if the drift of the device is known, rather conventional units may be used, the most common of which utilize some sort of a rotating vane. This may be a propeller, or a hemispherical cup as is used in Robinson's anemometer, or some other design of rotor, the speed of rotation being related to the current speed.

In recent years, instruments have been developed which measure rapidly fluctuating currents. This had not been possible in the past. With a rotating vane current meter it is difficult to measure a current which changes its magnitude or direction rapidly with time. The newer devices utilize the speed of sound in two directions to determine currents; these not only take a very small period of time to make a measurement but also have no mechanical inertia. Sound-speed is measured in one direction and compared with the sound-speed measured in the opposite direction, the difference between the two being the speed of water movement.*

Most of the devices discussed here have

* Sound energy is carried along with a moving medium.

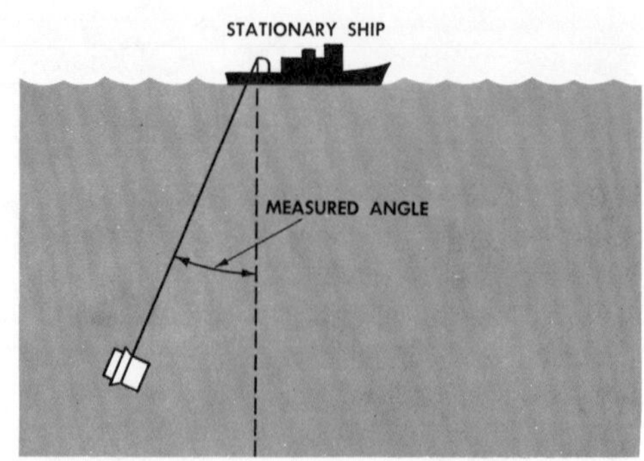


Figure 7-10. Using a current cross for current measurements.

been used with greater success in either shallow water or close to the bottom to measure bottom currents. There have been very few measurements made at sea for which great accuracies were claimed. However, a number of measurements have been made using very simple gear which have indicated the presence of currents where none had been measured before. For instance, a current cross may be lowered to the depth of interest, the angle which the line makes with the vertical is a function of the current speed (Figure 7-10). This was the case in the equatorial Pacific, for example, where the sub-surface Cromwell current was first detected in 1954 by the use of this type of current meter.

Another type of device which has been used in recent years for measuring subsurface currents is the *Swallow float.* This is a long cylinder designed to be buoyant at a particular density level, so that when it is released it will sink and remain at a particular depth. The float will then drift with the current at this level, and it may be tracked by means of acoustic gear. This has been quite successful and was utilized in affirming the previously predicted presence of a countercurrent underneath the Gulf Stream system.

Even though knowledge of currents at the present time is not complete, it is still sufficient for improving sailing times across the oceans. However, for navigational purposes, especially in certain areas, it is many times woefully inadequate. A basic knowledge of surface currents is especially important for such obvious problems as determination of: personnel lifeboat tracks, paths of manmade pollutants, and the movements of plankton populations with their associated larger marine animals.

## SUGGESTED READINGS

Chapin, H., and Smith, F. G. W., *The Ocean River,* Charles Scribner's Sons, 1952.

Cotter, C. H., *The Physical Geography of the Oceans,* American Elsevier Publishing Company, Inc., 1965.

Defant, A., *Physical Oceanography,* Vol. I, Pergamon Press, 1961.

Dietrich, G., *General Oceanography,* John Wiley & Sons, 1963.

Munk, Walter, "Ocean Currents," *Scientific American,* September 1955.

Neumann, G. and Pierson, W. J., *Principles of Physical Oceanography,* Prentice Hall, Inc., 1966.

Pickard, G. L., *Descriptive Physical Oceanography,* Pergamon Press, 1964.

# 8. The Kuroshio Current

RICHARD A. BARKLEY 1970

Every second the Kuroshio current carries some 50 million tons of sea water past Japan's southeast coast—a flow equal in volume to about 6000 rivers the size of the Danube or Volga. But even this massive current would take some 250 years to equal the total volume of the north Pacific. Thus, although the Kuroshio is one of the major currents in the world's oceans, and plays a vital role in the circulation of the north Pacific, it occupies only a small fraction (less than 0.1 per cent) of that ocean: a thin narrow band less than 100 km in width and about 1 km at maximum depth running for 3000 km along the western edge of the Pacific between the Philippines and the east coast of Japan (see Figure 8-1).

Asia's seamen have known the Kuroshio since ancient times. They named it Kuroshio (which means 'black stream' in the Japanese language) because of the deep ultramarine color of the warm, high salinity water which is found flowing north on the right hand side (looking downstream) of the current's axis. The heat which is carried north by this flow influences the weather throughout the northern hemisphere. The Kuroshio therefore plays an indirect but important part in the everyday life of the fishermen and farmers of eastern Asia and also, to a lesser extent, in the lives of most of the rest of mankind as well.

The first European chart to show the Kuroshio was Varenius' "Geographia Generalis" of 1650. Later, expeditions headed by Captains James Cook (1776-80) and Krusenstern (1804) added to western knowledge about the Kuroshio. Although Japanese scientists began to study the biology of the Kuroshio in 1880, it was not until 1893, when Wada started a series of drift bottle experiments, that systematic examination of its currents first began.

Today, in an attempt to learn more about the Kuroshio, scientists from China, Indonesia, Japan, Korea, Philippines, Singapore, Thailand, Hong Kong, United States, the Soviet Union and Vietnam are engaged in a major international project called the Cooperative Study of the Kuroshio (CSK). By

Dr. Richard A. Barkley is a physical oceanographer with the National Marine Fisheries Service's Southwest Fisheries Center, Honolulu Laboratory, Hawaii. He has compiled an oceanographic atlas of the Pacific Ocean, worked on the hydrodynamics of the Kuroshio-Oyashio front east of Japan, and is currently investigating boundary-layer phenomena associated with oceanic islands.

From *Science Journal*, Vol. 6, No. 3, pp. 54-60, 1970. Reprinted with author's revisions and light editing and by permission of the author and Syndication International Limited, London.

keeping a figurative finger on this pulse of the north Pacific, they hope to learn more about western boundary currents in general, the Kuroshio in particular, and the whole north Pacific Ocean as well. In the process, they should also learn more about the way in which both weather and climate respond to changes in conditions at sea, and the ways in which marine animals and plants are affected by their environment.

The influence exerted on ocean currents by the Earth's rotation was not generally appreciated until 1835, when G. de Coriolis, while studying equations of motion in a rotating frame of reference, discovered what is now called coriolis force. Coriolis showed how the effects of the Earth's rotation could be incorporated into the Newtonian equations of motion by adding two additional terms. One, the centrifugal force of the Earth's rotation, is usually absorbed into a redefined term for "gravitation," which includes gravity and centrifugal forces together and acts along a vertical defined by the direction of a plumb bob. By this definition there is no horizontal component of either force. The other term, the coriolis force, makes allowance for the effects of conservation of angular momentum on a particle which moves relative to the Earth's surface. Coriolis force acts at right angles to the Earth's axis of rotation, and thus has no effect on the energy of motion but only modifies its direction.

The vertical component of coriolis force is so small when compared to the force of gravitation that it can always be neglected in ocean current theory. In the sea, however, forces which act along the horizontal are generally weak. Indeed, frictional and inertial forces are far smaller than those we are accustomed to on land—by at least five orders of magnitude—and they have little or no effect on any but the fastest moving ocean currents. The forces exerted by wind stress are often even weaker. Thus the horizontal component of the weak coriolis force becomes an important factor when considering ocean currents.

In most ocean currents the horizontal pressure gradient is found to be in balance with coriolis force. Such currents are called geostrophic or "Earth-balanced" currents. To understand how this balance is achieved, consider a parcel of water in a region where sea level has been raised by a meter or so by convergent wind stress. This parcel of water tends to flow back toward a region of lower pressure. However, as soon as it begins to move at appreciable speeds, this motion generates coriolis force and the water is turned toward the right (in the northern hemisphere). Once it has turned 90° it cannot turn farther without flowing "uphill" and losing momentum, thus weakening the coriolis force. If it then turns slightly toward the left in response to pressure, it gains momentum, generating additional coriolis force and thus being forced to the right once again. In this way a balance is reached with horizontal pressure forces equal and opposite to horizontal coriolis forces, and the water flowing at right angles to both moving endlessly around centers of high (or low) pressure. At low latitudes the horizontal component of coriolis force is weaker than it is at high latitudes, and a relatively higher velocity is required to generate enough coriolis force to offset a given pressure gradient.

Since pressure gradients built up by wind stress are not relieved by this geostrophic flow, energy accumulates until the pressure gradient is large enough, and geostrophic flow fast enough, to generate appreciable friction in some parts of the ocean. Offshore this frictional force disrupts the geostrophic balance slightly, allowing some water to flow out of the high pressure cells back to the "lows." Along coasts friction dissipates energy by converting it to heat. Both processes counteract the effects of wind stress at the sea surface. Because of this near-equilibrium state, horizontal pressure gradients, coriolis force and geostrophic flow are closely linked; knowledge of one of these variables makes it possible to calculate the other two wherever friction can be neglected.

Thus it is possible to obtain a useful approximation (to within 15 per cent) to actual currents by making measurements of horizontal pressure gradients. To do this, a series of temperature and salinity measurements is made to depths of 1 km or more at several locations (called "stations") across a current. These observations define the field of density (which depends on temperature, salinity and pressure, or depth), from which

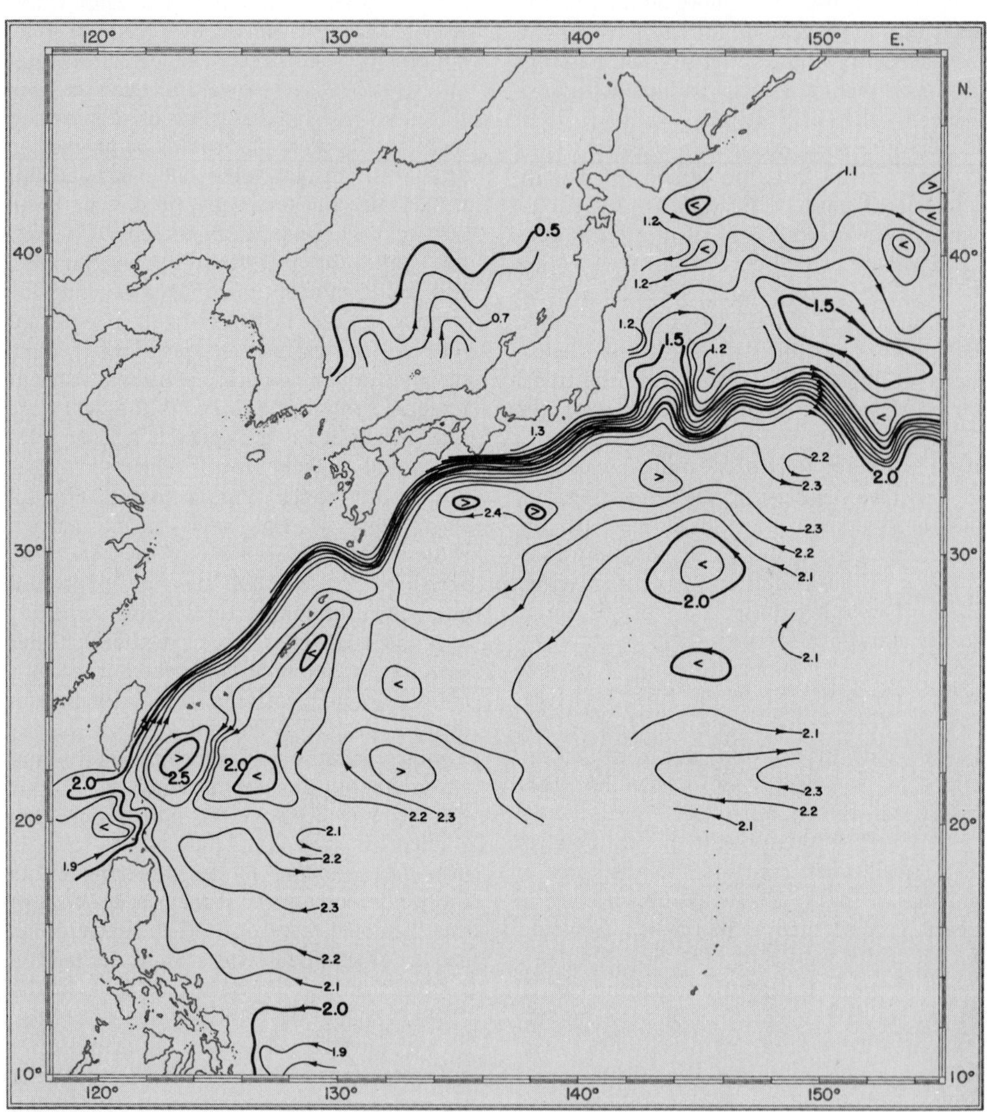


Figure 8-1. Path of the Kuroshio is shown by closely spaced contours on this chart of geostrophic flow at the sea surface. Contours show the elevation of the sea surface (pressure head in meters) or the potential energy (in dynamic meters) relative to an arbitrary horizontal reference plane. The region of narrow flow east of Japan is the Kuroshio Extension, which differs from the Kuroshio in that it has no land boundary to determine its path and absorb frictional stresses.

horizontal pressure gradients can be computed. A chart showing this field of pressure gradients is equivalent to a chart showing streamlines of geostrophic flow. This procedure is referred to as the dynamic method, and was first used by J. W. Sandstrom and B. Helland-Hansen in 1903. Unlike direct current measurements, which are more expensive and time consuming to make and more difficult to interpret, the dynamic method is little affected by transient motion due to surface waves, tides and winds, which are often much stronger than the movements of water in the permanent current system.

The theory of wind-driven ocean currents concerns itself primarily with the forces which generate, control and finally dissipate energy in the sea. Most of this energy appears in two forms: kinetic energy of motion—the currents *per se*—and potential energy of position—the "pressure head" due to slopes in the sea's surface and the internal density structure. There are also others, primarily thermal energy, which affect the distribution of density and thereby influence currents.

Those forces which carried Kuroshio water through nets set by Japanese fishermen this morning were generated weeks, months, or even years earlier by winds blowing over the entire north Pacific Ocean. Even a small gust of wind rippling the quiet waters off Baja California, for example, contributes to the oceanwide accumulation of energy which drives the inexorable flow of millions of tons of water past Asia's coasts. A major problem in ocean theory is to determine the way in which energy is transferred from the winds to the shallow wind-driven upper layers of the ocean; from there, into the geostrophic currents; and, finally, into the narrow shear zone on the left hand side of the Kuroshio, where energy is dissipated.

When V. W. Ekman provided, in 1905, a theoretical explanation for Nansen's observation that Arctic icebergs tend to drift to the right of the wind, he laid a major cornerstone for all subsequent studies of wind-driven flow. Ekman showed that a steady wind produces transport of water at right angles to the wind's direction (toward the right in the northern hemisphere, and to the left in the southern hemisphere). This movement of water is usually called Ekman transport. A balance is reached between coriolis force and wind stress at the sea surface, which is a precise analogy to the balance existing between coriolis force and the horizontal pressure gradient in geostrophic flow.

In 1947, H. U. Sverdrup, the Norwegian oceanographer and meteorologist, used Ekman's concepts to calculate the wind-driven transport in equatorial currents of the Pacific Ocean. The following year, H. Stommel showed that changes in the coriolis effect with latitude (the horizontal component of coriolis force varies as the sine of the latitude, so that it reaches a maximum value at the pole, and vanishes at the equator) were responsible for the narrow swift currents along the western boundaries.

A major advance in the theory of wind-driven circulation was made by W. H. Munk in his pioneer study of oceanwide transports. He pointed out the fundamental importance of wind shear or torque, which transmits angular momentum to the sea surface and thus generates the major circulation systems. Munk's study was based on a linear steady state mathematical model in which friction played a large part. K. Hidaka has explored such theoretical models extensively since 1949.

In more recent years the importance of large scale friction in currents such as the Kuroshio and Gulf Stream has been questioned by a number of theoreticians, who regard it as characteristic of the climatic-mean flow, but not of the instantaneous current. That is, meanders and eddies formed from time to time by the current could be considered as a form of turbulent friction of the magnitude required in Munk's and Hidaka's theories, if their effects were averaged over large areas over long periods of time. On a shorter time scale, and over smaller distances, such meanders and eddies must be treated individually, which requires the use of nonlinear time dependent mathematical models. Such models present formidable mathematical difficulties which in some cases can only be overcome by the use of numerical computer methods.

Prevailing surface winds over the north Pacific in summer describe a clockwise circulation around the mid-latitude high pressure cell, from which the air spirals outward, away from the high, towards the low pressure regions over Asia and Alaska, and towards the climatic Equator, the doldrums, near 5°N. Initially, this is cool, dry air which descends towards the sea surface and speeds up, removing both heat and moisture from the surface water layers as it goes. It then slows down as it reaches the convergent lows, where the air rises and much of the moisture returns to the sea as rain.

On streamline charts (such as Figure 8-2), constant amounts of water flow between any two streamlines (within the accuracy of the methods used), so velocity of flow is inversely proportional to the distance between adjacent streamlines. In addition, such charts show convergences and divergences, flow of water downward out of the layer in question, or upward from below, by showing streamlines terminating (convergence) or beginning (divergence) at a coast or in midocean. In the following discussion it will be convenient to use the term "Sverdrup unit" to indicate a flow of one million cubic meters per second.

According to the map (Figure 8-2), Ekman transport removes water from the equatorial currents and the northern gyre and transports it into the central gyre. Some 45 streamlines enter the gyre at its perimeter (from the coasts, between islands and across 10° and 50°N). What happens to this massive flow? Some of it—about 4 Sverdrup units—evaporates into the cool, dry air flowing out of the atmospheric high. But Ekman transport more than makes up for this loss; the excess "piles up" in the Subtropical Convergence and sinks to depths of 100 to 200 meters. From there, much of this water

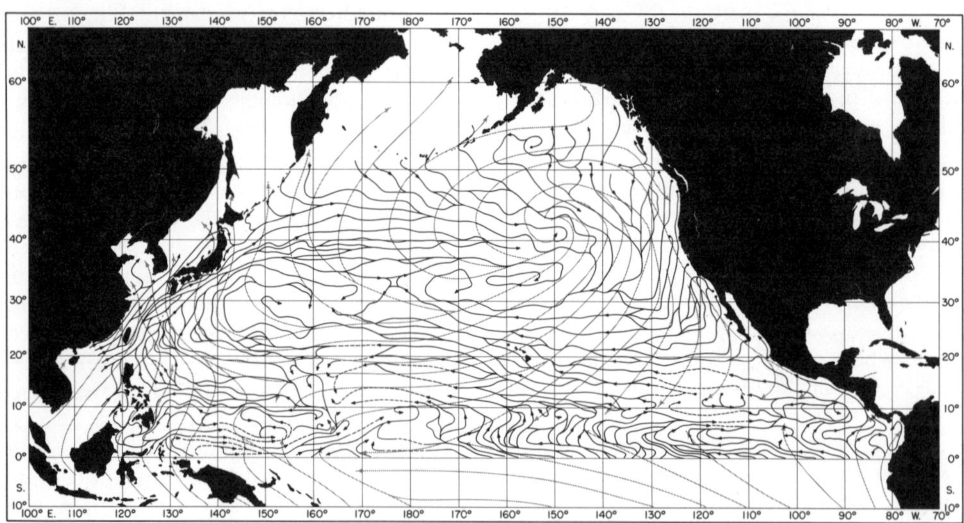


Figure 8-2. Surface current streamlines (black) and prevailing winds (heavy black) in the North Pacific during July. Off the coast of California, and the northeast coasts of China and Japan, winds blowing along the coast induce offshore Ekman transport of water. The opposite situation, where Ekman transport carried surface water toward the coast, can be seen on the northeast side of the Gulf of Alaska, and near the Gulf of Panama. Surface currents are determined primarily by the combined effects of wind-driven Ekman currents and geostrophic flow.

spreads radially outward but some of it is mixed downward, warming the underlying water. Over long periods of time, a "lens" of lower density water about one kilometer thick has accumulated in the center of the gyre. The low density layer is only one-quarter to one-tenth as thick at the perimeters of the gyre, and cold dense, deep water is found much closer to the surface there.

Density gradients due to convergence and divergence of the Ekman transport cause horizontal pressure gradients which generate the geostrophic flow shown on Figure 8-3. Such gradients are largest in the upper 100 to 200 meters and diminish to negligible values at 1 to 2 km depth, due to compensating displacements of denser, deep water.

The effectiveness of coriolis force in limiting the flow of water out of the thick, warm water lens at the convergence can be understood by comparing currents and horizontal pressure gradients in the central gyre with those at the Equator, where coriolis force vanishes. At the Equator a pressure gradient only one per cent as strong as that across the Kuroshio produces comparable current velocities. Why? Because flow at the Equator is not geostrophic and is therefore free to speed up until friction and inertia forces are large enough to balance the pressure gradient. At higher latitudes coriolis force allows much larger horizontal pressure gradients to build up before the flow reaches speeds where friction and inertia forces become important limiting factors.

The potential energy stored in the mid-latitude gyre is many hundreds of times greater than the kinetic energy of its currents, and represents an accumulation of energy five to ten times larger than the energy added by winds in a year. It is not surprising, then, that the ocean's density structure is remarkably constant, and that currents such as the Kuroshio hardly respond to changes in the local winds. Currents near the Equator, on the other hand, represent much smaller accumulations of energy and respond much more readily to changes in the wind.

After decades of effort by Japanese oceanographers, supplemented by studies made during international expeditions and by individuals from many countries, it is now possible to piece together a reasonably satisfactory description of the Kuroshio proper. Water enters the Kuroshio over a broad front 1000 km in width (13°N to about 23°N at longitude 125°E) then accelerates and narrows. Some water leaves the right hand side of the Kuroshio as soon as it begins to turn towards the east, but narrow, intense flow persists for 1500 to 2000 km after the current leaves Japan's east coast, after which there is a marked drop in velocity. This region of narrow intense flow east of Japan is called the Kuroshio extension, and it differs from the Kuroshio in that there is no land boundary on the left hand side to generate a frictional boundary layer.

Comparison of velocity profiles (plots of velocity across the surface current) of the Kuroshio and the Kuroshio extension shows that, although both have essentially identical velocity profiles on their right hand sides, the velocity gradient on the left hand side of the Kuroshio is at least six times greater (a change of 2m/s in 8 km) than that in the Kuroshio extension (2m/s in 50 km). Other things being equal, this would result in six times greater frictional stress on the left side of the Kuroshio. Such velocity profiles support the theoretical view that the Kuroshio and Kuroshio extension are the major non-geostrophic portions of the flow in the central and northern gyres, where important adjustments in the distribution of energy take place.

In the Kuroshio energy is dissipated through friction (on a small scale, since the frictional boundary layer is only about ten kilometers wide). On average, the dissipation rate must be in balance with the mean rate at which wind adds energy to the central gyre.

However, friction not only dissipates energy, it also generates counterclockwise angular momentum at a rate which more than compensates for the decrease in the

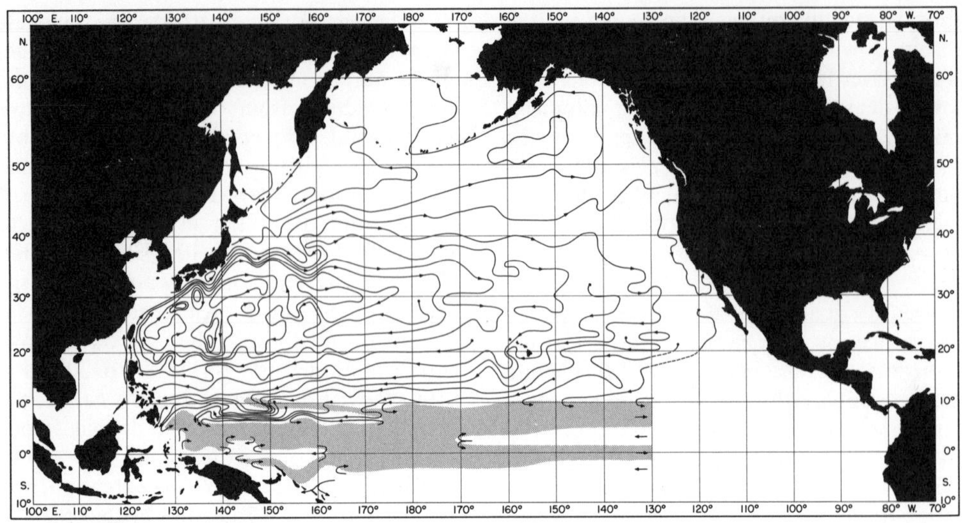


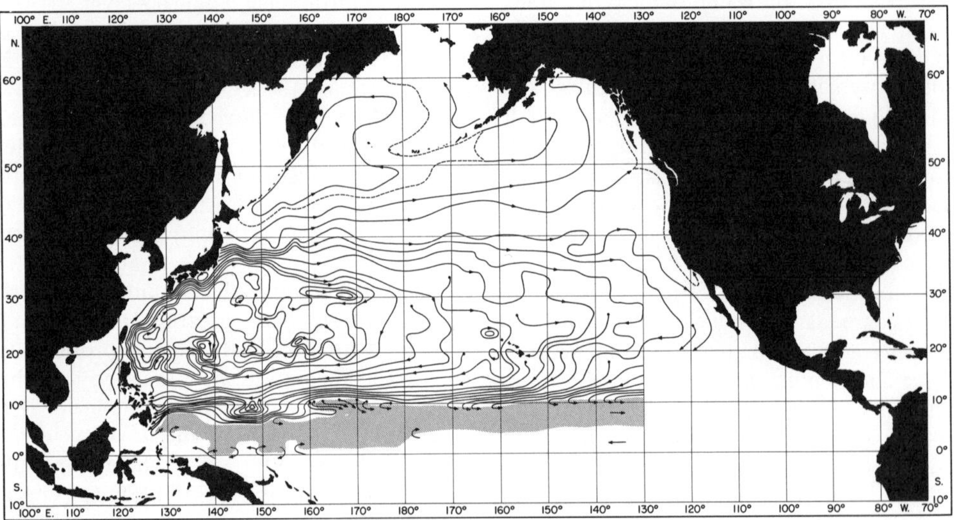


Figure 8-3. Volume transport by geostrophic currents in the North Pacific during the third quarter of the year, integrated from the sea surface down to 100 m depth (upper chart) and 1,000 m depth (lower chart). Each line represents 1 Sverdrup unit of flow on the upper chart, and 5 Sverdrup units on the lower chart. Both charts show the narrow intense flow along the western boundary, and the adjustment downstream to slower broad patterns of flow in mid-ocean. North of latitude 30°N there is little difference between the shallow and deep flows, but farther south the flow is more concentrated in the warmer upper layers, which are strongly influenced by surface winds, particularly the trade winds near 10° to 15°N. Much of the flow generated by trade winds in both hemispheres is relieved by eastward flowing currents in the countercurrent (5° to 10°N), which is caused by slack winds in the Doldrums, and by the Equatorial Undercurrent, which in the central Pacific flows along the equator at depths of 100 m or more. Note the tendency toward faster flow at lower latitudes, associated with decreased coriolis forces. The effects of Ekman transport on the surface currents can be seen by comparing these charts with the chart showing winds and surface currents.

Earth's (counterclockwise) angular momentum as the current flows north. To balance this excess, clockwise angular momentum is generated on the right hand side of the current, where the velocity decreases towards the right in what is sometimes termed an inertial boundary layer. As H. Stommel pointed out in 1948, this balance of angular momentum can only be attained on the western boundary, which accounts for the westward intensification in the current systems of the world oceans.

In the Kuroshio extension the flow adjusts to conditions in the ocean's interior, where large velocity gradients, and the concentrated angular momentum associated with such gradients, cannot persist. Friction is no longer concentrated at the boundary, nor are inertial forces restricted to the right hand side of the stream. Instead, large eddies and meanders dissipate kinetic energy throughout the path of the flow, and redistribute angular momentum at the same time. The transport decreases downstream as the flow fans out and becomes the broad, slow West Wind Drift between 155° and 160°E.

Fifty Sverdrup units of flow approach the east coast of Mindanao in the Philippines and half of this volume turns north into the Kuroshio. Most of this flow consists of warm (20°-28°C) water in the upper 200 meters; there is a layer with relatively high salinity (near 35 parts per thousand) between 100 and 200 meters with slightly more dilute water (34.5 parts per thousand) above that.

The depth of the high velocity flow increases from 200 to 400 meters, and the velocity goes up from a few tens of centimeters per second to one meter per second as the current narrows east of Taiwan. From Taiwan to Japan some dilute water from the Asian shelf, on the left of the current, is entrained by the flow, which speeds up even more, to velocities of 1.5 to 3m/s. Transport just off Japan's south coast amounts to 35 Sverdrup units, but there may be significant flow below 1000 meters since the current extends to considerable depths at that point, and so the total transport may be as high as 45 to 50 Sverdrup units.

Just as the current reaches Japan's southeast tip, it flows over the shallow Izu-Bonin Ridge which extends due south from Honshu, Japan's main island. The Kuroshio undergoes complex and little understood fluctuations near this ridge.

Once past the Izu-Bonin Ridge, the Kuroshio may turn north along Japan's east coast for a short distance, or it may continue to flow almost due east. In either case, it joins the Oyashio current, which flows southward from the Kamchatka Peninsula. Together these two currents leave the coast and form the Kuroshio extension. Transports here amount to about 45 Sverdrup units (up to 60 on occasion) though only 25 to 35 Sverdrup units are within the high velocity core of the Kuroshio extension, where speeds of two meters per second or more are often observed.

By the time the current has reached 160°E, towards the end of the Kuroshio extension, it consists of a mosaic of water types: warm saline water from the original source off the Philippines, coastal and shelf water of lower salinity, and cold dilute water from the Oyashio, with summer temperatures of 3° to 10° C, and salinities sometimes as low as 33.8 parts per thousand.

Some mixing occurs in the core of the Kuroshio extension, but on the whole there are two distinct types of water in the current: warm saline water on the right, and cold dilute water on the left. The convoluted front separating these two types of water is often very sharp and active, with strong velocity gradients and contrasts in the properties of the water on the two sides. Rich fishing grounds are located on both sides of the frontal zone in the Kuroshio extension, so this complex feature of the western north Pacific is of particular interest to Japan's fishing fleet. A pioneer in fisheries oceanography, Professor Michitaka Uda, has studied such fronts and the fisheries associated with them since 1930. He and his colleagues in

Japan's unique system of fisheries universities have contributed much to our knowledge of the sea as an environment. They have taken particular interest in variability in the occurrence of various kinds of fish, and changes in the environment which cause much of this variability.

The path of the Kuroshio as shown in Figure 8-1 is very nearly its average position, but the current can undergo marked and fairly rapid changes in speed and in the location of its axis. Apart from changes due to tides, short term changes due to major shifts in the axis of the Kuroshio can occur as it flows past southern Japan. Meanders develop in the current which occasionally bring high velocity flow unusually close to the coastline, and part of the Kuroshio's flow may be diverted into nearby bays, where it can flush out much of the coastal water within a matter of days. These sudden and as yet unpredictable events cause widespread damage to boats and fishing gear anchored in the normally quiet waters, as offshore currents move inshore at speeds of 1-2m/s, or more.

Meanders in the Kuroshio south of Japan have been studied intensively. The axis of the current may shift onshore or offshore 100 km or more in a matter of weeks. For example, in 1959 the Kuroshio off Japan's south coast (at 133°E) began to move offshore in March or April, shifting from its initial position 20 km offshore to a distance of 140 km in about one month. This meander also drifted rather slowly downstream, reaching the central portion of the south coast (136°E) by the end of May and the eastern portion (139°E) by early August, at which time the Kuroshio's axis was back within 25 km of the coast farther upstream (133°E), where the disturbance was first observed. Such meanders may appear and disappear within a few months, but they may also remain more or less stationary for more than a decade. When the meander develops, cold water is brought up toward the surface between the Kuroshio and the coast and temperatures drop to as much as 10°C below normal. This change has profound effects on coastal and offshore fisheries, since the area involved is fairly large–about the size of the Bay of Biscay. Familiar species of fish move away and are replaced by others, and so fishermen must either move to new grounds or market what they can catch on the old grounds.

The only nontidal changes in the Kuroshio which appear to be at all regular are annual changes in velocity and transport, which are easily obscured by the irregular variations discussed above. Japanese scientists generally agree that the speed is greatest from May until August, with a second maximum in January and February. But an analysis by Y. V. Pavlova has shown that the annual cycle is rather more complex, at least for geostrophic currents. Speed and transport not only vary with season, they vary in different ways from place to place along the Kuroshio. Off the southern tip of Japan, for example, maximum transport within the Kuroshio occurs in September and again in March or April, while maximum velocities are observed in July and January. Just east of Japan, according to Pavlova, maxima in transport occur during June and December, with velocity maxima in August and February.

What now remains to be learned about currents such as the Kuroshio? Perhaps most valuable would be information on fine structure and on fluctuations over periods of a month or less. To determine how fluctuations propagate from place to place, measurements must be made simultaneously at several points along the current, and at least a few direct measurements must be made of the currents at all depths. Many developments in ocean current theory await the results of such observations, which will also be needed for forecasts of conditions in and near the Kuroshio to serve the needs of fishermen and meteorologists. But the effort required, for a complete survey of the Kuroshio, in terms of ships, time and operating costs, is staggering and detailed rapid surveys of the Kuroshio must wait until more efficient tools, such as instrumented buoys, become commonly available.

Once routine monitoring of the marine environment becomes commonplace, we can expect marked improvements in long range weather forecasts and in catch rates of commercial fisheries, which will rapidly repay the original investment of effort and funds. Even rather minor improvements in weather forecasts can bring significant savings to farmers, public utilities, cargo ships, airlines and others who use forecasts in scheduling operations or planning routes.

Farmers in northern Japan may have good or poor harvests depending on the extent to which the Kuroshio flows north along Japan's east coast, before joining the cold Oyashio water, since water temperatures offshore strongly influence cloud cover and rainfall. Similarly, cold air from Siberia flows out over the Pacific in winter, to encounter warm water carried north by the Kuroshio; these temperature contrasts trigger formation of numerous cyclonic lows in the atmosphere over the Kuroshio. The lows carry stormy weather east to northeast across the northern Pacific Ocean towards the coasts of Alaska, Canada and the United States.

Improved knowledge of the ocean as an environment can help fishermen locate and catch protein-rich fish to feed an increasingly hungry world. Fishermen could make direct use of forecasts of the Kuroshio's flow, because the entire current system is a series of fishing grounds which move about with changes in the flow. Various species of tuna, sardine and anchovy, mackerel, squid and many other commercially important species are each found in specific zones in and near the Kuroshio. For example, fronts where coastal and offshore waters meet are often good fishing grounds. Species such as sardines are caught on the coastal side of these fronts, while mackerel and tuna occur in abundance in the warmer offshore waters. Changes in the marine environment appear to influence both the timing and the paths of fish migrations.

For more than 50 years, Kitahara, Uda and their fellow fisheries oceanographers in Japan have studied the response of fish to their environment. They have set up an extensive network for collecting and reporting temperatures at the sea surface and at various depths, movements of schools of fish near various fishing grounds, catch rates, and ocean current information for making fishing condition forecasts.

Six regional fisheries research laboratories and 38 prefectual fisheries experiment stations are responsible for collecting, analyzing and distributing information on individual fisheries, such as the salmon, sardine or albacore. Ships at sea send information on their catches and the environment to the appropriate laboratory by radio. There these reports are compiled and analyzed to produce charts of fishing conditions, conditions in the ocean, and forecasts of various kinds, which are sent to the fishing fleet by mail, radio and facsimile. Some charts and forecasts are prepared at 10 day intervals, and others are sent out once a month. Research and cargo ships also provide information on temperature, salinity, currents and other factors in the environment for use in the fishing condition broadcasts.

Forecasts are based on long term trends, the time when fishing begins or ends on various grounds, data on age and size composition of the catch, and on experience with changes in the ocean in various fishing areas and the consequences of such changes in the past. It is still too early to evaluate the system's effectiveness, except to note that the information provided to the fishermen is very much in demand.

The potential value of fishery forecasting systems can be judged from the fact that boats in some fisheries must spend 80 per cent or more of their time scouting for fish. If this time could be reduced by half, each ship in such a fishery could increase its catch as much as threefold.

We have seen that there are many reasons for undertakings such as the Cooperative Study of the Kuroshio. They range from the most abstract, through the coldly practical to the mundane–improvements in ocean current theory, better weather predictions, more efficient ways to catch fish, and improved charts of the oceans. All these and more will result from studies of the Kuroshio and other parts of the world ocean. But regardless of motive, form or content, the goal of these studies can be summarized in much simpler terms: the search for man's ultimate tool, knowledge.

## SUGGESTED READINGS

Water Characteristics of the Kuroshio, J. Masuzawa in *The Oceanographical Magazine,* **17**, 37, 1965.

The seasonal variation of the Kuroshio Current (In Russian), Y. V. Pavlova, in *Okeanologia,* **4**, 625, 1964.

Description of the Kuroshio (Physical aspect), D. Shoji, in *Proceedings of Symposium on the Kuroshio, Oceanographical Society of Japan and UNESCO, Tokyo, 1965.*

On the variability of the velocity of the Kuroshio Vol 1, D. Shoji and H. Nitani, in *The Journal of the Oceanographical Society of Japan,* **22**, 192 1966.

The influence of friction on inertial models of oceanic circulation, R. W. Stewart, in *Studies on Oceanography, Hidaka Jubilee Committee, Tokyo, 1964.*

On the nature of the Kuroshio, its origin and meanders, M. Uda, in *Studies on Oceanography, Hidaka Jubilee Committee, Tokyo, 1964.*

*An Introduction to Physical Oceanography,* W. S. von Arx. Addison-Wesley Publishing Co., Reading, Massachusetts, 1962.

# 9. Oceanic Water Masses and Their Circulation

JEROME WILLIAMS JOHN J. HIGGINSON JOHN D. ROHRBOUGH 1968

## THE UBIQUITOUS FLUIDS

All human life begins its existence enveloped in a mass of fluid. With birth, these babies are cast forth to spend the balance of their lives surrounded by other fluids. All human endeavors are partially, totally or in various combinations immersed in air or water, or in the interface region of the two. These fluids may arrange themselves in large bodies of relative homogeneity called *masses*.

## WATER MASSES

A *water mass* is defined as a large homogeneous body of water which has a particular characteristic range of temperature and salinity values. The density of the water, as specified by sigma *t*, is not sufficient to identify a water mass, since a combination of various temperatures and salinities can result in the same density value.

Note that since the sigma *t* curves are not straight lines, the mixing of two water masses having the same density will result in a new mass of *greater* density. This process is known as *caballing*. For example, in Figure 9-1 water mass *a* and water mass *b* are both shown to have the same sigma *t* value. When these are mixed in equal quantities water mass *c* results wherein $T_c=(T_a + T_b)/2$, and $S_c=(S_a + S_b)/2$, but $\sigma_{tc} \neq (\sigma_{ta} + \sigma_{tb})/2$. In general, when water masses mix, resulting temperatures and salinities may be obtained by simply averaging, but resulting densities may not.

Since water masses usually gain their temperature and salinity characteristics at the

Jerome Williams is associate chairman of the Environmental Sciences Department at the United States Naval Academy. He has also been associated with the Chesapeake Bay Institute of Johns Hopkins University, Maryland. His major research interests are underwater optics, instrumentation, and physical oceanography.

Commander John J. Higginson has been an instructor of oceanography at the United States Naval Academy. He has also been associated with the Apollo Recovery Program as operations officer in Helicopter ASW Squadron Four. He is presently in receipt of orders to Helicopter ASW Squadron Two at Naval Air Station, Imperial Beach, California.

Commander John D. Rohrbough is with the United States Navy and is on the staff of the Studies, Analysis, and Gaming Agency of the Office of the Joint Chiefs of Staff, the Pentagon, Washington. He has served as an instructor of oceanography and a member of the staff of the superintendent at the Naval Academy.

From *Sea and Air: The Naval Environment* by Jerome Williams, Lieutenant Commander John Higginson, U.S. Navy, and Lieutenant Commander John Rohrbough, U.S. Navy. Copyright © 1968 by the United States Naval Institute, Annapolis, Maryland. Reprinted by permission.

Table 9-1. Characteristics of Selected Water Masses.

| Mass | Ocean of Origin | Location Depth (m) | Salinity (0/00) and Temp. (°C) Range |
|---|---|---|---|
| 1. Antarctic Bottom | South Atlantic (Weddell Sea) | 4,000 to bottom | 34.66 (−)0.4[a] |
| 2. Antarctic Circumpolar | South Atlantic | 100-4.000 | 34.68-34.70 0.5° |
| 3. Antarctic Intermediate | South Atlantic | 500-1.000 | 33.8 2.2° |
| 4. South Atlantic Central | South Atlantic | 100-300 | 34.65-36.00 6° - 18° |
| 5. Arctic Deep and Bottom | North Atlantic | 1,300-4,000 as Deep 1,300-Bottom as Bottom | 34.90-34.97 2.2° - 3.5° |
| 6. North Atlantic Intermediate | North Atlantic | 300-1,000 | 34.73 4° - 8° |
| 7. North Atlantic Central | North Atlantic | 100-500 | 35.10-36.70 8° - 19° |
| 8. European Mediterranean | European Mediterranean | 1,400-1.600 | 37.75 13° |
| 9. Pacific Equatorial | Central Pacific | 200-1,000 | 34.60-35.15 8° - 15° |
| 10. Indian Central | Indian | 100-500 | 34.60-35.50 8° - 15° |
| 11. Red Sea | Red Sea | 2,900-3,100 | 40.00-41.00 18 |
| 12. Black Sea | Black Sea | 0-200 | 16.00 (average) various temp. |

[a]This is the only negative temperature in this table.

surface and then seek their own density level by thermohaline convection, water masses in the ocean are categorized by two factors: the depth at which they reach vertical equilibrium and the geographical source region. In order of increasing depth water masses are classified as being *surface, central, intermediate, deep,* and *bottom. Surface* waters extend down to about 100 meters, *central* to the base of the main thermocline, *intermediate* from below the central waters to about 3,000 meters, and the *deep* and *bottom* waters fill the lower portions of the ocean basins (see Table 9-1).

The surface water is unique in that it does not fall into a true water mass category since the variability of parameters is so great.

In general, it would be expected that waters at greater depth are formed at the higher latitudes, while those existing closer to the surface are formed nearer the equator.

## ATLANTIC OCEAN

In the immediate vicinity of the Antarctic Continent, particularly the Weddell Sea, waters reach extremely low temperatures in the winter. Due to this low temperature and high salinity resulting from ice formation, this water has the highest sigma *t* of any in the world ocean. As a consequence, having once gained these characteristics, it sinks and flows along the ocean floor in a direction toward the equator. In fact, traces of this water have been measured as far as 45° *North* latitude. This water mass is called *Antarctic Bottom Water,* obviously because of its location and formation area. The Ant-

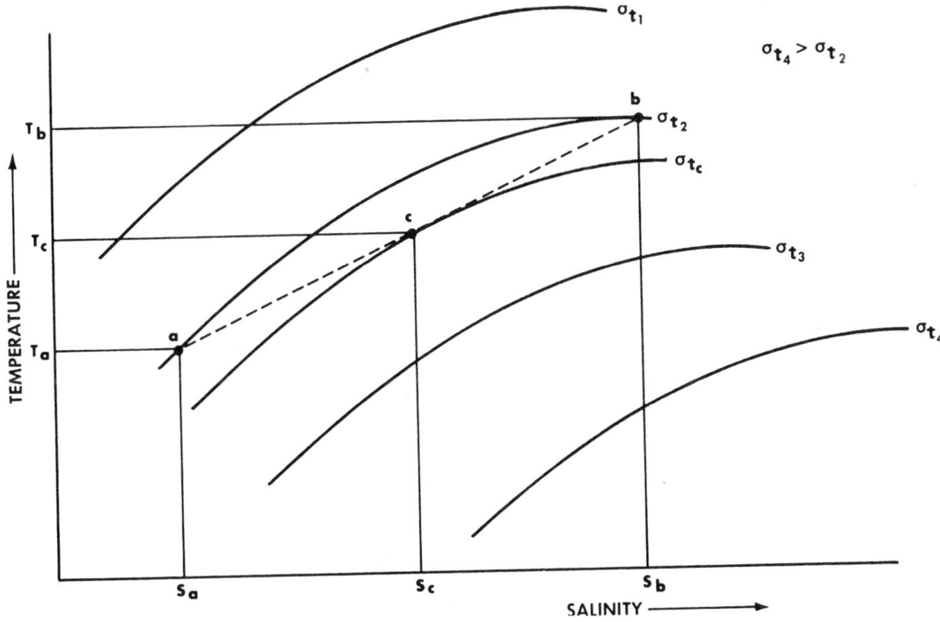


Figure 9-1. A T-S diagram showing simple mixing of two water masses.

arctic Bottom water mass also flows eastward around the Antarctic Continent due to the surprisingly deep-reaching effects of the surface West Wind Drift, mixes well below the surface with masses on its north edge, and becomes a separate, fairly homogeneous mass known as *Antarctic Circumpolar Water.* The deeper reaches of this mass, as it flows eastward, continuously provides deep water to the Indian and South Pacific Oceans. While it is true that some water circumnavigates the continent, it has been difficult to estimate the amount.

The *Arctic Deep and Bottom Water* (North Atlantic Deep and Bottom Water) is formed in relatively small areas off the coast of Greenland, one of which is the convergent region produced by the Irminger and East Greenland currents.* North Atlantic Deep and Bottom Water, less dense than Antarctic Bottom Water overrides Antarctic Bottom Water all the way to the South Atlantic reaching the surface south of 60°S (see Figure 9-2). The North Atlantic Deep Water is continuously modified in its transit by mixing with masses yet to be discussed.

The *Antarctic Convergence Zone,* located at approximately 60°S latitude, is primarily produced by the seasonal cooling of the Antarctic Intermediate Water as it sinks to its density level. This particular convergence zone is present at nearly all longitudes of the earth; however, similar convergence zones in the North Atlantic and North Pacific are somewhat discontinuous and at times can be difficult to locate. North Atlantic Intermediate Water flows south from the Arctic Convergence to approximately 20°N where it mixes with Antarctic Intermediate Water.

North and South Atlantic Central Waters

* Periodic overflows from the North Polar Sea across the Greenland-Scotland Ridge cascade down the southern slope with relatively high velocities due to the water's very cold (-1.4C) temperature (the coldest water anywhere in the deep sea); it is less dense, however, than North Atlantic Deep and Bottom Water because of a lower salt content.

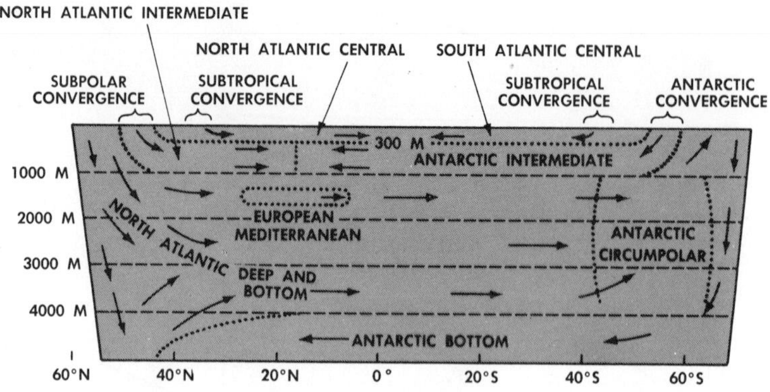


Figure 9-2. Atlantic Ocean: General subsurface movement.

form at the surface at their respective subtropical convergences during the winters. They sink and flow toward the equator losing their identities as they spread.

The one significant incursion of foreign waters is the large mass of European Mediterranean Water which finds its level at the average depth of 1,500 meters, after leaving through the Strait of Gibraltar. This water mass is continually formed in the northern area of western Mediterranean by winter cooling and evaporation by the dry air sweeping north from Africa. The cool, saline water sinks, flows south and west, and then spills out over the sill. On the surface in the Strait the less dense Atlantic waters flow in to maintain the balance, creating a two-layered stratification with each layer flowing in opposite directions (see Figure 9-3).

During World War II German submarines are said to have used the flows to transit the Strait undetected. They would dive deep or shallow depending on whether they desired to exit or enter, compensate for the required neutral buoyancy state, and then ride the flow quietly without use of their motors. This was a very ingenious use of environmental knowledge to circumvent detection.

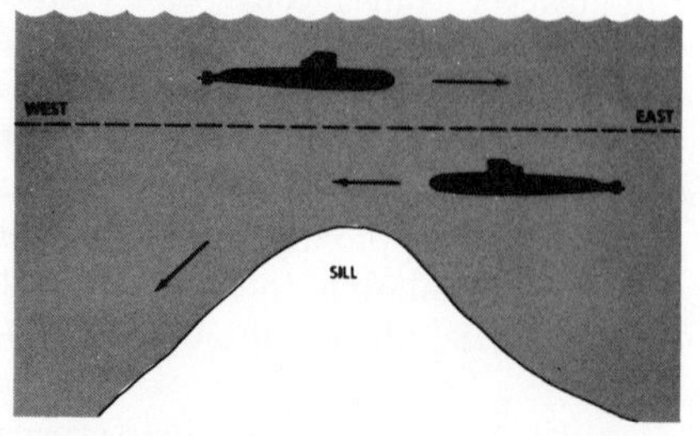


Figure 9-3. Water flow in the Straits of Gibraltar.

The Mediterranean Water, with its increased salinity, has strong effects on the upper section of the North Atlantic Deep Water mass. Although its influence is felt to the west and south predominately, its telltale salinity maximum has been traced to locations up to 1,500 miles from Gibraltar.

In conclusion, the Atlantic Ocean is constantly renewing itself at all depths although at a very slow rate. Recent analyses utilizing radioactive carbon measurements indicate that it has been about 750 years since Antarctic Bottom Water in the Atlantic was at the surface. In contrast to this, 1,500 years is estimated for the age of this water mass in the Pacific Ocean.

## PACIFIC OCEAN

The Pacific Ocean is noted for its generally sluggish deep water flow pattern when compared to the other oceans. However, the Antarctic Bottom Water, as it flows around the Antarctic Continent, provides a fairly

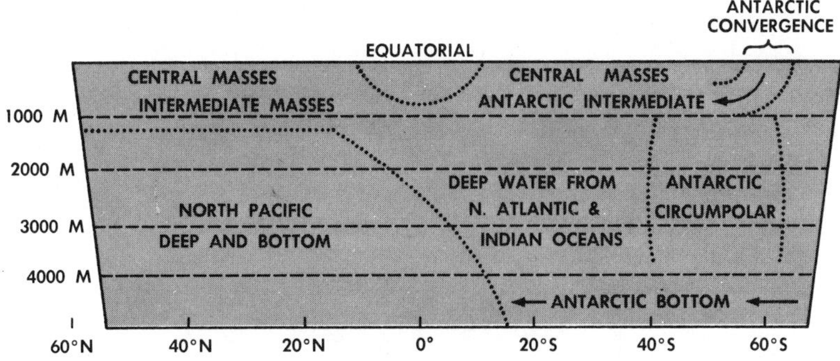


Figure 9-4. Pacific Ocean: General subsurface structure.

continuous input to the South Pacific Basin. On the other hand, Antarctic Circumpolar Water, which has been partially mixed with waters of the Atlantic and Indian Oceans, enters from the west to slowly but continuously push into the South Pacific deep layer (below 1,000 m).

The intermediate and central layers of the entire Pacific Ocean are diffuse and not well defined. The various convergence zones which would be analogous to those in the Atlantic are discontinuous and misplaced. Several masses existing at the same depth in different areas make a cross-sectional depiction difficult to construct. It is important to note that there is near surface mixing of masses from distant regions at the equator forming the Pacific Equatorial Water Mass—the only major water mass which does not receive any characteristics from the surface near the formation area.

The North Pacific is unique because no extremely dense water masses form in its most northerly reaches. The Deep and Bottom Water of the North Pacific experiences little interchange with other areas. Its origin is in doubt both in time and space, and it is characterized by an oxygen minimum due to the sluggish flow present.

Because of the slow movement of the subsurface mass, the surface current motion reaches deeper and has greater effect on the subsurface characteristics in the North Pacific than do the surface currents in other oceans. This is probably due to the general absence of vital thermohaline convective activity in the North Pacific Ocean (see Figure 9-4).

## INDIAN OCEAN

Of the three major oceans only the Indian Ocean does not extend into the North Hemisphere. There is no cold water sinking along its northern edge, causing the deep water mass to have a lesser movement than that in the North Atlantic Ocean. However, there is a well defined bottom flow in the South and, oceanographically speaking, it is like the South Atlantic south of the Subtropical Convergence Zone at about 40°S latitude.

The Antarctic Bottom Water is present at all latitudes of the Indian Ocean. The deep layer is that which is led around the south tip of Africa from the Atlantic; it is reasonably well oxygenated, especially considering the distance from its source region in the North Atlantic. The Antarctic Intermediate Water forms at the Antarctic Convergence Zone and spreads to the north. The Indian Central Water sinks at the Subtropical Convergence and flows north toward equatorial regions.

Bottom water from the Red Sea flows over the sill and on through the entrance at the Strait of Bab el Mandeb to spread and mix with deep layers of the Indian Ocean. Red Sea Water is characterized by its very

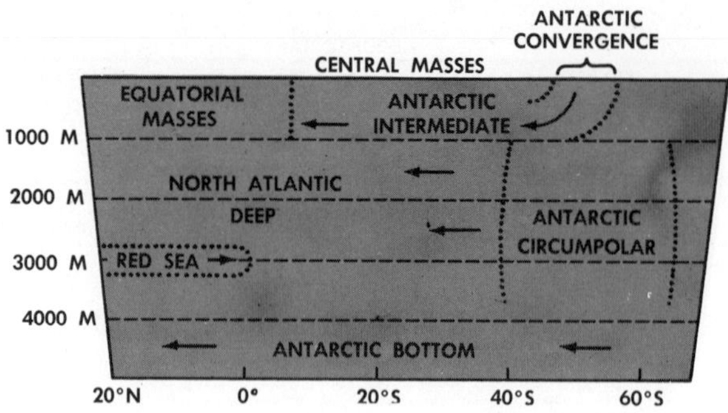


Figure 9-5. Indian Ocean: General subsurface structure.

high salinity of about 40°/oo to 41°/oo. This water mass is formed within the Sea by constant evaporation by dry air from Africa and by winter cooling periods in much the same manner as European Mediterranean Water. High salinity causes its density to be such that it spreads out in the Indian Ocean at depths near 3,000 meters. Traces have been identified as far as 1,250 miles south of the Gulf of Aden. Red Sea Water provides the only significant modifying effect in the entire deep Indian Ocean. As an aside, hot spots have been discovered recently at great depths (2,040 m) in the Red Sea. The anomalous temperatures measured thus far range from 22°C to 56°C; salinities have been determined to be in excess of 250°/oo. Their causes remain unexplained but future concerted investigations are planned to develop answers as to how the spots have been formed and how they continue to exist.

The Equatorial shallow layers of the Indian Ocean are not clearly defined. This is partially due to seasonal monsoon changes of surface currents. The water is being constantly overturned by changing winds and does not have significant characteristics. Little distinguishable subsurface flow is present (see Figure 9-5).

## BLACK SEA—A SEA APART

The Black Sea, with its complete lack of thermohaline convection, has a complete oxygen disappearance at all depths below 200 meters. Precipitation and runoff far exceed evaporation. The flow into the sea through the Bosphorus from the European Mediterranean is so meager that it would renew the waters below 30 meters only once in 500 years. Consequently, the deep waters have become stagnant; hydrogen sulfide is present; and only anaerobic bacteria can live in the blackened waters.

## CONCLUSION

The preceding discussion, at best, is only a very cursory qualitative treatment of deep water ocean circulation. Although the mechanisms producing subsurface flows were discussed, bottom topographic effects have been neglected. But to ignore the latter in a detailed study would be a serious omission. Only the most prominent of the marginal sea effects have been introduced.

Air can be subdivided into masses displaying similar identifiable characteristics just as the water masses of the oceans. In addition, there can be identified clear boundaries between these masses, both in the sea and in the air. Those in the sea have not achieved the importance that those in the atmosphere enjoy; however, the wall of the Gulf Stream has been clearly identified as a "front" in the ocean.

## SUGGESTED READINGS

Bailey, H. S., Jr., "The Voyage of the *Challenger*," *Scientific American*, May, 1953.

Dietrich, Gunter, *General Oceanography*, John Wiley and Sons, New York, 1963.

King, Cuchlaine, A. M., *An Introduction to Oceanography*, McGraw-Hill, Inc., 1963.

Kort, V. G., "The Antarctic Ocean," *Scientific American*, September, 1962.

Stommel, Henry, "The Anatomy of the Atlantic," *Scientific American*, January, 1955.

Sverdrup, H. V., Johnson, Martin, W., and Fleming, Richard, H., *The Oceans*, Prentice-Hall, Inc., 1942.

Williams, Jerome, *Oceanography*, Little, Brown and Company, Inc., Boston, 1962.

Yasso, Warren E., *Oceanography*, Holt, Rinehart and Winston, Inc., New York, 1965.

Special Issue: "Deep Ocean Engineering," *Naval Ship Systems Command Technical News*, January, 1967.

# 10. Ocean Waves

STEVE LISSAU 1975

Waves are the sculptors of coasts and the artisans of sand. They sing the song of the sea. Breaking on a beach, their heave and bellow tells of fierce distant storms and gale-force winds. Even the casual beachcomber finds a special significance in the breaking surf; for it is fearsome yet enticing, repetitious yet spellbinding.

Two distinct types of motion are combined within a wave: the circular orbits of the wave's component water molecules and the undulatory advance of the wave form itself. The circular orbits essentially close upon themselves and thus there is no actual transport of water as a wave rolls along in the open sea.

The high point of a wave is called the "crest," the low point is the "trough." All waves may be described in terms of their basic dimensions: "height," "length" and "period." Wave height is the vertical distance from crest to trough. Wave length is the distance from one crest to the next. The period is the amount of time (in seconds) required for two successive crests to pass a stationary point; in other words, the time for a crest to travel a distance of one wave length.

Wave length, period and velocity are directly related: the longer the period the longer the wave, and the longer the wave the greater its velocity (Figure 10-1). Since wave height has no relationship to either wave length, period or velocity, the period and height comprise the description of a wave.

Almost all ocean waves are generated by the eastwardly moving circular low pressure storms—called "extratropical cyclones" by meteorologists—that are born off the western side of the great oceans and mature as they travel across them. Areas of high pressure rarely build waves by themselves—the giant subtropical high causing the trade winds being a notable exception—but when a low, which is composed of warm, light air, passes near the cool, relatively heavy air of a high, air from the high rushes toward the low, attempting to mix with the warm air and thus equalize atmospheric pressure. In doing so wind is created and wind generates waves. Winter storms or lows can be exceptionally large, varying upwards from five thousand miles in diameter. The latter can occupy an area as big as the entire North Pacific.

Supplementing the waves generated by winter storms are the summer and fall swells created by tropical cyclones, better known as hurricanes when they are fully developed.

Steve Lissau is a part-time science teacher in Honolulu, Hawaii.

From *Oceans Magazine,* Vol. 8, No. 5, pp. 12-25, 1975. Reprinted with light editing and with permission of the author and *Oceans Magazine.*

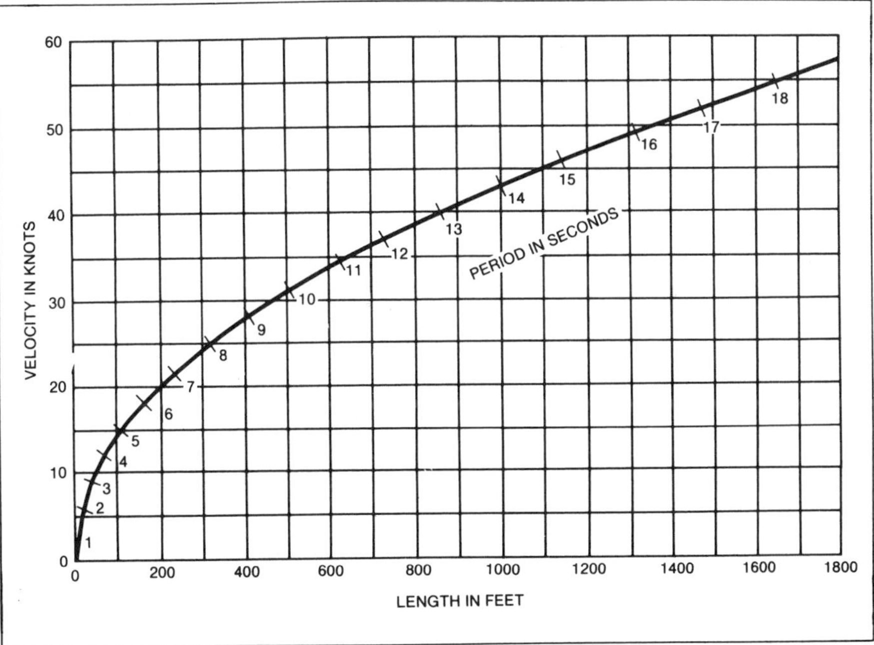


Figure 10-1. Graphic presentation of the theoretical relationship between wave lengths, velocities, and periods in deep water. A working rule is that the period (in seconds) multiplied by three gives the velocity in knots. The length is approximately equal to the period multiplied by 5.12. Wave velocity is equal to the length divided by the period. (After Bigelow and Edmundson)

But these are a different breed from the winter storms. For one thing they are much smaller, rarely exceeding three hundred miles in diameter, and they are capable of producing tremendous wind velocities at their centers. For example, a strong middle latitude winter storm might have winds of forty to fifty knots, but the winds at the center of a full-blown hurricane often exceed one hundred knots. Nevertheless, winter storms generate the biggest waves since their great size allows their winds to blow over hundreds of miles.

## WIND WAVES

As a passing cat's-paw first ruffles the smooth surface of a calm sea, the water becomes covered with tiny ripples. The ripples enlarge as the wind continues and small waves grow rapidly. Since wind always blows in irregular gusts, unequal pressures deform the water surface and waves of many different heights and lengths are simultaneously created. The wind pushes against the newly formed crests and its pull upon the water surface supplies energy to the waves and they enlarge.

Growing waves, still under the wind's influence, are referred to as a "sea." In the initial phases of wave formation, the sea will be choppy and difficult to describe. But as waves develop, they form a more regular series of crests and troughs moving in the same direction as the wind.

The height and length of growing waves is dependent upon four factors:

1. wind velocity
2. the distance of open water over which the wind has blown—called the "fetch"
3. the duration of the wind
4. the state of the sea (waves which were present when the wind started blowing)

The greater the wind velocity, duration and fetch distance, the greater the height

Table 10-1. Relationships Between Wind Velocity, Fetch, and Duration with Wave Height and Period.

| *Wind* | *Distance* | *Time* | *Waves* | | | |
|---|---|---|---|---|---|---|
| *Velocity in knots* | *Length of fetch (Nautical miles)* | *(Hours)* | *Average height (feet)* | *$H_3$ Significant height (feet)* | *$H_{10}$ Average of the highest 10% (feet)* | *Period where most of energy is concentrated (Seconds)* |
| 10 | 10 | 2.4 | 0.9 | 1.4 | 1.8 | 4 |
| 15 | 34 | 6 | 2.5 | 3.5 | 5 | 6 |
| 20 | 75 | 10 | 5 | 8 | 10 | 8 |
| 25 | 160 | 16 | 9 | 14 | 18 | 10 |
| 30 | 280 | 23 | 14 | 22 | 28 | 12 |
| 40 | 710 | 42 | 28 | 44 | 57 | 16 |
| 50 | 1420 | 69 | 48 | 78 | 99 | 20 |

**Conditions in fully developed seas. $H_3$ is the height of the highest 1/3 of the waves and $H_{10}$ represents the highest 10%. (After Bascom)**

and length of the waves. The length of "young waves" in a sea varies from about twelve to thirty-five times their height.

For any given wind velocity, there is a maximum fetch beyond which waves are incapable of further growth. This occurs when the waves reach the same speed as the wind. Extending the fetch or increasing the time the wind blows would not produce larger waves. A sea is called "fully developed" when the waves cannot absorb any more energy from the wind. Maximum fetches and wave heights for wind velocities of ten to fifty knots are given in Table 10-1.

Waves develop most rapidly during their early stages of growth. Growth becomes very slow once they have attained about seventy-five per cent of the maximum height possible under a given wind. Most storm waves reach close to their maximum heights within a fetch of six to seven hundred miles and a fetch of nine hundred miles is most likely sufficient for the generation of the largest storm waves yet reported. The vast majority of open sea waves are less than twelve feet high and those over twenty-five feet are considered large. The highest wave ever reported was encountered by the *U.S.S. Ramapo* in the North Pacific on February 7, 1933. It had a height of one hundred and twelve feet!

Besides these factors, one must always take "old seas" (waves generated earlier by winds blowing over other areas) into consideration in any discussion of wave generation. For the chances are there will be old seas present whenever the wind begins to blow over the ocean. These old seas will merge with the waves created by the new wind. If they are both going in the same direction the waves will enlarge. If they are traveling in opposite directions the waves will flatten each other. Accordingly, collisions of seas not moving in exactly the same or in opposite directions will have intermediate effects (Figure 10-2). Often there will be several intersecting series of waves present, which accounts for the choppy, irregular pattern of the sea. However, when waves cross in the open ocean, they can pass directly through each other without any permanent alteration.

From Table 10-1 we can see that as the wind velocity increases, waves become higher and are capable of storing more energy (energy is proportional to the square of the wave height). The periods increase as well. Note that there is a maximum fetch for any given wind velocity beyond which the wind will not further increase wave height.

Any sea exhibits great variation in wave

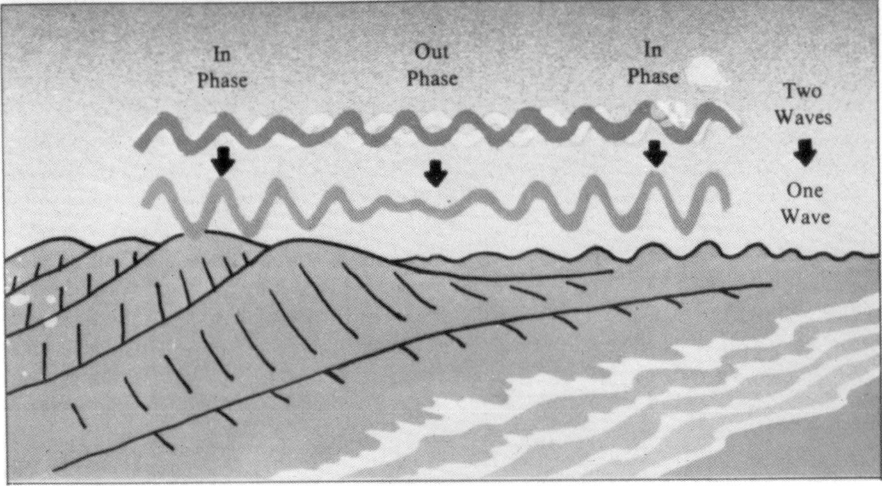


Figure 10-2. Interference creates wave sets. Interference of two waves of equal height and nearly equal length form wave groups. High waves resulting from in phase points alternate with low waves created by out of phase points. There are generally many more out of phase than in phase points. The wave period and direction of propagation are the critical variables determining whether waves will reinforce or flatten each other. (Illustration after Glenn Schot)

height and period and there is always a statistical chance of a wave far higher than the general run. For example, a thirty-knot wind will raise waves with an average height of fourteen feet, but the highest ten percent of these average twenty-eight feet, and the energy is concentrated within a twelve-second period.

## SWELL

As stormy waves move away from the winds that generated them, they undergo a transformation in which their crests expand sideways, become lower, more rounded and more symmetrical. Their form approximates that of a trochoid, and they move in groups of similar size. The entire wave train is then known as a "swell" and individual waves as "swells" (Figure 10-3). In this form, waves can travel through thousands of miles of open sea.

The low rounded crests, comparative smoothness of surface contours, great length from crest to crest, and the broad sideways expanse of swell, contrast markedly with the stormy seas from which it developed. A sea changes into swell because waves lose energy when the wind dies down. The shorter ones with the least energy become lower and finally disappear, leaving only the longer, more stable waves.

The alteration of seas into swells is a progressive process. Windy wave crests that rarely are more than a few times as wide as the wave length expand sideways as they become swell. A crest originally five hundred feet wide may expand to a swell of fifteen hundred or more feet. Swells half a mile wide have been observed. As a rule, the longer the wave period, the longer the crest.

The increase in crest length, however, is only one effect of the ubiquitous "sorting mechanism" based on wave length, which comes into play as swells move away from the generating area. Longer waves travel faster than shorter ones and may in fact overtake them. The immediate effect is that swells of similar lengths and periods tend to travel together, while longer ones move ahead. This process is called "dispersion." The farther a swell has traveled, the more "sorted out" and orderly it will be. A long period, well-sorted swell is referred to as

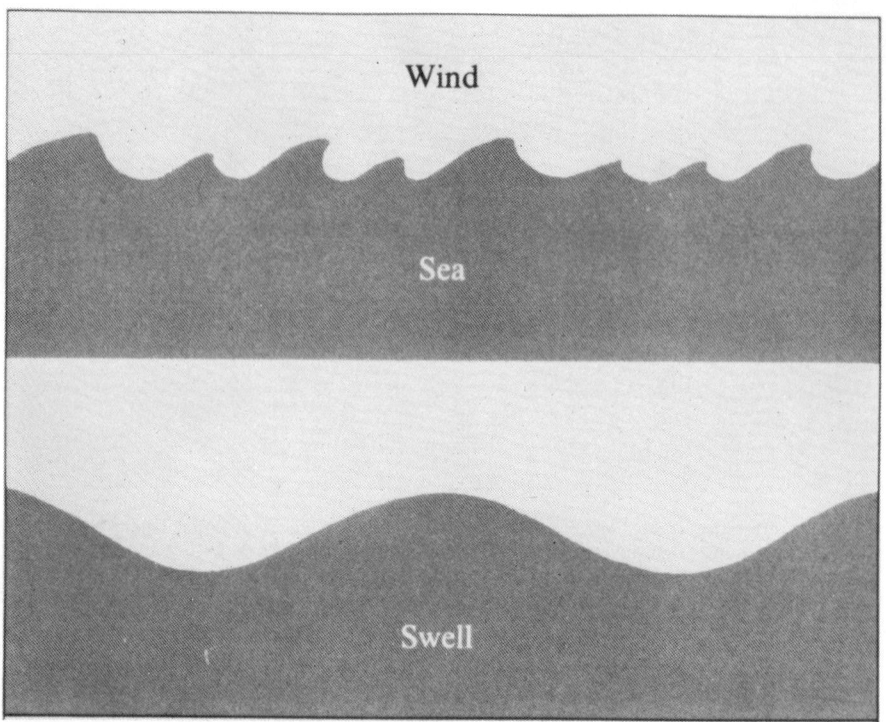


Figure 10-3. Contrast between sea and swell. A sea moves in the same direction as the surface wind, but swell may not necessarily correspond to it.

"old." Old swells are sometimes called "ground swells," to differentiate them from younger waves still in the process of sorting. The longest periods ever recorded for ordinary wind swells were twenty-six seconds on the south coast of England and thirty seconds in Long Beach, California.

Paradoxically, the velocity of a group of swells as a whole is only half as fast as its component swells, since each leading wave successively drops to the rear in the process of setting new water in motion.

123456
612345
561234
456123
345612
234561
123456

A swell group moves at only half the speed of its component individual swells. In each successive row the individual swells move forward two places while the group as a whole advances only one.

Out at sea, swells may be almost unnoticeable since their wave lengths are so long (a ratio of between thirty-five and two hundred) in proportion to their heights. But upon coming in contact with shallow water, swell-induced breakers come seemingly out of nowhere.

## WAVE SORTING

Swell gradually becomes segregated by wave length and spreads out over a greater area as a result of waves sorting themselves according to length.

Typically, the longest waves of a well-sorted swell are the first to reach the shore. Such waves often have periods close to twenty seconds and form breakers ranging in height from inches to three feet. These long low waves, which precede the arrival of the shorter high energy swells, are often called "forerunners." They are easily identified at a beach by the uncommonly long distances between waves and the great lengths of individual crests, both of which are atypical of small breakers. However, in the open sea, they would be virtually imperceptible. Forerunners are nature's warning that high waves will soon be coming, but often their message is obscured by the chaos of the sea.

As a rule the surf tends to build at a beach when the generating storm is moving in the same direction as the previously-formed waves. It falls as the storm moves away. The first sign of a declining swell comes when the larger sets begin to become inconsistent. As the inconsistency increases, the higher sets of waves disappear altogether. When steadily decreasing wave periods are observed, one can be sure that the swell is actually abating and is not just temporarily lulled.

The author has seen the waves along Oahu's north shore jump from virtually flat in the morning to twenty-five feet at dusk. Unexpected large sets invariably accompany a rising surf and occasionally a relentless onslaught of increasingly larger waves will put surfers and small craft in extreme jeopardy.

A famous tale in Hawaiian big wave lore concerns two surfers who were victims of a treacherous rising surf. On a seemingly normal day in the late 1940s, the surfers were riding ten-foot waves at Sunset Beach when the waves unexpectedly enlarged. Both men paddled hard and made it out past the huge "cleanup" sets. In comparative safety beyond the breakers, the surfers contemplated their fate. The surf had become so big, perhaps thirty to forty feet, that they knew it would be suicidal to even attempt paddling back in at Sunset Beach. In those days there were no convenient rescue helicopters and the matter of survival was entirely in their hands. With the veil of darkness rapidly approaching, the surfers decided to try to paddle in through the deep water of Waimea Bay, five miles to the south. As it turned out, one man was washed up on shore half-drowned, and the other was never seen again. Suffice it to say that surf from a powerful storm can rise very quickly and caution should be exercised whenever a big swell is due to hit.

## WAVE WINDOWS ON THE GLOBE

Once a swell has formed, it will continue traveling over the sea until it either breaks on a shore or is flattened by opposing winds. Frictional effects are negligible and a swell may easily roll from one hemisphere to the other.

On one occasion, a three-day swell arriving at Cornwall, England, was traced to Cape Horn, a distance of between 6,000 and 7,000 miles. Observers recorded the rate of decrease in the wave period, and by means of a mathematical process similar to that applied in judging the distance of a thunderstorm, they were astonished to discover that the swell had traveled nearly halfway around the earth. As it happened, weather data revealed that a storm had existed in the southern hemisphere, at just the right distance to have generated the swell.

Swell travels around the earth in "great circle paths." To verify their findings, the scientists had to check whether or not an open sea path between Cornwall and Cape Horn actually existed. Sure enough, they found that they could stretch a string between the two points on a conventional globe (a great circle path) without encountering any land obstacles. An open great circle path between any two points in or along the sea, is known as a "wave window." Wave windows reveal that swell from one area is capable of reaching another.

## SHALLOW WATER WAVES

When an open sea swell approaches a coast and moves into the relatively shallow waters of a continental shelf, the waves begin to feel bottom and undergo a series of changes. Initially they are affected at a depth just less than half the wave length. As they travel over an increasingly shoaling bottom, the waves slow down, their lengths get markedly shorter, and their heights decrease slightly at first, and then may increase. Along with the decrease in length comes an increase in steepness (the ratio of height to length). The period remains constant.

Waves progressively change direction as they advance into shoaling water through the mechanisms of "reflection," "diffraction" and "refraction." "Reflection" means that waves can be turned back by obstacles such as cliffs or walls, directly in their path. "Diffraction" implies a spreading of energy around islands or coastal projections. "Refraction," the bending of wave crests to conform to the bottom contours, is, however, the most important effect.

Refraction results from the drag of the bottom on incoming swell and the consequent decrease in wave velocity. When a wave either approaches shore at an angle, or over an irregular bottom contour, different portions of the same crest will travel through unequal depths. The segments in shallow water will slow down far more than those in deeper water, which advance ahead. As a result the swell bends in accordance with the bottom depth and the crest becomes roughly parallel to the underwater contour.

Variations in underwater topography may refract swell so as to concentrate its energy at one point on shore while leaving other areas relatively quiescent. This may explain why large waves appear at one place while at the same time only small waves are observed at nearby localities. Effects of refraction, however, are very much dependent upon the direction of the swell. A given coastal contour will not affect swells, coming from different directions, in the same way. This is one cause of variation in the breaking pattern of waves at a beach. For example, Laniakea on the north shore of Oahu, Hawaii, produces ridable surf on a north or northeast swell, while it "closes out" (breaks in a continuous wall) on a northwest swell of similar size.

## SIGNIFICANCE OF WAVE LENGTHS AND PERIOD

A relatively long wave suffers more deformation than a short one as it "feels bottom" since the alteration takes place throughout a greater range of depth. Accordingly a long wave will be refracted more gradually than a shorter one and this is one reason why longer waves are better for surfing.

Since the length and period of deep water waves are directly related, the wave period in shallow water is commonly used to denote the length of an open sea swell (remember, the length decreases in shallow water, while the period remains constant). For example, a period of five seconds would represent a relatively short wave, while twenty seconds would be a long one. Good surfing waves generally run about eight to sixteen seconds.

Besides being more susceptible to refraction, waves that are long compared to their heights in deep water may increase considerably in height before breaking. The magnitude of this increment would depend both on the bottom contour and the relative offshore steepness of the wave. A very long old swell, so low out at sea that it is hardly perceptible, may produce breakers several times the offshore height. Furthermore, the tendency for waves to "stretch" and lose height when they approach a coast at an angle may be countered by a possible increase in height before breaking. Conversely, deep water waves less than ten to fifteen times as long as they are high, would produce breakers no bigger than their offshore heights.

## BREAKING WAVES

As a swell reaches the end of its journey and approaches a beach, the subtle effects of a shoaling bottom become suddenly exaggerated. Wave length and velocity rapidly decrease as wave steepness increases. At a depth of about twice the offshore height, the crest suddenly "peaks up" which further increases wave steepness and instability. Finally, at an average depth of 1.3 times the wave height, the amount of water in the trough becomes insufficient to support the crest. The result is surf.

Depending on the wave period and bottom contour, waves may break at depths ranging anywhere from about half to three times their height. The bottom slope is all important in determining not only the depth at which a wave breaks, but also the manner in which it breaks. A steep bottom tends to make a wave retain all its energy until the last possible moment, when the crest suddenly peaks up and violently plunges forward into the trough. As the crest folds over it becomes concave, creating a "tube" or tunnel of air on the shoreward wave face. These are known as "plunging waves" (Figure 10-4).

A gradually shoaling bottom makes for a different sort of wave which releases its energy more slowly. When a crest finally becomes unstable, it gingerly rolls down or "spills" into the trough and the wave face remains gently sloped. Such "spilling waves" are characterized by the appearance of white water at the crest.

Figure 10-4. Plunging waves.

Many people refer to plunging waves as "crashers" or "dumpers" because of their ferocity. Hollow plungers are the most challenging waves for surfers because their steepness makes for a very fast ride, and it is often possible for them to crouch under the falling crest to be "locked in the tube." Perhaps the most famous plunging waves are those which curl over the dangerously shallow coral reefs of Hawaii's "Banzai Pipeline."

In general, long swells usually produce plunging breakers especially if the wind is blowing offshore; while relatively short waves tend to form spilling breakers, particularly if the wind is onshore. Any irregularity such as a rough bottom, stormy wind or interfering currents will tend to make waves spill rather than plunge. Moreover, we should note that even long period waves will break as spillers on a flat sloped beach (Waikiki is a perfect example) and any sudden shallow spots will cause most waves to "suck out" and plunge, regardless of their periods. Since most surf zones are in a state of constant change, one can usually observe a combination of plunging and spilling waves at the same beach.

## SURFING WAVES

Good surfing waves are those which peak at some point along an advancing wave front and peel off away from it as they break, creating a "curl" of unbroken water where a surfer can ride. In other words, the wave does not just topple over all at once in a continuous line.

Potential surfing waves have two major components: long range ground swells that roll in from far-off storms, and local seas produced by winds near shore. The local wind determines whether the surf will be smooth or blown out. Under windless or light offshore wind conditions at a beach, long range swells break unhampered by choppy local seas resulting in smooth glassy waves that are the best for surfing.

By far the majority of surfable waves are generated by the eastwardly moving low pressure winter storms that are born off the western side of the oceans. Supplementing the waves produced by these storms are the summer and fall swells created by hurricanes. But these waves are on the average lower and more infrequent.

Particularly large winter ocean storms occur in the vicinity of the Aleutian Islands. Here, North Pacific storms usually develop their maximum intensity. The situation in the Atlantic is analogous; storms reach maximum fury near Iceland. Meteorologists refer to these areas as the Aleutian and Icelandic lows. In winter, they are the focal points of almost constant storm activity.

Storm conditions in the Southern Hemisphere are different because of its lack of land and its great expanse of open ocean. Winter storms "down under" are usually not as large as those in the Northern Hemisphere. Because there is less land mass there is less differential heating of land and sea, and the stronger westerly winds tend to break up depressions. However, the westerlies themselves can be considered as a huge low rotating around the South Pole, probably building the greatest seas on earth.

For a coast to receive swells generated by winter storms, it must lie in an ocean that extends deep into the middle latitudes. The Pacific and Atlantic Oceans are affected by swells from both hemispheres. In winter, California surfers are able to ride the winter waves of the Northern Hemisphere and in summer they can ride the winter waves of the Southern Hemisphere. Of course the swells generated in the north are usually much larger than those generated in the south, since waves lose about half their height for every eight hundred miles that they travel.

Owing to the fact that winter storms typically develop on the western side of oceans and mature to maximum intensity as they move eastward, the east coasts of both Asia and North America have relatively light surf, while the west coasts of North America and Europe are besieged by heavy surf.

Rounding out the cycle of winter swells are the occasional surfs caused by hurricanes in the summer and autumn. Because of their extremely high winds, hurricanes are capable of rapidly raising good surfing waves—generally six to ten feet—over both large oceans and small bodies of water such as the Gulf of Mexico. The nice thing about hurricane surf is that it comes at a time when the weather is most conducive to surfing. In areas such as the east coast of the United States, hurricanes provide the best surfing waves of the year.

Knowing how storms make waves, one can learn to predict the surf. Ocean weather maps enable wave-wise surfers to forecast breaker heights with about seventy-five per cent accuracy, anywhere from a day to a week before the waves actually arrive.

## WAVE SETS

A casual observer at any beach soon notices a great deal of variation in the height of breakers. Many low waves may hit the beach followed by a series of several (generally two to five) larger ones, which are then followed by more low waves. In a few minutes another group of large waves may again appear. Such a series of large waves is called a "set."

Sets are the result of several factors: chaotic wind gusts in the storm which raised the waves; the sorting process (dispersion) that converts a sea to swell; and interference between swells, from different generating areas, simultaneously arriving at the same beach.

Wind squalls are of significance because, all other things being equal, stronger winds raise higher and longer waves. As swell moves away from its generating area, the long waves travel faster than shorter ones and soon overtake them. The result is that sets of high breakers follow each other in more regular succession.

If the crests of two or more different swells coincide, they will reinforce each other and form a set. If their crests are out of phase, that is, the crests of one swell coincide with the troughs of another, they will cancel each other and produce smaller swells. Since swells vary greatly in height, length, period and direction of propagation, two or more swells will rarely, if ever, be completely in or out of phase with each other. They are partially in phase at some points and thereby augment each other; and partially out of phase at other points and thereby reduce each other.

Since the height and period of waves arriving at a beach at any given time varies tremendously, most observers will consider only the largest one-third of the waves when reporting breaker height. This figure is known as the "significant height" and it roughly represents the average height of the higher waves.

As with most oceanographic sciences, the study of waves is in its infancy. For all the apparent regularity of the sound of breaking waves on the shore, each wave is a unique and mysterious composition of complex diverse forces.

# 11. Tsunami Warning Systems

MICHAEL J. MOONEY 1975

April 1, 1946, proved to be one of the cruelest April Fool's Days in recent memory for thousands of coastal dwellers in and around the vast 63-million-square-mile (163-million-square-kilometer) Pacific basin. Deep in the Aleutian Trench off Alaska's Unimak Island, gigantic undersea earth tremors triggered a series of seismic sea waves, or tsunamis, that radiated out relentlessly over the Pacific. The first to feel the impact of these giant waves was the five-man Coast Guard light station at Scotch Cap, which was obliterated by a foaming 100-foot (30-meter) juggernaut at 2:18 in the morning (*see* "Tragedy at Scotch Cap," *Sea Frontiers*, Vol. 21, No. 2, March-April, 1975).

Less than five hours later, the first of four successive monster waves surged unexpectedly into Hilo harbor on the island of Hawaii. Shortly after 7 a.m., horrified eyes beheld the spectacle of towering waves up to 45 feet (13 meters) high engulfing the waterfront and downtown sections of Hilo at regular 15 minute intervals. Death and destruction were everywhere. Great chunks of submerged coral were ripped from the harbor floor and swept ashore. Moored ships were wrenched free and smashed into piers and warehouses. An entire row of buildings was carried across a street into those on the other side. Highways were washed away, while railroad tracks were torn from their beds and twisted into fantastic shapes. Nearly 160 people died with more being hospitalized. More than 1,000 buildings were destroyed or damaged, and property damage exceeded $25 million. (*See* "Most Ominous Wave," *Sea Frontiers*, Vol. 4, No. 4, November, 1958.)

Though this was not the first time Hilo had been ravaged by the sea, it proved to be the last instance in which lack of advance warning would result in heavy loss of life. For the first time, it was decided that something had to be done to minimize the effects of these rampaging killers of the deep.

## FEARSOME SPECTERS

Like all waves, tsunamis are oscillations or vibrations of disturbances transmitted from

Michael J. Mooney is a freelance writer/photographer/cartographer who specializes in meteorology and oceanography. He is with CBS, Inc., New York, New York.

From *Sea Frontiers*, Vol. 21, No. 4, pp. 227-235, 1975. Reprinted with light editing and with permission of the author and *Sea Frontiers*, © 1975 by the International Oceanographic Foundation, 3979 Rickenbacker Causeway, Virginia Key, Miami, Florida 33149.

one part of the ocean to another and are usually generated by severe undersea earthquakes (7.5 Richter or greater), giant submarine avalanches, or underwater volcanic explosions. Unlike conventional wind waves, however, tsunamis are of extremely long length and period, measuring more than 100 miles (161 kilometers) between crests. Rising only a few feet at sea, they go unnoticed by passing ships and are completely undetectable from the air. When passing through deep water, tsunamis attain incredible speeds up to 500 miles per hour (805 kilometers per hour) or more. This forward velocity is related to the depth of water through which the wave travels—the greater the depth, the higher the speed.

Only when the tsunami approaches shallow coastal waters does its terrifying shape evolve. As bottom friction slows its forward speed, its energy becomes converted into height and the great wave rears up, transforming its momentum into the vertical specters dreaded around the Pacific.

## THE BIRTH OF A WARNING SYSTEM

The tsunami is usually not a single wave but rather a series of abnormally large surges, any one of which can pulverize an ill-fated coastline. Due to their long period, these giants arrive at intervals ranging from 15 minutes to an hour or more. Some coastal areas have been subjected to sustained tsunami attacks lasting many hours, even days.

Tsunamis exert fantastic pressure against resisting land masses. A "modest" 20-foot (6-meter) wave traveling at 45 miles per hour (72 kilometers per hour) produces a force of about 2 tons per square foot. Imagine the incredible power behind the 100-foot (30-meter) monster that destroyed Scotch Cap Light Station!

What made April 1, 1946, the turning point in the sea-old history of tsunamis was the fortuitous presence of several distinguished oceanographers visiting Hawaii en route to the atomic bomb tests at Bikini Atoll. When the unannounced tsunamis struck the Hawaiian Islands, these scientists were able to study firsthand the arrival of these waves and their immediate effects. After learning the time it took for the Unimak seaquake's waves to reach Hawaii, these men pondered the feasibility of predicting the arrival times of future tsunamis, based on similar seismic source data. Thus was born the idea that soon became the Seismic Sea-Wave Warning System (SSWWS).

## AN AUTOMATIC ALARM

Sponsorship of this embryonic program was assumed conditionally by the Coast and Geodetic Survey. The purpose was to detect and pinpoint an earthquake big enough and in the right place to cause a tsunami and to identify with the use of tide gauges the ocean waves generated by that earthquake (Figure 11-1). If the proper category earthquake were detected, a tsunami watch would be issued and, if the presence of seismic sea waves were confirmed, a tsunami warning would be issued. The warning would also include precise forecasts of the arrival times for the first tsunami wave at populated points in and around the Pacific basin.

In 1946, seismographs in the Pacific recorded their findings photographically and were not processed until the next day—too late for effective warning action against fast-moving tsunamis. A new device was soon developed, providing an instant, continuous seismic record that sounded an automatic alarm when the zigzags of a distant, severe earthquake were recorded.

Additional tide reporting stations augmented those already in existence around the Pacific. All of them were modified with a new seismic sea-wave detector that filtered out normal tide and wind-wave data, recording only those waves with distinctive tsunami characteristics. When sizable seismic activity was picked up by the detection stations, all tide-reporting stations were immediately alerted to watch for the passage of tsunamis.

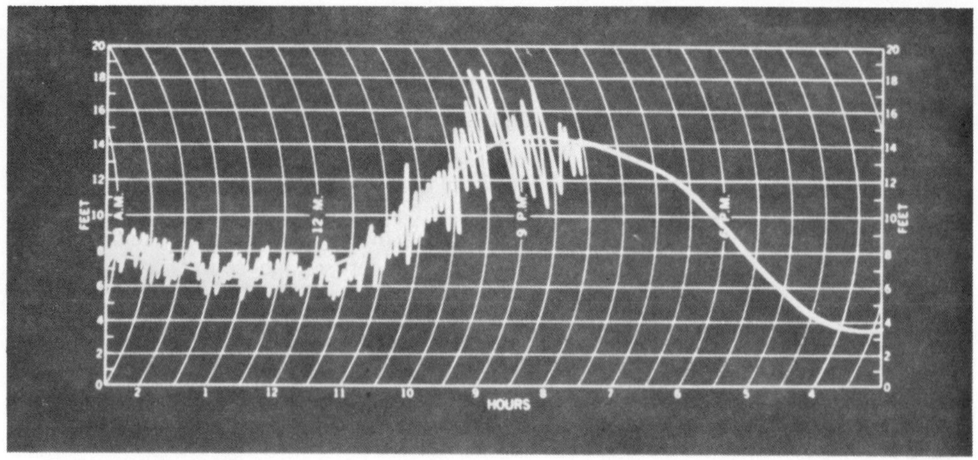


Figure 11-1. Continuous-recording tide chart shows the arrival of a tsunami just after 8:00 p.m.

## QUICK WARNINGS PAID OFF

Rounding out this widespread system was a newly devised travel-time chart consisting of roughly concentric curves centered on Hawaii and radiating to all corners of the Pacific (Figure 11-2). Each of these curves depicts a half hour's travel time of a given tsunami, depending on the topography of the seabed. (As bathymetric data are accumulated and checked for accuracy, these curves are adjusted accordingly.)

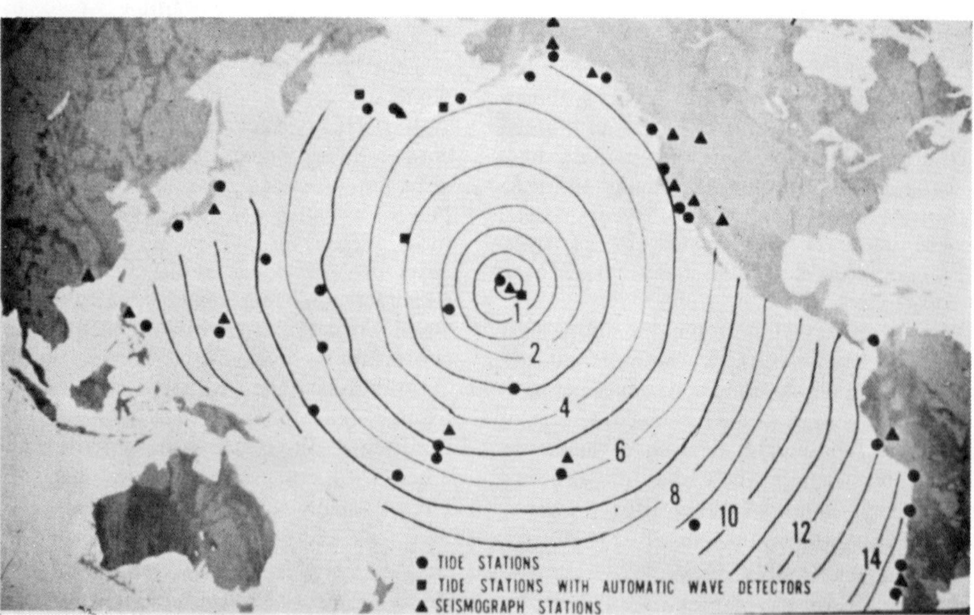


Figure 11-2. Travel-time chart which shows, for a given tsunami, hourly and half-hourly time curves centered on Honolulu.

Hindered by early skepticism and limited funds, the SSWWS did not become operational until 1948, with its initial goal the protection of Hawaii, the North American mainland, and the United States Trust Territories. Over the first four years, many submarine earthquakes were detected, but none were severe enough to trigger a serious tsunami. In November, 1952, however, a seaquake off Russia's Kamchatka Peninsula sent a series of great waves racing toward Hawaii. The SSWWS made it possible to warn the populace which responded accordingly and, when the waves struck, property damage totaled $800,000 with a casualty count of only six cows! In March, 1957, the notorious Aleutian Chain spawned another series of tsunamis which also struck Hawaii, causing $3 million damage, but again with no loss of human life, thanks to SSWWS warnings.

Three years later, the tsunami sirens wailed again, but some of the residents had grown lax through unintentional false alarms sounded in the early years of SSWWS operations and ignored the warnings. On that day in May, 1960, 61 people died beneath the giant, foaming waves from Chile while 282 more were injured—all this in spite of six hours' advance warning. Property losses stood at $22 million. Those who heeded the warnings and fled to higher ground—and stayed there—were saved.

In distant Japan and the Philippines, 200 people fell victim to these same waves. No local warnings had been issued in the Far East as it was not then known that a tsunami originating so far away could still be destructive. It was, and the Pacific-wide chaos wrought by the Chilean tsunamis prompted many nations and territories to join the SSWWS for mutual protection against future waves. This enlarged membership necessitated a more elaborate system of tide- and seismic-reporting stations along with additional basic research on tsunamis in general.

In March, 1964, one of the greatest earthquakes ever recorded in North America struck Prince William Sound off southern Alaska. On that Good Friday, the Richter scale read 8.5 (a magnitude of 8 indicates a "great" earthquake). Coastal communications were severely disrupted, slowing the transmission of local tsunami warnings. Within minutes of the initial shock, waves up to 135 feet (41 meters) high stormed ashore. No one within a 400-mile (644-kilometer) radius of the epicenter could have been warned in time via existing SSWWS facilities. Casualties from Alaska to California came to 131 dead and hundreds more were injured. Property damage approached $105 million.

## THE SOLUTION OF A DILEMMA

The events of Good Friday, 1964, revealed a glaring gap in the SSWWS: how to reduce the time-lapse between detection and warning for Alaskan-Aleutian coastal areas close to a seismic epicenter. In past practice, it took SSWWS headquarters at Honolulu at least an hour to determine an epicenter's location and up to three hours to confirm the existence of rampant tsunamis before issuing the appropriate warnings. To solve this dilemma, the Alaskan Regional Tsunami Warning System was established in 1967 with headquarters at Palmer Observatory near Anchorage. Now it was possible to respond almost immediately to tsunami-generating disturbances in the Alaskan-Aleutian region in a manner similar to the parent Pacific warning system without having to go through Honolulu. These two interlocking systems thus assured North Pacific residents of vastly improved warning response times, enabling the rapid evacuation of threatened coastal areas in advance of incoming tsunamis.

In addition to the Pacific and Alaskan tsunami warning systems, other nations have developed local warning systems to further guard their own shores. Japan, the perennial target for most of the Pacific's killer tsunamis, maintains an elaborate interisland network while the USSR has its own warning system guarding Kamchatka Peninsula and the Kurile Islands.

The SSWWS is now known as the Tsunami Warning System (TWS) and it is in the jurisdiction of the National Weather Service within the National Oceanic and Atmospheric Administration (NOAA). Though continuing progress is being made in perfecting the system, a number of deficiencies remain. This was evidenced in July, 1971, when an earthquake shook the Solomon Islands in the southwest Pacific, sending an unheralded wall of water into nearby Rabaul harbor where severe damage was wrought.

## IMPROVEMENTS AND PRECAUTIONS

To prevent future tsunamis from "slipping through the ranks," it is necessary to install many more seismic- and tide-reporting stations throughout the vast Pacific. In addition, better communications facilities are needed to prevent costly tie-ups and potentially tragic delays in getting vital messages through. At present, TWS must share time on heavily used Federal Aviation Agency and Defense Department circuits. This will be eased somewhat through the use of the geostationary operational environmental satellites in which several channels will be allotted for tsunami traffic.

In 1971, three deep-sea sensors were installed off three widely scattered Pacific islands. Each of these sentinels is anchored to the ocean floor by a 1,000-foot (305-meter) cable and can detect and record tsunamis of extremely small amplitude, thus setting future performance standards for the TWS. According to Robert A. Eppley, chief of NOAA's Tsunami Services Coordinating Branch, in the next five years, the network of tidal and seismic stations should be of sufficient density to detect any tsunami that threatens the Hawaiian Islands, Alaska, or the continental United States within a half-hour or less from the time of the earthquake.

NOAA recommends the following safety precautions for coastal dwellers in susceptible areas. When an earthquake has occurred, be prepared for a possible tsunami emergency. Do not stay in low-lying coastal areas, and never go to the beach to watch for a tsunami. Since a tsunami is not a single wave, but a series of waves, stay out of potentially dangerous areas until an all clear is issued by a competent authority such as local civil defense, police, or other emergency organizations.

The agency also points out that approaching tsunamis are sometimes heralded by a noticeable rise or fall of coastal water, and that a small tsunami at one beach can be a giant a few miles away. It is also stressed that the TWS does not issue false alarms. When a warning is issued, a tsunami exists, and all tsunamis—like hurricanes—are potentially dangerous.

## MAN'S EFFORTS ARE STILL DWARFED

Though the system has effectively reduced casualty figures over the years, property holdings remain vulnerable to the irresistible force of these great sea waves. No man-made sea defense in existence can stop an incoming tsunami though offshore coral reefs have reduced their destructive capabilities. To date, the only sure protection is to build on high ground a safe distance inland.

Coastal engineers have proposed the sinking of massive offshore breakwaters to nullify approaching tsunamis while urban planners have urged the relocation of vulnerable residential areas to higher ground. Both plans are quite ambitious and prohibitively expensive at the present time. To date, the tsunami still dwarfs man's best efforts at even partial control, but only through precautionary warning systems like TWS has man been able to fight back with some success against the ever-present tsunami challenge.

# 3

## *SEA LIFE*

# 12. The Ocean's Food Web, A Changing Paradigm

LAWRENCE R. POMEROY 1974

Few of us may ever live on the sea or under it, but all of us are making increasing use of it either as a source of food and other materials, or as a dump. As our demands upon the ocean increase, so does our need to understand the ocean as an ecosystem. Basic to the understanding of any ecosystem is knowledge of its food web, through which energy and materials flow. Flux of both energy and essential elements shapes or limits ecosystems, but only energy and organic compounds are considered here. The related problems of limiting supplies of essential elements (N, P, Si, Fe) will be considered elsewhere (Pomeroy[1]).

Although the ocean's food web has been studied for more than a century, several recent discoveries lead us to believe that the classical textbook description of a chain from diatoms through copepods and krill to fishes and whales may in fact be only a small part of the flow of energy. Recent studies of microorganisms, dissolved organic matter, and nonliving organic particles in the sea suggest the presence of other pathways through which a major part of the available energy may be flowing. Marine scientists have been approaching this view of the food web cautiously for decades, and caution is to be expected whenever an established paradigm is questioned (Kuhn 1962). Now there are many lines of evidence which suggest that a new paradigm of the ocean's food web is indeed emerging.

## THE ROLES OF MICROORGANISMS

### Photosynthesis

Photosynthesis is the best understood biological process in the ocean. Many thousands of measurements of photosynthesis have been made, fairly well distributed over the World Ocean. Ryther (1969) recognizes three regions of differing productivity. The open ocean, with 90% of the total area and

1. Pomeroy, L. R. Mineral cycling in marine ecosystems. *In* F. G. Howell, ed. Mineral Cycling in Southeastern Ecosystems. USAEC Conf. In press.

Dr. Lawrence R. Pomeroy is a Professor of Zoology with the Institute of Ecology at the University of Georgia. He presently serves on the advisory panel for Sea Grant (NOAA) projects and the editorial committee for the Annual Review of Ecology and Systematics. He has participated on a number of cruises in the Atlantic and Pacific Oceans.

From *BioScience*, Vol. 24, No. 9, pp. 499-504, 1974. Reprinted with light editing and with permission of the author and *BioScience*.

the lowest mean rate of photosynthesis, accounts for 81.5% of primary production. Coastal waters over the continental shelves, with 9.9% of the total area and twice the rate of photosynthesis of the open ocean, account for 18% of primary production. The major upwellings, with 0.1% of the total area and a rate of photosynthesis nearly 10 times that of the open ocean, account for 0.5% of primary production. The real accuracy of these estimates is not as good as the three digit numbers suggest. The usual methods of estimating the photosynthetic rate of phytoplankton do not measure all organic matter produced, and there is rarely enough replication to give us confidence limits for the values.

The most obvious plants in the sea are the seaweeds, but they probably are not the most significant primary producers. Ryther (1963) estimates that seaweeds account for 10% of the primary production of the ocean. Recent data on photosynthetic rates of kelp and other large seaweeds (Mann 1973) make that estimate seem high, although it is still difficult to make a good estimate on a planetary scale. Certainly, seaweeds and sea grasses are of major importance in the coastal zone.

On a planetary scale phytoplankton are the major producers. Phytoplankton have been divided into two size groups, net plankton and nannoplankton. The separation is arbitrary, based on the aperture of what was once the finest bolting cloth for making plankton nets. Net plankton (>60 μm) have received considerable attention and form the basis of the established paradigm of the food web, but nannoplankton (<60 μm) have proven more difficult to study and until recently they have been neglected. Like net plankton, they are so sparsely distributed in the water that it is necessary to concentrate them in some fashion to see them at all. Because many of them cannot be preserved well, they must be studied at sea while alive. Only recently has high magnification, oil-immersion microscopy at sea permitted the study of living nannoplankton aboard ships.

Efforts to understand the relative importance of net and nannoplankton have been made by several investigators, using the $^{14}C$ technique (Steeman-Nielsen 1952), by counting separately the radioactivity retained on discs of bolting cloth and on fine membrane filters. This was a crude separation. Some organisms larger than the aperture of the bolting cloth would be forced through it in fragments, and if a sufficiently thick layer of plankton accumulated on the bolting cloth, nannoplankton would be retained by it. In spite of these shortcomings, at least a dozen studies produced consistent results showing that the large diatoms and other net plankton, although highly visible and beautiful, account for a small fraction of total primary production. In a majority of cases nannoplankton account for more than 90% of total photosynthesis (Table 12-1). This is true not only in the central gyres of the ocean, but in upwellings, coastal waters, and estuaries. No one seems to have made the separation in polar regions. However, Digby (1953) found that in Scoresby Sound, Greenland, nannoplankton chlorophyll was always equal to and sometimes three times as abundant as net plankton chlorophyll. English (1961) found proportionately greater amounts of nannoplankton chlorophyll than net plankton chlorophyll at drift station Alpha in the arctic.

Some remaining doubts about the validity of the results of physical separation of net plankton from nannoplankton have been dispelled by Watt (1971) who measured the rates of photosynthesis of individual phytoplankters by $^{14}C$ autoradiography. He found that in most cases the large diatoms and dinoflagellates showed little photosynthetic activity while nannoplankton showed much activity. In the Sargasso Sea one nannoplankton species, *Coccolithus huxleyi*, appears to be responsible for most of the photosynthesis during most of the year. Far from being the grasses of the sea, net plankton appear to be the Sequoias of the sea,

Table 12-1. Estimates of the Relative Importance of Net Phytoplankton and Nannoplankton in Photosynthesis. Most of the Values are Medians of Sets of Observations.

| *Reference* | *Location* | *Photosynthesis net/nanno* |
|---|---|---|
| Malone 1971 | Mexico, Neritic Pacific | 0.5 |
| Malone 1971 | Peru Current (Equador) | 0.09 |
| Malone 1971 | E. tropical Pacific | 0.12 |
| Malone 1971 | Caribbean Sea | 0.10 |
| Watt 1971 | Atlantic slope, May | 0.6 |
| Watt 1971 | Grand Banks, August | 0.4 |
| Watt 1971 | Gulf Stream, 40° N, August | 0.05 |
| Anderson 1965 | Washington shelf | 0.04 |
| Anderson 1965 | Washington slope | 0.03 |
| Anderson 1965 | N. Pacific | 0.03 |
| Yentsch & Ryther 1959 | Vineyard Sound | 0.02 |
| Teixeira et al. 1967 | Mangrove estuary | 0.6 |
| Saijo 1964 | Central Indian Ocean | 0.04 |
| Saijo & Takesue 1965 | E. Indian Ocean | 0.07 |
| Gilmartin 1964 | Canadian fjord | 0.01 |
| Teixeira 1963 | Tropical Atlantic | 0.11 |
| Holmes & Anderson 1963 | Friday Harbor, Wash. | 0.4 |
| Holmes 1958 | E. tropical Pacific | 0.01 |

while the major part of photosynthesis is done by *C. huxleyi* and other nannoplankton.

The relative importance of nannoplankton is also suggested by recent studies of numerical abundance. Conventional methods of studying phytoplankton populations from preserved samples often result in descriptions of dominance by a succession of large diatom and dinoflagellate species. In reality there is usually a constant numerical dominance of nannoplankton which are less well preserved and often ignored (Bernard 1967, Semina 1972, Steidinger 1973). There is some evidence that within the nannoplankton (<60 μm) much of the photosynthesis is by organisms smaller than 30 μm (Holmes and Anderson 1963, Saijo 1964). However, these separations, which were made with membrane filters of different porosities, have been criticized because of the possibility of fragmentation of fragile nannoplankton. Verification of the results by microscopic methods such as Watt's autoradiography is needed.

## Respiration

We know much less about respiration in the ocean than about photosynthesis. Consumers in the ocean cover a much broader spectrum of sizes than producers do. Even if we dismiss as insignificant the respiration of all marine mammals (cf. Holdgate 1967), it is still impossible to collect all sizes of organisms in a single measurement of respiratory rate. Moreover, total respiratory rate is so low that it is necessary to concentrate the organisms from a large volume of water in order to achieve enough sensitivity to measure changes in dissolved oxygen or any other parameter of respiration in a short time. Any concentration process has inevitable uncertainties and difficulties.

Despite these difficulties, several investigators have made physical separations of two or more size classes of plankton and have measured various parameters of respiration of each size. Pomeroy and Johannes (1966) collected organisms with a No. 2 net (366 μm) and concentrated the smaller organisms (including phytoplankton) by reverse-flow filtration, comparing the respiration of net plankton and microorganisms. Several similar studies have since been made in various parts of the World Ocean (Pomeroy and Johannes 1968, Hobbie et al. 1972, Turner 1974). In virtually all cases respiration of microorganisms exceeds that of net plankton and is usually 10 times as great, suggesting that microorganisms are consuming most of the energy made available by primary production.

The numerical abundance of various size classes of heterotrophs has been examined by Beers, using a plankton pump which brings water aboard ship where it passes through a series of fine meshes (Beers et al. 1967, Beers and Stewart 1969), concentrating organisms in several size classes. This work focuses on the abundance and description of the smaller heterotrophs, but the results imply that the smaller plankton, especially the microorganisms, should be significant consumers of energy. Microorganisms as they are discussed in this paper include all Protista and not bacteria alone. Only when bacteria are considered specifically will they be so called.

New techniques for measuring in situ rates of respiration through biochemical techniques offer perhaps the greatest hope for measuring and understanding the metabolic processes of microorganisms in the sea. Two of these now in use are the measurement of the electron transport system (ETS) of plankton (Packard 1969) and the measurement of adenosine triphosphate (ATP) content of plankton (Holm-Hansen and Booth 1966). Both methods require concentration of organisms on a filter and do not necessarily give any indication of the size or identity of the respiring organisms. Sensitivity is achieved with enzyme assays. In its present form the ETS method measures potential activity in the presence of excess substrates, and a rather arbitrary factor is used to estimate actual electron transport from the observed potential. This introduces an error of unknown magnitude. The ATP method was originally proposed as a measure of microbial biomass, but it also shows promise as a parameter of respiration (Hobbie et al. 1972).

All of these approaches to measuring respiration, biochemical, microscopic, and respirometric, suggest that microorganisms are major consumers of energy in the sea. In the central oceanic gyres a significant component of this may be the respiration of the phytoplankton. In the gyres growth of phytoplankton is limited by the supply of essential elements, and the ratio of photosynthesis to respiration is low.

A different approach to the question of the relative significance of net plankton and microorganisms is that of Sheldon et al. (1972) who used a particle counter together with existing data on large organisms to suggest that the biomass of all size classes of organisms in the sea, from bacteria to whales, is about the same. There are problems to be resolved in discriminating living from dead particles counted. Some verification of the findings of Sheldon et al. by an independent method is needed. One such independent verification within the size range of net plankton and microorganisms seems to have been provided by Beers and Stewart (1969), albeit at a different time in a different part of the ocean. If the concept of uniform biomass distribution among size classes of organisms in the ocean is even approximately correct, the inverse relation between size and metabolic rate (Zeuthen 1947) makes the smallest organisms the largest consumers of energy.

If microorganisms are major consumers in the sea, we need to know what kinds are the metabolically important ones and how they fit into the food web. At present we do not even know the relative abundance of the various kinds of protists. Few investigators have examined freshly collected populations of living microorganisms at sea. Each investigator has used his own distinctive method with little collaboration or intercomparison.

What evidence we have is filled with contradictions. Large numbers of small palmelloid algae, or something of that general description, have been reported, even at considerable depth (Bernard 1967). Other investigators report large populations of bacteria (Kriss 1963, Seki 1972). Still other investigators have rarely found substantial populations of these or other recognizable microorganisms (Wiebe and Pomeroy 1972). Further studies of the systematics, abundance, and metabolic activity of the communities of microorganisms of the open sea are needed to resolve these conflicting reports.

## INDIRECT AND ABIOTIC PATHWAYS

### Other Sources of Particulate Organic Matter

The paradigm of the ocean's food web is also being changed through recognition of the potential importance of nonliving particulate organic matter which does not come directly from primary production. Nonliving particles of several types are more abundant than living organisms in the sea. Some resemble aggregates produced from natural sea water in the laboratory (Riley 1970, Gordon 1970a and 1970b, Wiebe and Pomeroy 1972). Several mechanisms of aggregate formation have been proposed (Nishizawa 1969, Riley 1970). Recent work suggests that some aggregates form as the result of the adherence of soluble organic molecules to the surface film of bubbles (Wheeler 1972). Other naturally occurring particles are flocculent and may be fecal or the remains of mucous nets. The proportion of particulate organic matter in the ocean which consists of authigenic aggregates, rather than fecal products or other materials, is not known, but most particulate organic matter represents secondary production of one sort or another. The fate of aggregates and other particles is uncertain, although aggregates produced in the laboratory from natural sea water can support the growth of zooplankton. It is not known whether bacteria or other protists can utilize them, but bacteria rarely are found attached to them in freshly collected samples of sea water (Wiebe and Pomeroy 1972).

### Heterotrophic Consumption of Dissolved Organic Material

The dissolved organic matter in the World Ocean is one of the largest reserves of organic carbon on the planet. Most of it is refractory, with a residence time of thousands of years (Williams et al. 1969). Yet we know that perhaps one-fourth of the organic matter synthesized by marine phytoplankton is lost as dissolved material (Anderson and Zeutschel 1970, Thomas 1971). Most of this material probably consists of early products of photosynthesis, such as glucose or glycolic acid. There is also a substantial release of dissolved organic material during digestion, defecation, and excretion all along the food web (Webb and Johannes 1967, Corner and Davies 1971). Some of this probably is refractory material or its precursors, but most of it is readily assimilable amino acids and larger protein fragments, lipids, and carbohydrates. The importance of the production of assimilable dissolved organic material has been suggested repeatedly (Khailov 1952, Strickland 1971). In a recent series of papers P.J. leB. Williams and his colleagues have shown that these assimilable compounds, which may be released by either plants or animals, are removed from sea water rapidly and efficiently. Williams (1970) suggests that the microgram amounts of glucose and amino acids that we find in the sea are the concentrations below which microorganisms can no longer remove them efficiently. As soon as photosynthetic or digestive activities of plankton increase the concentration of any assimilable organic compound, the microorganisms take it up, quickly bringing the concentration of the assimilable materials back to the basal concentration. According to Andrews and Williams (1971) direct consumption of dissolved organic matter may account for half of the total degradation of organic matter in the ocean. They estimate that the consumption of glucose and amino acids by microorganisms amounted to 35% of total annual primary production. When glycolate and other carbohydrates are included, the total could indeed by 50%. This is beginning to look like a much more significant pathway than we had suspected.

The identity of the microorganisms which may consume such a major share of available energy is uncertain, but the evidence points to bacteria or very small flagellates. Williams (1970) found that 80% of the microorganisms responsible for the utilization of soluble organic compounds would pass through an 8 μm membrane filter and 50% would pass a 1 μm filter. Here again there are questions about the validity of using membrane filters in this way which should be answered by autoradiography or electron microscopy.

The production of soluble organic compounds and utilization of them by microorganisms occurs in all parts of the ocean. The percentage of photosynthate that is lost by phytoplankton in dissolved form varies with their nutritional state. In the central gyres, where the supply of essential elements limits growth, as much as 40% of fixed carbon is lost as soluble organic compounds, while in nutrient-rich coastal waters and upwellings only 10% is lost (Thomas 1971). Although it may seem paradoxical, the largest rate of production of soluble organic compounds by phytoplankton is in the coastal waters and upwellings, because 10% of the photosynthesis in upwellings is greater than 40% of the photosynthesis in the central gyres. It is also in the highly productive regions of the ocean that respiration is highest (Pomeroy and Johannes 1966, 1968).

If small Protista are important both as primary producers and as primary consumers, this may have implications for the remainder of the food web, including fisheries. Actively growing bacteria have high assimilation efficiency. Payne (1970) found assimilation of individual substrates by bacteria to be around 60% in laboratory cultures (compared to 10-20% for many larger organisms). Andrews and Williams (1971) and others before them found that the assimilation efficiency for glucose in the sea is as much as 65%, and the efficiency for assimilation of individual amino acids is nearly 80%. This strongly suggests that the primary consumers are active bacteria, and that they are converting a substantial fraction of primary photosynthate, and secondarily produced dissolved organic materials as well, into microbial protoplasm. This could channel into higher trophic levels at least 30% more energy than we now estimate. However, if there are long periods when no substrates are available, microorganisms may ultimately respire all they have assimilated. In this case there would be a major shunt of high grade organic energy to heat.

The widely dispersed condition of bacteria and other small protists presents another problem. They can be consumed directly by other microorganisms, by mucus-net feeders such as salps or certain pteropods (Gilmer 1972), and according to laboratory experiments, by some copepods. However, the highly dispersed condition of the protists may provide an effective refuge for them from filter feeders, particularly for those under 5 μm and in the open sea where their absolute abundance is lowest. We have quite limited information on the mean residence time of Protista in the open sea. If it is very short (hours), then Protista probably are an active link in a major pathway in the food web. If it is long (days or weeks), the Protista may be consuming most of the energy they capture. In this case they will be a major energy sink. Jannasch's (1969) chemostat experiments with bacteria in natural sea water indicate a generation time for bacteria of several days. If something like half of the ocean's total primary production is really moving through this pathway, we need to find out whether it is going to consumers or is lost as $CO_2$.

## A NEW PARADIGM

### The Web of Consumers

In the classical paradigm of the ocean's food web (Figure 12-1) the primary consumers are thought to be net zooplankton, such as copepods, mysids, and euphausiids. The secondary and tertiary consumers are nekton, including fishes, cephalopods, and cetaceans. Microorganisms are assigned the role of decomposers (Strickland 1965, p. 585). Now there is increasing evidence that net zooplankton are not metabolically dominant. Microorganisms (whose biomass is approximately equal to that of the net plankton) are greater movers of energy and materials because of their higher metabolic rate per unit mass. The relative impact of microorganisms and macroorganisms on the flux of energy in the sea is still debated. Recent estimates of the microbial component of respiration vary from 50% (Riley 1972) to over 90% (Pomeroy and Johannes 1966). Both Strickland (1971) and Raymont (1971) suggest that microorganisms are a major metabolic component of the oceanic ecosystem, but they do not attempt to quantify their importance. Williams (1970) believes that the most active component has a size of less than 1 μm while Sheldon et al. (1973) present evidence that the most actively growing component has a size of around 4 μm.

### Unseen Strands in the Food Web

The new paradigm of the ocean's food web that is developing, as a result of recent studies of protistan activities and alternative pathways of organic matter, may contain many unseen strands. We are not certain how the long recognized food web of diatoms and copepods fits into the expanded web which is gradually appearing. Quantitatively, large diatoms seem to be minor contributors to production, and net plankton seem to be a minor component of respiration; but if this is not the major link of photosynthesis to nekton, what is? Are the communities of upwellings really more efficient producers of nekton, and is the

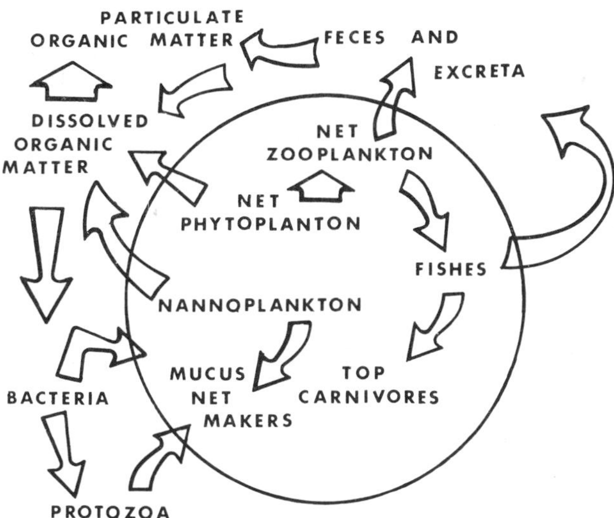


Figure 12-1. The classical paradigm of the ocean's food web in simplified form is enclosed within the circle. More recently conceived pathways are outside the circle. The possible relative magnitude of the pathways is discussed in the text.

food web really different in them? These questions are important not only to the basic ecologist but to the fisheries scientist. The flow of useful information from basic ecology to fisheries research has been sparse. Fisheries scientists can predict optimal yields and fish population dynamics with good success, but relating fish production to processes at lower trophic levels has been less successful. Strickland (1969) said, "I doubt if much has been learned [about marine productivity] of direct help to fishermen that could not have been deduced equally well from oceanographic data on currents, convergences, upwellings, and mixing."

While this may be an overly pessimistic view of the situation, one must admit that it is difficult to relate the production of tertiary consumers to unidentified primary consumers and controversial primary producers.

Better strategies for utilizing the productivity of the sea might be devised if we understood in more detail the pathways of energy transfer and whether they really differ in the productive and unproductive regions of the ocean. Hunting and catching methods for harvesting the wild populations of the sea have been perfected to the point where overfishing is possible, and less desirable populations will have to be exploited to expand or even sustain fishery yields. Nothing comparable to terrestrial agriculture has been developed in the sea, and there is little reason to believe that it is the best model on which to base new developments. Harvesting plants, other than coastal seaweeds, is out of the question. Monospecies animal cultures comparable to herds and flocks really do not exist, and only in circumstances where a species segregates itself (salmon, anchovies) is there immediate hope of intensive management. Only in salmon has there been significant progress in developing genetically defined populations.

Management of existing wild populations now consists at best of controlling fishing pressure to optimize yield, where legal and political considerations permit. Greater yields would be possible if we could harvest the lower trophic levels, such as the larger zooplankton. This is technologically possible, but at existing population densities it is probably a poor trade for the energy required to do it. Enhancement of productivity by creating artificial upwellings has been discussed for many years. The technology for accomplishing this still seems to be marginal and costly, and little consideration has been given to the problem of managing the resulting successional changes in natural communities. Our understanding of the marine food web and the basic principles of stability and diversity of natural ecosystems is not yet sufficient for such tasks (cf. Pomeroy[2]).

At the same time that we are approaching maximal yields from fisheries, we are forced to cope with increasing threats to the sea from pollution on a regional or even global scale. This creates a tendency to concentrate on expensive technological solutions to immediate problems while providing little support for a better understanding of how the system works. In the long run, more satisfactory and probably less costly solutions can be achieved through knowledge gained through basic research.

## ACKNOWLEDGMENTS

The viewpoint presented in this paper has developed over several years of research and discussion with colleagues, particularly Dirk Frankenberg, Robert E. Johannes, and William J. Wiebe. They also provided helpful criticism of the manuscript. Research contributing toward the development of this paper was supported by grants from the National Science Foundation.

## REFERENCES

Anderson, G. C. 1965. Fractionation of phytoplankton communities off the Washington and Oregon coasts. *Limnol. Oceanogr.* **10**: 477-480.

2. See footnote 1, p. 105.

Anderson, G. C., and R. P. Zeutschel. 1970. Release of dissolved organic matter by marine phytoplankton in coastal and offshore areas of the northeast Pacific Ocean. *Limnol. Oceanogr.* **15**: 402-407.

Andrews, P., and P. J. leB. Williams. 1971. Heterotrophic utilization of dissolved organic compounds in the sea. III. Measurement of the oxidation rates and concentrations of glucose and amino acids in sea water. *J. Mar. Biol. Assoc. U.K.* **51**: 111-125.

Beers, J. R., and G. L. Stewart. 1969. Microzooplankton and its abundance relative to the larger zooplankton and other seston components. *Mar. Biol.* **4**: 182-189.

Beers, J. R., G. L. Stewart, and J.D.H. Strickland. 1967. A pumping system for sampling small plankton. *J. Fish. Res. Board Can.* **24**: 1811-1818.

Bernard, F. 1967. Contribution à l'étude du nannoplancton de 0 à 3000 m, dans les zones atlantiques lusitanienne et mauritanienne (Campagnes de la "Calypso," 1960 et du "Coriolis," 1964). *Pelagos* **7**: 4-81.

Corner, E.D.S., and A. G. Davies. 1971. Plankton as a factor in the nitrogen and phosphorus cycles of the sea. *Adv. Mar. Biol.* **9**: 101–204.

Digby, P.S.B. 1953. Plankton production in Scoresby Sound, East Greenland. *J. Anim. Ecol.* **22**: 289–322.

English, T. S. 1961. Some biological oceanographic observations in the central North Polar Sea, Drift Station Alpha, 1957-1958. Arctic Institute of North America, Research Paper 13. 31 pp.

Gilmartin, M. 1964. The primary production of a British Columbia fjord. *J. Fish. Res. Board Can.* **21**: 505-538.

Gilmer, R. W., 1972. Free-floating mucus webs: a novel feeding adaptation for the open sea. *Science* **176**: 1239-1240.

Gordon, D. C. 1970a. A microscopic study of non-living organic particles in the North Atlantic Ocean. *Deep-Sea Res.* **17**: 175-185.

———. 1970b. Some studies on the distribution and composition of particulate organic carbon in the North Atlantic Ocean. *Deep-Sea Res.* **17**: 233-243.

Hobbie, J. E., O. Holm-Hansen, T. T. Packard, L. R. Pomeroy, R. W. Sheldon, J. P. Thomas, and W. J. Wiebe. 1972. A study of the distribution and activity of microorganisms in ocean water. *Limnol. Oceanogr.* **17**: 544-555.

Holdgate, M. W. 1967. The Antarctic ecosystem. *Phil. Trans. Roy. Soc. Lond.* **B252**: 363-383.

Holm-Hansen, O., and C. R. Booth. 1966. The measurement of adenosine triphosphate in the ocean and its ecological significance. *Limnol. Oceanogr.* **11**: 510-519.

Holmes, R. W. 1958. Size fractionation of photosynthetic phytoplankton. *U.S. Fish and Wildlife Ser., Spec. Sci. Rep't. Fish.* **279**: 69-71.

Holmes, R. W., and G. C. Anderson. 1963. Size fractionation of $C^{14}$-labelled natural phytoplankton communities. Pages 241-250 *in* C. H. Oppenheimer, ed. Symposium on Marine Biology. C. C. Thomas, Springfield, Ill.

Jannasch, H. W. 1969. Estimation of bacterial growth rates in natural waters. *J. Bacteriol.* **99**: 156-160.

Khailov, K. M. 1952. Dynamic marine biochemistry – development prospects. *Okeanologiya* **2**: 1-9.

Kriss, A. E. 1963. Marine Microbiology. Tran. J. M. Shewan and Z. Kabata. Oliver and Boyd, London.

Kuhn, T. S. 1962. The Structure of Scientific Revolutions. Univ. Chicago Press.

Malone, T. C. 1971. The relative importance of nannoplankton and net plankton as primary producers in tropical oceanic and neritic phytoplankton communities. *Limnol. Oceanogr.* **16**: 633-639.

Mann, K. H. 1973. Seaweeds: their productivity and strategy for growth. *Science* **182**: 975-981.

Nishizawa, S. 1969. Suspended material in the sea. II. Re-evaluation of the hypotheses. *Bull. Plankton Soc. Japan.* **16**: 1-42.

Packard, T. T. 1969. The estimation of oxygen utilization rate in sea water from the activity of the respiratory electron transport system in plankton. Ph.D. dissertation, Univ. Washington, Seattle.

Payne, W. J. 1970. Energy yields and growth of heterotrophs. *Annu. Rev. Microbiol.* **24**: 17-52.

Pomeroy, L. R., and R. E. Johannes. 1966. Total plankton respiration. *Deep-Sea Res.* **13**: 971-973.

——. 1968. Respiration of ultraplankton in the upper 500 meters of the ocean. *Deep-Sea Res.* **15**: 381-391.

Raymont, J.E.G. 1971. Alternative sources of food in the sea. Pages 383-399 *in* J. D. Costlow, Jr., ed. Fertility of the Sea, Vol. 2. Gordon and Breach, New York.

Riley, G. A. 1970. Particulate organic matter in sea water. *Rec. Adv. Mar. Biol.* **8**: 1-118.

——. 1972. Patterns of production in marine ecosystems. Pages 91-100 *in* J. A. Wiens, ed. Ecosystem Structure and Function. Oregon State University Annual Biology Colloquium 31.

Ryther, J. H. 1963. Geographic variations in productivity. Pages 347-380 *in* M. N. Hill, ed. The Sea, Vol. 2. Wiley, New York.

——. 1969. Photosynthesis and fish production in the sea. *Science* **166**: 72-76.

Saijo, Y. 1964. Size distribution of photosynthesizing phytoplankton in the Indian Ocean. *J. Oceanogr. Soc. Jap.* **19**: 19-21.

Saijo, Y., and K. Takesue. 1965. Further studies on the size distribution of photosynthesizing phytoplankton in the Indian Ocean. *J. Oceanogr. Soc. Jap.* **20**: 264-271.

Seki, H. 1972. The role of microorganisms in the marine food chain with reference to organic aggregates. Pages 245-259 *in* U. Melchiorri-Santolini and J. W. Hopton, eds. Detritus and its Role in Aquatic Ecosystems. *Mem. Ist. Ital. Idrobiol.* **28** (Suppl.).

Semina, H. J. 1972. The size of phytoplankton cells in the Pacific Ocean. *Int. Rev. ges. Hydrobiol.* **57**: 177-205.

Sheldon, R. W., A. Prakash, and W. H. Sutcliffe, Jr. 1972. The size distribution of particles in the ocean. *Limnol. Oceanogr.* **17**: 327-340.

Sheldon, R. W., W. H. Sutcliffe, Jr., and A. Prakash. 1973. The production of particles in the surface waters of the ocean with particular reference to the Sargasso Sea. *Limnol. Oceanogr.* **18**: 719-733.

Steeman-Nielsen, E. 1952. The use of radioactive carbon ($^{14}C$) for measuring organic production in the sea. *J. Cons. Perm. Int. Explor. Mer.* **18**: 117-140.

Steidinger, K. A. 1973. Phytoplankton ecology: a conceptual review based on Eastern Gulf of Mexico research. *Critical Reviews in Microbiology* **3**: 49-68. Chemical Rubber Co., Cleveland, Ohio.

Strickland, J.D.H. 1965. Production of organic matter in the primary stages of the marine food chain. Pages 477-610 *in* J. D. Riley and G. Skirrow, eds. Chemical Oceanography, Vol. 1. Academic Press, New York.

——. 1969. The marine food chain and its early stages; an assessment of present research, how well will it answer tomorrow's problems? Morning Review Lectures, 2nd Int. Oceanogr. Congr., Moscow 1966. UNESCO. pp. 93-102.

——. 1971. Microbial activity in aquatic environments. *Symp. Soc. Gen. Microbiol.* **21**: 231-253.

Teixeira, C. 1963. Relative rates of photosynthesis and standing stock of net phytoplankton and nannoplankton. *Bol. Inst. Oceanogr. São Paulo* **16**: 39-42.

Thomas, J. P. 1971. Release of dissolved organic matter from natural populations of marine phytoplankton. *Mar. Biol.* **11**: 311-323.

Turner, R. E. 1974. Community plankton respiration in a salt marsh tidal creek, estuary, and coastal waters of Georgia. Doctoral dissertation, University of Georgia, Athens.

Watt, W. D. 1971. Measuring the primary production rates of individual phytoplankton species in natural mixed populations. *Deep-Sea Res.* **18**: 329-339.

Webb, K. L., and R. E. Johannes. 1967. Studies of the release of dissolved free amino acids by marine zooplankton. *Limnol. Oceanogr.* **12**: 376-382.

Wheeler, J. 1972. Some effects of solar levels of ultraviolet radiation on lipids in artificial sea water. *J. Geophys. Res.* **77**: 5302-5306.

Wiebe, W. J., and L. R. Pomeroy. 1972. Microorganisms and their association with aggregates and detritus in the sea: a microscopic study. Pages 325-352 *in* U. Melchiorri-Santolini and J. W. Hopton, eds. Detritus and its Role in Aquatic Ecosystems. *Mem. Ist. Ital. Idrobiol.* **29** (Suppl.).

Williams, P. J. leB. 1970. Heterotrophic utilization of dissolved organic compounds in the sea. I. Size distribution of population and relationship between respiration and incorporation of growth substrates. *J. Mar. Biol. Assoc. U. K.* **50**: 859-870.

Williams, P. M., H. Oeschger, and P. Kinney. 1969. Natural radiocarbon activity of the dissolved organic carbon in the north-east Pacific Ocean. *Nature* **224**: 256-258.

Yentsch, C. S., and J. H. Ryther. 1959. Relative significance of the net phytoplankton and nannoplankton in the water of Vineyard Sound. *J. Cons. Int. Explor. Mer.* **24**: 231-239.

Zeuthen, E. 1947. Body size and metabolic rate in the animal kingdom with special regard to the marine micro-fauna. *C. R. Lab. Carlsberg, Ser. Chim.* **26**: 17-161.

# 13. Flashing Sea Pansies and Glowing Midshipmen

MILTON J. CORMIER 1974

Bioluminescence, the emission of light by living things, has probably intrigued man from his very beginnings. Chinese poets more than 3,000 years ago extolled the beauty of the firefly's glow, and Aristotle wrote in *De Anima* of things that "give light in the dark." In recent centuries, many outstanding philosophers and scientists—Francis Bacon, René Descartes, Benjamin Franklin, Louis Pasteur, Charles Darwin—were also enchanted by the soft glow of bioluminescent creatures.

The firefly is the best known example of bioluminescence, but the number of terrestrial biolominescent species is very small compared to the number found in the oceans. Until nearly the turn of this century scientists generally accepted the hypothesis that the ocean depths were completely devoid of life. But in the 1920s and 1930s this view was overturned by oceanographers who descended several thousand feet in bathyspheres to make man's first visual observations of the deep sea. These explorers discovered that not only is life abundant within certain deep layers of the ocean but that at 1,000 feet and below, nearly every living creature is bioluminescent.

Eternal darkness, great pressure, and uniform, near-freezing temperatures dominate these depths, and it is within this environment that evolutionary forces must have been highly selective for bioluminescent forms. Bioluminescence probably plays an important role in the survival of the species. The oceans also contain surface and shallow-water creatures that emit light, but they are relatively few compared to their deep-sea counterparts.

Most bioluminescent creatures produce light by similar chemical mechanisms; in a number of cases the chemical requirements for light emission are identical. In such cases light is produced by chemical oxidation in which an organic compound, luciferin, reacts with oxygen in the presence of an enzyme, luciferase. For most of the bioluminescent systems studied, the products of this oxidation are light, carbon dioxide, water, and oxyluciferin.

The oxidation of luciferin to oxyluciferin releases energy, which is held about one-

Dr. Milton J. Cormier is a research professor at the University of Georgia, where he studies bioluminescent marine organisms.

From *Natural History*, Vol. 83, No. 3, pp. 26-32, 1974. Reprinted with light editing and with permission of the author and *Natural History* Magazine, March, 1974. Copyright © The American Museum of Natural History, 1974.

billionth of a second within the oxyluciferin molecule. At this stage, oxyluciferin is in an electronically excited state, or very rich in energy; release of this energy produces light in the region of the spectrum visible to humans. Essentially none of the energy is liberated as heat—thus the term "cold light."

Bioluminescent creatures convert chemical energy into light energy, and some of them, such as the firefly, do it with nearly 100 percent efficiency. In contrast, an incandescent lamp operates with only 10 percent efficiency, with 90 percent of the energy wasted as heat. The present concern over the energy crisis makes the ability to understand how such efficient energy conversions take place more than merely academic.

While the chemical structures of luciferin and luciferase vary considerably from species to species, in a number of widely diverse species they are identical. Future analyses of these chemical structures will help scientists trace the evolution of bioluminescence, a phenomenon that occurs sporadically throughout the phylogenetic tree. Among the lower forms of life it occurs in bacteria, fungi, and protozoans and is found in about half of the animal phyla; fish are the only vertebrates to possess it. The late Prof. E. Newton Harvey, a Princeton University biologist, once said:

> It is apparent from the classification of bioluminescent species that no clear development of luminosity along evolutionary lines is to be detected but rather a cropping up of luminescence here and there, as if a handful of damp sand has been cast over the names of all living species written on a huge blackboard, with luminous species appearing whenever a grain of sand struck. . . . It is an extraordinary fact that one species in a genus may be luminous and another closely allied species may contain no trace of luminosity.

Indeed when the first few luciferin structures were analyzed, they were found to be quite diverse, and it appeared that not only was bioluminescence a randomly occurring phenomenon but also that the chemistry leading to light emission was different for each bioluminescent species. We now know from work on marine animals that this is not the case, and it is becoming increasingly clear that a strong thread of similarity exists in the chemistry of bioluminescence among marine animals.

Along the coast of Japan there abounds a pinhead-sized, luminous crustacean called *Cypridina.* This tiny animal's luciferin and luciferase are stored in separate gland cells. One type of cell is filled with colorless granules; the other, with yellow granules. When disturbed the animal simultaneously secretes both types of granules into the seawater where they mix and dissolve, forming a localized concentration of luciferin and luciferase that results in a brilliant cloud of bluish luminescence.

*Cypridina* luciferin has been synthesized in the laboratory. By mixing synthetic luciferin with luciferase isolated from *Cypridina,* biochemists can duplicate the animal's natural bioluminescence in a test tube.

The chemical structure of *Cypridina* luciferin is distinctly different from the luciferin structures of both luminous bacteria and the firefly, and *Cypridina* luciferin will not react with bacterial or firefly luciferase to make light. The enzymes that initiate the light reaction are very specific and generally will act only on specific types of molecules. For a long time no bioluminescent cross reactions were found between the luciferases and luciferins of different species.

Recently, however, researchers have made a surprising observation. They have found that the luciferin and luciferase from *Apogon* and *Parapriacanthus,* shallow-water fishes, which like *Cypridina* live in waters off Japan, will cross react with the luciferase and luciferin from *Cypridina* to produce a bluish luminescence identical to that produced by the *Cypridina* luciferase-luciferin reaction. The luciferin structures of *Apogon* and *Parapriacanthus* were found to be the same as that of *Cypridina.* This was the first example of apparently identical luciferins and luciferases being found in marine animals from different phyla: an interphylum luciferase-luciferin cross reaction.

These bioluminescent fishes, unlike many deep-sea forms with bizarre appearances and prominent light organs, possess no external peculiarities and appear to resemble ordinary, nonluminous fishes. But they are capable of emitting light indirectly from luminous organs inside their bodies. These organs are located within the coelomic cavity, and the light is emitted through translucent muscle tissue that serves as a lens. Chromatophores, or colored cells, within this tissue contract or expand to control the brightness of the light.

One of the major luminous organs housing most of the luciferin is connected to the gut by a small duct. Since these fish are known to eat live *Cypridina,* the question arose as to the origin of luciferin and luciferase in these glands. Do these fish naturally possess the ability to synthesize their own luciferin and luciferase or have they undergone an evolutionary adaptation in which an organ evolved to store luciferin and/or luciferase extracted from their food supply? Observations on other bioluminescent species helped to answer these questions.

A bioluminescent toadfish commonly called the midshipman (*Porichthys*) inhabits the Gulf of Mexico and the Pacific coastal waters of the United States. It gets its name from the beautiful array of more than 700 intradermal light-emitting organs, or photophores, located on its underside, which look like ornamental brass buttons. Luciferin and luciferase are located in these photophores, whose light-emitting capacity is under hormonal and neural control.

Luciferin and luciferase from the midshipman will cross react to produce light with luciferins and luciferases isolated from *Cypridina* and from bioluminescent fishes with internal light organs such as *Apogon* and *Parapriacanthus.* Thus, it is probable that all of these luciferins and luciferases are nearly identical.

The midshipman's intradermal photophores are not connected to the gut, and we might therefore conclude that the midshipman makes its own luciferin and luciferase. One of the midshipman's major food sources, however, is a small, bioluminescent shrimp, *Euphausia.* In addition, the luciferin and luciferase from this tiny shrimp appear to be identical with those of *Cypridina,* the midshipman *Porichthys, Apogon,* and *Parapriacanthus.* Furthermore, when the midshipman is in an environment devoid of euphausid shrimp, the luciferin disappears from its photophores and it loses the ability to bioluminesce. When these same midshipmen are fed live *Cypridina* or euphausid shrimp, luciferin is again found in the photophores and the ability to bioluminesce is restored.

Luciferin, but not luciferase, is found in all the tissues, as well as in the blood, of the midshipman, but it is most concentrated in the photophores. It thus appears that the midshipman derives its luciferin from its food source and that the luciferin is transported by the bloodstream and stored in the photophores. It is more difficult to transport large molecules like luciferase, so the animal must make its own.

Another diverse group of bioluminescent marine animals utilizes a luciferin that is structurally analogous to, but different from, that found in *Cypridina.* This most recently discovered luciferin has been found in the sea pansy, *Renilla.*

A pinkish violet, half-dollar-sized colonial coelenterate, the sea pansy lives on the ocean floor at depths of from twenty to fifty feet. (Figure 13-1) At the University of Georgia Marine Institute on Sapelo Island, Georgia, about one ton of these animals has been collected each summer for the past fourteen years, for use in research aimed at understanding how the animal produces light and how it controls its bioluminescent flash. When a sea pansy is stimulated by mechanical or electrical means, it sends a beautiful concentric wave of greenish light out from the point of stimulation, across its body surface and upward to the tip of each individual polyp. This wave of luminescence is controlled by some kind of elementary nerve network. Scientists do not yet know why sea pansies are bioluminescent.

The chemical structure of sea pansy luciferin has recently been determined, and like *Cypridina* luciferin, it can now be synthesized in the laboratory. Thus, by combining synthetic luciferin, sea pansy luciferase, and oxygen, we can duplicate in a test tube what the sea pansy does to make light.

Bioluminescence will not occur when sea pansy luciferin is mixed with the *Cypridina*-type luciferases. Sea pansy luciferin and *Cypridina* luciferin, however, have important structural similarities. The central portion of each animal's luciferin molecules, where the chemistry of light emission occurs, is identical.

When sea pansy luciferin and luciferase are mixed with oxygen in a test tube, the color of the emitted light is blue, but the color of light emitted by the live animal is a very characteristic green. This difference in light color is caused by a green fluorescent protein found in the sea pansy. This protein has an unknown chromophore attached to it that absorbs blue light and re-emits it as green light by a process called fluorescence.

The process of bioluminescence is actually analogous to the process of fluorescence. In fluorescence, light energy is pumped into a molecule and converted to a different color. In the case of bioluminescence, chemical energy is pumped into a molecule—as in the oxidation of luciferin by sea pansy luciferase—to produce blue light. In both cases an equivalent, short-lived product is produced—an electronically excited, or energy-rich, state of the molecule.

When the green fluorescent protein is added to a solution of sea pansy luciferase and luciferin in the laboratory, the color of light changes from blue to the same green light seen in live animals. When chemical energy is pumped into oxyluciferin by bioluminescence, this energy is utilized to create an electronically excited state of the green fluorescent protein by the process of energy transfer. Thus, the light emitted is green.

The flash of green light given off by a sea pansy is triggered by a nervelike impulse. Biochemists have isolated a luciferin-binding protein in the sea pansy that is apparently responsible for initiating and controlling the light flash. As long as luciferin is bound to this protein, it is prevented from reacting with luciferase. But when calcium is added, luciferin is released almost instantaneously from this protein, thus allowing the luciferin to produce light with luciferase. In the sea pansy all the proteins necessary for making and controlling green light—the luciferin-binding protein, luciferase, and the green fluorescent protein—are packaged together within a membrane-enclosed subcellular organelle called a lumisome. When the animal is stimulated by any means, a nervelike impulse triggers the sequential release of calcium within the lumisome. Because the light is controlled by the supply of calcium ions, it thus appears as a single flash.

The lumisomes and the other components that the sea pansy requires to produce green light have been found in all other bioluminescent coelenterates of the class Anthozoa that have been examined. These include the sea feather *Ptilosarcus,* the sea pens *Stylatula* and *Acanthoptilum* found on the ocean bottoms off the California coast, and another anthozoan, *Cavernularia,* found off the coast of Japan. These creatures produce the same quality of green light as the sea pansy.

The luciferins and luciferases found in these organisms are interchangeable with sea pansy luciferin and luciferase, suggesting identical structures. This same sea-pansy-type luciferin structure also appears to be involved in the bioluminescence of other coelenterates such as the jellyfish *Aequorea* found in Friday Harbor, Washington, and the hydrozoans *Obelia* and *Clytia* found in Woods Hole, Massachusetts.

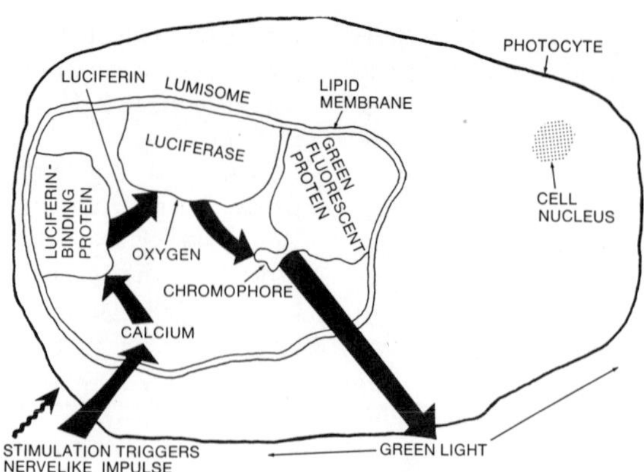


Figure 13-1. When the sea pansy is stimulated, a nervelike impulse releases calcium within the lumisome, an organelle one-fiftieth the size of the light-emitting cell, or photocyte. The calcium forces the luciferin-binding protein to release its luciferin to luciferase, where it oxidizes to form energy-rich oxyluciferin. The energy is transferred to a chromophore on the green fluorescent protein, producing the animal's green light. (Diagram not drawn to scale.)

A sea-pansy-type luciferin and luciferase have also been found in a bioluminescent fish, *Yarella,* in the Gulf of Mexico. Like the midshipman, *Yarella* also contains many intradermal photophores that house its luciferin and luciferase. Here is yet another example of an inter-phylum bioluminescent cross reaction—the sea pansy and a fish.

Because of the complexity of the molecules, there is precedence for the idea that some bioluminescent creatures may borrow luciferins from the environment rather than manufacture them. Some luminous fish selectively take in luminous bacteria from the environment and have developed highly complex light organs to house and maintain these bacteria. Certain photosynthetic marine slugs borrow photosynthetic organelles from the algae they eat. Many of nature's creatures take from the environment one component of a biological system and build the rest of the system around it.

Evolution at the molecular level proceeds by small changes in preexisting molecules, and it may well be that luciferases, as well as luciferins, have evolved from molecules that once had entirely different functions. Within a given environment, for example, evolutionary pressures—probably associated with recognition of the species, attraction of food, or protection from predators—could have been sufficient to have selected for a luciferase and an accompanying system for the purpose of making light. The associated luciferin could have been either created or borrowed from the environment. This kind of phenomenon might have happened many times during evolution. Biolominescence might have developed again and again in a sporadic fashion throughout the course of evolution. An analogous case would be the evolution of the power of flight, during which numerous animals such as insects, birds, reptiles, and mammals independently developed this capability at various times during their evolutionary development. This concept could help explain Professor Harvey's observation of the sporadic occurrence of bioluminescence among various species.

Biologists have long observed anatomical similarities between organs of vision and such organs of bioluminescence as are found in the photophores of deep-sea fish, squid, and shrimp. For example, many photophores contain a cornealike layer, or lens, and light-producing cells arranged in the manner of a retina, a reflector, and a nerve. There have been instances when biologists mistook photophores for eyes. Furthermore, the subcellular structures of some light-producing cells are arranged in a manner analogous to that of the rod and cone cells that absorb light in vision. The pigment responsible for light absorption for vision is concentrated within a membrane in one part of the cell, making light absorption more efficient. In bioluminescence, the pigment responsible for light emission—the green fluorescent protein—is concentrated within the lumisome membrane in one part of the cell so as to make light production more efficient.

Based on work with sea pansies, biochemists have extended the analogy between bioluminescence and vision to the molecular level. In vision, light absorption releases calcium, generating a nerve impulse. In bioluminescence, a nerve impulse releases calcium and light is generated.

As knowledge about bioluminescence accumulates, we are gradually learning how to use it. Research on possible applications is continuing for three specific reasons: first, many components of luminescence have been isolated and synthesized in the laboratory; second, highly sensitive devices for detecting light have been developed; and third, the measurement of light production is the most sensitive probe available to scientists for the specific detection of a variety of chemicals.

Because of their great sensitivity, swiftness, and reliability, luminescent reactions are especially valuable in detecting minute quantities (less than one part in a trillion) of an element or compound in a large mass. Bioluminescent components are—or can be made—specific to only one element or compound and will light up only in its presence. One such example is the firefly assay for ATP (adenosine triphosphate), a chemical found in all living cells. Because ATP is ubiquitous to all life, a sensitive technique has been worked out for counting bacterial cells using firefly luciferase and luciferin. The more cells, the brighter the light due to the increased amount of ATP. Such techniques are being used to expand medical research.

Tests for infectious bacteria in the urinary tract and in the bloodstream, which once took many hours, can now be done in minutes using the firefly system. The firefly ATP assay is also being examined as a possible technique for early detection of cancer because it has been found that the light intensity of the firefly system decreases in the presence of cancerous cells.

Another important chemical common to all animal and possibly to plant cells is PAPS, a sulfate derivative of adenosine diphospate. It is essential in metabolism, the buildup and breakdown of cellular material. The sea pansy bioluminescent system is now being used to detect PAPS, and the assay has proved just as sensitive as the firefly assay for ATP.

Certain other bioluminescent coelenterates, especially the jellyfish *Aequorea,* are being used to detect low levels of calcium in biological tissue. Calcium is important in muscle contraction and vision, and the *Aequorea* system is providing new information on how these important processes work.

Although scientists have unraveled some of the chemical processes of bioluminescence and have applied this knowledge to benefit mankind, in most cases they are mystified as to why the phenomenon exists and fascinated by the possibility of finding the answer.

# 14. Migration of the Spiny Lobster

WILLIAM F. HERRNKIND 1970

The migrations and mass movements of animals have long influenced man and stirred his curosity. He has wondered about the cause and purpose of the periodic exodus by lemmings and the incredible navigational capabilities of salmon returning to their home stream or adult eels returning to spawn at their birthplace a thousand miles out in the Sargasso Sea. I, too, have been intrigued by the appearance overhead of hundreds of Canada geese in V-formations and by the swirling masses of wormlike black elvers in the estuaries near my childhood home. However, while I had occasionally reflected on these phenomena, it was not until 1963 that I began to direct my scientific research toward comprehending such events, particularly one that is, curiously, both spectacular and virtually unknown.

As a graduate student assistant working on a bioacoustic research program at the Institute of Marine and Atmospheric Science, University of Miami, it was my job one October day to trace a breakdown in the underwater cable linking our hydrophones to The American Museum's Lerner Marine Laboratory in Bimini. The installation was located on the edge of the Florida Strait at a depth of 65 feet. Sea conditions, which had been intolerable owing to an autumnal squall, had improved enough to permit my co-worker and me to maneuver out in a skiff to the vicinity of a main junction in the cable. We donned SCUBA gear and dropped into the murky water to begin a search for the splice box. Particulate matter, stirred up and held in suspension by the rough seas, limited underwater visibility to 15 feet in an area where it is usually about 100 feet. Peering through the haze below me as I sank, I saw what I first believed to be long, dark furrows or waterlogged timbers lying on the bottom, but as I dropped farther they resolved into lines of dozens of spiny lobsters, *Panulirus argus,* marching head to tail in single-file.

I was surprised because this delectable creature is typified by its sparse numbers in the open sand areas where we located our acoustic array. As I settled onto the bottom,

Dr. William F. Herrnkind is an assistant professor with the Department of Biological Sciences at Florida State University. He is interested in the behavioral ecology of marine animals, and he has studied marine crustaceans, and especially spiny lobsters, in Florida, Bahamas, and the Caribbean.

From *Natural History,* Vol. 79, No. 5, pp. 36-43, 1970. Reprinted with author's revisions and light editing and by permission of the author and *Natural History* magazine. Copyright by *Natural History* magazine, 1970.

still another column marched steadily by without missing a step. I realized then that I was witnessing a "crawl," or "crawfish walk," long known to professional fishermen and other old salts, but poorly known and, in some cases, disbelieved by marine scientists. I first heard of these mass movements of thousands of lobsters from biologist William C. Cummings, who witnessed a similar event off Bimini in 1961. I also realized, as another column of twenty lobsters went by, that we would be unable to locate the splice box in such murky water, so we spent as much time as possible studying the lobsters.

These mass, single-file marches by spiny lobsters are unique, the only known formation movements by bottom-living crustaceans. Furthermore, the marches markedly contradict the established view of this species' behavior pattern. Spiny lobsters are nocturnally active; they wander about at night to feed on mollusks and crustaceans but return before daybreak to shelter in crevices on the reef, under rock ledges, or among dense fronds of sea whips. Why, then, do all the lobsters in a region become active each fall, moving by day, in formation, over exposed areas where they are never seen at other times?

Perhaps the most striking feature of the mass movements, aside from the sheer numbers involved, is the single-file formation, which I call a queue (Figure 14-1). Some other crustaceans travel in more or less definable groups: fiddler crabs and soldier crabs form great droves, or herds, which scour the beach for food at low tide, while King crabs aggregate in clusters. However, none approach a stable, spatial configuration to match the long straight queues of *Panulirus argus.* All queuing lobsters maintain the precise course and speed of the leader and move through turns as though they were on rails. More amazing is that all the queues, no matter how far apart, travel in equivalent or parallel headings! Just how do the lobsters organize themselves into queues, establish leadership, and maintain formation? What is the biological significance of the mass migrations? Where do the migrants come from and where are they going? The questions seem endless.

The difficulty of answering them lies in the necessity of performing much of the research in the sea at a relatively unpredictable time, at a relatively unpredictable location, under conditions that severely restrict visual studies. In studying the Arctic tern or indigo bunting, at least we know where they come from, where they go, and what they do when they get there (although we still don't know precisely *how* they navigate). After observing that marching horde of spiny lobsters, I felt irresistibly challenged to discover their secrets.

At first my lobster research proceeded slowly since I was committed to a doctoral research problem on a distant relative of the spiny lobster, the fiddler crab. This doctoral research provided useful background when I later tackled the more formidable problem of lobster migration and orientation.

Other sources of help were the numerous professional lobstermen, conservation officers, and skin divers I spoke with, who related their observations of similar marches in different regions. In all cases the general descriptions were similar—the events took place in the fall after intense storms and involved large numbers of lobsters of approximately the same size, traveling in long queues. Each queue in a given march headed in the same compass bearing, and the compass bearing was specific to each location. The stories told to me also suggested striking behavior I had never witnessed myself. For example, a fisheries officer from Florida described a marching column that extended, with few breaks in rank, for nearly one-quarter mile; that would conservatively comprise one thousand spiny lobsters. Several Biminites independently told of an immense number of lobsters that wandered into the Bimini Lagoon and, upon reaching a cul de sac along the shore, swirled about in a great mass with many individuals walking out of the water onto the beach. During 1969 in Bimini a migration occurred in which about

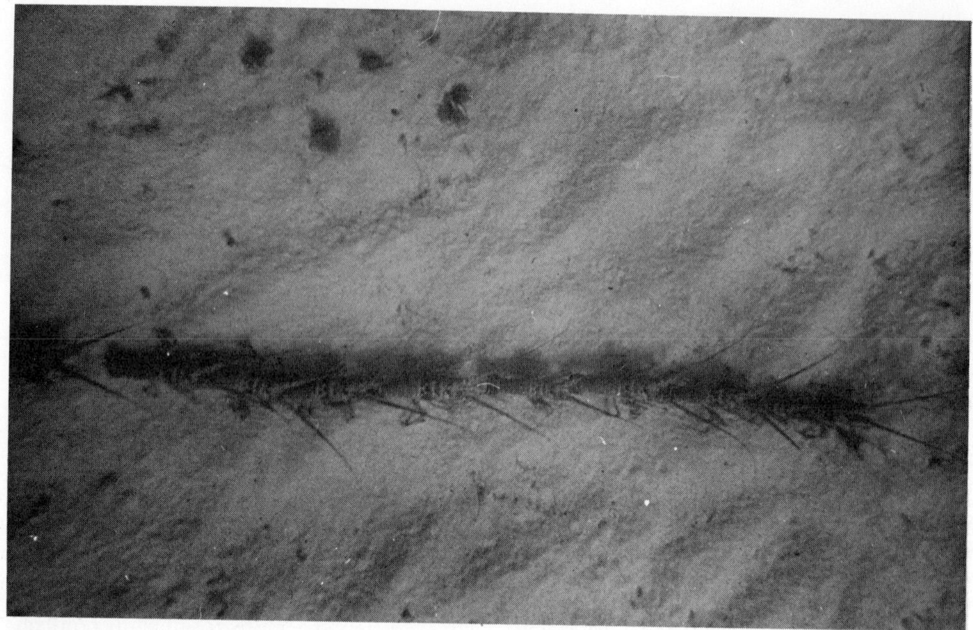

Figure 14-1. Single-file line, or queue, of spiny lobsters marching across open sand areas at a depth of nearly 35 feet near Bimini, Bahamas. Numbers of lobsters exceeding 100,000 take part in such autumnal mass movements. Each queue contains 2 to 50 individuals and travels with the same heading.

ten lobstermen captured an estimated 20,000 lobsters in five days. And they by no means caught them all, probably less than 10 per cent.

A colorful description of a march by one Bimini fisherman included the explanation that the lobsters migrate when they get "the spirit." I have subsequently found that this is a valid descriptive term for the internal state of the animals during these events. For my first opportunity to observe the persistence of this spirit I must thank a fellow student at Miami who called me at one o'clock one morning to invite me to witness a mass movement at Boca Raton. I gathered my diving paraphernalia and drove up in the wee hours to get overboard at daybreak. Sure enough, the columns of lobsters were marching alongshore and were literally piling up at a rock jetty, which looked from underwater like a pincushion of antennae. I mainly wanted some undamaged live specimens to bring back to the Marine Institute for study, but had overlooked bringing my hand nets. A feverish chase ensued, during which I captured some undamaged live specimens and hauled them back to a vinyl-lined sea water pool, 15 feet in diameter. Upon release, the group formed a queue and marched clockwise around the pool almost continuously, day and night, for the next two weeks. All in all, it was almost five weeks, and an estimated 500 miles, before the marching activity halted along the endless migratory pathway presented by the perimeter of the circular pool.

During that time I fed the lobsters and attempted to induce them to enter a concrete block shelter. However, they would eat only for brief periods interspersed with marching and would not take up residence in the shelters. This matches the behavior exhibited by lobsters while marching in the sea. There, certain members of a file stop occasionally and grasp such objects as starfish and small sea cucumbers, then move on, eating as they march. Columns also cluster under rock ledges for some minutes, as many as 200 in a 10 cubic foot space, with groups continually forming and moving off as others arrive. All these actions are in strong contrast to the responses of both captive and wild lobsters at other times, when feeding lasts much longer and the shelters are inhabited through the daylight hours.

The extraordinary behavior of captive migrating lobsters under artificial conditions suggests that their "spirit" is a modified internal state, or drive, responsible for the maintenance of the migratory activity. It might be likened to the internal processes that cause birds to become restless at the time of migration, a condition termed Zugunruhe. In some birds Zugunruhe is brought on by a modification of the hormonal system, the result of changes in day length or, more simply, photoperiod. Thus, as fall days shorten and nights lengthen in the North Temperate Zone, changes in birds' internal processes are manifested as a general increase in activity and a tendency to fly southward. A similar Zugunruhe occurs in the spring increase of photoperiod, but brings on a tendency to fly northward. The seasonal nature of the mass movements by spiny lobsters, and the continuous hyperactivity of captive specimens, suggests control by some internal process brought on previously by environmental changes associated with autumn.

The autumnal storms always reported to precede the marches seemed a strong possibility at first as a cause of the internal changes. But present evidence suggests that this is not so. Violent storms also occur at other times of year—particularly in the winter, spring, and in association with summer hurricanes and tropical depressions—but marches have been reported only during the September through November period. And, in the area off Bimini where I had made my original observation, a small march of brief duration occurred in October, 1969, during a two-week period of almost uninterrupted calm.

It appears, then, that some other factor brings on the internal state preparatory to migration, and that storms at that time act to trigger and synchronize the movement of the population.

This past summer I investigated some nutritive factors as possible causes. This was suggested by marine biologist Robert Schroeder, who mentioned that captive lobsters would begin to march around their enclosure shortly after being switched from a mollusk diet to fish, as though fish lacked some necessary substance that inhibited the Zugunruhe or, perhaps, contained some inductive substance lacking in mollusks. To test this effect I placed groups of ten lobsters in three pools provided with running seawater, sand substrate, and terra-cotta pipes for refuge. Except for the dietary regime, each group had nearly identical conditions. We fed the mollusk group surf clams, the fish group chopped fish, and the third group nothing, and monitored the activity patterns daily for any changes. By the fourth day the fish group became hyperactive and exhibited queuing during the day, while the others retained the normal pattern of inactivity by day, thus confirming Schroeder's observations. The situation remained the same through the following week indicating a relatively long-lasting effect.

At this time we switched the diets of the fish group and mollusk group. Activity decreased daily in the new mollusk group (former fish group) and increased in the new fish group (former mollusk group). Thus, a change in diet is a factor that can control activity and is a possible cause of migration. However, the animals given no food behaved in accord with the normal nocturnal pattern, leaving us in a quandary. If the lack of some substance in fish causes the migratory state, why doesn't the absence of food have the same effect? It may be that fish flesh contains an induction substance, but we feel that this would be a remote possibility as a cause of mass movements in nature since spiny lobsters probably seldom eat fish; they simply are not equipped to catch them.

Fish-fed lobsters, however, may continually add body tissues lacking in some necessary substance(s) found in mollusks, which must be kept in balance with the added body material for normal growth. The imbalance causes modifications in the metabolic system that subsequently result in the migratory state. Starved lobsters gain none of this substance either, but they are losing, not adding body material and, therefore, are not affected in the same way. More studies of the type described, along with studies of internal processes, must be conducted to define the role of nutrition as a causal factor.

Other factors may also work independently of, or in conjunction with, dietary modifications to bring on the migrations. For example, photoperiod seems a likely possibility: light exerts a strong influence on the hormonal physiology and behavior of many crustaceans, including *Panulirus argus.* And temperature flux may be involved, since temperature drops of several degrees centigrade often result from autumn storm activities. Another possibility is increase in population density, which most of you may have already thought of in connection with lemming and locust emigrations. Being gregarious, lobsters tend to cluster by day in habitable crevices, so an increase in immigrants or an increase in the living biomass of lobsters in the population, as occurs during synchronous molting, might produce a density effect culminating in emigration from that area.

We do not yet have conclusive evidence about where the lobsters come from or go. At present, I believe that migrant lobsters off Bimini originate in shallow areas well to the north and east of the island group. Finding their ultimate destination is a problem in tracking. Using a sonic pinger tag, which pulses a signal detectable by directional hydrophone, I was able to follow a lobster at Bimini by boat for several miles. The paths suggest that migrants disperse into suitable habitats along the west edge of the Bahama Bank five to ten miles south of Bimini. An expanded tracking program should clarify this in the future.

When we turn to the striking feature of queuing, we find that it is a basic component of this species' behavioral repertoire, since even young lobsters two to three inches long sometimes form single-file lines. Queues also occur at times other than the mass movements—whenever a group of lobsters is deprived of shelter or is introduced to a novel habitat situation. This tendency to congregate—even in the large circular pools of the laboratory—has enabled me to observe the sequence of queue formation and the sensory mechanisms used in maintaining it.

I recorded data on queuing by means of an event recorder. This device has separate, manual pushbuttons for each of twenty pens, which trace paths on a moving chart. Thus a button coded for each separate action was depressed by the observer whenever that action took place and for as long as it lasted. Afterward, the chart was reviewed to determine the number of times an action occurred, its duration, and its sequential relationship.

We found that an isolated, stationary lobster visually perceives, and directs its antennae toward, a moving individual up to several yards away. It then queues up by approaching the moving lobster from behind until antennal contact is made. At this point its antennules are brought into contact with each side of the lead lobster's abdomen, completing the alignment. The queue is maintained by the almost constant contact of the antennules or by the hooking of the tips of the pereiopods (walking legs) around the telson (tail) of the lead lobster. This tactile locking into place enables all the queue members to walk at the same speed and in the same direction, resulting in strikingly straight columns of up to 50 lobsters. The contact also permits the queue to maintain its integrity when the leader changes course to detour an obstruction. The significance of constant contact is suggested by the effort that separated individuals immediately make to close up any gaps.

But could lobsters deprived of their antennae, antennules, or anteriormost pereiopods still queue? Losses of these appendages are common in nature. To test this, we recorded and compared the performance of individuals deprived of one of these receptor-appendages either by forcing autotomy (self-release of appendages at certain joints) or by taping them up so they could not receive stimulation. In all three cases the lobsters could still queue since they substituted usage of one of the other remaining appendages. The lobsters, like the Apollo moonships, possess redundant back-up systems to take the place of any one that should fail.

The strongest evidence for concluding that tactile cues are the most important for aligning and maintaining the queue formation came from studies on lobsters blinded by opaque tape. These would queue up only after some tactile contact was made with another lobster, at which time the taped lobster turned neatly into alignment and maintained position as effectively as untaped individuals. It seems likely, then, that spiny lobsters can queue even in cloudy water and at night.

Since the queue involves a number of lobsters led by only one individual, it would seem that the leader should be outstanding for some noticeable attribute—perhaps size, indicative of age and experience, or peculiar behavior recognizable by the others. However, upon examination of over fifty "leaders" captured during one migration, we find them to fall by size and sex ratio right in the average for all the lobsters collected at that time. This, together with our laboratory studies, suggests that leadership is produced, not by exterior appearance, but by the behavioral manifestation of some inner drive.

Queues that I observed in the open sea formed in several ways, but the following was the most striking: Lobsters clustered together in a closely packed group or pod and turned about the center in a tight circle,

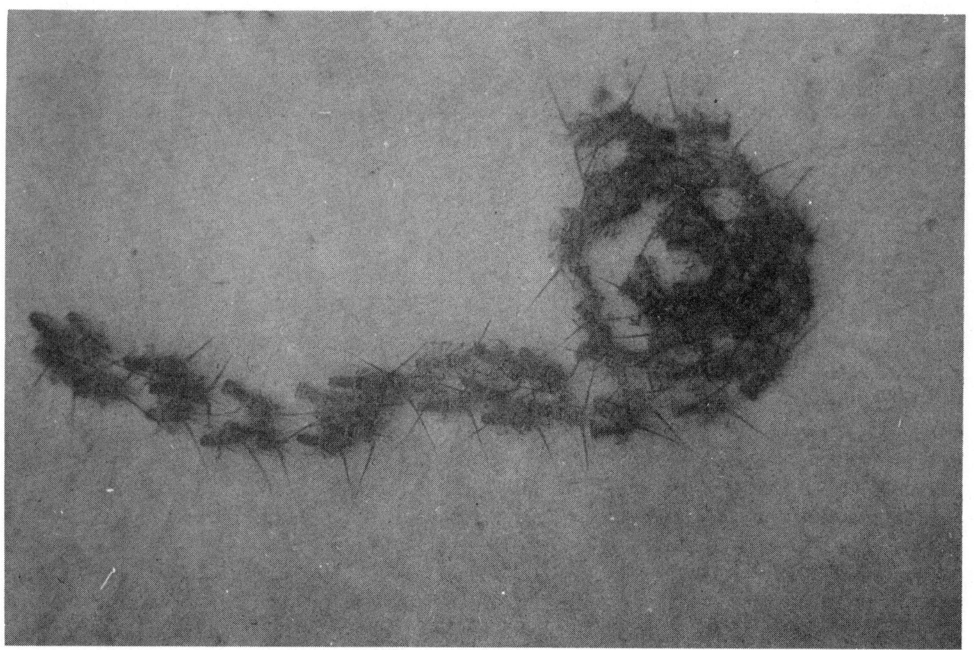

Figure 14-2. A queue may stop when the leader turns in a tight circle, the followers winding around one another in a spiral motion. Upon stopping, the individual lobsters rest facing the outside of the circle presenting a thicket of spiny antennae to an approaching diver or perhaps a predator. Locomotion resumes when one or more lobsters moves off and the rest fall into line.

giving the impression of rotation (Figure 14-2). At some point an individual moved off tangentially, pursued by the other lobsters. The formation then became a queue as individuals fell into single file. Moving queues form the pod in much the same way; i.e., the lead lobster turns in a tight circle and the followers wind about in an ever-widening spiral.

In the indoor pools, queues formed in back of those individuals that were most actively moving about the enclosure. Tests with "models" made from molted lobster carapaces mounted on glass rods proved that activity is the most crucial stimulus for leadership. I was able to induce queuing by merely moving the model about the test pool near the captive lobsters, in some cases even when they were inactive.

The question of the significance of queuing to survival arises. Answering this is far more difficult than determining the mechanism of queuing because it implies that the behavior has selective value in maintaining the species. As an educated guess, lobster queuing probably performs a defensive function. These lobsters are not offensive creatures of prey; they possess no claws or other weapons of attack. They rely on defense for their survival: hiding in a hard, horny armor, which deters all but the largest or hardest-mouth fishes; moving rapidly when in retreat, as the telson snaps forward propelling them backward; and keeping the abdomen, the least-protected portion of their anatomy, under a rock ledge. The pointed, hard front end is exposed to the predator, which usually gets either puncture wounds or a meal consisting of a spiny, almost hollow, autotomized antenna for its trouble. In open areas away from rock ledges, the abdomens of queuing lobsters are "protected" by the cephalothorax of the lobster behind. Of course, the last individual in line is at a decided disadvantage. Hiding under a rock doesn't always work either. My research assistant once came upon a lobster that had retreated from the open to the safety of a rock crevice only to find itself grasped tightly by a large *Octopus vulgaris* already in residence there.

The ability to move in a straight queue, whether or not the formation offers protection, seems of little value unless the movement is directed somewhere. This aspect of orientation brings up exciting problems because spiny lobsters are capable of feats that defy explanation. Witnesses of mass movements reported that all lobsters in a given area traveled in about the same direction although the direction varied from area to area: southerly at Bimini, northerly at Boca Raton, westerly at Grand Bahama. During the fall of 1969, at the Lerner Marine Laboratory in Bimini I observed a five-day mass movement and recorded the bearings of over 250 queues comprising some 2,000 spiny lobsters (Figure 14-3). The headings were strongly to the south over a distance of at least six miles. The lobsters maintained that bearing while moving over substrate of variable slope and at varying depths, in water visibility less than six feet, under completely overcast skies, and in areas of complex currents, all of which either occlude guidance cues or make them extremely variable. To appreciate this, consider yourself trying to walk on a direct course several miles through hill country, without a compass, in a dense London-style fog, while being buffeted by strong winds from different angles.

The most astounding performance by spiny lobsters occurred in experiments in Bermuda in 1949. Edwin Creaser and Dorothy Travis trapped and tagged lobsters, then released them at various distant locations. Afterward they regularly checked lobster traps located at the points of capture for any returns. Two lobsters released out at sea at a depth of 1,500 feet, two miles from the original point of capture, were retaken less than one week later! Since lobsters sink rapidly and are benthic creatures, it is unlikely they swam back near the surface. Returning two miles along the sea floor in virtually complete darkness suggests either a very effective guidance mechanism or a whole lot of luck. We have recently discovered that

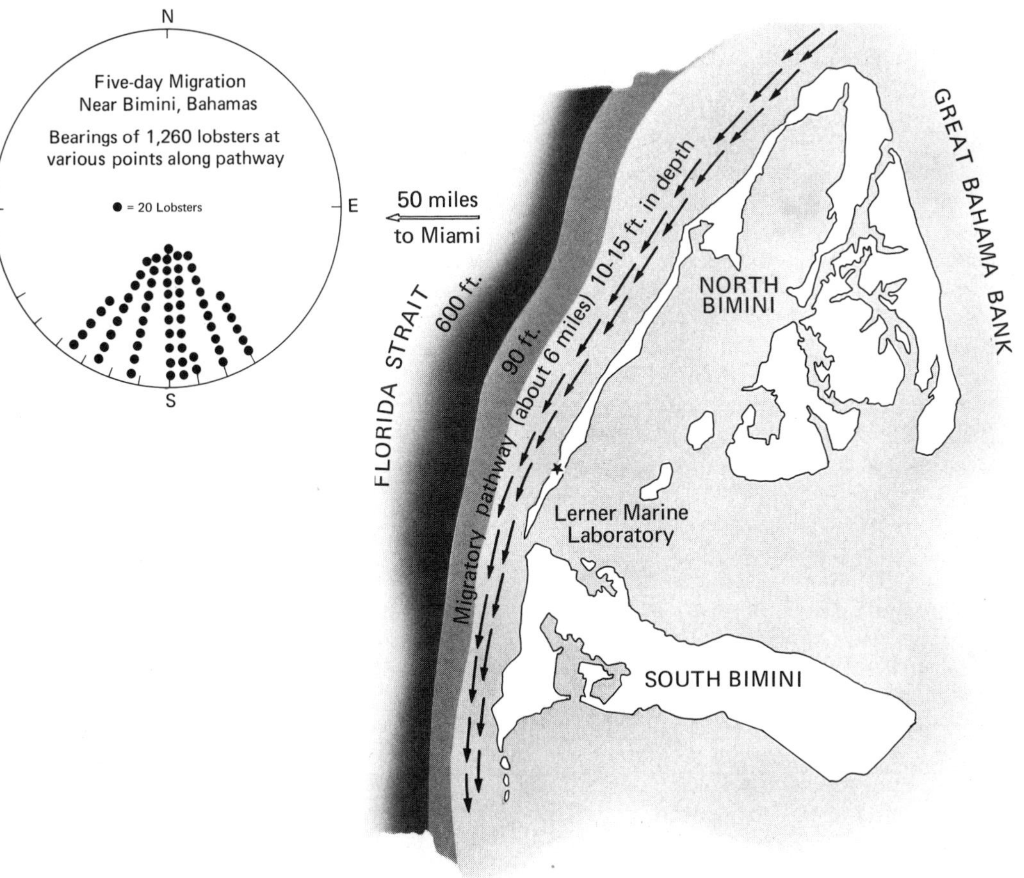


Figure 14-3. During November, 1969, migration, lobsters maintained strong southerly bearing, despite turbulent seas. Beginning and end of pathway are unknown.

reef lobsters typically live in a specific den for long periods, leaving by night to feed and returning before dawn. In addition, we corroborated the existence of homing ability by tracking the return of lobsters displaced up to 700 feet from their den.

To test for orientational mechanisms, I captured lobsters in nonmigratory condition from selected areas in the waters of Bimini. The animals were marked and released underwater at depths of 15 to 30 feet on level submarine sand plains devoid of vegetation. Each lobster's path was recorded on a plastic slate until it passed out of sight. The animal was then retrieved and released again to a total of eight times, each time at a compass heading 45 degress from the preceding one to control for any bias introduced by the direction the lobster was facing at the time of release.

The typical behavior of 26 lobsters after 208 releases was forward locomotion for a few yards, followed by a turn to a new heading, then direct movement over the underwater horizon. Twenty of the 26 lobsters distributed their runs in a nonuniform manner, that is, all eight runs fell in a specific range of compass bearings (within the 90 degree sector from west to north). Several individuals followed parallel paths on each release, crossing within 10 degrees or a few yards of a given point on three or four runs. We interpret this behavior as an indication of their ability to orient themselves and maintain a bearing in a relatively featureless area.

Convinced that spiny lobsters were capable of establishing a course in the open sea, we next wondered whether the process was effected visually. In further orientation experiments using lobsters blinded by opaque tape, twelve of fourteen lobsters exhibited parallel headings on each of the eight runs. In fact, several showed stronger orientation than the unblinded lobsters. It was particularly startling to release to the south a lobster that had previously run north and have it immediately turn 180 degrees and walk across my plastic slate. Doubtless, the spiny lobster can establish bearings without vision, which is not too surprising since they are nocturnal animals. But we are left with the question of what sensory mechanism and what environmental guidance cues are used to accomplish orientation under nonvisual conditions.

At this point we are not presuming that a single cue or mechanism is the only possible guidance factor. Rather we are alert to having several physical stimuli operating to guide the migration under different conditions. We feel this way for two reasons. First, it is becoming more and more apparent that other orienting animals, such as salmon, bees, pigeons, and fiddler crabs, respond to several types of cues. For instance, fiddlers can and do orient their movements by the sun and polarized sky when underwater, in tall grass, and under other conditions when only the sky is visible. However, if they are on the open beach, they orient by local landmarks even when the sun is clearly visible. So, if landmarks aren't available they use the sun-compass, if the sun isn't visible they use landmarks, and if neither is visible, as during rain or fog, we have some evidence that they don't bother to move more than a few yards away from the sanctuary of their burrows. The environment of the spiny lobster also has cues such as the sun, landmarks, and bottom slope available under some conditions, and these cannot be eliminated as possibilities.

A second reason is evident if one looks closely at the sensory capabilities of spiny lobsters. They have large eyes capable, at least, of recognizing other spiny lobsters; fine chemical and tactile sensors in each antennule, pereiopod tip, and also around the mouth; as well as tactile sensors in the telson and antennae. Internally there are proprioceptors, which sense not only movements of the appendages but also external forces such as gravity and uneven pressures. Additionally, there are indications of numerous receptors we have not yet characterized. If you look at the scanning electromicrographs taken of surface features, you will see numerous hairlike processes, clumps of setae, and pits in the chitin.

The functions of some of these are not yet known and one gets the strong impression that the spiny lobster is equipped as a walking undersea probe. Between the multitudinous physical cues of the ocean and the equally varied receptors, a self-contained guidance unit may be operating, exceeding any that man has yet devised.

## SUGGESTED READINGS

Allen, J. A. 1966. The rhythms and population dynamics of decapod crustacea. *Oceanography and Marine Biology, Annual Review* **4**, 247-265.

Herrnkind, William F. 1969. Queuing behavior of spiny lobsters. *Science* **164**, 1425-1427.

Herrnkind, William F., and R. McLean. 1971. Field studies of orientation homing and mass emigration in the spiny lobster, *Panulirus argus. New York Acad. Sci.* **188**, 359-377.

Waterman, T. H. (ed.) 1961. *The Physiology of Crustacea.* Academic Press, New York. Vol. 2.

Williams, A. B. 1965. Marine Decapod Crustaceans of the Carolinas. *U.S. Department of Interior Fishery Bulletin* **65**, 91-94.

# 15. Fish in Schools

EVELYN SHAW 1975

Schooling behavior is almost as prevalent as feeding and reproducing among the approximately 20,000 species of fish. About 16,000 species school as juveniles and about 4,000 of those continue to school throughout life. Schooling is found in a broad range of fish types, from the primitive, fragile anchovy to the advanced, powerful tuna. Schools of herring, cod, striped bass, and others make commercial fisheries feasible. Schooling is not only economically important, but it also provides animal behaviorists with endless puzzles about behavioral mechanisms and adaptive advantages.

Many schools are large, containing thousands of fish, but any number can compose a school—from two to the millions of individuals found in a seventeen-mile-long spawning run of herring. Schools have no leaders, and fish at the forward edge may suddenly find themselves at the rear when the school reverses direction. School members are usually of the same species and the same approximate size. Smaller fish are not able to maintain the right speed; larger fish swim too far ahead.

The tendency to school is certainly genetically programmed, for it appears when fish have had little or no experience with each other. Fish can "recognize" their own kind from the very beginning of their lives. For example, *Menidia*, or silverside, fry, when they are about one-quarter inch long, drift aimlessly with other plankton and are exposed to a variety of vertebrate and invertebrate species, but when they reach one-half inch in length, they come together and form schools. The newly formed schools contain a single species only. This specificity is dramatically demonstrated in laboratory experiments when two related schooling species are mixed. After a brief period of trying one another out through approaches and body vibrations, the young fry separate into two species-specific groups. Clearly, at the very earliest stages, the fish are able to distinguish appropriate peers and are mutually attracted to one another. Indeed, mutual attraction is the primary criterion used for designating true schooling types.

But schools have other characteristics as well. When fish in a school move forward,

Dr. Evelyn Shaw is an Adjunct Professor of animal behavior with the Department of Biological Sciences, Stanford University, California.

From *Natural History*, Vol. 84, No. 8, pp. 40-46, 1975. Reprinted with light editing and with permission of the author and *Natural History* Magazine. Copyright © The American Museum of Natural History, 1975.

they polarize, that is, they orient in parallel fashion—all individuals head in the same direction, swim at the same speed, and maintain fairly fixed distances from each other. When a school stops swimming, it depolarizes, but the fish remain together.

Parallel orientation and fish-to-fish spacing are distinctive qualities that give a school a characteristic three-dimensional structure—a geometry of its own. Fish in a school swim, not abreast, but in diagonal formation in a staggered pattern. When fish-to-fish spacing and diagonal positions change, the school looks quite different.

The most stunning feature of schooling is displayed when a school turns or changes direction. The fish then appear to be acting synchronously—turning together, increasing speed together, moving always in concert. This concurrent behavior entrances and baffles today's observers just as it mystified the scientists of the late nineteenth century, who postulated the existence of a "group mind" to explain the harmony of thousands of fish acting as one. The group mind concept had a short life, however, and twentieth-century scientists are discovering the biological mechanisms responsible for the synchrony and characteristic organization of schools.

In the 1920s experimenters identified vision as the sensory modality critical to schooling. Sightless fish do not approach other fish and consequently cannot school. Even though schooling fish must be able to see, they do not need to distinguish much detail for the school to maintain its coherence. A crescent moon, the stars, or phosphorescent organisms that cling to the skin of some species, all give sufficient light to enable schooling to continue. In one laboratory experiment, a school of jack mackerels maintained cohesion even when the light was so dim that it required ten minutes of adjustment before the observer could see the school. In the total absence of light, schools will disperse. Fish observed in the dark through a "snooperscope," were found to be swimming randomly inside a tank, seemingly unaware of each other's presence.

In addition to the visual sense, which is not only primary but which probably also serves as the major pathway of communication, other senses such as the olfactory and auditory may function in schooling. It is well known that fish have a fine ability to discriminate between even the faintest odors. It seems unlikely, however, that changes in the speed and direction of a school are communicated through a schooling pheromone, a chemical substance that conveys intraspecies information, but olfactory cues may operate in species discrimination, that is, in the recognition of similar types. Communication of changes in speed and direction through the production of sound is also unlikely. Schooling fish tend to be almost noiseless. Several experimenters have found that at night, when visual references are unavilable, some species produce sounds that may serve to keep the group together. These sounds are not detected, however, in the daytime in an actively moving school.

All fishes possess a special sensory system, called the lateral line, that detects changes in the movement and pressure of surrounding water. In many species the lateral line consists of a series of canals crisscrossing the head in a characteristic species-typical pattern. In addition, most fishes have a single canal that courses down the lateral body wall on each side. The basic sensor of the lateral line is the neuromast, a cluster of innervated hair cells capped by a gelatinous sheath known as a cupula. Neuromasts are spaced regularly along the canal. When water is displaced around a fish, the movement is detected by a neuromast through the bending of the cupula. Fish can see changes in the spacing, speed, and direction of schools, but because of the sensitivity of the lateral line system to movements and pressure changes in the surrounding water, it may serve as a prime source of information.

Exactly how the lateral line functions in schooling remains a mystery, but that it does function is suggested by the following experiments on tuna conducted by Phyllis Cahn, an acoustic physiologist at Long Island University, New York, and on jacks by the author. When jacks were artificially separated from each other by a transparent partition that blocked reception in the lateral line, the fish moved closer together than in a normal school and fish-to-fish spacing was markedly reduced. Tuna, on the other hand, will spread farther apart—from two to four times their normal distance—under similar experimental conditions. The loss of information from water displacements appears to upset the characteristic spacing maintained by schooling fish, and sight alone evidently cannot compensate for the lack of input derived from water movements.

In another experiment, John R. Hunter and Jon Van Olst, of the National Oceanic and Atmospheric Administration (NOAA) at La Jolla, California, showed that spacing and fish length are related. When they are young, jacks, mackerels, silversides, and anchovies swim in loosely structured schools, and the spaces between the fish measure about three to four body lengths. When the fish grow to three or four inches, the spacing shrinks to half a body length for all four species. Spacing of half a body length is also found in other species, which suggests that this may be the optimum distance for obtaining the most precise water displacement information through the lateral line sensors.

A last point about schooling and the senses concerns the relationship between speed of response and the visual system. Hunter found that a jack mackerel reacts more quickly to changes in a neighbor's activities if it sees the neighbor in certain areas of its visual field. By photographing one tethered fish and five freely swimming fish, he determined that the responding fish reacts more quickly to a neighbor's behavioral change if the neighbor is either directly ahead and can be seen with both eyes simultaneously or if the neighbor is at such an angle alongside that its image fills the entire visual field of one of the responder's eyes. The reaction time of the responder fish to changes in direction or speed is a mere 0.15 to 0.20 seconds, hardly more than a blink of an observer's eye. Indeed, the reaction time is so short that, to the unaided eye, an entire school of fish may seem to turn simultaneously in response to a change initiated by only a few individuals. This ability to react quickly is highly useful for survival.

All evidence indicates that it is beneficial for fish to be members of a school. Fish in schools swim for longer periods, cover greater distances, and tolerate colder temperatures than comparable fish swimming alone. Diverse experiments show that groups of schooling fish consume less oxygen per fish than an individual school member swimming alone. Goldfish in a group tolerate higher doses of toxins per fish than when alone, sunfish learn the pathways of a maze more quickly in groups than as singles, and groups of carp avoid a moving net more successfully than loners. An individual fish trained with a group and then removed regresses to poorer scores. The advantages of group life seemingly cannot be maintained by single fish.

From one point of view, schooling might be considered a form of social behavior in which the actions of a few benefit the many. For example, when a predator swoops out of the sky and plunges into a school of prey, the fish in the predator's immediate vicinity, reacting swiftly, alter their swimming course and speed in order to escape. Through visual signals and shifts in the water pattern, these changes are rapidly communicated to other fish in the school. A wave of disturbance will sweep through the school until the whole group diverges from its original path. The total elapsed time is perhaps half a second. In this case, the response of a few has benefited the entire group, and the school has escaped from the predator. A few individuals may have been consumed, but their loss is insignificant to the group.

Each member of a school can be thought of as a scanner of its own environment. In a randomly chosen school there may be hundreds, thousands, or even millions of scanners. Fish at the edges of the school become the "eyes" of the fish in the center, thereby enabling any fish to "see" beyond the limits of its actual field of vision. It is not necessary for fish in the center of the school to be constantly on the alert to potential danger; all they need do is respond rapidly to changes in their neighbors' behavior. The same holds true when a food supply is sighted; then too, the fish in the center are informed. When tuna sight prey, for example, dark bands form on their flanks, signaling other fish that food is nearby. In this manner, many fish can feast even though only a few have discovered the food.

Schooling has other attributes, depending on whether the school consists of prey fish or predators. A theoretical model, based on chance encounters during a given period of time within a large area, indicates that school prey should maintain a highly compact pattern and move very slowly in order to reduce the probability of an encounter with a group of predators. School predators, on the other hand, require encounters. The likelihood of detecting prey is theoretically enhanced if the predators move rapidly in looser schools so as to cover a large area. In fact, both types of schooling have been observed in nature.

When an encounter occurs, it is, of course, disadvantageous to be the prey, but single fish prey are at an even greater disadvantage than school prey. This was demonstrated by a Russian investigator who introduced young coalfish, alone and in schools of twenty-five to thirty-five, to predatory cod. Two and a half minutes elapsed before a cod consumed a single coalfish school member, but only a half minute elapsed before the cod consumed a coalfish introduced singly. The cod was unable to concentrate on any one fish in the school and was distracted again and again from its target fish, switching its pursuit from one individual to another until it finally focused on its victim. The school created a "confusion" effect, which provided time for all the fish to escape from pursuit except, ultimately, the victim.

As mentioned previously, schools generally contain only one species. Experiments confirm that there are advantages to acting and looking like your neighbor. Predators tend to select individuals that differ from their companions; they pursue the weak, the slow, the conspicuous. One experimenter marked prey fish with fluorescent dyes and found that the glowing fish provided brilliant targets for predators. Their shining hour came to a quick end. And, in nature, the flash of silver from the gill cover of an anchovy as it feeds pinpoints the fish as prey despite its membership in a school. Because a feeding anchovy no longer resembles its neighbors, it can be picked off.

Even regular spacing of fish in schools works to the advantage of the prey. Edmund Hobson of NOAA watched a grouper intently watching a school of herring. The grouper attacked only three times in two hours—when the school dispersed in response to a diving pelican. Herring that strayed too far from the aggregation were quickly gulped into the grouper's wide mouth. Dispersion also occurs when two prey schools encounter each other and their respective geometric patterns are temporarily disrupted. Before the schools can reassemble, individual fish are particularly vulnerable to predators.

Another survival feature of school geometry applies to prey and predators alike. Studies show that in fish-to-fish spacing, both the distances between individuals and their diagonal positions are important factors in the conservation of energy by a school, whether it be prey or predator. A diamond school pattern maximizes the energy available to the member fishes. Fish propel themselves forward by tail thrusts. As the tail sweeps from side to side, it creates vortices, or small whirls of water, in the fish's wake. Depending on its position in the school, one fish can coast on the vortices produced by another in front of it, thus spending less energy on swimming. Fish change position within the school with sufficient frequency to guarantee that no one fish must continuously work harder than any other. In this manner, one fish can utilize the energy expended by another—energy that would otherwise be dissipated and lost—and the over-all effect benefits the entire school.

It is apparent that many good things happen to fish when they take up a schooling life. They have constant companionship and readily available partners during the reproductive season, they make maximum use of available food, conserve their energy, and derive such social benefits as protection from predators and enhanced learning ability.

# 16. Sharks–The Oldest Living Predators

DOUGLAS MYLES 1974

Perhaps no other creature in the world is so feared by man as the shark. During all the centuries since mariners first put to sea the sight of the telltale dorsal fin cutting the water has frozen the limbs and struck terror to the heart. For in this fish man has instinctively recognized his mortal enemy, and has reacted with fright, hatred, and loathing.

Yet man knows little about his foe—surprisingly little, considering his fear. If asked about sharks the average person will do one of two things, either shake his head in ignorance, or proceed to answer from a monumental fund of misinformation. The facts of the matter are well authenticated, and should be known by every swimmer, skin diver, and yachtsman or anyone who loves the sea and wishes to sail it or enter it. For in knowledge there is protection. The record will show that the great majority of victims to shark attack have been ignorant of the creatures' habits.

We may begin by debunking all statements that sharks are relatively harmless to man, that they may be frightened away by shouting or thrashing the water surface. In World War II this fallacy was lent support by the United States Navy, whose training manual for men serving in shark-infested seas gave the impression that the man-eater was more myth than menace. Nothing could be further from the truth. There are 250 recognized species of shark, only a relatively few of which are known to be dangerous to man at all times, others being a hazard only when there is blood in the water. But all but one of the species which are deadly are quite prolific, so much so that sharks are very frequently encountered in all tropical and temperate seas. It is these creatures we discuss here. Their numbers alone make them the greatest living menace of the sea, the primary marine threat to man.

Can it be proved statistically? The answer is an unqualified affirmative. Every year throughout the world people are mutilated, crippled, and killed by shark attack. Australia is a case in point. On her east coast, particularly along the Great Barrier Reef, the past century and a half has seen recorded more than 200 authenticated shark strikes against humans. Nor are American waters by

Douglas Myles is a Marine Corps veteran of World War II. He is an avid scuba diver and a free-lance writer, primarily of novels.

From *Oceans Magazine*, Vol. 7, No. 5, pp. 64-69, 1974. Reprinted with light editing and with permission of the author and *Oceans Magazine*.

any means immune. In 1952 a seventeen-year-old boy, Barry Wilson, was fatally bitten while swimming at Monterey Bay, California. In 1959 a boy of eighteen, Albert Kogler, was killed at Baker's Beach near San Francisco's Golden Gate. In 1963 U.S. Navy Ensign John Gibson lost his life at Magens Bay, St. Thomas, Virgin Islands. And in 1968 movie stuntman Jose Marco fell victim to a great white shark off Mexico's Isla Mujeres, ironically, while making a film called *Shark* (see *Life* Magazine, June 7, 1968).

Figures for 1959 are about average: 36 proved attacks were recorded that year in both hemispheres, thirteen of them resulting in mortal wounds. Of this number, ten strikes were in American seas, three of them fatal. Young Kogler was one of the latter.

Of the four major groups of fishes, sharks and their relatives, the skates and rays, are the most primitive, having descended only superficially changed from the Devonian Period which began about 310 million years ago. Shark skeletons are cartilaginous, only the jaws and a few of the fin spines being of bone. Hence, these are the parts which alone may be preserved as fossils.

Owing to its extreme adaptability, the shark has survived where other marine species have become extinct. It developed much earlier than the bony fish, and in contrast to the latter's habit of laying eggs in the water at random, the young of most species of shark are spawned alive, a half dozen to sixty at once. In some species they will average eighteen inches at birth and can swim and seize their own food quite independently of the mother.

Anyone who is underwater and sees a shark approaching head on will observe three great fins, the vertical dorsal fin of the back, and the two pectoral fins projecting outward and downward at an angle from the sides. These are not used for swimming but for balance, as are the much smaller ventral fins, the anal, and the rudimentary posterior dorsal. It is the long caudal fin or tail that propels the creature by sweeping from side to side, and without its steadying thrust it is virtually immobilized. A few years ago, when the Norwegian Thor Heyerdahl and his comrades sailed across an ocean on the raft *Kon Tiki,* they boated dozens of sharks during their long voyage just to keep the area free of them should anyone go overboard. The system they used was simple. Slops were thrown in the sea to attract the sharks. As the big fish circled the raft, sometimes bumping it with their sides, the men caught hold of the caudal fins, pulling them tail-first from the water. Once the tails were lifted free of the surface the sharks were deprived of their great propulsive force. They were still difficult to subdue, but swim they could not.

Unlike the bony fishes of the world, sharks do not possess swim bladders. This means that if they cease all motion they will sink, as they invariably do in death. A shark may sleep on the surface while sunning itself, yet even in sleep some marvelous mechanism remains in operation. Slowly the powerful tail will move, the shark's body slipping almost imperceptibly through the sea. It is enough. All unknowing, the dozing killer remains afloat.

Sharks have been called both brave and cowardly. From the biological standpoint neither supposition has any validity. Bravery and cowardice are attributes of the intellect, entirely absent where the thinking process is absent. A shark cannot think, though it has highly developed instincts. Even in the largest of its species the brain will not exceed an inch and a half in length, and the nervous system is extremely primitive. It is this fact that makes it so hard to kill, for where severe wounds cause shock and hemorrhage in more advanced forms of life, the shark is virtually immune to both, having no equal for sheer durability. Jacques Yves Cousteau, renowned French underwater explorer and author of *The Silent World* and *The Shark: Splendid Savage of the Sea,* tells of firing an explosive harpoon through the head of a shark. Although he saw it detonate on the other side, the fish swam away without apparent harm. There are authenticated accounts of sharks being boated by whalers, then gutted and heaved overboard, after which they have swum to the harpooned whale whose carcass the sailors were protecting and attacked it, continuing to feed until the moment of death.

Short of blowing it to pieces there are very few ways of stopping a shark quickly, and the following method is not recommended as a diversion. On the remote island of Olosenga in American Samoa the natives hunt the creatures for sport, hunt them at night when their boats cast no shadows. From outrigger canoes they first lure them to the surface by trolling a longline baited with rotten fish (though they'll strike at fresh fish just as readily). As the pursuing shark breaks water the bait is pulled close alongside the outrigger. Then a native leaps on the shark's back, locks his legs around its body, grasps the dorsal fin, and rips a gaping hole in its belly with his knife. They say the trick is this: that long blade must find the liver, whose location the native well knows, so that salt water may paralyze the fish. Is this belief valid? It has never been scientifically tested, so far as the author knows. But, obviously, a shark with a torn liver isn't going very far.

It may seem a contradiction that the pain-insensitive shark has such keenly acute senses, but it is a fact. Its sense of smell is fantastic, its olfactory receptors guiding it unerringly to blood from an incredible distance. The careless skin diver trailing blood from a speared fish is asking for trouble, especially if a man-eater is in the area. And there is another thing. The swimmer thrashing on the surface may easily attract a lurking shark, who is very sensitive to sound vibrations. As Cousteau has observed, divers, though vulnerable, are less likely to be hit by sharks, who seem on the whole to become less aggressive with increasing depth. On the surface a human is a target. There is logic to this. The shark is an untiring seeker after food and will take it in the simplest possible manner. Surface prey is the easiest, for here is found the sick or dying gull, the crippled fish, garbage thrown from ships, the completely helpless human swimmer.

It is sometimes asked whether the shark has natural enemies. It greatest foe is man, of course, but the giant squid, giant octopus, and saltwater crocodile are all capable of killing it, as is the porcupine fish which inflates its body in the shark's mouth and causes asphyxiation. Its primary marine enemy is its own kind, for big sharks eat smaller ones readily, and the young are ever a prey to the adults. If a shark is injured and bleeding it can survive only if alone, for if others are nearby they will attack at once. Killer whales will defeat it, too. An adult male killer can destroy the most deadly shark, and the largest; it cannot cope with the mammal's keen intelligence, far greater bulk, unequaled ferocity, and *armored* defense of extremely thick blubber.

How does a giant octopus kill a shark? Such a fight has been filmed. The shark was observed to attack directly, going straight in to bite. Unable to avoid the snapping jaws which slashed into its mantle, the twenty-foot octopus girdled its enemy with powerful tentacles, fastening its suckers to the shark's gill slits and forcing them open. The octopus then drowned its antagonist by pulling it in a circle backwards through the water, a tactic apparently instinctive. The mechanism by which fish extract oxygen from water does not function in reverse.

Any African white hunter is aware of how the hippopotamus protects its young from crocodile attack. The members of the hippo herd simply turn on the croc and dispatch it by biting it in half. A similar thing happens when a shark follows a school of porpoise (misnamed "dolphin"), intent on snapping up a baby. When the mammals become aware of the tracking fish they immediately surround it. Then the shark is struck from all sides as the porpoise rush it, using their blunt heads like battering rams. They will pulverize the shark in this way, not ceasing their attacks against lower abdomen and gills until both are destroyed.

The shark's teeth are worth studying. Their method of replacement is particularly unique and fascinating. There are several sets, row behind row, those in the rear moving forward to replace the front ones as the latter break or wear down. In many species they are serrated to provide greater ripping power. So efficient are they as cutting instruments that a shark attacking a harpooned whale will remove up to twenty pounds of blubber at a time. It is widely believed that the position of the shark's lower jaw forces it to turn over to bite, but this is not true. The shark may occasionally do so, but never through necessity. It can attack with efficiency from any angle.

Comparatively little is known about shark breeding habits, something naturalists often cannot observe. An interesting aspect of it, however, is the phenomenon which occurs annually at Acapulco Bay in tropical Mexico. For eleven months of the year guests at the plush hotels there swim and frolic without incident, so long as they remain close to shore. But each September the warning signs go up and bathing is discouraged. And each September the sharks come in, as they have done every year for countless millennia. They are big makos, speedy acrobats of the undersea world, and they've come to breed. Many of them succeed in doing so, but others fall victim to the Mexican youths, who delight in attacking them with spears, often in no more than three feet of water.

Speaking of this, one is reminded of another very strange anomaly. Lake Nicaragua is in Central America, and like all lakes its waters are fresh. Yet, along with Lake Izabal in Guatemala, it has become the home of a species of shark so closely related to the bull shark that some authorities regard them as the same. How can such a thing happen? Do physical changes occur through evolution, the fish acclimatizing gradually over many generations? Apparently not. Most species of salmon, as well as some trout, are anadromous, migrating from the sea to freshwater rivers to spawn. Though not kindred to such bony fishes, the sharks too can seemingly adjust to these changes quickly. An incident is on record in Iran of a shark being found in a river nearly a hundred miles from the sea, while in India sharks have struck at bathers in the Ganges. Clearly, in a few sea creatures physiological mutations are unnecessary to allow migration from salt to fresh water. In the case of the Nicaragua sharks there is evidence that they enter the lake by way of the San Juan River.

A shark is a gastronomical monstrosity, one might say an impossibility were it not for proved accounts. There is almost nothing it will not eat—fish, lobster, crab, birds of all kinds, seals, sea lions, turtles, all mammals of whatever species, including man. The stomach contents of one shark taken in Australian waters were amazing. They included pieces of horseflesh, legs of mutton, part of a ham, a bulldog's head and forelegs and the rope that circled its neck, a pig's hindquarters, a ship's scraper, and a piece of cloth. This assortment was topped by that of another shark hooked in the Adriatic. Found in its belly were a car's license plate, three heavy overcoats, and a nylon raincoat.

Sharks do not chew their food. Among them only certain of the harmless dogfishes are equipped with teeth capable of grinding. Whatever it bites off the shark swallows whole, and apparently some species can store food in their stomachs for days or even weeks without digesting it. Human arms and legs have been found in sharks, as well as the mammalian remains mentioned above. Very often they are well preserved, a fact that must negate a belief in the potency of shark stomach acid.

Concerning its method of attack the shark has its own idiosyncrasies. One of the most characteristic is its habit of concentrating on a single target to the neglect of equally accessible ones. If it attacks one of a group of swimmers, it will return repeatedly to its first victim and disembowel or dismember him in their midst, ignoring the others. This happened in the Monterey Bay tragedy cited above, and in that at Baker's Beach, and has been often noted. The explanation? The first person hit is the bleeding one. Sharks go to blood like cats to catnip.

Sharkskin is very interesting stuff. Called shagreen, it is a substitute for scales, and consists of thousands of tiny placoid prominences, or denticles, very hard and rough in texture and of great durability. For centuries the fine swords carried by Japanese samurai have had their grips bound in sharkskin, and some of the oldest of them still show little sign of wear. But the very roughness of the hide can prove a swimmer's undoing. A blow from a big shark's tail will lacerate human skin. The resultant bleeding may then provoke the fatal attack.

It has been stated earlier that only a few of the 250 recognized species of shark are anthropophagous, or eaters of human flesh. Prominent among these are the great white, white pointer, or man-eater (*Carcharodon carcharias*); the great blue or, occasionally, blue-fin (*Prionace glauca*); the tiger (*Galeocerdo cuvieri*); the white-tip oceanic (*Carcharhinus longimanus*); the mako, blue pointer, or sharp-nosed mackerel shark (*Isurus oxyrinchus*); the gray nurse or Indo-Pacific sand shark (*Carcharias arenarius*); the black whaler (*Galeolamna macrurus*); and the great hammerhead (*Sphyrna mokarran*). Because their record of attacks on humans is notorious and extensive, these sharks will be discussed briefly. However, to the list might easily be added such dangerous species as the dusky shark (*Carcharhinus obscurus*); the Galapagos (*Carcharhinus galapagensis*); the bull shark (*Carcharhinus leucas*); the Atlantic sand shark (*Carcharias taurus*); the bay shark (*Carcharhinus lamiella*); the Ganges (*Carcharhinus gangeticus*); the Lake Nicaragua (*Carcharhinus nicaraguensis*); the great black-tip or spinner (*Carcharhinus maculipinnis*) (Figure 16-1); the lemon (*Negaprion brevirostris*); the porbeagle or mackerel

Figure 16-1. Great tip shark (*Carcharhinus maculipinnis*). Photograph by R. G. Pirie.

shark (*Lamna nasus*); the reef or gray reef shark (*Carcharhinus menisorrah*); the salmon shark (*Lamna ditropis*); the white-tip reef shark (*Carcharhinus albimarginatus*); the Zambesi (*Carcharhinus zambezensis*); the wobbegong (*Orectolobus maculatus*); the scalloped hammerhead (*Sphyrna lewini*); the smooth or common hammerhead (*Sphyrna zygaena*); and the bonito or Indo-Pacific mako (*Isurus glaucus*).

The great white shark is the largest of the killer fish, reportedly reaching a length of more than 36 feet and a weight approaching four tons. The color of the largest of them is lead-white, smaller ones being white only on the belly and a dark blackish-brown on the back and sides. The tips and edges of the pectoral fins are black. Fortunately, great whites are comparatively rare in all seas, even in the tropic zone, though they have recently been discovered in fairly large numbers at Dangerous Reef, 25 miles off Australia's south coast. They are incredibly aggressive, savage almost beyond belief.

The great blue shark is reported to reach a length of twenty feet, but sixteen feet is the largest this writer has found on record. It is light blue, steel blue, or grayish above, white below, and has a characteristically slender body, long pointed snout, and extremely long pectoral fins, affording great agility. This fish, called by Cousteau "the most beautiful shark of all," is also one of the speediest. Big ones will weigh about a thousand pounds. Like the great white it is pelagic, meaning it has a wide oceanic range, and, although a warm-water species, has been found as far north as Nova Scotia. All other sharks avoid the blue. When it glides effortlessly through the sea, the always open mouth taking in water forced through the gills, its deadly, serrated teeth flatly retracted within, it is, in the words of Colonel John D. Craig (who met a blue in its own element), "a blue and white torpedo of viciousness."

To the landsman, probably the best known of all sharks is the tiger. It is a blunt-nosed species, deriving its name from the numerous brown markings found on its back when young, spots or stripes that tend to fade with full adulthood. It is by far the most common of the group known as requiem sharks, is pelagic, and ranges throughout both tropic and temperate zones. Possibly the second largest of the man-eaters, it may reach a length of eighteen feet, though this is exceptional, and a weight in excess of two thousand pounds. In West Indian waters it is feared beyond all others.

Positive information on the white-tip oceanic shark has been comparatively late in being compiled. At first it was thought to be not very dangerous, but that view has changed in recent years. This pelagic species, twelve feet long at maturity, is gray, brown, or bluish on the back and sides, white or yellowish below, possessing the white-tipped pectoral and dorsal fins and similar caudal lobes which give it its name. Referring to both its great numbers and its savage nature, Cousteau calls it "the undisputed lord of the tropical oceans." He writes: "Every species of shark, even the most inoffensive, is anatomically a formidable source of potential danger. On paper, the most to be feared are the great white sharks (*Carcharodon carcharias*), with their enormous jaws and great, triangular teeth. But, in reality, this species is extremely rare. By far the most disturbing are the *Carcharhinus longimanus,* whose great rounded fins bear a large white circle at their extremities. These 'lords of the long hands' are encountered only in the open sea, but everywhere in warm waters. They are the only species of shark that is never frightened by the approach of a diver, and they are the most dangerous of all sharks."

The mako (or sharp-nosed mackerel shark or blue pointer) is the swiftest shark in the world, a species closely related to the great white. It is also the only shark reckoned as a game fish, being ardently sought by sportsmen because of the spectacular leaps it makes when hooked. It is dark bluish-gray above, white below, and may reach a length of over twelve feet and a weight of eight hundred pounds. It was originally called mako only in New Zealand, the word being of Maori origin, and in former times was believed to be no great menace. In recent years reports from the Red Sea and elsewhere have altered this opinion.

The gray nurse or Indo-Pacific sand shark (not to be confused with the inoffensive nurse shark–*Ginglymostoma cirratum*) is an Australian man-eater reaching fifteen feet in length and a slender thousand pounds. Its color is a slate gray, it has a smooth skin with small denticles, and its fins are of a distinctive, rounded configuration quite unlike those of most other sharks; they are quite similar in fact to the fins of some of the bony fishes. The teeth are shaped somewhat like those of the mako but are even more hideous in appearance, being curved in opposing directions and the longest of any shark of its size. This fish is a fast swimmer, much hunted for commercial purposes.

Indigenous primarily to Australian waters, but found also off the east coast of Africa, is the black whaler shark, related to the bronze whaler (*Carcharhinus brachyurus*) of New Zealand and the northern whaler (*Carcharhinus stevensi*) of Queensland. The reputation of this species is very bad, so much so that shark authorities V. M. Coppleson and Gilbert P. Whitley rate it on a par with the tiger shark as the deadliest fish found about Australia. Attaining a length of twelve feet and a weight of over seven hundred pounds, the black whaler's back and sides run from black to very dark gray, as do its fins, while its dentition is similar to that of the gray nurse and the mako. It is perhaps the most commercially valuable shark caught in Australia and provides a very fine grade of leather.

Lastly we come to the great hammerhead, one of the strangest creatures of the sea. It is close to the tiger in size, some specimens attaining over eighteen feet of length and more than seventeen hundred pounds in weight. This fish derives its name from the fantastic structure of its head, which joins its body like the top of the letter T. The eyes are at the ends of the head lobes, and these fleshy protuberances not only aid in the maintenance of balance but act like a vane, enabling the hammerhead to turn and maneuver with great speed. The teeth of this shark are comparatively small, and set at a very oblique angle. Its mouth too is small, considering the size of the fish. But if the hammerhead is one of nature's jokes, it is a very grim joke. Although a pelagic shark, it often frequents inshore waters, remaining much at or near the surface, and it is there it takes its toll of unwary swimmers. The first fatal shark attack in American waters was by a hammerhead. According to the records this was off Long Island in 1815. Since then the pattern has continued. The hammerhead's total for the slaughter of human beings stands close to the top.

Are there ways of stopping sharks, of putting an end to them as a menace? Many methods have been tried: chemical shark repellents, electrified nets, various types of noise-makers, even specially equipped ships and planes to hunt them down. Only the Australians have experienced any success. Their technique, which they call "meshing," is to seal off the bathing beaches with a series of slack-hanging nets strung during the night, very large nets in which sharks become easily entangled. Tested first at Sydney in 1937, the method netted more than fifteen hundred sharks in little over a year, more than half of them of dangerous species. The nets are in use at this writing. The average annual catch is now less than two hundred, and attacks on swimmers at protected beaches have practically ceased.

In World War II the U.S. Navy developed a copper acetate repellent called "Shark Chaser," theoretically having the power of driving sharks away. When it was tested off Brisbane the sharks made meals of whole packets of the chemical and showed not the least distaste for it. Only the dye it contained, called nigrosine, proved at all effective. Blue-black, like the ink of a squid or octopus, when it was released in the sea sharks gave it a wide berth.

But what can be done with sharks under

ordinary conditions is one thing. Their behavior during what is called a "feeding frenzy" is quite something else. This phenomenon has been observed when fish is cleaned aboard ship and the offal thrown overboard, staining the water with blood. Attracted by their marvelous sense of smell, sharks gather in great numbers on such occasions, become blood-maddened, and go literally berserk. They will strike at anything then, including each other, and once one of their number has been ripped open it is quickly torn apart.

A feeding frenzy may occur when a ship goes down; it is certain to do so if sharks are present. When it does it is one of the most terrible things possible to imagine. In 1942 the night attack of a submarine destroyed the troopship *Nova Scotia* off the South African coast, killing more than a thousand men. And on the following day the disaster area was littered with floating limbless bodies.

Is the shark then the only sea denizen dangerous to man? Practically speaking, yes, although certain other creatures definitely have a potential for menace, and are statistically insignificant only because seldom encountered. One of these is the sea snake, of which there exist about 55 species. Many sea snakes are found in Australian waters, off Malaya, in the Bay of Bengal, and generally throughout the eastern Indian Ocean, extending into Micronesia. One pelagic species, of a striking black and yellow coloration, ranges from Panama to Madagascar. *All* of these snakes are venomous, the most deadly being about one hundred times as toxic as the Australian tiger snake, possessor of the most virulent poison of any terrestrial reptile. But most are docile, disinclined to bite except when aroused.

Some small fish must be avoided. In the Indian and Pacific oceans are found the stonefish and the zebra fish (variously called turkeyfish and fire fish), the venom from whose hollow spines causes agonizing pain and frequently results in death or paralysis. Man need not worry about them unduly. They are not at all aggressive and the only victims they claim are those unlucky enough to touch them or step on them. Dozens of other small fish are dangerous, some having venomous spines, others flesh that is poisonous when eaten.

It is different with the great or king barracuda (*Sphyraena barracuda*). This thin, very fast fish, four to six feet in length, is clearly a hazard in West Indian and Florida waters, being on record as attacking humans. There have been fourteen confirmed attacks since 1884, and doubtlessly many others attributed to sharks. But one thing makes the barracuda much less dangerous than the shark. The shark strikes and then returns, strikes again, veers away and returns, as it tries to totally dismember its prey. Not so the barracuda. This fish strikes once, then, despite the blood of its victim in the water, it disappears. It leaves a ragged wound, utterly unlike the clean-cut, crescent-shaped bite of the shark.

As menaces to man, four large creatures may be quickly dismissed, these being the giant squid, the giant octopus, the saltwater crocodile, and the manta ray. Attaining a record length to date of 52 feet and a weight of around three tons, the giant squid is extremely formidable, possessing vast strength and a curved, razor-sharp beak capable of slicing a man to ribbons. But this huge invertebrate is very rarely met, and remains almost unknown. No man can say how long they live, how large they become, or how deep they may be found. They are known to be one of the principal foods of the sperm whale, and sperms have been taken with their bodies deeply scarred by the giant squid's powerful suckers.

From the tip of one tentacle to the tip of its opposite member the giant octopus has been known to reach a breadth of 28 feet. Equipped with a beak similar to that of the giant squid, it too can be a fearful opponent. But no octopus, large or small, is aggressive. They are shy creatures and if left unmolested will normally keep to themselves.

Saltwater crocodiles will reach a length of

twenty feet and weigh one hundred pounds to the foot. They have no fear of large sharks and kill them quite easily, but they are simply not widespread or numerous enough to be a serious threat to man.

In Mexican waters the manta, largest of the ray family, has an evil reputation among divers. Despite its dangerous appearance, great weight, and span of more than twenty feet, it is not a killer in the usual sense, nor does it ever attack man intentionally. But to "hard hat" divers with lifelines and air hoses it is often deadly. Projecting from the manta's head are twin curved, flipper-shaped antennae, sensory organs used to aid in feeding. They become covered with sea lice, which causes itching. The ray tries to dislodge them. To do this it may seize a frond of kelp and run with it, or a boat's anchor chain, or a diver's lines. When the latter occurs the diver is frequently killed.

Two warm-blooded marine mammals are dangerous to man, the sea leopard and the killer whale. Both are nearly unbelievably vicious, though specimens of the latter have actually been tamed. Both use similar tactics, such as following an animal on an ice floe by swimming beneath the ice and watching the intended victim's shadow. The sea leopard, a twelve-foot antarctic seal, derives its name from its spotted coat. Feeding mainly on fish, smaller seals, and penguins, it normally skins the latter as a man peels a banana, and nearly as quickly, nor does it hesitate to attack human beings.

The killer whale hunts in packs of from five or six to as many as thirty, and will reach about thirty feet in length and weigh at least twenty tons. It is the only natural enemy of the sea leopard and will devour one with relish. It also eats fish, penguins, seals of other species, walruses, sea lions, even a polar bear when it can seize one. The tongues of larger whales are a delicacy to the killer, which rips them out of its living victims' mouths and lets them bleed to death. Though indigenous to the polar regions, this black and white devil of the sea is pelagic in its range, having been sighted even in California waters. Fortunately, such occasions are comparatively rare: fortunately, too, not everyone is deceived by the benign appearance and docile behavior of the trained killers in aquariums and marine parks.

That, with a few minor exceptions (such as the moray eel), is about the lot. It is not a pretty rogue's gallery, but except for the man-eating sharks its members are statistically insignificant. And the human in the sea should remember these rules: (1) If on a life raft, air mattress, or surfboard, do not dangle the limbs over the side. (2) Never skin dive or go swimming in the sea alone. (3) Avoid swimming at night, or when water visibility is poor. (4) If you spear a fish, bring it to the surface at once and boat it. Don't tow its bleeding body at your belt. (5) If you are swimming and see a shark, don't thrash about. Swim to shore or to a boat quickly but quietly, preferably with a sidestroke or breast stroke. With the backstroke or crawl it is necessary to splash. (6) If a shark closes you, never try to hit it with your fist. The sharp denticles of the skin will make you bleed. Hit it hard on the sensitive snout with your knife butt or abalone iron. If you are wearing a breathing device, dive, keeping your eye on the shark, and gain twenty or thirty feet of depth. Then move toward shore or to a boat. (7) If you are bleeding, leave the water immediately. You are a target. If you cannot leave the water, try to hold the wound closed with your fingers, or bind it with cloth torn from your bathing suit or clothing. (8) If you are in the water and clothed, remain so. The material protects against laceration of the skin.

The author hopes this article may save lives. If it saves even one life, or prevents one person from being maimed, it is justified.

# 17. Deep Divers of the Antarctic

GERALD L. KOOYMAN 1976

Two large warm-blooded animals—the emperor penguin and the Weddell seal—have overcome the forbidding environment of Antarctica to make it their year-round home. Unlike the host of other birds and mammals that come to the continent only in the summer to breed and to feed on its abundant marine life and then depart for either the pack ice or lower latitudes, these animals stay throughout the severe winter.

The emperor penguin has been known as a species, *Aptenodytes forsteri,* only since 1844. Yet, it is one of the largest of all birds and is *the* largest extant aquatic bird. Males can be up to four feet tall and some weigh more than ninety pounds, although the average weight of the species is between fifty and sixty pounds. The emperor's nearest relative is the king penguin, *Aptenodytes patagonica,* which lives on and around the subantarctic islands, particularly on South Georgia Island. Both species are similarly striking in their markings, with black backs and white to yellow breasts. The long and slender bill, which the emperor frequently uses along with its flippers for helping to raise itself out of the water and from a prone to an upright position, is delicately marked with blue and pink borders on a black base. The feathers, except for those on the wings and tail, are uniformly one to one and a half inches in length. They are narrow, with a downy filament at the base, and give the superficial appearance of fur.

Emperor penguins feed mainly on fish and squid rather than on the surface-dwelling krill favored by many other penguin species. As a result, emperors must frequently dive under the ice and into deep water in their search for food. I am fortunate in having had the opportunity of making diving studies of these birds. These were probably the first such studies of any penguin, previous investigations having dealt primarily with penguin reproduction on land.

The procedure used was the same as that I had already employed in studying Weddell seals. An ice hole was cut well away from any other cracks or holes to which the diving birds might go. This forced them to return to our hole. A heated laboratory hut of

Dr. Gerald L. Kooyman is an Associate Research Physiologist at Scripps Institution of Oceanography, University of California, San Diego.

From *Natural History,* Vol. 85, No. 3, pp. 36-45, 1976. Reprinted with light editing and with permission of the author and *Natural History* Magazine, March, 1976. Copyright © the American Museum of Natural History, 1976.

sufficient size to provide researchers easy access to the deep sea below was placed over the hole. And an observation tower was lowered through the ice thirty feet away from the hut. The tower enabled us to sit about ten feet below the ice and observe much of the birds' diving activity. Although the six-foot-thick ice made it rather dark down there, the ice, in combination with the long winter night, suppresses plankton growth, and the result is perhaps the clearest surface water anywhere in the world. In some localities objects can be discerned underwater up to 600 feet away and meaningful light and dark areas can be distinguished at a distance of almost 1,000 feet. Under these circumstances, we released penguins, some wearing instrument packs, into the ice hole.

Because of the color pattern of the pen-

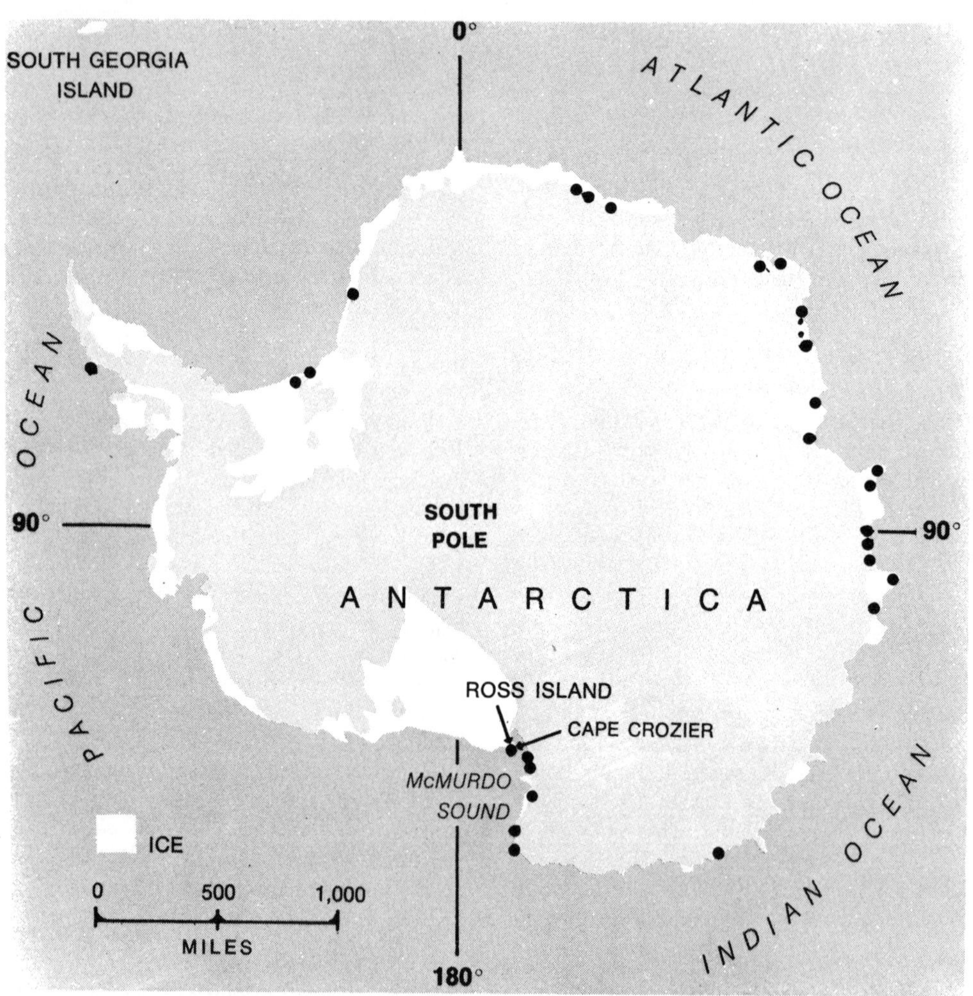


Figure 17-1. Twenty-nine emperor penguin breeding sites have been located by aerial survey along the Antarctic coast. They are shown here by dots. Although most of them are on sea ice or barrier ice, a few are on beaches.

Figure 17-2. Emperor penguin "flying" under the water. Photograph by the author.

guins, we lost sight of them at about 200 feet. Nevertheless, we did learn several interesting things from these experiments. By training some birds to swim between two holes spaced a known distance apart, we measured a maximum swimming speed of 5.2 mph, much slower than the illusion penguins give when maneuvering. We also discovered their acrobatic proclivities. I saw one bird virtually pinwheel on its wings and reverse swimming direction. The turn was so quick I could hardly follow it. The fastest ascent rate we measured was 400 feet per minute, an impressive figure considering the rapid pressure equilibration necessary if the ascent is made from a great depth. The longest dive in nearly 250 observations lasted eighteen minutes. This is considerably longer than the diving durations recorded for any other bird and longer than the dives of many marine mammals. The deepest dive measured was less than 130 feet, a surprisingly conservative figure probably influenced by our research methods and the fact that the birds were diving singly.

When released in the ice hole, a bird would spend all of its time seeking other exits or trying to make one by using its stout beak as a battering ram. Therefore, I organized a trip to Cape Crozier to measure the diving depths of birds at the ice edge, where I was sure they were feeding and their dives would, accordingly, be different. I knew from previous trips to the Cape that birds departing from the rookery wait in groups at the ice edge, dive together, and after several dives, return. Taking advantage of this behavior, we placed depth recorders on twenty-five birds. This device consists of a capillary tube in which the interior is dusted with a water-soluble dye. Any compression is indicated by a ring in the capillary. The instrument, devised in the mid-1800s by Lord Kelvin, the British mathematician and physicist, was a major innovation in that it permitted ships to make soundings while under way, rather than having to stop and drop a weighted line.

While we waited for the birds to return to their rookery, we watched them dive in groups as large as twenty-five to fifty. Their dives were literally made under our feet. The sea was glassy and we could see the penguins swimming vigorously as they disappeared from sight below us. They surfaced several minutes later, still in groups, breathing deeply in open-beaked gasps. On recovering our recorders, we were rewarded with a maximum depth measurement of 885 feet, probably the deepest dive ever recorded for a bird. (By comparison, according to the *Guinness Book of World Records,* the deepest dive made by a human being wearing scuba equipment is 437 feet.)

Impressive as these penguin statistics are, they pale alongside those of the Weddell seal, the other year-round resident of Antarctica, named for James Weddell, a British explorer who first collected specimens during his voyage to the Antarctic between the years 1822 to 1824. The species is large for seals; adults can exceed ten feet in body length and weigh more than 1,000 pounds. The chest and stomach are a mottled white and black or dark brown and the back is a uniform black or brown.

Weddells usually inhabit areas south of the Antarctic Convergence (the ocean boundary that separates the waters surrounding Antarctica into antarctic and subantarctic regions), although strays have been found as far north as South America, New Zealand, and Australia. The most northerly breeding ground is South Georgia Island, where a small number pup each year. Around Ross Island in McMurdo Sound, where my studies were made, several hundred pups are born from late September to early November—the antarctic spring. At birth the pups weigh about 55 pounds and are approximately 45 inches long. The mother provides them with one of the richest of milks, sometimes containing over 70 percent by weight of fat and protein. On this diet the pups gain weight rapidly, and after six to seven weeks, when they are weaned, they have gained as much as 200 pounds. The mother eats very little while nursing and endures a considerable weight loss of up to 300 pounds. She ends nursing by abruptly leaving the pup one day and not returning. After a few days of raucous bleating—and perhaps even attempting to get milk from another mother—the pup begins to move farther and farther from its birthplace. At this time of year, December—which is antarctic summer—the fast ice (solid sheets of ice fastened to the shore) is breaking up, there is much open water, sea food is in abundance, the weather is relatively mild, and circumstances are ideal for these young diving amateurs. Only an occasional killer whale pack is likely to disrupt their tranquility.

As winter sets in, although most adults remain, the young Weddell seals and some adults leave the southern regions of Ross Island for parts unknown. Those that stay continue to dive and feed under the newly forming ice that rapidly thickens to several feet, reaming breathing holes through the thinner areas as required. A secure ice platform containing spaced breathing holes made by the seals offers almost unlimited research opportunities, and for several years, beginning in the late antarctic winter and early spring, I conducted studies of Weddell seals in order to learn what I could about their diving behavior and physiology.

Following a procedure later copied in investigating the emperor penguin, a seal was released from an isolated hole. Because of the animal's size, the process was a little more complex with seals than with emperor penguins. A seal was towed to the hut in a large enclosed sled. The sled was backed up against the hut door and then opened. The seal usually crawled directly into the hut, entered the ice hole right away, and began diving. But occasionally a seal did not enter the water for several hours and then we were obliged to share our hut with the animal for the evening or the night—which reminded us of the joke about where does a 500-pound gorilla sleep.

A seal's first dives are usually short and shallow as the animal familiarizes itself with the under-ice surroundings of its new location. Soon, either deep-feeding dives or exploratory dives are begun. I was worried initially that a seal might become confused and drown under the ice. But it quickly became apparent that the animals have superior diving abilities with regard to depth and duration and can find their way around underwater. While feeding, they would commonly dive to depths of 600 to 1,200 feet. These dives lasted from eight to fifteen minutes. The deepest dive measured was to the bottom of McMurdo Sound at a depth of 1,970 feet. This is one of the deepest dives ever recorded for a marine mammal.

Especially interesting were the seals' exploratory dives. Unlike the deep dives, which were made directly below our hut, in exploratory dives the seals swam a considerable distance away from the hut and the vital breathing hole and never descended deeper than 600 feet. Presumably, those exertions were attempts to find other seals or other breathing holes. Because of recording equipment the seals occasionally carried, we know something of the nature of these dives. The longest exploratory dive recorded lasted seventy minutes. This is one of the longest natural dives recorded for any marine mammal, although sperm and bottlenose whales have remained submerged for even longer periods after being harpooned. Long-lasting dives were rare, but dives of twenty to forty minutes duration were common. All of these forays took place at depths of less than 600 feet as the seals swam possibly up to six miles from one breathing hole to another.

My observations of seals convinced me that there is almost nowhere in the Sound that they cannot reach. Any small break in the ice they can breathe through is likely to be found. Even in the most isolated areas, marine biologists making ice holes or scuba dives are likely to find a seal approaching from below.

The diving abilities of the emperor penguin and Weddell seal raise a variety of questions about how these animals function. For instance, what anatomical and physiological features enable the animals to withstand the enormous pressures they are exposed to when they dive deeply? And how are they able to hold their breath for so long? The most extensively studied aspect of the physiology of diving birds and mammals is the modifications that make extended breath-holds possible. Since breath-holding responses in both birds and mammals are similar, one explanation applies equally to both groups.

We know of two fundamental ways that enhance the capacity of animals to hold their breath. One is the increase of body oxygen stores; the other is the parsimonious utilization of those oxygen reserves. For example, the blood hemoglobin concentration of Weddell seals—and consequently the oxygen-carrying capacity of their blood—is 1.7 times greater than in humans. Similarly, the $O_2$ carrying capacity of the emperor penguin is 1.6 times greater than that of the domestic chicken. Furthermore, the total blood volume of the Weddell seal on a per weight basis is twice that of man. (But the blood volume of penguins on a per weight basis is no different from that of chickens.) The muscles of both penguins and seals contain a significantly higher concentration of myoglobin, an oxygen-binding molecule, than occurs in terrestrial birds and mammals. The net result is a larger total body oxygen store. However, the lungs of penguins and seals are not larger than those of terrestrial animals and contribute no more to the total oxygen store than the lungs of any other bird or mammal.

When penguins and seals dive, their large body oxygen stores are husbanded. This is accomplished by a major change in their blood circulation. Flow to tissues capable of periodic anaerobic or lowered metabolism, such as muscles, kidneys, or the gastrointestinal system, is decreased while flow to tissues of high aerobic and metabolic needs, such as the brain, are maintained. These flow changes are reflected in a lowered heart rate and cardiac output, which may drop to 10 percent of the predive level. The result is a significantly lowered consumption of oxygen during the dive and thus an ability to extend the breathhold.

Heart rates were measured during portions of Weddell seal dives. The usual method of measuring heartbeat rates is to place a positive and a negative electrode on opposite sides of the chest and connect them with three- or four-foot lengths of wire to a recorder. The recorder monitors the electropotential change that occurs within the body each time the heart muscles contract. We followed this conventional method, except that our wires were 200 feet long and had breakaway connectors. When the seal reached the end of the line, the connectors parted and terminated the recording until the next dive, when they could be plugged in again. This method permitted us to measure heartbeat rates during the entirety of some shallow dives and the early parts of deep and exploratory dives.

The recordings indicated that the degree of heart slowing depended on the type of dive. During shallow resting dives just below the ice hole, the heart rate dropped from a surface average of fifty-five beats per minute to a rate of twenty-five to forty. If the dive was deep, the rate dropped lower, and it was lowest of all on exploratory dives, when it sank to fifteen beats per minute. It seems quite logical that during the longest dives blood flow would be most restricted and oxygen stores be most slowly utilized. The heartbeat rate, however, is believed to be autonomic, or involuntary, yet the drop took place so quickly, it almost seemed to anticipate the dive. One can only wonder how that is achieved.

When Weddell seals and emperor penguins dive to great depths, those portions of the body that are most affected by mounting pressure are gas-filled spaces because their volume must change considerably as the animal descends. The largest gas-filled space in the body is the respiratory system, consisting of the trachea, or windpipe, and the lungs. The respiratory system of the Weddell seal, however, is structurally very different from that of the emperor penguin. And the seal's lungs are also somewhat different from those of terrestrial mammals. The airway system in the seal, which is the transport system of air to the gas-exchanging alveoli, or air cells of the lungs, is more extensively strengthened than in terrestrial mammals. The extra support consists of cartilage, muscle, and connective tissue. Experimental evidence indicates that the added reinforcement insures that when the animal descends, its lungs compress differentially. The alveoli, being more compliant—that is, capable of readily changing shape—than the airways, compress the most and the gas within them is forced into the airways. Since at great depth many or most alveoli are collapsed, there is very little gas exchange between alveoli and blood and the gas is sequestered in the non-exchanging airways. That this collapse will also occur at shallow depths is assured by the seal's behavior. As the seal dives it exhales one-half to two-thirds of its lung volume.

A stoppage of gas exchange at depth means that oxygen stored in the lungs is unavailable for consumption. However, it is a small amount of the total body $O_2$ store. More important is that nitrogen at high pressures is not taken up by the blood and accordingly does not expose the seal to decompression sickness—the bends—when the animal surfaces.

The penguin respiratory system is neither

as well studied nor as well understood as that of the seal. It consists of several air sacs distributed throughout the body and connected to the lungs by conducting tubes. The air sacs have a far larger volume than the bird's lungs. When the penguin dives it inhales deeply and most of the gas is stored in the air sacs. The volume of these sacs relative to body weight is up to eight times greater than the lung volume in the seal. The oxygen volume in the penguin's air sacs represents a large proportion of the bird's total body $O_2$ store; the rest is in the blood and muscles.

Under experimental conditions, Adélie and gentoo penguins have been put through simulated dives at pressures equivalent to those at 230 feet. In these circumstances, gas exchange between air sacs, the lungs, and the bloodstream continued and the tissues were exposed to high nitrogen tensions. But the birds did not get the bends, perhaps because the exposure to high pressure was brief. These two species of penguin cannot hold their breath for more than five minutes, and under natural conditions they rarely dive for more than one or two minutes. Similar experiments have not been done on emperor penguins but it is likely that tests would yield analogous results since the respiratory systems of all three species appear to be similar. This makes the emperor penguin something of an enigma. It commonly remains submerged for five or ten minutes while diving to great depths, and it is not clear how the bird avoids getting the bends when it surfaces.

The final and most frequently asked question about aquatic polar animals is, How do they maintain their body temperatures in the frigid air and water? When the penguin chick hatches it is covered with a fluffy coat of down. When the seal pup is born it is covered with a long fur called lanugo. The insulation of the penguin's down is only about one-half that of the fur coat of the arctic fox and the seal's lanugo is only about one-third as effective. These deficiencies, however, are not too important since adult plumage replaces the chick's down within a few months of hatching and the pup acquires another type of insulator one or two weeks after birth.

The tips of the feathers of the adult emperor penguin overlap like tiles on a roof, forming a waterproof shell, and the downy portion at the base traps a layer of air next to the body, conserving its heat. This plumage enables the bird to tolerate air temperatures as low as 14°F without making any effort to keep warm. That is no match for some arctic mammals whose thermoneutral zone extends to at least −60°F, but the emperor penguin's plumage represents a compromise—it has to be effective in water as well as air, and the requirements for a water-repellent, streamlined coat are different from one functional in air only.

The heat conductivity of water is more than twenty times that of air. Measurements of the metabolism of Adélie penguins show that it increases to three times the resting rate after they enter water. Presumably, a similar increase is necessary for the emperor penguin because when it remains inactive after entering the sea, it soon begins to shiver. In contrast, the adult Weddell seal does not rely on its pelt for insulation, but rather on a thick layer of subcutaneous blubber that begins to develop immediately after birth. This type of insulation, which conducts heat at about the same rate as asbestos, is so effective that the seal can rest comfortably in 28°F seawater. When a severe storm occurs, rather than be blown by winds that can achieve hurricane force and pelted with ice and snow on the surface, Weddells take shelter in the water until the storm subsides.

Two questions I have not answered are, Why don't deep-diving penguins suffer from decompression sickness on surfacing? And how do emperor penguins and Weddell seals navigate under the ice? On future visits to Antarctica, I plan to look into these matters, as well as other aspects of diving behavior and physiology, in the continuing search to learn how these animals function in one of the most hostile environments on earth.

# 4

# *MARINE GEOLOGY*

# 18. Plate Tectonics and Continental Drift

D. P. McKENZIE 1970

"The ruins of an older world are visible in the present structure of our planet; and the strata which now compose our continents have been once beneath the sea, and were formed out of the waste of pre-existing continents. The same forces are still destroying, by chemical decomposition or mechanical violence, even the hardest rocks, and transporting the materials to the sea, where they are spread out, and form strata analogous to those of more ancient date. Although loosely deposited along the bottom of the ocean, they become afterwards altered and consolidated by volcanic heat, and then heaved up, fractured, and contorted." This view of geology, expressed by Hutton in 1788, is still accepted today. What have, however, recently become better understood are the processes which transport sediments from the ocean floor to form mountain ranges. The first suggestion as to how this change might be accomplished came from detailed field mapping in the late nineteenth century in Scotland and in the Alps. Huge overthrust faults were discovered, some of which have been shown to have horizontal displacements of a hundred kilometers or more, and to pile up enormous thicknesses of sedimentary rock. Though such structures suggest crustal shortening on a vast scale, it is difficult to determine the total compression required to produce them. Further field work added an enormous mass of detail and classification, but little further understanding.

It was against this background that Wegener in 1912 put forward the hypothesis of continental drift. Though he was not the originator of this idea, his ardent espousal of it provoked a fierce and general discussion. Unfortunately a large number of the observations he used in support of his theory were in error, and the mechanism he suggested to maintain the motion was hopelessly inadequate. Though his ideas caused much debate, they did not provide a reliable theory of global tectonics. Even after it became clear that thermal convection in the Earth's mantle could provide enough energy to move the continents, for some years little serious use was made of Wegener's ideas.

During the past five years the hypothesis

Dr. Dan P. McKenzie is with the Department of Geodesy and Geophysics at the University of Cambridge, Great Britain. He was elected a Fellow of the Royal Society in 1976.

From *Endeavour*, Vol. 29, No. 106, pp. 39-44, 1970. Reprinted with light editing and with permission of the author and *Endeavour.*

of continental drift has been transformed from a highly controversial idea into a theory which is widely accepted by earth scientists. Though there is now overwhelming evidence in favor of large horizontal movements of entire continents, neither Wegener's original hypothesis nor an important later variant of it, known as "Sea Floor Spreading" (1), proved entirely successful. Recently a new version of these ideas was suggested (2, 3) which retains the satisfactory parts of both earlier theories. The new theory has become known as "plate tectonics" because it postulates that the outer 50-100 km of the Earth consists of a number of rigid plates in relative motion. Relative motion between plates produces earthquakes, and therefore the location of earthquakes can be used to determine the boundaries between plates. The concept of the rigidity and the importance of relative motion are the principal differences between the new theory and that of continental drift. Drift was often compared with the process of making jam. The Earth probably began as a mixture of its constituent materials without any continents. Convective motions must then have taken place to permit the lighter materials to float to the surface and form continents. The motion and deformation of the continents was believed to be directly related to the convective motions in the mantle beneath them. Similar convective motions in jam-making allow the scum to float to the surface and accumulate into lumps. Jam scum does not, however, form rigid plates, and though jam-making may illustrate the chemical processes involved during the Earth's evolution it is a poor analogy for plate tectonics. A much better one is the behaviour of floating ice, which moves and deforms in a remarkably similar fashion to the outer parts of the earth.

The motion of ice floes illustrates the importance of the rigidity and of relative motion. A man on an ice floe at sea cannot directly observe his motion relative to the ocean floor, and therefore cannot tell if his floe is drifting. The stability of his floe and his peace of mind both depend on the relative motion between his floe and surrounding ones. There are three possible types of motion between any two floes. If they separate, water will well up between them and freeze, forming new ice which is thinner than that of the main floes, and gradually thickens with time. If floes move towards each other one may override the other, or each may thicken to form a pressure ridge. Both types of deformation are observed in sea ice, the first being common in young thin ice, the second occurring in older thicker pack ice. The third type of motion involves one block of ice sliding past another, and can occur only if both edges are straight or are arcs of a circle. If the margins interlock, sliding cannot take place unless parts of one floe override the other. These three types of relative motion can best be illustrated by tearing a piece of paper and moving the two parts past each other.

The plates on the Earth are much larger than any ice flow, and their motion is much slower. Also many plate boundaries are beneath the sea, and therefore cannot be observed directly. For these reasons the plate boundaries cannot generally be mapped by geologists, but must be determined by indirect methods, of which the most important is the location of earthquakes. Various studies of large shallow earthquakes in many parts of the world have demonstrated that they are the result of sudden movements on large faults. Some of the measured displacements are very large, reaching 10 m in the Great Alaskan Earthquake in 1964. Such displacements are the direct expression of the motion of two plates, separated by the fault which is the boundary between them. Though not all earthquakes produce slip on faults at the Earth's surface, most are caused by surface displacement at the margin between plates which generally takes place by a succession of jumps, each of which is an earthquake, rather than by a steady creeping movement.

Figure 18-1 shows the positions of about 30,000 shallow earthquakes which have oc-

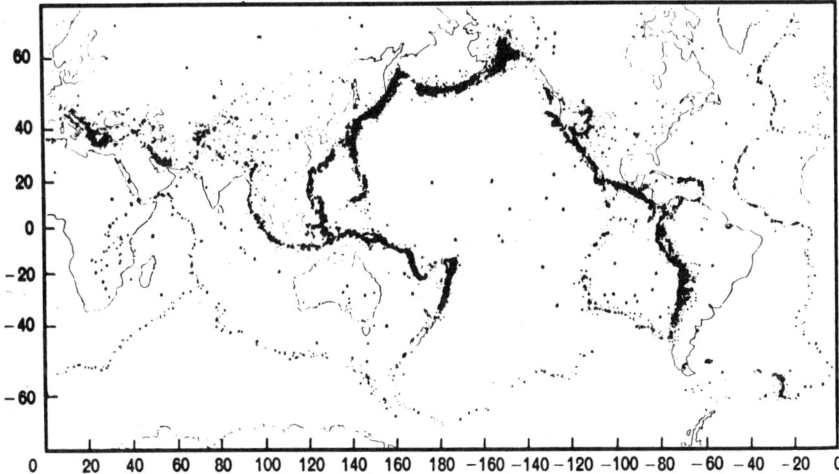


Figure 18-1. The location of shallow earthquakes from 1961 to 1967 as determined by the United States Coast and Geodetic Survey. Oceanic plate boundaries outlined by the earthquakes are narrow zones seldom wider than the location errors. In contrast the seismicity of the continents is spread over wide belts. (After (12).)

curred since 1960. Most earthquakes in oceanic regions take place in remarkably narrow belts associated with the major features of the ocean floor; ridges, trenches, and fracture zones. These features mark the boundaries between plates. However, since most of the ocean floor is not seismic, and is not now being deformed, it should move as rigid plates bounded by the earthquake belts. The belts are probably even narrower than Figure 18-1 suggests, since the error in location of most earthquakes is about 30 km, and therefore comparable with the apparent width. In some regions the plate margins cross continents and can be studied in the field. The slip between North America and the Pacific takes place on a single fault, the San Andreas. The sliding motion between the two plates is 6 cm a year, a rate which would carry a continent round the entire earth in 600 million years, or in the time that has elapsed since the Cambrian.

The positions of earthquakes on the continents are, however, generally much less localized than those of earthquakes beneath the oceans. Earthquakes in the Himalayas for instance are spread over a region about 1000 km wide (Figure 18-1). It is still not known whether rigid plate tectonics provides a useful model for understanding continental deformations. It is important to settle this question, since geology is concerned mainly with continental tectonics.

As in the case of ice floes, there are three possible types of motion between neighboring plates, shown diagrammatically in Figure 18-2. If two plates move apart, mantle material from beneath them wells up, cools, hardens and in this way regenerates the plates. Since the upwelling material is hot, it is less dense than the cold plates and therefore wells up above the deep ocean floor to form a linear ridge. There is no longer any reason to believe that each ridge marks the position of the rising limb of a convection cell within the mantle below the plates. Earthquakes occur along the axis of the ridge which is the boundary between the two separating plates. Another type of plate boundary can exist when two plates slide past each other without production or destruction of either, provided that the boundary between them is everywhere parallel to the direction of relative motion. Such boundaries are known as transform faults.

The most seismically active regions of the

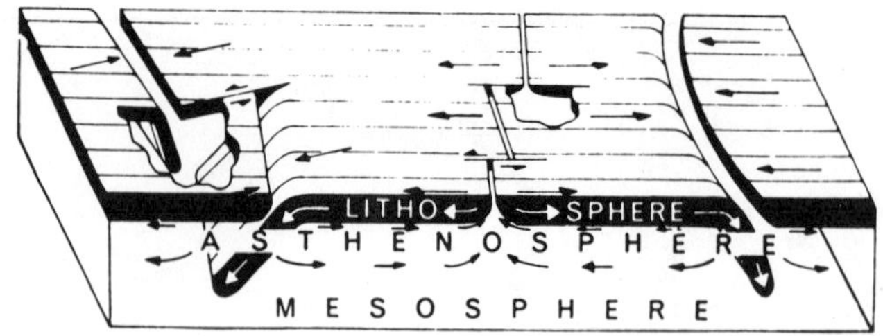


Figure 18-2. An illustration of the current theories of oceanic tectonics. Plates of lithosphere are formed symmetrically on spreading ridges, move horizontally as rigid blocks and are destroyed by underthrusting beneath island arcs. The arrows on the plates show the directions of relative motions. Arrows showing the flow in the asthenosphere serve merely to indicate that return flow must take place (10).

Earth are areas where two plates are moving towards each other. Here the plates behave as ice, with one plate overriding the other and driving it down into the mantle. There is, however, one important difference between the tectonics of ice floes and that of plates on the Earth. Since ice is less dense than water it must remain as a floating sheet even after it has been forced below another floe, whereas the cold plates are denser than the surrounding mantle and can therefore sink. As they sink they gradually warm up and their mechanical properties become indistinguishable from those of the surrounding mantle. The trenches and island arcs are the surface features associated with plate destruction, most of which is at present taking place on the Pacific margins. Nothing is yet known about the return flow which carries mantle material from beneath the island arcs to the ridges.

This simple model of the tectonics of the earth has now been tested in a variety of ways, though the most convincing evidence in its favor has come from seismology and paleomagnetism. All quantitative tests of the concepts of plate tectonics depend on a theorem of Euler. He proved that any movement of a rigid spherical cap on the surface of a sphere can be described by a rotation about an axis passing through the centre of the sphere. Thus the relative motion between two rigid plates must correspond to a rotation about some axis; if this is not so, the plates cannot be rigid.

E. C. Bullard, J. E. Everett, and A. G. Smith in 1965 were the first to use this theorem to fit together the continents surrounding the Atlantic (4). The fit of South America and Africa is particularly impressive (Figure 18-3) and shows that both continents have remained undeformed internally throughout the time that the South Atlantic has been opening. Since the present distance of separation of the two continents is 4000 km and has taken more than 80 million years to effect, this striking fit shows that the plates remain rigid for long periods of time while moving enormous horizontal distances.

It is also possible to test whether the plates move rigidly for short periods by using the field of elastic waves radiating from an earthquake to determine the direction of relative motion between plates. If an earthquake occurs on a plate boundary which is exposed on land, such as the San Andreas fault, the direction of slip on the fault between the two plates can be measured either by triangulation or by observing roads and ditches cut by the fault. However, neither of these methods can be used where the plate boundary is beneath the sea, as is commonly the case. But we can use the radiation field of earthquakes to discover the orientation of the fault and the motion between the two sides. Figure 18-4 is a drawing of a strike slip fault producing an earthquake at the point marked with a circle, radiating seismic waves in all directions. Four directions A, B, E, and F show four rays leaving the focus of the earthquake. The half arrows

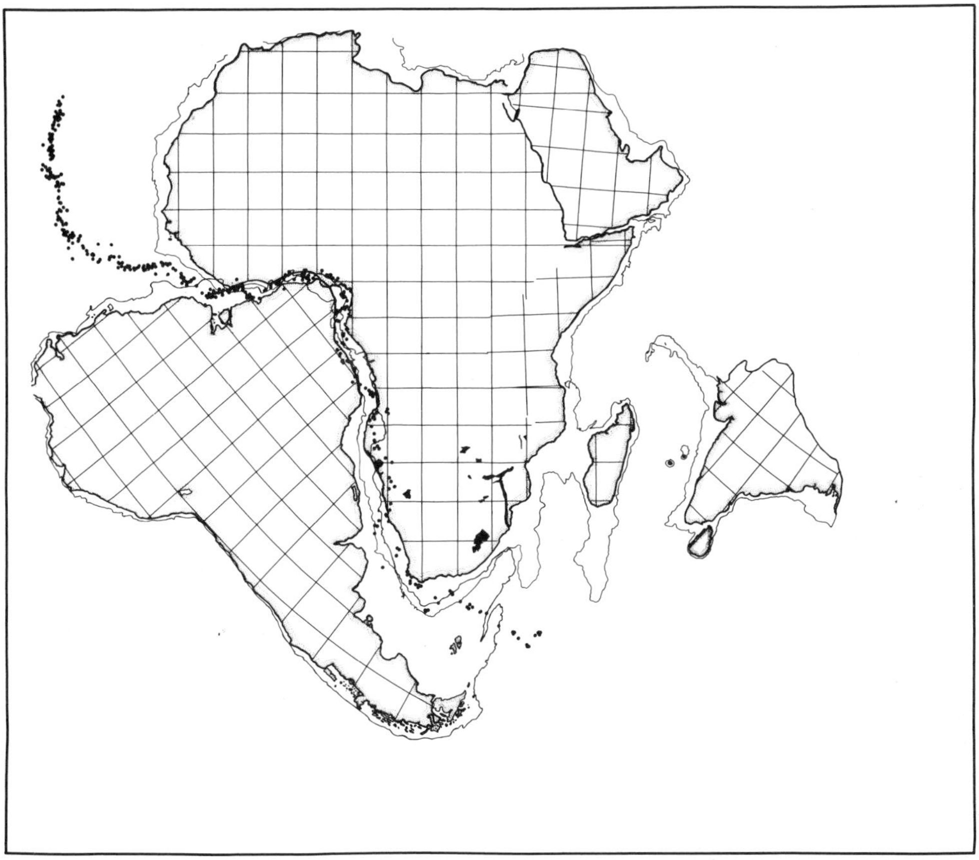

Figure 18-3. The fit of Africa and South America at the 500 fm contour produced by rigid rotations.

show the direction of the horizontal slip. In the direction of ray A the motion of the ground will first be towards the focus of the earthquake. Initial motions of this type towards the source are called dilatations, and all rays leaving the source in the quadrant 1 will have the same first motion as that of A. In quadrant 2, however, in the direction of

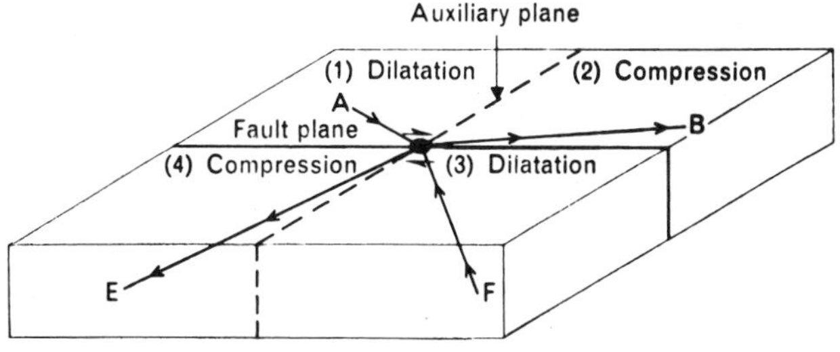


Figure 18-4. The radiation field from a strike slip earthquake. The arrows on the rays show the initial direction of motion of the Earth.

ray B, the ground will move away from the source of the earthquake, this being called a compressional motion. Similar motions occur on the other side of the fault, shown by the arrows on rays E and F. The radiation field of the earthquake thus consists of four quadrants separated by two planes, one of which is the fault plane and the other, at right angles to the fault plane, the auxiliary plane. The direction of slip on the fault is always the normal of the auxiliary plane; in this example the slip is horizontal and the auxiliary plane vertical. Rays such as A, B, E, and F travel through the Earth to reach the surface, where they are recorded on seismographs. To determine the orientation and direction of movement on a fault, seismograms have therefore to be collected from various stations throughout the world, where rays which set out from the focus in many different directions reached the surface of the Earth, and one must establish whether the first observed ground motion is towards or away from the station. If the rays which reached the stations are then traced back to the earthquake focus, the dilatations and compressions lie in four quadrants separated by the fault plane and the auxiliary plane. There is, however, no method of identifying any given plane from the radiation field alone, and other information must be used to decide between the two possibilities. Once this has been done the direction of slip in the fault plane is determined, since it is in the direction of the normal to the auxiliary plane. This procedure has been carried out for many earthquakes all over the world, and has permitted a detailed test of the concepts of plate tectonics (5, 6).

The simplest method of carrying out such a test is to utilize some of the special properties of Mercator's projection. A familiar example of a rigid rotation is the daily rotation of the Earth, which moves each point on the surface along lines of latitude. The axis of most Mercator maps is taken to be the rotational axis, and therefore in this projection the daily motion of points on the Earth become straight lines. Since the motion between two rigid plates may be de-

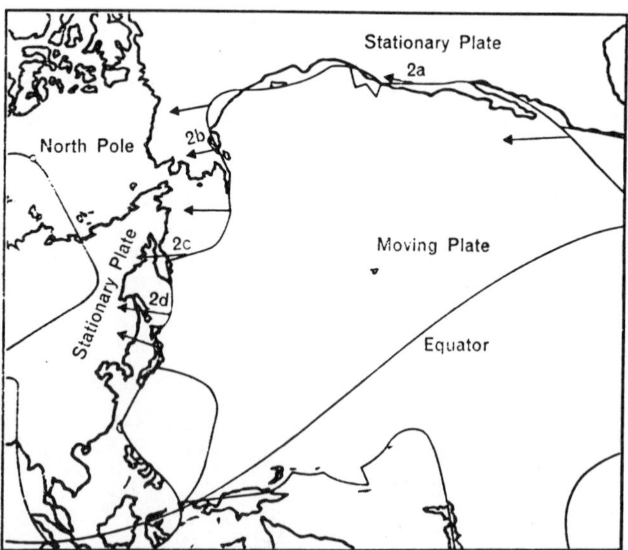


Figure 18-5. The arrows show the direction of motion of the Pacific plate relative to the American plate, and are obtained from the radiation field of earthquakes. Since the map is a Mercator projection about the pole of relative rotation, all arrows should be parallel to each other (2).

scribed by a rotation about an axis, the motion at all points along the boundary must be along lines of latitude with respect to this axis. If this axis of relative rotation is used as the axis for the Mercator projection, then the relative motion between the two plates must everywhere be parallel to the lines of latitude about the axis of rotation.

The first test of these ideas was made in the North Pacific (2), where there is a single boundary between the American Plate and the Pacific Plate from Baja California to Central Japan (Figure 18-5). Figure 5 is a Mercator projection of this region about the pole of relative rotation at 50°N, 85°W. The arrows show the direction of slip determined from the radiation field of various earthquakes in this region. If both the Pacific and American Plates are rigid, all these arrows should lie along lines of latitude about the rotational pole, and should therefore be parallel to each other and to the top and bottom of the figure in this special projection. It is clear that the arrows are indeed within 10° to 15° of being parallel to each other, which is within the limits of experimental error. This test shows therefore that the two plates involved in the tectonics of the Northern Pacific move as rigid spherical caps on the Earth's surface. Similar tests have since been applied to other regions with equal success. Hence we now possess a simple theory of tectonics applicable to the Earth as a whole. All tectonic activity must therefore be restricted to the plate margins, where the structures observed in ancient mountain belts are at present being produced. A careful study of deformation at present taking place at plate margins should lead to a more profound understanding of the tectonic history and development of the Earth.

Of the three types of plate boundary, ridges have been studied in greatest detail and probably have the least direct relevance to continental geology. One reason for this interest is that ridges have produced the floors of almost all the world's oceans in the last 200 million years, and as a result are relatively easy to study. More important, however, is the fact that they have left a complete record of their evolution in the sea floor they formed, as illustrated in Figure 18-6. Ridges form where plates are moving apart and hot mantle material wells up, becoming partially molten close to the sea floor as the confining pressure is released. The molten basalt produced in this way erupts through fissures along the ridge axis and rapidly cools in contact with the sea water. As it does so it becomes magnetized

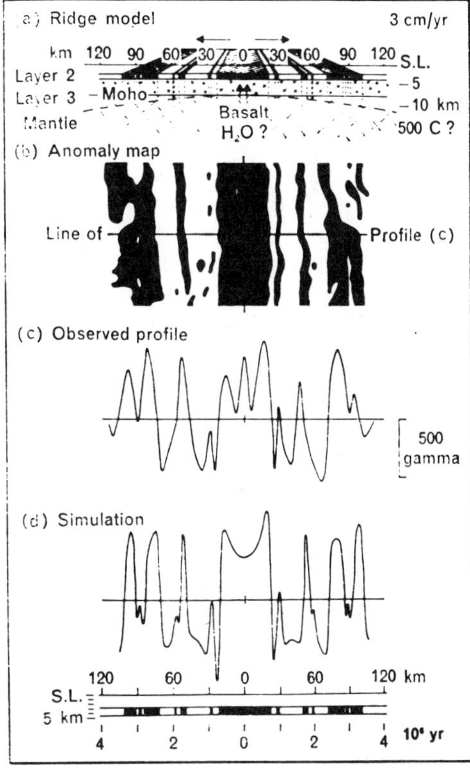


Figure 18-6. (a) Model for the production of sea floor along the ridge axis. Shaded material is normally magnetized, unshaded is reversely magnetized. (b) Part of a map of the magnetic anomalies over the Juan de Fuca Ridge in the north-east Pacific. The black regions are areas of positive anomalies, the white are negative. (c) A total-field magnetic anomaly profile along the line shown in (b). (d) A profile computed from the reversal time scale assuming the model in (a). (After (11).)

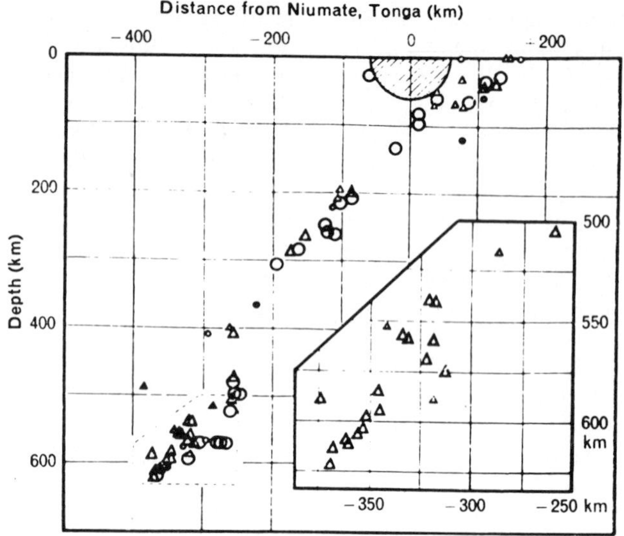


Figure 18-7. Section at right angles to the northern end of the Tonga trench, showing the locations of intermediate and deep focus earthquakes which lie within the sinking slab (10).

in the direction of the Earth's magnetic field. The polarity of the main field of the Earth is not constant, however, but changes sign causing the North pole to become the South pole. If such a reversal were to take place now, all magnetic compasses would turn to point south instead of north. Though the cause of these field reversals is not known, the reversal time scale for the last 5 million years has been worked out by observing the polarity of dated lava flows (7). This history of the magnetic field has been recorded by the spreading sea floor just as a tape recorder records on magnetic tape (Figure 18-6) (8). Since the magnetization of the basalts on the ocean floor contributes to the field intensity at the sea surface, the evolutionary history and spreading rate of a ridge can be obtained simply by towing a magnetometer behind a survey ship, and matching the records with those calculated from the reversal time scale. Such a survey has been made of the Reykjanes ridge to the south of Iceland (11). Here the symmetry of the anomaly pattern about the ridge axis requires material to be added to each plate at exactly the same rate of 1 cm/year on

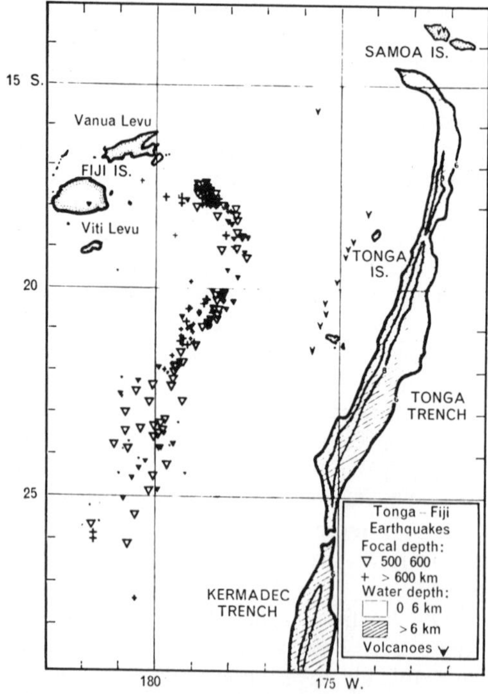


Figure 18-8. The distribution of deep earthquakes at the northern end of the Tongan Island arc mirrors the hook at the northern end of the trench (9).

each side of the ridge, and the shape of each anomaly records the shape of the ridge crest at the time that piece of sea floor was formed. Such magnetic anomalies have now been discovered in all the major oceans and are providing a detailed history of the evolution of oceanic ridges and hence of plate motions.

Unfortunately, there is no corresponding record of the evolution of trenches where plates are consumed, and rather little is yet known about their history. In contrast to ridges, however, their three-dimensional structure can be explored by locating earthquakes and studying their radiation fields (9, 10). Unlike earthquakes on ridges those associated with trenches are not confined to the crust and uppermost mantle, but occur to depths of almost 700 km. Where such deep earthquakes occur they are not spread through the mantle, but are confined to a thin planar volume which dips beneath the island arc and its volcanoes (Figure 18-7). At the northern end of the Tonga trench a bend in the trench is reflected in a corresponding bend in the deep earthquake distribution (Figure 18-8). There must therefore be an intimate connection between deep and shallow structures in such regions. This connection is the slab formed from the plate, which acquires the shape of the trench when it is underthrust beneath the island arc and remains cold as it sinks through the mantle. The deep earthquakes are produced within the sinking slab, and not by slip between it and the surrounding mantle, whereas the radiation patterns from shallow focus shocks near the trench show that they are caused by underthrusting of one plate by another (10).

The theory of plate tectonics that we here describe has at present two major shortcomings: it postulates no energy source to maintain the plate motions, and it is still uncertain whether it can be used as a description of continental tectonics. The problem of mechanism is likely to remain controversial until more relevant information is available. The same is not true for continental deformations, which probably resemble oceanic tectonics with some added complications. In the past three years extraordinary progress has been made, and it is to be hoped that the remaining problems of continental tectonics will be understood with only small modifications to existing theories. Should this be the case then we shall at last have a complete theory of global tectonics.

## ACKNOWLEDGEMENT

Figures 18-2, 18-7, and 18-8 are reproduced by kind permission of the *Journal of Geophysical Research.*

## REFERENCES

1. Hess, H. H. 'History of the Ocean Basins'. In 'Petrologic Studies Buddington Memorial Volume', p. 599. Geological Society of America, 1962.
2. McKenzie, D. P. and Parker, R. L. *Nature, Lond.,* **216,** 1276, 1967.
3. Morgan, W. J. *J. Geophys. Res.,* **72,** 4259, 1968.
4. Bullard, E. C., Everett, J. E., and Smith, A. G. *Phil. Trans.,* **250** *A,* 41, 1965.
5. Stauder, W. and Bollinger, G. A. *J. Geophys Res.,* **71,** 5283, 1966.
6. Sykes, L. R. *Ibid.,* **72,** 2131, 1967.
7. Cox, A., Doell, R. R., and Dalrymple, G. B. 'Time Scale for Geomagnetic Reversals'. In 'History of the Earth's Crust' (Ed.: R. L. Phinney). Princeton University Press, 1968.
8. Vine, F. J. *Science,* **154,** 1405, 1966.
9. Sykes, L. R. *J. Geophys. Res.,* **71,** 2981, 1966.
10. Isacks, B. L., Oliver, J., and Sykes, L. R. *Ibid.,* **73,** 5855, 1968.
11. Vine, F. J. 'Magnetic Anomalies Associated with Mid-Ocean Ridges'. In 'History of the Earth's Crust' (Ed.: R. L. Phinney). Princeton University Press, 1968.
12. Baronzangi, M. and Dorman, J. *Bull. Seis. Soc. Amer.,* **59,** 369, 1969.

# 19. Sea-Floor Spreading and Continental Drift

F. J. VINE 1970

Rather than attempt a further review of the vast subject matter now covered by the title of this paper, I shall endeavor to summarize developments and ideas not covered in my earlier short review in these pages (Vine, 1969).

As outlined in that article, the most specific and compelling evidence for sea-floor spreading in the past comes from the study of oceanic magnetic anomalies. The linear anomalies associated with ridge crests have been interpreted in terms of spreading of the sea floor accompanied by intermittent reversals of the earth's magnetic field. Since a reversal time-scale for the past few million years has been deduced by other independent techniques (Cox, Dayrymple, and Doell, 1967), spreading rates may be deduced at ridge crests and extrapolated across the flanks in an attempt to assign ages to the magnetic anomalies, underlying oceanic crust and reversals of the earth's magnetic field (Heirtzler, 1968). Clearly such an extrapolation is rather speculative and its validity was seriously questioned. However within the past year the results of the first phase of the JOIDES deep-sea drilling program have tended to confirm this magnetic time-scale.

On JOIDES leg III in the South Atlantic, eight sites were drilled across the Mid-Atlantic Ridge at approximately 30° S. These revealed a remarkably linear relationship between the age of the oldest sediment recovered, invariably immediately overlying or incorporated within basalt, and the distance of the site from the ridge axis (see Figure 19-1). This suggests continuous spreading throughout the Cenozoic at an essentially constant rate of 2 cm per year per ridge flank, precisely the rate assumed by Heirtzler *et al.* (1968) in calibrating the magnetic time-scale.

These points, together with similar results from leg V, on the flanks of the East Pacific Rise, and one fission track age from basalt

Dr. Frederick J. Vine is a reader with the School of Environmental Sciences at the University of East Anglia, Norwich, Great Britain. His well-known hypothesis on magnetic reversals has provided marine geologists and geophysicists with a key for determining the rate of continental movement and the relative ages of different parts of the ocean floor. He has written over twenty publications and in 1970 received the Henry Bryant Bigelow Medal in Oceanography from the Woods Hole Oceanographic Institution, Massachusetts.

From *Journal of Geological Education,* Vol. 18, No. 2, pp. 87-90, 1970. Reprinted by permission of the author and the *Journal of Geological Education.*

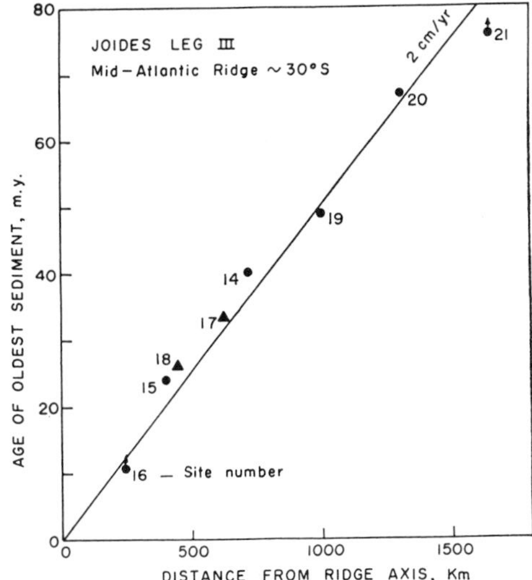


Figure 19-1. Age of oldest sediment substrate, "at drill site" plotted against distance of site from Mid-Atlantic Ridge axis, after Maxwell and Von Herzen (1969).

dredged beneath anomaly 10 in the Pacific (Luyendyk and Fisher, 1969), may be plotted on a graph of the age of the oldest sediment or hard rock against the age assigned on the basis of the magnetic anomalies (Figure 19-2). Clearly no points should lie significantly above the 45° line on such a plot if the magnetic time-scale is to be valid, but some points may be beneath it because the oldest material present has not been sampled. Thus although minor modification of the magnetic time-scale may ultimately be warranted, it now seems probable that it is essentially correct.

This geomagnetic time-scale is the best indication we have as yet of the timing and frequency of reversals during the Cenozoic. Ultimately, as a result of the JOIDES program, we should obtain an independent check on this time-scale from the magnetic stratigraphy of deep-sea sediments. Thus my earlier estimate of the extent of the present sea floor which was generated by spreading during Cenozoic time stands (Vine 1969, Figure 10), and it is rather sobering to note that this amounts to nearly 50 per cent of the area of the deep ocean basins. Alternatively one is maintaining that one-third of the present earth's crust has been created during the most recent one and one-half per cent of geologic time. It now seems very probable that all remaining oceanic areas are Mesozoic in age.

Recently, on the basis of paleomagnetic studies on land, it has been suggested that the Cretaceous is characterized by very few reversals and that throughout most of that period the earth's magnetic field was of normal polarity (Helsley and Steiner, 1969) (see Figure 19-3). This is in great contrast to the Tertiary, which is of essentially the same duration (i.e. 65-70 million years). Clearly if this is correct the magnetic signature of oceanic crust formed by spreading during the Cretaceous period should be very different to that formed during Cenozoic time. If we look beyond the oldest correlatable anomalies in the Pacific (Figure 19-4) or South Atlantic, where they are best documented, we do indeed find what have been termed magnetically "quiet zones" which appear to be devoid of the linear anomalies characteristic of Cenozoic crust. Actually

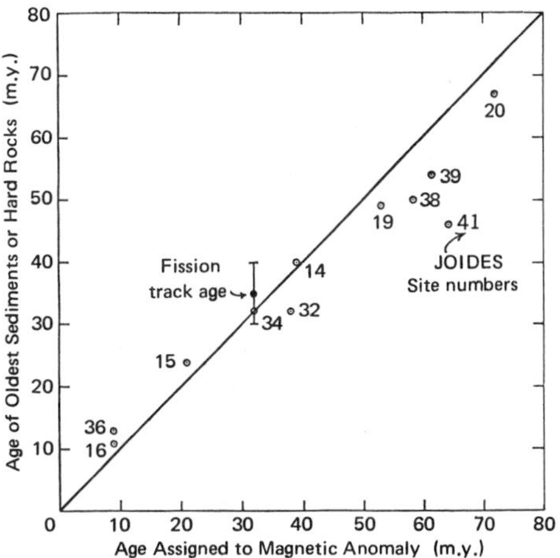


Figure 19-2. Fission track age from Luyendyk and Fisher (1969). JOIDES results from preliminary cruise reports. Magnetic time-scale assumed given by Hiertzler *et al.* (1968).

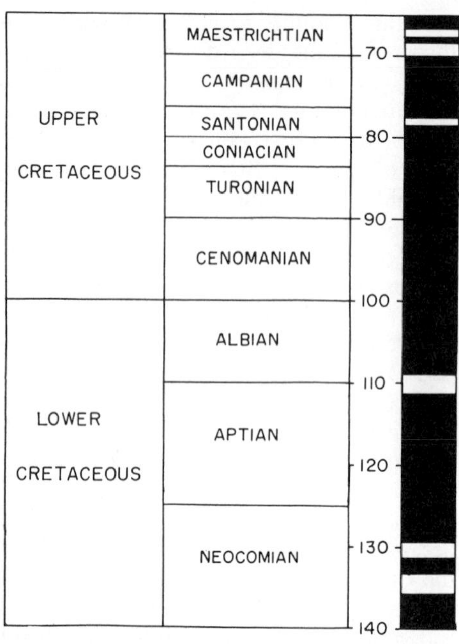


Figure 19-3. Suggested geomagnetic reversal time-scale for the Cretaceous period. Shaded intervals–normal polarity.

this transition is not exactly at the Mesozoic-Cenozoic boundary, and both the continental and oceanic magnetics suggest that there may be several reversals in the uppermost Cretaceous. Thus a consistent picture is emerging and such magnetically quiet areas may well be indicative of Cretaceous ocean floor. In the North Atlantic and Western Pacific even older oceanic crust is present and may eventually enable us to extend the geomagnetic reversal time-scale back to the uppermost Triassic or at least the Lower Jurassic.

In the Atlantic and Indian Oceans the magnetic "growth lines" parallel the trailing edges of the separating continents. In the North Pacific, however, the guidelines of separating continents are absent and the geometry of spreading revealed by the magnetic anomalies is less readily understood. Although complex, I do not see that it is necessarily incompatible with the global picture of spreading and plate tectonics.

Much of the Western Pacific is blanketed by the so-called "opaque layer" of reflection seismology. The upper surface of this layer is thought to approximate to the Mesozoic-Cenozoic boundary and its north-easterly extent is indicated by the pecked line on Figure 19-4 (Ewing *et al.,* 1968). Thus all crust to the southwest of this line must be at least Mesozoic in age, and again this is born out by the JOIDES results, although as yet the oldest material recovered is only Tithonian (uppermost Jurassic) in age. The Emperor Seamount Chain probably delineates a former transform fault, somewhat analogous to the Owen fracture zone in the northwest Indian Ocean at the present day. It must have accommodated a younger phase of spreading to the east. The Great Magnetic Bight at approximately 50°N 160°W was presumably formed at a triple junction of ridge crests, and again a present day analogy probably exists to the west of the Galapagos Islands (McKenzie and Morgan, 1969). It seems inconceivable that the Magnetic Bight could be formed in any other way, and it can be shown that the detailed geometry of the Bight is readily, and perhaps only, compatible with spreading from a triple junction (Vine and Hess, 1971). Finally one must remember that just as 50 per cent of the oceanic crust has been created at ridge crests during Cenozoic time, i.e. since the formation of this Bight, a similar area of oceanic crust has been destroyed in the trench systems, notably in the North and West Pacific. Paleomagnetic studies for the North Pacific (Vine, 1968) taken together with those for North America imply that as much as 5,000 km of oceanic crust may have been destroyed between the Alaskan peninsula and the Magnetic Bight during the Cenozoic. Clearly if resorption has gone on on this scale a great deal of the spreading geometry of the North Pacific has been lost, and it is perhaps no surprise that at present the Aleutian trench is consuming magnetic anomalies in the reverse order to what one might ex-

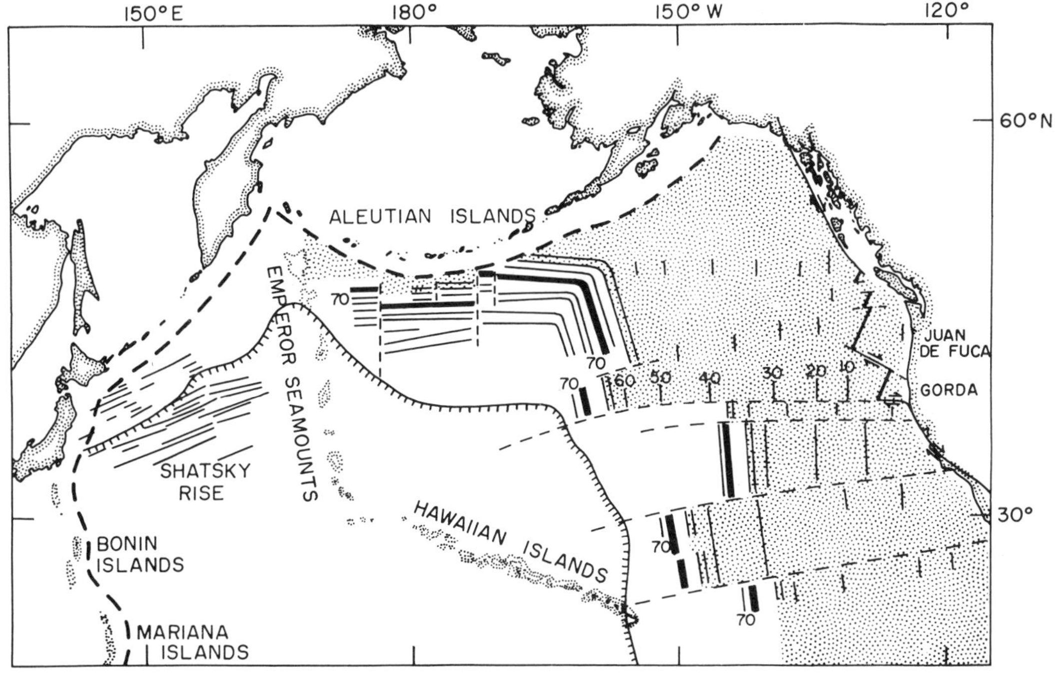


Figure 19-4. Summary of linear magnetic anomalies observed in the North Pacific (after Vine and Hess, in press). The extent of the "opaque layer" of reflection seismology, as given by Ewing *et al.* (1968), is indicated by the pecked line. The numbers refer to the age of the anomalies as suggested by Heirtzler *et al.* (1968). Crust formed by spreading during the Cenozoic (i.e., the past 65 million years) is shaded.

pect from the simplest formulation of spreading, i.e. younger anomalies first; although in some respects this is no different to the situation off California where presumably a trench system has overridden a ridge crest, and this explanation is fairly generally accepted.

To return to the gross picture of spreading and drift in the Atlantic and Indian Oceans, it is important to note that, as yet, we can trace the magnetic anomalies up to the continental margins, and hence date the initiation of drift, in only a few areas: in the extreme North Atlantic, south of Australia, and south of New Zealand. Thus in assigning an age to the initiation of drift in other areas one must turn to other criteria, particularly from the geologic record on the trailing margins of the continents. In drawing up the suggested time-table for the opening of the Atlantic and the fragmentation of Gondwanaland shown in Table 19-1, the extrusion and intrusion of tholeiitic basalts and quartz diabases, marine transgressions and the formation of evaporite basins have been assumed to be precursors of the initiation of drift in any particular area (Vine and Hess, 1971).

I think that the significance of sea-floor spreading, continental drift, and plate tectonics in earth science education goes without saying. These concepts are fundamental to virtually all aspects of our science. Also, since they should lead to a better understanding of the cause and distribution of earthquakes and igneous activity, of mountain building and flow in the mantle, of continental margins and likely settings for

Table 19-1. A Time-Table for Continental Drift.

| | *Opening of the Atlantic* | *Fragmentation of Gondwana* |
|---|---|---|
| — 0 — | | |
| Tertiary | (Opening of the Red Sea, Gulf of Aden, Gulf of California, and initiation of Galapagos Rise) | |
| | Opening of the extreme North Atlantic and the Arctic Ocean. | Separation of Australia from Antarctica and India from the Seychelle Bank. |
| **Upper Cretaceous** | **North Atlantic extends Northwards to from the Labrador Sea and Bay of Biscay.** | **Initiation of Pacific-Antarctic Ridge between New Zealand and West Antarctica.** |
| — 100 m.y. — | | |
| **Lower Cretaceous** | Opening of the South Atlantic | |
| | | |
| **Lower Jurassic** | Partial opening of North Atlantic between North America and Africa. | Separation of Australia + Antarctica from Africa + South America. |
| — 200 m.y. — | | |

the concentration of oil and mineral resources, I think one might also claim that they have some "relevance."

## REFERENCES


Cox, A., Dalrymple, G. B., and Doell, R. R., 1967, Reversals of the earth's magnetic field. *Sci. Amer.* **216**, 44-54.

Ewing, J., Ewing, M., Aitken, T., and Ludwig, W. J., 1968, North Pacific sediment layers measured by seismic profiling *in* The Crust and upper mantle of the Pacific area. *Geophys. Monogr.* **12**, *Amer. Geophys. Un.*, p. 147-173.

Heirtzler, J. R., 1968, Sea-floor spreading. *Sci. Amer.* **219**, 60-70.

Heirtzler, J. R., Dickson, G. O., Herron, E. M., Pitman, W. C., and Le Pichon, X., 1968, Marine magnetic anomalies, geomagnetic field reversals and motions of the ocean floor and continents. *Jour. Geophys. Res.* **73**, 2119-2136.

Helsley, C. E., and Steiner, M. B., 1969, Evidence for long intervals of normal polarity during the Cretaceous period. *Earth Planet. Sci. Letters* **5**, 325-332.

Luyendyk, B. P. and Fisher, D. E., 1969, Fission track age of magnetic anomaly 10: a new point on the sea-floor spreading curve. *Science* **164**, 1516-1517.

Maxwell, A. E., and Von Herzen, R., 1969, The Glomar Challenger completes Atlantic track–Highlights of Leg III. *Ocean Industry* **4**, 64-65.

McKenzie, D. P., and Morgan, W. J., 1969, Evolution of triple junctions. *Nature* **224**, 125-133.

Vine, F. J., 1968, Paleomagnetic evidence for the northward movement of the North Pacific basin during the past 100 m.y. [abstract]. *Trans. Amer. Geophys. Un.* **49**, 156.

Vine, F. J., 1969, Sea-floor spreading–new evidence. *Jour. Geol. Education* **17**, 6-16.

Vine, F. J., and Hess, H. H., 1971, Seafloor spreading, in *The Sea*, Vol. IV, pt. 2 Maxwell, A. E. (ed.), Wiley-Interscience, New York, pp. 587-622.

# 20. Continental Drift and Reserves of Oil and Natural Gas

DONALD H. TARLING 1973

Any new concept which is likely to assist in the location and assessment of the remaining reserves of oil and hydrocarbon gas is of obvious importance so it is opportune to use reviews[1,2] of the conditions of formation of the principal hydrocarbon sources and their subsequent migration and preservation in reservoirs to see how these are related to movements of the Earth's surface.

## DEPOSITION OF ORGANIC SUBSTANCES

The ability of hydrocarbons to migrate[3] and their complex chemical nature complicates matters but it is generally agreed that they are organically derived[4,5], 95% of the oil coming chiefly from animal proteins and gas from entirely vegetable proteins or heated oil.[1] Sources less than $10^7$ yr old are almost entirely deltaic and occur independently of latitude, the organic materials being trapped within the rapidly accumulating sediments. The rich terrestrial vegetation of tropical areas means that there may be some latitudinal control on the percentage of gas to oil, but this is unlikely to be significant. The location of deltas today is evident but somewhat older deltas exist which receive little or no drainage today and are therefore harder to distinguish physiographically as continental movements have separated the headwaters from deltas which now lie isolated and unexploited on other continents. The formation of mountain systems, along subduction zones or by continental collisions, also drastically changes the drainage pattern so that, for example, dispersed oil fields of the Andes may once have formed part of the proto-Amazon delta[6] when the Amazon drained from Africa. Deltaic areas older than

1. Halbouty, M. T., Meyerhoff, A. A., Dott, R., King, R. E., and Klemme, H., *Amer. Assoc. Petrol. Geol. Mem.*, 14, 502 (1970).
2. Radchenko, O. A., *Geochemical Regularities in the Distribution of the Oil-Bearing Regions of the World*, 312 (Israeli Prog. Sci. Trans., 1968).
3. Silverman, S. R., *Amer. Assoc. Petrol. Geol. Mem.*, 4, 53 (1965).
4. Dott, R. H., and Reynolds, M. J., *Amer. Assoc. Petrol. Geol. Mem.*, 5, 571 (1969).
5. Levorsen, A. I., *Geology of Petroleum*, 724 (Freeman, San Francisco, 1967).
6. McDowell, A. N., *Oil and Gas J.*, 69, 114 (1971).

Dr. Donald H. Tarling is with the Department of Geophysics and Planetary Physics, School of Physics, University of Newcastle upon Tyne, Great Britain.

From *Nature*, Vol. 243, No. 5405, pp. 277-279, 1973. Reprinted with author's revisions and light editing, with permission of the author and *Nature*.

200 m.y., which covers the "Wegenerian" phase of continental drift, are almost impossible to locate physiographically but are of less economic importance because most productive deltaic areas are less than 200 m.y. old and geological identification is possible, irrespective of age.

Shales are generally considered to have the highest initial organic content, followed by carbonates and finally sandstones–although sandstones are the principal rock type for major reservoirs[1] and can be a significant contributor to their own reservoirs. But the productivity of source rocks depends on the ease of migration of the hydrocarbons so that the most productive source rocks are the massive carbonates, unless the source rocks have been heated. Deep oceanic sediments accumulate slowly and are unable to trap significant protein matter before oxidation so that deep oceans are not potential oil or gas sources, except where shallower sediments have slumped into them, but much of the hydrocarbon is also likely to be lost at this time.

Because more than 90% of known oil and gas fields,[1,7-9] are associated with evaporite deposits the conditions for evaporite accumulation are relevant to the source, migration and preservation by hydrocarbons. Most marine evaporites are formed of anhydrite, with some gypsum, and contain only small amounts of the more soluble halite. Even when halite forms a large part of the deposit, it only represents temporary conditions as it was laid down some $10^2$ to $10^3$ times faster than anhydrite[10]. Significant deposits cannot therefore have formed by simple evaporation of seawater because halite would always predominate. Two depositional environments have been postulated to account for these features–the silled basin and the sabkha. The former[10-12] consists of a pool of water into which only surface waters can flow. As these surface waters evaporate, saline brines form and, being denser, sink to the bottom where the least soluble salts are eventually precipitated; but the salinity can only rarely increase to the concentration appropriate to halite deposition. "Sabkha" regions[13,14] form from the occasional flooding of supratidal flats which create extensive areas of shallow marine waters. As these waters evaporate and retreat, the least soluble salts are left behind. These deposits are greatest where the flats are bordered by lagoons in which the salinity is already higher than normal seawater. Such extensive flat regions would be more common when orogeny was less active than during the past 20 m.y. and when sealevel was more constant than during the eustatic changes of the most recent Ice Age.

In both environments the depositional area must sink relative to the barrier and sealevel to account for the observed thicknesses of evaporites. Rapid subsidence in areas of low evaporation would cause persistent flooding and the solution of previous salts, as would also happen with rare rainstorms in areas of low evaporation and slow subsidence. So although both types of environment could exist temporarily at any latitude, thick deposits could only form in regions with a very high rate of evaporation, that is where hot, dry conditions are accompanied by strong diurnal on-shore and off-shore winds. Cyclothems and structures in associated sediments indicate intermittent subsidence so that the evaporation rates would have to match the maximum rate of subsidence. Such prolonged subsidence implies movements of the lower crust and upper mantle, as occurs in response to isostatic

7. Martinez, J. D., *Amer. Assoc. Petrol. Geol. Bull.*, 55, 810 (1971).
8. Peterson, J. A., and Hite, R. J., *Amer. Assoc. Petrol. Geol. Bull.*, 53, 884 (1969).
9. Stöcklin, J., *Geol. Soc. Amer. Spec. Paper,* 88, 157 (1968).
10. Brongersma-Sanders, M., *Marine Geol.,* 11, 123 (1971).
11. Woolnough, W. G., *Amer. Assoc. Petrol. Geol. Bull.*, 21, 1101 (1937).
12. Raup, O. B., *Amer. Assoc. Petrol. Geol. Bull.*, 54, 2246 (1970).
13. Bush, P. R., *Trans. Inst. Min. Metall.*, B79, 137 (1970).
14. Kinsman, D. J. J., *Amer. Assoc. Petrol. Geol. Bull.*, 53, 830 (1969).

adjustments, for example during continental separation[15]. For continued deposition, the barriers of a silled basin and the shoreline of a sabkha must maintain their position relative to the subsiding depositional area. A fault-controlled structure, where very localized tectonic movements happen to cancel out regional movements, could create this situation, but it is more likely that such persistent barriers or shorelines would result from sedimentary or biological processes. Sandbars could be maintained relative to sea-level if marine currents and a sediment supply were unaffected by the subsidence, but the most persistent type of barrier/shoreline would be formed by shallow reef structures. Reefs in low latitudes would easily maintain their position relative to an intermittently deepening sea as their growth is optimized in shallow, warm, clear waters. These low latitude conditions, necessary for optimum evaporite formation, are bordered by those for the optimum production and preservation of hydrocarbon source materials as the concentration of nutrients in warm, saline waters results in rich organic blooms of microorganisms, the salinity restricts the entrance of larger organisms which could feed on them and the nearby anaerobic bottom conditions are ideal for the preservation of the organic debris[16-18].

## MIGRATION

The gradual freeing of hydrocarbons from the original organic matter occurs continuously but is accelerated by small temperature rises[19,20] to which plate tectonic theories and continental drift have varying degrees of significance. Tectonic heating during collision between two continental blocks is likely to be locally severe and drive off all hydrocarbons, but the less disturbed areas and margins of collision zones may be areas of significant oil and gas migration. Such areas can be located from paleomagnetic measurements of the angle and rate of collision but the shape of the original edges is also critical and this can only be detected by detailed geological and geophysical studies which, among other things, yield the information of sources, migration and reservoirs. Similarly, in subduction zones there is higher heat flow and igneous activity in a region up to 1,000 km wide, but the distribution of heat is not regular and the local controlling factors are only just becoming clear[21] and the estimation of heat flow in different areas, now and in the past, should become more precise as such interacting factors are considered further.

The igneous activity and high heat flow along spreading oceanic ridges are not of any importance within the oceans, where there are no source rocks, but become highly significant when these ridges intersect, or have intersected, continental plates. Local destruction of reserves is likely where significant igneous activity was involved, such as at previous plume centers, but these will also be rimmed by high gas pressures. In general, the high heat flow of the ridges will have been a major cause of migration as the hydrocarbons would move slowly from deep to shallow levels as the regional temperature increased. Thus the numerous, highly productive gas fields of north-west Siberia occur over the continental extension of the Arctic ridge; similarly the productive oil fields around Los Angeles[22] are where the East Pacific Rise underlies continental rocks. So the identification of present and past intersecting regions is of great importance.

As the Atlantic and Indian Oceans origi-

15. Bott, M. H. P., and Dean, D. S., *Nature Physical Science,* 235, 23 (1972).
16. Phleger, F. B., *Amer. Assoc. Petrol. Geol. Bull.,* 53, 824 (1969).
17. Fuller, J. G. C. M., and Porter, J. W., *Amer. Assoc. Petrol. Geol. Bull.,* **53,** 909 (1969).
18. Kendall, C. G. St. C., and Skipworth, P. A. D. E., *Amer. Assoc. Petrol. Geol. Bull.,* **53,** 841 (1969).
19. Philippi, H. W., *Geochim. Cosmochim. Acta,* **29,** 1021 (1965).
20. Welte, D. H., *Amer. Assoc. Petrol. Geol. Bull.,* **30,** 1830 (1965).
21. Tarling, D. H., *Nature,* **243,** 193 (1973).
22. McFarland, L. C., and Greutert, R. H., *Oil and Gas J.,* **69,** 112 (1971).

nated from the break up of the Gondwanan and Laurasian continents, the fractured edges must have been subjected to oceanic ridge heating at their inception. This heating would coincide with the accumulation and migration of organic materials in these areas as the persistent subsidence afforded troughs into which organic material could be trapped and also allowed a thick accumulation of sediments to develop in them, giving rise to burial heating of older sediments. In general, direct heat flow is likely to have been most significant along the margin[23] and burial heating would be dominant within a few hundred kilometers of the margin. This subsidence was usually along pre-existing fractures where these paralleled the opening margins and the deepest subsidence took place on the continental side of fault blocks as they respond to upper mantle and lower crustal flow. Seafloor spreading also seems to be the cause of the formation[24] of marginal basins, such as the Japanese Sea, which also contain shallow sedimentary rocks. Thus the availability of source rocks and heating by burial and elevated heat flow implies that these regions, particularly in the West and Southwest Pacific, are likely to be areas of high hydrocarbon potential.

On the plate tectonic model igneous activity and high heat flow are absent away from plate margins, with the minor exception of kimberlite-type intrusions[21]. Deep burial heating can still occur away from plate margins as a result of upper mantle/lower crustal movements, but significant heating in such areas presumably arises mainly from exothermic chemical and biochemical reactions which may accompany diagenesis and subsequent compaction. Most of these reactions are independent of plate tectonic concepts, but some important reactions, such as between organic materials and anhydrite[13], will occur chiefly in sediments originally deposited at low latitudes.

23. Sleep, N. H., *Geophys. J. Roy. Astron. Soc.*, **24**, 325 (1971).
24. Karig, D. E., *J. Geophys. Res.*, **76**, 2542 (1971).

The final composition of the reserves reflects the nature of the source materials, the temperature and organic activity in the source, during migration and after preservation in reservoirs, and the distance between source and the reservoir. So fatty, heavy grade oils are particularly associated with deltaic conditions[25] where migration has been restricted and the original organic material is often derived from brackish environments. Deltas also tend to have substantial gas. The variations of sulfur content within oils, or nitrogen within gas, are significant to extraction and refining techniques and prediction of the nature of the rocks through which the hydrocarbons have passed by determining their paleolatitudinal history will lead to a closer understanding of natural refining processes and therefore to a prediction of the quality of hydrocarbon reserves. Sulfur content[26,27], for example, seems to correlate broadly with the presence of evaporites in the source rocks, but the final composition is probably determined largely by bacterial activity, particularly within the reservoir rocks.

## RESERVOIRS

Various structures may trap oil and gas[5] and plate tectonic activity is involved in each, although some links are tenuous. Stratigraphic traps, for example, are related to the detailed local paleogeography, but the number of traps in any one region is controlled by broader considerations. For example, structural traps, such as anticlines and domes, are directly related to tectonic processes along subduction and continental collision zones. Thus the gas fields marginal to the Pyrenees owe their origin to the relative movements between Iberia and France and the Argentine fields possibly formed in re-

25. Biederman, E. W., *Amer. Assoc. Petrol. Geol. Bull.*, **53**, 1500 (1969).
26. Hood, A., and Gutjahr, C. C. M., *Abs. Geol. Soc. Amer.*, **4**, 542 (1972).
27. Ho, T. Y., Drushel, H. V., Koons, C. B., and Rogers, M. A., *Abs. Geol. Soc. Amer.*, **4**, 539 (1972).

sponse to movements of the Patagonian arc[6].

Evaporites are again significant because they lubricate tectonic movements, and afford an impervious seal for trapped hydrocarbons. Their ability to flow when the overburden exceeds some 600 m (ref. 28) means that they can create their own structural traps. The role of reefs and sand bars in evaporite formation also means that these offer potential reservoirs close to hydrocarbon sources. The margins of separating continents also provide structures, accompanying the faulting and folding movements, which may act as reservoirs.

## IMPLICATIONS FOR FUEL SUPPLIES

Concepts of continental drift and plate tectonics have a much more fundamental part to play in the evaluation of potential oil and gas reservoirs than in the mere matching of, for example, oil traps bordering the Atlantic. Physiographical location of deltaic sources deposited during the past 200 m.y. can be undertaken effectively only when continental movements are taken into account and similarly the structural evolution of an area should be related to the different distribution, movements, collisions and separations of the continents. The most striking feature is that paleoclimatic consideration plays a vital part in the origin, migration and accumulation of hydrocarbons. Paleomagnetic techniques, which offer a precise, economic measure of paleolatitude, are therefore likely to be of increasing significance.

As technology advances, it should be possible to extract oil and gas from some of the extensive tar shales as well as from inhospitable yet potentially productive areas such as the Labrador Sea, Newfoundland Shelf, northern Greenland and the Canadian Arctic Islands. Nonetheless, the fact that low paleolatitudes are so significant suggests that the southern continents which, as Gondwanaland, have mostly lain at high to intermediate paleolatitudes during the past 400 m.y., are unlikely to be as productive as the northern hemisphere—although the size of Gondwanaland implies that some areas must have been at low latitudes for appreciable periods of time. So something like two-thirds of the world's total reserves are likely to be in the present northern hemisphere, which are already the best known areas and the regions of highest exploitation. Major reserves which are largely undetected or unexploited must still exist, for instance, off north-western Australia, the south-west and western Pacific, as well as in uptapped Meso-zoic-Cenozoic deltas. It is also clear that the deep oceanic parts of the world are not likely to contribute to future needs for organic fuels. It should now be possible to make a realistic estimate of the world's hydrocarbon potential and thereby evaluate the optimum development of these resources for the benefit of mankind as a whole.

28. Brunstrom, R. G. W., and Walmsley, P. J., *Amer. Assoc. Petrol. Geol. Bull.*, 53, 870 (1969).

# 21. Seamounts: Keystones to the Earth

IGOR LOBANOV-ROSTOVSKY 1972

The long discussed theories of drifting continents, combined with the new science of Plate Tectonics, are rapidly filling in the gaps in the puzzle of the world mechanism and how it works. And the mountains of the sea may well be the key to the riddle of our evolving, very much alive planet.

Rising from the abyssal bottom of the great ocean basins are entire sunken mountain chains, some with peaks taller than the loftiest continental prominences. Sometimes the newest peaks in these ranges are still above sea level. The Hawaiian Islands, for example, are almost the only visible segment of a now-submerged mountain chain stretching northwest from Hawaii for over 2,700 nautical miles, with Midway Island jutting above the waves slightly past the halfway mark.

Unlike the land variety of mountains—such as the Rockies or Alps—which sprang largely from sediments folded by lateral pressure of landmasses, mid-ocean mountains are built from basalt, an igneous rock that emerged as molten magma from within the earth, then cooled and solidified.

The size and structural makeup of the sea's mountains are not their most salient factors, however. What is most significant toward understanding the earth is how these chains were formed, how former islands sank, where they are now, and especially how they have moved about on the earth's surface. Proof of this movement demonstrates clearly that great masses of the ocean floor are still very much in motion—carrying the water-bound peaks along pig-a-back.

Thus any discussion of seamounts involves the development, movement, and subsequent destruction of large plates of the earth's crust. Plate (or global) tectonics is a fairly recent geological concept that says the earth's crust is a massive mosaic of half a dozen large plates, plus numerous smaller ones; that these rigid crustal blocks, each about fifty to seventy miles thick, are in constant near-frictionless movement over the surface of the more plastic mantle.

The earth's crust—which can possibly be visualized as somewhat akin to the skin of an orange, except that it is far from smooth—is actually broken by a globe-girdling network

Igor Lobanov-Rostovsky was a U.S. Naval Reserve officer and has free-lanced as an editor/writer/photographer. He is currently managing editor of *Business Forum Magazine*.

From *Oceans Magazine*, Vol. 5, No. 3, pp. 66-75, 1972. Reprinted with light editing and with permission of the author and *Oceans Magazine*.

of cracks or rifts. From these rifts molten lava keeps pouring out to move across the ocean bottom in continent-sized plates. These plates meet a continental mass in a crunching edge-on encounter which sends the moving plate diving down into a trench in the ocean floor to be destroyed in the depths below.

Behind the trenches on the continent side is usually a "ring of fire" string of volcanoes in the classic Mt. Fuji shape. These steep-sided volcanoes differ markedly from the mid-ocean variety which usually have a shallower-slope structure. The "ring of fire" is perhaps most evident in Japan, but it is found along the edge of all other continents, especially around the Pacific. It is hardly surprising that these areas are also subject to frequent earthquakes.

Plate movement beneath the sea is actually splitting continents apart today in at least two obvious places: the Gulf of Aden, where the Mid-Indian Ocean Ridge enters the African continental mass, and the Gulf of California, where the East Pacific Rise is pushing northwestward into central California.

One strong objection to the entire theory of continental drift has been that there is no mechanism known which is capable of driving the continents. However, the recent studies of seamount chains, combined with a presumed group of "hot spots" well within the earth's mantle, may provide the answer. The key to the hot spots seems to be in the seamount chains. These strings of volcanoes may well represent a trace of the actual motion of a plate over the earth's mantle.

As noted earlier, the Hawaiian Ridge is the best example of such a chain. Other outstanding examples include the Emperor Seamounts—which run northward from the western tip of the Hawaiian chain—the Marshall-Gilbert-Austral chain, and the Line Islands—Tuamotu Archipelago, both in the south-central Pacific. Numerous other smaller chains have been located, primarily over much of the western and southwestern Pacific. And there are two short chains in the Gulf of Alaska.

Most of the chains have been found to progress in age from southeast to northwest. The Hawaiian Ridge, for example, as the youngest chain, goes from erupting volcanoes (on the island of Hawaii, the farthest southeast island) to volcanoes that have been extinct for over thirty million years on the far western tip. The sequence of island ages even appears in mythology. The Hawaiian goddess of fire, Pele, is said to have first come to the northernmost island, then traveled down the chain until she finally took up residence on the youngest island.

The Emperor Seamounts have been placed as 75 million years old at their distant end. Other ranges are apparently even older. However, much more data needs to be gathered on them before the age gradient and, in some cases, even the direction of travel are known accurately.

Undersea peaks occur in all oceans, but are probably most prominent in the Pacific. Since this body of water encompasses fully half of the earth's surface, it is a fertile area for study. The water depth makes marine mountain study difficult, but it has a mummifying effect that preserves ancient material which on the surface would long since have been eroded away by winds, waves, and streams.

A bench mark in seamount discoveries occurred when Professor H. H. Hess of Princeton was navigator (and subsequently commanding officer) of the *USS Cape Johnson* during World War II operations in the central Pacific. Hess recorded numerous sounding profiles of the bottom and discovered some thirty flat-topped mountains which he named guyots (Figure 21-1) after the nineteenth-century geographer Arnold Guyot. He published his findings in 1946, identifying the guyots as drowned ancient islands—cut off at sea level by wind and wave action—which had sunk from one to two kilometers below the surface.

Hess' report was a follow-up chapter to

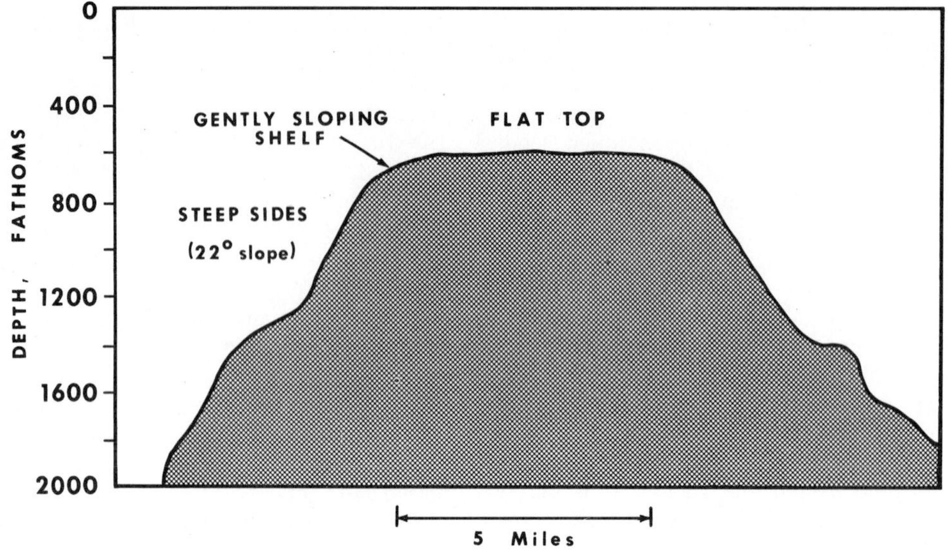


Figure 21-1. Bathymetric profile of a flat-topped seamount (guyot) discovered in the central Pacific Ocean. After Hess, H. H., *Amer. Jour. Sci.*, Vol. 244, 1946.

work done by Dr. H. W. Murray in 1941. Murray had published the first adequate description of seamounts, categorizing them as at least one kilometer high and having steep sides.

To date some 2,000 seamounts fitting this definition have been charted and at least 10,000 are believed to exist in the world ocean. As undersea volcanoes, they develop in a fairly set pattern usually including four major stages:

1. An explosive submarine stage in which the volcano emits a pillow lava (rounded blobs shaped roughly like pillows) and deposits of ash as it grows toward the surface.
2. The sea level state at which point there is a gentle outpouring, called a shield volcano, built from thin lava flows extruded from the summit crater and side rifts.
3. The collapse of the summit, forming a caldera (broad basin) and shallow depressions along the major rifts.
4. The caldera is filled in and a cinder cone is formed by later eruptions.

In some cases there is no first stage: the volcano begins and ends in the shield-building stage.

Currently all stages of volcanic development are found in the Pacific Basin—mostly in chains of peaks. Since the center of active volcanism usually travels along the chain, one end will have sunken mountains and atolls, while the other end may still contain active volcanoes.

Examples of this sequential development are evident in the Caroline, Hawaiian, Samoan, and Society island groups. A few areas, notably the Austral Island chain, display the results of disparate volcanic periods which left guyots and islands intermingled. However, these seem to be the exception.

The Pacific is thus literally a vast graveyard of volcanic chains. Why did the mountains drown? There have been many theories. Did the sea level rise and engulf the pinnacles? It is known that new water is constantly being added to the oceans from the interior of the planet. But this inflow is happening at a very slow rate; scientists estimate it has only boosted the ocean level by some forty to fifty feet since the Cretaceous

Period 100 million years ago. Sediment lost from continents also causes a slight rise in the sea level, but this too is relatively small. The theory that the lower sea level during the "lockup" of waters in the glacial age could have cut off the mountaintops is also unrealistic because the guyots were decapitated at various heights—with no consistent depth apparent—and at different times in prehistory.

During the summer of 1950 scientists aboard the Scripps Institution of Oceanography's *MV Horizon* conducted SIO's first large-scale deep-sea study when they explored the sunken Mid-Pacific Mountains. This abundant uprising extends from Necker Island in the Hawaiian chain southwest for 1,500 miles to near Wake Island. They surveyed several of the flattops—now resting at depths down to 5,700 feet—by making zigzag crossings, and found peaks rising to heights of 13,000 feet from the ocean floor. They then dredged up proof that the guyots had once been at the surface: reef fauna of the mid-Cretaceous Period and perfectly rounded and polished cobbles. The rocks were of homogeneous composition and had not been rounded as a result of volcanic explosions that produced falling lava "bombs" or by spheroidal weathering. These stones must have been rounded by wave action on a former shore, the scientists felt, since, even in mid-ocean, currents below the surface are not strong enough, as they pass over the rough tops of the guyots, to tumble rocks there to the degree necessary for rounding and smoothing them.

The discovery of deeply submerged reef coral—which cannot flourish below the light zone—at about 330 feet confirmed the sinking theory. Corals are active reef-builders only down to a depth of 25 fathoms, and cannot live beyond a depth of about 85 fathoms. In addition, they must have a water temperature of at least 68 degrees F.

The real irony of the light zone limit of growth is that the plants growing in this zone absorb much of the light themselves, thus effectively cutting the depth of the zone even further.

Drilling on many coral atolls has shown that the thickness of reef material is far greater than the depth of the light zone. The thickness of coral at Eniwetok, for example, is 4,600 feet. Seismic tests have shown that Bikini Atoll has 4,300 feet of coral, and that the reef on Kwajalein extends down from 3,300 to 6,600 feet.

Study of the basalt beneath the coral has further substantiated the sinking premise. The vesicles (small cavities produced by expanding air and gas bubbles formed during the molten stage) of basaltic rock now resting at a depth of 6,600 feet are much the same size as those found in surface volcanic rock on the island of Oahu. If the sunken rocks had never been above their present depth, the deep ocean water pressures would allow little of the gas to escape. The resulting cavities would thus be considerably smaller than those formed in the volcanoes on Oahu.

Extensive mapping of the deep ocean floor, its mountains, and other topography has only been possible in recent decades. Recording echo sounders came into wide use during World War II. Loran gear permitted accurate navigation in large areas, regardless of visibility, while the development of radar allowed precise navigation near shore or in the vicinity of a buoy. Magnetic Airborne Detection gear—used by naval aircraft to hunt submarines—was modified to be towed behind a steel ship for measuring the earth's magnetic field. Even nuclear weapon testing has contributed to ocean bottom knowledge. Such tests in the Marshall Islands were preceded by measurements of coral atoll thickness using both geophysical and drilling techniques.

Much mapping of ocean topography today is done with sound impulses. One quite useful device is the "air gun"—a compressed air cylinder that is towed submerged behind a ship and sends out low-frequency sound waves by means of explosions at regular intervals. The low frequency penetrates deeper into rock than the higher frequency sonar pings. Resulting charts of sea floor elevations show more detail below the surface of a seamount.

Such detail aids scientists in setting up dredging operations to recover fossils and rocks from the peaks. During the Aries Expedition in mid-1971, scientists aboard the 1,300-ton Scripps *R/V Thomas Washington* conducted some forty dredge hauls on nearly twenty seamounts scattered across the Mid-Pacific Mountains. They were also doing survey work for the deep drilling ship *Glomar Challenger,* looking at three sites in order to locate a thick layer of sediment suitable for drilling. So far, most of the drilling has been done between seamounts. So, to study the seamounts themselves, researchers must do as much as they can with dredging.

On log seven of the expedition, during a 10,000-mile survey track from Yokohama to Honolulu and at a point some 700 miles northwest of Midway, the ship's instruments charted one of the largest guyots known to man. This monumental truncated giant measured 70 miles long, 45 miles across, and 15,000 feet high. Its top proved to be within 1,500 feet of the surface. Coral and reef debris scraped from the guyot's surface indicated at one time it had been a coral atoll or island quite similar to Kwajalein in the Marshall Island group.

Dredge hauling from seamounts is harder than one might suspect. During the Scripps Institution's Styx Expedition in 1968, scientists aboard the *R/V Alexander Agassiz* sought samples of crustaceous life on the Mid-Pacific Mountains. According to Dr. William A. Newman, biological oceanographer who specialized in reef ecology at Scripps and one of the leaders in this study, the sea probers located a massive new seamount—which they promptly named after Charles Darwin (who in 1836 explained the grouping of atolls by concluding that a great mass of the sea floor had sunk).

"The principal problem," explained Dr. Newman, "was not in locating the seamount. Echo sounding did that. Our trouble came when we wanted to pull a trawl across the top. Imagine if you will our small ship moving along with three miles of cable strung out behind and trying to hit a mountain peak three-quarters of a mile wide and one mile down.

"We first had to resurvey the peak by making a series of echo sounding runs over it. Then we could determine the best angle and the spot to try and hit in order to drag our otter trawl to get a true surface sampling. The currents need only carry our craft a short distance, during the hour it took to put out the cable, in order for us to miss the target."

The otter trawl, developed from the beach seine, is basically a long net with wooden "barn doors" at the open end. If the doors happen to strike a rocky outcropping, the researchers could well lose both samples and the sampler.

The *Agassiz* trip was the first time scientists had sampled guyots using a net-type trawl. The traditional rock dredges had proved to be unwieldy for snagging swimming specimens, and the rigid bulky shapes would tend to bounce off any outcroppings. Most guyot tops contain both flat areas that have been smoothed off by silt deposits and some spots where current erosion has taken away great chunks of coral to leave a ragged outcropping.

Another biologist at Scripps, Dr. R. H. Rosenblatt, is interested in the theory of seamounts acting as stepping-stones for faunal migration. So far any evidence of such migration has been difficult to pin down. However, Dr. Rosenblatt believes the area of the Nasca Ridge off Peru may provide some clues, since strong evidence of progression has been shown there. Specifically, scientists have found one distinct subtropical species among these seamounts that is normally only seen in the waters off Australia and New Zealand. Since the prevailing direction of drift is westward, the "escape" of this one species from its family would indicate a counter-current transport. Chains of seamounts may have played a part in allowing the species to migrate, and such movement would be concurrent with the direction of newer volcanoes. Thus the age of the seamount is again important.

Oceanographers determine the age of a seamount in two ways:

1. The radiometric method—samples of the volcanic rock are tested to determine the amount of radiometric decay of certain isotopes that has taken place since the mineral was formed. Geologists know that at the time molten magma solidifies into solid rock, the elements in the mineral start changing at a known rate. Uranium, for example, decays to ultimately become lead. Thus the ratio between the parent material and the radiometric "daughter dependent" can reveal how much time has elapsed since decay began. This method does have drawbacks. Accuracy, for example, is only within a million-year span.
2. The fossil age method—whereby identifying and thus dating the material capping the seamount provides a minimum age for the volcano. Of course, all that is known then is that the seamount is older than whatever age is found for the cap.

By far the most important characteristic in the strings of seamounts is the chain effect and how the peaks moved out in a single direction. Therefore, a key bit of knowledge is the paleolatitude, or location of the seamount—with respect to the equator—at the time it was formed. Paleolatitude is calculated by measuring the magnetic inclination of the volcanic rock. The cooling lava, as it reached the Curie point, recorded the earth's magnetic field existing at that time and place.

To record the magnetic bearing of a single seamount, the survey ship tows a magnetometer through a flower-like pattern of transverse crossings above the inclination to the location of the magnetic pole during the cooling period of the volcano.

Determination of the latitude-at-birth often reveals that a seamount was formed at a great distance from its present location. Combining age and paleolatitude information, experts can begin to put together a history for undersea mountains—and for the earth.

For example, with the succeedingly older mountains of the Hawaiian chain, they know that the southeast end is "now" in age, or less than one million years old. Kauai, the oldest surviving island in the group, shows its greater age in many ways. It is, for example, the only island with established rivers, rather than ephemeral streams.

Midway Island, at about the halfway point in the entire ridge system, has been found by fossil and radiometric tests of drill cores to be 16 to 22 million years old (radiometry shows 16.9, while fossils indicate 15 to 22.5). Therefore, the age of the peaks on the far end of the ridge is probably about thirty million years.

The geologically young island of Hawaii—which is still coming out of the ground—has no paleolatitude. More exactly, its present and paleolatitudes are the same, since it has not had time to move on the earth's surface. Midway, on the other hand, has had time to migrate. And we do know that it was formed at another latitude. Thus, despite the lack of accuracy in age determination methods, we know that the older the seamount the farther it has been carried.

The dating and paleolatitude tests combine to bear out the premise that the Pacific Plate is moving northwest, since the older dates and greater apparent magnetic pole displacement show up the farther one travels in this direction. It is also believed that as the conveyor belt carries away a volcano, another is formed in its place.

Which brings us to the hot spots.

A Princeton University scientist, Dr. Jason Morgan, is one of the principal proponents of the hot spot theory. He has shown that if only the crust (lithosphere) is moving, then by charting its movement we may get the absolute motion of a plate with regard to the lower mantle.

In his recent paper entitled "Plate Motion and Deep Mantle Convection" (in press; to be published by the Geological Society of America), he proposes a series of narrow plumes (hot spots) of deep material which rise and spread out in the upper mantle. He concludes that all the seamount chains were produced by crustal plate motion over hot spots in the mantle. Thus the seamount and island chains (and also the aseismic ridges emanating from several points along the mid-ocean rises) indicate trajectories of plates over fixed points.

Dr. Morgan points to the remarkable parallelism in the three principal Pacific seamount chains: the Hawaiian-Emperor, the Tuamotu-Line Islands, and the Austral-Gilbert-Marshall groups; these he feels could well have been produced by motion of the Pacific Plate over the hot spots (Figure 21-2). There is presently active volcanism at the southeast end of each of these chains; at Hawaii at the end of the Hawaiian chain, at Macdonald Seamount at the southeastern tip of the Austral Islands chain, and at the East Pacific Rise near Easter Island at the southeastern end of the Tuamotu chain. Specifically, as the Pacific Plate moves over the upwelling hot spot beneath Hawaii, a continuous outpouring of basalt from below produces a linear basaltic ridge on the sea floor.

Accuracy of fit indicates to Morgan that the hot spots have stayed practically fixed in relation to one another through the past 100 million years. The rate of this motion of the plate has been calculated to be about 10 centimeters per year over the past five million years and five cm/yr prior to that time.

Morgan wonders why such motion does not produce a continuous ridge. In other words, why are the Hawaiian islands *islands*? The answer, he speculates, is the nature of the deep plume which flows upward only to be trapped in the interface between the crust and mantle. As it accumulates in pockets, the unstable situation causes vents to the surface to form—thus producing volcanoes. The plume may be spread over 100 square miles in the interface, declares Morgan, but a single vent taps the "reservoir" concentrating it in a surface upwelling. As the plate moves on, the vent is displaced and a new vent is formed, producing a new volcano.

Morgan also notes evidence of two minor hot spots in the Juan de Fuca Ridge region off Vancouver Island. These, he says, could be the cause of two lines of seamounts which extend northwest across the Gulf of Alaska. These seamounts, seamounts trending northwest from near the mouth of the Gulf of California, and seamounts between the Eltanin fracture zone and the Kermadec Islands, are all parallel to the Hawaii-Tuamotu-Austral trend. Other hot spots, according to Morgan, appear to be located beneath the Atlantic, Indian, and Antarctic oceans—for example Iceland, the Azores, Reunion Island.

Thus, Dr. Morgan presents evidence which ties in the parallelism of the Pacific seamount chains with the relative motion of the plates to—as he says—"make the hot spots a valid and useful concept."

He then proposes that the hot spots produce currents in the asthenosphere which drive the plates about—that is, provide the motive force for continental drift. Such a relationship is suggested by the nearness of most hot spots to a spreading ridge. Also, the rises and trenches do not seem to Morgan to be powerful enough to drive the plates—indicating that conceivably the massive currents in the mantle must provide the driving force.

Conceding the existence of great mantle currents, Morgan questions "are these great rolls—mirrors of the rise and trench system—or are they localized upwellings, i.e. hot spots? And how deep do such currents extend?"

Circumstantial evidence favors the hot spots, says Morgan, but more tests are

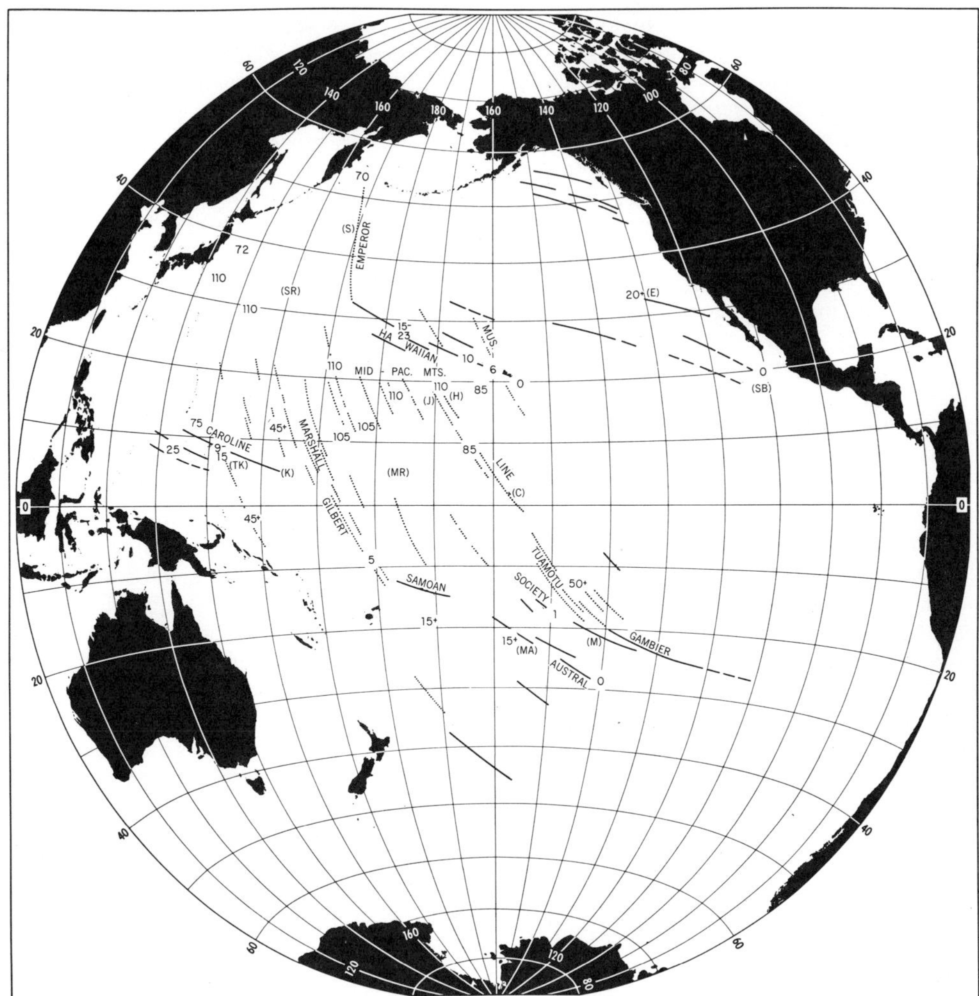


Figure 21-2. A charting of seamount chains shows the remarkable parallelisms which may indicate movements of the great plates on the earth's surface. The solid lines running northwest represent Neogene time (encompassing the four youngest epochs of the Cenozoic Era—Recent, Pleistocene, Pliocene, and Miocene)—from about zero to 25 million years ago.

The more steeply inclined dotted lines show seamount chains that are dated in the Paleogene (which includes the Paleocene and Oligocene epochs—25 to 75 million years ago), and Cretaceous time (70 to 135 million years).

The numbers represent the age of a seamount in millions of years. Note how the age increases as the mountains progress northwestward.

needed. One way, he notes, would be to seismically detect the "shadow" cast by a hot spot. A long-time delay in teleseismic events in Iceland (one of the Atlantic hot spots) could be caused by a deep plume effect. One could also, says Morgan, make assumptions on the plume magnitude together with stresses at rise, fault, and trench plate-to-plate boundaries to deduce the directions of resulting plate motions. Or further study of the heat flow in the mantle may provide clues. In conclusion, Dr. Morgan notes that major changes in the spreading pattern may be governed by the "turning on" or "turning off" of hot spots.

Dr. Edward Winterer, of Scripps Institution of Oceanography, is also seeking clues to plate movement and the relationship of hot spots. He believes that not only is the uppermost layer in movement, but that sections of the mantle beneath are also in motion—perhaps in an opposing direction. On the wall of his office, Dr. Winterer has charted directions of the major seamount chains in the Pacific Basin with strips of colored paper. He needs only two colors, since nearly all the chains seem to be running in one of two directions.

The 25 blue-coded chains, representing the Neocene Period, all run northwest to southeast. The oldest islands in the west are dated at about thirty million years.

An equal number of red-coded chains representing the Paleogene and Cretaceous time—including the Marshall and Gilbert island chains—are generally located in the mid-Pacific and are somewhat older. Their medium age is comparable to the oldest of the blue chains. The red chains are also more steeply inclined: they run from north-northwest to south-southeast. At this writing, the *Glomar Challenger* is drilling in these chains to see if the age increases as one moves northwest.

Few of Winterer's coded chains are farther east than Hawaii, since most of the eastern portion of the Pacific was not in existence when these chains were formed.

Why are these chains running remarkably parallel? Dr. Winterer concedes two prevalent theories:

1. Each chain is located over a crack in the crust which is growing and—as it splits—produces volcanic activity.
2. As the Pacific Plate moves over the mantle it passes over some old hot spots. Alternately, in line with Dr. Morgan's premise, perhaps it is the motion of plates over a sprinkling of very few stationary hot spots (scattered like freckles on the surface of the earth) which could produce a series of parallel fracture lines and in turn a spaced-out series of volcanoes.

Since a number of the largest known fractures run quite parallel in a north to northwest direction, the sprinkled hot spots premise seems to him more plausible.

While agreeing in general with the hot spot theory, Dr. Winterer feels that new evidence, based upon study of sediments in cores raised by the *Glomar Challenger*, substantiates the theory that the various earth layers may each be moving in a different direction.

Sediments can be both age and direction indicators. At any time in history the sediments being deposited on the sea floor beneath the equator tend to be rich in the fossils of chalky, limy, tropical microorganisms. After this material has been deposited, the whole plate moves—and carries along the fossil trace indicating the equator. Thus equatorial fossil chalk lines are found to be laid out in a progression as the plate has been moving northward. Another way to express this is to imagine that some (anti-ecology) person would drop a series of weighted beer cans at the equator. If he came back ten million years from now he would find that the row of metal was no longer beneath the equator but formed a line farther north. In truth, the fossil "lines" are a continuum—a solid wave of sediments that gets deeper as one goes north. A chart could indicate the location of these sediments at, say, ten million year intervals.

As the limy fossil sediment line is carried north, more sediments are piled on top. In other words, present-day sediments are now at the surface of the sea floor under the equator. But equatorial sediments forty million years old are found deep down in the drill hole to the north of the line. The farther north one goes the older the deposits and the deeper one has to drill to reach them.

A striking product of this sediment research technique has just been revealed. December 1971 saw results from corings into the oldest Pacific floor rock yet drilled by the scientists aboard the *Glomar Challenger* (as reported by Dr. Bruce C. Heezen of Lamont-Doherty Geological Observatory, Columbia University, and Dr. Ian D. MacGregor, University of California at Davis). They showed conclusively that the sea floor has moved northwestward over 2,000 miles during the past 125 million years. The drill cores from sedimentary rock southeast of Japan included layers of equatorial fossils. By comparing the sediment found in successive drill cores, Dr. Heezen and Dr. MacGregor not only clocked the movement, but found that the motion of the ocean floor was not steady; that it would at times temporarily reverse direction. Such reversal was indicated by thin films of abyssal clay separating the chalk and flint deposits being transported northward.

During the same drilling series, the men on *Challenger* measured the depth of layers of ash fallout from Asiatic volcanoes. They wanted to know how rapidly the ash was moving back toward the landmass. Calculations showed that the Pacific Plate is plunging beneath the Asian continent at the rate of four inches per year! These corings, incidentally, were the deepest ever accomplished on the Pacific floor—the drill bit passed down through 20,312 feet of water and then on down another 1,237 feet into the rock.

Dr. Jerry Matthews, a marine geologist at Scripps specializing in sedimentation studies, brought back from the western Pacific some of the oldest fossils and minerals yet scraped from seamounts. Estimated age of the fossils is 135 million years. These precious bits of the past are now being analyzed in an attempt to pin the age down more closely. "If we can gather enough well preserved material," Matthews declares, "we will know more about what is the oldest chain of seamounts we've yet sampled. It's possible we may find that these seamounts run in a completely different direction. We know that the fossils are Cretaceous, but that still gives us a period of some forty million years [from 100 to 140 million years ago] to play with. We need to get closer than that."

Using a petrographic microscope and polarized light to show optical properties, Dr. Matthews and his colleagues are also studying the origin of the samples of volcanic rock taken in the same dredge hauls. Further observation under a light microscope will show the texture and how the materials came together.

A postscript on the proof of plate movement is that not all sunken mountains have coral caps. Two possible explanations have been offered:

1. The peaks went down too fast for the coral reef to keep up, or
2. The seamounts moved out of the equatorial region of coral growth during the Cretaceous Period—when coral had temporarily ceased to grow.

"We need to know," says Dr. Winterer, "more about why they sink and the rate at which they go down. We think that as vulcanism heats up, then cools down, the plate may shrink as much as a few percent of its total thickness. The history of subsidence must then be a clue to the cooling of the plates.

"Our paleolatitude studies indicate that some volcanoes appear to have shifted 30 degrees north of the equator."

Questions that Dr. Winterer and his colleagues are now seeking to answer include:

1. What is the seamount chain's relationship to and movement over the convection plumes (hot spots) in the mantle?
2. What more can be learned about the sinking history of seamounts?
3. Where are the magmas formed? That is, are the molten lava cores created in the crust or below in the mantle?
4. Do the directions the seamounts have traveled provide positive clues to the motion of the Pacific Plate? and

5. The question that could complicate a lot of theories: does the underlying material also move—with the relative motion of both crust and mantle producing the journey of the seamount?

Dr. Winterer now has indications that whereas the volcanic chain is moving at a given rate, the underlying material may be moving at the same rate in the opposite direction. This latter movement could account for changes in latitude.

"We know," Winterer declares, "that crustal plates are moving at about one to 20 centimeters per year in various directions—apart from the ridges, together at the continental edge, or sideways, as along California's San Andreas Fault. The Western Hemisphere is moving away from Africa and Europe at about two inches per year. We believe that Africa and South America were one landmass only 130 million years ago.

"What I want to know now," he concludes, "is what motion the mantle is taking with respect to the spin axis of the earth?"

So it appears that seamounts offer a way of clocking the movements of our very active and continually shifting planetary surface.

Dr. Winterer and Dr. Matthews will be among the group of scientists due to be south of Christmas Island—almost on the equator—in late 1972 aboard the *Thomas Washington* as part of an expedition dubbed "South Tow." By using a wide variety of techniques—dredging, coring, (sound) reflection profiles, magnetic surveys, measurements of deep currents, and photographs of the deep bottom—they hope to find more pieces to fill in the seamount-earth movement puzzle.

Other researchers in the expedition will work with a deep tow vehicle called *FISH* (Fully Instrumented Submersible Housing) which will record echo soundings on the bottom; provide sonar soundings to chart bottom penetration and record sideways pinging, out to 1,200 feet from the sender; plus registering fine-scale magnetic anomalies; determining micro temperature structure across the bottom; and finally taking photographs of the deep sea floor geomorphology.

Deep drilling along the sides of seamounts in this area by the men on the *Glomar Challenger* is expected to produce needed supporting evidence.

The earth sciences are now in the midst of an explosive phase of increasing technology and rapidly mounting new data. Old theories are being buried (figuratively) in the recovered sediments, and new concepts are springing up in many quarters. The premise of our planet as a place whose component parts are still moving about extensively has been proved. With each answer, there are a dozen new questions. However, the pieces of the puzzle are being assembled.

The Annual Meeting of the Western Section of the Geological Society of America, held in Honolulu March 29 to April 1, 1972, had an entire section devoted to chains of islands, seamounts, and the hot spots. The various theories and speculations were presented and evaluated. One thing is clear: the sea harbors the ultimate answer to how our planet works.

# 5

# *OCEAN RESOURCES*

# 22. The Nation and the Sea–A New Awareness

ROBERT M. WHITE 1975

National policies reflect national concern. Nowhere is this currently more apparent than in the increasing attention being given to marine programs by the Administration and the Congress. This attention reflects the growing national awareness that oceanic resources promise at least partial solutions to some of the most pressing social and economic problems facing the nation and the world.

Man has reached a critical juncture in his relationship with his environment. His supply of both food and raw materials is threatened, and the threat will hang over him for a long time to come. Viewed against such needs, the fossil fuels, living resources, and minerals in and under the sea will play an increasingly large role in national efforts to cope with the problems facing mankind, now and in the future. Oceanic resources, however, must be developed with minimum harm to the marine environment.

## HIGH-LEVEL RECOGNITION

The need for a balanced approach is recognized at the highest levels of government, and has given new impetus to development of marine policies and programs designed to provide an effective national framework for both progress and conservation.

Recognizing the growing importance of the oceans, Congress in 1966 enacted legislation to establish the National Council on Marine Resources and Engineering Development and the Commission on Marine Sciences, Engineering, and Resources (known as the Stratton Commission).

Largely as a result of the Stratton Commission's report (published in 1969), the National Oceanic and Atmospheric Administration (NOAA) was established (in 1970) to provide a Federal focus for many civilian aspects of the nation's ocean activities. The following year, the National Advisory Committee on Oceans and Atmosphere was formed and the Federal Council for Science and Technology established the Interagency Committee on Marine Science and Engineering to succeed the National Council. Those steps represented a systematic evolution in the institutions for dealing with ocean policy considerations to meet national needs. Recent events, however, have led to further

Dr. Robert M. White is Administrator of the Commerce Department's National Oceanic and Atmospheric Administration (NOAA), Rockville, Maryland. He has also been Administrator of the Environmental Science Services Administration (ESSA) in the Department of Commerce and Chief of the U.S. Weather Bureau, now NOAA's National Weather Service. He has authored over thirty articles and papers.

From *Environmental Data Service,* March, pp. 3-11, 1975. Reprinted with light editing and with permission of the author and *Environmental Data Service,* NOAA, Rockville, Maryland.

action by Congress and the Executive Branch to strengthen and guide marine development.

The National Ocean Policy Study (NOPS) of the Senate was initiated in February 1974. Participants include the members of the Senate Committee on Commerce, representatives of other Senate committees responsible for ocean affairs, and other Senators who are members at large. To date, NOPS has focused on two areas: the impact of oil and gas exploration and drilling activities on the coastal zone environment, and Federal involvement in ocean affairs. In addition, NOPS has sponsored studies on ocean data and instrumentation, and on the economic value of ocean resources. Many other aspects of ocean affairs will also receive attention. The end result of the studies will be new legislation designed to improve the conduct of ocean science and the use of marine resources.

The Office of Technology Assessment (OTA), established as an advisory body to Congress early last year, is also studying the impact of offshore energy operations on coastal areas, including the effects of offshore oil drilling, and the construction of offshore nuclear plants and anchorages for supertankers. The areas chosen for study are off New Jersey and Delaware. OTA seeks to determine the direct and secondary impacts of multiple offshore activities on coastal States, and will compare them with the effects of alternative development plans. These efforts will be complemented by policy attention at the cabinet level in the Executive Branch.

## RECENT LEGISLATION

The evolution of national ocean policies and programs has been strongly influenced by recent legislation enacted to meet emerging national needs—specifically: the National Environmental Policy Act of 1969; the Federal Water Pollution Control Act Amendment of 1972; the Coastal Zone Management Act of 1972; the Marine Protection, Research and Sanctuaries Act of 1972 (ocean dumping); the Marine Mammal Protection Act of 1972; the Ports and Waterways Safety Act of 1972; the Endangered Species Act of 1973; the Special Energy Research and Development Appropriation Act of 1974; and the Solar Energy Research, Development, and Demonstration Act of 1974.

Major thrusts of the current national marine program concern development of marine energy and food resources, environmental protection and the preservation of endangered species, management of coastal zones, and cooperation with other nations in other areas of mutual interest and concern. The same program areas will continue to receive priority attention for years to come.

## ENERGY

The Outer Continental Shelf (OCS) continues to offer the greatest national potential for new oil and gas development, and the Federal Government is, therefore, accelerating a leasing schedule for marine lands. To hasten development of new OCS leases, Congress has directed reactivation of three NOAA oceanographic vessels that had been out of service for several years because of spending curtailments. The NOAA ships will be used in joint programs of the U.S. Geological Survey, Bureau of Land Management, and NOAA to gather baseline data needed to make critical environmental assessments in the OCS leasing program.

Providing docking facilities for supertankers is another way in which marine facilities are used to increase supplies of oil and natural gas. No existing U.S. port receiving crude petroleum shipments can accommodate the superships, and it appears that few, if any, can economically be deepened.

In December 1971, the U.S. Army Corps of Engineers began studying potential U.S. sites for three types of deepwater facilities—monobuoy arrays, mooring platforms, and artificial islands, all connected to shorebased storage tanks by submarine pipelines. In addition, the Maritime Administration has supported a detailed study of potential sites for artificial islands along the Atlantic and Gulf coasts.

In 1972, NOAA's Environmental Data Service published two special supertanker studies. The first, *"Environmental Guide for Seven U.S. Ports and Harbor Approaches,"* was prepared for the President's Council on Environmental Quality and examined coastal locations from Maine to Texas. Later, when the Gulf Coast area was chosen for initial development, the Army Corps of Engineers asked for a more detailed study of the potential sites selected. That request led to the *"Environmental Guide for the U.S. Gulf Coast."*

At present, monobuoy mooring appears to be the most promising type of facility. It reduces the risk of collision or grounding and permits unloading of larger tankers (thus reducing the number of transfer operations and possible spills). Oil industry groups are currently in advanced stages of planning for monobuoy facilities along the Gulf Coast and elsewhere.

Increasing petroleum supplies is essential. But, in the final analysis, the world's petroleum resources are finite and eventually new energy sources will be needed.

National energy requirements are expected to triple in the next 25 years, and the use of electricity to meet those growing needs is expected to increase even more rapidly. Conservation of energy resources by all users obviously becomes an urgent national need. Nuclear power, which now produces about 7 percent of the country's electricity, is expected to provide 50 percent of U.S. needs 25 years from now. As with oil and gas development, the most promising sites for nuclear powerplant construction are offshore.

The Atomic Energy Commission, in cooperation with the President's Council on Environmental Quality, NOAA, the Department of the Interior, and other agencies, is conducting comprehensive studies to provide the environmental baseline data and information needed to construct offshore nuclear facilities and to prevent damage to the ocean environment. The studies include assessments of potential damage resulting from hurricanes, storm surges, and other natural phenomena, during both construction and operation. They also examine the effect that such installations might have on other uses of the coastal zone.

The Ocean Thermal Energy Conversion Program, initiated by the National Science Foundation, is evaluating the technical and economic feasibility of ocean-based and near-shore powerplants capable of converting ocean heat into electric power. Developments in that area could offer new energy sources in the decades ahead.

## FOOD

Recent world food problems have led to greater appreciation of the role the coupled ocean-atmosphere system plays in global grain production. In 1974, severe food shortages caused widespread hunger in parts of Africa and India. Those shortages can be traced to climatic fluctuations that many scientists believe are associated with changes in the world's oceans, and give more urgency to development of global ocean monitoring programs.

Congress recently approved funding for SEASAT, NASA's ocean satellite, which should enormously enhance ocean-monitoring capabilities. SEASAT will be able to measure ocean topography, wave spectra, sea-surface temperatures, and ice conditions, as well as wind speeds and directions and atmospheric water vapor content. And it will collect all such data concurrently, routinely, and on a global basis.

Although the ocean, by influencing weather and climate, has an indirect effect on world grain supplies, improved management and use of fishery resources are more directly related. Fishery conservation and management traditionally have suffered from a lack of adequate biological data. A new program, MARMAP (Marine Resource

Monitoring and Prediction Program), now provides far more data to those charged with fishery conservation than they have ever had before. MARMAP data are currently being used as a basis for fishery management by the International Commission for the Northwest Atlantic Fisheries and other international fisheries commissions.

## MINERALS, MONITORING, AND MAMMALS

The United States is almost totally dependent on imports for manganese, nickel, and cobalt, yet extensive areas of the ocean floor are overlain with manganese nodules rich in those minerals. The technology for nodule recovery and processing is being developed to permit commercial operations by the end of the decade. To prevent possible environmental damage by deep sea mining activities, NOAA has initiated a Deep Ocean Mining Environmental Studies (DOMES) project, which will provide the information needed to develop environmental impact statements and to monitor environmental effects of prototype equipment tests.

Under the Marine Protection, Research, and Sanctuaries Act of 1972, the Department of Commerce is responsible for researching and monitoring programs concerned with the effects of ocean pollution and other man-induced changes on the marine environment. Those programs, developed and carried out by NOAA, are designed to provide the information needed by the Environmental Protection Agency to improve regulation and control of ocean dumping and pollution discharge. In March 1974, NOAA made its first report to Congress on Federal research concerning the effects of pollutants on the marine environment.

Marine Ecosystems Analysis (MESA) program efforts are concentrated in regional projects to develop information on the biological, physical, and chemical processes of selected coastal areas, to improve the ability to assess and predict the impact of man's activities. The New York Bight, first area selected for study, is one of the most complex and heavily used U.S. coastal areas. The MESA New York Bight Project is an integrated study involving NOAA and other Federal and State agencies, as well as industry and a number of universities.

Several agencies of the Department of the Interior also have developed programs concerned with preserving the quality of the marine environment. Among them are the Bureau of Land Management's Outer Continental Shelf environmental program, and the U.S. Geological Survey's "streamgaging" program, which provides data needed for pollution control in estuaries, bays, and nearshore areas.

The National Science Foundation's Research Applied to National Needs program supports regional studies of coastal zone pollutants. In one such project, a four-institution consortium in the Chesapeake Bay area is studying domestic waste problems to develop criteria for sewage effluent loading in Chesapeake Bay.

In 1973, the Environmental Protection Agency issued new regulations to govern ocean dumping of all wastes except dredge spoil, which is regulated by the Army Corps of Engineers. The Corps is currently engaged in a major program to develop techniques for determining and reducing the polluting effects of dredge materials.

In addition to pollution control, environmental protection encompasses the preservation of threatened species. Under the authority of the Marine Mammal Protection Act of 1972 and the Endangered Species Act of 1973, NOAA and the Department of the Interior are supporting regulatory and scientific programs for the conservation of whales, seals, and other marine mammals, as well as endangered species of fish, waterfowl, and other wildlife.

## COASTAL ZONE AND SEA GRANT

As indicated by recent and pending legislation, the United States is becoming increasingly concerned about the impact of development upon coastal areas. Vulnerable nursery and spawning grounds in coastal wetlands as well as the basic economic and labor patterns of coastal communities could be affected. To deal with the problem, the Coastal Zone Management Act of 1972 established the Coastal Zone Management Program, administered by NOAA, to provide a balance between economic development and the preservation of environmental quality in the coastal zone. The program is broad in scope and involves consideration of ecological, cultural, historical, and aesthetic values–as well as the requirements for economic development. The Federal Government provides guidance and support; state governments are responsible for coastal zone management.

By the end of 1974, 31 of 34 coastal states and territories, including the Great Lakes states, had been funded for development of coastal zone management programs. The Coastal Zone Management Program, together with the Sea Grant Program, provides the mechanisms needed for comprehensive planning and management of coastal zones.

The Sea Grant Program was established in 1966. It has a three-pronged mission involving (1) applied research, (2) education and training, and (3) providing of advisory and extension services across the whole range of ocean problems. Nearly 50 U.S. institutions now have Sea Grant programs, and some 600 important projects in mariculture, marine resource recovery, coastal zone management and protection, and other areas have been initiated or completed. Sea Grant advisory services have also developed rapidly, and currently about 200 agents work in 22 States. Last year the Secretary of Commerce designated the University of California as the seventh Sea Grant college. The other six are: Texas A&M, Oregon State University, and the Universities of Rhode Island, Washington, Hawaii, and Wisconsin.

## INTERNATIONAL DEVELOPMENTS

The United States firmly supports a comprehensive, broad-based treaty on the Law of the Sea and will continue to work toward a satisfactory international agreement on the oceans at the next session of the Third United Nations Law of the Sea Conference, to be held in Geneva in the spring. Such agreement should permit development of deep-sea marine mineral resources beyond the jurisdiction of any nation, with appropriate environmental safeguards, and should guarantee freedom of access for private companies, under reasonable conditions, coupled with security of tenure.

The United States also supports establishment of a 200-mile economic zone wherein coastal nations would have sovereign rights to develop seabed mineral resources (subject to certain international responsibilities, including environmental protection and the right to regulate offshore installations affecting their economic interests). Coastal nations would also have exclusive rights to manage living marine resources, subject to certain obligations. Special treatment would be given to anadromous species, such as salmon, and to highly migratory species, such as tuna.

Besides the Law of the Sea Conference, the United States has been an active participant in the work of UNESCO's Intergovernmental Oceanographic Commission and in a number of major, multinational oceanographic field experiments. For example, the recently completed Atlantic Tropical Experiment of the Global Atmospheric Research Program (GATE), a joint program of the World Meteorological Organization and the International Council of Scientific Unions, was an enormously successful 3-month air/sea study in the South Atlantic off Africa, and involving 40 vessels from 15 nations.

Project FAMOUS (French-American Mid-Ocean Underseas Study) is another exciting and productive cooperative international effort. Project FAMOUS field investigations, completed last summer, were conducted along the Mid-Atlantic Ridge some 300 miles southwest of the Azores. The investigations, which required 3 years of intensive planning and preparation, involved the ALVIN, a United States research submersible, and the ARCHIMEDES and CYANA, two French submersibles. In some 50 dives–to depths of

3,000 meters—it was possible for the first time to obtain evidence by direct human observation to confirm and advance contemporary concepts of plate tectonics and seafloor spreading. The observations provided new scientific insights on continental drift, earthquakes, geothermal energy, and evolution of minerals deep within the Earth.

In June 1973, the United States and USSR signed an agreement calling for bilateral cooperation in exploration of the global sea. A joint committee was established and, at its first meeting in February 1974, agreed on cooperative projects in six areas of ocean investigation: air/sea interaction; planetary-scale ocean currents and other aspects of ocean dynamics; geochemistry and marine chemistry of the world ocean; geological and geophysical investigations; biological productivity; and the intercalibration and standardization of oceanographic instrumentation and methodology.

## PROBLEMS AND PROSPECTS

There are, of course, serious obstacles that must be overcome in successfully meeting U.S. national needs for ocean services and resources. One of the most challenging involves the fisheries situation.

Mankind is rapidly reaching the point where the capacity of the world's fishing fleets will exceed the capacity of the oceans to sustain the fish stocks on which all depend. Several important species found off the coast of the United States have already been seriously depleted. To date, international efforts to develop satisfactory conservation measures have failed.

International Law of the Sea conferences may well provide a new opportunity to conserve such vital ocean resources. The proposed extension of national economic jurisdiction to a 200-mile zone would give the United States exclusive management authority over its own zone's living resources, many of which are now fished by foreign fleets.

In addition, NOAA, in cooperation with the Department of the Interior, State governments, and recreational and commercial fisheries organizations, is currently preparing a national fisheries plan. The plan will include contingency arrangements for fishery management in cooperative efforts of the States, regional groups, and the Federal Government.

Another serious problem facing the United States involves maintaining an oceanographic fleet adequate to provide the information needed to map and chart the oceans, survey their resources, assess and ameliorate environmental hazards, and conduct the basic research upon which future advances will be built. Ship support as a percentage of total program budgets is declining. Part of the decline can be compensated for by the use of other platforms, such as buoys and satellites, but eventually it will be necessary to make the investment required to continue needed ship operations and to replace vessels that are worn out.

Budget constraints of the last several years caused the retirement of 10 old ships without replacement. In addition, four NOAA ships, all less than 10 years old, were temporarily out of service last year. The pinch on ship-operating funds also is being aggravated by escalating fuel and maintenance costs. Like the rest of the nation, ship operating agencies will have to watch dollars closely and spend them where they are most needed.

Ships, satellites, aircraft, and buoys provide the most economical and efficient means of gathering much of the data needed about ocean features and processes. The national capability for ocean exploration is deficient, however, so long as it does not have adequate submersible and habitat facilities for manned undersea exploration.

In the 1960s, a great variety of submersibles and undersea habitats was built, but most were engineering experiments and are now "on the shelf." At present, the Navy is the only Federal agency owning a submersible, and NOAA, through its Manned Undersea Science and Technology Office, has assumed the task of coordinating civilian undersea operations. NOAA's efforts to help preserve the technology needed for underseas oceanographic exploration are expanding, but the United States well may face a future shortage of undersea platforms. It is to be hoped that NOAA, the Navy, and the National Science Foundation will be able to provide joint support for at least modest efforts to maintain the U.S. manned underseas capability.

Despite the problems which lie ahead, the U.S. marine program today is both healthy and growing. Ocean resources are no longer considered minor supplements to land resources but, rather, because of the rich potential of the sea, are viewed as part of the solution to some of the most serious national and international problems. The new national awareness which has developed will shape and structure marine programs for a long time to come. Priorities will have to be reassessed to serve the greatest national needs, and intensive interagency cooperation will be required to ensure maximum value for available resources.

The future promises discipline and hard choices, but also an increasingly important role for marine programs in the economic life of the nation.

# 23. Opportunities to Increase Food Production from the World's Oceans

DAYTON L. ALVERSON 1975

The potential of the oceans to provide food for mankind has been the subject of considerable debate, particularly during the last two decades. News coverage of this subject must be both confusing and frustrating to the public. Monday's "daily" may cast the ocean's living resources as the answer to the world's food need, but by Friday the same paper will carry a story discounting altogether the capacity of the oceans to contribute to the increasing world demand. Reality lies between these extremes. Because of a growing concern regarding food supplies throughout the world, exemplified by the recent U.N. World Food Conference, it is timely and appropriate to review the options available to increase fish production from the 70 percent of the world's surface that is covered by the ocean.

Much of the confusion over ocean food potentials has stemmed from different scientific views over (1) the efficiency by which carbon (fixed by plant photosynthesis) is transferred to higher levels in the food chain and (2) factors which have or will limit utilization of the biological material produced. Confusion regarding the ocean food potentials can be minimized if we examine the biological basis upon which fisheries may be further developed; and then evaluate technical, economic, and social-political factors which can influence future production trends.

## THE BIOLOGICAL BASIS FOR EXPANSION

Predictions regarding the ocean's potential to produce food have been based on extrapolations of total catch trends, biological surveys made in different regions of the world, and the amount of carbon fixed annually through photosynthesis. The forecasts of the total fish catches[1] based on production trends or biological sampling data have been relatively conservative, ranging from 55-80 million metric tons (Schaefer & Alverson, 1968). The lower of these values has already been exceeded. These conservative estimates, however, were generally based on the potential for traditionally exploited spe-

1. Estimates are usually concerned with expected yields from wild stocks including sharks, fishes, and shellfishes.

Dr. Dayton L. Alverson is a fisheries biologist with the National Marine Fisheries Service of the National Oceanic and Atmospheric Administration, Rockville, Maryland.

From *Marine Technology Society Journal*, Vol. 9, No. 5, pp. 33-40, 1975. Reprinted with light editing and with permission of the author and the *Marine Technology Society*.

cies (cods, tuna, flounders, herrings, shrimps, etc.). More interesting, forecasts of possible production have resulted from estimates based on primary production in the world's ocean. Authors who have dabbled in these mental gymnastics have come up with annual values ranging from 100-2,000 million metric tons (Gulland, 1971).

The wide range of forecasts may cast doubt on the validity of the latter technique; however, several factors account for the disparate values. The range is partially due to differences in the calculated total primary production, but in recent years calculations of the amount of organic carbon fixed annually through photosynthesis have converged; values ranging from 1.9-2.3 $\times$ $10^{10}$ tons annually (Moiseev, 1971) are now commonly accepted. The variation in the estimated amount of fish that might be produced from "fixed carbon" largely resulted from different views of the trophic level at which the harvest is or could be taken and coefficients associated with material transfer to higher trophic levels.

The pragmatist may feel estimates based on carbon production are academic and provide little in the way of useful information concerning species types or areas of the world where fisheries might be expanded. All in all, however, food chain dynamic studies have added more to our knowledge of biological production in the seas than other techniques; and those who find a certain fascination with theoretical approaches may wish to review the works of Dr. Vishniac of the University of Rochester (Anon., 1971). He has examined the problem, starting with radiant energy of the sun in watts; calculated the earth's calorie intercept; and, step by step, led us to a forecasted fish production of 240 million metric tons.

Although major portions of the world's oceans are frequently termed "biological deserts," the quantity of biological material produced is tremendous; and the amount of first-stage carnivores may exceed 1.9-2.3 $\times$ $10^9$ metric tons per year. But such a figure is of little help in understanding the potential for expansion of traditional marine fisheries. Most recent estimates associated with the biological basis for developing conventional marine fisheries range from 100-250 million metric tons—2-4 times the existing world catch.

Opportunities for further development of traditional fisheries appear best in the southern hemisphere. For demersal stocks, increases can be expected off the east and west coasts of South America, Australia, New Zealand, and Southeast Asia. Further growth of demersal fisheries should also occur off the west coast of Africa, and some expansion of reef fishes in the tropic and subtropic areas is feasible. Pelagic stocks, however (tunas, jacks, anchovies, sauries, etc.), constitute the largest underexploited resource available for increased production of traditional forms. Potential growth for fisheries based on these species is best in the coastal regions of the southern hemisphere and Indian Ocean.

If we consider the unconventional forms, the biological basis for expansion is enormous. The opportunities, however, appear best in several groups (i.e., krill, red crab, squid, lanternfish, and seaweed).

The most frequently mentioned unconventional form is the Antarctic krill (*Euphausia superba*). Over the past several years, Soviet and Japanese scientists have investigated the distribution, abundance, and utilization of Antarctic krill, which reaches a maximum size of about 70 mm and has a circumpolar distribution between the Antarctic convergence (50-60° S) and Antarctica (Anon., 1974). Krill are generally found in the upper layers to depths of 250 meters and swarm at or near the surface. Moiseev (1971) reports the swarms may attain a density of 10-16 kg per cubic meter. Investigations by Soviet and Japanese scientists have generally been concentrated within the arc intercepting Antarctica, from 60°W long. to 90°E long. Soviet scientists found highest concentrations in and around the Scotia Sea, while Japanese investigations have had somewhat better luck in waters further east.

Recent Soviet estimates of standing stock of Antarctic krill are from 800 to 5,000 million tons (Lyubimova et al., 1973) with an annual yield forecast of at least 100 million tons (Lagunov et al., 1973). This yield forecast seems small compared to the standing stock estimates, but it does closely fall within the range of forecasts made by other authors, e.g., Gulland (1971), 200 million tons, and Omura (1973), 100-200 million tons per year. These figures greatly exceed the present total annual world catch of all aquatic resources.

Another crustacean that reaches a moderate size is the red crab (*Pleuroncodes planipes*), one of the principal food items of tuna in the Eastern Tropical Pacific. Similar to, but slightly smaller than, the "langostino," which is heavily harvested off Chile for human consumption, red crabs frequently occur in large swarms near the surface. Longhurst (1968) suggests the use of the resource off the Pacific Coast of North America as food and estimates a potential annual production of 30-300 thousand tons of these crustaceans off lower California and Mexico. More recent studies (Anon., 1970) suggest the potential yield may be even larger.

The scientific basis for forecasting latent squid resources is of a more speculative nature. Voss (1973) suggests that the worldwide cephalopod catch from continental shelf waters alone could be increased from the present level of 1 million metric tons to about 8 million metric tons per year. Oceanic squid yield, estimated mainly on the basis of the predation by sperm whales, is suggested to be more than 50 times that amount. Moiseev (1971) lends some supporting evidence to squid abundance, noting their shells are common in marine sediments and that several species are widespread in the pelagic and neritic zones of tropical, subtropical, and boreal regions of the world.

Marine biologists have also speculated on the potential for developing fisheries for lanternfish. Gulland (1971) estimates they could provide a harvest up to 100 million metric tons per year. The Myctophid family is widespread throughout the world's ocean; and recent investigations of midwater fishes in the Atlantic Ocean (Krefft, 1974) have extended our knowledge of their distribution features. Although our knowledge of small, ubiquitous, pelagic fishes is still sparse, lanternfish, along with other small oceanic species, may produce a sustainable yield which exceeds 100-200 million metric tons per year.

The world harvest of seaweeds probably now exceeds one million metric tons per year. The potential for increase is not well known; and while no quantitative estimates have been attempted, Gulland (1971) notes that the majority of the existing production comes from a small area in the northwest Pacific. Unless natural production in other parts of the world is very much lower, the present world harvest could certainly be increased several-fold.

My conclusion, in terms of biological potential, may be summed up simply. The oceans do produce enormous quantities of biological material. Even in terms of conventional forms, the surplus biological production may be 2-4 times that which is now harvested. If one turns to unconventional forms, limited to species for which we have some basis for quantifying their potential, the biological basis for expansion is about an order of magnitude greater than the current world marine fish harvest.

The foregoing discussion of biological bases for expansion of fisheries was confined to wild stocks. Opportunities also exist to improve ocean production through ecological modifications, transplantations, and aquaculture.

## THE TECHNOLOGICAL-ECONOMIC BASIS FOR EXPANSION

Since World War II, there has been a rapid advancement in fishing technology, particularly as it concerns vessels, electronics, and materials used in fishing activities. Most of the fishing fleets that were destroyed during the war were rapidly replaced with modern vessels. Improvements in radar, sonar, radio navigational systems, etc., greatly enhanced the development of offshore fishing. Electronic advances were augmented by the introduction of synthetic fibers and the use of hydraulic power to operate a variety of deck machinery. These changes led to increased safety at sea, precision navigation, improved nets, reduced manual labor, and improved fish detection.

By the early 1970s, fishing had become a global activity. Japanese and Soviet vessels were investigating the Antarctic for the abundant krill; tuna fishing was being undertaken in the north and south Atlantic and Pacific Oceans and throughout most of the Indian Ocean; European fisheries had expanded north to the Arctic icepacks; and most of the productive continental shelf areas of the world were subject to intense fishing. In terms of both conventional and unconventional species, the fishing and support vessels currently used are capable of operating anywhere in the world.

Existing fish detection and extraction systems are adequate for expanded operations and for harvesting any unexploited concentrations of demersal or pelagic fishes. We might then be rather exuberant about the technological basis for increasing the harvest of conventional forms. The capacity of the existing technology, however, must be tempered by the fact that most large demersal and pelagic fish stocks are already under exploitation. Furthermore, although many stocks collectively may comprise large resources, they are sparsely distributed per unit volume of water and their effective utilization necessitates development of more efficient extraction systems.

Moiseev (1971), for example, notes that any further substantial increase in total catch will depend on man's ability to artificially concentrate fish, improve the efficiency of fishing gear, and learn to control the behavior of fish. Despite dramatic changes in the size and design of fishing vessels, propulsion engines, electronics, and materials, there have been no major alterations during this century in the basic techniques used to extract wild stocks from the ocean. Fishing gear used may have increased in size and become mechanized, but we still harvest most fish and shellfish from the sea with nets and hooks-and-lines.

The variety of exotic techniques that have been tried in the last two decades (electrofishing, lights, air-bubble curtains, etc.), have not contributed substantially to increased fish production. Major increases in harvesting conventional species will require a technological breakthrough to allow fishing at low-stock densities. Although some progress has been achieved in this area, one cannot be overly optimistic about solving the economic and technical problems confronting use of abundant species which are distributed sparsely over large geographic areas or throughout the water column.

The chances to resolve technological problems inhibiting use of some of the unconventional species appear better. Most of the unconventional species under consideration aggregate in a way that permits their detection and harvest with some minor modifications using traditional fishing techniques. In addition, progress has been made during the past several years in their processing and marketing.

Antarctic krill can be detected by sight at the sea surface or by acoustical methods and can be fished using midwater and surface trawls and purse seines. Recent catches have been promising, particularly with midwater trawls. In early 1974, a 1,500 gross ton Japanese freezer trawler reportedly caught 645 tons of krill in 2½ months of fishing. The catch taken with a midwater trawl, much like those used by small inshore boats, was about 1½ tons per hour trawling. The Soviets have had similar results using a small-framed net and midwater trawl (Anon., 1974).

Most experts feel considerable improvement in catching efficiency can be achieved by using larger and better-designed trawls. Problems, however, still plague the harvest of krill, especially those of location and detection. Although krill frequently swarm at the surface, recent studies show they may migrate to deeper waters where they are difficult to detect. Development of a special acoustical technique for detection is under consideration. If the fisheries are to prove successful, the variability in occurrence of swarms needs to be defined, and the environmental factors influencing their formation and distribution (temperature and currents) evaluated. The latter could be important in developing methods for locating good fishing areas.

Although major interest in fishing euphausiids has centered in the Antarctic region, a substantial euphausiid fishery was initiated by Japanese fishermen several decades ago in the western Pacific and annual production of *Euphausia pacifica* has reached a level of 10,000 tons (Komaki, 1974). The fishery is conducted around Kinkazan on the Pacific Coast of Japan and in nearshore waters of Yamaguchi-ken on the Japan Sea. Small scale euphausiid fisheries have also been established in the northeast Atlantic off Norway—the product being used as food for aquaculture projects.

Krill is processed in a number of ways. The Japanese have generally frozen the product in a raw state, after boiling, although they also have experimented with drying the product. The Soviets have produced a shrimp paste by squeezing the liquids and exoskeleton out of the tissue under pressure and coagulating the proteins contained in the liquid by heating. The yield of krill paste is between 17 percent and 25 percent, depending on size. The paste is frozen into blocks, transported to the Soviet Union, and sold directly as "Ocean Paste." It is generally mixed with cheese, butter, and other products. The paste contains 13 percent to 20 percent protein and is reportedly high in essential amino acids.

Similar studies have been conducted on the harvesting and processing of red crabs. In trawling for Pacific hake off Baja California, scientists had difficulty in obtaining fish samples without clogging their nets with quantities of red crab. Although some hake and other fishes were caught, the most prominent echotraces were found to result from pelagic crabs. Catch rates ranging from 1½ tons per 13 minutes of trawling and 5 tons per 30 minutes of trawling were reported. The scientists suggested that at least 20 tons per hour could be caught with appropriate midwater trawl gear. There are, however, the usual problems that must be resolved before we can expect their commercial production. The yield using current technology is low—from 8 percent to 10 percent of the body weight. This may be increased, however, by utilizing pressure techniques to recover edible portions. Chemical studies of galatheid crabs suggest a protein content of about 11 percent (Spinelli et al., 1974).

A variety of existing fishing techniques can be used to harvest squids and lanternfish. It is known that species of squid can be attracted to light, and an experimental light pump system has been successfully used in Monterey Bay, California. If the market demand for squid increases, it is quite likely that existing harvesting systems can be utilized in areas where concentrations are known to occur. Commercial exploitation of lanternfishes using trawls has already started off South Africa. The annual catch of this unconventional group has grown to over 20,000 tons.

There are several technological options available to increase food production from the oceans. We can develop the technology for improving extractive capabilities or we can also increase the amount of available protein through elimination of waste—that is, more efficient use of what we now catch.

One step towards this goal could be achieved by recovering higher yields of edible fish that are currently harvested. For example, flesh separating machines have recently been introduced that squeeze the flesh from the skin and bones of fish and pass the flesh through perforations on stainless steel plates or drums. The skin and bones do not pass through the perforation, and hence, are separated for the nonedible portions. Experiments on a variety of fish suggest that the technique may increase the usable yield 50 percent. The technique is currently employed on a fairly large scale in Japan and is finding a growing use in other areas of the world. Flesh separating machines are a classic example of a technological breakthrough which increases food supplies by eliminating waste and which may represent a large step forward in the total utilization of fisheries products (Miyauchi & Steinberg, 1970).

Other gains can be achieved through elimination of spoilage, transfer of fish from industrial products to human consumption, and utilization of species which are caught and discarded at sea.

Discards currently represent an unreported harvest which in some fisheries is substantial and which could be eaten themselves or used in products such as minced fish. In addition, catches which are used for production of fishmeal can be gradually transferred to human consumption. There is already a noticeable tendency to use less of the preferred food species, such as herring and mackerel, for fishmeal and more for human consumption. Such trends will have both economic and social advantages, particularly as it relates to improving the total quantity of protein available for direct consumption.

## SOCIAL-POLITICAL BASIS FOR EXPANSION

An obvious condition for continued growth and maintenance of the marine fisheries is a comprehensive arrangement for their international control based on sound research and logical management procedures (Holt, 1973). World fisheries are currently in a turmoil stemming from overfishing problems and changing jurisdictional philosophies which are under consideration at the United Nations Law of the Sea Conference. Although the character of the total package which may emerge from the Conference is difficult to predict, one can foresee major changes leading to coastal state jurisdiction over resources in a zone adjacent to their territorial sea—e.g., the 200-mile economic zone.

Achieving national jurisdictional aspirations, however, will not alone solve overfishing problems (Alverson & Paulik, 1973; Holt, 1973). A clarification of changing legal concepts as they deal with jurisdiction over resources or sections of the aquatic environment may be required before radical new management principles can surface. Nevertheless, fundamental management problems will remain; and the solution will depend on the power given the management agencies, their depth of understanding of the reaction of resources to natural and human events, and the willingness of governments to assume responsibilities delegated to them or acquired, including the promulgation and enforcement of appropriate regulations.

It is obvious that slicing the ocean into a series of ocean provinces may create new problems. Management could suffer, particularly if adjacent countries assume they can "go it alone." Evolution of appropriate regional or international institutions will be a requisite to improved management and improved production for the world's ocean. Without control of total fishing effort and its distribution by region, species, and among countries, improvements in technology may simply lead to more expensive and economically less efficient operations (Holt, 1973).

In a historical sense, fisheries management agencies have been concerned with resource depletion and the resolution of conflicts within one particular use of the sea—that is, fishing. We have tried to regulate competition between individuals, user groups, gears, fleets, etc., in an attempt to harmonize user interest in the potential resources and future use. This was probably appropriate inasmuch as the fishing industry was the major economic group exploiting the ocean resources. The situation, however, is changing rapidly. Both oil and minerals are being sought on the continental shelf and slope and deep seabed, estuaries are being used for a variety of industrial and recreational purposes, and the aquatic environment serves as a receptacle for disposal of industrial and human waste. It seems apparent that multiple use of the aquatic environment will become of increasing importance. Hence, in the near future, we may be as much concerned with another problem: harmonizing the fisheries use of the ocean and seabed with other uses and resolving competition between them (Holt, 1973).

## SUMMARY AND COMMENTS

In summary, there is evidence to support the belief that the oceans produce an enormous biological surplus upon which mankind could increase the amount of food produced from the world's oceans. There is, however, a great difference between what is produced and what can be realistically harvested. Although there may be a biological surplus for conventional species of 2-4 times that which is now harvested, technical and social-political constraints may limit catches for these species to no more than 100 mmt; and if we fail to establish effective national and international management institutions, we may never even approach this figure. In addition to the managerial problems, the maintenance and continued growth of fisheries could depend on an adequate resolution of energy problems. Should oil prices outrun the value of raw material, there could be major setbacks in production of food from the world's ocean.

Despite these difficulties, some modest increases in the catches of conventional species can be expected over the next 3½ decades (Table 23-1). With some improvement in managerial policies, we might expect an increased catch of at least 8 million tons of conventional species over the next decade. This is based on the premise that the Peruvian anchovy fishery will rebuild to a level of about 8 mmt; there will be a continued development of underutilized conventional species, particularly in the southern hemisphere and in the Indian Ocean; and fuller use will be made of the complex of species available for harvest. The rate of growth of conventional forms will, however, continue to decline; and perhaps no more than 14 million tons in addition to what is now caught will be produced before the end of this century.

Table 23-1. Opportunities for Increased Fish and Shellfish Production, 1985 and 2000.

| *Resource category* | *Potential increases (kilotons)* | |
|---|---|---|
| | *1985* | *2000* |
| Conventional | 8,000 | 14,000 |
| Unconventional | 5,000 | 35,000 |
| Waste elimination (equivalents) | 2,000 | 15,000 |
| Total | 15,000 | 64,000 |

The unconventional species offer the greatest opportunity for expansion. Changing coastal state jurisdiction may well focus increased use on the Antarctic and open ocean areas of the world. If the cost of locating and extracting krill can be resolved, we might expect production of unconventional forms to approach 5 million tons in 1985 and increase to 35 million tons by the year 2000.

In addition to increased catches which may come from geographical expansion of fisheries operations and exploitation of unconventional species, gains can be achieved through elimination of waste from species now harvested and through transfer of fish used for industrial purposes to products used for direct human consumption. For example, by 1985 the equivalent of 2 million extra tons of fish could be made available as a result of technological changes and utilization patterns of this type, and this value could be increased to approximately 15 million tons by the year 2000.

## REFERENCES

Alverson, D. L. and G. J. Paulik. Objectives and problems of managing aquatic living resources. *J. Fish. Res. Board Can.* 1973, 30:1936-1947.

Anon. Pelagic crabs in vast numbers present challenge to exploiters. *National Fisherman* (July) 1970, 50:16C.

Anon. Is the ocean an inexhaustible source of food for mankind? Office of Naval Res., London, European Scientific Notes, ESN-25-6:188-189, 1971.

Anon. Background paper for informal consultation on Antarctic krill. Food and Agriculture Organization of the United Nations, Dept. of Fisheries, Rome, Italy, 1974.

Gulland, J. A. *The Fish Resources of the Ocean.* 1971, Fishing News (Books) Ltd., England.

Holt, S. J. Marine fisheries and world food supplies. The Man/Food Equation Symposium, 20-21 Sept., London, 1973.

Joyner, T., Mahnken, C. V. W. & Clark, R. C., Jr. Salmon—future harvest from the Antarctic Ocean? *Marine Fisheries Review,* 1974, Vol. 36, No. 5.

Komaki, Y. A brief account of the Euphausiids, with special reference to *Euphausia pacifica* in the Japanese waters. *JAMARC,* 1974, No. 5, April.

Krefft, G. Investigations on midwater fish in the Atlantic Ocean. *Ber. dt. wiss. Kommn.* Meeresforsch. 1974, Verlag Paul Parey, Hamburg und Berlin. 23:226-254.

Lagunov, L. L., et al. Utilization of krill for human consumption. Paper presented to the Third Session FAO Technical Conference on Fishery Products, Tokyo, Dec. 1973. FAO, Rome.

Longhurst, A. R. The biology and mass occurrences of galatheid crustaceans and their utilization as a fishery resource. *FAO Fish.* 1968. Rep. 2:95-110.

Lyubimova, T. G., Naumov, A. G., & Lagunov, L. L. Prospects of the utilization of krill and other nonconventional resources of the world ocean. Paper presented to the Third Session FAO Technical Conference on Fishery Management and Development, Vancouver, B.C., 13-23 Feb. 1973, 9 p.

Miyauchi, D., & Steinberg, M. Machine separation of edible flesh from fish. *Fishery Industrial Research,* 1970, Vol. 6, No. 4.

Moiseev, P. A. The living resources of the world ocean (Biologicheskie resursy Mirovogo okeana). Translated from Russian by Israel Program for Scientific Translations, Keter Press, Jerusalem, 1971.

Omura, H. Whale and *Euphausia superba.* Tokyo Marine Resources Research and Development Center, 1973. (In Japanese.)

Schaefer, M. B., & Alverson, D. L. World fish potentials. In: *The Future of the Fishing Industry in the United States,* Univ. of Wash., Publ. in Fisheries Series, Vol. IV, 1968.

Spinelli, J. L., Lehman, L. & Weig, D. Composition, processing, and utilization of red crab (*Pleuroncodes planipes*) as an aquacultural feed ingredient. *J. Fish. Res. Board Can.,* 1974, 31:1025-1029.

Voss, G. L. Cephalopod resources of the world. *FAO Fish. Circular* No. 149, Rome, 1973.

# 24. Fish Meal and Fish Protein Concentrate

C. P. IDYLL 1970

In recent years world fish landings have increased twice as fast as human population (in contrast to the trends for other kinds of food), and from 1958 to 1964 fully 60 per cent of this increase consisted of varieties made into fish meal—species such as sardines, anchovies, and hakes.

For many decades fish meal was used largely as fertilizer and was referred to as "fish guano." Useful as it is for fertilizer, fish meal is now far too valuable to be used for this purpose. Instead, its enormously increased popularity is a consequence of the remarkable things it does in increasing the growth rates, the vigor, and the general health of farm animals at a cost much below that of most other supplements.

Farmers have known for centuries that their livestock relish—and thrive on—fish. In 325 B.C. Nearchus, one of Alexander the Great's generals, attacked a town on the Persian Gulf to restock his larder. According to the account given by the Greek historian Arrian, "the natives showed freely their flour, ground down from dried fish.... Even their flocks are fed on dried fish so that the mutton has a fishy taste like the flesh of sea birds." In the fourteenth century Marco Polo reported that some Asian peoples "accustom their cattle, cows, sheep, camels and horses to feed upon dried fish . . . of a small kind which they take in vast quantities during the months of March, April and May; and when dried they lay up in their houses for food for their cattle." Farmers in such far-flung places as Malaysia and the Shetland Islands of Scotland learned long ago to feed fish to pigs and sheep. The first bulletin issued by the United States fish commission in 1881 contained a letter from Isaac Hinkley describing the fish-eating cows of Provincetown, Massachusetts, which crowded around fishermen cleaning their catch to browse on the offal. Ling or blen-

Dr. C. P. Idyll is chairman and professor of the Division of Fishery Sciences and Applied Estuarine Ecology with the Rosenstiel School of Marine and Atmospheric Sciences, University of Miami, Florida. He is currently on sabbatical leave as senior consultant with the Food and Agricultural Organization of the United Nations in Rome, Italy. His research interests include ecology and fishery and estuarine biology. He is a member of the National Academy of Sciences' International Marine Science Affairs Panel. He has published nearly fifty books, articles, and reports.

From *The Sea Against Hunger*, pp. 128-144, 1970. Reprinted by permission of the author and the Thomas Y. Crowell Company, New York. Copyright 1970 by C. P. Idyll.

nies of three pounds and more were "freely eaten." Farmers taught cows to accept fish by mincing it and including it in their rations.

The use of fish meal for farm animals picked up momentum when its high content of nitrogen and phosphorus compounds was noticed in the early decades of this century. Feeding experiments met with remarkable success. Fish meal began to have general use as animal food in Europe, but this trend lagged in the United States until after World War I.

The American poultry industry has grown enormously with the aid of fish meal. More than a third of the United States broiler production can be attributed to it. More than half the fish landed in the United States goes to feed farm animals, and in 1968 this enormous bulk (more than 200,000 tons of fish meal) was supplemented by imports of 855,000 tons for the same purpose. In America turkeys and pigs also benefit from fish-supplemented diets. In Europe more meal is fed to swine than to chickens; in Germany, for example, 70 per cent goes to pigs.

For all farm animals—and for humans too—growth, vigor, and general health are dependent to a very important extent on the amount and quality of proteins available. These are the substances making up the muscle and other parts of the body mass. In addition, the minerals that are essential components of the skeleton and the vitamins that control the chemistry of the body are other important food constituents. Fish, whether fresh or reduced to meal, is one of the world's best sources of all three of these food groups.

Proteins occur in many kinds of foods, including plants: cereal grains, fruits, soybeans, and many more. They occur also in foods of animal origin: meat, milk, eggs, fish. The ruminants—cows and sheep—flourish with proteins derived from any of these sources. Other animals, including chickens, pigs, and man, may be undernourished on a diet high in protein if the sole source is cereals or other plants. The difference is related to the composition of the proteins from the two food sources.

Proteins are among the most complex of chemical substances. Their large molecules are made up of networks of smaller molecules of various amino acids. There are about eighteen amino acids, occurring in varying proportions in different kinds of protein. Nine or ten of these, called the essential amino acids, must be supplied ready manufactured, since most animals cannot synthesize them. Foods containing these essential amino acides are more nutritious than others in which some or all of them are deficient or out of balance.

Of all the essential amino acids three are likely to be missing in the grain rations of poultry. These are lysine and two sulfur-containing amino acids, methionine and cystine. For swine rations, lysine and tryptophan are those likely to be deficient. Cereal grains are low in all of these, so that chickens fed only with corn have to be fed larger amounts of grain to achieve optimum growth rate, maximum size, survival, and general health than if a better balance of amino acids can be supplied. Soybean meal does a better job than the grains, having ample quantities of lysine and tryptophan, but it is low in methionine and cystine. Sesame and sunflower meals, used increasingly in feeds in recent years, are rich in the sulfur amino acids but are low in lysine.

The rapidly rising use of fish meal for animal feeds has taken place because it is rich in all of these essential amino acids. One of the great strengths of fish meal is that only small amounts are required to supplement the essential nutrients available in cereal grains. Fish meal has by no means replaced the grains or soybean meal in animal feeds but instead has been used as a feed supplement. Soviet scientists have discovered that a metric ton (2,204 pounds) of fish meal added to the ration fed to pigs increased the yield of pork by 700 to 800 kilograms (1,540 to 1,760 pounds). When the same amount of fish meal was added to poultry feed, production of eggs increased by 25,000. In addition the meal replaced three tons of vegetable feeds. In Norwegian experiments, 7 per cent of fish meal added to the diet of chicks during their first six weeks increased their growth 11 per cent over that of animals fed only vegetable food. Pigs given a fish meal supplement to only their diet of grains increased in weight an extra 5 to 12 per cent by the time they reached market size. In Denmark the number of eggs per hen in ten months of production was 153 for birds fed 15 per cent fish meal compared to 126 for those on vegetable protein only. Soybean meal produced a 45 per cent hatch of eggs, but when the ration was supplemented by condensed fish solubles (the dissolved and suspended materials from fish reduction) the percentage rose to 74.

In the United States small portions of fish meal—ordinarily about 2 to 3 per cent but sometimes as much as 10 per cent—are used in the diet of chickens. More fish meal gives better results, but the cost rises when the fish replaces grain.

Meat, eggs, or milk fed to farm animals would give the same desirable effects as fish, and chemists have learned to synthesize methionine and other amino acids, as well as vitamins, in the laboratory. Hence it is possible to formulate fully balanced rations without fish meal. The modern poultry farmer lets a computer tell him what to use. The computer juggles the amino acid content of various components and comes up with a formulation that may include fish meal one day but exclude it the next because a cheaper protein source may be available. But fish meal is usually the cheapest source of high-grade animal protein.

Fish meals are rich in minerals, especially calcium and phosphorus, which are essential to the formation of bones. All such meals include iodine, copper, manganese, zinc, iron, and cobalt; they contain large quantities of the B vitamins, including $B_{12}$, riboflavin, niacin, and choline, all necessary for proper nutrition.

Finally, there is an air of pleasant mystery to the nutritional qualities of fish meal. After all the beneficial effects—the high protein content, the good amino acid balance, the high mineral and B vitamin content—have been accounted for, an additional value has been reported by some investigators. This has been called the "unidentified growth factor." It makes fish meal unique in nutritional value and has helped push it to its present heights of popularity.

There are a number of ways of making fish meal, but the largest quantities by far—some 95 per cent worldwide—are manufactured by the "wet reduction process." This is used when large volumes of oily fish are available. The fish are cooked with steam to denature the protein and break the cell walls to release the oil. The cooked mass is squeezed in a continuous screw-type press to remove water (up to 80 per cent of the raw fish) and oil (up to 20 per cent). The resulting "press cake" is dried and ground, an antioxidant is added, and the meal is bagged. Fish meal has a moisture content of 6 to 10 per cent, a fat content of 5 to 12 per cent, a protein content of 60 to 75 per cent, and an ash (mostly mineral) content of 10 to 20 per cent. It takes five pounds of raw fish to make a pound of fish meal; the difference is the water and oil removed.

This removal has two important results: it reduces the weight (and hence the shipping costs) to a fifth of the original fish weight, and it reduces spoilage, since bacteria must have moisture to operate. Hence fish meal can be stored at room temperature in simple containers such as bags, and can be shipped without expensive refrigeration.

Two other products, oil and solubles, result when fish meal is made this way. The oil-water mixture, called press liquor, is centrifuged, and oil and stickwater result. The stickwater is centrifuged again, to produce solubles. The market for these products is poor at present.

Fish oils are relatively unsaturated, meaning that their molecules are capable of picking up hydrogen atoms. This is of importance in human nutrition—and presumably for farm animals as well—and consumption of unsaturated instead of saturated fats may be a factor in the prevention of heart disease. Fish oils also have ready markets as ingredients for soap, paint, linoleum, lipstick, table and cooking fats, ink, and a surprising variety and number of other products.

Stickwater (or gluewater in Europe, both names describing its most obvious physical characteristic) is the residual liquid from the pressing of the cooked fish. It contains soluble and suspended materials—protein, minerals, and in particular, large amounts of the water-soluble B vitamins. Stickwater, once discarded, is now evaporated to about half its original volume to produce "condensed fish solubles." It is a valuable supplement to animal feeds, sometimes being added back to fish meal to produce "whole meat."

There has been a phenomenal rise in the use of fish meal throughout the world in recent years (Table 24-1). From a production of 571,000 metric tons in 1948, production increased eight and a half times by 1968 to about 4.8 million tons. The proportion of the world fish catch used for meal in 1948 was less than 8 per cent, rising to 14 per cent eight years later and to a level of about a third of the total catch in 1966. The price of fish meal before World War II was $30 to $40 per ton. By 1948 this had risen to $125, and in 1969 it ranged from about $150 to $195 per ton, depending on season and market.

This worldwide surge in demand for fish meal has been made against strong, sometimes bitter opposition. That this opposition should exist in the face of the obvious benefits in making better use of the desperately needed resources of the sea and in the creation of new food and new wealth, is only one more illustration that man is the world's most baffling and inconsistent animal.

Opposition to the use of fish for reduction to meal often takes this tack: By transforming fish into meal, costs are raised. More important, fish meal is fed to chickens and pigs, and only a fraction of the food value is passed on to human beings. It is cheaper and more efficient to feed fresh fish to people. Hence it is immoral and it should be illegal to manufacture fish meal.

This argument is a complex mixture of the truth and of blind sentimentality. It is true that costs are raised when fish is processed, and that there is loss of energy, protein, and other nutrients when it is cycled through chickens and pigs on its way to the

Table 24-1. World Production of Fish Meal in Metric Tons.[a]

| | |
|---|---|
| 1938 | 627,000 |
| 1948 | 571,000 |
| 1952, 1953, 1954 average | 995,500 |
| 1955, 1956, 1957 average | 1,198,400 |
| 1958 | 1,396,000 |
| 1960 | 1,955,800 |
| 1961 | 2,496,000 |
| 1962 | 2,885,000 |
| 1963 | 2,890,000 |
| 1964 | 3,660,000 |
| 1965 | 3,549,000 |
| 1966 | 4,196,500 |
| 1967 | 4,500,000 |
| 1968 | 4,802,000[b] |

[a]*Source: Food and Agriculture Organization of the United Nations.*
[b]Estimate.

human belly. But most of life's goals are reached by zigzag paths. The day will never come when mankind can use all fishes just as they come from the sea, wasting nothing by processing or by transforming the fishes to other kinds of flesh. The manufacture of fish meal permits the utilization of fishes that cannot be used in any other way at the present state of our skill.

The efficiency of conversion of food value by farm animals is already good and it is increasing as agricultural research progresses. When fish meal is added to a hen's ration, it lays eggs or grows to a plump broiler more rapidly, and with a recovery of food value higher than the rule-of-thumb 10 per cent usually used in calculations of transfer from one trophic level to another. A hen's recovery of energy from fish meal ranges from about 20 to 25 per cent of the calories; for proteins it is a high 40 to 50 per cent; and for the all-important essential amino acids it is even greater. Turkeys, pigs, and other farm animals also do good jobs of conversion.

It was pointed out earlier that more than a third of the broilers produced in the United States can be attributed to fish meal. In 1964, for example, fish were responsible for some 720,425 broilers on American tables; to this should be added substantial numbers of turkeys, pigs, and other food animals. Similar results are produced in Germany, in Japan, and in many other countries. In the face of such figures the argument that fish should be fed to humans instead of animals, implying that beasts are being fed at the expense of people, misses the point.

Humans probably will continue indefinitely to benefit from feeding fish to farm animals. Yet, in the face of a desperate and worsening shortage of food throughout the world, men should learn to use directly as human food as much as possible of the fish now fed to livestock. We may be on the threshold of such a development. It is possible now to produce high-quality fish meal and tasteless, odorless (or suitably flavored) fish protein concentrate (FPC) acceptable to many palates.

There are two principal barriers to rapid and widespread use of edible fish meal and FPC. The first of these is technological and economic: methods available are still relatively costly for most markets. The second barrier is psychological: they are unfamiliar foods, and therefore, in the minds of many people, unacceptable. Both of these situations can be changed—the first relatively easily and quickly, in direct proportion to the amount of effort put into research and development; the second only slowly and painfully, since human prejudice is far less amenable to manipulation than machines or chemicals.

Fish meal can be made for human food by the same methods as those used to make the meal now sold by the millions of tons for animal feed. But so much more care must be taken in its manufacture, and the cost is therefore so much higher, that this approach is probably not feasible. The raw material must be delivered fresher to the plants than is now usually done; the work must be conducted more hygienically and at a lower temperature than is common. Such edible fish meal is highly nutritious, but it has very little appeal to most palates, since its odor and flavor are strong. In the future it may be possible to improve the manufacture of fish meal sufficiently and to conduct energetic campaigns to persuade people to eat it. This would be a cheap and satisfactory method of improving the nutrition of mankind, but it will be long in coming, if it ever does.

A much more likely possibility is that the use of fish protein concentrate, or "fish flour," will be greatly increased. This is a whitish powder with high animal protein and mineral contents, a nutritionally well balanced amino acid composition, and a low fat content. It can be made tasteless and odorless if this is required by its consumers; it can have a fish flavor if this is preferred. It must be made with a process different from and more expensive than that used for fish meal.

FPC has some exceptionally weighty credentials as food for humans. It is nutritious and wholesome; two ounces contain as much animal protein as a twelve-ounce steak. It can be shipped and stored in cheap containers without refrigeration; in Canada herring flour has been stored in polyethylene bags for three years without noticeable change in flavor. It is acceptable in a variety of foods in many parts of the world. It is already moderately cheap and it will become cheaper.

At least 500 million people throughout the world are short of proteins, but 5 million tons of FPC could supply them with enough animal protein for a year. Made into fish protein concentrate, the unharvested fish of the United States coastal waters alone could raise significantly the nutritional standard of 1 billion people for 300 days.

Despite all this, there is no substantial commercial production of FPC anywhere in the world. This is largely because it is a new and unfamiliar material, and men are afraid of strange things.

FPC has had a difficult youth in the United States. Perhaps this is because ours is a country, unlike a considerable portion of the rest of the world, with very little need for new, cheap sources of animal protein.

The opposition of greatest consequence has been to the sale for human food of fish protein concentrate manufactured from whole fish. This opposition has been important because it came from the United States Food and Drug Administration, whose word on such matters is law and whose edicts produce repercussions in the rest of the world. The Food and Drug Administration has served the people of the United States well by protecting them against unscrupulous or careless manufacturers of drugs and processors of food; it has undoubtedly saved countless lives and dollars. But in the case of FPC made from whole fish the FDA has been wrong. Until early in 1967 it argued that such a product, containing as it does scales, fins, and entrails of fish, as well as the muscles and other parts of the body, would be "aesthetically unacceptable" and could not be sold in this country for human consumption. But the American public eats canned sardines and other fishes, entrails and all; it greedily swallows oysters and clams without cutting out any parts of them; it consumes a great many other foods that are truly "unaesthetic" if they are viewed in a detached and dispassionate manner. FPC, on the other hand, is wholesome and no more objectionable to the unprejudiced palate than a chicken leg or a spoonful of boiled spinach. The FDA came under heavy fire from nutritionists, biologists, members of Congress, and government groups for its stand, and it eventually retreated.

Research by scientists of the Bureau of Commercial Fisheries confirmed FPC's low level of toxicity (content of fluoride) and high nutritive value. These results were important in persuading the Food and Drug Administration to change its position, as was a strong stand taken by the Advisory Committee on Marine Protein Resources of the National Academy of Sciences.

One reason that FPC is more expensive to make than fish meal is that a great proportion of the fat must be removed. Fat and its decomposition products are the principal causes of objectionable odors and flavors, and the length of time the product can be stored before use depends heavily on low fat content to prevent it from becoming rancid. Thus, in the manufacture of FPC, processes must be employed to remove nearly all the fat. For example, the pioneer VioBin process uses ethylene dichloride, and the method developed by the Bureau of Commercial Fisheries (BCF) in its laboratory at College Park, Maryland, employs isopropyl alcohol. The fish used by the BCF is red hake, *Urophycis chuss,* a cheap and abundant species caught on the Atlantic coast of the United States. It is sold only in small amounts in this country, since it is too small and too soft to fillet, freeze, or can.

To make FPC by the Bureau process, whole fish are minced and treated three times with separate batches of isopropyl alcohol, once cold and twice hot. The alcohol extracts water as well as fat, and the residue of fish is dried, ground, and packaged. One hundred thousand pounds of raw hake yield 15,000 pounds of fish protein concentrate—a ratio of about 6 to 1. The concentrate is a white powder with a yellowish cast. It contains 80 per cent protein, 13.5 per cent ash (mostly calcium, phosphorus, and other minerals), and has virtually no odor or flavor. If the fish were bought for 1 cent a pound, a plant with a daily capacity of fifty tons of raw fish could probably produce this flour at 13.9 cents a pound and sell it at a profit for 20 cents a pound. If two extractions instead of three were sufficient (that is, if the market would accept a small residue of fat in the product and thus a faint fish taste) the selling price per pound would be about 13.5 cents. Canadian technologists estimate that FPC from herring would cost 15 cents a pound to manufacture in their country. In other parts of the world the selling price would be about the same as for dried skim milk, and in most countries fish protein concentrate could probably be produced more cheaply per unit of protein than any other animal material.

Fish protein concentrate is already highly acceptable to many people, especially children. Adults, with the usual stubborn adherence to the ways and tastes developed in youth, take to it much less readily, as they do to any other new product. But the Food and Agriculture Organization and the Children's Fund of the United Nations have carried out tests in thirty or more countries—often with encouraging success.

Fish protein concentrate can be used in a great many ways: in breads, pastas (that is, macaroni, spaghetti, and similar products), cakes, cookies, sauces, cereals, pastries, candy, soups, baby foods, and beverages. If a neutral bland product is required, without taste or odor (for markets in Europe, the Americas, and India), it can be produced; various strengths and kinds of fish flavors can be added for markets in central and southern African countries and those in Southeast Asia. With additives, fish flour can even be made to taste like cheese or beef.

Chile started testing FPC as early as 1958. Children in Santiago schools like bread made with an FPC content of 7 to 10 per cent. At the upper limit the color of the bread was affected, and above that the flavor was noticeable, but it will be remembered from the experiments with poultry that amounts of fish meal considerably less than 10 per cent were remarkably effective in improving nutrition, and with children similarly small proportions had beneficial effects.

In Kuala Lumpur, Malaya, children fed a standard diet enriched with skim-milk solids showed twice the rate of gain in growth as those without the milk; better still, those fed a standard diet supplemented with cookies made of FPC, cereal, sugar, and flavoring showed a *triple* gain. Moreover, the children (but not their parents) liked the cookies. In Senegal foods containing fish protein concentrate were successfully fed to children. In Burma it has been incorporated into soups, sauces, and vegetable dishes with high acceptability. In the Belgian Congo and in Ghana FPC was in good demand when the price was kept low by subsidy; later it was commercially successful at competitive prices.

In Mexico Dr. Federico Gomez carried out several years of experiments in the Hospital Infantil in Mexico City, and in Tlaltizipan, with impressive results. In 1960 he declared that "10 to 15 years after supplementation with 30-40 grams [about 1 to 1.5 ounces] of animal protein in the form of fish flour to the daily Mexican diet of corn, beans, and chili, the characteristics of Mexican people will change physically, mentally, and emotionally."

Sweden and the Union of South Africa have FPC plants in operation. The United States established a pilot-scale plant in Grays Harbor, Washington, in 1969.

The U. S. Agency for International Development (AID) has launched a vigorous campaign to persuade people in developing countries to eat FPC despite their reluctance to try strange foods. The first step in this program is to get an insight into consumer psychology in several countries (including Brazil, the Philippines, Korea, Thailand, and India), then to launch a campaign that will encourage voluntary use of FPC on a scale sufficient to support a profitable industry.

When the world is ready to accept it, immense amounts of FPC can be manufactured. A great proportion of the fish now landed and consumed in various fresh or processed forms is suitable for this purpose. Obviously no one is going to close the salmon canneries of British Columbia and Alaska, or the fillet and fish stick freezers of New England, and convert them into FPC factories, and highly regarded species such as halibut, sole, red snapper, shad, and others will continue to be marketed in their present forms. But more than a third of the world fish catch is now used to make fish meal, and all the same fish could theoretically be made into fish flour.

It is unlikely that all fish meal plants will be converted for fish protein concentrate, but once a demand is created and handling methods are improved, such huge stocks as the Peruvian anchovetta (now harvested at the rate of 22.5 billion pounds a year) would be suitable for making fish protein concentrate. Next door, Chile has produced 22 million pounds of anchovettas. At its peak the California sardine fishery produced 1.5 billion pounds. Whether it will ever do so again apparently depends on whether the ocean off California and adjacent areas warms up again to the sardines' liking, and whether they can shoulder their way back into a living space lost to the anchovies when their numbers dwindled. But if the sardines do come back, they would make millions of tons of good FPC. The menhaden industry of the United States Atlantic and Gulf of Mexico waters has produced as much as 2.25 billion pounds of fish. The Alaska herring populations produced 261 million pounds at their peak, and even this may have been less than the stocks could sustain. The British Columbia herring fishery peaked at 96 million pounds. In South Africa 880 million pounds of pilchard are landed in some years for the fish meal plants; in South-West Africa the peak amount has been nearly 1.5 billion pounds; in Angola, 238 million pounds. And so the roster grows.

These figures are taken from maximum catches of fisheries exploited now at varying levels: some fully exploited like that of the Peruvian anchovy, some overexploited like that of the California sardine, some underexploited to various unknown degrees. Of course, it is misleading to quote maximum catches as though these were the amounts available every year from their respective areas, and greatest catches may represent unusually favorable years instead of average years, or years when overfishing occurred. But some inkling of the immense total potential is gained in this way, and by no means all the fishable stocks have been included in the list above.

There are also stocks of fish whose existence is known but whose size can only be guessed, since fishing has not tested them. Estimates here may be very inaccurate, but judging from previous experience, assessments are more likely to err on the conservative side than otherwise. This is to be expected, since what is not seen is not counted.

In California alone there may be 30 billion pounds of anchovies, hake, lanternfishes, deep-sea smelt, and other species now unused. From one-quart to one-half—probably closer to the latter—of this quantity of fish is available on a sustained-yield basis. There are millions of pounds of hake and smaller but substantial quantities of other species to be taken off the coasts of Argentina and other southern South American coasts. West African nations are just beginning to exploit the fish off their coasts, and there are millions of pounds to be had there on a sustained basis. The total for these and dozens of other fish stocks over the world is impressive.

Another enormous resource, the squids, might also contribute great supplies of fish meal or FPC. Less is known about squids than about many other sea creatures; because relatively few people eat them, they have not been studied sufficiently. But it is clear from a few isolated fisheries and from limited scientific investigations that the sea contains enormous quantities of them.

Squids are popular food in some parts of the world, notably Japan and southern

Europe. Fisheries exist in waters off Hokkaido (the northern island of Japan), off Newfoundland, in the Mediterranean, and in a few other places. Japan landed 14.4 billion pounds in 1963, and its stocks of squids may be no larger than some others in various parts of the world. It is certain that vastly greater quantities could be caught worldwide. This is largely a matter of developing markets. One large market would be created by the manufacture of meal and protein concentrate from squids.

The protein of squids is of high quality, nearly equal to that of fish. They have a strong advantage over many other animals in the large proportion of edible parts of the whole body: 80 per cent compared to 40 to 70 per cent for fish. The water content of squid flesh is about the same as that of white fish meat, ranging from 70 to 80 per cent. The oil content of the flesh is low, ranging from 1 to 1.5 per cent.

On my desk I have meal made from squids by the American VioBin process, containing 77.6 per cent protein, 10.2 per cent ash, 9.0 per cent moisture and 1.9 per cent fat. It is a tan powder, like very fine beach sand, with a faint fishy odor. There is no reason to doubt that it would be an excellent supplement to either animal or human diets deficient in animal protein.

Of course, there is an eventual limit to the amount of fish, and even squids, that can be brought to shore. At that point the only place to go, if mankind is to get more food from the sea, is down one or more steps in the oceanic food pyramid, to exploit zooplankton. The quantities available are enormously larger than those of the nearly untouched squids, or even of the swarming little fishes that have formed the basis for the greatly expanded landings of recent years. In harvesting plankton the conclusion is reached that although it looks unlikely that man can soon make use of most of these resources, some of the larger animal-plankton organisms, notably the antarctic krill and the red crabs of the eastern Pacific, seems promising. Fantastic totals of millions of tons of krill may be available in far-southern waters, and the Soviets have shown that nutritious meal can be made from this raw material. Enormous quantities of red crabs are likewise available for capture off California and northern Mexico.

Thus we are not short of raw material for fish meal and fish flour. If we have the skill to produce acceptable products and to catch the animals cheaply, we have the opportunity to supply immense quantities of human food.

# 25. Time and Tide

F. L. LAWTON 1974

Tidal energy is abstracted from seawater at locations where estuaries or embayments and control structures permit utilization of the head.* Tidal-power plants operate on the continuously varying differences in level between the water in the basin constituted by the controlled estuary or embayment, on the landward side, and the water in the sea. The basin must be filled from the sea or emptied to the sea as required by the operating regime of the power plant, so that production can be matched with the demand on the power network to which the plant is connected.

It is technically feasible today to exploit much of the conservatively estimated 13,000 megawatts of the world's tidal-energy resources. Tidal energy, converted to electric energy, is free from any deleterious effect on the air, water, or land environment. Its exploitation rests on its economic competitiveness when all internal and external costs of competing energy resources are properly assessed. The uncertain availabilities and escalating costs of fossil fuels and, perhaps to a somewhat lesser extent, of fissionable fuels are inexorably advancing the time when tidal power will come into its own.

Records indicate that by the eleventh century tide mills were in use along the Atlantic coast of Europe, notably in Great Britain, France, and Spain. Even as late as the mid-nineteenth century, tidal energy was used widely in coastal areas where the tides attained a sufficient range. Twenty-foot waterwheels installed in 1580 under the arches of London Bridge were providing part of the city's water supply some two and a half centuries later. A tidal-power installation for pumping sewage was still in use in Hamburg in 1880. Other installations have been reported throughout this era in Russia, North America, and Italy. Some of the old structures were of impressive size. A tide mill in Rhode Island, built in the eighteenth century, used 20-ton wheels, 11 feet in diameter and 26 feet in width.

* Difference in elevation between two points in a body of seawater or other fluid.

F. L. Lawton is a Canadian engineer who has specialized in applications of tidal power. After his retirement in 1966, he worked three and one half years as Study Director of the Atlantic Tidal Power Programming Board's Engineering and Management Committee established by the Governments of Canada, New Brunswick, and Nova Scotia to investigate tidal power possibilities of the Canadian waters of the Bay of Fundy. He has authored and co-authored some forty articles.

From *Oceanus,* Vol. 17, Summer, pp. 30-37, 1974. Reprinted with light editing and with permission of the author and *Oceanus* Magazine.

Early tide mills produced small amounts of mechanical energy—about 30 to 100 kilowatts—generally used at the site. This was enough to satisfy demand before the advent of the electric motor and long-distance power transmission. The disappearance of tidal-power generation towards the end of the nineteenth century has been attributed to power economics. However, new concepts of construction and marked advances in large, better-adapted generating units have reawakened interest in the resource as a possible competitor with other forms of energy.

Engineers have examined a large number of locations potentially favorable to tidal-power development. These include sites in the estuaries and embayments of northeastern North America, the English Channel and North Sea coasts, the Irish Sea, Barents and White seas, the Gulf of Alaska, the Okhotsk Sea, and the coasts of Korea, China, the Gulf of Bengal, Pakistan, Western Australia, and Southern Argentina.

The USSR has slowly and methodically pursued work leading to the ultimate development of tidal-power generation, the principal proponent being L. B. Bernshtein. A small tidal-power plant was recently placed in service in Kislaya Bay, a deep basin with an area of one square kilometer, connected with the sea by a narrow estuary about 100 feet in width. The tidal range is something under 11 feet. Conceived as an experimental undertaking involving minimal expenditures, the basic concept entails the use of prefabricated caissons built under factory conditions at a suitable location, floated, towed to the site, and there sunk into prepared foundations.

In addition, the USSR is reported to be investigating a first-stage, 4000-megawatt development in the Mezen sector of the White Sea, with others to follow. They have in mind the possible development of a 320,000-kilowatt tidal-power plant at Lumbovskaya, where a bay with an area of 70 square kilometers can be cut off by a relatively short dam. Other tidal-power schemes, all in embayments of the White Sea and in estuaries of rivers flowing into it, would use flood tides of about 30 feet.

The French boast the world's only large modern tidal-power development. The facility lies across the estuary of the Rance River, which empties into the Atlantic Ocean between Saint-Malo and Dinard on the coast of Brittany. An average tidal range of 27 feet is utilized in 24 units, each rated at 10 megawatts, providing an annual production of 544 million kilowatt-hours. Inaugurated late in 1966, this power plant is notable for its development and use of the turbine, essentially a horizontal-axis propeller turbine with variable pitch runner blades. The turbine is connected to a generator enclosed in a nacelle or bulb upstream from the turbine in the passage by which water is conveyed to the turbine. The runner is so designed that it can operate as a turbine with flow from the basin to the sea or from the sea to the basin, and pump in either direction as well. It can also serve as an orifice, passing about 50 percent of its normal flow.

Electricité de France has also carried out extensive tidal-power investigations in L'Aber Vrach on the northwestern coast of Brittany and in the vicinity of Mont St. Michel near St. Malo.

In North America, studies of large-scale, tidal-power developments at various sites have been made during the last six decades by both Canadian and American agencies. Two only are discussed herein: the Bay of Fundy and its western arm, Passamaquoddy Bay. Both boast the exceptionally high tide ranges and large controllable embayments basic to economic tidal power. Tides in the Bay of Fundy are semi-diurnal. The interval between the transit of the moon and the occurrence of high water is nearly constant: the tides are extremely regular, there being two tides of nearly the same magnitude and pattern each 24 hour, 50 minute lunar day. Table 25-1 shows the range of tides encountered at several sites of interest. The tide is the so-called anomalistic type, the variation in range with the distance of the moon from perigee to apogee being the greatest varia-

Table 25-1. Tidal Ranges at Locations of Potential Tidal Power Developments.

| Site | Location | Tidal Range (ft.) | |
|---|---|---|---|
| | | *Maximum* | *Minimum* |
| 7.1 | Mary's Pt. to Grindstone Is. to Cape Maringouin | 43.7 | 19.1 |
| 7.2 | Ward Pt. to Joggins Head | 44.4 | 21.6 |
| 8.1 | Economy Pt. to Cape Tenny | 52.9 | 23.9 |

tion. The spring tides each month vary by a relatively small amount.

Reference has been made to the controlled estuary or embayment. Its importance lies in the phenomenon of tidal amplification, which under certain circumstances can materially modify the tidal range available at a given location and hence the head utilizable for power generation. The principal lunar, semi-diurnal, tide-producing component in the Bay of Fundy has a wavelength of about 745 miles.* The quarter-wavelength, then, is approximately 186 miles. Taking the mouth of the Bay of Fundy as a line running from Yarmouth, Nova Scotia, to Jonesport, Maine, the length of the bay is 159 miles to Cape Maringouin at the head of Chignecto Bay and 178 miles to a line from Economy Point to Cape Tenny. These lengths are sufficiently close to the quarter-wavelength to provide a partial explanation for the extremely high tides at the heads of the two arms of the bay. The vertical and lateral convergence of the bay from its mouth to its heads also plays an important role.

The International Passamaquoddy Engineering Board, in its report of October, 1959, recommended for specific design and costing a tidal-power project using Passamaquoddy Bay as the high pool, with Cobscook Bay in Maine and Friar Roads in New Brunswick as the low pool. The power plant, located at Carryingplace Cove, would have thirty 320-inch propeller-type, vertical axis turbines driving 10-megawatt, 13.8-kilovolt, 60-hertz generators at 40 rpm, operating under an average head of 11 feet. Connection with a hydroelectric plant was studied, as was a pumped-storage operation on a river emptying into Passamaquoddy. Though the investigation showed that the dependable capacity of the combination would amount to 323 megawatts and net annual generation to 1759 million kilowatt-hours, the scheme—and later variants—were found to be uneconomic.

In August, 1966, the governments of Canada, New Brunswick, and Nova Scotia set up the Atlantic Tidal Power Programming Board and the Atlantic Tidal Power Engineering and Management Committee, for which latter the author was the Study Director. Between November, 1966, and March, 1970, twenty-three sites—all in the Bay of Fundy—were looked over in a preliminary manner, and, after two series of evaluations, three were examined in detail (Figure 25-1). Investigations covered all relevant aspects of tides, geology, ecology, foundation conditions, ice formation, construction, generating equipment, transmission, production, and costs of tidal-power and alternative systems. A computer was used to help assess the significance of the implantation of tidal-power plants on the tidal regime of the Bay of Fundy.

Several practical power schemes received consideration during this study. These were selected from a range of proposals, many extremely complex and correspondingly costly. The intricacy often sprang from efforts to correct the basic weakness of tidal power: a variable production not necessarily in phase with human needs. Selected for special study were:

### The Single-Effect, Single-Basin Scheme

The oldest form of power generation, it was the basis of many tidal mills operating in

* Mean depth of the bay is 240 feet.

Figure 25-1. Three sites (7.1, 7.2, and 8.1) in Bay of Fundy selected for intensive study by Canadian experts.

Western Europe during the tenth and eleventh centuries. The basin is filled on the flood tide, and the sluice gates are closed at the high point of the cycle. Generation begins thereafter, the unit turbine operating on the difference in level of the water in the basin and that in the sea. In principle, operation in reverse is feasible, but production will be somewhat less. The single-effect, single-basin scheme can produce variable "slugs" of energy but no sustained power.

### The Double-Effect, Single-Basin Scheme

Exemplified by the Rance development, it utilizes civil works similar to those of the single-effect, single-basin concept, since it involves a single basin with double-effect generation and pumping plus use of the generating units as orifices to supplement sluiceway capacity. Power is generated during both filling and emptying phases. Starting with the point in the operating cycle of the single-effect, single-basin concept where the turbines are under the minimum head at which generation is feasible, the runner blades are feathered and the turbines function as orifices which, with or without the sluices, empty the basin to a level equal to that of the sea. After closure of the sluices and orifices, and after a suitable waiting period, during which the sea level rises above basin level, the generating units begin generation with flow from the sea to the basin. At the end of the generating phase the basin is filled, and subsequent operation with flow to the sea is similar to that in the single-effect, single-basin concept. The double-effect, single-basin concept is capable of producing dependable power at any desired time during the solar day. This is achieved at the expense of energy production, which is less than that of the single-effect, single-basin scheme.

### The Linked-Basin Concept

Suggested for Passamaquoddy, it entails the use of two more or less contiguous basins of suitable proportions. Such conditions exist at the mouths of Shepody Bay and Cumberland Basin. One basin can be operated as a high pool and the other as the low. The linked-basin concept was developed in response to the need for continuously available power. It requires less sophisticated generating units than some other schemes and may be economically attractive in the relatively few cases where two estuaries or embayments are physically close and suitable for development.

### The Paired-Basin Scheme

Consisting of two single-effect, single-basin schemes interconnected electrically, this arrangement affords somewhat more flexibility in operation to meet market demands. In certain cases where there is a difference in tidal phase, it may produce greater benefits than do other approaches.

Pumped storage was also considered as a supplementary power source for the Bay of Fundy sites. Although it requires additional capital investment, its ability to store low-value off-peak energy for subsequent use as high-quality, peak energy of maximum value makes it attractive. A hydraulic, pumped-storage facility provides flexibility in assigning energy to best advantage in meeting load requirements. The capacity and method of operation selected for the pumped-storage plant is determined by a number of factors, such as the volume of the storage reservoir, the characteristics of the output required by the system, and the installed capacity of the tidal-power plant.

The pumped-storage element at the three Bay of Fundy sites was predicated on both lower and upper basins using natural topographical features which could be enhanced by damming low sectors of the flow line, with either fresh or sea water serving as the working fluid. Where rock types and quality are suitable and a natural upper basin does not exist, the sea can substitute for the upper basin and underground chambers (or, in some cases, worked-out mines near the coast) for the lower basin.

Another means of upgrading the production of a single-effect, single-basin tidal-power plant (the type recommended for the Bay of Fundy sites) is the substitution of air compressors for the electric generators. The air is stored in underground caverns and released at peak periods of demand to drive gas turbine units feeding the power network.

Based on 1968 costs and seven percent money, costs of energy produced at our three sites from single-effect, single-basin schemes are indicated by Table 25-2, while Table 25-3 gives the costs of dependable peak and energy from double-effect single-basin schemes at the same three sites. These and other 1968 costs are currently under review by the sponsors of the Bay of Fundy tidal-power studies.

The optimized developments were determined on the assumption that all of the output from any of the schemes could be marketed. The unit costs of power and

Table 25-2. Cost of Energy At-Site from Single-Effect Single-Basin Schemes*

| *Item* | *Site 7.1* | *Site 7.2* | *Site 8.1* |
|---|---|---|---|
| Cost of energy at-site mills (kilowatt-hour) | 7.5 | 8.7 | 5.6 |

*No firm capacity is produced.

Table 25-3. Cost of Dependable Peak and Energy At-Site from Double-Effect Single-Basin Schemes

| *Item* | *Site 7.1* | *Site 7.2* | *Site 8.1* |
|---|---|---|---|
| Dependable peak* at site ($/kilowatt) | 32.65 | 40.29 | 25.20 |
| Energy credit (mills/kilowatt-hour) | 2.31 | 2.31 | 2.31 |

*Available 95% of time (total hour basis), 2 hours/day, 60 days/year.

energy were based on the total output, determined from power production studies. The unit costs of energy were computed by deducting from the annual costs a credit of $9.50 per kilowatt of dependable capacity. The at-site unit costs of dependable capacity for each of the schemes were computed by assuming an energy value of 2.31 mills per kilowatt-hour. The value was derived from a weighted averaging of displacement energy values in the regional power system and in the contiguous northeastern United States market, with due allowance for monetary exchange rates and the proportions of displacement energy which might be sold in the Maritimes and in the United States.

It has been conservatively estimated that the amount of tidal energy dissipated in the shallow seas, embayments and estuaries of the world is approximately $3 \times 10^6$ megawatts. The average potential power for the most interesting tidal-power projects in North and South America, Europe, and Asia has been estimated at 63,775 megawatts, of which about 13,000 megawatts might be abstracted. Federal Power Commission and Electrical World data place the total USA electric power industry capability at the end of last year at 438,492 megawatts, and hydroelectric capability, including pumped-storage, at 61,280 megawatts. The maximum probable world tidal-power capability would be, respectively, about 3.0 percent and 21.2 percent of these amounts. Thus tidal energy can be important, locally, if it cannot be a major contribution to national energy resources.

A good deal remains to be done before man can deal effectively with tidal power. The basic theory necessary for its development has been well established. However, substantial exploitation will require prior determination of the project's effect on the tidal regime of the waterway involved. Other necessary oceanographic work involves study of the tidal currents throughout the water column and the nature and movement of deposited and waterborne sediments. (Civil engineering features, relatively well advanced at this time, thanks to the experience with the Rance Development, the Dutch Delta Plan, and the Bay of Fundy studies, will benefit immensely from the North Sea oil and natural gas exploration and production.) The design, efficiency, and cost of generating equipment can also be improved, although much progress has been achieved with the bulb and straight-flow turbines. Considerable research on the pneumatic form of storage may well return appreciable economic benefits, as will work on the merits and demerits of a hydrogen-electricity energy source.

Our modern civilization is based on energy and, to a greater extent each year, on electric power. It is all too often forgotten that most sources of energy and electric power rely on fossil fuels (coal, oil, and natural gas) and on uranium—that is, on fuels which are depleted with use. When we consume them, we are dipping into our savings account provided by a beneficent Creator to serve the world for as long as it may exist. Evidence of approaching exhaustion of these depletable fuels is accumulating. Costs are increasing. Fortunately, there are a few sources of energy which are essentially income-type fuels—interest, as it were, on our inheritance. Of these sources—water power, geothermal power, ocean thermal power, solar power, and wind power—the tides are among the most accessible to the hand of man, with generation accurately predictable for decades.

# 26. Power, Fresh Water, and Food from Cold, Deep Sea Water

DONALD F. OTHMER OSWALD A. ROELS 1973

The sun's radiation is both the essential requirement of all life and the great source of man's energy. Besides keeping us warm, it supplies, directly or indirectly, (i) most of the energy we use, (ii) all of our food through photosynthesis in plants and many links of the food chains, and (iii) our fresh water supply from the cycle of evaporation from the sea, to clouds, to rain, to rivers.

The oceans contain 98 percent of the earth's water, over 1.3 thousand million cubic kilometers of that other great necessity of all life. With 71 percent of the earth's area, the oceans receive most of the sun's radiation to the earth. This radiation is absorbed on the hundreds of millions of square kilometers of the oceans and stored in vast amounts of living organisms stemming from photosynthesis and in the remains of this life—as organic and inorganic nutrients—and as vast amounts of heat in the surface waters of the tropic seas. These two resources—heat to supply energy and nutrients for food chains from single cells through all edible plants and animals up to man—are our greatest resources, as yet practically untapped. In the utilization of the heat, the third product, also from the usual radiation from the sun, fresh water, may be produced, often where needed most.

Sea water is always cold in the deeps, and often it approaches the temperature of its maximum density, near the freezing point. It is cooled in the Arctic and Antarctic where it settles to the depths and, by a grand thermosyphon system, moves on the bottom toward the tropics, where it is warmed, and moves again in tremendous currents toward the poles, to recycle. Photosynthesis in the upper layer penetrated by the sun produces single-cell organisms, thence bigger marine growths, and, by steps, up to the earth's largest plants and animals. Surface waters in the tropics may be crystal clear because pho-

Dr. Donald F. Othmer is a Distinguished Professor of Chemical Engineering at the Polytechnic Institute, Brooklyn, New York.

Dr. Oswald A. Roels is Director of the Port Aransas Marine Laboratory of the University of Texas Marine Science Institute in Port Aransas, Texas 78373.

From *Science*, Vol. 182, No. 4108, pp. 121-125, 1973. Reprinted with light editing and with permission of the authors and the American Association for the Advancement of Science. Copyright 1973 by the American Association for the Advancement of Science.

Supported by Sea Grant 1-36119. This article is Lamont-Doherty Geological Observatory contribution No. 2016 and City University of New York Institute of Oceanography contribution No. 21. The first engineering design was made by Alemco, Inc., a subsidiary of Viatech, both of Syosset, New York.

tosynthesis has utilized all nutrients; and larger living things have consumed all of the small organisms which cause haze, and thus have stripped the water of carbon, nitrogen, and phosphorus, the principal nutrients for life.

But this life, largely in surface water, dies, as does that in deeper water; and the remains settling slowly, as befits a burial, return to "dust," that of the ocean depths. Slowly these remains disintegrate; and, in solution and as particles, residues are carried in the deep currents back to particular areas of upwelling–only about 0.1 percent of the total area of the oceans. Here the great amount of nutrients causes an explosion of marine life. Just one major one, the upwelling of the Humboldt Current off Peru, supplies one-fifth of the world's total fish harvest.

## AVAILABILITY OF THERMAL ENERGY

Again with reference to energy (here heat), its concept implies the temperature of the "hot" substance being higher than that of another "cold" substance. Heat is only usable by its transfer to a colder body. Deep sea water may be from 15° to 25°C colder than surface water; but there is little conduction of heat, top to bottom, and little mixing because of density differences, except in notable upwellings.

While this temperature difference between surface and deep waters is small, considering usual sources of energy, the available heat is the product of this difference multiplied by the available masses of sea water which are infinite for all practical purposes. Means for the conversion of this available heat to electrical energy would give continuously very much more than mankind has found capability to use.

For example, the Gulf Stream, first studied scientifically by Benjamin Franklin, carries the heat absorbed in the Caribbean and the Gulf of Mexico past the coast of Florida. Some 2200 cubic kilometers of water per day may be as much as 25°C warmer than the cold, deep water which it was. To heat just 1 cubic kilometer of sea water per day 25°C would take six or eight times as much energy as all of the electrical energy produced in the United States. The reverse is staggering; it has been estimated that this heat in all of the Gulf Stream, if discharged to water colder by 25°C, could generate more than 75 times the entire electric power produced in all of the United States (*1*).

Both coasts of Africa, the west coast of both Americas, and the coasts of many islands, particularly in the Caribbean area, have places within a few miles of land where sea water has a surface temperature of 25° to 30°C, while at 750 to 1000 meters below the surface, the temperature may be 4° to 7°C (*2*). In some places, the ocean floor drops off from the shore line very steeply to an ocean deep within some hundreds of meters of land. The ideal location for a land-based power plant, using warm surface water on one side of a peninsula, would have a great sea depth close to shore on the other side of the peninsula. The contour of the bottom should be favorable to the installation of a large suction pipe to supply cold water.

## POTENTIAL VALUES

Both this energy and these nutrients are available, and they could supply all the world's power, light, and much of the protein food it uses; but so far they are locked away from us by the difficulty of their recovery from such dilute sources, compared to the relative ease of the utilization of other, more concentrated resources. With shortages of energy and food in the world, this utilization is a job for the present, and one well within the capabilities of technology now available. The dilution is indeed not prohibitive. The water brought up from the depths of tropical seas will absorb surface heat energy equal to the mechanical energy available from a 120-meter waterfall. Compared to other systems proposed for using solar energy, this utilizes a vast reservoir at any one of many places. Always the equipment for utilizing solar energy is large and expensive. And the mariculture using the nutrients can produce \$125,000 of product per year from each hectare of land converted to ponds [\$50,000 annually per acre].

Thus, if very large amounts of cold, deep sea water can be brought to the surface, warmed in receiving the heat discharged by a suitable power station, and passed to tropical ponds wherein its nutrients are used in photo- and biosynthesis by marine plant and animal food chains, the ultimate product is not fish meal or an artificial substance, but choice shellfish. The water is warmed in the pools to a temperature higher than surface sea water and is passed to the high temperature side of the power cycle. The simplest is direct production of very low pressure steam, turbine-generation of electricity, and condensation of the steam in warming the cold, deep sea water, giving fresh water as condensate.

## POWER CYCLE AND PROCESS ENGINEERING

Great minds backed by large sums of money, somewhat less large when the potential benefits are considered, have worked throughout almost a century to develop systems of utilizing the small difference of temperatures of surface and deep sea water to produce power (*3*). Claude made the most optimistic contributions 40 years ago (*4*), and the great problems which he recognized were principally two—the installation of the enormous pipeline to carry water from the depths and the removal of air from the evaporating warm water (*5*).

However, theoretically mechanical energy—and from it electrical energy—can be developed from heat from any body at any temperature being passed to any other body which can receive it, because of its lower temperature. Such energy is always more difficult and less efficient to produce, the lower this temperature difference is. Carnot showed the maximum efficiency to be $(T_1 - T_2)/T_1$ where $T_1$ is the temperature of the hot body and $T_2$ is the temperature of the cold body. These are measured above absolute zero.

This temperature difference for efficient heat engines may be many hundred or even a thousand degrees. The closer the temperature of the heat input approaches that of the output, the less the efficiency becomes. Here warm water is at 30°C and it is cooled, in producing very low pressure steam, to 25°C, the temperature of the steam. If this steam is condensed at 15°C by heating cold water from 5° to 10°C, with a 5°C loss in the condenser tubes, this temperature of 15°C may be regarded as the low temperature at which all heat is discharged.

Hence, if the steam supply is at 25°C, or 273° + 25° = 298°K, above absolute zero, and the corresponding temperature of the heat rejection is 15°C, or 273° + 15° = 288°K, then the maximum thermodynamic efficiency is (298 – 288)/298, or about 3.3 percent. Practically, because of many energy requirements in related machinery, and because of many losses, the efficiency obtainable could not be more than about 2 to 2.5 percent. Of equal importance usually, the amount and cost of equipment required always *increases* greatly with a decrease of the temperature difference. Thus, the heat in a cubic kilometer of warm sea water may be passed to colder sea water to develop mechanical energy, then electrical power. Necessarily, the heat available at this low temperature can be converted to power only with a large, costly plant, at a very low efficiency, and by the handling of extremely large amounts of the cold sea water to absorb the heat. However, the total amount of water to be handled may be less than the amount of water required to produce the same amount of power in a hydroelectric plant. Dams, penstocks, and machinery of a hydroelectric plant are also expensive in developing a "free kilowatt"; that is, free of cost of energy.

The cold water does not have to be lifted from the great depth by the pump; only the friction head must be considered, plus the small static head caused by the difference in density of the cold water and the average density of the water from the surface to the bottom of the pipe.

Various designs for floating power plants have been made with vertical suction pipes suspended from the vessel and with submerged power cables and fresh water lines carrying the products to the shore. However, these would make controlled mariculture more difficult.

Any plant for handling these large volumes of water and converting the available thermal energy to mechanical and then to electrical energy will be huge and expensive; and even the smallest one which would be worthwhile for demonstration purposes will involve many millions of dollars worth of equipment.

The simplest of many possible systems that have been studied depends on flash evaporating, in an evacuated chamber, a small amount of the warm water as it is partially cooled. This gives a maximum of 1 percent of the weight of the water as a very low pressure steam. This low pressure steam turns a turbine in cooling further and then is condensed on tubes through which the cold water from the deep is passing and being warmed. The condensate is fresh (distilled) water, almost always a valuable commodity on tropical coasts; and its sale adds to the revenue from the power produced by the generator turned by the steam turbine.

Because of the very low temperature and pressure of the steam, the turbine must be specially designed; and the condenser must be large. Some systems have not provided a surface condenser, but have depended on "open" condensation by sprays of the cold sea water. This produces no condensate fresh water, the sale of which is a valuable revenue for any system, unless a cooled fresh water spray were used (*6*).

A substantial plant using low pressure steam with a condenser for fresh water has been engineered (*7*). Several other designs were studied and discarded. The design for a 7180-kilowatt (net) power plant also showed an output of 6 million U.S. gallons of fresh water per day at a total installed cost of $18.4 million.

Several factors were considered in the economic analysis; and charts were made to show the interrelation of (i) the capacity factor, that is, actual production compared to maximum capacity, and (ii) the cost of power generation. Thus, for an investment of $18.4 million, a calculated maintenance and operating cost of $100,000 per year, at an assumed fixed cost of capital of 12 percent per year and a capacity factor of 0.9, fresh water would be produced for $1 per 1000 U.S. gallons, and electric power for 6 U.S. mills per kilowatt-hour; and, in general, total costs can be divided between the two products as desired, since total amounts of both are produced.

As another example, if the capital or fixed charges are taken as 16 percent per year at a capacity factor of 0.90; and if the cost of producing power is taken as 6 mills per kilowatt-hour, fresh water costs are $1.38 per 1000 gallons, or if power cost is taken as 1 cent per kilowatt-hour, then fresh water is $1.26 per 1000 gallons.

Under the economic conditions prevailing at the particular site, which changed during the program, the rate of return on private risk capital was not regarded as sufficiently attractive to private investors to warrant this investment to compete with power and fresh water from a combustion plant. The warm water was regarded as the more valuable stream—it contained the heat that was discharged to the equally necessary stream of cold water, brought up by the very expensive pipeline and pumping system.

In the case of a mariculture program, the valuable stream is that from the depths, with the nutrients therein. The warm water stream does nothing for the mariculture, except that its vapors condense and heat the cold water somewhat in passing through the condenser, and the higher temperature increases the rate of growth of marine life. However, it should be noted that, in passing through the sun-heated enclosed basins for mariculture, the effluent, when it is discharged back to the sea, may be warmer than the surface water from the open sea. If so, this effluent would be cycled through the flash evaporator or boiler of the electric power-fresh water system, and only one stream would be drawn from the sea. The process engineering, mechanical engineering design, and civil engineering design were completed along with the economic analysis which showed that this project was economically profitable. However, under other particular conditions pertaining at the site, it would be desirable to delay the construction of the plant for fresh water and electric power production. Some details may be of interest.

## PLANT LAYOUT AND EQUIPMENT AS FIRST DESIGNED

Because of an existing highway at the proposed site, the power and desalinating units were laid out about 140 feet from the shore line. Hydraulic losses and steam friction losses were minimized by short conduits with a minimum of bends. The warm surface water intake, a large subsurface conduit, supplies the boilers through trash racks and fine screen, then deaerators. Special design adapted from desalination evaporator practice minimized losses during flash-boiling of about 1 percent of the warm water supplied. A boiler discharge pump removes the cooled surface sea water.

A turbine with horizontal rotor is directly above each boiler and was designed to operate at a low speed because of its large diameter.

The two pipes for cold sea water intake were designed with a nominal diameter of 4.13 meters and to withstand the stresses imposed by the carefully planned system of installation and by the irregular sea bottom, the contour of which was explored from a small submarine. The section was located 4100 meters offshore at a depth of 975 meters.

## IMPROVEMENTS IN DESIGN OF PLANT AND EQUIPMENT

Improvements have been made in the newer design planned for installation as an integrated component with the mariculture unit at a demonstration plant. Various improvements and advantages will be included in the new design.

1) The water effluent from mariculture operations will be used, and it will be warmer than open sea water, thus a better efficiency should be achieved. Also there will be a considerable economy in almost eliminating the warm surface sea water circuit.

2) A greater ratio of surface water to deep sea water will use the latter more efficiently.

3) Improved design of the hydraulics of deep water systems should reduce installation and power costs.

4) Condenser cost will be greatly reduced if plastic tubes are used.

5) Boilers will use the controlled flash evaporation (CFE) system to reduce losses in pressure and temperature drops which will increase production of both water and power (*6, 8*). The CFE system also will reduce substantially the deaeration costs, which require 20 percent of power produced in previous plants.

6) In some locations where fresh water is unusually expensive, all of the available heat will be used for this production, with no power.

## MARICULTURE IN COLD, DEEP SEA WATER

Deep sea water which has absorbed the heat from warm surface water in producing power and fresh water has been brought to a temperature more favorable for biologic growth. It is rich in nutrients which often are exhausted almost completely by the high rate of photosynthesis in the sparkling clear surface tropic waters; and is practically free of organisms which produce disease in humans, predators and parasites of shellfish, fouling organisms, and manmade pollutants. By contrast, shellfish culture has had major pollution disasters in the past years along the continental Atlantic coast.

An experimental station has been operated on the north coast of St. Croix, one of the U.S. Virgin Islands, near Puerto Rico. Here the ocean floor slopes sharply to the Virgin Islands Basin (4000 meters deep) and reaches a depth of 1000 meters, 1500 meters offshore. Three [69-millimeter inside diameter (3 inches nominal)] polyethylene pipe lines, each 1800 meters (6000 feet) long, supply water from a 870-meter (2900 feet) depth in an amount of 159 liters (42 U.S. gallons) per minute. This water is warmed in being drawn up through the small pipes so that its cooling effect would be negligible but it is satisfactory for the mariculture work.

This water in January 1973 averaged (microgram atoms per liter) nitrate nitrogen, 32.1; nitrite nitrogen, 0.13; ammonia nitrogen, 1.1; phosphate phosphorus, 2.15; and silicon in silicates, 21.7. The salinity was 34,841 parts per million. While these amounts equal only a relatively small weight of synthetic nutrients which could be added, this clean, unpolluted water is free of parasites and hostile microorganisms which could endanger the cultured animals, or remain in their bodies to be passed to humans. Also the water, if used in a power and desalination cycle must be pumped up to gain its cooling value. It may also be fortified with additional amounts of added nutrients having components carefully chosen to give the greatest value in the particular mariculture used.

A development program is now in progress to determine the most desirable plant and animal species for a food chain to give optimum value of the produce species at the top of the chain with minimum cost in production. Two varieties of diatoms have been particularly satisfactory; and after inoculation the water develops up to 1 million diatoms per milliliter, when it is metered into the shellfish tanks.

Early work showed a 27-fold increase in unicellular algae (diatom) grown in water from a depth of 800 meters compared to that from the surface; and peak yields of 230 grams per cubic meter (1900 pounds per 1 million U.S. gallons) have been obtained. This amounts to 2.8 grams of algal protein per cubic meter of water.

Various types of shellfish feed on these unicellular animals by filtering them from the water they continually process; from previous work it appeared possible to obtain at least a 60 percent conversion of the diatoms to commercial foods. Thus, from an overall material balance, these nutrients of the deep sea water, basically the nitrogen, which would be utilized through the food chain to be explained, should give 1 kilogram of fresh clam meat per 300 cubic meters of deep sea water (27 pounds per 1 million gallons).

From the available marine life in nature, the most promising species are being chosen; there are hopes of improving the natural strains, as has been done by animal husbandry in every animal which has ever been bred for food. Greatly improved yields appear through proper control of (i) natural nutrient concentration—and possibly that of artificial nutrients, or other additives; (ii) solar radiation—by adjusting the depth of the ponds; (iii) water temperature; and (iv) still other variables as these first or axiomatic ones are optimized.

## ALGAL CULTURES

Many species of microscopic algae have been isolated, cultured, and studied as cultivated food for shellfish. Those preferred are fast-growing strains, readily accepted by shellfish and causing their rapid growth; they should be hardy against competitive organisms, against high summer temperatures, 32° to 33°C of the pools, and against the excessive sunlight radiation which prevails in shallow pools. Some have developed weight increases of young oysters (3 millimeters) of more than 75 percent in 3 weeks.

Extensive experiments in all sizes of tanks and pools up to 45 cubic meters (12,000 gallons) of 1.2 meters (40 inches) depth, with many variables, have indicated that dependable production of large amounts of algae satisfactory for shellfish food can be maintained. This work to improve the breed and production of algae continues because of the promise of considerable improvements in the development of better, more stable, and hardier strains. Also the geometry of the pools is being optimized; and continuous operation has been developed.

## SHELLFISH

Oysters and clams from cultures stemming from Long Island (New York), Japan, and various tropical locations have been worked with as brood stock and for growth studies.

Experimentation with the shellfish has indicated that certain species grow very rapidly indeed in this "artificial upwelling" system: thus, hybrid clams were grown to market size in 6 months. Similarly, the European oyster and the bay scallop were grown from spat to market size in 6 months (*9*). This is considerably faster than generally occurs in nature. Clams, European oysters, and bay scallops of commercial size grown in this system were submitted to a panel of seafood experts for taste testing, and judged to be of excellent taste and superior to those harvested in natural waters. Thus, hybrid clams averaging 8 grams, on introduction, increased in weight almost five times to 38.5 grams in 6 months so they could be marketed in the littleneck size.

Scallops multiplied their weight 60 times in 145 days, from an average single weight of 0.24 gram at an age of 8 days to 14.42 grams. Average lengths of the scallops were, respectively, 9 and 40.7 millimeters.

Oysters have grown from 3 millimeters to market size in a little more than 8 months; and one species of oysters grew from an average live weight of 1 gram when introduced to 70 grams in 74 days.

Shellfish filter the microorganisms from the water for food; their filtering efficiencies for gathering and retaining the food cells from the pools have varied from 49 percent without culling of the shellfish to over 90 percent when the small shellfish have been periodically harvested to stimulate the growth of the larger ones remaining. These harvesting techniques are now being optimized.

## CRUSTACEANS

A great variation in the growth rates of shellfish has been observed; one long-term objective is to improve the strain by selective breeding of the fastest growing individuals, which also have other desirable characteristics. Thus a large number of small clams at different ages would always be culled to minimize competition of the faster growing animals; and the culls may be used as a very acceptable food for crustaceans. First tried were adult spiny lobsters, native to St. Croix in the Virgin Islands. The best of these showed an average weight gain (in an 89-day period between moltings) of 55 percent, while eating 5.2 times as much food weight as its gain in weight.

Similar experiments are under way with cold water lobsters from the Massachusetts coast which are growing at a greatly accelerated rate in the warm waters of the mariculture ponds.

## SEAWEED

If the effluent from the shellfish and lobster growing operation were returned directly to the sea, the animal wastes might constitute a source of pollution. Therefore, experiments are under way with commercially useful seaweeds which can be processed to obtain either agar or carrageen. These seaweeds are grown in the effluent from the animal tanks, to optimize the nutrient utilization in the system, and to purify the discharged waters before returning them to the sea.

## CHAIN OF NUTRIENT UTILIZATION

The water from the deep will have been substantially warmed in the plant for production of energy and fresh water; and the optimum utilization of its nutrients appears now to be via (i) single cell algae; (ii) filter-feeding shellfish, such as oysters and clams, which feed on the algae; (iii) lobsters, shrimp, and possibly other crustaceans which feed on culls of the shellfish; and (iv) specialized seaweed, which grows in effluent water containing the solubilized body wastes of the shellfish and crustacea, and has several important markets.

## MARICULTURE PONDS AND OPERATION

The mariculture will be done in a series of shallow concrete pools of optimized depth. The deep sea water flows through slowly to permit residence times, not widely different, for (i) algal growth, (ii) shellfish growth, (iii) crustacean growth, and (iv) seaweed growth. The apportionment of the time periods for the different growths has not been established exactly to date but will be optimized insofar as possible to give the greatest financial return with the minimum of land and pool area.

For the demonstration plant now being planned, it is expected that 25,000 gallons (95 cubic meters) of deep sea water per minute will be available and that there may be a total of 6 hectares (15 acres) of ponds required with a total time of water in transit of about 2 days. This area may be divided approximately as follows: (i) 50 percent for algal growth, (ii) 10 percent for shellfish growth, (iii) 10 percent for crustacea growth, (iv) 20 percent for seaweed growth. It is impossible as yet to estimate the optimum operational yields of different products; but it is expected that, at an average annual yield, an average value at the plant will be about 340,000 pounds of shellfish at \$2.25 to \$2.50 per pound of meat. This works out to be an average of over \$50,000 annual revenue per acre of ponds without credit for values that cannot yet be optimized.

For a larger plant, handling 870,000 gallons (3390 cubic meters) per minute, a somewhat lower unit price for shellfish may have to be taken; and the total annual revenue has been projected to be between \$20 and \$25 million.

## SUMMARY

Many times more solar heat energy accumulates in the vast volume of warm tropic seas than that produced by all of our power plants. The looming energy crisis causes a renewal of interest in utilizing this stored solar heat to give, in addition to electric power, vast quantities of fresh water. Warm surface water, when evaporated, generates steam, to power a turbine, then fresh water when the steam is condensed by the cold water.

A great increase in revenues over that from power and fresh water is shown by a substantial mariculture pilot plant. Deep sea water contains large quantities of nutrients. These feed algae which feed shellfish, ultimately shrimps and lobsters, in shallow ponds. Wastes grow seaweed of value; and combined revenues from desalination, power generation, and mariculture will give substantial profit.

## REFERENCES

1. D. F. Othmer, in *Encyclopedia of Marine Resources*, F. E. Firth, Ed. (Van Nostrand, Reinhold, New York, 1969), p. 298.
2. R. D. Gerard and O. A. Roels, *Marine Technol. Soc. J.* **4** (No. 5), 69 (1970).
3. S. Walters, *Mech. Eng.* **93** (No. 10), 21 (1971).
4. G. Claude was developing support in the United States in 1925-26 for the pilot plant which he then built in Cuba. He gave a

demonstration lecture in the laboratories of the University of Michigan where D. R. Othmer was then a graduate assistant. Claude's equipment included a small tank for warm water and one for cold, a vessel to which the warm water was admitted to undergo flash evaporation (about 1 percent), a small steam turbine driven by the low pressure steam that was forming, a condenser having the cold water in direct contact with the turbine exhaust steam, and a vacuum pump for air removal. A small generator was driven by the turbine and was wired to a small electric bulb, which lit as the house lights went off—and the audience cheered.

5. G. Claude, *Mech. Eng.* **52** (No. 12), 1039 (1930).

6. The vapor reheat system of multistage flash evaporation uses a separately cooled fresh water stream to condense vapors for fresh water production and has been described [R. E. Kirk and D. F. Othmer, *Encyclopedia of Chemical Technology* (Wiley, New York, ed. **2**, 1970), vol. 22, pp. 39-48].

7. The sea water power and fresh water plant was engineered by Alemco, Inc., now a division of Viatech, Inc., Syosset, New York. One of us (D.F.O.) is a consulting engineer to and director of both corporations. The plant was designed for another island site in the Caribbean which was then regarded as eminently suitable.

8. R. C. Roe and D. F. Othmer, *Mech. Eng.* **93** (No. 5), 27 (1971).

9. J. S. Baad, G. L. Hamm, K. C. Haines, A. Chu, O. A. Roels, *Proc. Nat. Shellfish. Ass.* **63** (No. 6), 63 (1973).

# 27. Riches of the Ocean Floor

D. S. CRONAN 1976

There are many instances of minerals lying in shallow water near land, usually in the form of unconsolidated mineral aggregates known as placers. Important examples of these continental margin deposits are tin off Indonesia and South West England, titanium off Mozambique, diamonds off South West Africa and gold off Alaska. The deposits are formed through the erosion of minerals from the nearby land masses and they are concentrated either in old buried river channels, now submerged because of the post-glacial rise in sea level, or on the sea floor as a result of marine processes in shallow water. Because they are unconsolidated, they are relatively easy to raise. Minerals are found also in veins and lodes exposed where the rocks outcrop on the sea floor, but they are of less commercial interest than placers because they are much more difficult to extract.

Another mineral resource found in continental margin areas is phosphorite, which may be in the form of nodules, bedded deposits or grains spread throughout sediments. It lies mostly in deeper water than placers do, in many instances close to the edge of the continental shelf. The deposits consist largely of calcium phosphate, which is a valuable fertilizer, and their distribution is rather restricted, appearing to be related to the upwelling of cold water rich in nutrients along continental margins as, for example, off the West coasts of Africa and the Americas. How the phosphorus is precipitated is still a subject of research, but evidence is accumulating that it replaces carbonate ions in calcium carbonate, which is abundant on the sea floor in many shallow-water regions. Because there are extensive deposits of phosphate on land, marine phosphates are unlikely to be mined on a large scale for some considerable time.

## DEEP-SEA DEPOSITS

In deep sea areas two main types of mineral deposit are economically important, manganese nodules (Figure 27-1) and metalliferous sediments. They are related in origin but are usually found in different areas of the ocean floor, as shown in Figure 27-2. Manganese nodules are most abundant in the deepest parts of the oceans, other than the trenches, whereas metalliferous sediments are associ-

Dr. D. S. Cronan is the Director of the Marine Chemistry Program in the Applied Geochemistry Research Group with the Department of Geology, Imperial College of Science and Technology, London.

From *Spectrum,* No. 137, pp. 10-12, 1976. Reprinted with author's revisions and light editing, and with permission of the author and *Spectrum* (British Science News).

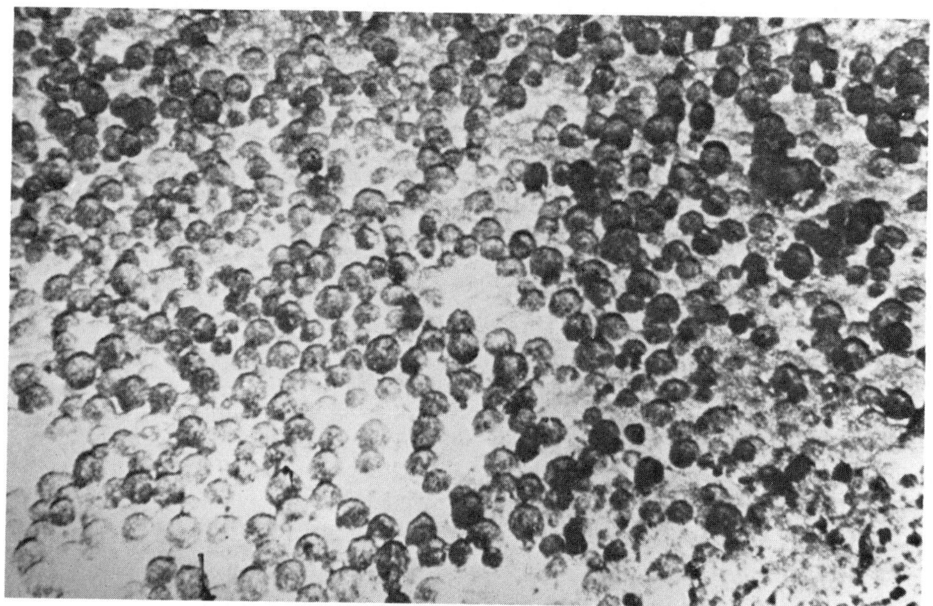

Figure 27-1. Manganese nodules on the ocean floor.

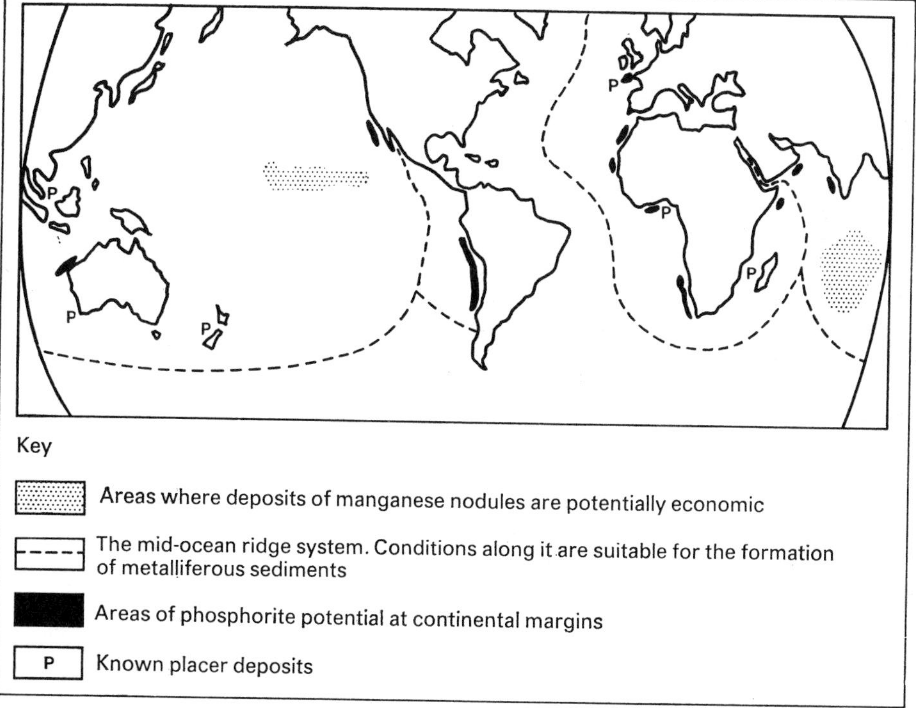


Figure 27-2. Distribution of mineral deposits in the oceans.

ated with submarine volcanic activity on mid-ocean ridges or in island arcs and their marginal seas.

Manganese nodules are the most valuable deep-sea mineral resource at present because they are abundant, they occur as unconsolidated deposits at the sediment surface and they contain concentrations of valuable metals such as nickel, copper, cobalt, lead and zinc, all precipitated from seawater. The deposits are mostly outside areas of national jurisdiction and therefore pose an ownership problem. They are developed to the greatest extent in the North Pacific, the central Indian Ocean and parts of the South Pacific, where small amounts of silts and clays are accumulating. The nodules usually grow around a nucleus of foreign matter such as pumice, shark's teeth or whale's earbones; detrital matter, that is matter from the land worn down by erosion, flowing into the sea inhibits nodule growth because it can bury the nuclei. Away from deep water, towards land, manganese nodules become sparser and sparser and are almost entirely absent on continental shelves.

The elements of most economic value in manganese nodules, nickel and copper, occur because the deposits grow very slowly and they scavenge these metals from seawater. However, not all nodules are equally enriched with these metals. Those with the highest nickel and copper content are found mainly in the North East equatorial Pacific and the central Indian Ocean. Why their distribution should be restricted in this way is being studied. In the applied geochemistry research group at Imperial College, research into the development of geochemical methods for locating nodules rich in nickel and copper have indicated that the mineral make-up of the nodules has a big effect on the rates at which these elements are extracted from the sea.

## TODOROKITE

We have found that there are two main minerals in manganese nodules: todorokite, which is a mixed oxide of divalent and quadrivalent manganese and which has a structure suitable for the inclusion of nickel and copper, and $\delta MnO_2$, which is almost all manganese dioxide and does not have a structure as suitable. Todorokite appears to be the principal mineral in nodules from the North East equatorial Pacific and the central Indian Ocean, and this may be part of the reason for the greater enrichment in nickel and copper there.

Another factor which could also be responsible for it is the occurrence of the nodules in the equatorial zone, where planktonic organisms are much more abundant than elsewhere. They can extract nickel and copper from the surface waters and transfer them to the ocean bottom when they die and sink. The physiochemical conditions prevailing at depths of more than 4500 meters, below which nodules rich in nickel and copper are most abundant, are such that most organisms dissolve, so liberating the metals into the bottom waters where they can be incorporated into the nodules. However, evidence is accumulating that some organisms that live on the bottom, benthonic foraminifera for example, may actually live on the growing nodules. They are thought to extract nickel and copper from seawater as part of their life processes, the metals becoming incorporated into the nodules as the deposits grow. Completely different factors are thought to affect the enrichment of the deposits in other metals such as cobalt and lead, and the enrichment of economically important elements in manganese nodules is likely to be a fruitful field of research for some time to come.

## ATLANTIS II DEEP

Metalliferous sediments in the oceans are less well known than manganese nodules, partly because their potential economic importance has only recently been recognized. The best examples described so far are in a series of deeps in the central valley of the Red Sea, where new ocean crust is being formed by volcanic processes. Such deposits are formed by the volcanic discharge of hot solutions containing metal into the sea. The reactions that take place on mixing cause sulfides, silicates and iron-manganese oxides to be precipitated, most of the valuable metals such as copper, zinc and lead being concentrated in the sulfides.

The Atlantis II Deep contains the best example of metalliferous sediment formation going on now in the Red Sea, and contains the most valuable deposits found so far. Within and around the deep, the sequential precipitation of metal sulfides, silicates and oxides takes place. The sulfides are restricted to the deep itself, where they precipitate first. Iron oxides precipitate when conditions become sufficiently oxidizing for $Fe^{2+}$ to be oxidized to $Fe^{3+}$; manganese precipitates last, under the higher pH and oxidation potential needed to oxidize $Mn^{2+}$ to $Mn^{4+}$.

This selective dispersion of hydrothermally introduced metals on mixing with seawater has been investigated at Imperial College using a series of sediment cores collected at increasing distances from the Atlantis II Deep. We have found a pattern of geochemical zones in the sediments around the deep, with an inner iron-rich halo and an outer manganese-rich halo, the latter extending as much as 10 km from the Deep. This knowledge is important in exploration elsewhere for deposits similar to those in the Atlantis II Deep. The economically valuable sulfides may have a small lateral spread but, if manganese from the same source can be widely dispersed around the deposit, exploration for areas of manganese enrichment in other submarine volcanic regions could find more deposits like those in the Atlantis II Deep.

## MID-OCEAN RIDGES

The central valley of the Red Sea is just a small part of the volcanically active mid-ocean ridge system which extends for many thousands of miles throughout all the oceans of the world, as shown in Figure 27-2, so the processes leading to metalliferous sediment formation in the Red Sea may be duplicated in other mid-ocean ridge areas. Metalliferous sediments rich in iron and manganese oxides have been found at many places on the ridge but, as yet, no associated sulfides rich in copper, lead or zinc.

A clue to the whereabouts of such deposits may be provided by analogy with the sequence of precipitates around the Atlantis II Deep, where the sulfides are early-formed precipitates from the hydrothermal solutions caused by volcanic action. The later precipitates include the iron and manganese oxides, similar to those on mid-ocean ridges elsewhere, so it may be that these other deposits are equivalents of the widely-dispersed precipitates around Atlantis II.

If this is so, the early precipitates, possibly including metal-rich sulfides, may have been concentrated in small restricted hollows next to the submarine hydrothermal vents or may be within the rocks through which the hydrothermal solutions have passed. Available evidence indicates the latter to be more likely. Owing to open ocean circulation over most parts of the mid-ocean ridge, conditions similar to those in which metal-rich sulfides are deposited in the Red Sea are unlikely on the sea floor but might occur in fractures and fissures within the rocks of the oceanic crust. Nevertheless, it is possible that the complete sequence of metalliferous deposits from sulfides to manganese oxides occur on the sea floor in areas of mid-ocean ridge similar to the Red Sea. The great fracture zones which cut across the mid-ocean ridge system in all the oceans have a combination of volcanic activity that could supply the metals and deep basins to entrap them.

## ISLAND ARCS

Another kind of region of submarine volcanic activity where metalliferous sediments similar to those in the Red Sea may be found is in marginal basins behind island arcs. The origin of island arcs and their marginal seas has not yet been fully explained but it is well known that they include areas where there are active submarine volcanoes. This activity, coupled with the possibility of the right conditions in some of the basins, could cause high-grade metalliferous sediments to be deposited. Ancient marginal seas around island arcs are thought to have been the places where some massive sulfide deposits now exposed on land were formed. Traces of sediments rich in iron and manganese have been found in existing island-arc marginal seas, particularly in the South West Pacific; more detailed exploration may reveal metal-rich sulfides of ore grade.

The genetic relationship between manganese nodules and metalliferous sediments is illustrated in Figure 27-3 and can most simply be explained in terms of the ratio of iron to manganese in the deposits. This ratio varies from metalliferous sediments very rich in iron at mid-ocean ridge crests to nodules very rich in manganese near some continental margins. Within this range are the iron-rich and manganese-rich metalliferous sediments typical of mid-ocean ridge crests, with a ratio of about 3, the ferromanganese oxide encrustations typical of mid-ocean ridge flanks with a ratio of between about 1·0 and 1·6, and the manganese-rich nodules typical of abyssal plains with ratios down to about 0·2. The reason for the differences in iron-to-manganese ratio of these deposits may be ascribed to the two elements having come from different sources, iron mainly being derived from volcanic sources at the ridge

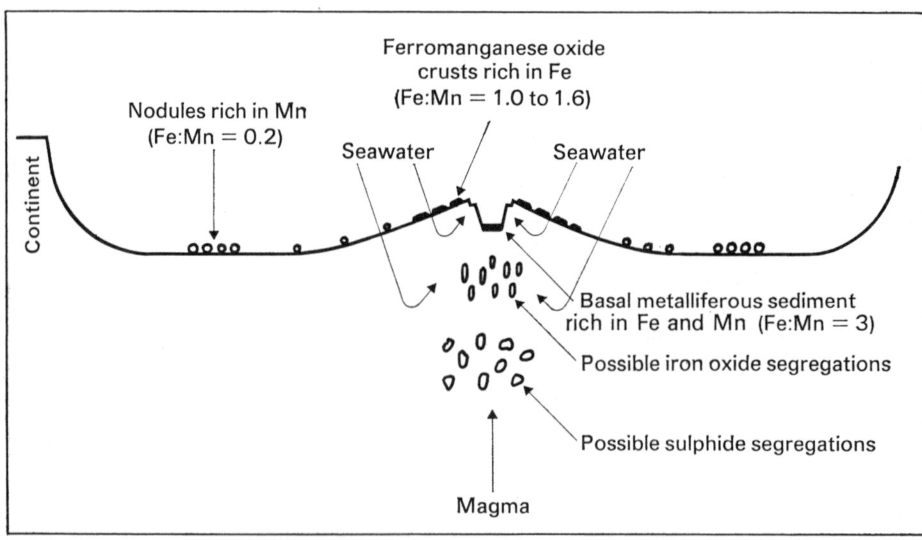


Figure 27-3. Idealized hypothetical section of mid-ocean ridge showing possible sequence of mineral deposition (not to scale).

crest and manganese from seawater. At the mid-ocean ridge crest, iron and some manganese, from volcanic sources, probably precipitate fairly rapidly on contact with seawater, possibly having a catalytic effect on the precipitation of more manganese from seawater. At greater distances from the ridge crest the proportion of volcanically-derived iron is less (although some can be supplied through the slow alteration of volcanic rocks exposed on the sea floor) and the proportion of manganese derived by slow precipitation from seawater is greater.

## EXPLOITATION

Obviously there is more to the exploitation of undersea mineral deposits than simply finding them. They have to be mined, processed and marketed. Processing and marketing probably do not present any great difficulties, but some hard technological problems will have to be solved before all the different types of deposits can be mined successfully. Placers have been exploited for some time and their extraction is relatively easy, using dredging and suction devices. Nobody has attempted to mine offshore phosphorite, so no system has been developed for it. By contrast, two systems are under development for mining manganese nodules, a hydraulic suction device similar in some respects to a vacuum cleaner and a system consisting of a large number of buckets which are lowered to the bottom on a chain-like conveyor belt. Each system has been tested at sea but neither is fully operational at present. The retrieval of metalliferous brines and sediments will most likely involve some sort of pumping.

In any undersea mining operation, vast amounts of sediment and bottom water are going to be disturbed and could create a pollution problem which may be particularly severe in enclosed basins like the Red Sea, where metal-rich brines will have to be brought to the surface so that the metals can be extracted. Ultimately, however, legal and financial considerations will probably fix the pace at which undersea mining progresses. The large sums of money that will have to be spent to set up commercial operation are unlikely to be forthcoming until there is internationally-accepted law for the ocean floors.

# 28. Minerals from the Deep Sea

SIR EDWARD BULLARD 1974

Ten years ago it seemed unlikely that the deep oceans contained mineral deposits of economic importance. The sea floor was known to be composed almost entirely of basaltic lava flows partly or entirely buried by sediments. The sediments were formed, in large part, by the slow accumulation of the skeletons of minute animals that had lived and died in the sea. The specimens brought up by coring tubes and dredges were of the greatest scientific interest, but did not promise a direct economic return.

The only hopeful feature was the occurrence of the manganese nodules discovered a hundred years ago by the Challenger Expedition (1, 2). These have been described in a recent article (3) and will not be discussed in detail here. Even if efficient methods of recovering them from the sea floor can be devised, it will be difficult to develop sufficiently cheap methods for separating the copper and nickel that they contain from the larger amounts of manganese and iron. It may be that other mineralized deposits of the deep sea floor will, in the long run, prove economically more attractive.

## THE "HOT HOLES" OF THE RED SEA

In 1948, the Swedish research vessel *Albatross* found unusually high temperatures at a point in the middle of the Red Sea, about half-way between Port Sudan and Jidda. For several years this remained an isolated observation, until in 1963-65 the American, British, and German ships *Atlantis II, Discovery,* and *Meteor* respectively made measurements of temperature and salinity and collected water samples in the neighborhood of the anomaly found by *Albatross.* The results were truly remarkable and led to a detailed study in 1966 by the research vessel *Chain* of the Woods Hole Oceanographic Institution (Figure 28-1). Most of our knowledge of the hot holes comes from the results of this cruise and particularly from the work of J. L. Bischoff and his collaborators (4). Very recently an elaborate study of both the water and the sediments has been made by the German ships *Valdivia* and *Wando River* (5).

Three closed basins were found; the largest, called Atlantis II Deep, is about 15

Sir Edward Bullard is Professor of Geophysics with the Department of Geodesy and Geophysics at the University of Cambridge, Great Britain, and has done experimental work on gravity, seismology, and the measurement of heat flow on land and at sea. He has written on the origin of the Earth's magnetic field and on magneto-hydrodynamics.

From *Endeavour,* Vol. 33, No. 119, pp. 80-85, 1974. Reprinted with light editing and with permission of the author and *Endeavour.*

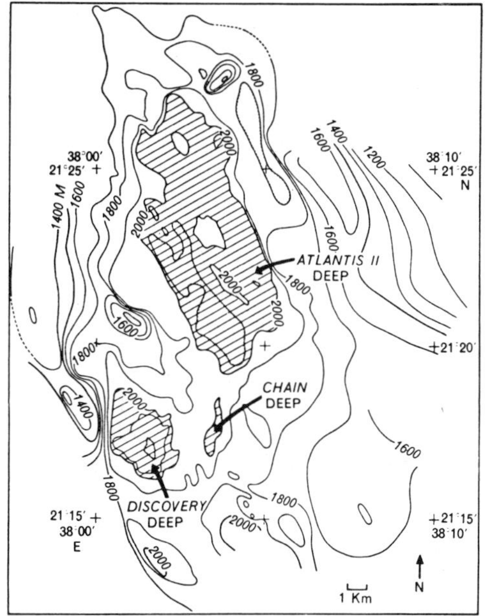


Figure 28-1. A chart of the hot holes; the area of hot brine is shaded. The deeps are named after three research ships which have worked in the area. (Reproduced from [4] by permission of the Editors.)

km long and 5 km wide. In each of the basins the water depth exceeds 3600 m; they are separated by sills with depths of less than 3000 m. The basins are filled with water at a temperature of 56°C, overlain by a thin layer of cooler water (about 40 m thick) at 44°C. The hot water is about seven times as saline as normal Red Sea water, which is itself a good deal saltier than the rest of the oceans. The sediments below the hot water contain layers of yellow, red, and blue clay. These layers contain a great variety of metals including sulphides of copper and zinc (see Figure 28-2). If they were found on land they would be regarded as valuable ores.

If, for the moment, we leave aside all questions of the practicability of recovering the ore and extracting the metals, the value of what lies in the hot holes is impressive. Dried material from the colored layers contains about 4 per cent of copper, 9 per cent of zinc, and traces of silver and gold. The dark material higher up contains smaller proportions of the metals but is thicker. In all, the upper 8½ m of sediment in Atlantis II

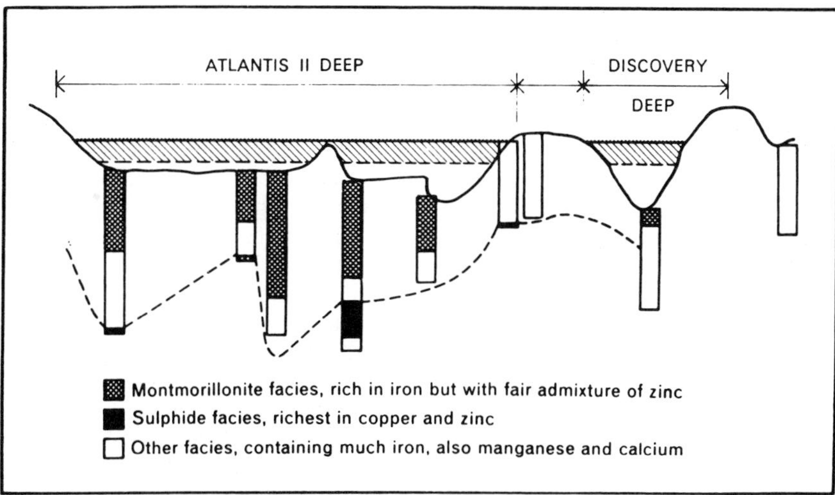


Figure 28-2. A section across the Atlantis II Deep and the neighboring Discovery Deep showing the hot water and the mineralized sediments. The part of the sediment shown shaded is richest in iron, and contains some zinc. The parts shown in black are richest in copper and zinc; the unshaded areas contain iron with some manganese, calcium and other light metals. The greatest depth penetrated by the corer was 8 m. It is not known how far below this the mineralized zone extends. The vertical scale of the topography is exaggerated 16 times; that of the cores beneath the bottom 870 times. (Based on [4] by permission of Dr. J. L. Bischoff and Prof. E. T. Degens.)

Deep, which is all that has been examined, contains 1.1 million tons of copper and 2.9 million tons of zinc spread through sediment which, when dried and freed from salt, would weigh 83 million tons. If the copper and zinc could be extracted they would, at January 1974 prices, be worth £2500 million, that is £30 per ton of dried sediment. How much lies below the depth that has been sampled is unknown, perhaps nothing, perhaps several million tons of metal. Longer cores have been recovered by *Valdivia,* but the published account of them gives no details of the copper and zinc sulfides.

Such calculations are often entirely misleading; for example, it is easy to show that there is more gold dissolved in the water of the Gulf of Mexico than there is in Fort Knox but, in the absence of an economical method of extraction, no one is any the richer. The object of the calculation is to show that there are important mineral resources beneath the floor of the deep sea and that it is worth considering how we might find and work them. First, we need some background knowledge of the Red Sea ores.

## THE RED SEA AND ITS ORES

The recent revolution in our knowledge of the history of the oceans makes it worthwhile to stand back a little and take a broad look at the surroundings of the hot holes. If we can understand them in terms of the new theories, perhaps we can tell where to look for other similar ore-bodies.

The Red Sea has been formed by the separation of Arabia and Africa during the past 20 million years. At first the crust was stretched and a depression was formed, then a crack appeared through which molten rock welled up and formed lava flows on the floor of the depression. As the valley was widening the sea was intermittently able to break in, at first from the Mediterranean to the north and later from the Indian Ocean at the southern end. Even today, when the valley is a sea 150 miles wide, the connection with the open ocean is not very secure. In the past this connection has often been cut, the water in the Red Sea has evaporated, and salt has been deposited. Drilling on the shores shows up to 4 km of salt and seismic shooting at sea suggests that the salt extends over a large part of the whole depression. To get a layer of salt even 1 km thick, the Red Sea would have to be evaporated and refilled about 100 times. We can thus imagine the thick layer of salt building up intermittently through most of the last 20 million years at an average rate of a few centimeters per thousand years. While it was building up it would have been continually split by the separation of Arabia and Africa and penetrated and overlain by lavas.

Sea water would penetrate through the cracks in the salt and would come in contact with the hot lavas beneath; it would then rise to the surface in the central valleys and form brine pools. Some such process must have occurred, since the water in the brines has isotope ratios characteristic of sea water. The salt in the brine has presumably come from the layers of salt through which the water has travelled. The copper and zinc have probably come from the lavas; in the solidification of an igneous rock such things are often excluded from the crystallizing solid and carried away in the hot water, steam, and volcanic gases.

The brine in the hot holes does not retain the metals in solution; they are precipitated as sulfides and form sedimentary ores at the bottom of the holes. Just why or how the precipitation takes place is not very clear; perhaps there are separate streams of hot water carrying hydrogen sulfide to the holes (it is common in volcanic gases); there may be sulfates in the water, derived from the salt deposits, which are reduced by aqueous bacteria to form $H_2S$. A study of the ratios of the light and heavy sulphur atoms ($^{32}S$ and $^{34}S$) suggests that the first process is the more important in Atlantis II Deep and the second in the other deeps.

The time taken to form the sediments in the hot holes has been measured by carbon

14 and other methods and is only some 10-20 thousand years; the rate of deposition is 10 to 30 cm in a thousand years and is many times greater than is usual in deep water. We therefore have a picture of a rather temporary phenomenon. We have cracking and lava flows on the axis of the Red Sea, a flow of water down through the cracks in the salt to the hot lava and then out again into the hot holes where the sulfides are deposited. After a few tens of thousands of years the lavas will cool and the cracks will be filled and the process will stop. The ordinary processes of sedimentation will slowly cover the ore with skeletons of minute marine plants and animals and there will be nothing to show that the ore is there. Meanwhile the cracking will start somewhere else along the axis of the sea and a new brine pool will be formed. As the sea widens the ore bodies will be carried away from the axis by the motion of the African and Arabian plates.

We shall therefore expect to find actively forming ore bodies in the central valley of the Red Sea. In fact, another deep filled with hot brine has been found by German workers (6); it seems to contain no mineralized sediment. On each side we may hope to find 'fossil' hot holes which are no longer hot and are buried under a few inches or a few feet of normal marine sediment. Sometimes they may be covered by lava flows.

Embryo oceans, such as the Red Sea, are rare; in fact, the only other clear examples are the Gulf of Aden, which is an extension of the Red Sea, and the Gulf of California. Neither of these is known to possess hot holes or sulfide ores, but it would be surprising if drilling did not reveal them. It is very desirable that a thorough study be made of the Gulf of California.

The Imperial Valley is a northward extension of the Gulf of California and differs from it only in being above sea level. Near the Salton Sea there are bore holes yielding hot mineralized water generally similar to that in the hot holes of the Red Sea, but containing a higher concentration of metals and more lead and silver relative to copper than do the Red Sea brines. It is disappointing that no major discovery of ore has been made in the Imperial Valley, but the large thickness of sediments renders search difficult.

The Afar region of Ethiopia is also to be regarded as an extension of the Red Sea. Its numerous hot springs and steam vents should be examined for signs of mineralization.

## MINERALS IN THE MAJOR OCEANS

If the Atlantic Ocean started as a narrow crack comparable to the Red Sea, then we may expect that, in the early stages, salt will have been deposited and holes filled with hot mineralized brine will have been formed just as they have been in the Red Sea. The mineral deposits in the holes will move away from the axis of the widening ocean and will be buried under sediments. Thus we may expect a ring of mineralized sediment to surround the Atlantic, lying somewhat above the basement of basaltic lava flows and underlying the sediments at the foot of the continental slope.

The JOIDES project, a joint undertaking by five U.S. universities for drilling in the floor of the deep sea, has discovered mineralized sediment in the Atlantic in just these circumstances. Their hole number 105 was drilled 500 miles south-east of New York in water 5251 m deep (7) (Figure 28-3). Six hundred metres of sediment were found overlying typical oceanic basalt. The lowest sediment, just above the basalt, was 153 million years old, and at the time of its origin this part of the Atlantic was probably about 900 km wide. About 10 m above the basalt there was a thin vein of tiny crystals of metallic copper; higher up, in material deposited about 100 million years ago (the date is uncertain from lack of suitable fossils), there is a layer 60 m thick which resembles the mineralized zone in the Red Sea. The sediment contains zinc sulfide which, in patches, constitutes 50 per cent of the mate-

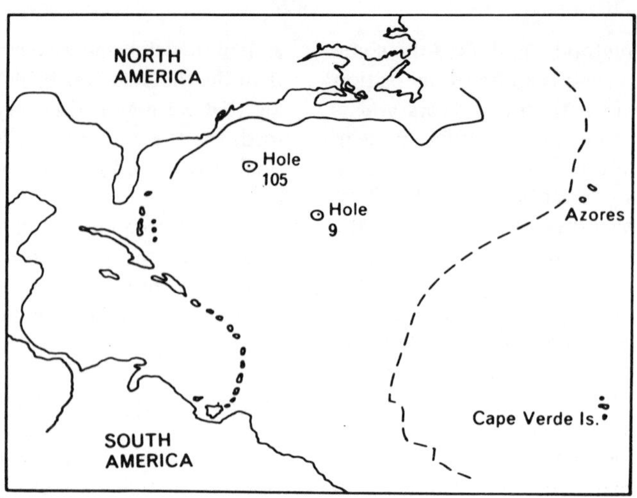


Figure 28-3. Positions of JOIDES holes 105 and 9 both of which show mineralization. The axis of the mid-ocean ridge is shown as – – – and the edge of the continental shelf as ——.

rial; the amount of copper in the samples so far analysed is less than 0.1 per cent though, rather surprisingly, there was enough to turn the drilling gear green. No salt was found in this hole though it is known at other places on the edge of the Atlantic. The sediments in hole 105 are of no possible commercial significance since they are only slightly mineralized and are deeply buried. Their discovery is mainly of interest in showing that the Red Sea ores are not a rarity peculiar to a given site and time, but are an example of a general process.

The next and critical question is: are such ores formed only in the early stages of ocean growth and are they therefore confined to the edges of the major oceans or are they formed all the time as an ocean splits along its central valley? We do not know the answer. Salt deposits will be formed only so long as the ocean is a narrow valley intermittently connected to the open ocean. Perhaps the salt and the resulting brine are essential to ore formation; perhaps in the absence of the heavy brine, the ore-bearing solutions from the volcanic rocks are carried away by ocean currents instead of being held and precipitated as sulfides in hot holes. Perhaps the ore is usually covered by lava flows.

There is some evidence for ore formation, or at any rate for mineralization of sediments in the open ocean. Hole number 9 of the JOIDES project was drilled 500 miles further out to sea than hole 105 and two years earlier. Black specks were noticed in the sediment and were thought to be magnetite. After the discovery of mineralization in hole 105, the cores from hole 9 were re-examined and it was found that the specks consisted of zinc sulfide. Thus in this part of the Atlantic, the ore is not confined to the edge of the ocean. On the other hand, it was not found in several other holes drilled between the coast of the U.S.A. and the mid-ocean ridge and therefore does not occur everywhere. A Russian expedition found a boulder of nickel ore in the central valley of the mid-Atlantic Ridge. There is little sediment in the central valley of the Atlantic and few cores have been taken and few of these examined for metals. We may have missed something important.

On the axis of the East Pacific Rise there is no central valley and more sediment than in the Atlantic. Melvin Peterson of the

Scripps Institution has shown that the sediment on the axis is mineralized though not to the extent that would make it interesting as an ore body.

A quite separate line of evidence comes from Cyprus. The geological history of this island has long been a puzzle but, thanks to the work of Gass and others, it is now clear that the southern part of the island is a piece of ocean floor. In the valleys of the Troodos Mountains we can see the upper mantle overlain by lavas that were poured out under water and then covered by sediments. The whole sequence has been pushed above sea level, perhaps as an incident in the on-going collision of Africa and southern Europe. Among the sediments and in the lavas are important copper deposits which have been worked for 2000 years and are now nearing exhaustion. Drummond Matthews has suggested that these deposits were formed on the ocean floor by processes similar to those that have produced the Red Sea ores. At the time they were formed the Mediterranean was a wide ocean, part of the Tethys Sea which separated Europe and Asia from the southern continent of Gondwanaland. Here there is further evidence, perhaps a little speculative, that ore can be formed in the open ocean. The main doubt is whether Cyprus was part of the main Tethys ocean floor or was part of some narrow arm of the sea. A. Miyashiro (8) believes that they were formed near an island arc and not on the axis of a mid-ocean ridge.

## PROSPECTING IN THE DEEP SEA

If we believe that the deep sea contains ore then we need methods of finding it. As a start we might try to look for ore containing a few per cent of the sulfides of copper and zinc mixed with iron oxides, clay and finely-divided calcium carbonate either exposed on the sea floor or buried under a few feet of deep-sea calcareous ooze. Such ore would be easier to find and more likely to be workable than more deeply-buried material. It might or might not be associated with hot brine. It would be likely to be found in closed basins near the axis of a mid-ocean ridge, particularly in embryo oceans.

In such circumstances the study of variations in gravity or of the Earth's magnetic field are unlikely to be helpful. The rugged topography of the lava flows will mask small effects associated with the ores. The measurement of the electrical resistance of the sediments is unlikely to detect the ore but might detect brine. The most helpful physical methods appear to be to search for places where the water near the bottom is abnormally hot and to look for potential differences in the water. Sulfides are fairly reactive chemically and, in the presence of sea water or brine, may be expected to be slowly oxidized and to act as electric batteries producing currents and differences of potential in the sediments and in the overlying sea water. Another possibility is geochemical prospecting. Samples of water and sediments would be examined for traces of copper and zinc and also for volcanic gases, particularly $SO_2$ and $H_2S$.

The physical methods are, in principle, rather simple. A recording thermometer and a pair of electrodes would be towed along the sea floor and the temperature and the potential difference recorded on a recorder towed with the thermometer and electrodes. Such a device would reveal whether there was anything interesting to record, but would not be an efficient prospecting tool. For this purpose, one would need to transmit the results by cable to the ship and record them on board. Also needed would be cameras to photograph the bottom, acoustic responders to find the position of the instruments relative to the ship and devices to sample the water and sediments, either at regular intervals or on command. All this could be done with existing technology, though some development would be needed in sample collection. The ideal vehicle to carry the gear along the bottom would be the "Troika" developed by

Jacques Cousteau about fifteen years ago and unaccountably neglected by the major oceanographic institutions. This is a sledge which is towed along the bottom and is so designed that it can surmount most obstacles and is self righting if accidentally overturned. The Troika could carry the cameras, the thermometer, the sampling equipment, the responder and one of the electrodes. The other electrode would be towed a hundred meters or so astern. At a later stage one could conceive of analytical equipment capable of continuously monitoring trace elements in the water and sediment, but this would be a project of a different order of difficulty and expense. Naturally, anomalies found by geophysical or geochemical means would need to be followed up by coring of the sediments and ultimately by drilling.

There appears to be here an almost unexplored field of marine geology and geophysics which is neither very expensive nor very difficult to enter and which might have important practical consequences. C. Brewitt-Taylor has recently shown measurements of potential on the deep-sea floor from a moving ship to be practicable and the noise level to be around 1 mV for electrodes 50 m apart.

## METHODS OF PRODUCTION

The ore on the floor of the deep ocean is useless unless economical methods can be found for recovering it and extracting its metal. The difficulties are obvious and do not need to be stressed. To mine in the deep sea is to work in a new environment in ways to which miners are not accustomed. It involves not merely taking traditional methods to sea but developing new methods appropriate to the changed circumstances. No one knows what such an enterprise would cost or whether it would be profitable. Perhaps it is better, at the start, to consider, in a rather optimistic frame of mind, how one might set about the task and maximize the advantages of the marine environment, rather than to stress its difficulties and hazards.

The Red Sea ores are soft muds. It is likely that they could be converted to a fluid by a little agitation and pumped to the surface. Here we have a great advantage over most metalliferous mining on land. Nature provides us with a slurry and we have no need to drill, sink shafts, excavate rock or to crush and grind ore to separate the mineral particles.

The techniques for keeping a platform stationary in deep water and of lowering tubes to the bottom have been developed by the JOIDES drilling project and now present no great problems. The platform need not be anchored and can be kept in place by means of its propellers, relative to acoustic responders placed on the bottom. When the material comes on board it would be necessary to remove most of the brine and as much as possible of the clay and calcium carbonate. Some kind of centrifugal separator seems attractive. The volumes to be handled are large—for example, if the top 8½ m of Atlantis II Deep were to be mined in five years, 400,000 tons of wet sediment would be removed daily.

The output from the centrifuge would be copper and zinc sulphides mixed with a larger amount of iron oxides and some sand. The traditional method of smelting such an ore does not seem well adapted for use at sea. The provision of fuel, flux and material for relining furnaces would be expensive and inconvenient. If the traditional process were to be used it would probably be best to remove the partially dried ore from the centrifuge and ship it to a refinery on land. It is not clear that this is the ultimate solution. Perhaps a wet process can be devised using chemicals derived from air and sea water. Among the substances that are, in principle, available are hydrogen, oxygen, hydrochloric acid, ammonia, nitric acid, and caustic soda. Whether such schemes will, ultimately, be attractive is difficult to say. The cost of development would be high, partly because of the problems of avoiding widespread contamination of the ocean.

## POLITICS AND THE FUTURE

It can reasonably be hoped that we are about to discover major mineral resources of whose existence no one dreamt a few years ago. The situation is somewhat similar to that in the late 1930s, when the great thickness of the sediments on the continental shelves was discovered. At first the oil companies were quite uninterested; the development of a new technology to tap a resource which might be too small to be economic and which was not essential to their operations seemed too daunting. Gradually, however, they became used to the idea and began to dip their toes in the water. The lure of politically secure oil became stronger as the sheiks became more demanding.

Will the same story repeat itself in the deep ocean? There seems to be little doubt that, whether the mining companies are interested or not, the oceanographic institutes, the universities and government establishments will continue to study the ocean floor, to make geophysical surveys and to drill. In 10 years we should know, in outline, what is available. A series of most difficult questions then arises. How can a company operate in a perfectly lawless environment? How can anyone be expected to set up a platform in the Red Sea when there is no one from whom he can obtain valid permission to prospect and mine and who will assume an obligation to give protection from other claimants and interlopers? Over most of the deep ocean no development can take place without new international agreements. There are exceptions to this; for example, no one is likely to deny that Mexico has sole rights over mining in the Gulf of California, even though it would be difficult to point to any agreed principle of international law that establishes the rights.

It seems that the only body of law remotely applicable to the subject is the 1958 treaty on the continental shelf. This provides that, on the shelf, prospecting and mining of minerals are under the control of the country that owns the nearest land. This treaty has formed the basis for a fairly amicable division of oil rights in the North Sea and seems a reasonable basis for such purposes. Unfortunately, the "continental shelf" to which it applies is defined in the treaty as "the seabed and subsoil of the submarine areas adjacent to the coast but outside the area of the territorial sea, to a depth of 200 m or, beyond that limit, to where the depth of the superjacent waters admits the exploitation of the natural resources". The final words might be thought to extend the area to the whole of the deep ocean, except that the deep ocean is not the continental shelf and most of it cannot be reasonably said to be "adjacent" to any land.

An extension of the principles of the 1958 treaty to the deep oceans would lead to absurd conclusions and would sterilize indefinitely what may prove to be important resources. Consider, for example, the northwest Indian Ocean. Here the "nearest land" rule gives control of almost all the area to the governments of the Seychelles, Mauritius, the Maldive and Laccadive Islands, and the Chagos Archipelago, the coastal states being largely excluded. In the South Pacific, control would be fragmented among the owners of thousands of atolls, many of them uninhabited.

Clearly no rational man will invest money where the rights to control and the obligation to protect are so ill-defined and, if substantial development is to occur, some new agreement is needed. The only solution seems to be a system of licenses from some international body for all production beyond some depth and some distance from shore. Such a proposal has been made in the United Nations and is at present the subject of negotiations.

Any agreements on prospecting and mining carry serious risks of hampering oceanographic investigations of all sorts. The 1958 treaty has already had this effect on the continental shelf and it is to be hoped that those conducting the present negotiations at the U.N. will attach due importance to this in drafting their treaties.

## REFERENCES

1. Murray, J. and Renard, A. F. 'Report on deep-sea deposits,' in Report on the scientific results of the voyage of HMS Challenger during the years 1873-1876, Vol. 5. Eyre & Spottiswoode, London. 1891.
2. Horn, D. R. (editor). Papers from a conference on ferromanganese deposits on the ocean floor. National Science Foundation, Washington. 1972.
3. Tooms, J. S., *Endeavour,* **31**, 113, 1972.
4. Bischoff, J. L. In 'Hot brines and recent heavy metal deposits in the Red Sea'. E. T. Degens and D. A. Ross (Editors). Springer, New York. 1969.
5. Backer, H. and Richter, H. *Geol. Rundschau,* **62**, 697, 1973.
6. Baumann, A., Richter, H., and Schoell, M. *Geol. Rundschau,* **62**, 684, 1973.
7. Hollister, C. D. *et al.* 'Initial Reports of the Deep Sea Drilling Project'. Vol. 11. U.S. Govt. Printing Office, Washington. 1972.
8. Miyashiro, A. *Earth Planet. Sci. Lett.,* **19**, 218, 1973.

# 29. Ocean Boundaries and Petroleum Resources

HOLLIS D. HEDBERG 1976

During the last decades, the focus of world interest and activity in exploration for petroleum has been moving more and more into the oceans. In the highly competitive petroleum industry, rewards have traditionally gone to those who were willing and able to be the first to brave the hazards of strange and forbidding environments in order to preempt the choice petroleum areas they might contain. Thus, exploration has advanced through the mountains, the deserts, the jungles, the swamps, and the arctic tundras on land, and is already widespread in the coastal waters of the seas and oceans.

The entry to each new environment has been made possible only as specialized equipment and technology could be developed to meet the special problems of each. The complexities of resource extraction offshore once seemed completely prohibitive, but the development of marine geophysical prospecting and various types of marine drilling installations suited to various water depths has now made exploration and production in shallow and moderately deep offshore waters of the continental shelf entirely feasible and, in some respects, less difficult than in some land areas. Currently, there are hundreds of offshore fields producing oil and gas in the world; 17 percent of U.S. production and 18 percent of world production in 1973 came from these offshore sources (*1*).

Progress into deeper waters of the outer shelf, the slope, and beyond still presents formidable obstacles. However, exploration holes for petroleum now have been drilled in water depths of as much as 655 meters (2150 feet), and production has been established in water depths of more than 125 meters (about 400 feet). The latest record of the Joint Oceanographic Institutions for Deep Earth Sampling Deep Sea Drilling Program is a hole penetrating 1411 meters (4656 feet) below the ocean floor in a water depth of 4975 meters (16,417 feet).

Costs of offshore petroleum drilling and production operations are extremely high, and in waters as deep as 1000 meters or more would be fantastically so. However, there is now little doubt that drilling and production at these and greater depths can and will be accomplished eventually if the prospective returns are great enough.

Dr. Hollis D. Hedberg is Professor Emeritus of Geology at Princeton University, Princeton, New Jersey.

From *Science,* Vol. 191, No. 4231, pp. 1009-1018, 1976. Reprinted with light editing and with permission of the author and the American Association for the Advancement of Science. Copyright 1976 by the American Association for the Advancement of Science.

## POLITICAL-ECONOMIC SETTING

Apart from matters of technology, two factors during the last few years have drastically altered the situation with respect to petroleum from the deep offshore waters. (i) The recent multifold increase in the price of crude oil on world markets and the recent emphasis on an inevitable future shortage of supplies of hydrocarbon energy have escalated the values attributed to potential offshore petroleum properties. (ii) The wave of nationalization of the petroleum industry, together with the increased prices of crude oil and the energy crisis, has stimulated a keener sense of national proprietorship in the ocean beds by those countries with ocean coastlines. In contrast with this latter point has been the appeal so eloquently voiced by U.N. Ambassador Pardo from Malta in 1967 and endorsed in word if not in spirit by many others since—the doctrine that the oceans are the heritage of all mankind and that the resources of the deep-ocean floor belong to the community of nations rather than simply to those nations who happen to control coastlines adjacent to them.

## NATIONAL-INTERNATIONAL BOUNDARY

The result of the interplay of these factors has been the impasse at meetings of the U.N. Committee on the Peaceful Uses of the Seabed and the Ocean Floor Beyond the Limits of National Jurisdiction, starting in New York in 1968 and most recently held in Geneva during the spring of 1975, on the question of to whom the ocean floors belong. Another meeting is scheduled for March 1976 in New York but a solution satisfactory to the various parties concerned is dubious.

Nearly everyone recognizes that there should be an outer limit to the areal extent of a coastal state's jurisdiction over the ocean floor extending outward from its shores. Also, it is generally agreed that the great central regions of the deep ocean floor should be under international jurisdiction. The big problem is just how far out the boundary between national and international domains should be drawn.

It is critically important that the position of this boundary be decided promptly. It is equally important that it be decided wisely. Once petroleum exploration drilling has progressed out to water depths which may bring it close to this boundary, and the position of particularly attractive areas for petroleum development begins to be known, the problem of attaining any boundary agreement based on principle rather than on self-interest, greed, or military power will have become infinitely more difficult.

Various boundaries based on depth of water or distance from shore, or a combination of the two, have been proposed but none have been adopted. At the moment, the proposal which is said to have the most support is that of a national-international boundary 200 nautical miles (1 nautical mile = 1852 meters) from shore. However, for subocean resources this proposal lacks any basis in nature or logic; it is largely an inheritance from the fishing claims of certain South American countries. As applied to petroleum (and other mineral resources) such a boundary would be unacceptable to many countries who would lose much potentially valuable territory naturally pertaining to them, whereas others would needlessly be given huge tracts of ultra-deep ocean bed which would more appropriately have been assigned to an international oceanic regime.

Moreover, although the 200-mile boundary superficially has a simple and definite sound, there appears to be little realization of the many problems involved in its practical implementation. One of these is the lack of any uniform rule among nations for determining the coastal base lines from which the 200-mile distance would be measured. Another is the unsettled question of whether the 200 miles should be measured from the mainland coast only, or whether any or all of the myriad reefs, islets, and islands of the continental shelves, far from shore but belonging to coastal nations, might also be used to extend their 200-mile limits farther seaward. Furthermore, probably few have considered how difficult accurate definition on the ocean floor of 200-mile limits measured off from an irregular coastline might be, although the time might come when such precise and detailed definition of the national-international boundary would be of the greatest economic and political consequence.

## REQUIREMENTS FOR BOUNDARY

Any plan for a boundary between national and international jurisdiction that could, in the long run, prove acceptable to the nations of the world would be so in proportion as it satisfied the following conditions.

1) It should be a plan with a logical or natural reason behind it rather than one that is purely artificial.

2) As a minimum, it should give to each nation what appears to be the natural prolongation of its land mass—continental or insular—beneath the oceans.

3) It should allow each coastal nation a substantial maritime zone of ocean bottom adjacent to its shores, regardless of the narrowness of its shelf or the steepness of its slope.

4) It should be a plan which it would be equitable to impose uniformly on all nations without exception or special modification for any.

5) It should be a plan that provides for the boundary problems of islands, whether on the shelf or in the deep sea and whether isolated or in archipelagos.

6) It is desirable that it allow each coastal nation to be represented in the fixing of its own precise boundary, which should be defined by coordinates of latitude and longitude within internationally agreed guidelines.

7) It should be a plan which can accomplish uniformly for all nations whatever turns out to be the agreed wishes of the nations with respect to a national-international division of the ocean bottom out beyond the minimum coastal state limits.

8) Finally, it should be a plan which, while recognizing the natural oceanward extent of the coastal state domain, at the same time leaves some substantial part of the potentially valuable resources of the ocean bottom to the international domain.

## CONTINENTAL MARGIN BOUNDARY GUIDE

In contrast to the many artificial distance boundaries and the even more artificial and impractical water-depth boundaries that have been proposed, there is one obvious, natural, and logical guide to a division between national and international jurisdiction over the ocean floor. This is based on the difference between the topographically high-standing continental and island blocks of the earth's surface—the traditional domain of mankind and the nations—and the topographically low-lying deep-ocean floor which has been conventionally international territory (*2*).

The line of division between the two is at the continental margin (or insular margin), and the boundary problem should have been approached from the very beginning with the recognition that the margin is the natural reference base or guide for any boundary between coastal state and international jurisdiction.

The term "continental margin," as used here, is simply the now-submerged *edge* of the continent, as the word margin itself implies. Its position and breadth depend entirely on how sharply one defines that edge. The edge may be considered to be the frontal face of the submerged continental mass (or insular mass) as it faces the deep oceans; and as such it is the continental slope (or the insular slope). Most exactly, however, it is

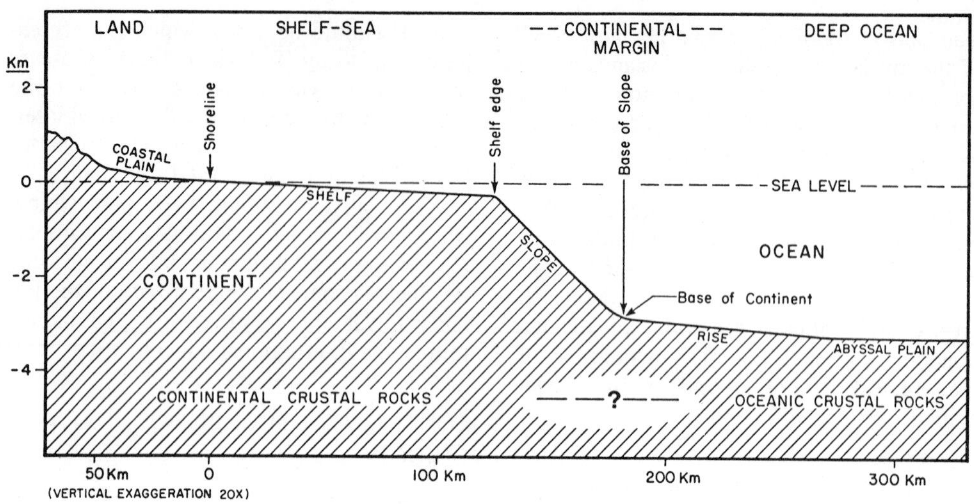


Figure 29-1. Geomorphic features of the continental margin. [Drawn originally for (*1*)]

the *base* of that slope that marks the outer limit or base of the continent (or island). (The true inclination of the margin features is far more gentle than the exaggerated scale in Figure 29-1 might suggest.)

The continental margin as thus defined coincides in a very general way with a geological change from a relatively light but thick continental crust to a relatively dense but thin oceanic crust—a change that is probably fundamentally responsible for the difference in elevation between the continents and the deep-ocean floors. The continental masses of relatively low-density rock tend to float high in the heavier oceanic crust. However, this geologic change, although scientifically important, is too ill-defined and uncertain in position to be of much help in drawing a political boundary.

The most practical basis for the definition of the outer limits of continent and island masses is not geologic but geomorphic. It is based on the simply and directly observable surface form of these earth features and is readily identifiable by anyone at least in a general way. This outer geomorphic limit of the continents and islands—the boundary separating these high-standing masses from the intervening vast and deep ocean basins—is the most natural and most logical guide to where the political boundary between national and international jurisdiction over the resources beneath the ocean floor should lie.

## BASE-OF-SLOPE BOUNDARY ZONE PLAN

The only boundary scheme that appears to meet closely the eight requirements listed above is one which calls for the base of the continental slope (or the insular slope) to serve as a general guide to an internationally prescribed boundary zone, within which the exact position of the boundary between national and international jurisdiction over mineral resources beneath the ocean floor would be designated by the coastal state itself.

The continental slope is probably the single most impressive and most extensive feature of the earth's surface, with a linear extent of 300,000 kilometers on the ocean floor and a height of as much as several kilometers. The slopes of islands are almost equally impressive. However, although the base of the slope is a remarkably widespread and distinctive feature well suited to serve as a general guide to a boundary, it is not definable sharply enough to serve as the boundary itself. Hence an essential feature

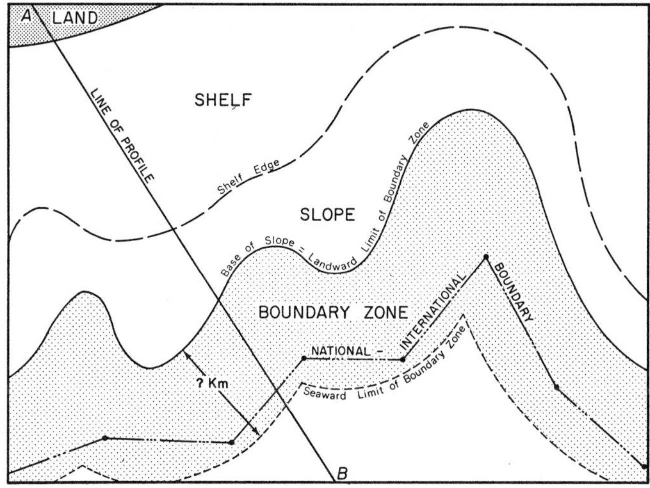


Figure 29-2. Base of slope, boundary zone, and national-international boundary. [Drawn originally for (*1*)]

of any proposed plan that uses the base of slope as a guide is the creation of a boundary zone that would extend oceanward from the approximate position of the base of the slope for an internationally agreed distance within which the precise boundary would be drawn by the coastal state itself (Figures 29-2 and 29-3). It would seem impracticable for the standard width of the boundary zone to be less than 100 kilometers (54 nautical miles), although it might be as much wider as the consensus of nations considered desirable.

The principal reasons for the boundary zone are to take care of uncertainties in precise identification of the base of the slope, as well as to guarantee to all coastal nations as a minimum the submerged part of the continental or island mass adjacent to their shores and naturally pertaining to them and to allow them uniformly such additional area as the nations in joint consultation might agree to be desirable. An additional advantage of the boundary zone scheme is that it would allow the final designation of the precise boundary to be made by the

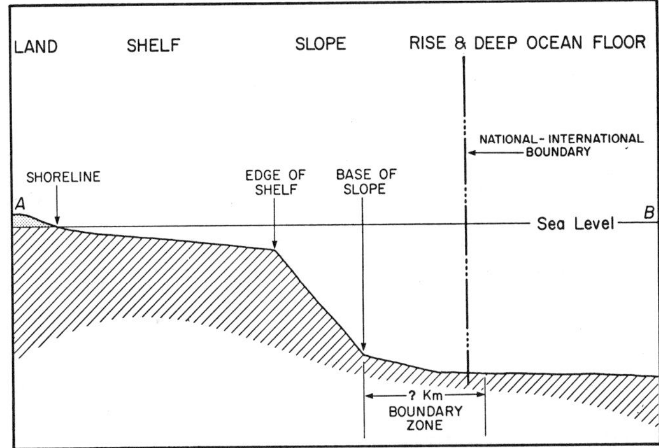


Figure 29-3. Profile across area of Figure 29-2. [Drawn originally for (*1*)]

coastal country itself, although within internationally agreed boundary zone limits. Finally, the boundary zone concept carries the added advantage of allowing the final boundary to be drawn by simple straight lines connecting fixed points of latitude and longitude, which makes it a practical, precise, and readily determined boundary—a feature quite lacking in a 200-mile-from-shore boundary.

As must be the case with respect to the application of any boundary formula, the establishment of an international boundary commission with qualified technical personnel would be necessary to make certain that the precise boundaries drawn by the coastal states fell within the internationally prescribed limits. This body, working in conjunction with individual advisory national oceanographic committees, would determine in advance the approximate position of the base of the slope (or its reasonable projection through areas of uncertainty) for each coastal state. Based on this approximate base-of-slope line and the standard distance adopted by the nations-in-concert for the width of the boundary zone, the coastal state would itself proceed to draw its own precise boundary. This would then be submitted to the international boundary commission for approval, for linking with the boundaries proposed by adjacent countries, and for recommendation for acceptance by the nations-in-concert.

This, in essence, is what seems to be the simplest, most equitable, and most practical procedure for choosing and defining boundaries between coastal state and international jurisdiction over the mineral resources beneath the ocean floor. Details of the scheme have been explained elsewhere (*2*). Some years ago, using the best bathymetric maps available to me, I tentatively tried out the feasibility of drawing an approximate base-of-slope line around most of the continental and insular areas of the world, and believe that it could be done quite satisfactorily by a group of experienced oceanographers working for the international boundary commission. Some examples showing the approximate position of the base-of-slope line in various parts of the world, boundary zones of alternative widths of 100, 200, and 300 kilometers, and supporting profiles were published in 1973 in order to illustrate the method and its feasibility (*2*, attachments 1-8). Further experience and information indicate that some of these initial attempts require modification.

It should be stressed that the proposed plan is recommended only for a national-international division of jurisdiction for *mineral resources* beneath the oceans. It is not a plan for a division of jurisdiction over oceanic waters for navigational purposes, nor is it necessarily a plan for division of fishing rights. These purposes involve other factors and should be settled accordingly. It might not even be a plan for minerals *on* the ocean floor (such as manganese nodules), although it could be. It is rather a plan that concerns only mineral resources *beneath* the ocean floor requiring drilling or mining and fixed ocean floor installations for their recovery—principally petroleum resources.

## DEFECTS OF 200-MILE BOUNDARY SCHEME

Some of the practical difficulties in application of a 200-mile-from-shore boundary formula have been mentioned above. However, in view of the publicity that has been given to the 200-mile proposal, it may be well to consider also some of its more fundamental defects.

Just as there is no logical or natural basis for an arbitrary 200-mile-from-shore limit, so also the distribution of mineral resources is much less related to the very superficial feature of the present shoreline than to the more fundamental base of slope, or base of continent. The world's great thicknesses of sediments with promising petroleum prospects are more closely related to the base of the slope than to some fixed distance from shoreline.

Adoption of a 200-mile-from-shore formula would cause many "wide-margin" countries to lose large potential petroleum-bearing areas situated on the natural seaward projection of their lands. These would be countries whose base-of-slope line is more than 200 miles from shore, such as Argentina, Australia, Canada, People's Republic of China, Ireland, Great Britain, the United States, and the Soviet Union. At the same time, many countries with narrow shelves and slopes would by the 200-mile formula be given vast tracts of deep-ocean bottom of little or no value to them and in no way an apparent prolongation of their lands beneath the sea. Examples are such countries as Chile, Peru, Portugal, Liberia, and Malagasy.

In contrast, the base-of-slope formula would assure to all countries all adjacent ocean floor naturally pertaining to them, and only so much more as the nations agreed to allot uniformly to all coastal states. If the extent given by the 200-mile formula were considered a desirable minimum, this could be attained by making the standard width of the boundary zone great enough (for example, 300 kilometers, or 162 nautical miles) to always allow the drawing of a boundary at least 200 miles from shore. Moreover, this could be done without robbing the wide-margin countries of their natural rights or without the complication of having to establish different formulas for wide-margin countries than for narrow-margin countries. Conversely, the international oceanic domain could be adjusted readily to whatever size the nations-in-concert might wish, simply through the standard width assigned to the boundary zone.

The base-of-slope formula, as compared with the 200-mile formula, provides a much readier means of expressing the wishes of the nations-in-concert and relating them to essential issues, foremost of which is the wish of each nation to be assured of the sub-ocean bottom minerals that it feels naturally belong to it.

## PETROLEUM PROSPECTS BENEATH OCEANS

Critical to any wise decision on jurisdiction over the mineral resources beneath the ocean floor is a proper understanding of the nature of their occurrence. Aside from manganese nodules, phosphate deposits, and other surface deposits on the ocean floor, it seems clear that petroleum is by far the most important sub-ocean bottom resource to be considered. It also seems clear that thoughts of petroleum resources have been a dominating factor in the attitude of the nations with respect to proposed boundaries between national and international jurisdiction.

We know from the geology of existing oil-field areas that marine geological environments of the type that we can associate with the continental margins constitute some of the world's most favorable settings for the genesis and accumulation of petroleum. This is in part because of the abundant supply of organic matter there, which is derived from both terrestrial and marine sources by drainage from the land and from marine life fed by upwelling, nutrient-rich waters from the ocean depths. In part, it is because of the restricted bottom circulation and rapid sedimentation rate of many of the margin seas which have been conducive to the preservation of organic matter. And in part, it is because the extraordinary crustal mobility of these margin belts adjacent to the continents has allowed the thick accumulation of a variety of sediments, the gradual cooking of the organic matter under sedimentary overburden, the collection of the generated hydrocarbons in reservoir beds, and the development of abundant trapping features through folding, faulting, unconformities, and stratigraphic changes.

Although a very substantial part of the world's petroleum is already coming from accumulations beneath the ocean floor, almost all is from the landward, relatively shallow waters near shore on the continental shelves. We still know little or nothing directly from actual drilling for petroleum about the prospects of strata beneath the deeper waters adjacent to the margin—those of the continental slope and beyond the base of the slope.

Such information as we have suggests that much of this deeper water area associated with the margins may also have a good petroleum potential. Geophysical surveys and the very limited amount of deep-sea drilling and sampling done for scientific purposes indicate that under much of this deep water lie sequences of sediments deposited, not under bathyal conditions as might offhand have been expected, but under all the favorable shallow-water sedimentary and structural environments of the sediments of the known oil-field areas of the present coastal plains and continental shelves.

However, about as far as we can justifiably go in appraising the prospects of this deep-ocean floor is to recognize that in general it has petroleum potential and that much of it is worthy of drilling exploration for petroleum when the need and incentive are great enough to compensate for the tremendous costs involved in operations in deep, open oceanic waters far from shore bases. Furthermore, in considering the prospects of entirely undrilled ocean areas, it should be recognized that they are truly unknowns. At this stage we can only speculate as to how well they may meet the geological requirements that experience and the progress of the science have shown are necessary for the creation of commercial petroleum accumulations.

The principal requirements for the development of a geological setting favorable to petroleum prospects may be summarized briefly as follows.

1) There must be a rich source of organic matter of the right kind.

2) Conditions must be favorable for the preservation of the organic matter until it can be buried by sediments.

3) Conditions must be favorable for the thermochemical conversion of the organic matter in the sediments to fluid petroleum (oil or gas). This requires an adequate thickness of blanketing sediments (1000 meters or more) so that, with the local geothermal gradient, favorable generating temperatures (50° to 150°C) may have been attained in the buried sediments, but not exceeded to such point as would have destroyed the fluid petroleum generated.

4) Conditions must be favorable for the movement of petroleum from source rocks to carrier beds. This presupposes the presence, in or adjacent to the fine-grained, organic-rich source rock sediments, of porous and permeable rock layers into which the newly generated petroleum can migrate in response to compaction pressure and other expulsive forces, and along which it can move to accumulation centers.

5) Accumulation traps must be present. These are structural or stratigraphic features where petroleum moving along carrier beds might be concentrated to form commercial accumulations.

6) There must be impermeable cover rocks to prevent the escape of petroleum and its dissipation at the surface. Thick shales and evaporites in the section are commonly effective cover rocks.

7) Proper timing in the development of the various conditions mentioned above is necessary; for example, traps formed after the petroleum has departed are of course worthless.

The more nearly an area promises to qualify with respect to the factors listed above, the better are its prospects. However, failure in any one factor may nullify promise in all the others, and until extensive drilling is done in an area it is rarely possible to evaluate all of the critical factors with assurance.

In some ways it is much easier to eliminate areas of little or no prospects than it is to determine how good are those with some prospects. One factor stands out as essential to the fulfillment of almost every one of the requirements listed, and that is the presence of an adequate thickness of sediments. Of course, mere thickness of sediments does not necessarily mean favorable petroleum prospects, but the lack of an adequate thickness to give temperatures sufficient to convert organic matter into petroleum, or to give pressures necessary to have caused its migration to accumulation centers, is sufficient in itself to condemn the prospects of many areas.

Geophysical surveys have already effectively eliminated vast areas of the ocean floor from serious consideration for petroleum by showing that they have only a few hundred meters of sediment. They have also shown that particularly thick sections of sediments commonly exist along the margins of the continents (and in associated seas and small ocean basins) and in some regions extend far out beyond the base of the slope. A thickness of about 1000 meters has commonly been used to separate areas of no promise from those that may have some promise, depending on the character of the rocks. Figure 29-4 shows estimated thicknesses of sediments above basement in the Atlantic Ocean as interpreted from seismic surveys (*3*).

Unfortunately, there is no reliable answer to the demand for quantitative estimates of the magnitude of petroleum resources in unknown and undrilled areas such as those beneath the deep oceans. Many persons have yielded to the pleas of the public, governments, or the United Nations and have come out with figures. This is perhaps good, because there is a variety in these estimates which tells its own story and because, taken as a whole and in application to large enough regions, such estimates probably do give a worthwhile order of magnitude answer. However, the truth is that the estimators do not know, nor does anyone know before drilling. Quantitative estimates of petroleum resources in new undrilled areas should probably be prefaced by a zero so that a true impression of the estimator's justified assurance may be given(*4*).

## RELATION OF BOUNDARY TO PETROLEUM

The margins of continents and islands appear to have constituted a generally favorable environment for petroleum accumulation. Abundant petroleum production already comes from the landward edge of the margin—the near-shore continental shelf—and even most of the production from petroleum fields on land comes from uplifted sediments which were once deposited in close association with the continental margins of past geologic time.

A dividing line between national and international jurisdiction drawn at today's base of continental slope would leave a large share of this promising belt of potential petroleum-bearing sediments on either side. The landward side of course has the better-known potential, is in shallower water, and is more accessible. However, some of the thickest sedimentary deposits known lie just seaward of the base-of-slope line and constitute the so-called continental rises—huge sediment-filled sumps which, although somewhat questionable as regards adequate reservoirs and traps, must certainly have been good generators of petroleum. The oceanward side of the base of slope may thus have a high petroleum potential although it has the disadvantages of its remoteness from land and the great depths of water in which any operations would have to be carried out.

However, it is not the base of the slope itself but a boundary zone adjacent on its oceanward side that is recommended as the site for the national-international boundary. Thus, the width adopted as standard for this boundary zone would be of critical importance. A boundary drawn near the outer edge of a boundary zone of minimum width (100 kilometers) would still leave much of the areas of thick sediment in the international zone, although in very deep water. On the other hand, the nations-in-concert might decide that a wider boundary zone was desirable—200 or 300 kilometers, perhaps—expressly in order to give the coastal states more of the possible petroleum resources of the so-called rises, or perhaps in order to give complete continuity to the sea floor areas between the islands of archipelagic countries like Indonesia, Philippines, or Mauritius, or to completely divide up the very promising seas and small ocean basins, such as the Gulf of

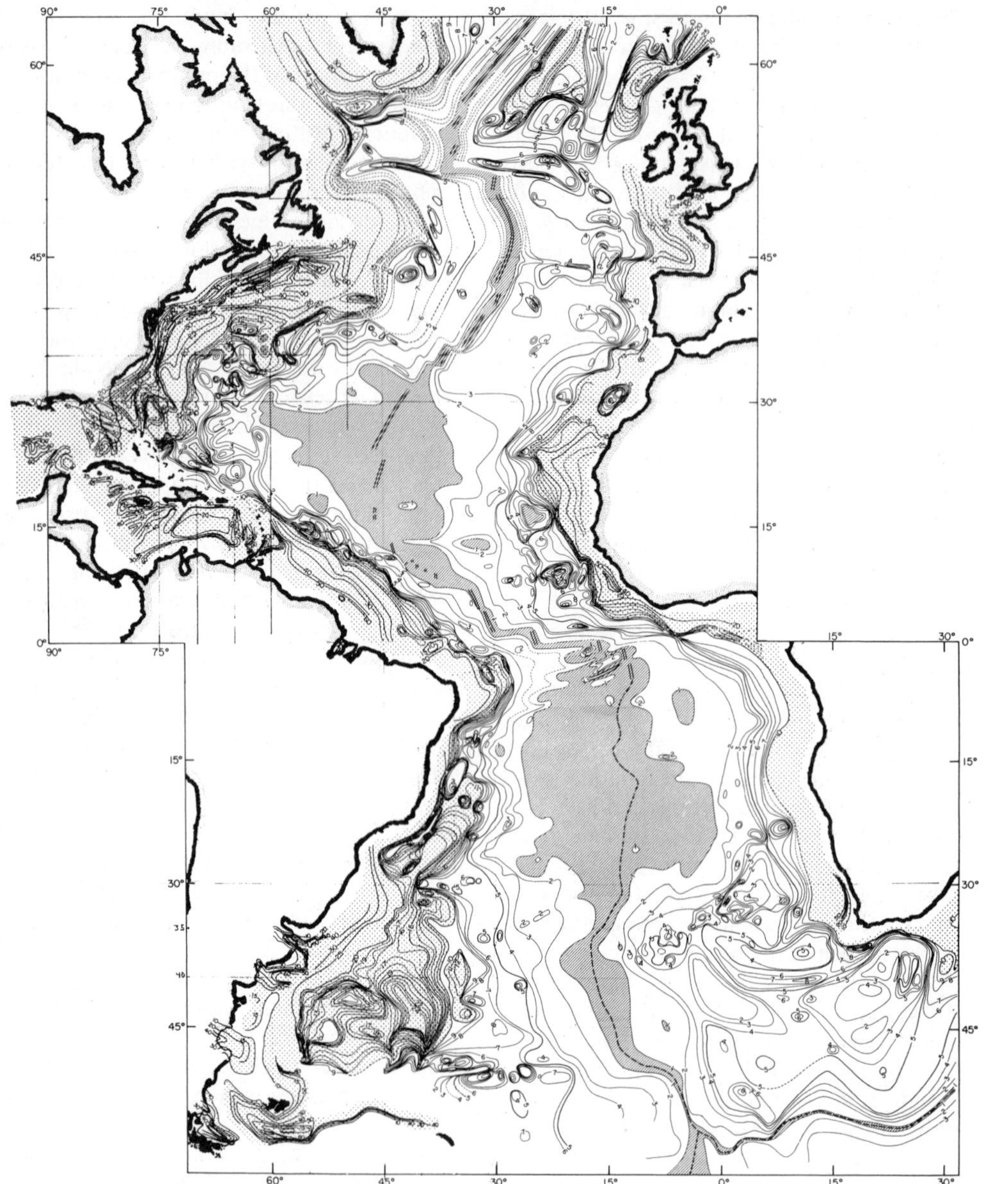


Figure 29-4. Thicknesses of sediment above basement in Atlantic Ocean (*3*). Diagonal hachuring indicates areas of less than 100 meters of sediment. Dotted pattern indicates areas of more than 1000 meters of sediment. Numbered contour lines show thicknesses of sediment in hundreds of meters.

Mexico, the Bering Sea, or the Black Sea, among the adjacent bordering states.

Obviously, any increases in the width of the boundary zone would leave less and less to the international regime and give more and more to the coastal states. However, even with a boundary 300 kilometers oceanward from the base of the slope there would still be some large ocean floor areas with more than 1 kilometer of sediment thickness left in the international zone (for example, off of Argentina, Canada, India, the United States, and the Soviet Union, among others). The boundary zone concept leaves a flexibility in decision to the nations-in-concert as to how much of the world's prospective petroleum territory they wish to make international, while at the same time guaranteeing by the base-of-slope guideline that the coastal nations shall have at a minimum all that naturally belongs to them.

I am optimistic about the eventual petroleum production prospects of the outer continental margins, but certainly with a boundary beyond the base of slope the ocean territory that would go to the international regime would have little prospect of early petroleum development regardless of how good its ultimate potential might be.

The problems of drilling and development in the extreme water depths and remote locations of the outer margin may be so great and the costs so overwhelming that many of these areas may never even be given a chance to yield actual production. Certainly, only extremely lush reservoirs in this environment could be economic in the near future. And certainly, any areas beyond the base of the slope could not be a great source of international revenue in the next few years, as many seem to have hoped.

Moreover, the plan, once envisioned by some, to immediately benefit the developing countries through the proceeds of petroleum production beyond a national-international ocean floor boundary can no longer practically be carried out, because firm coastal state claims have already preempted the sea bottom out beyond any water depths that will be attractive for petroleum development for many years to come.

If it is the serious will of the nations to assign some part of the world's sea floor resources for the benefit of developing nations, a much more expeditious and practical procedure would be for the nations-in-concert to agree to dedicate to this purpose a certain percentage of coastal state government revenue from all ocean installations actually producing petroleum from water depths greater than a specified number of meters or at distances from shore greater than a specified number of kilometers. Accurate determination of such depths or distances could readily be carried out for each producing installation. International revenue from such sources, however, should of course come entirely from the coastal government's share and not from private entrepreneurs, because the development of even moderately deep and distant water areas will require maximum financial incentives, not additional tax burdens, in order to stimulate interest and compensate for the huge financial risks involved.

## PROPOSED BOUNDARY OFF EASTERN UNITED STATES

Figure 29-5 is a bathymetric map of the ocean floor off the eastern (Atlantic) coast of the United States, including adjacent offshores of Bahamas, Bermuda, and Canada (*5*). The base-of-slope boundary guide and alternative zones, as well as the 200-mile-from-shore line, are shown. The base-of-slope line does not coincide with the conventional boundary between slope and rise provinces off eastern United States but has been drawn farther offshore to make it correspond approximately with the outermost principal flattening of the seaward gradient of the ocean floor at the continental edge. More detailed or revised bathymetry might change its position somewhat, but to have used the conventional slope-rise boundary would have put the base-of-slope line at a water depth of about 2000 meters, high up

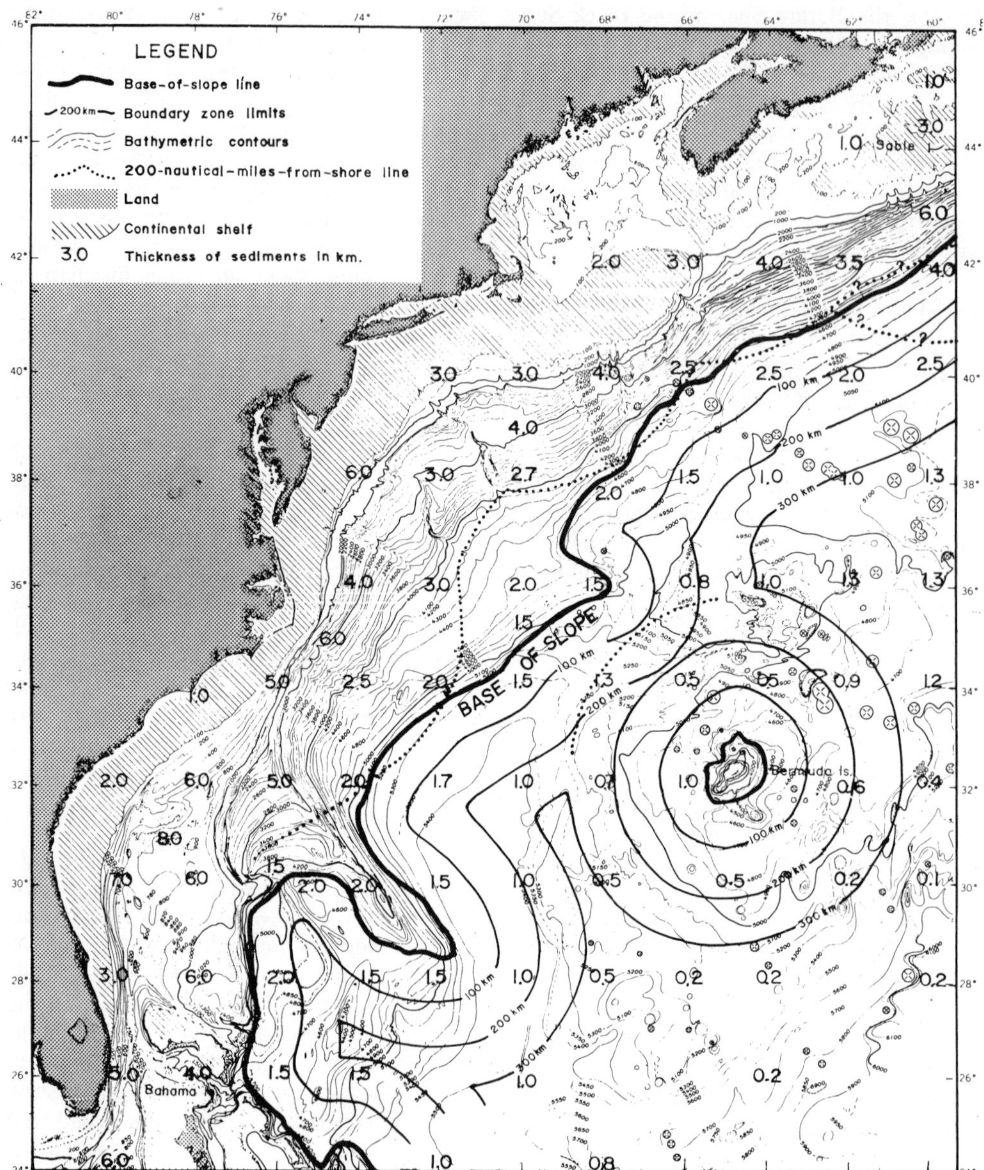


Figure 29-5. Bathymetry (meters), sediment thickness (kilometers), and effect of various boundary proposals off the Atlantic Coast of the United States. The approximate base-of-slope boundary guide is shown with three alternative boundary zones on its oceanward side (black lines to right of and parallel to base-of-slope line). These lines indicate possible zone widths of 100 kilometers (54 nautical miles), 200 kilometers (108 nautical miles), and 300 kilometers (162 nautical miles). The thickness (in kilometers) of sediments is measured above acoustic basement (*3*).

on the edge of the geomorphic continent rather than at its base.

Thicknesses of sediments (in kilometers) from the isopach map of Figure 29-4 (*3*) have been transposed roughly to Figure 29-5 where they are shown as numbers. However, more recent investigations have indicated that maximum thicknesses of sediment near the axis of the sediment-filled trough adjacent to the continent are somewhat greater than previously supposed and in several areas exceed 10 kilometers.

Assuming that a sediment column of a minimum thickness of 1 kilometer is necessary to make petroleum prospects interesting, it is evident that all of the offshore area out to the base-of-slope line qualifies in that respect. The 100-kilometer boundary zone beyond the base of slope also appears to have an adequate sedimentary thickness for petroleum prospects. Boundary zones of 200 and 300 kilometers would include successively less interesting thicknesses of sediment but even a 300-kilometer boundary zone would leave some sediment thicknesses greater than 1 kilometer on its oceanward side.

Figure 29-5 illustrates differences that would result from the proposed 200-mile-from-shore boundary between national and international jurisdiction as compared with a boundary related to the base of slope.

North of latitude 38°, the 200-mile line would coincide quite closely with the base of slope if the 200 nautical miles were measured from the mainland of Nova Scotia. However, if the position of the 200-mile line were also influenced by Sable Island (a small Canadian island at the edge of the shelf southeast of Nova Scotia), a quite different boundary would result. Both possibilities are shown in Figure 29-5. This is an example of one of the problems with the 200-mile scheme—the question of how small shelf islands should be treated in determining a base from which the 200 nautical miles should be measured. In contrast, using the base-of-slope guide there would be no such ambiguity.

Between latitudes 34° and 38°N, there is a large divergence between the 200-mile line and the base-of-slope line. The 200-mile line fails to include for the United States most of a broad terrace area which is underlain by a substantial sediment thickness. Likewise, between 29° and 32°N, the 200-mile line fails to include in national territory the interesting Blake Ridge, which has thick sediments and has already shown evidence of gas hydrates (*6*). South of latitude 30°N the 200-mile line is not shown because it is uncertain how it might be measured in this area of both United States and Bahama islands shorelines.

## PETROLEUM PROSPECTS OFF EASTERN UNITED STATES

In evaluating the significance of proposed national-international boundaries to ownership of petroleum resources off the East Coast of the United States, three cautions need to be emphasized. They are: (i) the unreliability of attempts at quantitative estimates of the petroleum resources of this area; (ii) the tremendous costs of any drilling and production operations in the remote deep waters beyond the edge of the continental shelf; and (iii) the remoteness in time when technology and economics might unite to make such areas practically commercial.

There have been many estimates of the petroleum resources off the Atlantic Coast of the United States during the last few years. Some have been very sanguine, others less so; all have one thing in common—they are necessarily based on little or no drilling knowledge and so are of little quantitative reliability. Such estimates, with the false impressions of accuracy which they too often give, may actually be a hindrance to good planning and may impede realization of our true need—the need to find out.

Probably the best (and most conservative) job of appraisal (*7*) is that which, however, applies to the offshore only out to a water depth of 200 meters. This estimate is based on the coordinated studies of a large group of specialists and is given as a range from 0 to 9 billion barrels plotted against a scale of probabilities (for example, 75 percent probability that there will be more than 1.5 billion barrels, 25 percent probability that there will be more than 4 billion barrels, and so on). However, even with this estimate, perhaps another probability factor needs to be applied—the probability that any estimate in a previously undrilled region will not be even close to the truth. What group of specialists, however skilled, would have come close to estimating the petroleum resources of the North Slope of Alaska before Prudhoe Bay, even with the most thorough study and after several wells had been drilled?

The important initial task is not a quantitative estimate but a careful and thorough appraisal of all geological, geochemical, geophysical, and economic data available, with the purpose of answering the only pertinent and practical question at this stage, which is: Do the prospects of the region, in the light of all the knowns and unknowns, reasonably justify exploratory drilling? In the case of the Atlantic offshore, the answer is Yes. The sooner we get on with the job of drilling exploration the better, regardless of quantitative estimates, optimistic or pessimistic (*8*).

To some extent the concern shown about the division of petroleum resources under the deep-ocean waters far from shore may seem a tempest in a teapot, so far removed is their utilization from present reality. With the tremendous costs and marginal economics of many current offshore petroleum exploration and development projects even at very moderate water depths, it may be completely impractical to think of ever producing oil and gas from deep-ocean environments. It may also seem only a barren academic exercise to argue about schemes for national-international boundaries in these remote areas that are so difficult to exploit.

However, the same things were once said about shallow-water offshore drilling; yet in only a few decades this has become commonplace. Offshore oil and gas now occupy an important position in our world economy. With inevitable progress toward the exhaustion of our petroleum reserves on land and in shallow coastal waters, the already steady march of exploratory drilling into deeper and deeper waters farther from land may see no limits as far out as geological possibilities of petroleum accumulations exist. It seems true that if the productive possibilities are good enough, there is scarcely a place on the earth where either technology or economics will be allowed to be a permanent barrier.

In view of this trend, the prudent time to settle matters of jurisdiction is *now,* before actual discoveries in the far offshore make it more and more difficult to peaceably establish boundaries on the basis of uniform and equitable principles without the complicating factor of selfish interest in acquiring specific local areas. The principle on which the boundary is to be established should be decided now, even if, locally, implementation into precise and definitely defined boundaries is delayed somewhat by needs for more accurate bathymetric data.

Even assuming that deep water and remoteness from land may not be permanent barriers to petroleum exploration and development, realistically it is still necessary to recognize that petroleum resources near the base of the slope are resources only for the far future. Many years of improving technology and increasing demand must intervene before such resources can be utilized. Moreover, the chimera of a rapid and enormous payoff from an internationally owned and sponsored petroleum development, to be used for the benefit of developing nations, must be abandoned, even in only moderately deep waters. A much more effective alternative was suggested above, but perhaps it should be considered whether a more practical way for all to benefit from petroleum resources under the deep oceans may not be simply to create stable conditions of national ownership of the ocean floor naturally pertaining to each coastal state so that these resources may be developed as rapidly and efficiently as possible, as the need for them arises, by those having the special skills, equipment, and geographic location to do so. A more abundant supply of petroleum more widely distributed among the coastal nations of the world would relieve present monopolies and inevitably work out to the advantage of all countries.

## BOUNDARIES OFF OTHER U.S. COASTS

The possible effect of proposed national-international boundaries on the U.S. petroleum position off the Atlantic shore has been discussed in detail. It may be of interest to briefly consider three other U.S. coasts similarly affected. It is also worth mentioning that the U.S. Pacific Coast, including Alaska, has a base of slope such that with a 100-kilometer boundary zone all areas of important petroleum promise would probably go to the United States. This would also be true for a 200-mile-from-shore boundary which would, however, result in the needless inclusion also of a broad band of deep-ocean bottom without petroleum prospects and with no other known subbottom values.

1) *Gulf of Mexico.* Geologically the whole Gulf of Mexico may be considered prospective petroleum territory. Extensive offshore production has long been established off the Louisiana, Texas, and Mexican coasts. The base of slope is quite clearly indicated or can be reasonably interpolated around most of the periphery of the Gulf and would serve to mark the limits of *minimum* areas to be assigned to the three bordering countries. With a 100-kilometer boundary zone a thin, elongate international zone would still be left in the middle of the Gulf, but with a boundary zone as wide as 200 kilometers this would be eliminated and the whole Gulf area would be divided between the United States, Mexico, and Cuba (*2,* attachment 3-B).

Use of the 200-mile-from-shore boundary would also leave a small central portion of the Gulf in the international zone, but again, the mode of application of this scheme would be uncertain because of the presence of several small Mexican reef islets at the edge of the shelf about 100 miles off the Yucatan shore. If the 200 nautical miles were measured from these islets rather than from the Yucatan mainland, Mexico's share of the Gulf would be greatly increased at the expense of the international zone and in part at the expense of the United States.

2) *Alaska: Bering Sea.* The Bering Sea not only has a thick sediment cover (locally as much as 10 kilometers) over its very broad shelf area, but also has thick sediments and petroleum potential throughout its whole deep-water area beyond the base of the slope. A base-of-slope boundary would of course assure to the United States all of the broad eastern shelf of the Bering Sea, and the use of a 300-kilometer boundary zone would probably give essentially all of the deep-water sea floor to coastal state (United States and Soviet Union) jurisdiction.

A 200-mile limit measured from the mainland coast of Alaska and the Aleutian islands would leave much of the potential petroliferous area of the Bering basins, both on the shelf and in deeper water, under international jurisdiction. However, if the 200-mile distance were measured from the small U.S. shelf islands of St. Matthew, St. Paul, and St. George, far distant from the mainland, the United States could claim the entire eastern shelf area and also a substantial part of the deep-water area beyond the base of the slope under this boundary formula. Even so, it would lose much of the deep-sea, potentially petroliferous area that it would have received from the base-of-slope plan with a 300-kilometer boundary zone.

3) *Alaska: Arctic Coast.* Probably nowhere on U.S. coasts does the importance of the base-of-slope boundary stand out more than off the north coast of Alaska. Here the huge shallow-water areas of the Chukchi Shelf extend far out into the Arctic and are underlain by a thick (up to 6 kilometers) section of potentially petroliferous sediments. The situation with respect to the

Chukchi Shelf is shown in Figure 29-6. (*9*). The proximity of the great North Slope petroleum discoveries adds interest to the Chukchi region.

With a base-of-slope guide and a minimum (100-kilometer) boundary zone, a large part of this extensive and potentially petroliferous shallow to moderate water depth area would come under U.S. jurisdiction, whereas with a 200-mile-from-shore boundary, much of this part would go to the international zone.

## CONCLUSIONS

In conclusion, the United States has everything to gain and nothing to lose by supporting a boundary formula that gives it its natural subsea territory out to the base of the adjacent continental slope, plus such additional selvage as may be provided by whatever width boundary zone the nations-in-concert decide is desirable. Conversely, the United States would definitely lose by accepting a 200-mile limit. In several places this would deprive it of potential petroleum territory which naturally should belong to it, while in other places it would give it an excess of deep-ocean bottom poor in sediments.

Similarly, for all coastal countries, the base-of-slope formula could give them as a minimum all the potential petroleum territory which they would receive by the 200-mile formula, without the unnecessary addition of inutile deep-ocean bottom better assignable to the international sphere, with the advantage to broad-shelf countries of

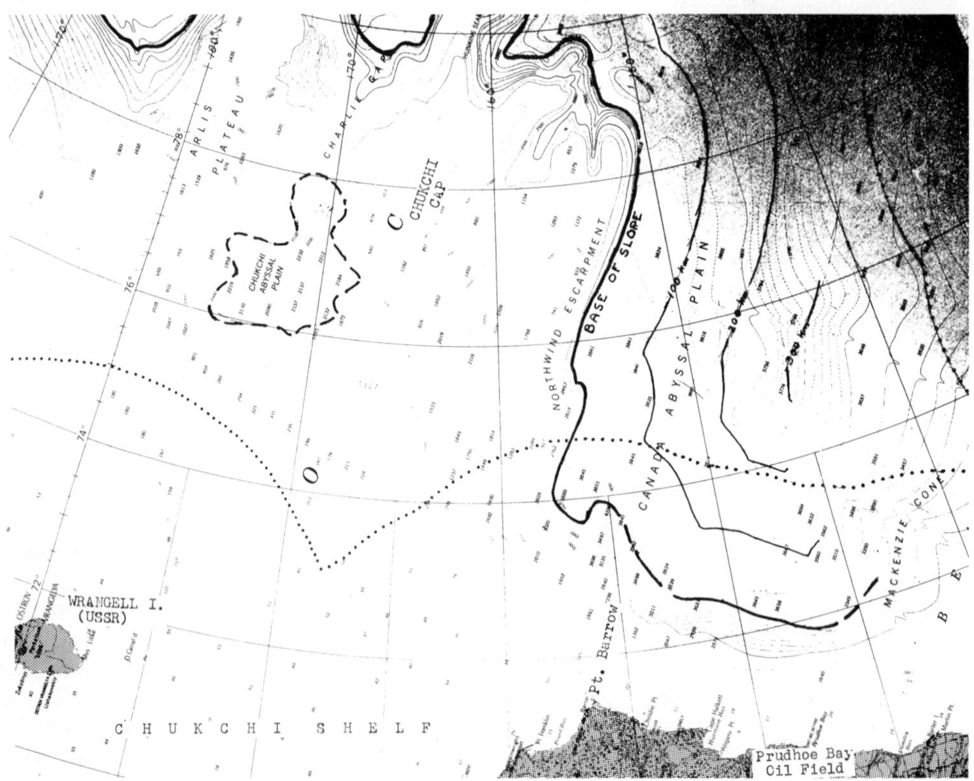


Figure 29-6. Bathymetry (meters) and effect of various boundary proposals, Chukchi Shelf, north of Alaska (*9*) (conventions as for Figure 29-5).

giving them also all of their rightful petroleum resources beyond the 200-mile limit.

It is of course conceivable that the United States and other broad-margin countries may wish, for political or altruistic reasons, to go along with the 200-mile boundary proposal and donate what may be important potential petroleum resources of the far future to an international regime; but if so, they should know in advance what they are doing, and that they alone of the world's nations are doing it. Another alternative may be for the nations-in-concert to adopt one formula for the narrow-margin countries and another for the broad-margin countries (although differentiation between the two groups might be very difficult); or to adopt a combination of the two proposals, such as 200 nautical miles from shore or the outer edge of the margin, whichever is greater (although implementation of such a plan might be very complicated). Finally, perhaps, the United States and other countries may yet be willing to speak out for the simpler, more effective principle that gives all nations the sub-sea bottom resources that naturally belong to them through the natural prolongation of their land masses beneath the oceans, which treats all coastal states alike, and which still leaves some substantial areas of thick sediment in an international zone.

## REFERENCES

1. *Ocean Petroleum Resources* (National Petroleum Council, Washington, D.C., 1975).

2. H. D. Hedberg, *Ocean Manage.* **1**, 83 (1973).

3. M. Ewing, G. Carpenter, C. Windisch, J. Ewing, *Geol. Soc. Am. Bull.* **84**, 71 (1973).

4. H. D. Hedberg, in *Methods of Estimating the Volume of Undiscovered Oil and Gas Resources*, J. D. Haun, Ed. (American Association of Petroleum Geologists, Tulsa, Okla., 1975), p. 160.

5. R. M. Pratt, *U.S. Geol. Surv. Prof. Pap. 529-B* (1968). This map was used because it was the only one available to me showing bathymetric contours down to 100-meter intervals all the way across the margin. Offshore boundaries between the United States and Canada and the United States and the Bahamas are not shown because they are still controversial.

6. C. D. Hollister, J. I. Ewing, *et al., Initial Reports of Deep Sea Drilling Project* (Deep Sea Drilling Project, Washington, D.C., 1972), vol. 11, pp. 791-799 and 958-966.

7. B. M. Miller *et al., U.S. Geol. Surv. Circ. 725* (1975).

8. An initial exploratory stratigraphic test well for stratigraphic information only, sponsored by a large group of companies and scheduled for a 16,000-foot depth, is reported to have started drilling on 14 December 1975 in 290 feet of water some 75 miles off the New Jersey coast.

9. *Map of Arctic Region, 1:5,000,000* (American Geographical Society, New York, 1975).

# 30. Oil, Superships, and the Oceans

JOHN FRYE 1974

Among facts of life for all who care about the oceans and this country's seas and shores for what's left of the twentieth century are these:

Superships, many needing depths more than double those of almost all existing American ports, are here, even though many were laid up in the middle and late 1970s in a confused energy situation.

Some are loaded with 100,000 to 475,000 tons of crude oil from the Middle East when they can get a charter. Others haul up to 125,000 cubic meters of liquefied natural gas at −162°C (−260°F) from Algeria, Libya, and other still unexploited fields. Still others carry iron, bauxite, or other ores from South America, Africa, and the Caribbean, and some haul coal to Japan and Italy, and grain to Russia.

There are no present United States ports that can handle the biggest—the supertankers, the VLCCs or Very Large Crude Carriers—but some superports are in the making.

Up to 1974, it seemed inevitable that the world-wide surge toward supertankers would go on, and that we would soon see crude oil carried at a million tons a load. Such a ship was, and presumably still is, on paper in Japan. Then came the Middle East oil embargo and rising prices, with consequent conservation measures by industry all over the world—though not by individual consumers, who continued to gas up their cars with little apparent concern for the thought that the world might be drained dry of oil within half a century.

Suddenly a great surplus of ships developed. By mid-1976 estimates ran to 80 million tons deadweight of tankers either idle or on "slow steaming," running at half or two-thirds speed to save their own bunker oil and to serve as slow-moving storage tanks for a commodity being priced out of many markets. Shipyards all over the world which had been bidding gaily for new contracts in the early 1970s found themselves trying to cancel. Owners found themselves with more ships than they could find cargos for.

How long the situation would last no one could say as the second half of the decade got under way. The London firm of ship brokers, Eggar Forrester, Ltd., and its research affiliate, Terminal Operators, Ltd., first to forecast the crisis and consistently right with their analyses, thought that by the

John Frye is Associate Editor of *National Fisherman* and a free-lance writer/photographer.

From *Oceans Magazine*, Vol. 7, No. 1, pp. 48-55, 1974. Reprinted with author's revisions and light editing and with permission of the author and *Oceans Magazine*.

1980s the shipping picture could right itself. However, this was conditional on provisos, including conversion of many VLCCs to grain hauling and other uses, faster retirement and scrapping of older vessels, reduction in non-cancellable backlog orders, and stabilization of Middle Eastern political dynamics.

Whatever the future, so many of the great ships are already afloat that it is certain that some use will be found. Discovery of new oil fields could put them to their original use, and oil men, wildcatters at heart, always hope for this.

The environmental considerations in use of supertankers are great. Conservation alarm bells have been sounding from Valdez, Alaska, where the pipeline is to end, to Eastport, Maine, where a proposed deepwater terminal and refinery has been blocked only by Canada's refusal to permit supertankers to navigate its adjacent narrow and turbulent territorial waters to get there.

The familiar specter of the *Torrey Canyon* is invoked and too often brought to mind by such later disasters as the grounding of the Dutch supertanker *Metula* in the Strait of Magellan August 9, 1974, with loss of more than 53,000 tons of crude and bunker oil; the grounding and explosion of the Danish *Jakob Maersk* off Oporto, Portugal, with loss of her entire 85,000 tons of crude January 29, 1975; and the grounding and explosion of the 111,200-dwt Spanish *Urquiola* May 12, 1976, at the entrance to the harbor of La Coruña, Spain, with loss of 25,000 tons.

There are also warnings of potential ecological disturbances from harbor dredging, port construction, and even movement of such ships in harbors, bays, estuaries, and sounds. However, present thinking, at least in this country, tends toward establishing offshore monobuoy or artificial island terminals rather than attempting, as in Europe, to create new ports ashore.

Industry and government promise that many millions will be spent to prevent disaster and ecological disturbance, although officials of seaside resort towns, already edgy about drilling off the Atlantic Coast, may be skeptical about offshore terminals. Government and industry also warn that any interference with what the oil industry wants may cause a "backlash" of public sentiment. Those of us who must have our beer cans, second cars, air conditioning, electric toothbrushes, and other comforts are to be rallied in the cause of energy and let the next century take care of itself.

The great ships already have been calling on North American if not United States shores. Gulf Oil Corporation operates a fleet of Universe-class 326,000-dwt ton tankers, each with a capacity of 312,482 tons of Kuwait crude (Figure 30-1). They draw 80 feet or more and need 90 feet in protected water, 100 in open. They are in shoal water the minute they come over any continental shelf. They deliver now to Nova Scotia, less than 300 miles from Maine.

Nor are the Universe ships the largest. The pioneer Japanese have launched the 369,000-dwt *Nisseki Maru* (Figure 30-2) of Tokyo Tankers, Ltd., the 484,000-dwt *Globtik Tokyo* for Globtik Tanker Co. of Great Britain, and have contracted for a 500,000-dwt tanker for Stratis Andreadis of Greece. Preliminary contracts have been signed with Globtik for a 700,000-dwt ship. And among ships of mammoth size—even if dwarfed by these and the Universe fleet—are the 15 Exxon ships of 250,000-dwt each, already in service. All major oil companies, American or international, have or are getting similar vessels. Kockums, the big Swedish shipbuilder, reported recently it was finishing a series of twenty, each of 255,000; was ready to start work on 355,000-dwt ships; and could build, outfit, and deliver a giant tanker in 110 working days.

In June 1972 our Maritime Administration let subsidy contracts for six supertankers, three of 265,000-dwt (the first completed in late 1976), the largest ever ordered in this country, and three of 225,000. This could be done only in expectation that, by the time the first is ready for service, we will

Figure 30-1. *Universe Ireland* under way.

have at least the makings of a superport to unload them closer than Nova Scotia, Freeport in the Bahamas, where another port has been built, Haiti's Fort Liberté Bay, or Mona Island between Puerto Rico and Hispaniola, where others are proposed.

Thus it is too late to ask if there isn't another way. There probably isn't. We can thank the Egyptians and Israelis for the closure of the Suez Canal which forced hauling from the Persian Gulf, source of one-third of the free world's crude and site of an estimated two-thirds of its reserves, to go around the Cape of Good Hope. The oil companies had to have huge ships to make the haul economical.

Nor can the supertankers use the Panama Canal with its 110-foot lock widths, something that Panamanian nationalists might consult with the ghost of Nasser about. If a need develops to haul oil from Valdez to the East Coast before any practical way of using the Northwest Passage is worked out, or a new canal is built, or a trans-Canada pipeline, that oil will come via Cape Horn. Even such comparatively small ships as three

Figure 30-2. This, for the time being, is the world's second largest tanker, the *Nisseki Maru,* 369,000 dwt. Last winter the Japanese launched what, again for the time being, is the largest, the *Globtik Tokyo,* 477,000 dwt. A 500,000-dwt ship has been ordered, and preliminary contracts have been signed for one of 700,000 dwt.

120,000-dwt tankers being built at Baltimore for West Coast service must be delivered around the Horn.

All this came about so fast during the late 1960s and early 1970s that it was hard to accept the great change. According to Maritime Administration figures, the average tanker in the world fleet was 47,000-dwt as late as 1970. In 1974 the average under construction was 200,000-dwt. MARAD also reported that of the 234 tankers then in the U.S. fleet, only 27 were of more than 45,000-dwt, and the average was 30,000. According to the Corps of Engineers, only Seattle and Long Beach, Calif., can receive ships of more than 100,000-dwt (Table 30-1). Much thought has gone into the situation being created, in part possibly to make sure the situation *is* created, but in substantial part to see what can be done to make it tolerable if inevitable. There are so many factors—ranging from the "energy crisis," to

Table 30-1. Port and Harbor Capabilities in the United States.

| Port or Harbor Area | *Maximum Draft Vessel Using Area (feet)** 1969 | 1970 | *Controlling Depth (feet)* | *Aver. Tidal Variation (feet)* | *Approx. Max. Dredgable Depth (feet)* | *Expansions Contemplated (Depths)* |
|---|---|---|---|---|---|---|
| Portland, Me. | 51 | 51 | 45 | 9.0 | 60 | Indefinite |
| Boston | 41 | 42 | 40 | 9.0 | 40/60 | 45 |
| New York (Ambrose) | 45 | 44 | 45 | 4.5 | 60 (Narrows) | Indefinite |
| New York (Kill Van Kull) | 40 | 40 | 35 | 5.0 | 38 | 47 (rock), 45 (soft) |
| Delaware Bay to Philadelphia | 46 | 46 | 40 | 4.1 to 5.9 | 41 | 50 |
| Philadelphia, Pa. | 40 | 41 | 40 | 6.0 | 41 | 50 |
| Baltimore, Md. | 40 | 40 | 42 | 1.2 | 60 | 50 |
| Hampton Roads, Va. | 44 | 47 | 45 | 2.5 | 60 | 58 to 60 |
| Jacksonville, Fla. | 35 | 35 | 40 | 2.5 | 44 | Indefinite |
| Port Everglades, Fla. | 38 | 39 | 40 | 2.5 | 42 | Indefinite |
| Tampa, Fla. | 35 | 35 | 34 | 2.0 | >40 | 44 |
| Mobile, Ala. | 40 | 40 | 40 | 1.5 | 45 | 50 |
| Pascagoula, Miss. | 38 | 39 | 38 | 1.6 | 50 | Indefinite |
| New Orleans, La. | 40 | 39 | 40 | 1.0 | 45 | 50 |
| Baton Rouge, La. | 40 | 40 | 40 | 1.0 | 40 | Indefinite |
| Beaumont, Tex. | 37 | 39 | 40 | 1.0 | 47 | Indefinite |
| Galveston, Tex. | 39 | 40 | 36 | 2.0 | 52 | Indefinite |
| Houston Ship Channel | 40 | 40 | 40 | 1.0 | 45 | 45 |
| Corpus Christi, Tex. | 40 | 39 | 45 | 1.0 | 50 | 45 (in progress) |
| Los Angeles, Calif. | 52 | 45 | 51 | 5.4 | >80 | 80 (1975) (Outer Harbor) |
| Long Beach, Calif. | 46 | 51 | 52 | 5.5 | >80 | Indefinite |
| San Francisco Bay Entrance, Calif. | 50 | 51 | 50 | 5.7 | >100 50 (Interior) | 55 (Outer Bay) |
| Columbia River Entrance | 38 | 38 | 42 | 2.0 | 48 | Indefinite |
| Puget Sound | 39 | 39 | 100-500 | 11.1 | >100 | Indefinite |

*Source: Waterborne Commerce of the U.S., Corps of Engineers, U.S. Army

rebuilding our merchant marine, to our balance of payments, to world economy and our devalued dollar—that at best environmental considerations can only share in the give and take, or trade-offs, as the jargon goes.

Yet environmental considerations are not being neglected. The oil companies are aware of the damage done to *them* as well as to the environment by the *Torrey Canyon*, the *Wafra* and lesser wrecks, the Santa Barbara blowoff, fires in the Gulf of Mexico, and spills large and small that constantly afflict our harbors and waterways. Aside from soiling the industry image, lately of concern, there is economic waste: a ship lost is $50 to $100 million lost. Every gallon in an oil slick cost money to get it there, plus a possible fine. Even recently developed procedures such as "load-on-top," by which what's left in pumped-out tanks is recovered rather than dumped, have been found to pay for themselves and better. (Still, too many ships go on cleaning tanks at sea, at least fifty miles off our shores unless nobody is looking.)

Further, oil companies have found public resistance to shore expansion projects—refineries, tank farms, terminals—makes it necessary to promise, and mostly perform, whatever must be done to end water pollution and other environmental damage. The new measures and corporate attitudes carry over to the marine phases.

The changing attitudes extend into some but not all branches of government. The Corps of Engineers, possibly smarting or at least chastened by frustration of porkish jobs like the Florida Barge Canal and delay on the Tennessee-Tombigbee Waterway, lately have been seeking to show long-time, even historic, concern for the environment. Top officers have been stumping the country to shuck the pork barrel image. One of the better examples of "thinking ahead" on the specific problem of bringing oil here with least risk of disaster, or of merely continuing damage, is in studies (published in late 1971) the Corps' Institute for Water Resources ordered, analyzing potential problems and reviewing experience elsewhere.

Both reports had to be written keeping in mind the lack of concrete experience available in this country. Except for people in government, industry, and international trade who have seen—and in some cases helped promote—the developing situation, plus a few concerned about the environment, we have not had to think about it.

We have not had to realize that among elements of "future shock" is to be urgent provision for ships. . . .

That need 60 to 120 feet of water just to float.

That may range up to 1,500 feet in length and 300 in beam (the hull as wide as the flight deck of an aircraft carrier) and need a quarter mile or more in channel width just to pass.

That may operate at moderate speeds of 15 to 17 knots but can't steer at less than five or six.

That need between one and four miles to turn around and 20 to 25 minutes to stop from cruising speed. An Arthur D. Little, Inc., report gave these estimates for a 500,000-dwt ship in calm, slack water. At eight knots she could stop in 15 minutes in six times her 1,370-foot length, at four knots in five minutes in a length and a half. There was no guess for the one million-dwt planned, beyond the estimate of her 120-foot draft.

Yet there has been enough experience gained elsewhere, by at least one American company, to provide starting guidelines. Love it or hate it, Gulf Oil Corporation has been in both the supertanker and superport business since 1968 with its fleet of Universe and similar tankers, and with its "sea island" deepwater loading facilities in the Persian Gulf and its three transshipment ports. The first is on Whiddy Island in Bantry Bay, Ireland, the second at Point Tupper, Nova Scotia, the third at Heianza, Okinawa, in Japan's Ryukyu Islands. The ships and the ports are designed to handle more than four million tons of crude on each tanker cycle.

A common factor of all four ports has been water deep enough for little dredging or similar environmental disturbance, except in building piers. Such water is available here only at Valdez, Alaska, and in Puget Sound on the West Coast, and in one or two Maine bays on the East, although oil companies contend that they can create a deepwater terminal in lower Delaware Bay, off Big Stone Beach, with minimum disturbance. (That project was shot down, at least for a while, by Delaware's 1971 coastal zone law forbidding further heavy industry along the state's bay or ocean shores.)

The Bantry Bay port was completed in October 1968, and while Gulf officials concede that a number of small spills have had to be cleaned up, the Little report made a special point of praising its ballasting and deballasting and bilge pumping facilities as "worthy of reproduction at any marine terminals in the U.S."

"More generally," the report added, "Gulf's conservative approach in vessel and terminal design is technically and environmentally sounder than many taken since.

"Environmental planning, whether on Gulf's own volition, or spurred by the Irish Tourism Board and Department of Fisheries, seems to have been serious. . . .

"There were no baseline studies, only

borings for pile driving, but neither dredging nor fill was needed and there are no traces of irreversible damage by operations such as pipelaying, and island dock construction. . . ."

The tankers retain ship sewage and garbage in holding tanks while in the bay, and port tugs have garbage and sewage processing equipment. The report listed only four small spills up to November 1971, one costing a $300 fine.

Fishing was reported mostly outside the bay, for scallops, herring, cod, and salmon, and the report said no fishing complaints had been received. Regular water quality tests are made, at Gulf's expense, by an Irish University student using a small laboratory in an old construction shack.

The Little report noted that the Universe ships had 24 tanks in eight compartments, of maximum size of 12,000 cubic meters, against 15,000 "asked by conservationists." Gulf had an option of adding 15,000 tons of steel over shipyard design and "exercised it entirely." This and maneuverability due to twin screws and rudders, plus traffic-free routes and the performance to date, has resulted in "excellent insurance rates."

A description of piloting and docking procedures is given in an article in Gulf's house quarterly, the *Orange Disc,* with additional detail in the Little report.

"Tankers approaching Bantry Bay are in radio contact with the terminal control room for two hours before they arrive off Sheep's Head at the mouth of the bay," the article said. "Gulf control informs the skipper of berthing conditions, and if immediate berthing is not possible, the tanker is requested to anchor at one of two pilot stations within the bay."

Eleven channel buoys, including a mid-channel line with in-and-out separation, guide the ships, with supplementary markers ashore. When a ship reaches buoy 2, twelve miles from the "sea island" loading jetty 1,200 feet off Whiddy Island, four tugs and a pilot are sent out. At buoy 5, halfway up the bay, two tugs go to the port side, one of the bow, one to the stern. Speed is held to three to four knots. When the tanker is broadside to the pier and about 1,000 feet off, two tugs push on starboard, two pull on the port side for a pier approach at 0.6 feet per second. The pulling tugs join the two pushing in the final approach.

The ship's engines line up ship and pier manifolds. Mooring lines are handled by the tanker's fifty-ton-capacity tension automatic winches. In normal weather four bow lines, four stern, two breast, and two spring are used. Additional spring and breast lines are used in bad weather. Oil is unloaded through hydraulically operated, articulated loading arms rather than flexible hoses. Ballast and remaining oil cargo must be kept in balance so the ship can sail quickly if necessary, with up to 120,000 tons of ballast needed to maintain proper draft of at least forty feet while unloading.

"Should a storm blow up, or any other emergency arise," the *Orange Disc* said, "the unloading operation would cease immediately and the ship would be required to move away. . . ." Meanwhile, two tugs, also equipped for fire fighting and detergent spraying, remain on hand.

Even with these precautions, Gulf has had some spills there. On October 22, 1974, the 93,000-dwt *Universe Leader,* loading crude for transshipment, leaked nearly 2,600 tons from a valve nine meters below the waterline—left open by accident. On January 10, 1975, a tug with inadequate bow fendering punched a four-by-four-inch hole in the 228,000-dwt *Afran Zodiac* while undocking her for a return light to the Persian Gulf. The tanker lost 391 tons of bunker oil, with the company pilot ordering her to sea to trail the oil on the water instead of getting a boom around the ship quickly.

Dirty ballast water from smaller tankers goes into two 500,000-gallon tanks ashore for use by the big ships discharging. Any excess accumulating is cleared of oil, treated chemically, piped to a storage pond, then allowed to drain to the bay. Oil remaining is reported below five parts per million. Dirty ballast water taken by the supertankers goes through the standard load-on-top procedure. Oil is held only briefly in the 14 partially hidden storage and bunker tanks ashore, for transshipment in smaller tankers to European terminals.

Similar facilities were developed for the new Point Tupper terminal and refinery of Gulf Oil Canada, which opened in August 1971 with arrival of the 253,000-dwt CP Ships tanker *T.G. Shaughnessy,* the largest to cross the Atlantic up to then. The dock provides more than 100-foot depth only 750 feet from shore on protected Canso Strait separating the island of Cape Breton from the Nova Scotia mainland.

Gulf reported that $5 million had been spent on specific anti-pollution measures in the refinery, and that air cooling made water use "extremely low." Holding ponds and separators retain and treat both waste process water and ballast from tankers. Oil handling and cleanup equipment and procedures match those of Bantry Bay. The $18 million dock, unloading crude through two 42-inch pipelines at 100,000 barrels per hour for 24-hour turnaround, provides an outer berth nearly 1,000 feet long and an inner berth of 620 feet. Construction involved driving 337 pilings, some through silt into bedrock to be anchored by drilling in the rock, inserting an anchoring system, and grouting the holes with concrete.

The Gulf complex, along with other industrial facilities including a huge pulpmill, set off a $1.5 million federal program of improving navigational aids. The harbor is now described as one of the world's best in terms of navigation and docking aids.

Neither terminal "just growed." Both had to be designed and engineered. Gulf cited as typical of its superports the problems and solutions involved in creation of its third, the Heianza terminal which opened in July 1971 with arrival of *Universe Iran.*

Studies for a Far Eastern facility started in 1966. A first decision was to build the terminal on the small island of Miyagi. "A small but quite vocal minority" of residents protested while those of adjacent Heianza wanted it, the *Orange Disc* reported. Construction started December 9, 1968. Ashore more than 100 graves had to be moved at a cost of $233,000, plus $82,500 for crops being grown on land needed. On the water, $145,000 was paid for fishing rights "to insure that no one would be penalized if construction of the offshore berth interfered with fishing, and to keep small boats and nets out of the shipping lanes, minimizing the danger of accidents."

A hydrographic survey of Kin Wan Bay was made, with continuous depth recordings and wire dragging of twelve square miles of approaches and turning areas to a depth of 100 feet. Tidal currents were found to be less than one knot, and depth contours disclosed maneuvering space for Universe tankers and a berth site 9,000 feet offshore, in water deep enough for ships of up to 500,000-dwt when they become available.

Piles were driven in bad, foggy weather, with laser beams cutting through the mists to spot exact locations, to create an outside berth for supertankers and an inside berth for ships of 20,000- to 150,000-dwt for transshipment. Six pipelines connect the pier to the shore refinery, one 48-inch and one 42-inch for crude, a 30-inch line for black oil, two 20-inch lines for intermediate products, and a 26-inch line for ships' ballast, pumped ashore for separation and return of oil residues in load-on-top procedures.

Again safety and pollution control equipment follows the pattern of Bantry Bay and Point Tupper, with such later improvements as hydraulic couplers to eliminate flanging on unloading arms and thus "drastically reduce the danger of oil spillage."

The "sea island" loading dock at Mina-al-Ahmadi, off the Kuwait coast on the western shore of the upper Persian Gulf, was developed by Gulf and British Petroleum just for the Universe tankers. The artificial island is nine miles offshore, with a depth of 95 feet. This presumably will just barely enable it to handle 500,000-dwt ships, which are expected to draw 92.5 feet. Along with oil pipelines from the shore, the platform is provided with water, air, diesel oil, fire fighting foam, and power. The Kuwait Oil Co., which operates it, receives eight-day notice of approach of a tanker, and the master confirms 72 hours from his estimated time of arrival. Upon sighting, the tanker is called on VHF or signal lamp and given an estimated berthing time. A pilot then boards to bring her alongside with tug assistance.

"Cargo loading rate is automatically adjusted from the shore," the Little report said, "and is reduced gradually when nearing completion, or at the request of the duty officer, to minimize the possibility of an overflow during the final 'topping off,' which is conducted on gravity flow alone.

"The port nautical surveyor then inspects the loaded draft . . . to make sure she is not overloaded. Before the loading hoses are disconnected, they are emptied. . . ."

In 1969 the island loaded 208 tankers, including the six Universe ships, one taking a full cargo of 312,482 tons "at a record average rate of 14,204 tons per hour in December 1970."

The Little report found little pollution. Ships must retain dirty ballast or risk large fines. "Minor spills do occur, but apparently are readily dispersed, due to warm-water conditions and the fresh-water inflow from the Shatt-al Arab," the report said. "The usual detergents are used to clean spills.

"There were no baseline studies, but no adverse effect on the local marine life has yet been noted in the vicinity of the piers or the sea island on the dredged channel. Kuwait has an active program of shrimp and fish trawling, and no complaints have been heard about odor or taste." The report said oil spills had been a general Persian Gulf problem "but the largest volume by far comes from offshore wells."

"Some parts of the southern coast of the Gulf . . . are uniformly coated with a thin mixture of oil and sand, resembling dark volcanic or mineral sands," the report said. "However, only scattered damage is visible and clear blue waters, white sands, and good fish and shrimp catches can be enjoyed almost everywhere—including around large terminals.

"Faulty equipment or human error are responsible for the minor spills. . . . Hydraulic valves (overflow) and underwater pipeline control valves (leaks) are somewhat troublesome. . . . Flexible hoses and aluminum chicksan (loading) arms have been known to fail, and drainage of connections and manifolds must be efficient. Strong enforcement action is being taken by several countries . . . but there is no deballasting equipment available, as tankers have much time on long voyages to clean their ballast."

What is the result of these studies and reports? Whether the IWR effort has any influence on what is done remains to be seen. It is particularly doubtful that a five-year study as recommended by the Little report ever will be started.

Assuming that the mid-1970s tanker surplus ends in time and the approach of supertankers and development of superports to receive them again become imminent, it might be well to seek ways to make the impact on our coastal waters and shores as light as possible. Blind opposition will be futile. People who want superports and all that goes or may go with them outnumber those who don't and can outshout them in Congress, the White House, and the Departments of Interior and Transportation.

Few Americans now are willing to make sacrifices to cut down the growing demand for energy. If blackouts or mere brownouts come because a power plant runs out of fuel, or because a nuclear plant is far behind schedule as a result of environmental problems, we will suffer the inconveniences with little grace and much loud demanding of action.

Nor can people living far from the shores be expected to be greatly concerned over oil-soaked beaches and dying seabirds. They *will* be concerned if the lights go out and the air conditioner shuts down, or if the car has to stay in the garage until the filling station gets gasoline.

The technology for safe and environmentally acceptable operation of supertankers and superports seems available and in limited use. There are laws aplenty, starting with the Refuse Act of 1899, a law so simple it baffles lawyers, and continuing through various oil pollution and water quality acts. The concept of coastal zoning, pioneered by Delaware and being explored elsewhere, offers a means of control. In October 1972 Congress passed a Coastal Zone Act to encourage state programs (but failed to appropriate any money, an action quickly matched by President Nixon in putting nothing in his budget!).

Other efforts are under way to find ways to haul oil safely, though not without controversy. The Coast Guard rewrote its tanker safety regulations, but promptly was challenged in court by an environmental coalition charging that the actual rewriting was done by a committee dominated by the oil and shipping industries, largely to embody existing practices. Failure to include requirements for double bottoms or segregated ballast tanks was cited specifically, and the Coast Guard undertook further work on the latter.

The need for segregated ballast tanks, located along the sides of a tanker and used only for ballast water, never for cargo, was demonstrated early November 14, 1975. The Onassis tanker *Olympic Alliance,* with more than 200,000 tons of Arabian crude for Hamburg, was rammed in heavy fog in crowded Dover Strait by the Royal Navy frigate *Achilles.* Two to three thousand tons spilled out of one tank to wash on British beaches, close to those once blackened by the *Torrey Canyon.* If the tanker had had only water in the side tanks, only water would have been spilled.

The Maritime Administration and tanker owners and builders are reviewing "design studies of novel tanker configurations" for better protection against spills in collisions and strandings and for elimination, as far as possible, of ballast water in cargo tanks. The suggestions include use of double bottoms or double sides, or both, the voids to serve as ballast tanks sealed off from the cargo, or placement of separate ballast tanks along the sides in the forward two-thirds of the hull, where most grounding and collision damage is suffered. Thus a rupture would spill water, not oil.

Design problems get into intricate areas of stability, and equally intricate ones of economics. Deviations from convention cost more and the required freight rate to amortize costs must go up. Even so, Mobil Oil Co. now has a class of 210,000-dwt ships with double bottoms.

The greater gain, when problems are solved, will be in ships with minimum need to dispose of the inevitable oil-water mix, or dirty ballast water, either to shipboard or shoreside treatment equipment, or pumped out at sea—so-called "intentional spills." The industry doesn't like the term, contending that a tanker master frequently has no choice but to dump dirty ballast water to maintain trim and seaworthiness. However, this practice, dating to the first days of tankers, and tank cleaning are probably the source of at least as much oil on the oceans as accidental spills and probably the reason Thor Heyerdahl could report blobs of tar floating far at sea during his crossing in his papyrus boat *Ra II.* A National Oceanic and Atmospheric Administration research cruise last year confirmed the report and expanded it to cover 500,000 square miles of the Atlantic.

The design proposals were part of this country's effort to help meet a 1975 goal of the United Nations Intergovernmental Consultative Organization for an end to all "wilful and intentional pollution of the seas by oil and other noxious substances." MARAD officials said representatives of the shipbuilding and oil transport industries cooperating in the studies seemed "reasonably satisfied with the results to date," although no formal preference poll had been taken.

Meanwhile a new Ports and Waterways Safety Act empowers the Secretary of Transportation to set standards governing design, construction, maintenance, and operation of tankers, with consultation from the Environmental Protection Agency. New rules on design and construction are to become effective after January 1, 1974, and no later than January 1, 1976.

The National Transportation Safety Board, reporting on the March 1971 sinking of the tanker *Texaco Oklahoma* off Cape Hatteras with a full cargo of fuel oil and loss of 31 men, blamed high stresses on a lightly constructed hull, plus a practice of considering Cape Hatteras seas as a "summer zone" all year, permitting full loads.

The board, a Transportation Department investigative arm, urged the Coast Guard and NOAA to develop methods of calculating wave effects on ships and vessel resistance to seas in Cape Hatteras storms. The Coast Guard was told it should require tanker operators to furnish means of making short-term predictions of wave effects, and work with the Federal Communications Commission on a mandatory casualty alerting system unless an international system was started within a year.

Such measures are more urgent for supertankers. For all Gulf's good experience, and its discovery that a Universe tanker was rolled only 17° in a Pacific typhoon, there have been heavy losses elsewhere. In addition to the *Metula, Jakob Maersk,* and *Urquiola* disasters already mentioned, others have included, in the bad year of 1969, the loss of the *Marpessa,* a 207,000-dwt ship which exploded and sank off the east coast of Africa on her maiden voyage, fortunately with no cargo. An explosion seriously damaged a sister ship, the *Mactra,* and the 105,000-dwt Norwegian *Silja* exploded and sank in a collision off Marseilles; then the 98,000-dwt Swedish *Seven Skies* exploded and sank off Singapore. Lloyds' shipping underwriters soon raised rates.

And in December 1972 the second worst known spill occurred in the Indian Ocean when the Liberian-registered *Seastar* lost 115,000 tons—the *Torrey Canyon* lost only 2,000 more—in a disaster on which little has become public. The Smithsonian Institution's Center for Natural Phenomena, which reported the spill in its "Second Generation Directory of Spills," could get no further information.

There have been lesser disasters. In 1971 the 68,600-dwt *Wafra* became disabled and went aground near Cape Agulhas, Africa's southernmost point, to spill more than 63,000 tons of oil on shores and beaches. But, as with the *Torrey Canyon* wreck, anything of this magnitude overwhelms all emergency measures and only nature's ability to overcome the worst man can do, in time, gives hope.

Here the Navy and private interests are trying to help nature with research on stimulation of bacteria to consume spilled oil. At least one oil company, Humble, is trying compounds to jell oil in cargo holds if they are ruptured. MARAD and NOAA are working on a research program on the "fate and behavior of oil on the oceans," intended to find the "maximum permissible level of oil considered to be harmless to marine life." This would enable the Coast Guard and the EPA to establish "reasonable purity standards for ships' discharges."

None of this can be as good as simple prevention of disaster—keeping tankers and other ships from bumping into each other, even though some of a captain's authority may have to be limited, and keeping them out of dangerous waters, the kind that ended the *Torrey Canyon* and the career of her master.

# 31. Deep-Water Archeology

WILLARD BASCOM 1971

## INTRODUCTION

The greatest remaining treasure-house of information about the ancient world—the bottom of the Mediterranean—is about to become accessible. In this article I explain why I believe that there may be many ancient wooden ships in reasonably good condition on the deep-sea floor, how these ships can be located and recovered, why they sank, and why their cargoes are clearly worth a substantial search and recovery effort. In addition, I present the rationale for deciding where to search in order to optimize the chances of finding long-lost ships.

A new form of underwater archeology will begin when a new kind of scientific ship and new techniques are used to explore the deep-sea floor for sunken ancient ships. The *Alcoa Seaprobe*[1] is such a ship—capable of reaching down with its sensors, which are in a pod at the tip of a pipe, and making a detailed examination of the bottom in water several thousand meters deep (Figure 31-1). It is equipped with sonar to systematically search the sea floor at a rate of about 1 square nautical mile every 6 hours (1 square nautical mile = 3.4 square kilometers). Men at the surface will be able to inspect objects on the bottom with television, dusting away sediment by means of jets and propellers. Photographs can be taken and objects of interest identified (and perhaps recovered) by means of grasping devices. Because *Alcoa Seaprobe* will be capable of lifting from deep water loads weighing 200 metric tons, it may be possible, under some circumstances, to recover entire small ships in one piece. The overall capability of this new ship will be substantially greater than that of any previous device for search and recovery in deep water.

I deal here only with ships that sailed the Mediterranean Sea during the pre-Christian era, but it is evident that there are many

1. *Alcoa Seaprobe* is owned by the Aluminum Corporation of America and operated by Ocean Science and Engineering, Inc., for Ocean Search, Inc., a wholly owned subsidiary of Alcoa. It was designed by Ocean Science and Engineering, Inc., and built by Peterson Builders, Inc., in Sturgeon Bay, Wisconsin. It has just begun operations.

Willard Bascom is president and chairman of Ocean Science Engineering, Inc., California. He is also director of Ocean Mining, Inc., Deep Oil Technology, and Oil Search, Inc. He is former director of the National Academy of Sciences' Mohole Project. He has written numerous scientific and popular books and articles.

From *Science*, Vol. 174, No. 4006, pp. 261-269, 1971. Reprinted with light editing and by permission of the author and the American Association for the Advancement of Science. Copyright 1971 by the American Association for the Advancement of Science.

Figure 31-1. The *Alcoa Seaprobe.* (Photograph courtesy of Ocean Science and Engineering, Inc.)

other, more recent (but still very old) ships in that sea, and elsewhere in the world, to which these search and salvage methods can be applied.

Every ship is a small sample of the life and times during which it sails. On ancient ships, as on today's ships, the people aboard had all the utensils required for living, the weapons for fighting, and the tools for working. Much of this hardware and part of the cargo is virtually imperishable. Some of these objects can be dated and associated with peoples and ports to give information about the culture and commerce of the period. The hulls of the ships reveal the state of the art of marine technology in naval architecture and shipbuilding. Since each ship represents the surrounding civilization, and since most sink quickly, carrying down everything except minor flotsam, a complete ancient ship in good condition is the marine archeologist's dream—a sort of undersea Pompeii, in which dark, cold water instead of hot ashes has preserved a moment in time.

Until now, most of the old ships excavated have been represented mainly by piles of amphorae and the part of the ship's bottom structure that was protected by being submerged in mud. Most of these ships were wrecked on reefs in shallow water, and only the most resistant materials, such as ceramics, bronze, and glass, have survived.[2] Ex-

2. The following objects can survive under the sea for 2000 years. General: metal ingots (bronze, tin, copper, and silver), tools, coins, amphorae, pottery, glass, and inscribed stone tablets. Ship's gear: anchors, bronze tools, tiles, utensils, metal fasteners, ballast rock, firepots, leg-irons, navigational

posed wood rarely survives the attacks of boring animals and waves for more than a dozen years. Only the wood buried safely beneath mud and sand can be studied and recovered.

Our picture of ancient shipping is, therefore, somewhat skewed by the materials that survive and by the corresponding blank spots in recorded history. A great deal is known about some aspects of the old ships, but virtually nothing is known about others;[3] for example, knowledge of the upper structure is derived primarily from the generally inadequate renderings on bas-reliefs and vases. The scientific argument about how the rowers and oars were arranged on warships is still active after 100 years of debate. Although we are not certain what it meant to say a ship was an "eight" or a "thirteen," details such as the cost and length of oars are known. No example of the trireme, the most common warship for some 400 years, has yet been found and excavated, although the sinking of thousands of them has been recorded.[4] Much remains to be learned about how ancient ships fought, were constructed, sailed, loaded, and crewed.

## SURVIVAL OF WOODEN HULLS IN DEEP WATER

In deep water (more than 1000 meters below the surface), the chance of survival of both the wooden and the fragile parts of a ship should be enormously improved; the temperature on the bottom is near freezing, and chemical reactions proceed slowly. It is dark, and the currents are usually minimal, thus allowing protective silt to accumulate on the upper surface. A ship lying there will be well beneath wave action, trawl nets, and divers. Since the cargo will not have moved after its original landing, it should not be scattered about nearly as much as it is in ships wrecked in shallow water.

The most uncertain aspect of wreck preservation in deep water has to do with the possible damaging effects of marine borers. Teredos are not known to go deeper than 200 meters, but in some places *Xylophaga* a borer clam, lives at 2000 meters.[5] Old wood untouched by borers has been found on the Pacific continental slope south of Panama, and an old ship was seen in deep water off Gibraltar by a small submarine looking for the lost H-bomb. In one Atlantic location off the coast of Florida, exposed wood from a Spanish wreck, 400 meters deep and about 300 years old, has not been attacked.[6] Probably the reason that some hulks have borers and others do not is because of local variations in oxygen, nutrients, metallic ions, or currents. The very action of a ship landing on the sea floor might cause a cloud of mud to swirl up and around, falling back on the ship as a protective cover. Some ships had resistant wood, lead sheathing, paint, copper parts, and tarred decks or seams, all of which may have helped protect against borers, especially where currents are low. A wooden ship landing in an anaerobic area, such as the Black Sea, should endure indefinitely.

The amount of mud that accumulates on a ship because of normal sedimentation will vary considerably, since the rate of sedimentation depends on distance from a land mass, amount of runoff, and local currents. In the central basins of the Mediterranean where the water is 4000 meters deep, the rate of sedimentation is believed to be about 10

equipment, and lead sheeting. Military equipment (if bronze): armor, swords, spears, shields, helmets, chariots, axes, boarding grapples, Greek fire tubes, and ramming beaks. Art: sarcophagi; columns; obelisks; statues of bronze, stone, or clay; bracelets, rings, and other jewelry; and musical instruments.

3. L. Casson, *The Ancient Mariners* (Minerva New York, 1959).

4. H. Frost is excavating a hull of Sicily, believed to be that of a trireme.

5. J. S. Muroka, *Deep Ocean Biodeterioration of Materials—Six Months at 6,000 feet* (Technical Note N-1081, U.S. Naval Civil Engineering Laboratory, Port Hueneme, Calif., 1970); R. D. Turner, *Some Results of Deep-Water Testing* (Annual reports, 1965, American Malacological Union, Allen, Lawrence, Kans., 1965).

6. R. Marx, personal communication. In deep water off Florida, Marx found a Spanish wreck with the wood in good condition.

centimeters per 1000 years.[7] In embayments close to shore, the rate may be more than ten times that amount;[8] but intermediate depths, say 1000 meters, where muds, clays, and calcareous oozes are deposited, 20 centimeters per 1000 years is a reasonable estimate. Forty centimeters of sea dust since the start of the Christian era should give an ancient ship, if otherwise whole, the blurred appearance of a wagon after a snowstorm.

The degree of preservation of a ship in shallow water apparently becomes stabilized after about a dozen years, and then seems to remain unchanged for centuries.[8,9] One has good reason to hope for much less deterioration in deep water, both in those first years and afterward.

Almost certainly, special circumstances exist in the many places beneath the sea where very old ships have not decayed substantially where they still sit upright on the bottom and have barely changed from the way they looked when they first sank.

## SALVAGING WRECKS IN SHALLOW WATER

The salvage of ancient ships and cargoes for their archeological information and art treasures is not new. In 1832, the 5th century bronze Apollo which is now in the Louvre was brought up by a trawler from the waters off the island of Elba. In 1901 a wreck at Antikythera was accidentally discovered by sponge fishermen who had made an exploratory dive while waiting for the weather to moderate and found a spectacular collection of bronze and marble statues. They reported their find to the government, and an expedition was launched. Many statues were salvaged, along with an astronomical computer which set the date of the voyage at 80 B.C., suggesting that this special cargo was probably loot from Greek cities en route to Rome. This wreck was on top of an undersea cliff, and some of the cargo had slid off into water of far greater than diving depth before it was found.

Greek sponge divers also found a wreck at Mahdia in the Bay of Tunis in 1907. An entire temple was aboard, as well as many bronzes. Greek trawlermen—fishermen who drag nets along the bottom in water somewhat deeper than that divers work—brought up parts of bronze statues from Cape Artemision in 1926. An expedition was begun to recover other statues (including the larger-than-life bronze of a naked Zeus casting a spear—a replica of which stands at the entrance to the United Nations building in New York), but the water was too deep for the diving technology of the day, and after several serious accidents the site was abandoned and perhaps lost.

These finds of truly great statuary were, of course, tremendously exciting to the art world; but they were of less significance to classical archeologists, who did not feel that random finds of ships carrying art objects were very important in defining societies and cultures. It is also possible that much of the early undersea work was ignored because of its technical crudity in mapping, dating, and processing of finds. Peter Throckmorton[10] quotes a Turkish official in the Department of Antiquities in 1960 as saying: ". . . underwater archaeology is not very important or interesting. We archaeologists are interested in the culture of the people, not in minor details of ship construction, which is of interest only to a few specialists."

The beginnings of recent activity in salvaging old ships from shallow water seems to have begun with Jacques Y. Cousteau, who organized a team of divers in 1952 to excavate a wreck at Gran Congloué, not far from Marseilles. It was an exciting adventure, widely reported in the press and enhanced somewhat by Cousteau's colorful descriptions and motion pictures. In this exca-

7. Y. Herman, *Late Quaternary Mediterranean Sediments,* in press.
8. P. Throckmorton, *Shipwrecks and Archaeology* (Little, Brown, Boston, 1970), pp. 152-155.
9. H. Frost, *Under the Mediterranean* (Routledge, London, 1963), pp. 122-129.

10. P. Throckmorton, personal communication.

vation, which followed an undersea slope downward as deep as 50 meters, the Cousteau group pioneered many techniques that have since been greatly refined, including the use (for archeological purposes) of television, air lift, and the Aqualung.[11] The excavators worked in the glare of publicity and could not be expected to foresee many technical problems of wreck excavation. Looking back on the work, it now seems possible that there were at the site two wrecks, one above the other, which got confused. This does not seem quite as serious now as it did at the time, when that site was thought to be unique.

The Congloué operation was a good beginning in the sense that it attracted the world's attention to a new source of historical material that has since revealed a great deal about ancient times. That excavation was followed by a flurry of artifact hunting by scuba divers, mostly along the French Mediterranean coast. These hunts were characterized by confusion of purpose and numerous diving accidents. In the early days, divers were not archeologists, nor vice versa. As wrecks were destroyed in the search for artifacts, few careful drawings were made and most of the data were lost forever. But in 1958, Throckmorton and, shortly afterward, George Bass, decided that classically correct underwater excavations were technically feasible and that a Bronze-Age wreck off Cape Geledonia, Turkey, was a good place to attempt one. This very successful archeological work, in which the first precision, three-dimensional surveys of ship and cargo were made, has been described in detail by Bass.[12] It was followed by a similar work by Throckmorton[8] in Italy and Greece, and Katzev[13] in Cyprus; thus a technology for precise excavation of wrecks in shallow water has been established.

11. J. Y. Cousteau, *Nat. Geogr.*, January 1954, p. 125.
12. G. F. Bass and P. Throckmorton, *Archaeology* 14, No. 2 (1961), p. 728; G. F. Bass, *Expedition* 3, No. 2 (Winter 1961), p. 131.
13. M. L. Katzev, *Nat. Geogr.*, June 1970, p. 841.

However, the depth at which such work is practicable is set by the usual physiological problems of diving. Even today, in doing extended work deeper than, say, 50 meters, there is a real chance of diver-archeologists getting the bends or having other kinds of diving trouble. True, it is possible to put down living quarters and remain at depth for weeks at a time, to use complex mixed-gas apparatus, or to use a saturated diving system, in which one lives under pressure at the surface and is carried to and from the depths in a pressure chamber. Doubtless these methods will eventually be used and the archeological diving work will be extended as deep as perhaps 200 meters; but the costs and problems increase greatly, while the archeological advantages do not improve at the same rate.

Bass and others successfully used side-looking sonar for detecting wrecks off the coast of Turkey in water depths to 130 meters; they identified the targets with television.[14] Bass also used the small submarine *Asherah*, equipped with stereophotographic mapping cameras, to take overlapping photographs from which accurate maps could be made. Although further development of the equipment was said to be required, these techniques were effective. However, they are not known to be in use at the present time. Throckmorton and others have used bottom-penetrating sonar to find wrecks beneath harbor muds.

So much for the history of undersea work and the present state of work in shallow water. The operations in deep water will be quite different.

## WHERE TO LOOK FOR SUNKEN SHIPS

There will be an essential difference in the

14. G. F. Bass, *A Diversified Program for the Study of Shallow Water Searching and Mapping Techniques* (University of Pennsylvania Museum, Philadelphia, 1968); M. S. McGehee, B. P. Luydendyk, D. E. Boegman, *Location of Ancient Roman Shipwreck by Modern Acoustic Techniques* (Report No. MPL-U-98/67, Marine Physical Laboratory, Univ. of California, San Diego, 1967).

means of finding deep-water wrecks. Wrecks in shallow water have generally been found accidentally by sponge divers, trawlers, or sport divers. Throckmorton, who probably has located more wrecks in the Mediterranean than anyone else, has relied largely on talking to sponge divers in waterfront bars. He pleasantly engages them in Turkish, Greek, or Italian over auzo or raki and eventually turns the conversation to "old pots in the sea"–amphorae. Every sponge diver in the Mediterranean knows where there are a few mounds of such pots marking the site of an old wreck. Eventually, they tell him and he records the location. He has personally checked many of these, and his charts show hundreds of sites.

In deep water there is no similar mechanism for getting a lead on a promising wreck. Instead, it will be necessary to rely on statistics that are based on knowledge of the ancient ports and population centers, the kinds of cargoes and location of trade routes, and the nature of the old ships and the way they were sailed. Probably the last of these is the most important, since the mariners of old did not sail in straight lines between ports as a modern ship would. The ships were small and they sailed between protected bays, sometimes stopping to avoid the strong afternoon winds. They would minimize runs in the open sea by sailing within a few miles of the coast, anchoring during the calm, and sailing with the favoring winds as much as possible. Often the outward voyage would follow a different route from the return, and both might change seasonally or stop entirely during the months of November to March because of the increased risk during bad weather. The size of the ship and the way it was rigged, as well as the destination of its cargo, also influenced the route.

The story of what is known about the ancient ships is well told in the works of Lionel Casson[15] and others, but there is also much that is not known about the many varieties of ships and cargoes over a period of several thousand years.

15. L. Casson, *Ships and Seamanship in the Ancient World* (Princeton Univ. Press, Princeton, N.J., 1971).

A very brief review of the history of Mediterranean shipping before the Christian era is appropriate. This was an age when empires were formed, established their colonies, collapsed, and were replaced. Because rough terrain and unsettled political situations made land travel very difficult and risky, there may have been more ships afloat in some periods than there are now. The objective is to find places along well-traveled sea lanes where ships would have troubles that would cause them to sink in deep water. Then a search for sunken ships can be conducted where the statistics are more favorable.

Egyptian ships were trading along the eastern Mediterranean at least as early as 2500 B.C., one of their first imports being cedar from Lebanon for shipbuilding. Minoan Crete was the first great sea power in the Mediterranean. In the years 1800 to 1500 B.C., its ships explored the Aegean and Black seas and pioneered the trade routes, as far west as Sicily, that were destined to last for centuries. By 1500 B.C., the Mycenaeans controlled the seas, giving way in about 1200 B.C., to the Phoenicians, who extended the trade routes into the western basin and built colonies at least as far west as Cadiz, which is beyond Gibraltar. Their sailing technology was remarkable, and some people think that they may have sailed on across the Atlantic. On their return eastward, they carried metals–tin, silver, lead, and iron–mainly from the mines of Spain.

Gradually, by about 800 B.C., dominance of the sea shifted to Greek shippers, who dealt more in such bulk commodities as olive oil, wine, wheat, pottery, and hides. The Greeks founded hundreds of colonies and linked these to the homeland by ship traffic; thus, by 500 B.C., Athens (Piraeus) was a major trade center. Its influence gave way to that of Rhodes and Alexandria, until, in the century before Christ, the Romans dominated the sea (Figure 31-2). Presumably all

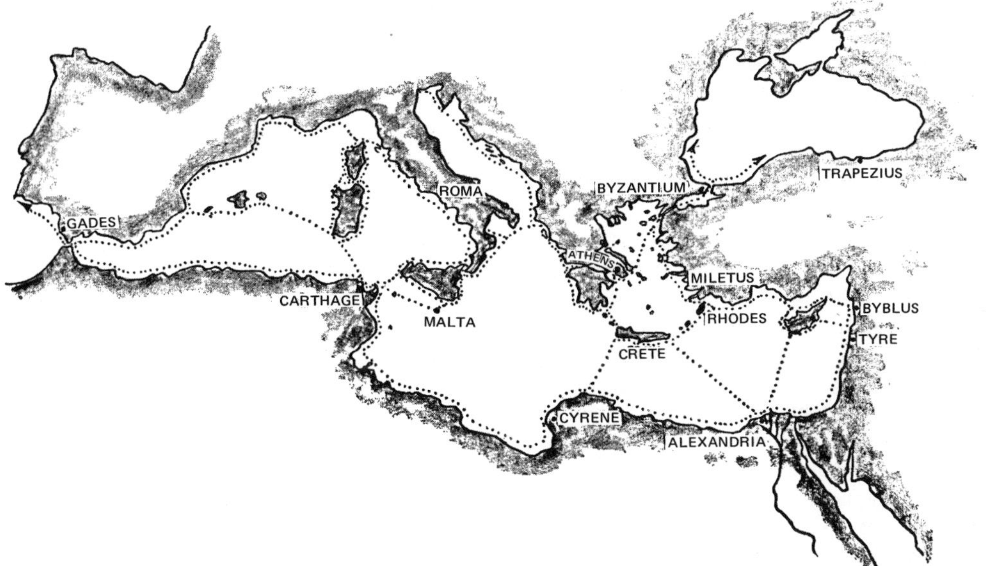


Figure 31-2. Trade routes in the Mediterranean, from about 500 to 200 B.C.[24]

of the countries around the sea had ships that were involved to some extent in trading, piracy, and intermittent wars. The point is that there were a great many different kinds of ships at sea, manned by crews of different nations, during the millennium B.C. The routes they followed remained virtually unchanged for thousands of years.

## WHY SHIPS SANK IN DEEP WATER

Why would a ship suddenly sink in deep water—especially considering the fact that the routes they followed were generally near shore and that risks were minimized by anchoring in protected waters when the weather was bad? There were accidents of many kinds. The weather in the Mediterranean is known for sudden, violent change, and the old ships could not respond rapidly or sail into the wind very well. In the Aegean, they feared the meltime, a northerly, afternoon wind that has gusts to gale force and that dies down again, to leave the sea calm by midnight.[16] It would be very easy for a ship to be blown well offshore and sunk in a sudden squall. In the Adriatic these northerly gales are called boras, and they reach force 10.[17] In the late fall and winter there is the sirocco, which can blow at a steady force 6 for a week, with gusts to force 8 or more. In 1966, a modern steamer went down in one, with a loss of 166 people. These violent and unexpected winds are known to have been the principal cause of losses of sailing ships in the eastern Mediterranean in the 19th century A.D.—and they doubtles were in previous centuries as well.

The ancient ships were generally small (less than 40 meters long) and made of wooden planks held edge to edge, caravel

16. H. M. Denham, *The Aegean* (Murray, London, 1963), p. 63.

17. Force 10 is a whole gale with winds of 50 knots; it can make (fully developed) waves 7 to 10 meters high. Force 6 is a strong breeze with winds of 25 knots; it can make (fully developed) waves 3 to 4 meters high.

style, with mortised joints. If the planks came apart, the weight of cargo and ballast would take a ship down in a few minutes. This kind of accident might be aggravated by a shift of cargo, a weakening of the wood by marine borers, or by one large wave. Generally the ships did not have much freeboard, and many were not completely decked. In heavy weather they could take water over the sides and quickly founder or capsize.

Pirates were the scourge of shipping for many hundreds of years; they doubtless sank many of the vessels they caught. Fire was also a frequent cause of loss–coals would fall from the galley stove as the ship pitched, or a carelessly held torch would start a blaze. Some nations had strict safety laws about fire on shipboard. In later centuries, there were several occasions when whole fleets were lost by fire. Besides the other hazards, warships had a chance of being rammed in battle or being scuttled after capture.

One concludes that ships sank in ancient times for the same reasons they did in the 19th century. Because the old ships were smaller, less well built and rigged, and sailed by less well-trained crews, the statistics must have been worse. Throckmorton[8, p. 34] points out that, in the years from 1964 to 1869, 10,000 insured merchant ships were lost–1000 without a trace. Of the 372 British naval ships lost by mishap between 1793 and 1850, nearly half were lost by running onto unmarked shoals, and 78 of them, or 21 per cent foundered at sea, usually in deep water with all hands. He also notes that on a single reef at Yassi Ada he and Bass found more than 15 wrecks, ranging from 3rd century B.C. to the 1930's.

The number of ships involved in commercial traffic during the millenium B.C. can be used to estimate the number of wrecks lying in deep water. Yalouris[18] believes there were over 300 active ports by the 4th century B.C., with an average capacity of 40 ships each, and that half of these ships were at sea. If so, the standing crop of ships was

18. F. Yalouris, unpublished data.

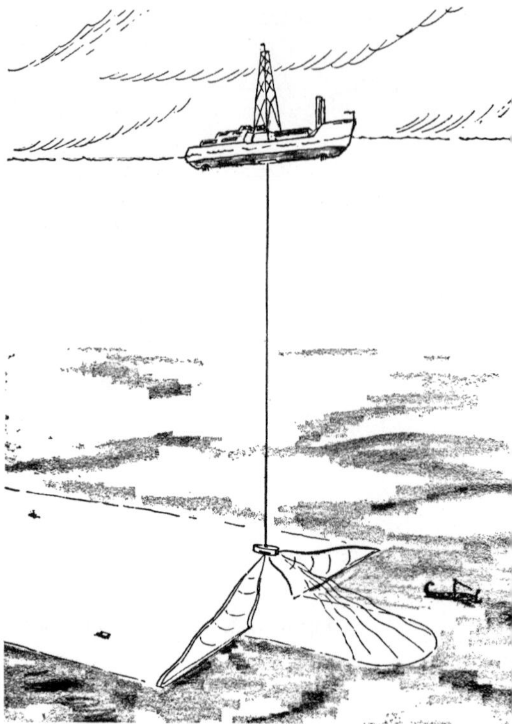

Figure 31-3. Searching with *Alcoa Seaprobe.* A pod containing both a forward and a side-looking sonar, as well as television, is attached to the tip of a weighted pipe. Together the sonars sweep a pathway about 400 meters wide at a speed of about 1 meter every 2 seconds.

about 12,000. This number increased markedly in Roman times, although it was much less at the beginning; therefore, a conservative estimate would probably be that there were, on the average, 6000 ships in trade over the 1000-year period. If one judges the average life of a merchant ship to be 40 years, some 150,000 ships were built.

Being guided by the statistics of ship losses during the 1800's, one can guess that half eventually retired safely and the other half were lost on voyages. If, of those lost, 20 per cent foundered, then there are 15,000 ships down offshore–many in deep water. If the total length of the trade routes in the eastern Mediterranean were 6000 nautical miles (1 nautical mile = 1.9 kilometers) and the average width 10 nautical miles, there is a reasonable chance of one ship in every 4 square nautical miles of bottom along those routes. By selecting specific areas were ships were known to get into trouble, it is possible to improve the chances considerably. There are numerous high-probability sites in the straits between islands, between islands and mainland, and at major "jumping off points," where ships left the security of nearby land and set out into open waters. Such sites exist between the Peloponnesus and Crete, east of Crete to Rhodes and Turkey, between Italy and Yugoslavia, between Tunis and Sicily, around Malta, near Gibraltar, and along the coasts of Lebanon, Israel, and Cyprus.

Somewhat more is known about the losses of military ships in the same period, and there are more fixed points to guide estimates in this case. There are literally hundreds of historical references to sea battles in which astonishing numbers of ships were involved. For example, at the battle of Economus in 255 B.C., 250 Roman ships faced 200 Carthaginian ships; only 16 ships were lost in the battle (which Rome won), but in a storm off Camarina shortly afterward, 250 of the remaining ships were wrecked. When Agrippa fought Sextus at Naulochus in 42 B.C., 600 ships were engaged. When Anthony and Cleopatra met Augustus at Actium in 37 B.C., about 100 ships of the 900 involved were lost.

The life-span of a trireme is estimated at 20 to 30 years,[18] if it were not destroyed by warfare or storm. Thus a force of 300 ships would be maintained by building ships at the rate of 10 to 15 a year. A law of Themistocles decreed that 20 ships should be constructed each year, in order to ensure replacement of the old ships. We do not know how long it was enforced, but the total number of warships built in Athens in the 5th and 4th centuries B.C. was around 1200. Considering the number of states with fleets, the size of the fleets, the rapidity of the replacement, and the life expectancy and survival chances of the ships, I estimate that 25,000 warships may have been built before the time of Christ.

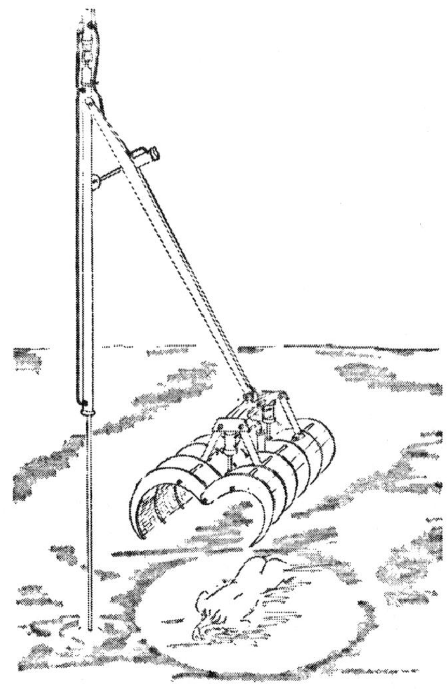

Figure 31-4. The exploratory tongs are guided by television and powered by a sea water hydraulic system. They are supported by an adjustable arm and are held steady by a pin 10 meters long. The pin can be driven into the bottom when the object to be recovered is seen. Tongs open to about 3 by 3 meters and can lift 5 metric tons. This system can perform delicate operations of lowering, rotating, and closing. It retracts through the center well into the ship.

If one figures battle losses at 10 per cent and losses at sea for another 10 per cent [Casson (reference 3, p. 157) says the Romans lost four ships to weather for every one to enemy action], then there may have been 5000 warships sunk–many of them in deep water. The locations of the battles are often known within a few miles.

Although I have used the millennium B.C. in this discussion of ship losses, it is obvious that the sinkings continued, at least through the age of sail, at about the same rates. The ships were larger, better built, and easier to sail, but the storms and wars and accidents went on. Ships that sank much later than the ancient ones may be even more interesting. For example, the Battle of Lepanto was fought not far from Actium 1608 years after Anthony and Augustus fought there; another 100-odd ships went down, this time with a very different array of artifacts. Sunken ships have been accumulating in the Mediterranean for 4000 years. Sorting through them on the bottom and identifying those of interest to archeological salvors may be a bit of a problem.

## THE SHIP AND ITS EQUIPMENT

Having decided that very old ships and their cargoes were among the most valuable objects to be found on the sea floor, and knowing the limitations of other possible methods, I proposed in 1962 the search and recovery system described here.[19] With few changes it has been developed into the *Alcoa Seaprobe.*

*Alcoa Seaprobe* is like a drilling ship with a center well and is propelled and maneuvered by two Voith-Schneider vertical-axis propellers, fore and aft. It is 75 meters long, 17 meters beam, and draws about 4 meters. The ship is all electric, with a power plant forward; it has quarters for 50 persons aft. (It is the world's largest aluminum structure—constructed mainly of 5456 aluminum, to demonstrate the excellent marine properties of that material.) The ship is steered by means of a console on the bridge, which controls the propellers and makes it possible to exert thrust in any direction almost instantaneously. Thus it can be dynamically positioned[20] manually or, with certain navigational inputs, automatically.

Above the 4 by 12 meter center well, there is an aluminum derrick that can lift up to 400,000 kilograms. The available working load of the derrick and draw works will be 200,000 kilograms (200 metric tons, with a safety factor of 2).

The derrick and pipe-handling system is capable of lowering or recovering drill pipe at an average rate of about 0.25 meter per second, to a depth of 6000 meters (although only about 2400 meters of pipe will normally be aboard). Depending on the operational situation and the depth, the lower end of the pipe will be weighted with up to 20 metric tons of drill collars. The drill pipe ordinarily carried is 11.5 centimeters in diameter, in 10-meter joints; it is handled as pairs, or "doubles," 20 meters long. It can be raised or lowered with precision a centimeter at a time, or rapidly at several meters a second (if necessary to avoid obstacles). The pipe can be rotated slowly to change the orientation of the instrument pod or tools at its lower tip.[21]

The information and control cable that connects the instrument pod to the scientific control center is attached to the outside of the pipe by special clips at 20-meter intervals. Within that cable, sonar and television signals come up coaxial conductors; power and instructions go down adjacent pairs. The information is recorded on paper recorders and on television tape; because precise position and time are recorded marginally at short intervals, it is possible to refind objects on the bottom.

The principal searching instruments are two sonars mounted in the pod; one scans directly ahead, and the other sees the bottom on each side at right angles to the motion of the pod (Figure 31-3). The side-looking sonar has a frequency of 177.5 kilo-

19. W. Bascom, U.S. Patent No. 3,215,976 (2 November 1965).

20. Dynamic positioning is a phrase first used by the author in 1960 to describe the process of equipping a ship with multiple propellers whose net thrust can be controlled from a central console, enabling the ship to hold position in deep water, relative to a fixed marker, in spite of winds, waves, and currents.

21. In addition to search and recovery, the *Alcoa Seaprobe* is capable of drilling for geological cores in deep water, generally following the method devised by the author and his associates in 1960 (W. Bascom, Ed., *Experimental Drilling in Deep Water* Publication No. 914, National Academy of Sciences, Washington, D.C., 1961).

hertz and a beam width of 0.3 degree. It sends and receives sound pulses in such a fashion that objects that project above the bottom (such as a rock or a ship) will better reflect the sound and produce a darker spot on the record. Because the sea floor immediately beyond an object is in the sonic shadow, the record of that area remains white. As the ship (and the pod) moves, the line-by-line record of a succession of pings builds a sonic picture of the bottom; thus, the size and position of any object can be determined within a few meters, as can the approximate height of the object. The resolution is such that, at a distance of 200 meters, the sonar can distinguish between two objects that are more than 1 meter apart.

Since the principal information obtained is a white shadow, it is evident that the sonar beam must strike the bottom at a substantial angle (there are no shadows near the nadir). This means that a pathway immediately beneath the pod must be searched by the forward-scanning sonar. This sonar works in a similar fashion; but, because it scans an area rather than a thin slice of bottom, it is not practical to record this information. Instead, any objects seen on its plan-presentation scope are noted for time and position; later they are plotted by hand on the record from the side-looking sonar.

The necessary precise navigation will be done in one of several ways, depending on the distance from land, the depth of the water, and the size of the area to be searched. For short-range work in depths to 2000 meters when an area of up to 50 square nautical miles is to be searched, the following method will ordinarily be used. Two taut-moored, subsurface buoys will be installed some 10 miles apart outside the search area; a surface buoy with radar transponder will be tied to each. Under most circumstances, the movement of a transponder buoy relative to a point on the surface above its anchor will be less than 20 meters. The ship will then obtain its position relative to these fixed buoys by ranging on them with radar. The digitized distance to each buoy will be recorded at 1-minute intervals, which are also coded automatically on the margin of the recordings. The maximum uncertainty of position will be about 40 meters (half the length of the ship).

## SEARCHING, INSPECTION, AND RECOVERY

When the ship arrives at a site selected for search, the transponder buoys are installed and the area is surveyed with an ordinary echo sounder, in order that the search can be conducted approximately along contour lines. The instrument pod is lowered on the weighted pipe until it is about 60 meters above the bottom. Then the ship begins to move along the planned course at a speed of about 0.8 meter per second. At this height above the bottom, the sonar scans a pathway about 400 meters wide. At this velocity, it searches an area of about 20,000 square meters per minute, a square kilometer every hour, and a square nautical mile every 4 hours. Allowing for an overlap in pathways of 50 meters, to make up for the navigational uncertainty, and allowing time for turns and adjusting pipe length, the average time needed to search 1 square nautical mile will be about 6 hours.

Doubtless, many objects will be detected in each square nautical mile searched. These will be given priorities for inspection, based on experience in interpreting such records. Ships that rest upright on the bottom should be relatively easy to identify as ships. Deciding whether or not they are valuable as salvage targets is a more difficult problem.

The pod that holds the sonars also holds the television camera and lights, but the sonar height of 60 meters above the bottom is beyond the range of the television (about 15 meters is the maximum range in clear water).

Therefore, when a visual inspection is to be made of the objects found with sonar, the pod is lowered until it is a few meters above the bottom. The ship navigates by radar back to the priority site, and a more localized search begins. While the ship holds position, the tip of the pipe is maneuvered by means of a propeller just above the pod. This propeller, driven by sea water pumped down the pipe, is capable of moving the pod up to 50 meters in any direction (depending on depth and pipe weight). Watchers on the ship will look for and attempt to identify the object and, if it is a ship, to determine the approximate kind and age. All wrecks would be carefully photographed for whatever information they contain.

If the ship is worth close inspection, the next step would be to retract the pod and replace it with the exploratory tongs shown in Figure 31-4. The tongs are a grasping tool guided by television. They are supported by a movable arm that extends out from a cylinder containing a 10-meter-long, hydraulically driven pin. This pin is used to fasten the tip of the pipe to the bottom adjacent to the wreck, and to give a fixed point about which the tongs can be rotated. The tongs can thus make slow, sure movements, in spite of small movements of the ship above. Watchers on *Alcoa Seaprobe* can wait for the dust to settle without the ship's drifting off course. Each of the tong tips has a pipe through which clear sea water is pumped to wash sediment away so that a better inspection can be made. Objects weighing less than 5 metric tons can be grasped and lifted with considerable delicacy. Specific objects of art or items of cargo can be recovered with these tongs and withdrawn through the center well into the ship.

When an entire ship suitable for recovery is located, the super-tongs will be towed to the site. These tongs would weigh about 50 metric tons and would be supported on the surface by their own pontoons, whose buoyancy can be adjusted. On site, the tongs may be slung beneath the ship, secured to the tip of the pipe, and lowered. As with the exploratory tongs, these will have television equipment mounted so that those on the ship can see the object to be seized. When fully closed, these tongs will surround a cylinder about 100 meters in diameter and 12 meters long. They are closed by a hydraulic system worked by leverage, which exerts increasingly greater force, up to about 10 metric tons per double tine (60 metric tons for six double tines). This should be sufficient to penetrate the mud beneath a hull and to close without touching the old ship.

The dimensions were selected with the sizes of ancient ships in mind. Figure 31-5 shows the super-tongs holding a small Phoenician-like trading ship of 1000 B.C. The ship is about 16 meters long and 7 meters beam. (Half full of mud, this would approach the weight-lifting capacity of the *Alcoa Seaprobe.*) Depending somewhat on the amount of mud and cargo in the hull, the remaining structural strength of the wood,[22] and the shape, ships up to the rated capacity of 200 metric tons could be lifted. Much longer ships would be neatly cut into two or more pieces with a hydraulically driven chain saw, and the lifting process repeated. These pieces can be reassembled later, probably with less difficulty than the fragments of ships found in shallow water to date.

When the super-tongs have been retracted to a position just below the ship, the *Alcoa Seaprobe* will slowly move into quiet, shallow water and set the burden on the sea floor. There the mud, ballast, and cargo can be removed by divers, thus lightening and strengthening the hull for its final move.

A special museum barge (Figure 31-6) would then be brought in, and an ordinary, large capacity marine derrick will lift tongs and hull from the sea bottom to the barge's tank, which is a few meters deep and filled with water. The super-tongs are removed

22. R. Marx, personal communication. Marx found the complete lower ribs of a 300-year-old galleon covered with sand in shallow water. The oak ribs were 20 centimeters square; beneath the outermost 1 centimeter, they "looked like new" and were in a condition so good that furniture could be made of them. He notes that this is unusual but not unique, and that the Spanish wreck he found in deep water[6] seems to be equally sound.

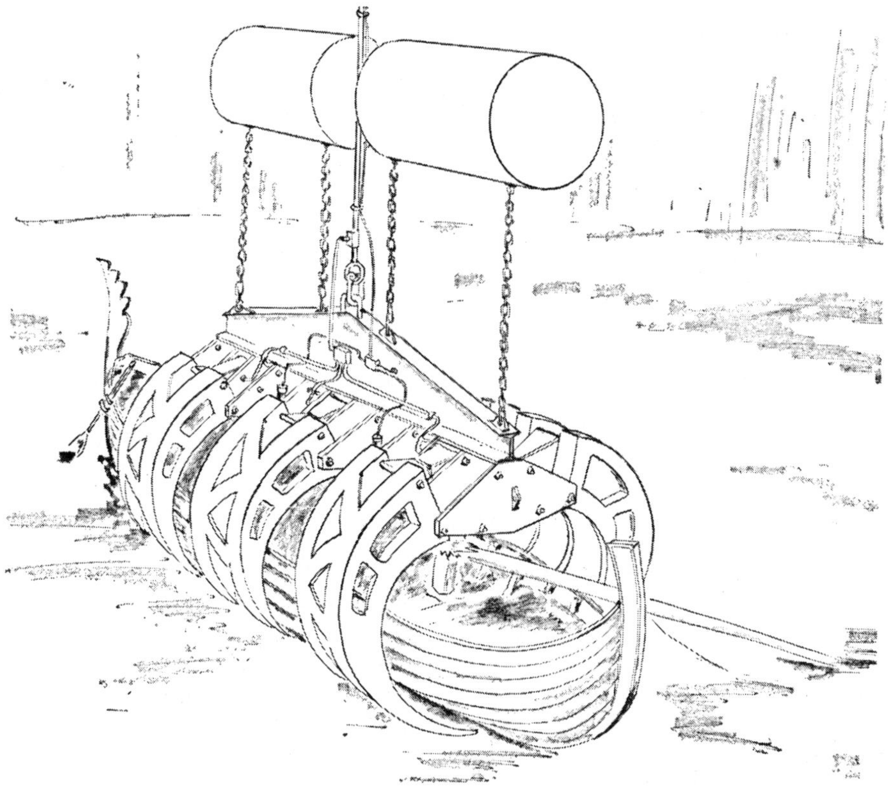

Figure 31-5. The super-tongs shown are lifting a small vessel from deep water. Guidance is by television; closing power comes from sea water pumped down the pipe at high pressures. These tongs (which weigh 50 metric tons) would be towed to the salvage site on their own flotation and used in a nearly neutral condition of buoyancy.

Figure 31-6. A museum barge could be constructed to support a tank in which an ancient ship could be carefully rebuilt underwater and displayed. A crane that can lift 200 metric tons (and that is available around most major ports) would be used to lift the super-tongs and the ship from shallow sea water into the tank and then return the tongs to the sea.

(and possibly sent back for the rest of the hull), and the archeologists can complete the reconstruction underwater, with controlled conditions of light and chemicals. The ancient ship will be visible to the public, but will remain submerged in a controlled environment. Because the barge would be mobile, it can be conveniently moved about the world for display.

## LEGAL CONSIDERATIONS

The objects being considered for salvage are clearly part of the general heritage of our civilization and should eventually become the property of the world's great museums. Since the countries and kingdoms that once owned these ships are long gone, it may not be easy to say who owns them, and it may not even be possible to determine what flag the ship sailed under. However, in most cases the following general principle will apply.

Many countries subscribe to those Law of the Sea conventions that specify a 3-mile zone of territorial waters (measured from a baseline drawn between promontories) and, beyond that, a contiguous zone to 12 nautical miles. The laws of most countries would prohibit ships of a foreign power from conducting salvage operations within these zones without specific permits.

Beyond the 12-mile limit are the high seas, where a vessel may generally be said to possess the right to conduct scientific research and to search for sunken property. Private vessels drive the right of the country whose flag they fly.

A coastal state may lay special claims to the sea floor on the continental shelf (whose limit is generally considered to be 200 meters). This kind of claim is intended to protect a state's natural resources to the limits of exploitability, but sunken property can hardly be considered a natural resource. Since the depths of greatest interest for *Alcoa Seaprobe* are well outside both the 12-mile limit and the 200-meter contour, it would seem that the ship will clearly be operating on the high seas. This would be true under U.S. law, off our own coast.

However, as a matter of scientific courtesy, one might invite archeologists from nearby states to participate. In some cases, the ship may be invited into territorial waters to perform search and recovery in the interest of international science or for a local government. Depending on the nature of the material salvaged and its origin, it should be possible to negotiate a reasonable arrangement for distributing the finds among the appropriate museums. The unique capability of the *Alcoa Seaprobe* makes it likely that several of the countries around the Mediterranean will be interested in cooperative archeological ventures.

## CONCLUSION

Obviously this kind of work is expensive; so is any work in modern science, compared to what it cost a few years ago. But the results will justify the expense. Salvaging one ancient ship from deep water will probably cost no more, for example, than salvaging the *Maine,* or the *Vasa,* or the Roskilde Viking ships. The daily cost of *Alcoa Seaprobe* will be about half that of an ordinary tanker, destroyer, or deep-sea drilling ship. The preservation and maintenance of the ship salvaged will be a fraction of similar costs for the *Texas* or the *Queen Mary.*[23] It

23. The *Maine,* sunk in 1898, was salvaged from the floor of Havana harbor in 1911; the *Vasa,* sunk in 1628, was raised from Stockholm harbor in 1961; the Roskilde Viking ships, sunk about 1400, were raised from a Danish harbor in 1962. The cost of each of these was several million dollars. Daily charter rates for a medium-sized tanker of 50,000 tons are now about $20,000; rates for destoyer, if computed on the same basis as those for a civilian ship, would be about $22,000 per day, plus depreciation and shore support. The day rate of the *Glomar Challenger* is about $16,000. The battleship *Texas,* now on public display at San Jacinto battlefield, was made into a presentable monument for a cost of about $1 million. The *Queen Mary,* now a convention center-museum at Long Beach, California, has a cost over $50 million to date.

is quite possible that a museum of ancient ships can be made self-supporting. Certainly it will attract the general public as well as the scholars, the tourists as well as the natives.

Who can say what a Roman trireme, or a Phoenician trader, or a Cyprean pirate ship is worth in terms of a better understanding of history? By these standards, it would seem that our civilization can afford to recover those ancient ships that can provide insights into the living and working conditions of another civilization, especially when they are not discoverable by other means. A new intellectual adventure that is understandable by the public and that generates interest and excitement can contribute to the appreciation and support of science as a whole.

## SUMMARY

There is reason to believe that some old wooden ships on the deep-sea floor have survived for thousands of years without much change. They will not be covered with much sediment, and it will be possible to find them using new searching techniques. These are embodied in the system of the *Alcoa Seaprobe,* which is also equipped to identify and raise old ships.

24. A. A. M. Van der Hyden and H. H. Scullard, Eds., *Atlas of the Classical World* (Nelson, London, 1959).

# 6

# *MARINE POLLUTION*

# 32. Mankind's New Target: The Vulnerable Oceans

BARBARA WARD 1974

Over 350 years ago, when cockle shell boats, weighing no more than 180 tons, were beginning to carry settlers to the Americas, Hugo Grotius formulated the legal doctrine of the freedom of the seas—a doctrine that has been the main assumption of maritime law virtually ever since. For him—as, no doubt, for the passengers of the *Mayflower*, enduring week after week of the strange and terrifying Atlantic passage—the sheer power, extent and majesty of the oceans seemed, not unreasonably, to express their fundamental nature. Grotius wrote of

"The ocean, which although surrounding this earth, the home of the human race, with the ebb and flow of its tides, can be neither seized nor enclosed; nay, which rather possesses the earth than is by it possessed."

There is, therefore, an appropriate logic behind the U.N. Conference on the Law of the Sea, which is likely, whatever else it does, to redefine Grotius's law to an unrecognizable degree. For the conference coincides with a quantum jump in man's ability and determination to "seize and enclose" the watery commons which cover three-fourths of his planet.

This change, which amounts to the extension to ocean space of the modern technological order, has been building up for some time—just as Newcomen's pump and Darby's coking ovens and even James Watts' steam engine long preceded the full-scale industrial revolution that lay ahead. But at a certain point in the extensions of technology, the processes become cumulative, the pace accelerates formidably and men are suddenly shaken awake into the realization that their whole way of life and work has been transformed. This was how the process evolved on land. It begins to look as though we are witnessing the same process of critical acceleration, this time as it takes place on the planet's oceans.

We can perhaps define five traditional uses of ocean space—as a means of transport, as a source of wealth (which in the past has

Dr. Barbara Ward (Lady Jackson) is a distinguished British economist, author, and educator. She is President of the International Institute for Environment and Development.

From *Living Wilderness*, Vol. 38, No. 127, pp. 7-15, 1974. This article has appeared in *The Economist* and as the introduction to a report, "Toward an Environmentally Sound Law of the Sea," by Robert Hallman, published by the International Institute for Environment and Development. Reprinted with light editing and with permission from *Living Wilderness* and the International Institute for Environment and Development.

mainly meant fishing and whaling), as an area for fixed installations (piers, lighthouses, telegraph cables), as an area of recreation and as an ultimate dump or sink for all the wastes of human society and indeed of everything else. In all these categories, change is now formidably speeding up. Take transport, first of all. The transfer of goods by sea is expanding by eight percent a year. In the sixties, the weight of world cargo doubled—from 1,110 million tons to 2,280 million. At the same time, the size of cargo ships is expanding faster still. As recently as 1948, no cargo ship weighed more than 26,000 dead weight tons. By 1973, over 400 oil tankers, each 200,000 dead weight tons or more in size (with cargo capacity of 60,000,000 gallons or more) were in operation, under construction or on order; a 477,000 DWT tanker was afloat; and plans had reached the drawing board for the million-ton tanker. The possible impact of these monsters can be gauged from the estimate that an accident 20 miles offshore to a 400,000 DWT oil-carrying supertanker could cause $3 billion worth of damage. Another type of fuel transporter—the carriers of liquid natural gas—will quadruple in numbers between 1971 and 1975. At the same time their carrying capacity is increasing from the 58,000 cubic meters of today to the 130,000 cubic meters forecast for 1985.

When we turn to the exploitation of the ocean's resources, it is a question today not simply, as with transport, of a vast expansion of a traditional activity. Fishing and whaling have, it is true, grown to an unprecedented degree. But the development of new, largely mineral resources is, if anything, more remarkable still. The frantic drive to increase man's hold on both the living and the inanimate resources of the oceans has a common root—the explosive growth of world population by 2.5 percent a year and the even more explosive determination of these increasing numbers to employ ever more energy—energy use grows by six percent a year. Whether the search is for protein or fuel or minerals, the scale of exploitation is already without precedent and increases at exponential rates.

Between 1950 and 1970, the world fish catch grew from 20 million metric tons to 70 million. Such a vast expansion was made possible by radical changes in fishing technology. Shoals are traced by sonar and by helicopter. Factory ships, weighing up to 44,000 tons, often equipped with the oceanic equivalent of giant vacuum cleaners, suck up all forms of marine life, dump back into the sea the unwanted material—a whale can be flensed and melted down in just half an hour—and then refrigerate on the spot fish destined for markets on land. Such mass methods are indiscriminate. Porpoises, for instance, are freely caught in nets trawling for tuna and look like they are endangered. On these ships, too, the use of energy is often remarkably high—one ton of fuel for each ton of usable fish. But this is simply another facet of the industrialization of the whole process.

The big break with the past comes with the growth of mineral exploitation. In the last decade, the extraction of oil and natural gas from the continental shelves has all but caught up, in value, with the world's entire fish catch. At present, it provides 18 percent of the 15 billion barrels of oil produced each year. But the energy crisis has both accelerated the pace of exploration and taken some inhibitions off the exploitation of known reserves—for instance off the coasts of California, where the memory of the Santa Barbara oil spill has been overlaid by more urgent preoccupations with oil at $11 a barrel. By 1980, it is estimated that the level of world production will be between 25 and 30 billion barrels a year with offshore oil accounting for 30 to 40 percent. By the end of the century, the percentage could be nearly half of an annual total of some 70 billion barrels.

So far, offshore oil has come from the continental shelves at depths of less than 100 meters of water. But here, too, high technology is moving in to open up deeper and more difficult reserves. These may lie on the continental slope beyond the shelf, on the millenial jumble of fallen rock at the bottom of the slope—the so-called "rise"—and even in the ocean bed itself, including the abyssal plains (from 5,000 to 7,000 meters in depth) to the deepest parts of the ocean, 8,000 meters and more below the surface of the seas. An American research ship, the *Glomar Challenger,* has done some successful drilling at 5,000 meters. A new commercial oil rig, the so-called SEDCO 702, is said to be able to drill at 1,000 meters under water in spite of 80-foot waves, 100-mile-an-hour gales and a freezing temperature. The extension of such technologies makes it possible to envisage tapping such sources of oil as are believed to exist beneath so-called "salt domes" on the ocean bed at a depth of 4-5,000 meters.

Technological breakthroughs are even more decisive in opening up wholly new fields of mineral exploitation in the ocean depths. The first signals of possible exhaustion of some land-based minerals have speeded up the search and it has been rewarded with a number of possibilities. One of the richest may follow from the discovery that there is an upwelling of hot sediment, full of valuable minerals, at the underwater line where continental "plates" come together. Such pools or sinks have, for instance, been located along the Red Sea and could lie at the foot of the 40,000 miles of undersea mountain ranges where the continents are piled up against each other.

The largest discovery so far lies on the deep ocean bed in the form of unexplained but highly exploitable reserves of so-called nodules, varying in size from ping-pong balls to footballs, made largely of manganese, cobalt, nickel and copper, and able, according to some estimates, to provide 400 million tons of ore annually *ad infinitum* since they obligingly renew themselves either because they are organic systems, like coral, or because some obscure process of ionization is at work on the sea bed. They also seem to be dredgeable from the ocean floor. All in all, they are interesting enough to have persuaded Howard Hughes to commission a 35,000-ton mining ship to put the dredges to work in the Pacific depths by 1975.

A vast increase in the number of fixed installations in the seas follows inevitably from this expansion of mineral exploitation. Ships in the Gulf of Mexico already have to follow carefully defined shipping lanes to avoid collisions with the platforms and rigs for offshore oil development. Pipelines will increasingly link the wells with onshore facilities. At Forcados in Western Nigeria there is already a 14-mile, 48-inch pipline out to the area of exploitation. North Sea installations are and will be longer (ranging between 115 and 225 miles) and in deeper waters (ranging from 230 to 400 feet).

The age of the undersea oil storage tank dawned in the Persian Gulf when in 1969 Abu Dhabi installed a 500,000-barrel-capacity steel tank in 155 feet of water, and two identical tanks have since been added to the complex. There is now a concrete undersea storage tank of the order of a million-barrel capacity in 230 feet of water in the Norwegian oil fields. The increasing size of tankers also dictates more construction out to sea. There are only nine on-shore ports in the world that can handle the 200,000-ton tanker and none of them are on the east coast of the United States. Offshore terminals ranging from single-point moorings to full-service island complexes are increasingly seen as the answer.

But such permanent extensions of human work to the seas are simplicity itself compared with some of the ventures already in the inventors' sights. Some construction firms believe that low-cost stable ocean platforms installed near the source of seabed minerals will make it economic to mine, beneficiate and load the ores in mid-ocean. Energy, in the larger flights of technological fancy, could be provided by nuclear reactors. Westinghouse-Tenneco believes that such plants, using seawater to produce oxygen and hydrogen by electrolysis, could produce liquid hydrogen and methanol at competitive prices for transshipment to the shore. Technical advantages such as unrestricted access to cooling water and relative separation from centers of population have already led to plans—by Offshore Power Systems—to build a nuclear plant about 2.8 miles off the shores of New Jersey and have it in commission by 1975.

Nor are these the only plans for energy. If the fusion process comes to be mankind's major source of nuclear power, the deuterium in the oceans will provide a virtually inexhaustible fuel. Meanwhile, scientists are interested in the potential energy that could be tapped from tides and currents and "heat gradients"—the interchange between cold and warm water levels in the oceans which could in theory be harnessed to deep sea turbines. One such area for possible experiment is in the Straits of Florida where the line of Bahamian islands diverts the flowing Gulf Stream to the North Atlantic.

Installations at sea are also in the dreams of the more imaginative tour directors, those modern impresarios of planned mass recreation. Floating villages with every form of aquatic sport could be an answer to the relentless growth of the tourist industry. The postwar coming of the two-to-three-week annual holiday in the industrialized world tripled the flow of international tourists in the 1960s—it stood at nearly 160 million in 1970, dotted every Mediterranean or Caribbean island with concrete Hiltons and provided wall-to-wall hotels round every promising bay. When the shores are used up, so goes the argument, the whole industry must move to sea.

But the biggest quantum jump in the use of the seas is where all the other expansions come together in a single gargantuan exercise shared by them all—the disposal of waste in the ocean deeps. Since the oceans are ultimately the receptacle without any outlet of everything that runs off the land or is dissolved from the skies, the problem of estimating what accumulation of wastes is actually taking place seems insoluble. Take one example only—oil wastes. The amount reaching the oceans from land-based sources such as refineries sited on rivers or estuaries, from the tankers at sea voiding their bilges and dirty ballast water or hitting a reef, from port installations where transshipment takes place, from carelessly sealed underwater oil wells is variously estimated at between 2.5 and 5 million tons a year. However, oil is also known to well up along the fault lines of the continental plates. In addition, a vast unmeasured precipitation first blown into the air and then dropped back into the ocean takes place from the exhausts of millions of automobiles. Some scientists believe the annual rate of pollution may be nearer 100 million tons.

Our ignorance is as great for other substances—DDT, plastics, heavy metals, radioactive wastes, concentrated sewage from coastal megalopolises growing by four to eight percent a year. We can say with certainty that all forms of waste are increasing. We can say with equal certainty that the coming surge of oceanic industrialization will multiply the effluents by an order of magnitude. What we cannot say is by how much. And, which is a far more dire and disturbing ignorance, we do not know how the oceans will respond, how much overloading and disruption they, as natural and therefore vulnerable systems, can continue to absorb. Thus the Law of the Sea Conference coincides not only with a quantum jump towards the "seizing and enclosing" of the oceans. It could also mark the beginning of their end.

Such a statement easily revives all the citizen's distrust in the inveterate doomsayer. It seems contrary to all reason and common sense to suppose that a body of water which is estimated at 1,349,929 million cubic kilometers cannot absorb, dissolve and dispense the rubbish of man. It took only a stricter control of atmospheric and other pollutions in London after 1952 to allow the dolphins to swim back up the Thames a couple of decades later; yet the Thames is a minute body of water to be able to cope with all London's filth. How many Londons could not the oceans cleanse without lasting damage?

The arguments for caution are, however, hardly negligible. Take first the general reasons for a careful approach. Oceans that are capable of supporting organic life are an integral part of the general maintenance of existence for all the planet's species, including man. Seventy percent of the world's oxygen is renewed through the biological action of minute phytoplankton near the ocean's surface—where 90 percent of its organic life is to be found. Scientists are reasonably certain that billennia of photosynthesis by plants and algae have built up so large a terrestrial supply of oxygen that the oceans' contribution is no longer critical. Yet to dispense with 70 percent of the breatheable atmosphere's renewal mechanism in a planet filling up with internal combustion engines seems a little foolhardy, to say the least, especially for the species that have evolved from gills to lungs.

But men live not only by oxygen but by the interactions of the total system. Climate, rainfall, radiation, cloud cover, the movements of winds and tides—all these are directly affected by seas and oceans and all could be unpredictably disrupted if careless, violent change occurs in the planet's watery sphere. Three features of the total system have particular significance for the impact upon it of man's activities. The first is precisely this complete and unavoidable interconnectedness. Without citing that well-known Antarctic penguin found with DDT in its fatty tissues, one can point to the worldwide distribution by wind and current of virtually any reasonably long-lasting substance that enters the "moving waters" anywhere. In the United States, dumping of wastes has multiplied five times over in the last two decades and the concentrated gunk emitted by the high technology of the eastern seaboard has not only dirtied local beaches. Added to the oil discharges of passing tankers, it has, according to the latest monitoring surveys conducted by the United States National Oceanographic and Atmospheric Administration (NOAA), befouled with large concentrations of oil and indestructible plastics one million square miles out into the Atlantic and down into the Caribbean as far as the Yucatan Peninsula. Thor Heyerdahl, crossing the South Atlantic on his raft, *Ra,* found similar discards spreading literally from shore to shore. When such wastes include radioactive carcinogenic substances or strong poisons like mercury or cadmium—or indeed worn-out old canisters of somebody's discarded poison gas—the emissions of one land mass can turn up to destroy the health and life of species half a world away.

But the most potentially devastating effects of freely spreading wastes would follow on a vast increase in the generation of nuclear energy, particularly if plants are sited at sea. Cooling systems already produce and dispense tritiated water—the radioactive isotope of hydrogen. Other forms of seepage and leakage include effluents that are uniquely lethal. Strontium 90, with a half-life of 28 years, builds up in the bone to induce cancer. Plutonium, with a horrifying 25,000 years' half-life, is so cancer-inducing that scientists reckon a concentration no larger than an orange could, sufficiently dispersed, threaten human survival. As for accidents—which can hardly be excluded—it is estimated that a 1,000 megawatt nuclear power reactor has an annual output of radioactive materials equal to a 23 megaton bomb. Occurring under or near water, accidents to reactors (whether floating or on the ocean bottom) would have totally unpredictable and indiscriminate spread effects. So, it need hardly be said, would major accidents to nuclear submarines.

The second feature of the system is synergism—the tendency of chemicals and processes to come together to form unforeseen combinations which may have a wholly new or markedly more powerful effect than the substances or processes taken separately.

Smog is a particularly irritating instance occurring in atmospheric pollution. A vast increase in the scale and versatility of modern chemical manufacture adds to the stock every year more than a thousand new and untested materials which can reappear in the flood of industrial effluents. Most of them are not in any case biodegradable. In addition, the likelihood that their mixture in the oceans could produce unexpectedly lethal synergistic effects is not to be easily dismissed, especially if, as with both DDT and mercury, a substance can be ingested by seabirds or fish, and increasing in concentration as it goes up the foodchain, end by poisoning the final predator, man.

The synergistic effect can also link different elements in the total biosphere. One of the fears aroused by oil spills in arctic waters is not simply that, in such freezing temperatures, the pollution will be long lasting. It is also possible that sustained exposure to oil will stain the bottom of the icefloes. Then, when melting above brings the black ice to the surface, the ability of the polar ice to throw back the sun's rays will be sharply diminished. More violent melting could follow, with unpredictable consequences for water levels everywhere.

Another instance of multiple, unpredictable and cumulative results from supposedly local events could follow if Gulf Stream currents are mobilized for energy use off the Florida coast. The heat and current profiles might be sufficiently modified for the British to be much less sure of a temperate water mass sufficient to spare them the fate of Labrador.

Finally, the threshold—the third general feature of the biosphere—is both the most unpredictable and the most alarming symbol of possibly irreversible damage. Basically, the concept is simple. Natural systems, including the oceans, are incredibly resistant. They can take any amount of punishment and yet recover from their wounds and infections. Regeneration is a special property of water and it is exercised on an inconceivably massive and majestic scale by the oceans, the healers and cleansers of the whole terrestrial globe. But the system is nonetheless an organic system. As such it is still capable of death.

The point—or threshold—comes at which regenerative powers are irretrievably lost. If giant vacuum cleaners attached to superships suck everything out of the oceans, not only the fish but the spawn may be lost and the species itself extinguished. Since 1970, the world's fish catch has started to fall. Has the "threshold" of a number of species already been crossed by indiscriminate and brutal factory fishing? The whales, we know, are endangered in the wake of the half-hour process from catch to melted fat. How many more species are at risk?

Inland seas can lose most of their dissolved oxygen if excessive waste disposal stimulates the growth and then the death of oxygen-absorbing algae. Then nothing can live. The sturgeon catch in the Caspian has fallen by 80 percent since the war. Parts of the Baltic are already anaerobic. The seas round Italy are threatened by a degree of pollution that kills the fish and turns molluscs into cholera-spreaders for the unlucky tourists. Admittedly, these are enclosed waters. But ultimately the oceans, too, are enclosed. There is no outlet. They are the ultimate sump. How much more can they carry? We do not know now. How much less can we estimate the coming impact of the furious drive to exploit and industrialize ocean space.

Not all these risks are certainties. One of the profound problems posed by nature's "thresholds" is that the approach to the point of no return may give few if any danger signals. Red lights do not flash on in the deeps as one more species—of whose role in the total ecosystem we are completely ignorant—heads for death. Perhaps its survival did not matter. But perhaps it was the catalyst of an entire feeding system on which other species depend. So another threshold approaches. But, again, there is no blowing of sirens or rockets in the sky. One more piece of the biosphere falls away. We do not even know what we are losing. Even if we did, it would be too late.

The Law of the Sea Conference thus confronts two relatively unfamiliar but inescapable realities each in potential conflict with the other. The first is man's surge forward to the "seizing and enclosing" of the oceans in order to submit them to the full rigors of technological development. The other is his deepening understanding of the totally interdependent biosphere, vast but vulnerable, life-giving and life-destroying, of which the oceans are the most interdependent, the most vulnerable, the most life-determining part. The possibilities of conflict are too obvious to require much detail. Man has fought steadily and bitterly over his land frontiers. He will not necessarily change his habits when the frontiers he tries to establish are on the indiscernible, deceptive, floating tides of the high seas. The Greeks and the Turks are already reviving an ancient enmity over oil reserves in the Aegean. Britain and Iceland have conducted a mini-war over cod. And short of armed conflict, there can be fundamental divergences of perspective and interest between developing states which may well look on all talk of environmental risks as a rich-nation ploy to keep them poor and developed nations which have both created most of the pollution and now worry most about its possible consequences. Nor are all the difficulties political. How can states reconcile totally incompatible uses for the same ocean space? National parks to preserve oceanic breeding grounds set against a coastal drive for massive industrialization, controlled shipping lanes and environmental protection measures in narrow waters versus the right of unrestricted navigation through the world's straits, maximum exploitation of local shoals even if it threatens the survival of a species that all fleets want to fish, cut-price municipal dumping at sea with the effluents washing up on distant tourist beaches—the contradictions are endless and with them the possibility of another quantum jump, this time into renewed and enflamed nationalist conflict.

In theory, one can spell out the principles of environmental jurisdiction and action which should be achieved by the Law of the Sea Conference. The fundamental requirement is a system of overall environmental management in which governments, international authorities and private interests can all join provided they recognize its role in reflecting the complete interdependence of the ocean system. Some aspects of this management would be global in nature—for instance, oversight over planet-wide winds and currents and the pollutants they may carry. Others would have a regional and local focus and imply special regimes for subsystems like the China Sea or the Caribbean. A chief tool of management would be a very greatly strengthened system of monitoring and assessment based upon comparable methods of collecting and analyzing relevant data—the kind of system of which the Earthwatch program now embarked on by the United Nations Environment Program is a preliminary model. This flow of information should underpin a set of international and regional measures and standards for environmental protection which would be seen to be in no way arbitrary but to reflect genuine needs and imperatives in the biosphere. And once these regulations were promulgated—whether for permissible limits on a particular fish catch or standards of protection at nuclear power stations or control on discharges into the ocean from shore, ship and fixed installations or measures to prevent disruption of areas of critical natural significance—the management system would require powers to see that the regulations were effectively applied, sanctions imposed in the event of their being flouted, and poorer states given subsidies and technical aid to enable them to control levels of pollution for which, in global terms, they are not now much responsible.

One has only to establish these minimum criteria to see how far governments are still removed from any viable system to contain and guide the new ocean-based technological revolution. In politics, they are divided between two versions of exclusive sovereignty—the old "freedom of the seas" which allowed sovereign governments to do what they pleased outside other peoples' three-mile limits and the new varieties of extended territorial waters or exclusive economic zones which could transfer most of the useful ocean space to more or less unrelieved local national sovereignty. Beyond the new limits, the remaining seabed may come under some kind of international regime, but it looks at present as though its "powers" might be restricted to licensing the technologically competent—in other words, the rich states and corporations—to develop their interests on a first-come, first-served basis—with little (if any) consideration given to the environmental implications of seabed exploitation, let alone other activities on the horizon. In any case, it is in coastal waters that the greatest use—and abuse—of the maritime environment occurs, but pressures are strong to cede exclusive control over pollution here to the exploiters, the coastal states and maritime interests.

That this minimal arrangement would offer no safeguard against disruptive exploitation is shown by the almost total disregard in present economic practice for anything but the most immediate and narrow cost-benefit analysis, including a discount rate for which ten years is too long a prospect and excluding environmental and social costs. The fact that this myopia can allow whole species to be fished out or reefs cleaned out with no regard for future needs or present disruptions does not register in strict economic calculus. Nor does the switch from private to public capitalism affect the outcome. The Russians have pursued the whale with quite as much predatory single-mindedness as the Japanese.

Even when the grosser forms of environmental insult and pollution have occurred—for instance in the *Torrey Canyon* disaster—the counter measures have been ineffective and ad hoc. There are now, among others, conventions on civil liability for oil pollution damage, on the maritime carriage of nuclear materials, and on ocean dumping. But the present array of international agreements aimed at pollution control and living resource conservation do not add up to a comprehensive system. They avoid fundamental problems of juristiction to set and enforce regulations, as well as liability and compensation for damages, and few, indeed, have even been ratified, let alone enforced.

Must we then assume that the Law of the Sea Conference will, to adapt Tom Paine's cry of anguish, divide "the plumages and forget the dying bird," carve up ocean sovereignties and forget that the seas themselves are at risk? Hopefully not. Several governments have submitted proposals which indicate some support for environmental management and acceptance of the oceans as "the common heritage of mankind." Also, passionate conflicts, which few governments relish, may become unavoidable unless there is some rationale—and some machinery—for impartially mediating disputes. The overriding need to preserve the ocean environment could be such a rationale; the functional machinery to carry out that protection could grow into the needed instrument of global mediation. In the last analysis, the modern Canutes and all their courtiers cannot divide or stem the moving oceans. But perhaps they can begin to learn how to live with them—and let them live—instead.

It may be asked why, with urgent and enflamed non-environmental issues under discussion, any emphasis should be put on environmental matters. Surely the future of the oceans is much more likely to depend on the definition of the international regime for the seabed or of the extent of territorial waters or the powers and privileges to be secured in the exclusive economic zones proposed for coastal states. Difficulties are far more likely to arise over the need to combine free passage through straits with the controls demanded by local sovereignty or over the claim to define the limits of economic zones by including contiguous islands—a "solution" which would transfer a massive amount of ocean territory and resources to a mere score of coastal states.

But the primacy of the environmental issue is rooted in inescapable physical fact. No political arrangements will alter the fundamental biological interdependence of the watery sphere. No drawing of zones or limits will prevent pollution spreading throughout the marine ecosystem. The whole biological background is *given,* in a way in which no political and economic arrangements can ever be. In fact, the most important, the most far-reaching, the most fateful and unavoidable decisions taken by the Law of the Sea Conference will be precisely in the area of environment.

This is because the governments have in fact no choice. Either by acting or by not acting, they help to determine the oceans' viability. A decision to have no environmental safeguards—even if it is taken by default—is a decision which affects the nature of future ocean use as directly and inescapably as the decision to set up a rigorous system of environmental controls. Thus, in a double sense, the Law of the Sea Conference is fundamentally about the maritime environment. All the decisions on exploiting living resources in the oceans depend upon there being living resources to exploit. All the plans for regulating the uses of the ocean depend upon the continuance of a biosphere in which users can live and work. And in this context, the non-decision is precisely equivalent to a decision. There is no evading the issue of the environment. It can be handled well. It can be handled badly. But there is no way of not handling it; it simply cannot be removed from its central place as the ultimate determinant of everything else.

It follows that a major responsibility of governments is to accept a number of broad principles which underlie any effective system of environmental safeguards and then to devise a strategy or system which incorporates these principles.

The main principles are (1) the acceptance of the need to treat the marine environment as a common heritage of mankind; (2) the need to halt the taking of unilateral actions which would foreclose the possibility of developing a responsible international system; and (3) the necessity of establishing such a system in time to prevent the kind of acceleration of conflict and danger of abuse which must flow from man's violently increasing use and exploitation of the oceans.

# 33. Marine Pollution: Action and Reaction Times

EDWARD D. GOLDBERG 1974

Thousands of substances used or produced by human society now move through the oceans. Some of these substances, such as the pesticides DDT and dieldrin and the artificial radioactive materials produced in nuclear reactors, are alien to the marine system. Others, such as lead, occur naturally; but their concentrations are altered by man's activities. For example, the concentrations of lead in coastal waters have been increased by the entry of antiknock agents and the products of their combustion in automobiles.

Only a few of these many compounds are likely to have negative effects, such as the contamination of seafood, the alteration of communities of marine organisms, and the loss or restricted use of nonliving resources, such as recreational areas. Nevertheless, we must be prepared to counteract the destructive impact of pollutants on the marine environment and to develop strategies for managing toxic materials. Toward this end, it is necessary to understand the time scales involved in both natural processes and societal responses.

## OCEANIC TIME SCALES

The times that chemicals spend in seawater may be estimated by means of simple mathematical models in which the oceans are depicted as a vast reservoir for continental materials mobilized by winds, rivers, and glaciers. Substances involved in these estimates are usually considered to have time-invariant concentrations in the oceans. The amount of a material entering the oceans in a given period of time is compensated by the same amount of the material falling to the sediments or undergoing radioactive decay or microbial degradation. Thus, the time a chemical spends in the oceans is given by the total amount in the oceans divided by the total flux into or out of the oceans. This period is known as the residence time. (The assumption is made that there is complete mixing of the substance within the reservoir in a time span that is short with respect to its residence time there.)

Several characteristics of these models are important to pollution studies. First, a pollutant will reach a steady-state level in a period

Dr. Edward D. Goldberg is a chemical oceanographer with Scripps Institution of Oceanography, University of California, San Diego.

From *Oceanus*, Vol. 18, No. 1, pp. 6-16, 1974. Reprinted with light editing and with permission of the author and *Oceanus* Magazine.

equal to approximately four residence times. If the release of the pollutant stops after the steady-state concentration is reached, original conditions will prevail after the same period—four residence times. Second, the residence time of a chemical is inversely related to its level of reactivity in the reservoir. Persistent (low-reactivity) chemicals will have longer residence times, whereas more reactive chemicals will be removed more quickly by either breakdown or precipitation to the sediments. Use of these two concepts may allow the prediction of pollutant levels in the ocean environment where the residence time of a naturally occuring substance or of a previously studied pollutant with similar chemical properties is known.

## COASTAL OCEAN

The world ocean can be conveniently divided into two zones for the purposes of both scientific and societal inquiries: the coastal ocean and the open ocean. The coastal ocean constitutes about 10 percent of the total oceanic area and includes estuaries, lagoons, inshore waters, and many marginal seas and waters over the continental shelves and slopes. The North Sea, Chesapeake Bay, Persian Gulf, and Sea of Japan are examples of coastal waters. Their properties are strongly influenced by boundaries with the continents and the sea floor. The coastal ocean receives direct injections of continental materials via rivers, direct terrestrial runoff and drainage, and the atmosphere, and through such mobilizing agents of man as domestic and industrial outfalls and ships.

Coastal waters are the sites of high rates of biological activity. The marine primary production of organic material—photosynthesis, which is the base of the food chain that ends in fish, birds, and marine mammals—takes place predominantly in these waters. The open ocean areas, with a few exceptions, such as some productive equatorial waters, are the marine deserts. Within the coastal zone there are some especially productive waters—upwelling areas—where a coupling of strong offshore winds with prevailing boundary currents brings nutrient-rich deep waters to the surface. Here, with even higher levels of primary productivity, fish stocks are large. These most important upwelling areas are off Peru, California, and the western coast of Africa. Although they are estimated to constitute only 0.1 percent of oceanic areas, they are responsible for about 50 percent of fish production (the other 50 percent occurs in the remainder of the coastal zone).

High rates of biological activity in coastal seas affect materials introduced from the continents. Some organisms have a remarkable ability to accumulate substances from seawater, even where the materials are in extremely low concentrations (parts per billion or parts per trillion). For example, vanadium, at levels of about one part per billion in seawater, is enriched in the blood of tunicates to levels of parts per thousand. DDT and its residues are found in surface seawaters in concentrations of parts per trillion; yet in the fish, levels of parts or tens of parts per million are not uncommon. Organisms living in coastal waters may therefore act as conveyors of man's wastes. They can move substances from surface waters to the sea floor through their death or the discharge of metabolic waste products. Or they may return such materials to man in the form of food.

The persistence of chemicals in coastal waters—before removal by sedimentation, degradation, mixing with the open ocean, or harvesting of living organisms—may extend from months to decades. Estuaries exchange their waters with the open ocean in such periods of time. Recent work at the Scripps Institution of Oceanography showed that the residence times of radium and lead isotopes in the highly productive Gulf of California were a few months and almost one month, respectively. Calculations such as these may not be applicable to many pollution problems, because they assume a steady-state situation in which the concentration of the substance in the water is invariant with time. For most pollution problems, however, there is a gradual accumulation of the material. The time from initial entry of a pollutant to awareness of a problem may be measured in decades. In the case of the brown pelican colony on Anacapa Island, off the California coast, failures to reproduce during the period 1969-72 were attributed to extensive DDT pollution that had first appeared in sediments in 1952.

## OPEN OCEAN

The open ocean, which constitutes approximately 90 percent of the world ocean, differs from coastal waters in its time scales and its relationships with the continents and sediments. Whereas time spans describing natural processes in coastal waters extend from months to decades, periods associated with the open ocean are between hundreds and hundreds of millions of years. For example, aluminum species, which enter the ocean as a result of weathering processes on the continents, spend almost one hundred years in the open-ocean waters before precipitating to the sediments. Sodium, one of the principal elements in seawater, remains in the open ocean for perhaps a hundred million years before accommodation in the sediments.

Deeper waters of the open ocean, those below 100 meters or so, are out of contact with coastal or surface waters for periods that average between a few hundred and a thousand years, depending upon the ocean basin. Herein lie not only the present value of these waters as accepters of man's wastes, but also the future perils that can arise from the small, but continuous, introductions of highly toxic substances. For example, open-ocean waters contain about 100 million tons of mercury, an amount far greater than the hundredth of a million tons mined annually by man. Thus, the deep ocean can today safely accept low-level mercury wastes, especially in the inorganic forms, and similar arguments can be made for the disposal of such toxic metals as arsenic and antimony.

On the other hand, the long residence times of chemicals in the open ocean may lead to the formation of a toxic broth through the slow accumulation of man's wastes. There is taking place today in the deep waters of the open ocean a gradual, but continuous, build-up of halogenated hydrocarbons—synthetic organic chemicals, some of which contain chlorine atoms. They enter the coastal ocean through sewer outfalls, and the surface waters of the open ocean as gases via the atmosphere; they are transferred by physical and biological processes to the deep ocean in less than a decade. Some of these chemicals are known to interfere with metabolic processes of living organisms. The heavier compounds, such as DDT and its degradation products, and polychlorinated biphenyl (PCB), affect the calcium metabolism of marine birds, with the result that their eggs have thin shells. The lower-molecular-weight species, such as the chlorofluorocarbons, which are used as aerosol propellants, may inhibit the fermentation activities of microorganisms.

Of major concern is the possibility that a toxic material can reach such levels that the exposure of organisms in the open ocean, as well as the coastal ocean, to these levels will result in widespread mortalities or morbidities. The great volume of the open ocean makes removal of a toxic substance, identified by a catastrophic event, impossible with the technologies of today or the foreseeable future.

Open-ocean sediments accumulate natural debris a thousand or so times more slowly than do coastal deposits. The fluxes of solids that are mobilized during weathering processes and carried to the open ocean primarily through the atmosphere are much smaller than those that enter coastal waters from rivers and direct terrestrial runoff. Also, since biological activity is less intense in the surface waters of the open ocean than in those of the coastal ocean, there is a lesser potential for the downward transport of pollutants through biological activities. Most of the materials dispersed to the open-ocean environment through man's activities are still in the water column. Only a very few have been taken up by the sediments.

Today the open-ocean water column contains many signatures of our technological society. Radioactive isotopes of strontium and cesium, produced primarily in nuclear bomb detonations, have been found to depths of 1000 meters or so, approximately one-fourth of the way down to the sea floor. Other radioactive isotopes, such as those of cerium and promethium, which are chemically more reactive, have been found at even greater depths, although in smaller concentrations than those in surface waters. DDT and its degradation products have been found in all open-ocean species sampled over the past five years.

The surface of the open ocean is soiled with petroleum products in the forms of tar balls and coatings (oil slicks) whose thicknesses have molecular dimensions. In addition, ocean currents carry litter, plastics, glass, wood products, and metals, many of which are used to contain products of commerce. These visible alterations of the surface signal the need for continual measurement and assessment of the invisible pollutants below.

## SOCIETAL TIME SCALES

The scientific community or a catastrophic event alerts governing bodies to regulate the release to the environment of substances that can jeopardize marine resources. The possibility that the discharge of high levels of radioactivity from nuclear power reactors or from nuclear detonations could harm public health and the vitality of marine organisms prompted scientists to action during the years following World War II. The primary concern was the return of ionizing radiation to man through food or through direct exposure by swimming or recreational activities on beaches. There was the sense that it would be convenient, and perhaps necessary, to deliberately dispose of some amounts of radioactive nuclides in the seas. The complexities of chemical processes in the oceans did not allow prediction of the fate of a specific chemical introduced to a particular place. Thus, the initial recommendations for sea disposal of radioactive wastes contained an explicit sense of caution, control, and limitation. They were intended to be experimental. Since that time, the amounts of radioactivity introduced to the oceans have been strictly limited under national regulations based on internationally promulgated standards (primarily by the International Atomic Energy Agency and the International Commission on Radiological Protection).

The policies of the United Kingdom are an example of the national management of radioactive materials. Minimum risk to its citizenry is sought in the area of both somatic and genetic effects. Of primary importance is the identification of potentially significant pathways along which radioactive substances released by man can return to man. Once identified, they provide the basis for the "critical pathway approach," a management strategy that provides an adequate and economic surveillance of the return routes. (These pathways usually involve the ingestion of foods or the inhalation of atmospheric constituents. For any specific isotope, the routes are few; in many cases only one has been found to exist.)

How quickly can governments respond to an unexpected catastrophe resulting from the unregulated discharge of an unknown toxic substance into the marine environment? The Minimata Bay incident in Japan and subsequent events provide a time scale that may reflect a unique social-economic framework rather than a general set of reaction times that may be expected in the future. Still, it is worthy of review because it may provide a guide for better and faster responses.

The Minimata Bay incident started in the late 1930s when the Chisso Corporation, one of the leading chemical industries in Japan, began to produce vinyl chlorides and formaldehyde at its factory on the shores of Minimata Bay. Spent catalysts containing mercury were discharged into the bay, and fish and shellfish accumulated the mercury in the form of methyl-mercury chloride. Their consumption by the inhabitants of the area, primarily the fishermen and their families, resulted in an epidemic of neurological disease. The first occurrence of the disease was reported in 1953, about 15 years after the wastes first entered the bay. It was not until 1959, after some 80 cases of neurological disorders had been diagnosed, that mercury was associated with these afflictions.

In 1960, articles describing both the disease and the circumstances under which it developed began to appear in environmental and medical journals throughout the world. At this time the prevailing opinion was that a still-unidentified organic compound of mercury was the cause. During this early period, the Chisso factory was making every effort to avoid an association with or a responsibility for the disease. The company had gathered together a group of scientists who refuted the evidence of the workers at the Kumamoto Prefecture University, who had established the relationship between mercury and the disease. The company then found new waste-discharge sites in a northern area, where, soon thereafter, several new cases of the disease were reported. By this time, the citizens of Minimata Bay had become aware that local seafood was the source of the epidemic. Strong animosities developed between the fishermen and the Chisso Company as the demand for fish by the local inhabitants fell to zero. The fishermen became violent and stormed and destroyed the factory offices. Through such actions the Minimata Bay disease became known throughout Japan. Eventually, the company paid very small compensations to the fishermen for the loss of their livelihood and to the victims of the disease. For a few years the problem was forgotten. However, in 1965, a second outbreak occurred, this time in a new location along the Agano River in Niigata. Here the source of the pollution was attributed to an acetaldehyde factory of the Show Denko Company that discharged its spent mercury catalysts into the river. The victims of the second outbreak initiated a civil action in the court in June 1967; this is presumed to be the first large civil suit brought against a polluter in the history of modern Japan.

In 1963, ten years after the first cases were diagnosed, the active agent causing the disease was identified as methyl-mercury chloride. This discovery introduced a new dimension into the marine chemistry of mercury. Before this time it was thought that only inorganic forms of mercury were involved in natural processes. But further surprises were in the offing. In Sweden, as a consequence of some disastrous impacts of mercurial pesticides on wildlife, a group of scientists was working on the environmental chemistry of mercury. Their analyses of mercury in uncontaminated fish indicated that nearly all the mercury was in the form of an organic compound, methyl-mercury. The toxic form causing the Minimata Bay disease was similar to the naturally occurring form. These unexpected results were eventually confirmed by Japanese scientists.

The first group to systematically evaluate the risks involved in the consumption of fish containing mercury—at naturally occurring levels or at higher levels caused by man's activities—was appointed in 1968 by the Swedish National Institute of Public Health in conjunction with the Swedish National Board of Health and the Swedish National Veterinary Board. The group assessed the toxicological evidence from the Japanese epidemic and the fish-eating habits of both the Japanese and the Scandinavian populations. It was found that in Sweden there was a small number of persons who had no symptoms of Minimata Bay disease but who had consumed fish to such an extent that mercury concentrations in their hair and blood were the same as those of Japanese who had shown neurological symptoms of poisoning. These results emphasized the varying sensitivity of peoples to methylmercury poisoning and the differences in their eating habits.

Although the group was not charged with the formulation of allowable methylmercury levels in fish, they did consider the problem in their report, published in 1971. Subsequently, Sweden adopted the level of 0.5 parts per million. Several other countries followed, including the United States, where the average daily consumption of fish is 17 grams, less than one-third that of Sweden. These levels apply not only to coastal fish, whose mercury levels may have been raised by man's activities, but also to deep-sea fish, such as tuna, whose mercury levels appear to have remained unchanged during the past century.

It took more than two decades for the Japanese government to halt the discharge of mercury into the marine coastal zone and for other countries to determine what are acceptable mercury levels in seafood. Recently, mercury has been blacklisted by the ocean-dumping convention. What the mercury episodes have shown is that the time periods required by scientists to get to the root of a problem and by environmental managers to formulate measures to protect coastal resources are similar to those involving reactive chemicals in near-shore systems.

## SOCIETAL RESTRAINTS

There are several impediments, each with an economic root, to the development of a scientific basis for the description and forecasting of ocean pollution problems. The first involves the difficulties in acquiring a knowledge of past, present, and predicted production and use data for chemicals that may insult the marine system. A continual assessment by scientists of the production and uses of chemicals and energy can provide a means to predict which substances, if released to the environment, might jeopardize the continued uses of marine resources. Such evaluations usually involve estimates of toxicity and the construction of mass balance models—schematization to understand the flow patterns of materials from the site of release to the environmental reservoirs. However, there are obstacles to such undertakings: the production and use data are often maintained as privileged information by manufacturers or sovereign nations. For example, in the United States, where a chemical is produced by no more than two companies, the production and use figures are proprietary information. The rationale that prohibits the release of such data is economic. Governments have an obligation to protect their manufacturers from being placed at an economic disadvantage through the publication of production and use data. Yet it is in the interest of their citizenry that there be a continual assessment of the state of marine resources, for which such data are essential.

New concerns are evolving for which production and use figures are urgently needed. For example, there is a geographical shift in the applications of DDT in agriculture and public health. Most DDT was initially used at mid-latitudes of the northern hemisphere. It now appears that the center of usage is shifting southward as more industrial countries ban DDT. However, the details of this change are not available to the scientists to assess the possible impact on marine life. As another example, a group of marine scientists wants specific information about the discharges of transuranics from nuclear reactors and reprocessing plants. For military and economic reasons, much of this data is classified.

As a result of a general lack of production and use data, in early 1974 the Intergovernmental Oceanographic Commission formed an ad hoc group of experts (POOL—Pollution of the Ocean Originating on Land) who have been directed to "suggest practicable and effective means for obtaining information on the quantities of important pollutants, present and potential, introduced into the ocean from land-based sources by whatever route." The charge is well defined, the task formidable.

Of greater concern than either the chemical manufacturer or the sovereign nation are the multinational corporations (MNCs), whose activities compete with those of major nations in the utilization of materials and energy. Effective controls on their actions still have not been formulated by international organizations (debate has now begun in the United Nations), yet concern for the environment in the prosecution of their activities seems to be minimal.

The global influences of MNCs can be seen in terms of their annual products. For example, General Motors in 1970 had an annual product of $24 billion (the gross national product of Switzerland was $20 billion, of Denmark $15.5 billion). Of the first fifty institutions or nations ranked in order of annual product value, nine are MNCs. But what is more foreboding is that their annual rate of growth exceeds that of national states. Most probably there will be more transnational mergers of firms, with an increase in the number of MNCs. Clearly, one of the problems facing the international community of nations is to find ways of dealing with the MNCs, especially as they impinge on common environmental resources. The weak link in plans to protect the world ocean may be the country willing to negotiate the quality of its coastal environment for short-term economic gains.

## FUTURE STRATEGIES

Strategies for the management of highly toxic marine pollutants must be formulated by the major producers. One cannot expect a large group of nations, such as the United Nations and its family, to address itself to the pollution problems that plague the technologically advanced societies when there are basic problems of survival for the populations of developing member countries. Bilateral and multilateral agreements to deal with these problems seem to be the best approach. Recent agreements between the United States and Canada to protect the Great Lakes; among the North Sea countries, through the International Council for the Exploration of the Sea, to understand their pollution problems; and between the United States and Russia to exchange scientists and jointly publish a periodical dedicated to marine quality problems are some of the steps necessary to recognize potentially dangerous leakages to the environment and to propose remedial actions. Efforts to solve the first-order problems of marine pollution by large international organizations have, in general, been both noble and futile. Information needed for the statement and solution of problems has usually been unavailable, because economic and social concerns have overridden environmental ones. The starting point is acknowledgment of a problem by political leaders and scientists alike.

# 34. Plastics in the Marine Environment

ANTHONY M. CUNDELL 1974

A visit to the seashore almost anywhere nowadays will acquaint even the casual observer with the prevalence of discarded plastic materials in the coastal environment. Reports are appearing in the literature which suggest that both coastal and oceanic waters are polluted by plastics. Oceanographers have found plastics in plankton tows (Carpenter & Smith 1972; Carpenter *et al.*, 1972) and have made visual sightings of floating plastic objects from research vessels in mid-ocean, far from major shipping lanes (Heyerdahl, 1971; Venrick *et al.*, 1973).

## NATURE OF PLASTIC MATERIALS

Plastics have been defined by the Society of the Plastics Industry (USA) as 'materials that contain, as an essential ingredient, an organic substance of large molecular weight, and that, at some stage in their manufacture or processing into finished articles, can be shaped by flow' (Arnold, 1968).

In terms of this discussion, it would be useful to pinpoint plastic materials which, because of their volume of manufacture, density, and applications, have the greatest potential for marine pollution. The most common plastic materials are polyethylene, polystyrene, polyvinyl chloride, polypropylene, and acrylonitrile butadiene styrene, which had sales in the United States of 5.8, 2.8, 3.1, 0.9, and 0.5, $\times 10^9$ lb,* respectively, in 1970 (Anon., 1971*a*). Of these, polyethylene (specific gravity 0.91 to 0.96) constitutes a particular hazard because it will float on sea water. However, polystyrene foam (specific gravity 0.8) will also be represented in flotsam.

What are the chemical compositions of the common plastics? The term resin is usually applied to the long chains of repeating units in the polymeric material. These resins may be linear, branched, or cross-linked. Other constituents of the plastics are plasticizers which improve the flexibility of the plastic, colored pigments, antioxidants, ultraviolet light stabilizers, lubricants, mold-release agents, and occasionally biocides to inhibit microbiological deterioration.

These other constituents influence the physical properties and age-resistance of the plastic material. For example, the properties

Dr. Anthony M. Cundell is a Fellow in Applied Biology, Engineering Sciences Laboratory, Harvard University, Cambridge, Massachusetts.

From *Environmental Conservation,* Vol. 1, No. 1, pp. 63-68, 1974. Reprinted with light editing and with permission of the author and the Foundation for Environmental Conservation, Switzerland.

of polyethylene can be greatly improved by the incorporation of an antioxidant that is used to prevent degradation of the resin during high-temperature processing such as the blow-molding of bottles, and also gives it protection during its service life. Ultraviolet radiation stabilizers protect polyethylene from damage by sunlight in outdoor situations; similarly, carbon black is included in polyethylene mulching film to block the penetration of radiation. With thin polyethylene films, slip agents can be used to decrease the frictional properties of the plastic, anti-block agents can be employed to prevent sheets of film from sticking together, while antistatic agents may be used to dissipate electrostatic charge build-up (Joyner, 1971).

## POTENTIAL PLASTIC POLLUTANTS

It seems pertinent to discuss plastic materials which may be found accumulating in the marine environment. A survey recently conducted by the author in Narragansett Bay, Rhode Island, indicated that plastic objects manufactured from polyethylene made up the bulk of the flotsam on a private beach at the entrance to the East Passage, Conanicut Island (at the mouth of Narragansett Bay). The ubiquity of polyethylene is illustrated by Table 34-1, which lists some of its major applications.

Table 34-1. Applications and Quantities of Polyethylene Used in the United States in 1970.

| *Application* | *Quantity of all types of plastic used (millions of lb*)* | *Quantity of polyethylene (millions of lb*)* |
|---|---|---|
| Houseware | 967 | 490 |
| Agricultural use | 197 | 111 |
| Packaging film | 1,595 | 1,250 |
| Blow-molded containers | 707 | 584 |

* 1 lb = 0.454 kg.

Common objects manufactured from polyethylene include houseware items such as buckets, dustpans, measuring jugs, and colanders; blow-molded bottles such as squeeze-out bottles and bleach containers; wire and cable coverings; black film for agricultural mulching, pond liners, and construction sheeting; packaging film; and plastic shipping pallets. A noticeable trend is the replacement of a natural material with a synthetic material. Traditionally, pallets for transporting freight which are readily loaded by forklift vehicles were made of wood; now, pallets are increasingly being made of polyethylene. Predictably, this trend will result in an increased incidence of the pollution of the marine environment by plastic materials.

Another seaborne plastic material is expanded polystyrene, produced by the addition of a foaming agent. This type of polystyrene can be molded into foamboard for insulation, contouring board for pouring reinforced concrete, spaghetti-like polystyrene strands used as a packaging material, and the popular disposable drinking cups. Polystyrene and polyurethane foams are commonly used in flotation materials such as life preservers, buoys, and fishing-net floats, and can be expected to accumulate in the marine environment.

Polyvinyl chloride, by virtue of its density (specific gravity 1.4), will not float on sea water. Unplasticized polyvinyl chloride is used in the manufacture of phonograph records, toothbrush handles, cosmetic containers, and waste-water pipes. Plasticized polyvinyl chloride is a suitable product for rainwear, shower curtains, baby pants, upholstery, tubing, and electric insulating parts.

Other plastic products which, because of their everyday use, may accumulate, are: a co-polymer of vinylidene chloride and vinyl chloride manufactured under the trade name of Saran; nylon (polyhexamethylene adipamide), which can be used for such diverse products as safety helmets, outboard motor propellers, unbreakable tumblers, and fishing lines; and cellulose acetate film used for food packaging, photographic film, lampshades, and 'blisters' used for packaging small consumer items. Melamine-formaldehyde tableware, which combines resistance to breakage with light weight, is preferred to chinaware in airplanes, naval ships, and institutions serving large numbers of people; hence it may cause a potential pollution problem.

The introduction of all-plastic soda and beer bottles, which seem destined to replace glass bottles and aluminum cans during the latter part of this decade, will create a litter problem. The Coca-Cola Corporation successfully test-marketed high-barrier nitrile resin 10-oz. bottles in the Providence, R.I., area in 1972. There is a $4.4 \times 10^{10}$ unit market for plastic bottles in the United States if they ever fully displace glass and metal in packaging carbonated beverages (Anon., 1973*a*).

## DISTRIBUTION AND IMPACT OF PLASTICS

The distribution of plastics in the marine environment is most likely to be uneven. Plastic products are readily sighted along the foreshore—especially in areas of dense population, such as the coastline ranging from Boston, Massachusetts, to Norfolk, Virginia. Plastic bottles, sheeting, and fragments arising from the wave destruction of larger objects, accumulate in the high-tide area along with seaweeds, tarballs, and other waterborne flotsam and jetsam (Figure 34-1). Coastal currents, wind direction, and tidal excursions, will naturally influence the distribution of plastic pollutants. However, sightings in the North Pacific Ocean, 600 miles (960 km) from Hawaii and outside the major shipping lanes, of plastic bottles and fragments (Venrick *et al.*, 1973), suggest that oceanic waters probably contain considerable quantities of plastic materials. Ocean currents would appear to concentrate plastics in such areas as the Sargasso Sea (Carpenter & Smith, 1972) and convey seaborne plastic pollutants to isolated stretches of the shoreline in Scotland (Scott, 1972).

Figure 34-1. High density polyethylene bottles and caps on the high-tide mark on a beach north of La Jolla, California. Photograph by R. G. Pirie.

The plastics industry recognizes that plastics represent a small but highly visible part of the solid-waste disposal problem. Solid wastes may be disposed of by incineration, sanitary landfill, open dumping, composting, or salvage. The relative dominance of these disposal methods is indicated in Table 34-2 (after Darnay & Franklin, 1969). Poorly-managed landfill areas in coastal regions are potential sources of marine pollution. Ocean disposal of municipal refuse is not practised in the United States because of the danger of fouling beaches. However, the dumping of baled garbage has received serious consideration by such major U.S. coastal cities as New York, Philadelphia, and San Francisco, since 1970 (Smith & Brown, 1971). Another solid-waste disposal system which is gaining in popularity is that involving incineration. Conventional burning of plastic materials in incinerators leads to the gumming of grates

Table 34-2. Relative Dominance of Disposal Methods in the United States: 1966 and 1976 (estimated).

| | *Percentage of solid waste tonnage handled* | |
|---|---|---|
| *Disposal method* | *1966* | *1976* |
| Incineration | 14.0 | 18.0 |
| Sanitary landfill | 5.0 | 13.0 |
| Open dumping | 77.5 | 64.0 |
| Composting | 0.5 | 1.0 |
| Salvage | 3.0 | 4.0 |
| Total | 100.0 | 100.0 |

by molten plastics,* while the combustion of polyvinyl chloride produces metal-corroding and air-polluting hydrogen chloride. Reclamation and reuse of plastic materials is not technologically feasible and economically attractive, as plastics are difficult to separate from garbage, and only polystyrene can be successfully reconverted to its monomer styrene (Wood, 1970).†

The authors of a recent report on the biological effects of ocean disposal of solid wastes predict that there will be considerable pressure to dump baled garbage off the Atlantic seaboard of the United States in the near future (Pratt *et al.,* 1973). The economic aspects of the alternative garbage disposal methods for New York City are summarized in Table 34-3. These figures suggest that, as land near coastal urban areas becomes scarce, it is almost inevitable that such cities as New York City will dispose of their garbage at sea. Arguments can be advanced for the disposal of baled refuse at both continental shelf and deep ocean sites. Shallower sites are closer to land and reduce the probability of forced dumping if a storm occurs, while the bales can be monitored on the bottom and may be used to form reefs to attract fish. Decomposition can be

* A referee writes that 'Gumming of grates has been solved.' –Ed., *Environmental Conservation.*
† A referee writes that 'Reclamation *is* successful and should not be ignored.' –Ed., *Environmental Conservation.*

Table 34-3. Unit Cost of Garbage Disposal Methods in New York City (exclusive of a $28 per ton collection cost).

| *Method* | *Cost per ton* |
|---|---|
| 50-miles (80 km) rail-haul and sanitary landfill | $ 7.62 |
| Incineration | 11.00 |
| 80-miles (128 km) ocean tow to dump compacted bales | 8.09 |

expected to be more rapid on the shelf than in deeper, cooler waters. In fact, the low rates of microbial activity found in deeper waters will lead to very slow rates of conversion of organic materials to dissolved substances (Jannasch *et al.,* 1971). However, the reduced waste compaction by hydrostatic pressure, possible bottom currents, and possible introduction of toxic hydrogen sulphide, ammonia, and heavy-metal ions, into pollution-sensitive coastal waters, are good reasons for not disposing of baled refuse on the continental shelf (Pratt *et al.,* 1973).

Plastics in the form of raw material—especially pellets of polystyrene which are shipped to fabricators—were found to be prevalent in the North Atlantic Ocean and Caribbean Sea. The U.S. National Oceanic and Atmospheric Administration monitoring service revealed the presence of white plastic scraps or opaque spheres, from mere specks to pea-sized, which were ingested by larval fish (Anon., 1973*b*). These findings are yet to be evaluated, and the environmental impact of the plastic pollutants needs to be determined.

A number of problems exist when it comes to the identification of plastic materials. Simple properties such as density, flame resistance, and solvent resistance, as well as more difficult infra-red spectrometry of the plastic resin, can, however, be employed as identification procedures. A knowledge of the material of construction of common plastic objects can also be applied in the manner of a detective.

What is the biological impact of plastics on the marine environment? Some plastic particles have been found to contain polychlorinated biphenyls (PCBs), apparently absorbed from the surrounding sea water; they may range up to 5 parts per million in the plastic particles. These include polystyrene spherules which are ingested by fish larvae and may be responsible for their death (Carpenter *et al.*, 1972). Predation of these fish larvae by larger fish and sea-birds would lead to the consumption of plastic materials. This may make a minor contribution as an entry-point for PCBs into marine food-chains.

## PERSISTANCE AND ULTIMATE FATE OF PLASTICS

How persistent will plastics be in the marine environment? Plastics floating in the euphotic zone will be subject to oxidative degradation. This involves free-radical chain-reactions leading to cleavage of the polymer with the introduction of carboxyl groups. The mechanism is ill-defined; for example, hydroperoxide groups that arise from oxidative attack are photolyzed by ultraviolet light to form free radicals which initiate chain scission. The plastics become brittle as the molecular weight of the polymer is reduced. High-density polyethylene, which consists of linear chains and is used in blow-molded bottles, is more prone to oxidative ageing than is low-density polyethylene sheeting, which consists of highly-branched chains. However, very thin plastic film, unless protected by carbon black and peroxide-decomposing antioxidants, will be degraded within months by photooxidation.

Besides weathering, microbial degradation may be responsible for the loss of plastic materials in the sea. However, a review of the literature suggests that plastics are not susceptible to biodegradation (Heap & Morrell, 1968). Polyvinyl chloride, polyethylene, polystyrene, polyvinylidene chloride, nylon, and cellulose acetate, have been reported as resistant to microbial attack. Work by Cundell & Mulcock (1973) showed that synthetic rubbers (neoprene, nitrile, butyl, polybutadiene, and styrene butadiene rubber) are not attacked, whereas a naturally-occurring polymer such as natural rubber is attacked by microorganisms. This suggests that, generally, synthetic polymers are immune from the metabolic activities of microorganisms. However, an investigation by Mills & Eggins (1970) indicates that low-molecular-weight oxidation products from polyethylene boiled in concentrated nitric acid, will support the growth of thermophilic Fungi; hence plastics which have been subjected to prior oxidative ageing may be susceptible to biodegradation.

An exception to the above discussion is the susceptibility of polyester-based polyurethane to microbial degradation (Darby & Kaplan, 1968; Evans & Levisohn, 1968; Jones & LeCampion-Alsumard, 1970). This particular polymer has peptide bonds which are apparently prone to enzymic hydrolysis.

Can plastics be manufactured to be biodegradable? As n-alkanes with a molecular weight below 500 are metabolized by microorganisms, a programed cleavage of the chains of polyethylene by photo-decomposition has been suggested. Gerald Scott, of the University of Aston in Birmingham, England, claims that the inclusion of chromophoric groups within the plastic, which produce free radicals on the absorption of ultraviolet light, will disintegrate polyethylene to chain-lengths suitable for microbial degradation (Scott, 1973). Another approach is the manufacture of light-susceptible plastics, such as polybutene-1, to which only sufficient anti-ageing agents are added to maintain the integrity of the plastic during a predetermined service life (Anon., 1971*b*).

Little work has been published on the biodegradation of plastics in the marine environment. Muraoka (1969) has investigated the effect of a deep-ocean environment on plastics, but he was mainly interested in damage by marine borers. A number of workers found that polyurethane coatings and panels were degraded by marine Ascomycetes and members of the Fungi Imperfecti

(Bellan-Santini *et al.*, 1970; Jones & LeCampion-Alsumard, 1970; LeCampion-Alsumard, 1970). Workers at the Bell Laboratories, Murray Hill, New Jersey, investigated the persistence of polymeric materials in marine sediments and generally found they were not degraded by microorganisms but were penetrated by marine borers (Coscarelli, 1964).

It is possible that the time during which floating plastic materials have been in the water can be determined by the degree of biotic colonization of the plastic surface and the age of the colonizers. A succession on a newly-immersed plastic surface progresses from a bacterial film, through the colonization by diatoms, coelenterates, hydroids, tunicates, encrusting bryozoans, green and brown Algae, and barnacles. However, fouling communities show seasonal changes in species abundance, and colonization varies with the time of the year at which a substrate is exposed (Sutherland, 1972).

In conclusion, as plastic materials are relatively resistant to oxidative ageing and are generally not degraded by microorganisms, they will accumulate in coastal and oceanic waters. However, the technology is available to manufacture plastics with a programed service life which, if widely adopted, would reduce the accumulation of plastic materials in the sea. More information on the extent of pollution of the marine environment by plastic materials is required. A more complete knowledge of the origin of plastic pollutants, their distribution, environmental impact, and ultimate fate, will only be gained when more research is undertaken. Meanwhile, the random distribution of plastics should be discouraged.

## ACKNOWLEDGEMENTS

The author is indebted to his colleagues Drs R. W. Traxler and R. H. Pierce, Jr, for reading an early draft of this paper and making a number of helpful suggestions. This publication is Contribution No. 1520 from the Rhode Island Agricultural Experiment Station, to whom grateful thanks are also due.

## SUMMARY

The pollution of the marine environment by plastics such as polyethylene, polyvinyl chloride, polystyrene, and polyurethane, is discussed. As plastic materials are relatively resistant to oxidative ageing and are generally not degraded by microorganisms, they will accumulate in coastal and oceanic waters. The origin of plastic pollutants, their distribution in the marine environment, and their persistence and ultimate fate, are largely unknown. The technology is available to manufacture plastic materials with a programed service life which, if widely adopted, would reduce the accumulation of plastics in the sea. But their random distribution should be discouraged on behalf of the marine environment.

## REFERENCES

Anon. (1971*a*). Trends in the plastics industry. *Modern Plastics,* **45**, pp. 5-9.

Anon. (1971*b*). Biodegradability: lofty goal for plastics. *Chem. & Eng. News,* **50**, pp. 37-8.

Anon. (1973*a*). Clearing the shelves for all-plastic soda and beer bottles. *Modern Packaging,* October, pp. 22-5.

Anon. (1973*b*). Plastic wastes are a burning issue. *Chemical Week,* February 28, p. 51.

Arnold, L. K. (1968). *Introduction to Plastics.* Iowa State University Press, Ames: 287 pp.

Bellan-Santini, D., Arnaud, F., Arnaud, P., Bellan, G., Harmelin, J. G., LeCampion-Alsumard, T., Kit, L. T., Picard, J., Pouliquen, L. & Zibrowius, H. (1970). Etude qualitative et quantitative des salissures biologiques de plaques expérimentales immergées en pleine eau. 1. Conditions de l'expérience. *Tethys,* **1**, pp. 709-14.

Carpenter, E. J. & Smith, K. L. (1972). Plastics on the Sargasso Sea surface. *Science,* **178**, pp. 1240-1.

Carpenter, E. J., Anderson, S. J., Harvey, G. R., Miklas, H. P. & Peck, B. B. (1972). Polystyrene spherules in coastal waters. *Science,* **178**, pp. 749-50.

Coscarelli, W. (1964). Deterioration of organic materials by marine organisms. Pp. 113-47 in *Principles and Application of Aquatic Microbiology* (Ed. H. Heukelekian & N. C. Dondero). John Wiley, New York: xxxiii + 452 pp., illustr.

Cundell, A. M. & Mulcock, A. P. (1973). Measurement of the microbiological deterioration of vulcanized rubber. *Material u. Organismen,* **8**, pp. 1-15.

Darby, R. J. & Kaplan, A. M. (1968). Fungal susceptibility of polyurethanes. *Appl. Microbiol.,* **16**, pp. 900-5.

Darnay, A., & Franklin, W. E. (1969). The role of packaging in solid waste management, 1966 to 1976. *Publ. SW-5c U.S. Dept of Health, Education and Welfare,* Rockville, Maryland, p. 120.

Evans, D. M. & Levisohn, I. (1968). Biodeterioration of polyester-based polyurethane. *Int. Biodetn Bull.,* **4**, pp. 89-92.

Heap, W. M. & Morrell, S. H. (1968). Microbiological deterioration of rubbers and plastics. *J. Appl. Chem.,* **18**, pp. 189-94.

Heyerdahl, T. (1971). Atlantic Ocean pollution and biota observed by the 'Ra' Expeditions. *Biological Conservation,* **3**(3), pp. 164-7, map.

Jannasch, H. W., Eimhjellen, K., Wirsen, C. O. & Farmanfarmaian, A. (1971). Microbial degradation of organic matter in the deep sea. *Science,* **171**, pp. 672-5.

Jones, E. B. G. & LeCampion-Alsumard, T. (1970). The biodeterioration of polyurethane by marine Fungi. *Int. Biodetn Bull.,* **6**, pp. 119-24.

Joyner, R. S. (1971). Polyethylene. *Modern Plastics,* **48**, pp. 72, 77, and 80.

LeCampion-Alsumard, T. (1970). Etude qualitative et quantitative des salissures biologiques de plaques expérimentales immergées en pleine eau. 2. Etude préliminaire de quelques pyrénomycetes marins récoltés sur des plaques de polyurethane. *Tethys,* **1**, pp. 715-8.

Mills, J. & Eggins, H. O. W. (1970). Growth of thermophilic Fungi on oxidation products of polyethylene. *Int. Biodetn Bull.,* **6**, pp. 13-7.

Muraoka, J. S. (1969). Effect of deep-ocean environment on plastics. Pp. 5-19 in *Materials Performance and the Deep Sea.* American Society for Testing Materials, Philadelphia: 445 pp.

Pratt, S. D., Saila, S. B., Gaines, A. G. & Krout, J. E. (1973). Biological effects of ocean disposal of solid waste. *Marine Technical Report Series, University of Rhode Island,* No. 9, 52 pp.

Scott, G. (1972). Plastics packaging and coastal pollution. *Intern. J. Environ. Stud.,* **3**, pp. 35-6.

Scott, G. (1973). Improving the environment: Chemistry and plastic waste. *New Scientist,* pp. 267-72.

Smith, D. D. & Brown, R. P. (1971). Ocean disposal of barge-delivered liquid and solid wastes from U.S. coastal cities. *Publ. SW-19c, Solid Waste Management Office, U.S. Environmental Protection Agency,* pp. 33-41.

Sutherland, J. P. (1972). Quantitative analyses of seasonal progression in the fouling community at Beaufort, North Carolina. Pp. 176-7 in *Abstracts, Third International Congress on Marine Corrosion and Fouling,* National Bureau of Standards, Gaithersburg, Maryland, 2-6 October 1972.

Venrick, E. L., Backman, T. W., Bartram, W. C., Plah, C. J., Thornhill, M. S. & Yates, R. E. (1973). Man-made objects on the surface of the central North Pacific Ocean. *Nature,* London, **241**, p. 271.

Wood, A. S. (1970). Plastics challenge in packaging: Disposability. *Modern Plastics,* **47**, pp. 50-4.

# 35. Icebergs and Oil Tankers

LUTHER J. CARTER 1975

The potential environmental problems associated with transporting oil from Alaska's North Slope to U.S. markets have been under discussion for so long that it is surprising for a worrisome new problem to turn up now, but it looks as though one has. A recent U.S. Geological Survey report—warning that icebergs from the huge, 425-square-mile Columbia Glacier near the port of Valdez (Figure 35-1) may pose a menace to the supertankers that will soon be calling daily to take on oil from the Trans-Alaska Pipeline System (TAPS)—has stirred concern enough at the U.S. Coast Guard headquarters in Washington for one of the admirals to send for the glaciologists.

What the glaciologists are saying is that the glacier, which juts into Prince William Sound just west of the Valdez Arm, may be on the verge of a "drastic retreat" and could discharge up to 50 cubic miles of ice into the sound over the next 30 to 50 years. Moreover, the fact that dangerous icebergs—which are not always readily detectable—could be borne by winds and currents from the vicinity of the glacier into the shipping lanes is already compellingly evident in the northern end of the sound and especially at the entrance to the Valdez Arm.

Alyeska, the consortium that will operate TAPS, has said that even if the glacial retreat does occur, the consequences for the tanker fleet would be minimal, involving no more than occasional delays in the movement of ships in and out of Valdez. El Paso Alaska, the company which is seeking permission to build a trans-Alaska natural gas pipeline and run a fleet of 11 liquefied natural gas (LNG) tankers from a terminal at Gravina Point, some 40 miles from the glacier, has as yet given no indication that it sees any potential problem at all.

But the Coast Guard's Office of Marine Environment and Systems, headed by Rear Admiral Robert I. Price, has asked for the two glaciologists who have led the Columbia Glacier study to meet with the admiral on 6 November. These scientists are Mark F. Meier, the USGS project chief for glaciology, and Austin Post, author of the as yet unpublished "open file" report on the glacier. They are based in Tacoma, Washington.

Luther J. Carter is a science writer for the American Association for the Advancement of Science.

From *Science*, Vol. 190, No. 4215, pp. 641-643, 1975. Reprinted with light editing and with permission of the author and the American Association for the Advancement of Science. Copyright 1975 by the American Association for the Advancement of Science.

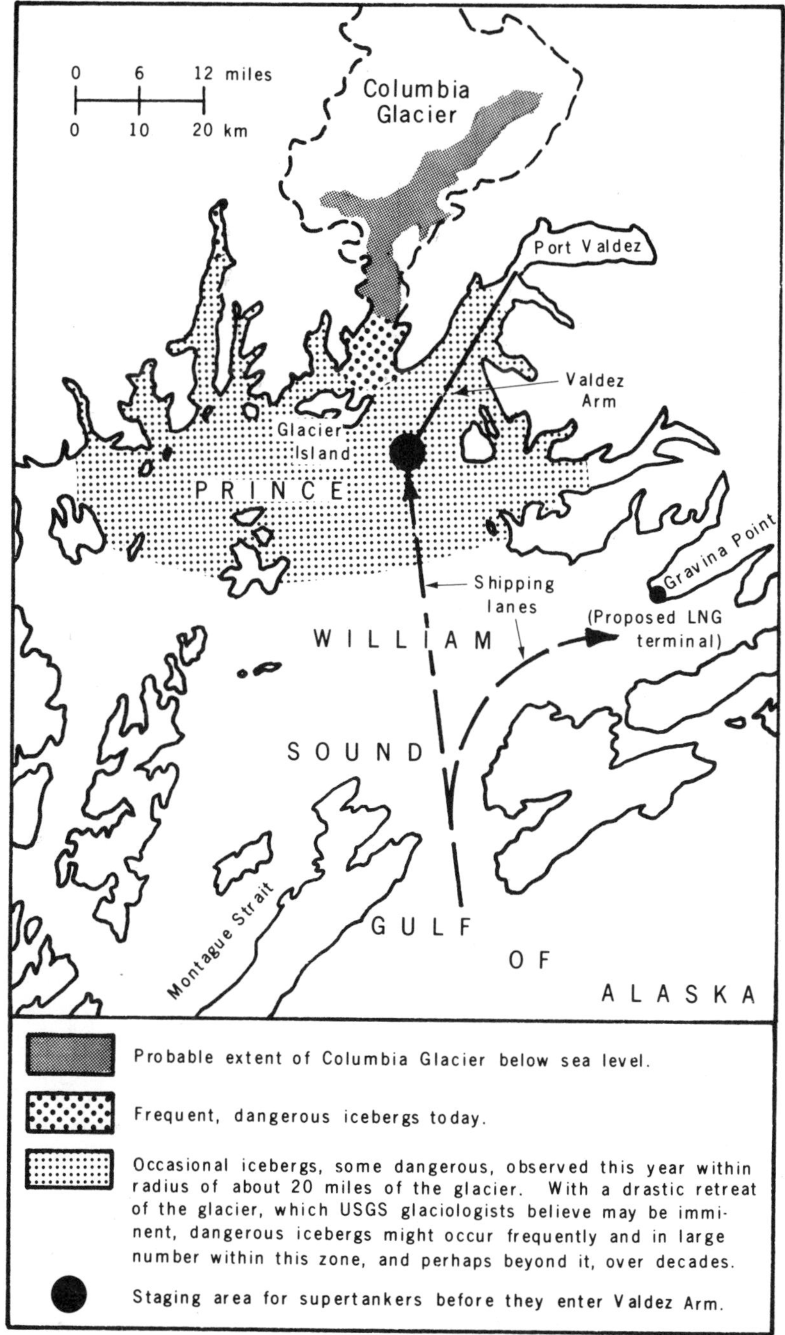


Figure 35-1. Columbia Glacier and shipping lanes in Prince William Sound, Alaska. Map by Eleanor Warner.

From the discussion with these scientists, Admiral Price hopes that the potential iceberg problem can be better defined with a view to devising whatever special navigation safeguards might be necessary. The movement of supertankers in and out of the port of Valdez will begin in late 1977 or early 1978, as the first oil from Prudhoe Bay begins to flow. The Coast Guard will be responsible for controlling this tanker traffic, and, to that end, it plans to invest about $7 million in such new facilities as a radar station on the Valdez Arm and a microwave communications relay.

Meier and Post will explain to the admiral why they suspect that the glacier is now at a point of critical instability—and why, at the present stage of their investigation, they can't offer firm predictions as to its behavior. What follows here pretty much sums up what they know about the glacier, and what they are still trying to find out.

At its terminus on Prince William Sound, the Columbia Glacier is about 4 miles wide and presents a towering ice cliff which, in places, is as much as 300 feet or more above the sound. The glacier has remained in a relatively stable condition during this century, in that its advances and retreats have tended to offset one another, with the changes in the position and configuration of its terminus being relatively minor. In this it has been unique, because the other tidal glaciers in North America have all made retreats from extended positions. For instance, the Muir Glacier, in what is now the Glacier Bay National Monument (about 100 miles east of Juneau), has retreated 21 miles since 1900.

It was in the summer of 1973 that Austin Post first began to suspect that the Columbia Glacier, too, might now be on the verge of an abrupt and drastic retreat. So extensive were the embayments existing along the west side of the terminus, it appeared that a good half of this part of the glacier was not resting on the moraine shoal that had supported and confined it. Being subject to "plastic flow" as well as sliding and melting, glacial ice will not stand up unless supported, and Post wondered if conditions were now such as to cause a rapid break up of the glacier.

In his judgment, three key questions had to be answered. First, he wanted to know whether the moraine shoal was comparatively narrow, occurring only along the terminus, without reaching "upstream" beneath the glacier. Second, was much of this great river of ice below sea level—or, to put it another way, was it confined in a deep fiord, with the ice extending down hundreds, if not thousands of feet? If so, as the glacier fell back from its extended position on the moraine, an immensely high ice face would be left exposed and unsupported. Third, was the glacier in a declining "state of health"? That is, was the annual "wastage" of snow and ice greater than the annual accumulation?

If all these questions could be answered affirmatively, then Post believed that he would be able to predict that a drastic retreat of the glacier was in fact imminent and inevitable.

In the summer of 1974, a team of USGS glaciologists headed by Mark Meier began taking some of the critical measurements. By deploying a small, unmanned, remote-controlled boat from the University of Alaska's 85-foot research vessel, the *Acona,* they were able to take fathometer readings along the face of the glacier which confirmed that the moraine shoal is indeed narrow and does not extend much beneath the ice. From these readings, together with other available information, they concluded that, within embayments extending no more than a quarter of a mile or so into the ice face, the water might be as much as 300 feet deep, compared to the depths of about 10 to 150 feet found along the shoal.

Also, by means of a radar device which they were able to deploy at various points along the glacier, the team obtained readings on the thickness of the ice which showed that the glacier extends below sea level for more than 20 miles of its length and that in some places it reaches as much as 2000 feet below. But they were not able to take enough measurements to draw firm conclusions as to the glacier's state of health, and this key question remains unanswered today.

The occurrence of unusually heavy calving near the center of the terminus during the past 2 months has, however, reinforced the USGS investigators' belief that a drastic retreat of the glacier may be at hand. One embayment now measures fully a mile both in width and lateral depth, and at least two-thirds of the entire west side of the terminus is believed to be off the shoal. If the retreat occurs, it could progress at an astonishing rate, with the terminus withdrawing a mile or more each year until it reaches a stable retracted position at the head of the fiord.

Besides meeting with Admiral Price of the Coast Guard on their trip to Washington, Meier and Post will also give a special briefing to the top staff of the USGS. In this briefing, requested by Vincent E. McKelvey, director of the USGS, the glaciologists will point out that $100,000 or more will be required for each year over the next several years to continue the Columbia Glacier research project.

Much of the money would be spent on chartering helicopters. USGS crews and their snow toboggans, radar, and drilling and digging equipment must be transported about the surface of the glacier to permit the taking of further measurements. In addition to determining the glacier's state of health, the glaciologists want to map the shape of the fiord and thus be better able to say whether there are shoals or "islands" beneath the glacier that might slow down movement of the ice.

Although such research is of scientific interest, its primary justification—especially now, at a time when the USGS faces a tight budget—is that it could give the Coast Guard, Alyeska, and other navigation interests better information as to what, literally and figuratively, may be lying ahead. In fact, the possibility that the Coast Guard might be willing to support the research, either financially or by providing a helicopter or other services, is sure to be explored.

Any mention of icebergs always calls to mind the loss of the *Titanic.* But, actually, since that famous disaster of 1912, there seem to have been relatively few major maritime losses attributed to icebergs. The last one that a Coast Guard officer formerly with the International Ice Patrol in the North Atlantic recalls was the loss of the Danish motorship *Hedtoft,* which disappeared off the southern tip of Greenland in early 1959. In more than a century of operations in Alaskan waters, the Coast Guard has not found icebergs to be much of a problem there.

Nevertheless, icebergs are treated with respect, even small ones. An iceberg that is, say, 90 feet long, 60 feet wide, and 10 feet vertically represents a 6000-ton mass that the skipper of a heavily laden, 165,000 dead-weight-ton tanker cruising at 16 knots across Prince William Sound will not want to run into.

Icebergs of up to 100 feet or more in draft could escape over the moraine shoals and be carried by the prevailing currents out into the entrance of Valdez Arm and on into the main body of the sound. The Coast Guard, the glaciologists, and the captain of the excursion boat *Glacier Queen* have all observed icebergs in or around the shipping lanes during the past 2 months. A small iceberg normally melts within about a week, and thus is not likely ever to reach the lower region of the sound where it could be a menace to tankers calling at a liquefied natural gas terminal at Gravina Point, should such a facility ever be approved and built. Some larger bergs might well enter these waters, however.

Various safeguards against icebergs are of course available. The tankers that will call at Valdez will all be radar equipped, and shore-based radar operated by the Coast Guard will provide coverage over the entrance to the Valdez Arm and that part of Prince William Sound adjoining it. Also, regular iceberg patrols could be carried out by Coast

Guard vessels and aircraft should this appear necessary. "We will take whatever management and monitoring measures necessary to ensure safety," says Lieutenant Commander Kenneth W. Thompson, chief of port safety for the 17th Coast Guard District, Juneau.

Yet, while any iceberg problem that arises may well be manageable, the safeguards will not be foolproof. For, the fact is, some dangerous icebergs, particularly the smaller ones, can be hard to detect. If the water surface is agitated from high winds, a small berg may escape surveillance by either radar or the human eye. Furthermore, if an iceberg's natural buoyancy has been reduced by rock enclosed within the ice, the top of the berg may be barely awash or may even be hidden slightly below the surface.

All in all, the glaciologists' finding of a possible iceberg threat to the tanker traffic offers another illustration of the special, and sometimes unexpected, problems encountered as oil exploration and development is carried to increasingly difficult environments.

# 36. Ocean Pollution Seen from Rafts

THOR HEYERDAHL 1971

There are times when an observation is made by someone who is looking for something else. This was the case when the present speaker experimented with prehistoric types of watercraft to travel back into man's past, and yet stumbled upon three practical observations which have a bearing upon man's future:

1. The ocean is not endless.
2. There is no such thing as territorial waters for more than days at a time.
3. Pollution caused by man has already reached the farthest section of the world ocean.

It may seem superfluous to state that the ocean is not endless, something the world has known since Columbus crossed the Atlantic in 1492. Yet I dare insist that this fact has not sufficiently penetrated our minds, we all subconsciously act as if the ocean has horizons running into the endless blue sky. When we build our city sewers in pipes far enough into the sea, when we dump poisonous refuse outside territorial borders, we feel we dispose of it for ever in a boundless abyss. We have known for centuries that our planet has no edges and that the oceans interlock in a never-ending curve around the world, but perhaps it is this uninterrupted curve that gives us the feeling of endlessness, this feeling that the ocean somehow continues to curve into space. From all continents we keep on sending our refuse into the presumably endless ocean almost with the impression that we send it away into space. Rarely do we stop and think of the fact that the ocean is nothing but a very big lake, landlocked if we go far enough in any direction. Other than being the largest body of water on earth, its main distinction from other lakes is that they usually have an out-

Dr. Thor Heyerdahl is an internationally known ethnologist and explorer. He is perhaps best known for his *Kon-Tiki* expedition on which six Norwegian scientists drifted westward on a model of a prehistoric Inca balsa-wood raft from Peru to the Polynesian atoll Raroia in the Tuamotu Archipelago—a distance of 4300 miles. This expedition tested the theory that some inhabitants of these islands came from South America. More recently, his *Ra I* and *II* expeditions gained worldwide attention when his international crew of seven men traveled in papyrus rafts from Africa to the Caribbean Islands. These expeditions tested the theory that the pyramid builders of the Western Hemisphere, particularly in Mexico and Central America, were influenced by the pyramid builders in Egypt.

From a statement read before the United States Senate Committee on Ocean and Atmosphere on November 8, 1971. Reprinted with permission of the author.

let to carry away excessive natural solutions and pollution, whereas the ocean has none. Through a worldwide, non-stop flow, all the excess waste and refuse that run from lakes and land assemble in the ocean, and only clean water evaporates back into the atmosphere. There were days not far back when our ancestors would laugh at the idea that man could pollute and kill a lake so big that nobody could see across it. Today Lake Erie is only one of a long series of lakes destroyed by man in the most different parts of the world. Place ten Lake Eries end to end and they span the ocean from Africa to America. True, the ocean is deeper than any lake, but we all know that due to photosynthesis the bulk of life is restricted to the thin upper layer, and we also know that an estimated 90 per cent of all marine life happens to be on the continental shelves which represent only 10 per cent of the total ocean area. Add to this that if half a dozen towns send their refuse into Lake Erie, all the cities, all the farmlands, all the rivers and ships of the world channel their refuse into the ocean, directly or in a roundabout way. No wonder then, that a time has come when even the world ocean has begun to become visibly polluted.

This discovery, which was first forced upon me while drifting at surface level in the mid-Atlantic in 1969, helped to open my own eyes to the fact that the ocean has its limits, and the closer one gets to know it the more easily this can be perceived. When we rush across it with engine-driven craft we feel that it is thanks to the modern traveling speed that the continents seem to be not so immensely far apart. But when you place yourself on a primitive raft and find that, entirely without engine or modern means of propulsion, you drift across the largest oceans in a matter of weeks, then you realize that you made it, not because of modern technique but quite simply because the ocean is not at all endless. With a speed slightly faster than that of average surface pollution, I crossed the Pacific from South America to Polynesia on nine balsa logs in 1947, and, on bundles of reeds, from Africa to the Caribbean Islands almost twice within a year in 1969-70. Each of these oversea voyages on an aboriginal type of watercraft was intended as an eye-opener for fellow anthropologists who, like the average layman, have retained the universal concept of the ocean as an endless waste, unsurmountable by pre-Columbian craft because of its boundless dimensions. This concept is wrong, and we run the risk of harming ourselves dearly unless we abandon this medieval concept of the endless sea and accept the fact that the ocean itself is nothing more than a big, salt lake, limited in extent and vulnerable as all the smaller bodies of water.

A second dangerous illusion equally hard-to-die is the image of territorial water. We draw a line parallel to the coast, three miles, ten miles, or a hundred miles off shore, and declare the inside as territorial water. There is no such thing as territorial water, the ocean is in constant motion, like the air. We can draw a line on the ocean floor and lay claims to the static land on the bottom, but the body of water above it is as independant of the map as is the atmosphere above dry land: wind and currents disregard any national border lines. Refuse dumped inside Peruvian territorial waters equals refuse dumped around the shores of Polynesia; refuse dumped inside Moroccan territorial waters equals refuse dumped in the Caribbean Sea. Any liquid piped into the port of Safi in Morocco, and any buoyant material dumped outside the local breakwaters just where our papyrus bundle-boat was let adrift, will run along as on a river straight to tropic America where some will wash against the beaches and some will move on up along the east coast of the United States. Moroccan territorial waters in a matter of weeks or months become American territorial waters, with all the good and evil this may involve. The salt sea is a common human heritage, we can divide the ocean floor between us, but we shall for ever be deemed to share the common water which rotates like soup in a boiling kettle: the spices one nation puts in will be tasted by all the consumers.

Only when we abandon the almost superstitious awe for the immensity of the sea, and the misconception of coastal water as a stagnant body, can we fully understand what is happening when visible pollution is scattered the full length of the North Atlantic surface current which flows perpetually from northwest Africa to tropical America. This entire span of the ocean, from continent to continent, contain among other modern refuse an immeasurable quantity of small drifting oil clots. They were accidentally noticed during the crossing with the papyrus raft-ship *Ra I* in 1969 and deliberately surveyed and sampled the next year during the crossing with *Ra II*.

In fact, in organizing our marine experiment with the first papyrus vessel ever to be tested at sea in modern times, our expedition group was initially unprepared for pollution studies. The objectives of the enterprise were to investigate the sea-going abilities and geographical range of the oldest type of watercraft used by man's earliest civilizations in the Mediterranean world as well as in Mexico and Peru, and furthermore to test the effects of multi-national cooperation in cramped quarters and under stress. We were seven men from seven nations on *Ra I* and eight from eight nations on *Ra II*. At sea, however, early in the voyage of *Ra I*, pollution observations were forced upon all the expedition members by the conspicuous presence of oil clots and undoubtedly also because of our own proximity to the ocean surface and slow progress through the water.

Departing from the Moroccan port of Safi on the northwest coast of Africa on May 25th, 1969, the seven men on board *Ra I* became aware of traveling in polluted water for the first time on June 6th, at 24°38′N and 17°06′W, or about a hundred miles (160 km) off the coast of Mauritania. The sea was now rolling calmly and we noticed the surface to be densely scattered with brownish to pitch-black lumps of asphalt-like material as big as gravel and floating at close intervals on and just below the surface. The clots were drifting with the surface current in our direction, but benefiting more from the tradewinds we moved considerably faster, averaging a speed of about 2 to 2.5 knots. The local current speed is about 0.5 knots. Knowing that our reed-vessel was near the circum-African shipping lane, we climbed the mast and began to scout for ships, being convinced that we had entered the wake of some nearby oil tanker that had just cleaned its tanks. No ship was seen. On June 8th, having advanced about a hundred miles farther to the southwest, we found ourselves again sailing through similarly polluted water, still without any ship in sight. The following day we sailed into an area of the ocean where the same flotsam included pieces of larger size, some appearing as thick, black flakes of irregular shape up to 5-6 inches in diameter. The local ocean water itself gradually turned into an opaque and greyish-green color instead of being transparent and clear blue; it was recorded in the expedition journal as resembling harbor water at the outlet of city sewers.

Although sporadic lumps were noted, no specific entry was made in the expedition log until June 30th, when our position was at 15°45′N and 35°08′W, that is virtually in the mid-Atlantic with Africa and America almost at the same distance. Here once more we suddenly entered an area so polluted that we had to be attentive in washing ourselves or dipping our toothbrushes into the water, to avoid the seemingly endless quantities of oil clots of sizes ranging from that of a grain of rice to that of a sandwich.

*Ra I* covered 2700 nautical miles (*ca* 5000 km) in 54 days, and on July 15th and 16th, shortly before abandoning the test vessel we found ourselves again in the same general type of polluted water. Our position was now 13°32′N and 47°20′W, or some six hundred miles (960 km) east of the island of Barbados and slightly closer to the mainland coast of South America. Many of the clots had an eroded or pitted surface, and small barnacles as well as algae were occasionally seen growing on them.

Some samples were collected and at the end of the voyage delivered with a brief report to the Permanent Norwegian Delegation at the United Nations. Although no deliberate or preconceived observations were made, the voyage with *Ra I* resulted in the involuntary recording of six day's traveling through visibly strongly polluted water in the course of eight weeks of trans-Atlantic sailing. Thus, more than 10 per cent of the surface water traversed by *Ra I* was visibly polluted by a rich flotsam of nonorganic material of rather homogeneous appearance and undoubtedly resulting from modern commercial activity.

Our report to the United Nations in 1969 aroused a general interest, not least among scientists and shipping authorities, and prepared for what we might again encounter, we decided to keep a systematic record of daily observations when we embarked on the voyage of *Ra II* the following year. *Ra II* was again launched outside the breakwaters of the same ancient port of Safi in Morocco, this time on May 17th, 1970. As the water along the west coast of Africa and in the latitudes where we were to undertake the Atlantic crossing is not at all stagnant, but moves toward America with a speed of 0.5 knots or more, it is clear that we did not voyage through the same surface water this second time. In fact, the surface water observed by us from *Ra I* had been displaced more than four thousand miles during the year that had passed between the departures of the two consecutive raft expeditions. In other words, the water which we traversed along the African coast in May 1969, had long since deposited its flotsam along the Caribbean shores or else carried it into the initial part of the Gulf Stream, by the time we embarked on the second voyage in 1970. Correspondingly, the water seen around us as we abandoned *Ra I* short of Barbados in July 1969, would this subsequent year be on its return flow with the Gulf Stream back across the North Atlantic, heading for Europe. Nothing could impede this eternal circulation of ocean water, westward near the Equator and eastward in the far north, caused by the rotation of the earth itself. Thus the pollution we saw during *Ra II* was wholly independent of anything we observed on *Ra I*.

During our experiment with *Ra II,* in addition to the regular entries in the expedition log, a special pollution record was kept by Madani Ait Ouhanni, who also at reasonable intervals collected samples of the asphalt-like clots which, toward the end of the voyage, were handed to the United Nations' research vessel *Calamar* for subsequent transfer to the Norwegian UN Delegation. The samples were taken by means of a fine-meshed dip-net. It should be noted that in the rippled seas oil-clots were difficult to detect unless washed on board or drifting past very close to our papyrus deck. Only when the wave surface was smooth, or the floating objects were of conspicuous size, was it possible to detect and record pollutants passing more than six or eight feet away from the *Ra*. Thus, the considerable quantities of oil clots and other floating refuse which were found to float close alongside our papyrus bundles reflect the true dimensions of the problem is estimated in a broader geographical scope. It should also be noted that the route followed by *Ra II* was straighter and somewhat more northerly than that of *Ra I* which constantly broke the rudders and was forced on a drift voyage down beyond the latitude of the Cape Verde Islands.

On the background of these facts, it is disheartening to report that drifting oil clots were observed forty out of the fifty-seven days it took *Ra II* to cross from Safi to Barbados. This is 72 per cent of the traveling time spent in water where oil clots could be seen. From May 17, 1970 when we left the port in Morocco (at 32°20′N and 9°20′W) until and including June 28 when we had reached 15°54′N and 45°56′W, we recorded oil pollution on forty days out of forty-three. On the three days when pelagic oil lumps were not seen, Ouhanni's entries in the pollution record state that the sea was too rough for proper observation. It may thus be safely assumed that the 2407 nautical miles (4350 km) covered by *Ra II* during the initial 43 days of its voyage represented an uninterrupted stretch of polluted surface water, the degree of visible pollution varying from slight to very grave. It is slightly encouraging to note, however, that with the exception of some sporadic lumps observed on July 30th, no record of such particles was made during the remaining 700 miles to Barbados. This curious fact should not delude us through, since this was the very area where we noted extreme pollution the previous year. Also, on our arrival in Barbados, the owner of our east coast hotel reported that oil clots were sometimes so common on this beach that it was a problem to keep carpets clean from lumps that had stuck to his clients' feet.

Perhaps the sudden disappearance of oil clots in front of the Caribbean Islands during the 1970 crossing can be ascribed to a temporal irregularity in the local movement of water. The disappearance of the clots coincided with the sudden arrival of feeders from northbound branches of the South Equatorial Current, which were noticed both in our own displacement and simultaneously indicated by sudden changes in water temperature. Nevertheless, although the seemingly ever-present oil lumps disappeared this time, plastic containers and other imperishable manmade objects were observed sporadically until the last day of our crossing.

The average extent of oil pollution recorded during the voyage of *Ra II* amounted to lumps of asphalt-like material the size of finger-tips or smaller, scattered far apart in otherwise clean water. There would be days when only a very few such lumps could be seen from sunrise to sunset, whereas in exceptional cases the water was so polluted that a bucket could not be filled without some floating clots being caught at the same time.

The first very seriously polluted water was entered by *Ra II* four days after departure, on May 21st, at 29°26′N and 11°40′W, about 100 nautical miles off the African coast before we entered the passage between the Canary Islands and Morrocco. From early that morning until the evening of the following day, *Ra II* was drifting very slowly through calm water that was thickly polluted by clusters of solidified oil lumps commonly of the size of prunes or even potatoes. Many of these lumps were dark-brown, mousy, and pitted, more or less covered by marine growth, whereas others were smooth and black, with the appearance of being quite fresh. For a duration of two days, the surface water, containing large quantities of these lumps, was also covered intermittently by a shallow white foam such as develops from soap or synthetic washing powder, while occasionally the ocean's surface was even shining in rainbow-colors as from gasoline. The sea was smooth and a vast quantity of dead coelenterates could be seen for considerable distances on both sides of our track. The expedition journal recorded that "the degree of pollution is shocking."

The following week only sporadic lumps were noticed, until on May 29th, at 25°43′N and 16°23′W, when our records again show that "the pollution is terrible." During the previous night, oil lumps, of which the biggest were the size of a large fist, had been washed on board during darkness, to remain as the water filtered through the papyrus as through the fringes of whalebone. Barnacles, marine worms, crustaceans, and sometimes bird feathers, were found attached to the oil lumps. The high degree of pollution was this time witnessed for three consecutive days, when swimming inevitably meant colliding with the sticky clots. On May 31st, at 25° 00′N and 17°07′W, the expedition journal has the following entry: "An incredible quantity of shell-covered asphalt lumps today, big as horse-droppings and in clusters everywhere. One plastic bottle and one metal oil-can also observed, plus a large cluster of greenish rope, and nylon-like material besides a wooden box and a carton. It is shocking to see how the Atlantic is getting polluted by Man." No ships were seen in the vicinity.

The next entry into seriously polluted waters was on June 16th. At 18°26′N and 34°28′W, again virtually in the mid-Atlantic, the surface of the waves and as far as we could see below contained endless quantities of large and small oil lumps.

*Ra II* completed its Atlantic crossing on July 12th, 1970, landing on Barbados after covering 3270 nautical miles (*ca* 6100 km) in fifty-seven days. Although pelagic oil clots represented the most consistently recurring type of visible pollution during the two *Ra* voyages, it should be made clear that other debris from man of a rather heterogeneous kind was also common, even where oil was absent. Thus, in 1970, pollution in the form of plastic containers, metal cans, glass bottles, nylon objects, and other perishable and nonperishable products of man, representing refuse from ships and shores, passed close by the sides of our raft at intervals from the day of departure to the day of landing.

This was in marked contrast to our experience during the voyage of the raft *Kon-Tiki* two decades earlier. A noted aspect of that voyage, which then took place in the Pacific, was that not a single oil clot, in fact not a single sign of Man's activities, was seen during the 4300 miles crossing. From the day we left Callao in Peru until we landed on Raroia atoll in Polynesia 101 days later, we were constantly impressed by the perfect purity of the sea. The first trace of other human beings observed was the wreck of an old sailing vessel thrown up on the reef where we landed. Although, in fact, the contrast refers to two different oceans, the currents rotate between them and the difference between observations in 1947 and 1970 is so marked that it probably has some bearing on the rapidity with which we pollute the sea.

Through the State Department of Norway, a meeting was arranged between representatives from different scientific institutions and the oil industry who were invited to discuss an analytic program for the oil clot samples collected by the *Ra II* expedition. The analytic program was designed to determine whether the samples represented crude or refined oil, and also to estimate the origin, whether it could be leakage from drill, scattered oil from a single wrecked super-tanker like *Torrey Canyon,* oil from marine organisms, or mixed discharges from many different vessels. The analytic work was carried out by the Central Institute for Industrial Research in Oslo, and their findings can be summarized as follows:

The results of the infrared spectras show that the samples consist mainly of saturated hydrocarbons or mineral oil. Some samples seem to contain compounds from decomposed crude oil or heavy fuel oil. Vegetable and animal oils are apparently absent. According to the results of a gas chromatographic analysis, the saturated hydrocarbons were normal paraffins (n-paraffins) with 14 to 40 carbon atoms in each molecule with maximum around 20 and 30 carbon atoms. Such n-paraffins are generally, but not exclusively, the major fractions in mineral oil from the U.S.A. and North Africa. The samples showed a wide range in their contents of nickel and vanadium which indicate that they have derived from geographically different sources. In short, the conclusion was that the countless oil clots drifting about from continent to continent represent crude oil pollutants not from one leakage or one wreck, but from different sources. We are hardly far off then if we suspect the major part of the oil clots to be the scattered refuse from the numerous tankers which daily discard their ballast water at sea before entering a port of loading.

It was not an objective of the *Ra* expeditions to draw biological or ecological conclusions from our observations. Our aim is merely to call attention to observations that were virtually forced upon us by our prolonged proximity to the surface of the sea. Yet, one cannot refrain from certain deductions. Clearly, the time has passed when ocean pollution was a mere offense to human aesthetics because the surf throws oil and rubbish upon the holiday-makers' beaches. Much has been written about the tendency of oil molecules to expand in thin layers over wide areas of water, thus impeding the photosynthesis needed by the oxygen-producing phytoplankton. Those of us who sat on the two *RA*s observing fishes, large and small, nibbling at any floating particle wonder how the almost ever-present oil clots can avoid affecting the metabolism of the marine fauna and flora; not least the filter-feeding fishes and whales which swim with open mouth and, like the reed-bundles of *Ra,* let the water sieve through whereas plankton and oil clots alike get stuck in gills, whalebones or intestines. Small fish may get wise to the presence in their own element of unpaletable oil clots, but larger marine species have no way of gaping over plankton without taking in nonorganic material floating alongside as well. In addition, the oil lumps examined showed that they very frequently provided a foothold for live organisms which ride along as a sort of bait attracting the attention of bypassing fish. I am referring here to the fact that small *Cirripedia,* or edible barnacles (identified as *Lepas pectinata*) were very commonly sitting in regular clusters on the lumps. Various edible crustaceans were also frequently found clinging to the lumps, notably an isopod (*Idothea metallica*) and a small pelagic crab (*Planes minutus*). Marine worms hid in the pitted surface, and the shell of a tiny dead cuttlefish (*Spirula spirula*) was found in one sample.

In closing, I may be permitted a personal remark. A much more far-reaching study than our improvised sampling will be needed before we can judge the durability and effects of this steadily increasing flotsam of oil and debris. Perhaps bacterial activity and disintegration will finally sink or efface the oil from the ocean's surface, but certainly not before a large percentage is washed up against the continental and island shores. Having first personally witnessed the almost uninterrupted host of clots rotating about in the mid-ocean, I have subsequently visited some shorelines of the three continents bordering on the land-locked Mediterranean Sea and found a belt ranging in color from grey to black along the waterline of cliffs exposed to the polluted surf. In certain areas, like on the otherwise attractive island of Malta, it is as if the entire coastline to a height of six or eight feet above water-level has been smeared by a black impregnation. Where the invisible marine paintbrush has been at work there is no sign of life, neither algae nor molluscs, crustaceans or any other marine species naturally at home on such rocks. The coastal cliffs and reefs represent, as we know, a major breeding place for pelagic plankton and a necessary stepping stone in the life cycle of a great many of the species of paramount importance to Man.

I stress again, there are few things as illusive as the concept of territorial waters. What others dump at sea will come to your shores, and what you dump at home will travel abroad irrespective of national legislation. We must start at national level, but we must quickly move on to international agreements if we shall be able to protect our common ocean for future generations.

# 37. Scientific Aspects of the Oil Spill Problem

MAX BLUMER 1971

## THE EXTENT OF MARINE OIL POLLUTION

Oil pollution is the almost inevitable consequence of our dependence on an oil-based technology. The use of a natural resource without losses is nearly impossible and environmental pollution occurs through intentional disposal or through inadvertent losses in production, transportation, refining and use. How large is the oil influx to the ocean? The washing of cargo tanks at sea, according to the director of Shell International, Marine Ltd.[1] had the potential in 1967 of introducing 2.8 million tons into the ocean, assuming that no use was made of the Load on Top (LOT) technique. With the increase in ocean oil transport from 1967 to 1970 this potential has grown to 6 million tons. The LOT technique is not being applied to one quarter of the oil tonnage moved by tankers; consequently, these vessels introduce about 1.5 million tons of oil into the sea. The limitations of the LOT technique have been described by E. S. Dillon[2]: the technique is not always used even if the equipment exists, the equipment may be inadequate, shore receiving facilities may be lacking and principal limitations lie in the formation of emulsions in heavy seas or with heavy crude oils. Insufficient time may be available for the separation of the emulsion or the oil water interface may not be readily recognized. In addition the most toxic components of oil are also readily soluble in water and their disposal into the ocean could be avoided only if clean ballasting were substituted for the LOT technique. For these reasons it is estimated that the present practices in tanker ballasting introduce about 3 mil-

1. Statement by J. H. Kirby, quoted by J. R. Wiggins, Washington Post, March 15, 1970.

2. Dillon, E. Scott, "Ship Construction and Operation Standards for Oil Pollution Abatement," presented to a Conference on Ocean Oil Spills, held by the NATO Committee on Challenges of Modern Society, Brussels, November 2-6, 1970.

Dr. Max Blumer is an organic geochemist and senior scientist with Woods Hole Oceanographic Institution, Massachusetts. He studies natural hydrocarbons and pigments.

From *Environmental Affairs,* Vol. 1, No. 1, pp. 54-73, 1971. Reprinted with light editing and by permission of the author and the Environmental Law Center of the Boston College Law School. This paper was presented to a Conference on Ocean Oil Spills, held by the NATO Committee on Challenges of Modern Society, Brussels, November 2-6, 1970. Contribution No. 2616 of the Woods Hole Oceanographic Institution.

lion tons of petroleum into the ocean. The pumping of bilges by vessels other than tankers contributes another 500,000 tons.[3] In addition, in-port losses from collisions and during loading and unloading contribute an estimated 1 million tons.[4]

Oil enters the ocean from many other sources whose magnitude is much less readily assessed. Among these are accidents on the high seas (*Torrey Canyon*) or near shore, outside of harbors (West Falmouth, Mass.), losses during exploration (oil based drilling mud) and production (Santa Barbara, Gulf of Mexico), in storage (submarine storage tanks) and in pipeline breaks, and spent marine lubricants and incompletely burned fuels. A major contribution may come from untreated domestic and industrial wastes; it is estimated that nearly 2 million tons of used lubricating oil is unaccounted for each year in the United States alone, and, a significant portion of this reaches our coastal waters.[5,6]

Thus, the total annual oil influx to the ocean lies probably between 5 and 10 million tons. A more accurate assessment of the oil pollution of the oceans and of the relative contribution of different oils to the different marine environments is urgently needed. Such an assessment might well lie within the role of the NATO Committee on Challenges of the Modern Society.

With the anticipated increase in foreign and domestic oil production, with increased oil transport and with the shift of production to more hazardous regions (Alaska, continental shelf, deep ocean), we can expect a rapid increase of the spillage rate and of the oil influx to the ocean. Floating masses of crude oil ("tar") are now commonly encountered on the oceans and crude oil is present on most beaches. Oil occurs in the stomach of surface feeding fishes[7] and finely dispersed hydrocarbons occur in marine plants (e.g. sargassum[8]) and in the fat of fish and shellfish.[6,9a,b] Hydrocarbons from a relatively small and restricted oil spill in the coastal waters of Massachusetts, U.S.A., have spread, nine months after the accident to an area occupying 5000 acres (20 $km^2$) offshore and 500 acres (2 $km^2$) in tidal rivers and marshes. The effect on the natural populations in this area has been catastrophic. The full extent of the coverage of the ocean bottom by petroleum hydrocarbons is unknown; chemical analyses are scarce or nonexistent.

## EVALUATION OF THE THREAT

### Oil: Immediate Toxicity

All crude oils and all oil fractions except highly purified and pure materials are poisonous to all marine organisms. This is not a new finding. The wreck of the *Tampico* in Baja, California, Mexico (1957) "created a situation where a completely natural area was almost totally destroyed suddenly on a large scale. . . . Among the dead species were lobsters, abalone, sea urchins, starfish, mussels, clams and hosts of smaller forms."[10] Similarly, the spill of fuel oil in West Falmouth, Massachusetts, U.S.A., has virtually extinguished life in a productive coastal and intertidal area, with a complete kill extend-

3. Statement by C. Cortelyou, Mobil Oil Company, quoted by W. D. Smith, The *New York Times*, April 19, 1970.
4. Blumer, M., "Oil Pollution of the Ocean," in *Oil on the Sea*, D. P. Hoult, ed., Plenum Press, 1969.
5. Anon., "Final Report of the Task Force on Used Oil Disposal," American Petroleum Institute, New York, N.Y., 1970.
6. Murphy, T. A., "Environmental Effects of Oil Pollution," Paper presented to the Session on Oil Pollution Control, American Society of Civil Engineers, Boston, Mass., July 13, 1970.
7. Horn, M. H., Teal, J. H. and Backus, R. H., "Petroleum Lumps on the Surface of the Sea," *Science* 168, 245, 1970.
8. Youngblood, W. W. and Blumer, M., unpublished data, 1970.
9a. Blumer, M., Souza, G., and Sass, J., "Hydrocarbon Pollution of Edible Shellfish by an Oil Spill," *Marine Biology* 5, 195-202, 1970.
9b. Blumer, M., Testimony before the Conservation and Natural Resources Subcommittee, Washington, D.C., July 22, 1970.
10. North, W. J., "Tampico, a Study of Destruction and Restoration," *Sea Frontiers* 13, 212-217, 1967.

ing over all phyla represented in that habitat (Hampson and Sanders[11] and unpublished data). Toxicity is immediate and leads to death within minutes or hours.[12]

Principally responsible for this immediate toxicity are three complex fractions. The *low boiling saturated hydrocarbons* have, until quite recently, been considered harmless to the marine environment. It has now been found that this fraction, which is rather readily soluble in sea water, produces at low concentration anaesthesia and narcosis and at greater concentration cell damage and death in a wide variety of lower animals; it may be especially damaging to the young forms of marine life.[13] The *low boiling aromatic hydrocarbons* are the most immediately toxic fraction. Benzene, toluene and xylene are acute poisons for man as well as for other organisms; naphthalene and phenanthrene are even more toxic to fishes than benzene, toluene and xylene.[14] These hydrocarbons and substituted one-, two-, and three-ring hydrocarbons of similar toxicity are abundant in all oils and most, especially the lower boiling, oil products. Low boiling aromatics are even more water soluble than the saturates and can kill marine organisms either by direct contact or through contact with dilute solutions. *Olefinic hydrocarbons,* intermediate in structure and properties, and probably in toxicity, between saturated and aromatic hydrocarbons are absent in crude oil but occur in refining products (*e.g.*, gasoline and cracked products) and are in part responsible for their immediate toxicity.

Numerous other components of crude oils are toxic. Among those named by Speers and Whithead,[15] cresols, xylenols, naphthols, quinoline and substituted quinolines and pyridines and hydroxybenzoquinolines are of special concern here because of their great toxicity and their solubility in water. It is unfortunate that statements which disclaim this established toxicity are still being circulated. Simpson[16] claimed that "there is no evidence that oil spilt round the British Isles has ever killed any of these (mussels, cockles, winkles, oysters, shrimps, lobsters, crabs) shellfish." It was obvious when this statement was made that such animals were indeed killed by the accident of the *Torrey Canyon* as well as by earlier accidents; work since then has confirmed the earlier investigation. In addition, this statement, by its emphasis only on the adult forms, implies wrongly that juvenile forms were also unaffected.

## Oil and Cancer

The higher boiling crude oil fractions are rich in multiring aromatic compounds. It was at one time thought that only a few of these compounds, mainly 3,4-benzopyrene, were capable of inducing cancer. As R. A. Dean[17] of British Petroleum Company stated, "no 3,4-benzopyrene has been detected in any crude oil . . .. [I]t therefore seems that the risk to the health of a member of the public by spillage of oil at sea is probably far less than that which he normally encounters by eating the foods he enjoys." However, at the time this statement was made, carcinogenic fractions containing 1,2-benzanthracene and alkylbenzanthracenes had already been isolated by Car-

11. Hampson, G. R., and Sanders, H. L., "Local Oil Spill," *Oceanus* 15, 8-10, 1969.
12. Sanders, H. L., Testimony before the Conservation and Natural Resources Subcommittee, Washington, D.C., July 22, 1970.
13. Goldacre, R. J., "The Effects of Detergents and Oils on the Cell Membrane," Suppl. to Vol. 2 of Field Studies, Field Studies Council London, 131-137, 1968.
14. Wilber, C. G., *The Biological Aspects of Water Pollution,* Charles C. Thomas, Publisher, Springfield, Ill., 1969.
15. Speers, G. C. and Whithead, E. V., "Crude Petroleum," in *Organic Geochemistry,* Eglinton, G. and Murphy, M. R. J., eds., Springer, Berlin, 638-675, 1969.
16. Simpson, A. C., "Oil, Emulsifiers and Commercial Shell Fish," Suppl. to Vol. 2 of Field Studies, Field Studies Council, London, 91-98, 1968.
17. Dean, R. A., "The Chemistry of Crude Oils in Relation to their Spillage on the Sea," Suppl. to Vol. 2 of Field Studies, Field Studies Council, London, 1-6, 1968.

ruthers, Stewart and Watkins[18] and it was known that "biological tests have shown that the extracts obtained from high-boiling fractions of the Kuwait oil . . . (method) . . . are carcinogenic." Further, "Benzanthracene derivatives, however, are evidently not the only type of carcinogen in the oil. . . ." In 1968, the year when Dean claimed the absence of the powerful carcinogen 3,4 benzopyrene in crude oil, this hydrocarbon was isolated in crude oil from Libya, Venezuela, and the Persian Gulf.[19] The amounts measured were between 450 and 1800 milligrams per ton of the crude oil.

Thus, we know that chemicals responsible for cancer in animals and man occur in petroleum. The causation of cancer in man by crude oil and oil products was observed some years ago, when a high incidence of skin cancer in some refinery personnel was observed. The cause was traced to prolonged skin contact by these persons with petroleum and with refinery products. Better plant design and education, aimed at preventing the contact, have since reduced or eliminated this hazard.[20] However, these incidents have demonstrated that oil and oil products can cause cancer in man, and have supported the conclusions based on the finding of known carcinogens in oil. These references and a general knowledge of the composition of crude oils suggest that all crude oils and all oil products containing high boiling aromatic hydrocarbons should be viewed as potential cancer inducers.

Safeguards in plant operations protect the public from this hazard. However, when oil is spilled into the environment we loose control over it and should again be concerned about the possible public health hazard from cancer-causing chemicals in the oil. We have shown that marine organisms ingest and retain hydrocarbons to which they are exposed. These are transferred to and retained by predators. In this way even animals that were not directly exposed to a spill can become polluted by eating contaminated chemicals. This has severe implications for commercial fisheries and for human health. It suggests that marketing and eating of oil contaminated fish and shellfish at the very least increases the body burden of carcinogenic chemicals and may constitute a public health hazard.

Other questions suggest themselves: Floating masses of crude oil now cover all oceans and are being washed up on shores. It has been thought that such stranded lumps are of little consequence ecologically. It has been shown that such lumps, even after considerable weathering, still contain nearly the full range of hydrocarbons of the original crude oil, extending in boiling point as low as 100°C. Thus such lumps still contain some of the immediately toxic lower boiling hydrocarbons. In addition, the oil lumps contain all of the potentially carcinogenic material in the 300-500° boiling fraction. The presence of oil lumps ("tar") or finely dispersed oil on recreational beaches may well constitute a severe public health hazard, through continued skin contact.

## Low Level Effects of Oil Pollution

The short-term toxicity of crude oil and of oil products and their carcinogenic properties are fairly well understood. In contrast to this we are rather ignorant about the long term and low level effects of oil pollution. These may well be far more serious and long lasting than the more obvious short term effects. Let us look at low level interference of oil pollution with the marine ecology.

Many biological processes which are important for the survival of marine organisms and which occupy key positions in their life processes are mediated by extremely low concentration of chemical messengers in the sea water. We have demonstrated that marine predators are attracted to their prey

18. Carruthers, W., Stewart, H. N. M. and Watkins, D. A. M., "1,2-Benzanthracene Derivatives in a Kuwait Mineral Oil," *Nature* 213, 691-692, 1967.
19. Graef, W. and Winter, C., "3,4 Benzopyrene in Erdoel," *Arch. Hyg.* 152/4, 289-293, 1968.
20. Eckardt, R. E., "Cancer Prevention in the Petroleum Industry," *Int. J. Cancer* 3, 656-661, 1967.

by organic compounds at concentrations below the part per billion level.[21] Such chemical attraction—and in a similar way repulsion—plays a role in the finding of food, the escape from predators, in homing of many commercially important species of fishes, in the selection of habitats and in sex attraction. There is good reason to believe that pollution interferes with these processes in two ways, by blocking the taste receptors and by mimicking for natural stimuli. The latter leads to false response. Those crude oil fractions likely to interfere with such processes are the high boiling saturated and aromatic hydrocarbons and the full range of the olefinic hydrocarbons. It is obvious that a very simple—and seemingly innocuous—interference at extremely low concentration levels may have a disastrous effect on the survival of any marine species and on many other species to which it is tied by the marine food chain.

Research in this critical area is urgently needed. The experience with DDT has shown that low level effects are unpredictable and may suddenly become an ecological threat of unanticipated magnitude.

### The Persistence of Oil in the Environment

Hydrocarbons are among the most persistent organic chemicals in the marine environment. It has been demonstrated that hydrocarbons are transferred from prey to predator and that they may be retained in organisms for long time periods, if not for life. Thus, a coastal spill near Cape Cod, Massachusetts, U.S.A., has led to the pollution of shellfish by fuel oil. Transplanting of the shellfish to clean water does not remove the hydrocarbons from the tissues. Oil may contaminate organisms not only at the time of the spill; hydrocarbon-loaded sediments continue to be a source of pollution for many months after the accident.

21. Whittle, K. J. and Blumer, M., "Chemotaxis in Starfish, Symposium on Organic Chemistry of Natural Waters," University of Alaska, Fairbanks, Alaska, 1968 (in press).

Oil, though lighter than water, does not remain at the sea surface alone; storms, or the uptake by organisms or minerals, sink the oil. Oil at the sea bottom has been found after the accidents of the *Torrey Canyon,* at Santa Barbara, and near Cape Cod. Clay minerals with absorbed organic matter are an excellent adsorbent for hydrocarbons; they retain oil and may transport it to areas distant from the primary spill. Thus, ten months after the accident at Cape Cod, the pollution of the bottom sediments covers an area that is much larger than that immediately after the spill. In sediments, especially if they are anaerobic, oil is stable for long time periods. Indeed, it is a key fact of organic geochemistry that hydrocarbons in anaerobic recent sediments survive for millions of years until they eventually contribute to the formation of petroleum.

## COUNTERMEASURES

Compared to the number and size of accidents and disasters the present countermeasures are inadequate. Thus, in spite of considerable improvement in skimming efficiency since the Santa Barbara accident, only 10% of the oil spilled from the Chevron well in the Gulf of Mexico was recovered.[22] From an ecological point of view this gain is nearly meaningless. While we may remain hopeful that the gross esthetic damage from oil spills may be avoided in the future, there is no reason to be hopeful that existing or planned countermeasures will eliminate the biological impact of oil pollution.

The most immediately toxic fractions of oil and oil products are soluble in sea water; therefore, biological damage will occur at the very moment of the accident. Water currents will immediately spread the toxic plume of dissolved oil components and, if the accident occurs in inshore waters, the whole water column will be poisoned even if

22. Wayland, R. G., Federal Regulations and Pollution Controls on the U.S. Offshore Oil Industry, this conference.

the bulk of the oil floats on the surface. The speed with which the oil dissolves is increased by agitation, and in storms the oil will partly emulsify and will then present a much larger surface area to the water; consequently, the toxic fractions dissolve more rapidly and reach higher concentrations. From the point of view of avoiding the immediate biological effect of oil spills, countermeasures are completely effective only if *all of the oil is recovered immediately* after the spill. *The technology to achieve this goal does not exist.*

Oil spills damage many coastal and marine values: water fowl, fisheries, and recreational resources; they lead to increased erosion; they diminish the water quality and may threaten human life or property through fire hazard. A judicious choice has to be made in each case: which–if any–of the existing but imperfect countermeasures to apply to minimize the overall damage or the damage to the most valuable resources. Guidelines for the use of countermeasures, especially of chemical countermeasures, exist[23] and are being improved.[24] Some comments on the ecological effects and desirability of the existing countermeasures appear appropriate.

### Detergents and Dispersants

The toxic, solvent-based detergents which did so much damage in the clean-up after the *Torrey Canyon* accident are presently only in limited use. However, so-called "nontoxic dispersants" have been developed. The term "nontoxic" is misleading; these chemicals may be nontoxic to a limited number of often quite resistant test organisms but they are rarely tested in their effects upon a wide spectrum of marine organisms including their juvenile forms, preferably in their normal habitat. Further, in actual use all dispersant-oil mixtures are severely toxic, because of the inherent toxicity of the oil, and bacterial degradation of "nontoxic" detergents may lead to toxic breakdown products.

The effect of a dispersant is to lower the surface tension of the oil to a point where it will disperse in the form of small droplets. It is recommended that the breakup of the oil slick be aided by agitation, natural or mechanical. Thus, the purpose of the detergent is essentially a cosmetic one. However, the recommendation to apply dispersants is often made in disregard of their ecological effects. Instead of removing the oil, dispersants push the oil actively into the marine environment; because of the finer degree of dispersion, the immediately toxic fraction dissolves rapidly and reaches a higher concentration in the sea water than it would if natural dispersal were allowed. The long term poisons (e.g. the carcinogens) are made available to and are ingested by marine filter feeders, and they can eventually return to man incorporated into the food he recovers from the ocean.

For these reasons I feel that the use of dispersants is unacceptable, inshore or offshore, except under special circumstances, *e.g.*, extreme fire hazard from spillage of gasoline, as outlined in the Contingency Plan for Oil Spills, Federal Water Quality Administration, 1969.[23,24]

### Physical Sinking

Sinking has been recommended. "The long term effects on marine life will not be as disastrous as previously envisaged. Sinking of oil may result in the mobile bottom dwellers moving to new locations for several years; however, conditions may return to normal as the oil decays."[25] Again, these conclusions

23. Contingency Plan for Spills of Oil and Other Hazardous Materials in New England, U.S. Dept. Interior, Federal Water Quality Administration, Draft, 1969.
24. Schedule of Dispersants and Other Chemicals to Treat Oil Spills, May 15, 1970, Interim Schedule, Federal Water Quality Administration, 1970.

25. Little, A. D., Inc., "Combating Pollution Created by Oil Spills," Report to the Dept. of Transportation, U.S. Coast Guard, Vol. 1: Methods, p. 71386 (R), June 30, 1969.

disregard our present knowledge of the effect of oil spills.

Sunken oil will kill the bottom faunas rapidly, before most mobile dwellers have time to move away. The sessile forms of commercial importance (oysters, scallops, etc.) will be killed and other mobile organisms (lobsters) may be attracted into the direction of the spill where the exposure will contaminate or kill them. The persistent fraction of the oil which is not readily attacked by bacteria contains the long term poisons, *e.g.*, the carcinogens, and they will remain on the sea bottom for very long periods of time. Exposure to these compounds may damage organisms or render them unfit for human nutrition even after the area has been repopulated.

The bacterial degradation of sunken oil requires much oxygen. As a result, sediments loaded with oil become anaerobic and bacterial degradation and reworking of the sediments by aerobic benthic organisms is arrested. It is one of the key principles of organic geochemistry that hydrocarbons in anaerobic sediments persist for million of years. Similarly, sunken oil will remain; it will slow down the resettlement of the polluted area; and it may constitute a source for the pollution of the water column and of fisheries resources for a long time after the original accident.

For these reasons I believe that sinking of oil is unacceptable in the productive coastal and offshore regions. Before we apply this technique to the deep ocean with its limited oxygen supply and its fragile faunas we should gather more information about the interplay of the deep marine life with the commercial species of shallower waters.

### Combustion

Burning the oil through the addition of wicks or oxidants appears more attractive from the point of view of avoiding biological damage than dispersion and sinking. However, it will be effective only if burning can start immediately after a spill. For complete combustion, the entire spill must be covered by the combustion promoters, since burning will not extend to the untreated areas; in practice, in stormy conditions, this may be impossible to achieve.

### Mechanical Containment and Removal

Containment and removal appear ideal from the point of avoiding biological damage. However, they can be effective only if applied immediately after the accident. Under severe weather conditions floating booms and barriers are ineffective. Booms were applied during the West Falmouth oil spill; however, the biological damage in the sealed-off harbors was severe and was caused probably by the oil which bypassed the booms in solution in sea water and in the form of wind-dispersed droplets.

### Bacterial Degradation

Hydrocarbons in the sea are naturally degraded by marine microorganisms. Many hope to make this the basis of an oil removal technology through bacterial seeding and fertilization of oil slicks. However, great obstacles and many unknowns stand in the way of the application of this attractive idea.

No single microbial species will degrade any whole crude oil; bacteria are highly selective and complete degradation requires many different bacterial species. Bacterial oxidation of hydrocarbons produces many intermediates which may be more toxic than the hydrocarbons; therefore, organisms are also required that will further attack the hydrocarbon decomposition products.

Hydrocarbons and other compounds in crude oil may be bacteriostatic or bacteriocidal; this may reduce the rate of degradation, where it is most urgently needed. The fraction of crude oil that is most readily attacked by bacteria is the least toxic one, the normal paraffins; the toxic aromatic hydrocarbons, especially the carcinogenic polynuclear aromatics, are not rapidly attacked.

The oxygen requirement in bacterial oil degradation is severe; the complete oxidation of 1 gallon of crude oil requires all the dissolved oxygen in 320,000 gallons of air saturated sea water. Therefore, oxidation may be slow in areas where the oxygen content has been lowered by previous pollution and the bacterial degradation may cause additional ecological damage through oxygen depletion.

### Cost Effectiveness

The high value of fisheries resources, which exceeds that of the oil recovery from the sea, and the importance of marine proteins for human nutrition demand that cost effectiveness analysis of oil spill countermeasures consider the cost of direct and indirect ecological damage. It is disappointing that existing studies completely neglect to consider these real values.[17] A similarly one-sided approach would be, for instance, a demand by fisheries concerns that all marine oil production and shipping be terminated, since it clearly interferes with fisheries interests.

We must start to realize that we are paying for the damage to the environment, especially if the damage is as tangible as that of oil pollution to fisheries resources and to recreation. Experience has shown that cleaning up a polluted aquatic environment is much more expensive than it would have been to keep the environment clean from the beginning.[26] In terms of minimizing the environmental damage, spill prevention will produce far greater returns than cleanup—and we believe that this relationship will hold in a *realistic* analysis of the overall cost effectiveness of prevention or cleanup costs.

## THE RISK OF MARINE OIL POLLUTION

### The Risk to Marine Life

Our knowledge of crude oil composition and of the effects of petroleum on marine organisms in the laboratory and in the marine environment force the conclusion that petroleum and petroleum products are toxic to most or all marine organisms. Petroleum hydrocarbons are persistent poisons. They enter the marine food chain, they are stabilized in the lipids of marine organisms, and they are transferred from prey to predator. The persistence is especially severe for the most poisonous compounds of oil; most of these do not normally occur in organisms and natural pathways for their biodegradation are missing.

Pollution with crude oil and oil fractions *damages the marine ecology* through different effects:

1. Direct kill of organisms through coating and asphyxiation.[27]
2. Direct kill through contact poisoning of organisms.
3. Direct kill through exposure to the water soluble toxic components of oil at some distance in space and time from the accident.
4. Destruction of the generally more sensitive juvenile forms of organisms.
5. Destruction of the food sources of higher species.
6. Incorporation of sublethal amounts of oil and oil products into organisms resulting in reduced resistance to infection and other stresses (the principal cause of death in birds surviving the immediate exposure to oil[28]).
7. Incorporation of carcinogenic and potentially mutagenic chemicals into marine organisms.
8. Low level effects that may interrupt any of the numerous events necessary for the propagation of marine species and for the survival of those species which stand higher in the marine food web.

26. Ketchum, B. H., *Biological Effects of Pollution of Estuaries and Coastal Waters,* Boston Univ. Press, 1970 (in press).

27. Arthur D. R., "The Biological Problems of Littoral Pollution by Oil and Emulsifiers—a Summing up," Suppl. to Vol. 2 of Field Studies, Field Studies Council, London, 159-164, 1968.

28. Beer, J. V., "Post-Mortem Findings in Oiled Auks during Attempted Rehabilitation," Suppl. to Vol. 2 of Field Studies, Field Studies Council, London, 123-129, 1968.

The degree of toxicity of oil to marine organisms and the mode of action are fairly well understood. On the other hand, we are still far from understanding the effect of the existing and increasing oil pollution on the marine ecology on a large, especially worldwide, scale.

Few, if any, comprehensive studies of the effects of oil spills on the marine ecology have been undertaken. Petroleum and petroleum products are toxic *chemicals;* the long term biological effect of oil and its persistence cannot be studied without chemical analyses. Unfortunately, chemical analysis has not been used to support such studies in the past and conclusions on the persistence of oil in the environment have been arrived at solely by visual inspection. This is not sufficient; a sediment can be uninhabitable to marine bottom organisms because of the presence of finely divided oil, but the oil may not be visually evident. Marine foods may be polluted by petroleum and may be hazardous to man but neither taste nor visual observation may disclose the presence of the toxic hydrocarbons.

A coordinated biological and chemical study of the long-term effect and fate of a coastal oil spill in West Falmouth, Massachusetts, U.S.A. has shown that even a relatively low boiling, soluble and volatile oil persists and damages the ecology for many months after the spill. In this instance about 650 tons of #2 fuel oil were accidentally discharged into the coastal waters off the Massachusetts coast. I wish to summarize our present findings of the effect of this accident.

### Persistence and Spread of the Pollution[9a,b,29]

Oil from the accident has been incorporated into the sediments of the tidal rivers and marshes and into the offshore sediments, down to 42 feet, the greatest water depth in the sea. The fuel oil is still present in inshore and offshore sediments, eight months after the accident. The pollution has been spreading on the sea bottom and now covers at least 5000 acres offshore and 500 acres of marshes and tidal rivers. This is a much larger area than that affected immediately after the accident. Bacterial degradation of the oil is slow; degradation is still negligible in the most heavily polluted areas and the more rapid degradation in outlying, less affected, areas has been reversed by the influx of less degraded oil from the more polluted regions. The kill of bottom plants and animals has reduced the stability of marshland and sea bottom; increased erosion results and may be responsible for the spread of the pollution along the sea bottom.

Bacterial degradation first attacks the least toxic hydrocarbons. The hydrocarbons remaining in the sediments are now more toxic on an equal weight basis than immediately after the spill. Oil has penetrated the marshes to a depth of at least 1-2 feet; bacterial degradation within the marsh sediment is still negligible eight months after the accident.

### Biological Effects of the Pollution[11,12]

Where oil can be detected in the sediments there has been a kill of animals; in the most polluted areas the kill has been almost total. Control stations outside the area contain normal, healthy bottom faunas. The kill associated with the presence of oil is detected down to the maximum water depth in the area. A massive, immediate kill occurred offshore during the first few days after the

29. This and the next two sections of the paper were written nine months after the West Falmouth oil spill. The following reports, giving the status after two years, are now available:

(a) The Persistence and Degradation of Spilled Fuel Oil. *Science.* (1972) 176, 1120-1122.

(b) The West Falmouth Oil Spill. I. Biology. Howard L. Sanders, J. Frederick Grassle, and George R. Hampson. WHOI 72-20.

(c) The West Falmouth Oil Spill. II. Chemistry. Data Available in November, 1971. M. Blumer and J. Sass. WHOI 72-19.

These reports are available from the National Technical Information Service, Springfield, Va. 22151.

accident. Affected were a wide range of fish, shellfish, worms, crabs and other crustaceans and invertebrates. Bottom living fishes and lobsters were killed and washed up on the beaches. Trawls in 10 feet of water showed 95% of the animals dead and many still dying. The bottom sediments contained many dead clams, crustaceans and snails. Fish, crabs, shellfish and invertebrates were killed in the tidal Wild Harbor River; and in the most heavily polluted locations of the river almost no animals have survived.

The affected areas have not been repopulated, nine months after the accident. Mussels that survived last year's spill as juveniles have developed almost no eggs and sperm.

### Effect on Commercial Shellfish Values[9a,b]

Oil from the spill was incorporated into oysters, scallops, softshell clams and quahaugs. As a result, the area had to be closed to the taking of shellfish.

The 1970 crop of shellfish is as heavily contaminated as was last year's crop. Closure will have to be maintained at least through this second year and will have to be extended to areas more distant from the spill than last year. Oysters that were removed from the polluted area and that were maintained in clean water for as long as 6 months retained the oil without change in composition or quantity. Thus, once contaminated, shellfish cannot cleanse themselves of oil pollution.

The tidal Wild Harbor River, a productive shellfish area of about 22 acres, contains an estimated 4 tons of the fuel oil. This amount has destroyed the shellfish harvest for two years. The severe biological damage to the area and the slow rate of biodegradation of the oil suggest that the productivity will be ruined for a longer time.

Some have commented to us that the effects measured in the West Falmouth oil spill are not representative of those from a crude oil spill and that #2 fuel oil is more toxic than petroleum. However, the fuel oil is a typical refinery product that is involved in marine shipping and in many marine spillages; also, the fuel oil is a part of petroleum and as such it is contained within petroleum. Therefore, its effect is typical, both for unrefined oil and for refinery products. In terms of chemical composition crude oils span a wide range; many lighter crude oils have a composition very similar to those of the fuel oils and their toxicity and environmental danger corresponds respectively. However, many crude oils contain more of the persistent, long term poisons, including the carcinogens, than the fuel oils. Therefore, crude oils can be expected to have even more serious long term effects than the lower boiling fuel oils.

The pollution of fisheries resources in the West Falmouth oil spill is independent of the molecular size of the hydrocarbons; the oil taken up reflects exactly the boiling point distribution of the spilled oil. Thus, spills by other oils of different boiling point distributions can be expected to destroy fisheries resources in the same manner.

We believe that the environmental hazard of oil and oil products has been widely underestimated, because of the lack of thorough and extended investigations. The toxicity and persistence of the oil and the destruction of the fisheries resources observed in West Falmouth are typical for the effects of marine oil pollution.

### The Risk to Human Use of Marine Resources

The destruction of marine organisms, of their habitats and food sources directly affects man and his intent to utilize marine proteins for the nutrition of an expanding population. However, the presence in oil of toxic and carcinogenic compounds combined with the persistence of hydrocarbons in the marine food chain poses an even more direct threat to human health. The magnitude of this problem is difficult to assess at this time. Our knowledge of the occurrence of carcinogens in oil is recent and their relative concentrations have been measured in very few oils. Also, our understanding of the fate of hydrocarbons, especially of carcinogens, in the marine food chain needs to be expanded.

Methods for the analysis of fisheries products for the presence of hazardous hydrocarbons exist and are relatively simple and the analyses are inexpensive. In spite of this no public laboratory in the United States—and probably in the world—can routinely perform such analysis for public health authorities. There is increasing evidence that fish and shellfish have been and are now being marketed which are hazardous from a public health point of view. Taste tests, which are commonly used to test for the presence of oil pollutants in fish or shellfish, are inconclusive. Only a small fraction of petroleum has a pronounced odor; this may be lost while the more harmful long term poisons are retained. Boiling or frying may remove the odor but will not eliminate the toxicity.

### The Risk to the Recreational use of Marine Resources

The presence of petroleum, petroleum products and petroleum residue ("tar," "beach tar") is now common on most recreational beaches. Toxic hydrocarbons contained in crude oil can pass through the barrier of the human skin and the prolonged skin contact with carcinogenic hydrocarbons constitutes a public health hazard. Intense solar radiation is known to be one of the contributing factors for skin cancer. The presence of carcinogens in beach tar may increase the risk to the public in a situation where a severe stress from solar radiation already exists.

### The Risk to Water Utilization

Many of the toxic petroleum hydrocarbons are also water soluble. Water treatment plants, especially those using distillation, may transfer or concentrate the steam-volatile toxic hydrocarbons into the refined water streams, especially if dissolved hydrocarbons are present in the feed streams or if particulate oil finds its way into the plant intake.

## CONCLUSIONS

1. Oil and oil products must be recognized as poisons that damage the marine ecology and that are dangerous to man. Fisheries resources are destroyed through direct kill of commercially valuable species, through sub-lethal damage and through the destruction of food sources. Fisheries products that are contaminated by oil must be considered as a public health hazard.

2. Only crude estimates exist of the extent of marine oil pollution. We need surveys that can assess the influx of petroleum and petroleum products into the ocean. They should be world-wide and special attention should be paid to the productive regions of the ocean; data are needed on the oil influx from tankers and non-tanker vessels, on losses in ports, on offshore and inshore accidents from shipping, exploration and production and on the influx of oil from domestic and industrial wastes.

3. The marine ecology is changing rapidly in many areas as a result of man's activities. We need to establish baseline information on composition and densities of marine faunas and floras and on the hydrocarbon levels and concentrations encountered in marine organisms, sediments and in the water masses.

4. All precautions must be taken to prevent oil spills. Prevention measures must be aimed at eliminating human error, at the present time the principal cause of oil spills.

5. Spill prevention must be backed by effective surveillance and law enforcement. *In terms of cost effectiveness spill prevention is far superior to cleanup.*

6. Perfection and further extension of the use of the Load on Top methods is promising as a first step in reduction of the oil pollution from tankers. The effectiveness of the technique should be more closely assessed and improvements are necessary in interface detection, separation and measure-

ment of hydrocarbon content in the effluent, both in the dispersed and dissolved state. On a longer time scale, clean ballast techniques should supersede the Load on Top technique.

7. The impact of oil pollution on marine organisms and on sources of human food from the ocean has been underestimated because of the lack of coordinated chemical and biological investigations. Studies of the effect of oil spills on organisms in different geographic and climatic regions are needed. The persistence of hydrocarbon pollution in sea water, sediments and organisms should be studied.

8. Research is urgently needed on the low-level and long term effects of oil pollution. Does oil pollution interfere with feeding and life processes at concentrations below those where effects are immediately measured? Are hydrocarbons concentrated in the marine food chain?

9. Carcinogens have been isolated for crude oil but additional efforts are needed to define further the concentrations and types of carcinogens in different crude oils and oil products.

10. The public health hazard from oil derived carcinogens must be studied. What are the levels of oil derived carcinogens ingested by man and how wide is the exposure of the population? How much does this increase the present body burden with carcinogens? Is there direct evidence for the causation of cancer in man by petroleum and petroleum products outside of oil refinery operations?

11. Public laboratories must be established for the analysis of fisheries products for toxic and carcinogenic chemicals derived from oil and oil products, and tolerance levels will have to be set.

12. The ocean has a limited tolerance for hydrocarbon pollution. The tolerance varies with the composition of the hydrocarbons and is different in different regions and in different ecological sub-systems. The tolerance of the water column may be greater than that of the sediments and of organisms. An assessment of this inherent tolerance is necessary to determine the maximum pollution load that can be imposed on the environment.

13. Countermeasures which remove the oil from the environment reduce the ecological impact and danger to fisheries resources. All efforts should be aimed at the most rapid and complete removal since the extent of the biological damage increases with extended exposure of the oil to sea water.

14. Countermeasures that introduce the entire, undegraded oil into the environment should be used only as a last resort in situations such as those outlined in the Contingency Plan of the Federal Water Quality Administration, involving extreme hazard to a major segment of a vulnerable species of waterfowl or to prevent hazard to life and limb or substantial hazard of fire to property. Even in those cases assessment of the long term ecological hazard must enter into the decision whether to use these countermeasures (detergents, dispersants, sinking agents).

15. As other countermeasures become more effective, the use of detergents, dispersants and sinking agents should be further curtailed or abolished.

16. Efforts to intensify the natural bacterial degradation of oil in the environment appear promising and should be supported by basic research and development.

17. Ecological damage and damage to fisheries resources are direct consequences of oil spills. In the future, the cost of oil leases should include a fee for environmental protection.

18. Environmental protection funds derived from oil leases should be used to accomplish the necessary research and education in the oil pollution field.

## ACKNOWLEDGMENTS

The author expresses his gratitude for continued support to the National Science Foundation, to the Office of Naval Research and to the Federal Water Quality Administration.

# 38. Potential Effects of Aquaculture on Inshore Coastal Waters

WILLIAM E. ODUM 1974

The possibility that the construction and operation of aquaculture facilities might affect surrounding natural areas has been generally overlooked. This review is an examination of some cases which have been documented, with speculation concerning problems that may arise. At this point the goal is to obtain an idea, though admittedly rough, of the kinds of changes which might occur, so that measures can be devised to mitigate their impact.

## AQUACULTURE AS A POLLUTION SOURCE

Aquaculture, like any other industry, has the potential to generate pollutants which may be intentionally or accidentally released into the natural environment. The United States, along with many other countries, regards the aquaculture practitioner as legally responsible for effluents which adversely affect water quality. Thus some years ago, a minnow farmer in Arkansas (U.S.A.) was taken to court for discharging toxic pond-water containing sodium cyanide and Endrin into a public stream and causing the destruction of fish for 70 kilometers downstream (Anon., 1970*a*).

For convenience, the following discussion is divided into two sections. The first deals with excess organic matter resulting from the aquaculturist's attempts to maximize production; the second concerns the release of chemicals that are used to reduce competition with the culture species.

### Organic Effluents

In certain special cases, the effluents from intensive aquaculture, like those from cattle feed-lots or duck farms, may contain enough nutrients and unoxidized organic matter to affect near-by bodies of water adversely. Potential alterations include changes in the composition of animal and plant populations, increased or decreased primary production, pH changes, and lowered dissolved oxygen concentrations. The water leaving salmonid fish hatcheries has been reported by Liao (1970) to be degraded in respect to taste, odor, and concentrations of Bacteria,

Dr. William E. Odum is an Associate Professor with the Department of Environmental Sciences at the University of Virginia. He has authored or co-authored thirty scientific publications on the subjects of estuarine ecology and conservation.

From *Environmental Conservation*, Vol. 1, No. 3, pp. 225-230, 1974. Reprinted with light editing and with permission of the author and the Foundation for Environmental Conservation, Switzerland.

fecal matter, and residual food. Hinshaw's study (1973) of the effect of the discharges from six trout hatcheries found significant adverse changes in biochemical oxygen demand (B.O.D. 12-59-fold increase), most probable number (M.P.N.) Coliform counts (28-fold increase), suspended solids, nitrate, and dissolved oxygen, below the hatchery outfalls. In addition, he reported large decreases of pollution-intolerant benthic invertebrates below outfalls.

This potential to degrade water-quality has prompted at least one investigator (Yee, 1972) to suggest that primary—and perhaps secondary—treatment will be necessary for water discharged from intensive culture operations such as those proposed for oyster-, shrimp-, and catfish-rearing. Culley (1973) has pointed out that confining aquaculture waste-water in lagoons may result in periodic, large-volume releases containing toxic blue-green Algae and lowered oxygen content.

Documented cases of alterations resulting directly from aquaculture in neighboring systems are rare and restricted to situations in which the effluent has been dumped into confined bodies of water. For example, it has been suggested that intensive fish-culture using fertilizers, feedstuffs, and manure, in the arid region surrounding Lake Kinnereth, Israel, has resulted in an increased rate of eutrophication of the Lake. One investigator, however, who has studied the Lake, found little evidence to support this idea (B. Hepher, pers. comm.). In fact, he has suggested that fish-ponds actually serve as nutrient traps, because most of the organic compounds are either precipitated, lost to the atmosphere, bound by the sediments, or tied-up in fish flesh—so that little leaves the pond when it is drained.

### Beneficial Use of Organic Effluents

One interesting possibility concerns the utilization of enriched effluents from intensive aquaculture for additional culture of organisms capable of utilizing low levels of dissolved organic matter. A pilot study along these lines is being conducted as part of the Virgin Islands artificial upwelling project; it consists of taking water which has passed through tanks of oysters and using it to grow Algae in additional tanks (O. Roels, pers. comm.). Although this water has been filtered thoroughly and contains few phytoplanktonic organisms, it is rich in dissolved organic matter excreted by the inefficient oysters. The final effluent from the algal tanks is returned to the sea with about the same nutrient concentration and at the same temperature as the waters that receive it.

### Special Problems Created by Raft Culture

Probably the highest densities of organisms in present aquaculture practice are found in hanging or 'raft' culture of oysters and mussels. Maximum annual yields (meat weight) per hectare approach 50,000 kilograms in Japanese oyster culture and 500,000 kilograms for Spanish mussel rafts (Ryther, 1969). These rafts, through their sheer numbers of filter-feeders, have the ability significantly to lower downstream oxygen and phytoplankton concentrations as evidenced by lower growth-rates on the downstream sides of the rafts.

Production figures from raft culture are misleading because they do not represent the true production per hectare of estuary. The rafts are placed so that they filter a large volume of water, and the food which supports the oyster or mussel growth is actually derived from primary production over a much larger portion of the estuary than that covered by the raft. If the density of rafts is great enough, they may compete for food with natural populations of filter-feeders. It is conceivable that future intensive raft-culture could seriously affect production of natural estuarine organisms by limiting growth and causing reduced survival of larvae due to low phytoplankton densities.

Another problem associated with raft culture is the increased sedimentation rate under the raft. This results both from the baffling effect caused by impeding the flow provided by the raft and its hanging organisms, and by the continual filtering, packaging, and precipitation, of suspended particles as pseudo-feces and feces. Japanese oyster culturists have found that large rafts floating in areas of limited circulation cannot be maintained successfully for long periods of time unless the raft is moved about. This is apparently due to growth-inhibiting substances emanating from the layers of feces and pseudofeces which are deposited on the benthos under the rafts (Uyeno *et al.*, 1970). In the Philippines, hanging and stick cultures have increased sedimentation rates along some littoral and shoal-water coasts to the point that progradation of coastlines has occurred in a few places (Davis, 1956). This is particularly noticeable along the southeast shore of Manila Bay, where increased accumulation of sediments and decreased current velocities can be found (Iversen, 1968).

### Release of Toxic Chemicals

To reduce competition in culture ponds between the culture organism and unwanted animals and plants, a number of toxic chemicals are routinely employed. Included are herbicides such as sodium arsenite, chlorinated hydrocarbon and chlorinated benzene pesticides, and the fish poisons Antimycin and Rotenone. Diseases are often controlled with compounds that are only slightly less toxic than the disease itself. Lindane, Endrin, and Malathion, have all been used for control of *Argulus* parasites in carp ponds (Lahave *et al.*, 1962).

Problems arise when effluents containing residues of these chemicals are released into natural bodies of water. For example, Rotenone and Antimycin may be applied to shrimp ponds at levels sufficient to kill predaceous fishes but not affect the shrimps. If the contaminated water is then pumped out of the ponds a short time later, a massive fish-kill in the receiving body of water may result. Cases of fish-kills are particularly common after a fish-pond has been harvested by using a fish poison and then quickly emptied. Problems also arise when the culture organism is resistant to the chemical in use. This may lull the aquaculturist into believing that the water in his pond is perfectly safe when in fact it may be lethal to other, less resistant wild species (note the previously mentioned case in Arkansas).

## PHYSICAL ALTERATION OF THE ENVIRONMENT

Another potential threat from future aquaculture projects is large-scale physical alterations of the environment. Activities such as construction of ponds, diking, and blocking-off of sections of estuaries, should be carefully planned so that they do not adversely affect other, naturally productive regions.

### Changes in Circulation Patterns Within Estuaries

As Copeland (1968) has observed, small embayments depend upon large bodies of water for maintenance of circulation. This is because sufficient wave-energy for adequate flushing often cannot be generated in the short distances offered by the surface of a restricted body of water. For this reason any project which involves the construction of a permanent, solid barrier within an estuary should be planned so that (1) the enclosed area will have adequate circulation either by natural or artificial means, and (2) no natural area is disconnected from a larger body of water upon which it depends for generation of circulation.

In the first case, adverse effects are restricted to the area under cultivation: Loch Craiglin in Scotland provides an example. An attempt to close off the Loch with a permanent dam for aquaculture purposes failed owing to greatly reduced circulation, resultant stratification, and the formation of a surface layer of warm, relatively sterile water which ruined the Loch as a fish-farm (Idyll, 1970).

South Bay of the Laguna Madre in Texas provides an example of the second type of alteration to be avoided. Although in this case aquaculture was not involved, the results could be expected from badly conceived dredging and diking for culture ponds. Poorly placed spoil-banks from dredging operations associated with construction of the Brownsville ship channel effectively served to isolate South Bay from the remainder of the Laguna Madre. This was quickly followed by a decrease in circulation, an increase in sedimentation rates, smothering of the benthic sea-grass beds, drastically lowered primary production, and the creation of a shallow, practically worthless embayment (Breuer, 1962; H. T. Odum & Wilson, 1962). A few kilometers north of this Bay, a spoil-bank was constructed between the Laguna Madre and a large mud-flat. This spoil-bank, not unlike the dikes constructed for fish-ponds, prevented circulation from the lagoon over the mud-flats during normal tides. Occasionally, during autumn and spring storm-tides, the flats were flooded; but as the tide receded, water became trapped behind the spoil-bank and eventually evaporated, leaving a layer of salt. Subsequent strong winds blew this salt over near-by pasturelands, destroying several thousand acres of grass (Price, 1968).

### Increased Sedimentation from Poorly-designed Dredging and Filling

Construction of aquaculture ponds which involves dredging and filling adjacent to estuaries, should be designed so that a minimal amount of suspended particulate matter—especially of oxidizable particles—is released into the estuary. D. Frankenberg & Westerfield (1969) found that sediments, when suspended in estuarine waters, are capable of removing 535 times their own volume of oxygen from the water. D. Frankenberg (1968) has estimated that the construction in a Georgia salt-marsh of a dike three feet (91 cm) high and 12 feet (3.7 m) wide at the base would liberate enough sediment into the water to remove 334,385 milligrams of oxygen for each foot (30.5 cm) of dike constructed. This would completely remove the oxygen from 2,437 cubic feet (69,006 l) of water having a dissolved oxygen content of 4.8 mg/l.

### Interference with Freshwater Input to the Estuary

Among the most logical locations for the construction of aquaculture ponds is the strip of generally unproductive, marginal land lying behind regularly flooded estuarine marshes. Unfortunately, construction in this area, if too extensive, may block the transport of fresh water into the estuary.

Such a blockage was caused by the construction of a highway through coastal Louisiana and Mississippi (Copeland, 1968). This highway, which served effectively as a dam, formed a barrier between inland freshwater marshes and the outer estuarine marshes. The result was complete alteration of circulation patterns within the entire marsh system, saltwater intrusion into the outer marsh because of reduced flow of fresh water from inland sources and, ultimately, lowered production of commercially valuable organisms. Effects such as these from aquaculture-related construction could be avoided by spacing and arranging ponds and service roads so that serious disruptions of natural drainage patterns do not occur.

### Destruction of Productive Land Peripheral to the Estuary

As many shallow estuaries depend upon marshes for much of their input of primary production, through plant detritus introduction, destruction of these areas leads to decreased secondary production within the estuary (Odum, 1970). In the case of aquaculture, this destruction might result from the replacement of marshes by ponds, dikes, service roads, or buildings. Even when the marsh is left relatively untouched except for diking, serious alteration may occur. Diking can lead to reduction or elimination of water fluctuation, which in turn causes alteration or elimination of marsh grasses and sedges, etc. The construction of dikes in New Jersey marshes (U.S.A.) resulted in reduced tidal amplitudes and the replacement of *Spartina alterniflora* by the less productive *S. patens* (Copeland, 1968).

### Permanent Removal of Productive Estuary by Aquaculture

The diking or fencing off of estuarine areas which are already naturally fertile should be regarded with suspicion. The removal of such areas from production may adversely affect natural stocks of organisms which support traditional commercial and sport fisheries. This problem could prove especially critical for those species which depend upon estuarine refuges during their early life-histories.

One solution to this problem may be to require the aquaculture facility to release the equivalent amount of juveniles which would have been produced if the estuary had not been closed. An agreement of this sort was reached between the state of Florida and Marifarms, Inc., which leased 2,000 acres (810 ha) of public estuary near Panama City, Florida, for shrimp-raising purposes. A stipulated percentage of hatchery-reared juveniles were to be released outside the Marifarms enclosures; this does not guarantee, however, that survival of the hatchery shrimps will be of the same order of magnitude as survival of natural shrimps.

### Schemes to Raise Nutrient-rich Cold Water to the Surface

A number of projects have been proposed which would create artificial upwelling by lifting cold, nutritionally-enriched water from ocean depths to the surface. These projects range from pumping up small quantities of water through pipes into ponds, to creating extensive areas of upwelling in the open ocean by placing nuclear reactors on the sea-bed. Idyll (1970) has pointed out a number of potential ecological problems which might result from large-scale projects: (1) increased phytoplankton production and creation of murky conditions in areas where clear water normally occurs, (2) destruction of coral reefs by lowering of water temperatures, (3) changes in beaches, and (4) climatic changes.

The magnitude of potential damage from artificial upwelling would be proportional to the size of the project. Extensive upwelling created by a number of nuclear reactors might cause widespread alterations; smaller projects, such as the experimental installation at St. Croix, U.S. Virgin Islands, appear to present no serious side-effects because of (1) relatively low volumes of water, (2) the tendency of the water to warm up as it is slowly raised to the surface, and (3) the almost complete utilization of nutrients in carefully controlled aquaculture ponds.

## LIVING POLLUTANTS: INTRODUCTION OF EXOTIC ORGANISMS

As aquaculture methods become more refined and widely practiced, an increasing number of species with superior growth and food qualities will be utilized in areas outside of their natural ranges. In regions which provide suitable habitat, this may result in escapement and permanent establishment of both the culture organism and its attached parasites, predators, and pathogens. This is not a new phenomenon, of course, as attempts to improve conventional fisheries have often included intentional introduction of commercial and game species. Although these introductions have been well-intended, the transplants have frequently become harmful pests which seriously alter the biological structure of their new environment (examples are reviewed by Laycock, 1966). One reason for disruption is that the introduced species may occupy a different trophic niche from that occupied in its native habitat (Regier, 1968). In extreme cases this can result in displacement or extinction of one or more species (Allen, 1949; R. Frankenberg, 1966).

Even beneficial, intentionally-introduced species often bring unwanted travellers with them. The oyster is a case in point. As Cronin (1967) has remarked, "It is possible that the transplantation of oysters, oyster shells, and seed, has modified the distribution of more aquatic species than any other human activity." The oyster shell alone provides a habitat for a remarkable variety of protozoans, Algae, sponges, worms, coelenterates, hydrozoans, snails, and the eggs and spores of other types. Once in their new habitat, these attached organisms may create unexpected problems. The barnacle *Elminius modestus,* introduced into English waters from the southern hemisphere, has reduced oyster production by competing with oyster larvae for settling-space. Another unwelcome import in the same waters is the Oyster Drill (*Urosalpinx cinerea*), which accompanied the introduction of *Crassostrea virginica* from the east coast of North America. *Urosalpinx* has also been accidentally introduced on the west coast of North America, where it competes for oysters with another recent arrival, *Tritonalia japonica,* a drill inadvertently introduced with the Japanese Oyster, *Crassostrea gigas* (Cronin, 1967).

### Introduction of Disease Organisms

Although it is recognized that Bacteria, Fungi, and viruses, have been transferred into new areas with shipments of live fishes and invertebrates, almost nothing is known of their effect on native organisms. The introduction of animal parasites, however, because of their greater size and potential for routine identification, is much better documented (Lindroth, 1957); at least 48 aquatic parasites are known to have been transferred and established in new continents (Hoffman, 1970). Included are five species of Protozoa, 31 monogenetic trematodes, five digenetic trematodes, three nematodes, one acanthocephalan, and three copepods.

One example of a parasite which has been disseminated widely by fish culturists is *Myxosoma cerebralis,* which causes cartilage degeneration and the so-called 'whirling disease' in salmonids. Hoffman (1970) has reconstructed the probable spread of this parasite by shipments of live fishes to France, Poland, Czechoslovakia, Italy, Bulgaria, the United States, Sweden, Scotland, and South Africa. Evidence that the disease was transferred with live fish is provided by the fact that it has not been found in countries which currently prohibit the importation of salmonids, including Australia, New Zealand, Japan, England, and Canada.

Disease organisms may also be transported in the water accompanying imported fishes or invertebrates. W. R. Courtenay & C. R. Robins (pers. comm.) estimate that a minimum of three million U.S. gallons (11,355,000 l) of water per year enter the United States in this manner. They point out the great danger of introducing schistosomiasis (bilharzia) into areas where it does not currently occur, as has happened already in some areas of the Caribbean.

### Southern Florida: a Case-history of Environmental Disruption by Introduced Fishes

Southern Florida (U.S.A.) provides an example of a situation in which aquaculture, in this case the aquarium-fish industry, has permanently altered the native fish fauna (discussed at length by Lachner *et al.,* 1970). Of the 450 tropical aquarium fish-farms and importers in the United States, most are located in Florida (Axelrod, 1971). These fish-farms generally cover ten to twenty or more acres (4-8 or more ha) and are often built upon land which is subject to periodic flooding. Effluents from these ponds are frequently dumped into adjacent canals and streams, usually through open, unscreened pipes. Little effort has been expended to prevent accidental escape, and often entire ponds, including all of their fishes, are flushed into adjacent bodies of water.

It is not surprising to find that waterways

in the vicinity of these fish-farms often contain more species of exotic fishes than native forms (Ogilvie, 1969). W. R. Courtenay & C. R. Robins (pers. comm.) list as established Florida residents 16 species of exotic fishes, 8 of which are known to have been introduced from fish-farms. Included in the latter group are several species which have proved to be especially destructive. The Pike Killifish (*Belonesox belizanus*), which is well established and widely distributed in Florida, is an active predator that is capable of removing all small fishes from restricted bodies of water (Lachner *et al.*, 1970). But perhaps the most harmful introduction to date is that of the Walking Catfish (*Clarias batrachus*) (*see* Buckow, 1969; Idyll, 1969), which competes with and may deplete native fishes—especially the centrarchids.

### Regulation

Regulations restricting the movement of diseased fishes are not new (FAO, 1968), although full recognition of the dangers inherent in transplantation of even apparently healthy fishes has developed slowly and has often been hindered by the aquaculture industry. The United States, for example, recently enacted the U.S. Import Law of 1967 (Title 50—Wildlife and Fisheries, Part 13) which restricts the import of trout from areas where two serious salmonid diseases, whirling disease and viral haemorrhagic septicaemia, are endemic. Shortly thereafter, Senate Bill 1151, which would have given the Secretary of the Interior power to control (inspect) interstate movement of fish and shellfish suspected of carrying diseases, was prevented from reaching committee action because of opposition from fish farmers (Anon., 1970*b*).

### Aquaculture Operations as Disease Generators

The densely-packed conditions created by aquaculture encourage a greater incidence of disease than that found in natural populations. An aquaculture pond can be shown to have many similarities with a culture flask or test-tube, suggesting an ability to produce extreme concentrations and, possibly, new strains of Bacteria and viruses in a relatively short time. These in turn could be spread to natural populations.

Evidence for such occurrences is admittedly limited, although whirling disease, which is usually restricted to hatcheries and ponds, has been known to escape into wild populations (Hoffman, 1970). Unusually high concentrations of oysters, such as are found in culture operations, have been shown by Andrews (1965) to stimulate epizootics of *Dermocystidium marinum* which then spread to areas of lower host concentrations.

Finally, it should be pointed out that construction of aquaculture ponds provides additional habitat for certain disease organisms that are dangerous to Man—particularly schistosomiasis. W. R. Courtenay & C. R. Robins (pers. comm.) mention that the construction of ponds for *Tilapia* culture in Puerto Rico have increased the habitat for the fluke responsible for schistosomiasis and its intermediate snail host.

## SUMMARY

Aquaculture, like any other industry, has the potential to generate pollutants for which the aquaculturist may be held legally responsible. Some of the pollutants created by aquaculture operations include both organic materials originating from excess primary production or inefficient supplemental feeding and toxic compounds such as herbicides, pesticides, and fish poisons. It is possible to utilize excess organic effluents for beneficial purposes such as culturing additional algal and animal species.

Construction of aquaculture facilities can result in physical alteration of the environment—including changes in circulation patterns, increased sedimentation, interference with freshwater input to the estuary, and direct destruction of productive areas. Intensive raft-culture may interfere with natural estuarine production.

Finally, the potentially serious threat from widespread dissemination of culture species is discussed. Possible problems include introduction of pathogens and all of the ecological problems that are commonly associated with introduced species.

## REFERENCES


Allen, K. R. (1949). The New Zealand Grayling, a vanishing species. *Tuatara,* **2**(1), pp. 22-7.

Andrews, J. D. (1965). Infection experiments in Nature with *Dermocystidium marinum* in Chesapeake Bay. *Chesapeake Science,* **6**(1), pp. 60-7.

Anon. (1970*a*). Minnow farmer faces Arkansas pollution charge. *American Fish Farmer,* September, p. 21.

Anon. (1970*b*). Aquaculture legislation dies with adjournment. *American Fish Farmer,* October, p. 24.

Axelrod, H. R. (1971). *The Aquarium Fish Industry–1971.* T.F.H. Publications, Jersey City, N.J.: 7 pp.

Breuer, J. P. (1962). An ecological survey of the lower Laguna Madre of Texas, 1953-1959. *Univ. Texas Inst. Marine Science Publications,* **8**, pp. 153-83.

Buckow, E. (1969). Exotics: New threat to U.S. waters. *Field and Stream,* May, pp. 16-28.

Copeland, B. J. (1968). Impoundment systems. Pp. 1101-12 in *Coastal Ecological Systems of the United States.* Unpublished report to the U.S. Federal Water Pollution Control Administration (FWPCA), 1878 pp., illustr.

Cronin, L. E. (1967). The role of Man in estuarine processes. Pp. 667-89 in *Estuaries* (Ed. G. Lauff). Amer. Assoc. Adv. Sci., Washington, D.C.: xv + 757 pp., illustr.

Culley, D. C. (1973). Raceways; exotic species most affected by proposed E.P.A. discharge permits. *American Fish Farmer,* July, pp. 9-12.

Davis, J. H. (1956). Influences of man upon coast lines. Pp. 504-21 in *Man's Role in Changing the Face of the Earth* (Ed. W. L. Thomas). Univ. of Chicago Press, Chicago: 714 pp., illustr.

FAO (1968). Comparative study of laws and regulations governing the international traffic in live fish and fish eggs. *FAO Legislative Branch,* FI/EIFAC 68/SC, pp. 11-7.

Frankenberg, D. (1968). *Oxygen Depletion Effects.* In a report to the State of Georgia on the proposed leasing of state-owned lands for phosphate mining: C-16-C-18, 27 pp. (mimeogr.).

Frankenberg, D. & Westerfield, C. W. (1969). Oxygen demand and oxygen depletion capacity of sediments from Wassaw Sound, Georgia. *Bulletin Georgia Academy of Sciences,* 1969, pp. 29-36.

Frankenberg, R. (1966). Fishes of the family Galaxiidae. *Australian Natural History,* **15**(5), pp. 161-4.

Hinshaw, R. N. (1973). Pollution as a result of fish cultural activities. *E.P.A. Report No. EPA-R3-73-009.* U.S. Government Printing Office, Washington, D.C.: 209 pp.

Hoffman, G. L. (1970). Intercontinental and transcontinental dissemination and transfaunation of fish parasites with emphasis on whirling disease (*Myxosoma cerebralis*). Pp. 69-81 in *A Symposium on Diseases of Fishes and Shellfishes* (Ed. S. F. Snieszko). Special Publication No. 5, American Fisheries Society, Washington: 528 pp., illustr.

Idyll, C. P. (1969). New Florida resident, the Walking Catfish. *National Geographic Magazine,* **135**(6), pp. 846-51.

Idyll, C. P. (1970). *The Sea Against Hunger.* Thomas Y. Crowell, New York: 315 pp., illustr.

Iversen, E. S. (1968). *Farming the Edge of the Sea.* Fishing News (Books), London: 301 pp., illustr.

Lachner, E. A., Robins, C. R. & Courtenay, W. R., Jr. (1970). Exotic fishes and other aquatic organisms introduced into North America. *Smithsonian Contributions to Zoology,* **59**, 29 pp.

Lahave, M., Shilo, M. & Sarig, S. (1962). Development of resistance to Lindane in *Argulus* populations of fish-ponds. *Bamidgeh,* **14**(4), pp. 67-76.

Laycock, G. (1966). *The Alien Animals: The*

*Story of Imported Wildlife*. Natural History Press, Garden City, N.Y.: 240 pp.

Liao, P. D. (1970). Pollution potential of salmonid fish hatcheries. *Water and Sewage Works*, **117**(12), pp. 291-7.

Lindroth, C. H. (1957). *The Faunal Connections Between Europe and North America*. Wiley, New York: 228 pp.

Odum, H. T. & Wilson, R. F. (1962). Further studies on reaeration and metabolism of Texas bays, 1958-1960. *Univ. Texas Inst. Marine Science Publications*, **8**, pp. 23-5.

Odum, W. E. (1970). Insidious alteration of the estuarine environment. *Trans. Amer. Fisheries Society*, **99**(4), pp. 836-47.

Ogilvie, V. E. (1969). *Illustrated Checklist of Fishes Collected from the L-15 Canal in Palm Beach County, Florida*. Unpublished report to the Florida Game and Fresh Water Fish Comm., 11 pp. (mimeogr.).

Price, W. A. (1968). *Abatement of Blowing Salt Conditions Inland from Laguna Madre, Texas*. Report to Coastal Bend Regional Planning Comm., 27 pp. (mimeogr.).

Regier, H. A. (1968). The potential misuse of exotic fishes as introductions. *A Symposium on Introductions of Exotic Species*. Department of Lands and Forests, Ottawa, Research Report, **82**, pp. 91-111.

Ryther, J. H. (1969). The potential of the estuary for shellfish production. *Proc. National Shellfisheries Assoc.*, **59**, pp. 18-22.

Uyeno, F., Kawaguchi, K., Terada, N. & Okada, T. (1970). Decomposition, effluent and deposition of phytoplankton in an estuarine pearl oyster area. *Reports of the Faculty of Fisheries, Prefectural University of Mie*, **7**(1), pp. 7-41.

Yee, W. C. (1972). Thermal aquaculture: engineering and economics. *Environmental Science & Technology*, **6**(3), pp. 232-7.

# 39. Control of Estuarine Pollution

JEROME B. GILBERT   RONALD B. ROBIE*   1971

## INTRODUCTION

In the area of environmental concern, there is a growing awareness that nearly every one of man's activities affects the environment. Our history has shown that many seemingly innocuous decisions which do not have immediate adverse effects have proven to be damaging over extended periods of time. The present condition of our nation's estuaries serves as a glaring example of this reality.

Estuaries[1] are one of the nation's most important assets. They are utilized for a wide range of commercial, industrial, and recreational activities while simultaneously serving a vital role in the natural cycles of fish, animal and plant life.

Because of the natural mixing of fresh and salt waters, the estuarine environment produces a wide variety of living organisms, from microscopic species to large numbers of fish and shellfish, birds, and mammals. Many species, such as clams and oysters, spend their entire life cycles in the estuaries. Others, particularly shrimp, migrate from the sea to estuarine nursery areas. In these rich waters, they grow to sub-adult size before returning to the sea to complete their life cycles. The anadromous species, such as salmon and striped bass, pass through the estuaries to their spawning grounds farther upstream, and the young return through the estuaries to the ocean. At least two-thirds of the animal populations in the oceans spend an essential portion of their life cycle in

* The authors are indebted to James Wernecke for his research assistance. The views expressed herein, however, are those of the authors and not of the State of California.

1. For the purposes of this article an estuary will be defined as a body of water which has a free connection to the sea and within which sea water is mixed with fresh water derived from land drainage. See Pritchard, *What is an Estuary: Physical Viewpoint*, in Estuaries (G. Lauff ed. 1967).

Jerome B. Gilbert is a civil engineer and consultant with offices in Sacramento, California; he also teaches at the University of California at Davis. He was executive officer of the State Water Resources Control Board in California from 1969 to 1972.

Ronald B. Robie is a lawyer and adjunct professor at the University of the Pacific (McGeorge School of Law) and has been a member of the State Water Resources Control Board in California since 1969. Before that, he was a consultant to the Assembly Water Committee, California Legislature.

From *Natural Resources Journal*, Vol. 11, No. 2, pp. 256-273, 1971. Reprinted with authors' revisions and light editing and by permission from the authors and *Natural Resources Journal* published by the University of New Mexico School of Law, Albuquerque, New Mexico.

estuarine waters or are dependent on species that do. Innumerable waterfowl and shorebirds depend on the plant and animal organisms of the coastal zone for their food. Many winter and nest in these waters.

The base for all animal life in estuaries is the abundant variety of plant growth, from mangroves to eelgrass and algae. They are supported by the mixing and flushing action of the tides and the organic nutrients which collect to produce the rich bottoms and wetlands.[2]

Estuaries' role in the support of fish and wildlife is inconsistent with their intensive use by man. This inconsistency extends to both competition between resource use and resource protection. Rivers bring accumulations of municipal and industrial waste[3] and urban runoff adds fertilizers and nutrients. Excessive siltation from upstream land use practices and reclamation activities of adjacent land owners have resulted in the filling of extensive water areas.[4] Upstream diversions may change the position of the fresh water-salt water interface in the estuarine zone, thereby affecting fish and wildlife habitats.[5]

Concurrent with public determination to end pollution of the environment has been rising concern over the fate of our nation's estuaries[6]—concern that ranges in direction from the serious effects of such pollutants as chlorinated hydrocarbons[7] to the increasingly demonstrated adverse effects of numerous toxic substances upon the estuarine environment.[8] Due to the complex nature of the estuarine environment,[9] and the fact estuarine areas are population centers,[10] there is a tendency to suggest they must be considered and managed as individual environmental units. But, estuaries are not "the problem." It is the watershed, it is regional, it is metropolitan. Estuaries depend on land and water management; they are assaulted from all sides by organic and sediment im-

2. U.S. President's Council on Environmental Quality, First Annual Report on Environmental Quality 176 (1970) [hereinafter cited as Council Report].
3. For example, a limited investigation of pesticides undertaken as part of the San Francisco Bay-Delta Water Quality Control Program found that between 10,000 and 20,000 pounds of chlorinated hydrocarbons entered the Bay-Delta system in 1965. The data indicated that from twenty to forty per cent of the chlorinated hydrocarbons entering the system were discharged in municipal and industrial wastes. Kaiser Engineers and Assoc. Firms, Final Report to the State of California, San Francisco Bay-Delta Water Quality Control Program, at II-8, XII-23 (1969).
4. A recent study rated 62 per cent of California estuaries as severely modified by landfill activity. U.S. Department of the Interior, Fish and Wildlife Service, 1 National Estuary Study 25 (1970).
5. Migrating birds, anadromous fish, shellfish and a wide variety of aquatic life depend upon a sometimes delicate balance for their survival. An alteration in the chemical or physical characteristics of environmental zones can severely alter the number and variety of species.
6. Estuarine problems have been the subject of a number of Congressional Committee Hearings. See, *Hearings on the Nation's Estuaries: San Francisco Bay and Delta, California Before the Subcommittee on Conservation and Natural Resources of the House Committee on Government Operations,* 91st Cong., 1st Sess., (1969); *Hearings on the National Oceanographic Program Before the Subcommittee on Oceanography of the House Committee on Merchant Marine and Fisheries,* 91st Cong., 1st Sess., pts 1 & 2 (1969). Estuaries have also been the subject of several recent federal studies. See U.S. Dept. of the Interior, National Estuary Study (1970), and U.S. Fed. Water Pollution Control Admin., National Estuarine Pollution Study (1968).
7. Chlorinated hydrocarbon pesticides are a group of insecticides that contain at least carbon, hydrogen and chlorine. In general, they are persistent in the environment, have an affinity for fatty tissue and are toxic to numerous insects. Examples are DDT, Dieldrin, Endrin, Chlordane and Toxaphene.
8. Manufacturing processes are becoming more complex creating greater amounts of exotic wastes potentially toxic to humans and aquatic life; and the effects of current levels of such substances as cadmium, lead and mercury are still not fully understood. Council Report, *supra* note 2, at 52.
9. The estuarine environment is continually in a state of change. Salt and fresh water concentrations are subject to any variation in the level of fresh water input. In turn, fresh water input is determined by upstream use, seasonal variation in the weather, and variances in the year to year precipitation levels. *See* U.S. Fed. Water Pollution Control Admin., Marine Biology and Pollution Ecology Training Manual, at C23-1, (1970).
10. Eight of our most populous metropolitan areas are located in estuarine zones and Great Lakes areas, as are 15 of the largest U.S. cities. National Estuary Study, *supra* note 4, at 50.

balances, toxic substance accumulation, and salinity intrusion.[11]

Water pollution control efforts until recently were designed primarily to protect the quality of water used for consumptive purposes, and since estuarine waters are not generally sources of domestic water, the control of estuarine pollution has lagged behind the control of pollution in entirely fresh water areas.[12] A number of other factors have contributed to the estuaries' falling behind in the race for environmental protection and enhancement, including problems regarding the effectiveness of pollution control efforts as well as difficulties in efforts to measure pollution in an estuarine environment. This article will attempt to shed light on some of these problems.

## THE LEGAL BASIS FOR CONTROL

The scientific problems associated with water quality control in estuaries, which are discussed elsewhere in this article, are more than matched by the problems caused by the nation's intricate governmental systems and by the political values relating to estuarine management. Governmental responsibility is divided between federal, state and local jurisdictions.[13] Various laws dealing with estuarine management are often times conflicting, and unsettled public use rights,[14] disputed titles and overlapping provisions of law make difficult the orderly administration of our estuarine resources. This section will discuss the estuarine control activities of the several levels of government.

### Federal Government

#### Constitutional Basis of Authority

The federal role in estuarine management is supported by a number of broad congressional grants of authority. Because estuarine areas are often extensively involved in commerce, the "Commerce Power"[15] affords the federal government its most significant basis from which to regulate estuarine-related activities. The Federal Water Pollution Control Act,[16] which applies to interstate and coastal waters,[17] and the regulation of navigation, principally by the United States Army Corps of Engineers,[18] are the primary federal activities based on this power.

Under the "Property Power,"[19] the federal government exercises influence in estuaries through control of property owned by the United States. Similarly, under the General Welfare Clause,[20] the United States, through the Department of the Interior's

11. Salinity intrusion extends to the movement of saltwater into groundwater basins as well as up streams that flow into the estuary. For a more complete discussion of this problem see Gindler and Holburt, *Water Salinity Problems: Approaches to Legal and Engineering Solutions,* 9 Natural Resources J. 329 (1969).

12. President's Commission on Marine Science, Engineering and Resources, Our Nation and the Sea, A Plan for National Action 74 (1969).

13. U.S. Dept. of Interior, Fish and Wildlife Service, 2 National Estuary Study 212 (1970).

14. This is a cause of confusion to many states. Recently, the California Supreme Court held that historic use of shoreline areas is to be a major consideration in determining public use. The Court also stated that the courts should encourage public use of shoreline areas whenever that can be done consistently with the federal Constitution. Gion v. Santa Cruz, 2 Cal. App.3d 29, 465 P.2d 50, (1970). For a discussion of the subject see Sax, *The Public Trust Doctrine in Natural Resources Law: Effective Judicial Intervention,* 68 Mich. L. Rev. 473 (1970).

15. U.S. Const. art. I, § 8, para. 3–to regulate commerce with foreign nations and among the several states. Extended to include activities "affecting commerce." See County of Mobile v. Kimball, 102 U.S. 691 (1881).

16. Water Pollution Control Act, 62 Stat. 1155 (1948), *as amended* 33 U.S.C. 1151 et seq. [hereinafter the Federal Water Pollution Control Act in its amended form is cited as F.W.P.C.A.].

17. F.W.P.C.A. § 10(a) "The pollution of interstate or navigable waters . . . shall be subject to abatement as provided by this Act."

18. In 1935 Congress provided generally that investigations and improvements of rivers, harbors and other waterways shall be under the jurisdiction and prosecuted by the Department of the Army under the direction of its Secretary and supervision of the Chief of Engineers. Act of Aug. 30, 1935, § 1, 49 Stat. 1028, 33 U.S.C. 540.

19. U.S. Const. art. IV § 3, para. 2.

20. U.S. Const. art. I, § 8, para. 1.

Bureau of Reclamation, constructs water storage projects on the tributaries of estuaries. The operation of these projects can have a significant impact upon the estuaries and the land and water resources that surround them.[21]

The "Treaty Power"[22] provides an interesting basis for authority inasmuch as the United States is a party to two major multilateral treaties relating to pollution of the sea by oil[23] and to a number of treaties and agreements with Mexico and Canada that affect the quality and use of boundary waters.[24]

### Administrative Regulation

With constitutionally vested powers and the broad interpretation thereof forming a base, Congress has assigned authority for a number of estuarine-related activities to various federal agencies.[25]

The Department of the Interior has major administrative responsibilities in the estuarine zone. The Estuarine Areas Act of 1968[26] gives the Secretary of the Interior review authority over federal development activities affecting estuarine resources. Furthermore, numerous agencies within the Department have administrative responsibilities ranging from the study and protection of wildlife to the development of water resources that will eventually affect the estuary.

The recently formed Environmental Protection Agency,[27] which houses the principal federal regulatory functions in the environmental field, is significantly involved in estuarine management. The Agency's Water Quality Office oversees the establishment and enforcement of federal water quality standards for interstate and coastal waters. It also administers grant programs to assist states and public agencies in the administration of water quality programs, research, and construction of water quality control facilities.[28] The construction of treatment facilities with federal financial assistance has been the major factor in the upgrading of the quality of waste discharges to estuarine waters in many parts of the country.[29]

21. For example, the massive Central Valley Project in California, undertaken as a reclamation project, significantly affects the flow of water through the Sacramento/San Joaquin Delta and the full effect of this project upon fish and wildlife and water quality is not yet known. See United States v. Gerlach Livestock Co., 339 U.S. 725 (1950).

22. U.S. Const. art. II, § 2, para. 2. Treaties made under the authority of the United States shall be the supreme law of the land. U.S. Const. art. VI, para. 2.

23. The International Convention for the Prevention of Pollution of the Seas by Oil. 12 U.S.T. 2989 (1961). The United States Convention of the High Seas, [1962] 13 U.S.T. 2313. Recently, President Nixon made a proposal for a new treaty that would, among other things, protect the ocean from pollution. Wkly. Comp. Presidential Docs., May 25, 1970, 677-678.

24. The International Boundary and Water Commission, United States and Mexico. Rio Grande, Colo., and Tijuana Treaty, 59 Stat. 1219, T.S. No. 994. The Boundary Waters Treaty, 1909, 36 Stat. 2448, T.S. No. 548, authorized the creation of the International Joint Commission of the United States and Canada.

25. This has resulted in some confusion between agencies. Activities of one agency will often conflict or cancel the efforts of another. See *Federal Pollution Attack Gains Steam, But Long-Term Outlook Remains Cloudy*, 2 Government Executive 50-52 (1970).

26. 16 U.S.C. § § 1221-26 (1968). The Act authorized a general study and inventory of estuaries (See § 1222), and requires all federal agencies in planning for water and land resource use and development to give consideration to estuaries, their natural resources, and their importance for commercial and industrial developments (See § 1224).

27. See Reorganization Plan No. 3 (H.R. Doc. No. 91-364) Operative Dec. 2, 1970. The Agency has assumed responsibilities formerly held by the Atomic Energy Commission regulating radioactivity from nuclear installations, which often are or will be located adjacent to or within estuaries. In addition, the Agency has also assumed responsibilities formerly held by the Dept. of Health, Education and Welfare and administered through the Environmental Health Service including functions exercised by: The National Air Pollution Control Administration, the Environmental Control Administration and the Air Quality Advisory Board, also the functions in regard to establishing tolerances for pesticide chemicals and the functions of the Bureaus of: Solid Waste Management, Water Hygiene, and Radiological Health.

28. F.W.P.C.A. § § 6-8.

29. The nation's municipal waste-handling systems show an investment of $880 million for the year

The Defense Department has considerable influence in estuarine areas due to the presence of a number of military installations in these areas and the active role the Army Corps of Engineers has played through its civil works program.

Through activities of the Coast Guard, the Department of Transportation also performs a number of service activities directed at the beneficial use of estuarine waters. The Coast Guard is charged with the enforcement of federal laws in the navigable waters of the United States, and with the maintenance and operation of aids to navigation.[30]

Many federal agencies and laws also indirectly affect estuarine areas.[31] For example, a recently enacted provision of the Federal Water Pollution Control Act[32] adds the consideration of environmental factors to the existing statutory authority of many federal agencies, the most prominent of which is the Corps of Engineers.[33] Furthermore, considerable federal control is exercised over state and local actions through the review responsibilities in assorted federal grant programs other than those contained in the Federal Water Pollution Control Act.[34]

### State and Local Government

Generally, state and local governments have the most direct authority in estuarine areas. The most substantial basis for their regulation of estuarine activities falls under the so-called police power.[35] This power supports state water quality regulation and land-use controls.

Many states have delegated significant authority[36] in estuarine management and land use to local government,[37] and in some cases these local controls are protected from state legislative interference by so-called "home rule" provisions under which municipal affairs or matters not of statewide significance are constitutionally protected powers of local government.[38]

1969. This amount, however, did little more than cover replacement and growth needs developed in the same year. Total investment requirements will conservatively amount to $10 billion over the years 1970-74 if all existing deficiencies are corrected and no new deficiencies incurred. U.S. Department of the Interior, Federal Water Pollution Control Administration, The Economics of Clear Water, Summary Report 5 (1970). Recent estimates prepared during Congressional action on amendments to the Federal Water Pollution Control Act range from $15-25 billion between 1972 and 1977.

30. See 14 US.C., Ch. 5 (Supp. III), 33 U.S.C., Ch. 7, 33 U.S.C. 157. Also, F.W.P.C.A. § 13 provides that the secretary of the department in which the Coast Guard is operating is charged with the enforcement of federal standards in respect to the control of sewage from vessels.

31. For instance, the U.S. Forest Service, Department of Agriculture, manages the forestry aspect of watershed protection and 12 national forests involve lands that drain directly into estuarine areas. U.S. Department of the Interior, 3 National Estuarine Pollution Study, at V-27 (1969). Presently, under the Environmental Policy Act of 1969 (Pub. L. No. 91-190, Jan. 1, 1970), all federal agencies are required to submit reports regarding the environmental impact of their proposed actions. See § 102.

32. F.W.P.C.A. § 21(b). Applicants for a federal license or permit to conduct any activity that may result in a discharge into the navigable waters of the United States are required to submit a certification from the state in which the discharge will originate to the effect that activity will not violate applicable water quality standards.

33. Also, F.W.P.C.A. § 21(a) requires each federal agency having jurisdiction over any real property, a facility, or engaged in any federal public works project to insure compliance with applicable water quality standards.

34. A number of grant programs administered by the Departments of the Interior, Defense, Agriculture, and Housing and Urban Development directly affect estuarine management. For example, see California Assembly Committee on Water, Handbook of Federal and State Programs of Financial Assistance for Water Development (1972 ed.).

35. The inherent and plenary power in states over persons and property which enables the people to prohibit all things inimical to comfort, safety, health, and welfare of society. Drysdale v. Prudden, 195 N.C. 722, 143 S.E. 530, 536 (1928).

36. Generally, local government authority stems entirely from powers delegated by the parent state.

37. Notably, a few states have maintained or reasserted their land-use powers. See Hawaii Rev. Laws § 205-10 (1968) and [6] Me. Rev. Stat. Ann. Tit. 12 § 681-89 (Supp. 1970).

38. Article XI, § § 6 and 8(j) of California's Constitution gives charter cities the power to "make and enforce all laws and regulations in respect to municipal affairs, subject only to the restrictions and limitations provided in their several charters."

Generally, state activities in estuarine management are concentrated in state water pollution control agencies.[39] For the most part, these pollution control efforts have been designed to regulate municipal and industrial waste discharges.

There has been a trend toward establishing special purpose governmental agencies devoted to specialized problems affecting estuaries or a particular estuary. One of the most notable examples of the latter was the establishment in California of the San Francisco Bay Conservation and Development Commission.[40] The basic function of the Commission is to control the filling of San Francisco Bay, an activity which has already reduced the surface area of the Bay from 700 square miles to slightly over 400 square miles. The remarkable support the Commission received from the California public was shown in 1969 when the California Legislature made the Commission permanent and expanded its jurisdiction to include all the territory located between the shoreline of San Francisco Bay and a line 100 feet landward.[41]

39. A discussion of those rights, remedies and defenses relating to water quality is presented in 3 Gindler, Waters and Water Rights 37-195 (1967). For a summary of state water pollution control agencies see Hines, *Nor Any Drop To Drink: Public Regulation of Water Quality,* 52 Iowa L. Rev. 186 (1966-67). However, the California Water Code provides that, "In acting upon applications to appropriate water, the board shall consider water quality control plans which have been established . . . and may subject such appropriations to such terms and conditions as it finds are necessary to carry out such plans." (Sec. 1258) West. Supp. 1970. Thus water quality considerations are an integral part of water rights administration.

40. Created in 1965 by the McAteer-Petris Act Cal. Govt. Code § § 66600-66653 [West 1966], the Commission is charged with responsibility for preparing "a comprehensive and enforceable plan for the conservation of the water of the bay and the development of its shoreline." For background on the Commission and its activities see: Committee on Government Operations, Protecting America's Estuaries: The San Francisco Bay-Delta 7-12 (1970).

41. Cal Govt. Code § 66610(b) (West Supp. 1970).

## Conflicts and Limitations

### Federal–State

Much of the active disagreement between state and federal governments concerns the ownership of submerged lands.[42] In 1953, Congress attempted to resolve this conflict with passage of the Submerged Lands Act,[43] which placed title in the coastal states to the submerged lands within their boundaries, defined their seaward boundaries as extending three geographical miles from the coastline (three marine leagues into the Gulf of Mexico), and placed these lands and their resources under applicable state law.[44] However, because coastlines consist of numerous indentations and extensions and because many coastal states have developed and extended authority over coastal islands, the definition and design of coastline boundary standards and the seaward extension of state authority are still the subject of debate.[45]

President Nixon's treaty proposal of May 23, 1970[46] includes a recommendation that would establish a 12-mile territorial sea. This proposal could have a direct effect upon the regulation of estuarine pollution. Pollution of the sea is subject to the action of the tide, currents and winds. Discharges into the sea will, in many instances, float toward the coastal zone and result in degradation of the estuarine environment just as discharges into the coastal zone will have an effect on the sea. Because the President's proposal would extend United States' jurisdiction over a 12-mile area, pollution standards and regulations that include estuarine considerations could be initiated. However, the questions of

42. See United States v. California, 332 U.S. 19 (1947); also United States v. Louisiana, 394 U.S. 11 (1969).

43. 43 U.S.C. § § 1301-15 (1953).

44. *Id.* § 1311.

45. See United States v. California, 381 U.S. 139 (1965); also United States v. Louisiana, 394 U.S. 11 (1969).

46. See The International Convention for the Prevention of Pollution of the Seas by Oil, *supra* note 23.

authority allocations between the federal and state governments would still be unresolved. Proposed legislation was introduced in the 91st Congress providing for state planning jurisdiction over offshore areas in which the concerned states have a legitimate interest.[47]

Another conflict has been the scope of regulation which the federal government could exercise under the Federal Water Pollution Control Act. Estuarine waters are covered by the Act because they are defined as "interstate waters."[48] The Act provides that state water quality standards for estuaries are subject to federal approval,[49] and if they are unsatisfactory the federal government may impose standards.[50]

In 1970 acting under Executive order 11574 (December 23, 1970), the U.S. Army Corps of Engineers began to require waste discharge permits of all U.S. industries discharging to navigable waters and their tributaries. This directly duplicated the programs of many states including California, Michigan, New York and others. But it added uniformity on a national basis potentially strengthening some weak state and local efforts. The statutory authority for this program is the Rivers and Harbors Act of 1899 (33 U.S.C. 401-413; Sec. 407 is referred to as the "Refuse Act"). The act is not designed to cope with modern pollution problems and Congress appears ready to supplant the whole Corps effort (few permits had been issued by the end of 1971) with a comprehensive national regulation program administered by EPA and the states. See S. 2770 and HR 11896, 92nd Congress, 1st Session.

### State-Local

Probably of more concern from a practical standpoint than federal/state conflicts are the self-imposed limitations on state ability to regulate estuarine areas. For example, despite the "public trust doctrine,"[51] many coastal states have transferred ownership of submerged lands to private individuals or local government[52] with the result that the most direct state basis for regulating the use of these lands has been lost. Only a few states have provided comprehensive state regulations covering coastal activity and development, including the placing of structures.[53] However, as with any exercise of the police power, a governmental agency must be able to meet changing judicial interpretations as to what constitutes the taking of property without just compensation.[54] This question was raised during the consideration of legislation to extend the San Francisco Bay Conservation and Development Commission's authority to include the regulation of structures on the shoreline.[55]

47. S.2802, S.3183 and S.3460, 91st Cong. (1969-70). Only one of these bills would cover the proposed 12-mile territorial sea extension (S.3183 which defines coastal zone as extending "seaward to the outer limit of the United States territorial sea"). All of these bills reserve in the Federal Government the right to review and approve the states' planning or operating programs for their coastal zones.

48. 6 U.S. Dept. of the Interior, Fish and Wildlife Service, National Estuary Study, at E-2 (1970).

49. F.W.P.C.A. § 10.

50. *Id.*

51. Under this doctrine title to the tidelands is held in trust by the state to be used by the people. The state is obligated to protect the public rights of navigation, fishing and commerce. See Pollard's Lessee v. Hagon, 44 U.S. (3 How.) 212,229 (1844). See also Council Report, *supra* note 2 at 176.

52. Exceptions include Hawaii, Texas and Alaska which own their estuarine zones. National Estuarine Pollution Study, *supra* note 31, at V-133-34.

53. Massachusetts, Connecticut and North Carolina have wetlands protection laws while Hawaii, Wisconsin, and to some extent Oregon have exercised statewide powers over the contiguous dry lands. Council Report, *supra* note 2, at 178. In 1972, several attempts were made to provide for state regulation of California's coastal activities, but they failed to gain legislative approval. See California Senate Bills. Also California Assembly Bills.

54. U.S. Const. amend. V commands that "private property [shall not] be taken for public use, without just compensation." The problem of what constitutes a compensable taking of property has long been a source of confusion to scholars and courts.

55. San Francisco Bay Conservation and Development Commission, San Francisco Bay Plan 3-4, 37-38 (1969).

Maine's Wetlands Act,[56] which was designed to protect the ecology of coastal areas, recently failed to meet the test of substantive due process.[57]

Problems are also created by the frequent reluctance of local governments to establish and implement land-use plans which maximize environmental protection in estuarine areas. A local government's most important legal tools in this regard are zoning and taxation. However, local agencies are frequently restricted by a relatively small tax base and are thus prevented from the purchase of estuarine areas. This situation also tends to encourage local planning bodies to accept industrial development (which increases employment and tax revenues) at the expense of environmental protection. Frequently, even when estuarine areas are zoned for protection of environmental values, special-use allocations or subsequent rezoning for industrial and commercial activities result in degradation of the environment.[58] Clearly, local government has given priority to its tax base and lip service to conservation. It would appear that significant state or federal financial assistance to local government will be necessary if local efforts at limiting land use in estuarine areas are to be successful. As an alternative, special tax treatment of the lands involved could be considered.

In addition to being limited by financial and special interest pressures, local government is frequently limited in its ability to manage an estuary because of areal limitations in governmental jurisdiction. Typically, an estuarine area is under the jurisdiction of numerous cities, counties and other special-purpose governmental agencies which frequently have differing tax bases, powers and estuary-related priorities. Under the best of circumstances, even a limited degree of coordination among local government concerns in estuarine areas is difficult to obtain.[59] More difficulty arises when an estuary involves more than one state. The northeastern United States has witnessed the development of several compacts designed to administer a cooperative multi-state effort of estuary protection. Of these, the Tri-State[60] Compact and the Delaware River Basin Compact[61] have the broadest range of activities in relation to estuarine water quality. Although these compacts recognize the need for state-level administrative cooperation, studies have indicated their effectiveness has been limited and that many of the signatory states continue to provide administrative controls outside the framework of their respective compacts.[62]

56. Me. Rev. Stats. Ann. Tit. 12 § § 4701-09 (1970).
57. See Maine v. Johnson, 265 A.2d 711 (1970).
58. National Estuarine Pollution Study, *supra* note 31, at V-147, V-155.

## California: A Case in Point

The San Francisco Bay-Delta Estuary, located at the confluence of the Sacramento and San Joaquin rivers at the head of Suisun and San Francisco Bays, is the most important estuary in the state. The Central Valley of California, which comprises nearly 40 per cent of the state's total area, is tributary to the Delta and more than 5.75 million people reside in the adjacent counties.[63]

California has a comprehensive and broadly interpreted[64] state water quality control act[65] designed to protect the quality

59. This situation prompted the Planning and Conservation League of California to comment: "The odds against a thousand city governments regulating an end to boosterism in the coastal zone of California are roughly equivalent to the classic probability of a million monkeys pecking away at typewriters and someday producing 'Hamlet.' " The Riverside Press Enterprise, Sept. 20, 1970.
60. New Jersey, New York and Connecticut.
61. Delaware, New Jersey, New York, Pennsylvania and the U.S.
62. National Estuarine Pollution Study, *supra* note 31, at V-201.
63. Final Report to the State of California, San Francisco Bay Delta Water Quality Program, *supra* note 3, at XIV-1 to XIV-35.
64. See 26 Op. Cal. Att'y Gen. 88 (1956); 27 Op. Cal. Att'y Gen. 482 (1956) and 43 Op. Cal. Att'y Gen. 302 (1964).
65. The Porter-Cologne Water Quality Control Act, Cal. Water Code § § 13000-13951 (West Supp. 1970).

of state waters[66] from the discharge of waste[67] from all sources.[68] Administration of water quality control is carried out by a five-member, full-time State Water Resources Control Board,[69] and nine, nine-member[70] decentralized regional boards which act on an area wide basis. Supervision, budgetary review, approval of regional water quality plans, resolution of disputes between regional boards,[71] and appeal responsibility are placed in the State Board.[72]

Other state agencies which affect the San Francisco Bay-Delta Estuary include the State Lands Commission, custodian of approximately 634,653 acres of state-owned land, a large portion of which is tide and submerged lands in the estuarine zones,[73] the Department of Water Resources, which is concerned primarily with water resources investigations and the development of fresh water supplies;[74] the Department of Fish and Game, which has enforcement authority concerning fish kills and is the State's scientific arm for investigating the effects of water pollution on marine life;[75] the Department of Health, which regulates public health aspects of water use;[76] and the Department of Conservation's Divisions of Forestry, Mines and Geology, Oil and Gas.[77] Each of these agencies exerts considerable influence in regard to management and maintenance of the water quality in the estuarine area.

Much of California's fresh water supply is concentrated in the northern part of the State and involves the extensive watershed of the San Francisco Bay-Delta Estuary. Diversions of this water supply from the Estuary to other portions of the State by the Federal Central Valley Project[78] and the State Water Project[79] affect the extent of salinity intrusion in the Delta which in turn affects the ecology.[80] Delta water users are protected by statutory provisions requiring the State Water Project, in coordination with

66. Cal. Water Code § 13000 (West Supp. 1970).
67. "Waste" includes sewage and any and all other waste substances . . . associated with human habitation, or of human or animal origin, or from any producing, manufacturing, or processing operation of whatever nature. Cal. Water Code § 13050(d) (West Supp. 1970).
68. See for example, State Water Resources Control Board Resolution 70-23, Aug. 6, 1970 (Cal.).
69. Cal. Water Code § § 174-188.5 (West Supp. 1970).
70. Cal. Water Code § § 13200-13207 (West Supp. 1970).
71. Cal. Water Code § 13320(d) (West Supp. 1970).
72. Cal. Water Code § § 13168, 13320(a) (West Supp. 1970).
73. The Commission has exclusive jurisdiction over all ungranted tidelands and submerged lands owned by the state including the authority to lease or otherwise dispose of such lands. Cal. Pub. Res. Code § 6301 (West 1956).
74. Cal. Water Code § 150 (West Supp. 1956).
75. The provision most used by the department in its enforcement activities is Cal. Fish & Game Code § 5650 (West 1968). See also § 5652.
76. The department is given responsibility for the maintenance of pure water for domestic use [Cal. Health & Safety Code § 203 (West Supp. 1956)], the authority to revoke permits issued to any person supplying water for domestic use (§ 4011), and also the authority to regulate the disposal of many wastes ( § § 4401, 4400).
77. See Cal. Pub. Res. Code § § 630-647, 2002-2322, 3001-3234 (West Supp. 1970).
78. The Federal Central Valley Project was authorized in 1935 under provisions of the Emergency Relief Act as a reclamation project. It is a multipurpose development to supply water for irrigation, municipal, industrial, and other uses, improve navigation on the Sacramento River, control floods in the Central Valley, and produce hydroelectric energy. It includes 16 dams and some 900 miles of conduits, tunnels, and canals.

Major reservoirs include Lake Shasta on the Sacramento River, Folsom Lake and Auburn Reservoir on the American River, Millerton Lake on the San Joaquin River, and New Melones Reservoir on the Stanislaus River. Major aqueduct systems are the Delta-Mendota Canal, Friant-Kern Canal, Madera Canal, and Corning Canal. Other key features are the San Felipe Division, Trinity Division, and San Luis Division.

79. The California State Water Project is a multipurpose water development that conserves and distributes water, produces electrical energy and provides flood control, recreation, and fish and wildlife enhancement. The initial facilities of the Project—now 95 per cent completed or under construction—include 18 reservoirs, 15 pumping plants, 5 powerplants and 580 miles of aqueducts. Parts of the Project have been in service since 1962; water deliveries will be made from the southern terminus in 1972.
80. See California State Water Resources Control Board water rights Decision 1379 (July 28, 1971) for a discussion of these factors in relation to the State Water Project and Central Valley Project.

the Federal Central Valley Project to provide salinity control and an adequate water supply[81] and also by the State's recognition of the sensitive interrelationship between water quality and water quantity as expressed through water rights allocation.[82] California law recognizes both the riparian[83] and appropriative[84] doctrines of allocation of water resources. Under this latter doctrine, permits for appropriation of water are issued by the State Water Resources Control Board.[85]

The development and implementation of land-use planning programs in the San Francisco Bay-Delta Estuary is typical of the confusion and difficulties which arise on the local level. The San Francisco Bay-Delta Estuary consists of 12 counties, 104 cities and numerous limited-purpose special districts which have powers affecting the environment of the estuary;[86] there is no single- or multi-purpose agency covering the entire estuary. The San Francisco Bay Conservation and Development Commission[87] is the only agency approximating areawide jurisdiction.

Even the readily isolated problem of waste disposal is fragmented among many separate jurisdictions. Although a three-year comprehensive study of pollution of the San Francisco Bay-Delta area recommended in 1969 that an areawide agency be established to handle waste disposal in the area the initial response was negative both in the Legislature and within the area itself. However, in 1971 the Legislature finally created the Bay Area Sewer Services Agency and more detailed studies of subregional parts of the Bay area were underway. But the determination to justify piecemeal solutions to pollution on technical, financial, and, most importantly, local autonomy grounds remains, despite a clear state and national interest in this estuary. The critical problem of achieving local action for environmental protection remains.[88]

## PLANNING FOR WATER RESOURCES MANAGEMENT

Failure to provide nationwide guidance of land use has complicated the problem. Local agencies empowered to decide how land is used have continued to operate within their

81. Cal. Water Code § § 12202-05, 12220 (West Supp. 1970).

82. In California the Water Resources Control Board has the authority to approve appropriations by storage of water to be released for the purpose of protecting or enhancing the quality of other waters put to beneficial use [Cal. Water Code § 1242.5 (West Supp. 1970)], to take into account the amounts of water needed to remain in the source for the protection of beneficial uses, including any uses specified to be protected in any relevant water quality control plan [Cal. Water Code § 1243.5 (West Supp. 1970)], and to institute necessary court actions to adjudicate rights or to further the physical solutions necessary for the protection of the quality of groundwater [Cal. Water Code § 2100 (West Supp. 1970)]. For a discussion of water quality and water rights see Robie, *Relationship Between Water Quality and Water Rights,* Contemporary Developments in Water Law 73-83 (Water Resources Symposium No. 4, C. Johnson and Lewis S. eds. University of Texas 1970).

83. Under this doctrine the law recognizes that each riparian owner has a right to the reasonable use of water on land riparian to a watercourse. It is a judically oriented common law system concerning the rights of one riparian vis-a-vis other riparians.

84. The doctrine of prior appropriation states that the first in time to use the water beneficially is the first in right.

85. Cal. Water Code § 1250 (West Supp. 1970).

86. More than 275 local public entities in the 12-county study area perform functions related to the provisions of water or sewer service. Of the 104 cities located in the 12-county Bay-Delta area, 68 provide sewer service and 48 provide water service. Sewerage functions are performed by 155 public entities in the 12 counties. In addition to the 68 cities, 44 entities operate pursuant to the Sanitary District Act. The remaining 18 entities operate pursuant to one of 10 other acts which meet the specific needs of the service area. A total of 103 public entities provide domestic water service in the 12 counties. In addition to the 48 cities which provide water service, there are 40 districts which operate pursuant to the county water district law and 15 other entities providing water service under nine special district acts. There are 17 special flood control and water conservation districts in the 12-county Bay-Delta area. Final Report to the State of California, San Francisco Bay-Delta Water Quality Control Program, *supra* note 63, at 2.

87. See Cal. Govt. Code, note 40 *supra.*

88. California Stats. 1971, Ch. 909. See also State Water Resources Control Board *Clean Water For San Francisco Bay,* January 1971.

narrow areas of authority while ignoring the regionwide results of their fragmented decisions.[89] Only recently has there been a general realization that communities were neglecting long-term resource protection to achieve short-run improvements in the tax base or economic situation. This last-minute awareness has dramatized the need for proper land-use planning techniques that can insure a predictable rate and direction of development compatible with environmental goals.[90]

## Water Quality Controls

To a limited extent, water quality controls have been used to indirectly fill the void created by the lack of adequate land-use plans. For instance, in recent years there has been an acceleration in the planning and construction of waste treatment facilities on an areawide basis.[91] Because of the absence of land-use planning, such water quality planning may be subject to criticism as accomplishing only a limited purpose. Appropriate predictions of land use and consideration of other environmental factors must necessarily supplement water quality plans. Recent federal regulations emphasize the land-use planning responsibilities expected from water quality management by requiring area-wide planning as a prerequisite to federal construction grants.[92]

## Adequacy of Water Quality Controls

The past few years have seen significant progress in the development and implementation of state water pollution control programs[93] through programs of indirect or direct control of waste disposal.[94] However, the effectiveness of existing and proposed waste treatment facilities is being questioned.[95] In addition there is no general acceptance in the scientific community of new planning needs, particularly as they relate to waste treatment facility design. Although it is technically simple and relatively inexpensive to reduce the oxygen-demanding characteristics of waste, it is more difficult to reduce the wide range of toxic chemicals, heavy metals, and nutrients that are discharged from most types of today's treatment plants.

Also evident are the limitations inherent in current waste discharge regulations. For example, the traditional methods of measuring pollution[96] are no longer adequate. They do not consider problems of toxicity or the long-term cumulative effects (such as increased productivity[97] ) of the discharge of

89. Council Report, *supra* note 2, at 184.
90. There has been some federal recognition of the need to coordinate land use planning activities with environmental considerations. See The Natural Land Use Policy Act, S. 3354, 91st Cong. (1970) which calls for ecological factors to be used as criteria in land use planning. For a discussion see Caldwell, *The Ecosystem as a Criterion for Public Land Policy*, 10 Natural Resources J. 203 (1970).
91. For example, the regional systems in San Diego, Seattle and Toronto were forerunners in the construction to accommodate areawide considerations.
92. See 35 Fed. Reg. 10756 (1970).

93. Council Report, *supra* note 2, at 50.
94. These include such measures or the construction of public waste treatment facilities, judicial or administrative orders requiring dischargers to either cease or correct deficiencies, and tax incentives awarded industries to bring their discharges into compliance with acceptable standards.
95. In the last few years, communities around the nation have invested large sums in improvement of waste treatment facilities but in many streams the degree of treatment needed is far beyond the technical capability of existing or proposed facilities.

There are many types of pollutants that cannot be effectively controlled by treatment such as pesticides and products that contain phosphates. Both of these pollution sources and other similar products must be controlled at the source and new federal authority is needed to assure rapid elimination of dangerous products from the market. See Final Report, San Francisco Bay-Delta Water Quality Control Program, *supra* note 3, at XX-31 to XX-40 and X-1 to X-10.
96. Traditional water pollution parameters include Biochemical Oxygen Demand (BOD), Chemical Oxygen Demand (COD), suspended solids and coliform counts. These parameters measure the oxygen depleting characteristics, the particulate matter content and the numbers of coliform bacteria respectively in wastewaters or the receiving water.
97. Production can be defined as the total amount of cellular organic matter that is formed within a certain time from the raw material nutrients sup-

nutrients into confined portions of the estuary.

Certain rigid governmental policies also tend to complicate the problem and may in some cases increase the already existing problems of estuarine productivity.[98]

The discharge of heated wastes, primarily industrial and power plant cooling water, provides another threat to the estuarine environment. Small increases in the temperature can have serious effects, particularly in estuaries that support anadromous fish runs.[99] Protection from this source of pollution requires either the elimination of heated waste discharges or their rigid control.

Problems in maintenance of water quality in the estuary also encompass the difficulties involved by depletion of freshwater supplies caused by upstream diversions and storage projects. This is a critical problem in the coastal areas of the arid west, and it is becoming an increasingly significant problem in the estuaries of the Eastern United States where rainfall is more evenly divided throughout the year. Water stored primarily to meet consumptive purposes can be released in natural channels to meet environmental demands as well as the water supply needs for domestic, agricultural, and industrial uses.[100] But this would mean substantially increased magnitude and scope of water quality planning efforts, fully coordinated with planning for the protection and development of other natural resources. Considerations such as these suggest that protection of our nation's waters should depend less upon programs limited to the regulation of waste discharges and more upon management programs which include water quantity, water quality, and land-use controls.

## A CHOICE FOR THE FUTURE

The ability to provide effective environmental management programs depends upon the implementation of comprehensive development plans supported by the enforcement of land-use controls. Existing regulatory efforts of federal, state, and local government can reduce pollution loads of waters and contribute to the protection and enhancement of our nation's natural assets. But, until the use of land is controlled within a framework of areawide or statewide planning programs (in some instances, this must be multi-state), these efforts cannot prevent the continuing degradation of the total environment.

The complex nature of estuaries demonstrates the need for programs that can regulate pollution control activities at their source. Estuaries are an inseparable part of an upstream watershed. Any upstream development will have a dramatic impact on the estuaries' sensitive environmental characteristics. Controls must extend not only to waste discharges but also to the development activities in the total watershed or basin of which the estuary is an integral part.

Since it may be many years before adequate plans can be developed, it is essential that existing and fragmented regulatory and planning efforts be simplified and consolidated. The wave of environmental concern

plied. In aquatic terminology, "Production" or "Productivity" usually expresses the rate of algal growth in the body of water. This is often referred to as "algal primary productivity." See Calif. State Water Quality Control Board, Eutrophication—A Review, Pub. No. 34, (1967).

98. For example, the Federal Government supports the concept that secondary treatment (85% BOD removal) be provided for all communities (with limited exceptions) regardless of individual local water conditions. See proposed rule at 35 Fed. Reg. 8942 (1970).

99. In his presentation entitled "Research on Thermal Pollution Report on the Columbia River and Estuary" presented at the Annual Pacific Marine Fisheries Commission meeting held at Coeur d'Alene, Idaho, Nov. 21, 1968, George R. Snyder reported that anadromous fish have been blocked in the Okanogan River, Washington by high water temperatures and that temperature blocks to fish migration have been observed near the confluence of the Snake and Columbia Rivers.

100. McCullough and Vayder, *Delta-Suisun Bay Water Quality and Hydraulic Study*, Journal of the Sanitary Engineering Division 801-27 (Proceedings of the American Society of Civil Engineers, Oct. 1968).

has the capability of generating environmental bureaucracy of unprecedented proportions. Many federal and state agencies have strengthened their role in enforcing pollution standards, but they often compete with each other to do the most environmental good. As a result of this interagency competition many massive projects which might further degrade the environment and those projects that are needed to correct environmental damage are caught up in a web of paperwork, hearings and controversy.

The federal role in estuaries should be limited to technical support and financial assistance administered by one central agency. Although the creation of the Environmental Protection Agency is a positive step in this direction, residual power in other federal agencies[101] creates external conflicts. Because the federal government is too far removed from the geographically and politically scattered estuaries, quality control can be most effectively exercised at the state level.[102] Municipal governments on the other hand have limited financial resources, and their attempts at controlling the extensive estuarine area are often faced with a wealth of private interests that frustrate conservation-related regulations. The states in partnership with local governments have both the legal basis and the administrative ability to provide the means by which the estuarine environment can be protected and enhanced. The federal government could by example and by deed greatly alleviate estuarine pollution. The Corps of Engineers through control of the placement of polluted dredging spoils and the Navy through control and removal of toxic painting wastes and shipboard sewage could end damages from what will constitute the last remaining sources of pollution in many estuaries.

Recent examples in California have shown that estuaries can be effectively managed.[103] Single-minded, single-purpose programs that attempt to separate them from the total environment and assign responsibility for their management to the federal government will result in nothing more than a continuation of the present situation. State controlled management programs based on land-use planning and consideration of the total effect on the environment can be administered within a framework of cooperation between state and local government to produce maximum protection and enhancement of the estuary.

101. For instance, the Department of Housing and Urban Development is involved with land-use planning, The Environmental Protection Agency is concerned with envrionmental controls, and the Corps of Engineers and Bureau of Reclamation is concerned with public works projects.

102. The unanimous conclusion of three federal studies was that responsibility for the management of estuaries should reside with the states. See National Estuarine Pollution Study, *supra* note 31, at V-259; The National Estuary Study, *supra* note 4, at 73; and Our Nation and the Sea, A Plan for National Action, *supra* note 12, at 8.

103. Except for the persistent problem of vessel waste pollution, San Diego Bay is a clean bay as a result of an areawide waste treatment and disposal system. Water quality control programs have substantially improved the quality of the Los Angeles Harbor and the variety and number of marine organisms are increasing in San Francisco Bay.

# 7

# OCEAN LAWS AND MANAGEMENT

# 40. Ecology, Law, and the "Marine Revolution"

CARLETON RAY 1970

## INTRODUCTION

Man has not yet solved the age-old paradox upon which his civilizations have many times foundered; namely, that high population numbers with high cultural levels demand high environmental productivity, yet exploitation of Nature produces environmental destruction and ecological collapse. When the numbers of humans will come to exceed the total carrying capacity on Earth, as is already the case in many nations, no one can say; but if Man does not learn the lessons of history, there is no doubt that this catastrophic situation will occur relatively soon. The survival of Man, or anyway of civilization as we now know it, will surely depend upon how he handles this challenge.

There are two dominant features of the marine part of this challenge: first, the development of international law with enforcement for exploitation of the sea, and, second, the development of ecosystem-based conservation practices. The latter includes the cessation of existing destructive practices, the assessment of marine environments relative to the carrying capacity of Earth for Man, and the creation of marine parks, sanctuaries, and control areas for research. These ecological aspects have to date been attacked in a piecemeal fashion. Ultimately, the answers will depend upon value judgements about what sort of a world we choose to live in. The late Fairfield Osborn (1953) asked: "Is the purpose of our civilization really to see how much the earth and human spirit can sustain?"

This paper considers biology and law as they reflect upon what we may call the Marine Revolution. Biology and law require different approaches. The body of law by which we exercise control and responsibility is of Man's creation. It should reflect common sense and be capable of rational alteration. Natural phenomena may make no "sense" at all, and their complexities are

Dr. G. Carleton Ray is an associate professor with the Department of Pathobiology, School of Hygiene and Public Health at Johns Hopkins University, Maryland. He is director of the International Biological Program on Marine Mammals and serves on the National Academy of Sciences' Panel on Marine Aquatic Life and Wildlife. Physiology and acoustical mechanisms of seals and walruses are his research interests. He has published over fifty technical and popular articles.

From *Biological Conservation,* Vol. 3, No. 1, pp. 7-17, 1970. Reprinted with author's revisions and light editing and by permission of the author and *Biological Conservation,* Elsevier Publishing Company, Ltd., England.

infinite. It has been stated that the ecosystem is not only more complex than we think it is; it is also more complex than we can think. The ecologist can rarely be definitive. He often experiences great difficulty in explaining, even to some fellow scientists and especially to engineers and technicians, the real nature of the ecological crisis. Ehrlich's (1969) "Eco-catastrophe" sounds to many like alarmist stuff, yet it has a fundamental basis of perception.

To a great extent we are slaves of our own history. The *laissez faire* spirit of exploitation, the goal of economic growth, Man's socio-religious beliefs which separate him from Nature, and the conflict and case-history methods of law make little sense when applied to the environment. The emerging "Marine Revolution" poses to those concepts a challenge which magnifies the importance of the sea far beyond its resource value. The wide recognition that this is so is reflected by the numbers of recent symposia and reports on the exploration, use, and legal régimes of the sea. Unfortunately, meetings of the American Bar Association and the Marine Technology Society, among others, have been composed almost entirely of industry representatives, lawyers, and a scattering of government officials, naval personnel, and fisheries biologists–the last mostly representing mission-oriented government agencies or industry. Marine ecologists have been virtually absent!

In spite of this, the intensifying debate has produced the beginnings of workable ideas. The ecosystem approach may be just over the horizon, the greatest present need being for marine ecologists to make their voices heard. If consideration for the ecosystem be added to the debate, it is possible that non-destructive and cooperative exploitation on an international basis will result, and perhaps then marine ecosystems will not suffer further.

## THE MARINE REVOLUTION

Man's massive entry into "inner space" initiates what we are calling the Marine Revolution. It is resulting in increased resource utilization and new régimes for law, politics, and socio-economics, as Man investigates, uses, and hopefully will conserve, that three-quarters of the world's surface which has been mostly foreign to him.

### Agricultural and Industrial Revolutions

Some thousands of years ago, Man began to grow his own food. This change from the hunter-gatherer to the agriculturalist comprized the Agricultural Revolution. It led to the diversity of occupations which marks present urban culture. The Agricultural Revolution produced more food in a more accessible form than was available to the hunter-gatherer. Food, which presumably had been a limiting factor, was limiting no more. The carrying capacity of land for humans rose and the population grew accordingly.

The Industrial Revolution has been going on for the last two centuries or more. It has been marked by the growth of science and technology, by increased resource-use, and by expanded diversity and efficiency of human skills. It has meant a turning away from the agricultural way of life to an increasingly urbanized and "artificial" one. It once again increased the carrying capacity of the land for human beings and led to a spectacular decrease in death control without concomitant birth control. Most significantly of all, the Industrial Revolution, in its greed for resources, has produced environmental destruction at an astounding and dangerous pace. Forests have been cut, land has been eroded and stripped, bays have been polluted and filled, and the result of all of these and other activities has been to lower the long-term carrying capacity of land for future human populations, notwithstanding the temporary increase which technology has made possible. Such environmental wastage makes our wish to provide a better life for our children seem to be sheer hypocrisy.

### The Marine Revolution

Thus does Man turn to the seas which become increasingly vital for his resources. However, the Marine Revolution is not totally a consequence of the exhaustion of the land. Man also turns to the sea as it lies before him in the form of a challenge which he is now becoming technologically able to accept. "Products are sold on an open world market that cares nothing about the origin of the material; one competes only against price" (Bascom, 1966).

Thus, we accept the challenge of the sea, being not a little starry-eyed over our technology. But we must remind ourselves that Man remains a hunter-gatherer in the oceans; in only an insignificant few places does he farm the sea. This contrast between developing technology and the inadequacies of cultural and legal frameworks for regulation is a characteristic of "revolution."

The Marine Revolution is, to my mind, quite as important a development as the previous Agricultural and Industrial Revolutions. It is no more obvious on a day-to-day basis than the Agricultural and Industrial Revolutions were in their time. Future Man will clearly see this Revolution as his inner-space logistics and utilization increase.

## ECOSYSTEMS AND HOMEOSTASIS

The ecosystem is the fundamental functional unit of the natural world. It is comprised of all the living and non-living components of an environment and the totality of their interrelationships. An ecosystem has properties of self-sustainment. Solar energy must be added, but nutrients and other materials are recycled. Examples are a lake, a forest, an estuary, and a coral reef.

### Carrying Capacity, Limiting Factors, and Synergisms

Carrying capacity may be defined as the number of individuals of a species within a particular ecosystem beyond which no major increase in numbers may occur. It fluctuates about an equilibrium level and may change seasonally or even daily. It is regulated according to Liebig's "law" of the minimum and Shelford's "law" of tolerance, which together state that the presence or abundance of an organism locally is determined by the amounts of critical materials available or by the local levels of environmental factors such as salinity or temperature.

It is typical of ecology that "laws" are easy to state but difficult to prove. A major reason for this is *synergism;* that is, environmental factors often act together to produce effects which are different quantitatively or qualitatively from the effects expected separately or additively. Carrying capacity and limiting factors apply to all living things. The foolish assumption is that technology may negate them for Man. Technology cannot alter ecological laws, though it can redirect utilization in limited ways.

### Productivity

Productivity is determined by turnover rate. The standing crop or biomass is a poor indicator of this, as it tells little about how often materials are recycled. Plants absorb about one per cent of solar energy for photosynthesis. An examination of trophic levels from these producers to primary, secondary, or tertiary consumers, reveals that each step involves about a 90 per cent loss of energy. Thus, food-chains are usually short and each trophic level shows much lower total production than its predecessor.

Nutrients, unlike energy, are recycled. The biogeochemical cycles of gases, salts, and minerals, are most efficient in complex ecosystems. Man can occasionally increase productivity through the addition of substances which once were limiting. More often, his "making the desert bloom" fails in the long run through failure to recognize the interrelationships of these cycles.

Primary productivity varies widely.

Deserts and the waters of the deep oceans, which together cover most of the Earth, produce less than one gram of dry organic matter per square meter per day. Grasslands, waters over the continental shelf, and marginal agriculture produce 0.5 to 3 gm; moist forests and agriculture produce 3 to 10 gm; estuaries, inshore seas, and intensive agriculture produce 10 to 25 gm (Odum, 1959).

Owing to their large total productive area and volume, the seas contain more living material than the land supports. However, Man's utilization is at a higher trophic level in the sea: land = sun → grass → cow; sea = sun → phytoplankton → zooplankton → primary carnivore (e.g. herring) → secondary carnivore (e.g. tunny). The seas contain a much greater total diversity of life in terms of classes of animals than does the land, but owing to the lower oxygen content of water than air, the seas are dominated by animals of lower metabolic rate, but higher ecological efficiency than birds and mammals. Lastly, the sea provides a more stable environment than the land; in it, the "weather" is mild and the productive season is long. For all these reasons, marine productivity is not equivalent to that of land.

### Homeostasis, Simplification, and Pollution

Homeostasis defines the "balance of nature." All ecosystems depend upon recycling for sustainment and upon complexity for stability. These involve intricate mechanisms analogous to (but more complex than) the heat-producing, dissipating, and conserving mechanisms which regulate human body temperature. Ecosystems are never perfectly balanced, but homeostatic mechanisms give them recuperative power which, when exceeded, leads to breakdown; the eutrophication of Lake Erie is a classic example of such excess.

A major part of homeostasis lies in complexity which insures both productivity and stability, and also has aesthetic value for Man (Elton, 1958; Dasmann, 1968). Man is a simplifier of ecosystems and thus reduces their recuperative power. The many forms of pollution are the most serious stresses in this regard. Historically, Man has depended upon maximum homeostatic capacities of the environment to endure pollution; but in simplifying and polluting at the same time, he attacks with a two-edged sword.

Is the ocean too large to disrupt? I think not. According to the Task Force on Environmental Health and Related Problems (1967), the American people and their enviornment are being exposed to half-a-million different alien substances with 20,000 new ones being added each year. Some of these go to sea. For instance, pesticides have been distributed throughout the world's oceans through the vectors of air and precipitation (Frost, 1969). Polikarpov (1966) suggests that radionuclide pollution of the seas may already be at a dangerous level for some organisms. Hedgpeth (in press) remarks that our standards for waste disposal are anthropocentric and that laboratory tests on pollutants are "interesting, but possibly academic as far as the real world is concerned"—in other words, waste-level standards set for Man are not necessarily those which ecosystems will tolerate.

## MAN'S USE OF THE SEA

Only recently has Man begun to explore the sea throughout its three dimensions. The first extensive exploration of the deep sea was in 1873-76 by *H.M.S. Challenger.* Not quite a century later, Man has visited the ocean's deepest place in a research submarine and knows that all marine waters are capable of supporting life.

The Marine Revolution consists of five major aspects, which are related to, but by no means coincidental with, its dominating challenges mentioned in the Introduction. These aspects are: fisheries, minerals and mining, military interests, science and technology, and conservation and recreation. Emery (1966) gives world values of marine resources in 1964 as follows: biological—US

$6.4 \times 10^9$; geological–US $3.6 \times 10^9$; and chemical–US $1.3 \times 10^9$. Biological resources will always be the most valuable, even if surpassed economically, for Man cannot exist without them, and they are largely renewable.

## Fisheries

Fisheries remain the most difficult aspect of international law of the sea. This is due mainly to the fact that most commercially important marine animals move and cannot be claimed. It is ludicrous to discover that certain benthic organisms are, in fact, classified as "minerals" under the Convention of the Continental Shelf. In some cases it is of advantage to the exploiter that they should be so classified, an instance being the Alaska king crab (Oda, 1968); in other cases the reverse is true, instances including some shrimps (Neblett, 1966). Fisheries resources include various algae, plankton, shellfish, fishes, turtles, and mammals (Walford, 1958); but, as has been pointed out above, Man's utilization represents only a fraction of total marine productivity.

Over-utilization continues to dominate fisheries, especially off-shore ones. Clark (1967) states that Japanese long-lining accounted for almost a million billfishes in 1965. Even larger quantities of tunny were taken. Evidence is accumulating that such utilization cannot be sustained. Perhaps even more serious than overfishing is inshore habitat destruction. Over two-thirds of all commercial and sport fishes of the eastern United States depend upon inshore environments at some critical time of their life-cycle. The most effective way to extirpate a species is by environmental disruption, and this is being done inshore at a rapid pace.

Consideration of energetics lead many to propose exploitation at lower trophic levels. Complex size/metabolic factors and fishing efficiency strongly indicate, however, that higher-order consumers are more effective fishermen and converters of energy than Man is. A total "plankton" fishery should be considered as a last, and none too satisfactory, resort. Those who have taste-tested swordfish and plankton might agree! The choice, however, should not be between swordfish and plankton; given proper management, we could have both.

The concept of "yield" is vital biologically and legally. Fisheries biologists have emphasized the asymptotic attainment of maximum biomass through controlled utilization. Such a yield may or may not conform to economic efficiency or to local market value–hence the preference of "optimum" over "maximum" yield (Crutchfield, 1968).

W. M. Chapman (1966) states an exploitive point of view: "When the fishing effort has increased beyond the point of maximum sustainable yield, the fishing can ordinarily be permitted to expand without serious damage to the resource." He ignores Allee's principle (Odum, 1959), which is that density is in itself a limiting factor for population growth and survival. Relative abundance of the species in a community is a contributor to homeostasis. Thus, it is biologically most sound to change population size as little as possible in natural systems.

Christy (1966) considers broader aspects of utilization: ". . . somehow or other it will be necessary to limit the number of fishermen that can participate in a fishery. Such limitations can be achieved only by further restricting the 'freedom of the seas'; and this clearly raises questions about the meaning of this freedom and about the distribution of wealth." This approach appears to me more susceptible to ecological application than Chapman's more narrowly-stated views.

Aquaculture presents different sorts of problems from hunter-gathering, and may be the dominant provider of the future. Aquaculture is a major concern of the U.S. Sea Grant Program (Abel, 1968). Ryther and Bardach (1968) and Bardach and Ryther (1968) review aquaculture and make the point that it will be carried out largely along coasts–exactly the areas currently most stressed at the hand of Man. To reconstitute coastal environments, or to fertilize them artifically, is difficult or impossible. The key to aquaculture is clearly the maintenance of natural productivity.

### Minerals and Mining

Reading in this field often leaves one impressed with the viewpoint that somehow we are slaves to "economic growth." Close (1968) speaks of "the care and feeding of a gigantic industrial complex." One hopes that only a segment of industry would speak so carelessly, but it does appear true that an awareness of ecology and a willingness to exploit the non-living resources at little or no expense to the living are indeed rare. If mineral exploitation continues by sea as it has by land, the predicatable results are frightening to contemplate. Strip mining is one parallel example.

Mero (1966, 1968), Luce (1968), and Young (1968), review the diversity of mineral resources in the sea. Inshore mineral exploitation is already heavy, but a consensus exists that only a few minerals, such as oil and gas, are currently feasible of exploitation. This is evidently based upon the lack of a favorable legal and economic climate, not upon the lack of technological capability. Further, it is not true that exploitation will progress from shallower to deeper water, any such progress being a function of the resource sought (Wilkey, 1969).

Off-shore mineral production in 1968 was 6 per cent of the world total and of it oil and gas accounted for 84 per cent (Economic Associates, 1968). In 1965, 16 per cent of the free world's oil was produced off-shore, the result of the work of 325 rigs which have drilled many thousands of wells (Dozier, 1966); oil has been produced from wells in as much as 104 m of water (Wilkey, 1969), and exploratory drilling was carried out in 1968 in the Gulf of Mexico in over 3600 m. At any one time, about 30,000,000 tons of oil are at sea in tankers. From U.S. off-shore wells alone the production of oil has so far been $2 \times 10^9$ barrels,* and of gas $5.5 \times 10^{12}$ ft$^3$,* at an investment of U.S. $6 thousand million, and with the ultimate potential of 15-35 thousand million barrels of oil and 90-170 $\times 10^{12}$ ft$^3$ of gas (Nelson and Burk, 1966). The massive pollution potential of the oil industry has been previewed by the tragic *Torrey Canyon* and Santa Barbara disasters. We can be certain that these episodes are not the last of their kind, and probably there will be far bigger ones.

* 1 barrel = *ca* 200 liters; 1 cubic meter = *ca* 30 cubic feet.

### Military Interests

Military activities in the oceans are shrouded in secrecy. It would, for instance, be interesting to know what the degree of radionuclide pollution is from Soviet and U.S. nuclear-powered submarines. Both Harlow (1966) and Hearn (1968) give as the U.S. Navy's viewpoint the contention that maximum freedom to use all dimensions of the sea must be maintained in order to exploit naval strength to the fullest in the best national interest. I think it fair to state that such a position is shared by the military of other major powers. The effect is to raise a serious obstacle to internationalization, to expanded territorial management, and to peaceful use of the sea-floor.

It is difficult for me to understand why putting the sea-bed under a "peaceful purposes only" treaty, as has already been done for outer space and Antarctica, is not in the "best national interst." Evidently, military influence was a major factor in preventing that principle from being accepted at the 1967 United Nations debate on the subject (Eichelberger, 1968). As yet the sea-bed is not much utilized militarily, though the waters over the floor of the sea certainly are. Thus, it is particularly disturbing to read that "military strategists . . . have been looking for better ways to put the sea to use for the purposes of national defense" (New York Times, 1969).

It must be pointed out that military interests are not necessarily contrary to fishing or mineral exploitation. In any case, international progress on these last should not be held up by conflicts with the military authorities.

### Science and Technology

The United States, among other nations, is heavily committed to marine exploration, science, development, and conservation. Reports on the highest level are numerous, including: Interagency Committee on Oceanography (1963, 1967); National Academy of Sciences (1964, 1967, 1969); Panel on Oceanography, President's Science Advisory Committee (1966); National Council on Marine Resources and Engineering Development (1967, 1968*a*, 1968*b*); and the Commission on Marine Science, Engineering and Resources (1969).

The last-mentioned, the so-called Stratton Commission Report, departs courageously from—while also building upon—the baseline established by its predecessors and is no doubt that most significant of them all. It is broadly ecological and international in nature, and recommends a U.S. National Oceanographic and Atmospheric Agency for centralization of U.S. research, exploration, data collection, and education. Further, it proposes an International Registry Authority for ocean claims—with régimes for ocean bottoms, a delineated continental shelf, and an intermediate zone. The Commission also stresses optimal use of coastlines on a long-term basis in which industry, water quality, and aquaculture would be regulated under Federal law to guard against deterioration of the inshore marine environment. A useful review of this Report, including both the pros and the cons, is provided by the Program of Policy Studies in Science and Technology (1969).

Looking not at reports, but at budgets, produces some dismay. Ocean Science News (1969) states the current U.S. Federal commitment to marine matters to be $528 million per annum, of which only $150.6 million is in basic and applied research, $143 million being in national security—and this in the very year of Man's travel to the moon and continued development of supersonic transport! The overall oceanic budget has grown 22 per cent since 1968, when Economic Associates, Inc. (1968) remarked: "what remains to be pointed out is the very low level of Federal expenditure on . . . resources and their environment, compared with Federal oceanologic programs in general and, decidedly so, with the Federal effort in such a field as outer space."

The International Biological Programme's Marine Productivity section deserves mention. The IBP theme of "The biological basis of productivity and human welfare" is ideally suited to the needs of Man during the initial period of the Marine Revolution. However, at the current level of funding (only U.S. $7 million for all U.S. IBP sections in fiscal year 1970), it is certain that IBP cannot fulfil its goals.

### Conservation and Recreation

To many, conservation and recreation involve *inter alia* the establishment of parks, sanctuaries, and control areas for research (Ray, 1961, 1965, 1966, 1968; V. J. Chapman, 1968; Randall, 1969). However, conservation and recreation must not be confined to protected areas. Both must principally be concerned with the maintenance of ecosystem homeostasis on a worldwide basis, and this is a large order indeed.

The concepts of conservation have been developed for terrestrial environments and are only vaguely applicable to the sea. The oceans together occupy a vastly larger part of the biosphere than does the land, and they are more continuous. The sea's rate of change, its biotic complexity, and our ignorance of its three-dimensional hydrosphere, are of a different order of magnitude from their counterparts on the more familiar land. For both land and sea, modern conservationists have become less concerned with the placing of "fences" about sea or landscape, valuable as protective measures are, than with an ecological concept of the total ecosystem of which Man forms a part. A good basis of conservation policy exists for land and, in part, for inshore seas. For the high seas, this is not the case.

## LEGAL RÉGIME OF THE SEA

Ultimately, Man's marine activities of all kinds must be legally regulated. Griffin (1967) states: "To a large extent, a period of legal conjecture is ending." The problem is ". . . to evolve policies and a legal régime which will maximize all beneficial uses of ocean space. . . . Under no circumstances, we believe, must we ever allow the prospects of rich harvest and mineral wealth to create a new form of colonial competition among the maritime nations." A contrary view is that of Ely (1967*a*): "Above all, we should not now cede to any international agency whatsoever the power to veto American exploration of areas of the deep sea which are presently open to American initiative. We can give away later what we now keep, but the converse is sadly false." Ely (1967*b*, 1968) later extended these views.

Basically, the argument concerns whether the sea and sea-floor are *res nullius* (belonging to no one but subject to claim) or *res communis* (property of the world community).

Eichelberger (1968) puts the matter another way when he says: "Either [the sea] opens up another threat of conflict or another area of cooperation." Of course, the argument is not so simple. As Friedham (1966) and Belman (1968) point out, traditional law of the sea is imperfect, but there is legitimate hesitancy towards creating new modes when our experience with the sea and our ignorance of its resources are both still great.

### Historical Background

In 1609, Grotius wrote *Mare Liberum* as a challenge to national jurisdiction of areas of ocean. This brief for the Dutch Government was directed toward breaking the Portuguese monopoly of the East Indies spice trade. Gradually, and in partial response to struggles for supremacy between Britain and Spain, the principle of "freedom of the high seas" was accepted.

The concept of a territorial sea was born when Bijnkershoek wrote *De Comino Maris* in 1702. A territorial width of three nautical miles (*ca* 6 km) has been attributed to the distance of a cannon-ball shot, but the range of cannon at the time was only a single nautical mile. Probably the three-mile limit began with a British instruction to her Ambassadors, in 1672, that control should be exercised one marine league ( = 3 nautical miles) from shore (Weber, 1966). Three nautical miles was never adopted as a limit universally; claims of up to 12 such miles (*ca* 24 km) have always been valid.

A Convention of 1884 sustained all states' rights to lay cable on the deep sea-floor; but it was not until the Treaty of Paria, between Britain and Venezuela in 1942, and the Truman Proclamation of 1945, that any state claimed jurisdiction and control over any part of the sea-floor. By its important action, the United States effectively laid claim to an area of shelf larger than Alaska and Texas combined.

Three-and-a-half centuries of precedent thus led to recognition of the following zones: (1) internal waters and bays within the control of the coastal state; (2) territorial sea under the control of the coastal state; (3) continental shelf over which the coastal state might claim control; (4) contiguous zones for special purposes; (5) the high seas, held to be *res communis;* and (6) the deep sea-floor, held to be *res nullius.* New technology for ocean research and exploitation after World War II indicated obvious conflict under this system.

The International Law Commission had been created in 1947 under the United Nations. It proposed in 1956 that a Conference on Law of the Sea be held. This occurred in 1958 at Geneva and adopted four Conventions as follows:

(1) Territorial Sea and the Contiguous Zone: ratified 10 September 1964. This Convention confirmed the control of the coastal state over all resources within a territorial sea. In addition, the coastal state might declare control over a contiguous zone

for security, fishery, fiscal, immigration, or sanitary purposes, but not to interfere with the right of innocent passage. The width of the fisheries zone is still undecided. Of 91 coastal states, 49 declare 12 nautical miles, 17 declare more than 12, 10 declare between 3 and 12, and 15 declare 3 miles in 1966 (Oda, 1968). A narrow territorial sea is favored by military interests and by states with international fishing fleets; Japan is the only major fishing nation which adheres to three miles. A wide territorial sea is favored by states wishing to protect a coastal fishery. Obviously, the U.S. has been in a delicate position and only recently declared 12 nautical miles to be the width of its fisheries zone, the territorial width remaining 3.

(2) High Seas: ratified 30 September 1962. This includes all waters outside territorial ones and declares freedoms of navigation, overflight, fishing, and the laying of submarine cables and pipelines. Also included are regulations on piracy and pollution.

(3) Continental Shelf: ratified 10 June 1964. This Convention is mainly concerned with the sea-floor and does not include the water lying above. It has already been pointed out that certain living resources are included. The most serious contention concerns the extent of the shelf, which is defined in the Convention as extending: ". . . to the sea-bed and subsoil of the submarine area adjacent to the coast, but outside the area of the territorial sea, to a depth of 200 meters or, beyond that limit, to where the depth of the superjacent waters admit of the exploitation of the natural resources of the said areas." Two schools of thought prevail here. One contends that as this Convention is entitled "Continental Shelf," the sea bottom beyond its geographic limits of about 200 m depth is not included. The other contends that the exploitability provision defines a "juridical shelf" which could include the slope or even the whole ocean bottom. It should be kept in mind that the shelf area is a huge one; without the slope it comprises $10 \times 10^6$ mi$^2$ (about $28 \times 10^6$ km$^2$), which is equal to 20 per cent of the total land area on Earth (Mero, 1966, 1968). An excellent review of the problem is that of Tubman (1966).

(4) Fishing and Conservation of Living Resources of the High Seas: ratified 20 March 1966. This remains the most controversial of the Conventions, being the only one which did not more or less standardize a body of existing custom but which contained genuine innovation. The problem that one non-cooperating state could vitiate fishery conservation efforts was a major reason for calling the Geneva Conference. This Convention "virtually forces consideration of the need for conservation of a fish stock by all participating nations if only one (or an adjacent coastal state) insists on it," but "it says nothing about the principles to be followed, nor, more fundamentally, about the objectives sought" (Crutchfield, 1968). It does not treat allocations or provide more than case-by-case consideration of conservation.

## Prognosis

Christy (1968) outlines four approaches to the developing law of the sea. The "wait and see" approach leaves exploitation to chance. Support for wait-and-see comes in part from proponents of case law who heed the dictum of Oliver Wendell Holmes: "The life of the law is not logic, but experience." Additional support accrues from those who note our lack of knowledge and experience in the sea.

The second approach is that of the "national lake." The obstacle here is that the division of the sea would be highly inequitable. The U.S.S.R. would get little, whereas tiny oceanic islands would gain title to huge territories.

The "flag" approach is the third. It is supported mainly by mineral and military interests of powerful nations. Burke (1966*a*, 1966*b*, 1968, 1969), McDougal (1968), and Wilkey (1969), all defend this point of view, emphasizing traditional processes of mineral claim on and under a sea-bed held to be *res nullius*. Some are willing to make concessions on an international registry or towards cooperation in pollution and security. On the other hand, Young (1968), Krueger (1968), and Eichelberger (1968), hasten to point out that the flag approach is but a form of neocolonialism which would rapidly lead to a gold-rush. Nor does the flag approach, with its unavoidable competitive nature, make much sense ecologically.

The United Nations has shown its resolve by a series of resolutions. One of 31 December 1968, designated Resolution 2467A-2467D (XXIII), includes the following points: (1) promotion of international cooperation; (2) exploitation for the benefit of mankind; (3) prevention of pollution; (4) desirability of peaceful use of the sea-bed; and (5) endorsement of an International Decade of Ocean Exploration.

I find it impossible to argue against any of these goals, and equally impossible to see an alternative to internationalism in achieving any of them. Precedents of treaties on Antarctica and outer space exist though both Young (1968) and Eichelberger (1968) point out that the ocean floor is not *tabula rasa* (i.e. a "blank slate") as were in some senses both Antarctica and outer space. However, they do not point out that virtually all of Antarctica was under territorial claim, and that nuclear testing and exploration had been carried on in outer space before those treaties were signed. Both treaties involved a yielding of claims and nullifications of military interests. It is difficult to sea why such yielding could not also take place for the sea-floor, the superjacent waters, and even some sections of shelf. One thing is certain; under no reasonable circumstances would the exploiter lose by international control. All that might ensue would be more efficient utilization and a cleaner sea.

Gargantuan problems exist with regard to internationalism. Burke (1966*a*, 1966*b*, 1968, 1969), Alexander (1966), and Griffin (1967), review the problems of disarmament, bilateral and multilateral agreements, the extent of off-shore claims, scientific freedom in research, and many others. Burke (1969), particularly, examines difficulties in applying the Stratton Commission Report. However, one should not be deterred from a path simply because it is stony.

## CONCLUSION

The sea lies today like a huge plum which Man is ready to pluck, but toward which he gropes in quandary. This paper emphasizes the application of ecology to this Marine Revolution. We see that historically we have grown to treat the sea as the land–exploitively and as a "frontier" to be conquered. There is no longer room for doubt that this is a collision course and that the "conquest" of Nature threatens Man's existence as a species with high "culture."

Much as we might wish it so, the sea is not a placebo for our destruction of the land. The very existence of Conventions on the sea are cause for optimism and proof of awareness of the need for change. To the international lawyers belongs most of the credit. However, there persist such items as the "house" lawyer's fear of loss of proprietary rights, the industrialist's fear of loss of claim, and the fisherman's fear of loss of *laissez faire* exploitation. Many maintain that we do not yet know enough about the sea, nor do we have sufficient experience with it, to change our *modus operandi.* Nevertheless, one must agree with Belman (1968): "If law awaits developments, it loses the ability to shape them."

The ecosystem principle must serve as the overriding guide for shaping our future resource use. We simply do not dare exceed limits of homeostasis in the sea. Ripley (1966) states: "The basic problem therefore is to acquire sufficient knowledge about or ecosystems to provide feedback controls essential to homeostasis." It is true that we do not as yet have all the knowledge we might desire, but it is also true that we know enough now to be able intelligently to monitor our actions. We *can* assume that every one of our actions puts some stress on the environment. We *can* put aside expediency, tradition, and false economic idols. We *can* negate flimsy and obsolescent national boundaries. We *can* shift the burden of proof for ecological damage from the plaintiff-community to the defendant-exploiter. The problem is not the ability to change; it is the desire and necessary understanding.

A new brand of environmental biologist must become increasingly involved in the Marine Revolution; without him, no purely political or legal solution will suffice. Nonbiologists, even lay conservationists, have too rarely shown comprehension of the complexities of the living world and they are not equipped to deal with the sophistication of ecosystem ecology. However, the biologists have been largely unwilling to commit themselves. Darling (1967) has pinpointed part of the problem: "... public policy has to be ahead of public consensus ... ecology and conservation can move surely into the hurly-burly without losing scholarly integrity, a course most of us must be prepared to follow. ..." Biology must to a new degree achieve interaction with politics and the law. Scientific integrity must be defended and this is not in conflict with a willingness to "stick one's neck out."

There is apparently no end in sight either to Man's reproductive potential or to his infinite conceit that he shall inherit the (still productive?) Earth. Yet there is a limit to the sea as to the land. The uniqueness of the Marine Revolution lies in part in the fact that Man is recognizing the limits of the Earth as he is developing exploitation of its most remote and unknown region—the oceans and seas. It also lies in the fact that the oceans' and seas' uncertain ownership forces Man at last to consider alternatives to provincialism and nationalism. Indeed it may be said that the Marine Revolution, for the first time in Man's history, ties survival with international cooperation.

## ACKNOWLEDGMENTS

To the following I owe thanks for helpful comments on this paper: Eugenie Clark, University of Maryland; Raymond F. Dasmann, Conservation Foundation; Sidney R. Galler, Smithsonian Institution; Roger M. Herriott, The Johns Hopkins University; A. Starker Leopold, University of California (Berkeley); Nicholas Polunin, *Biological Conservation*; John E. Randall, Bishop Museum, Honolulu, Hawaii; George W. Ray, Jr., private lawyer; Frank M. Potter, Jr., Environmental Clearinghouse; Charles H. Southwick, The Johns Hopkins University; Richard Young, private lawyer. I am indebted to all these persons, for their very constructive criticism.

## REFERENCES

Abel, Robert B. (1968). A history of federal involvement in marine sciences: emergence of the National Sea Grant Program. *Natural Resources Lawyer* **1**, 105-14.

Alexander, Lewis M. (1966). Offshore claims of the world. Mimeo. for *Law of the Sea Institute.* University of Rhode Island, June-July, 8 pp.

Bardach, John E. and Ryther, John H. (1968). *The Status and Potential of Aquaculture. Vol. II: Particularly Fish Culture.* Amer. Inst. Biol. Sci., Clearinghouse for Fed. Sci. & Tech. Information, Springfield, Virginia, 225 pp., illustr.

Bascom, Willard (1966). Mining in the sea. Mimeo. for *Law of the Sea Institute,* University of Rhode Island, June-July, 1 p.

Belman, Murray J. (1968). The role of the State Department in formulating federal policy regarding marine resources. *Natural Resources Lawyer* **1**, 14-22.

Burke, William T. (1966*a*). Technological development and the law of the sea. Mimeo. for *Law of the Sea Institute,* University of Rhode Island, June-July, 18 pp.

Burke, William T. (1966*b*). Legal aspects of ocean exploitation—status and outlook. Pp. 1-23 in *Exploiting the Ocean. Trans. Second Annual Mar. Tech. Soc. Conf. & Exhibit.,* Mar. Tech. Soc., Washington, D.C.

Burke, William T. (1968). A negative view of a proposal for United Nations ownership of ocean mineral resources. *Natural Resources Lawyer* **1**, 42-62.

Burke, William T. (1969). Law, Science and the ocean. Mimeo. for *Law of the Sea Institute,* University of Rhode Island, August, 34 pp.

Chapman, V. J. (1968). Underwater reserves and parks. *Biol. Conserv.* **1**, 53.

Chapman, Wilbert M. (1966). Fishery resources in offshore waters. Mimeo for *Law of the Sea Institute,* University of Rhode Island, June-July, 18 pp.

Christy, Francis T., Jr. (1966). The distribution of the seas' fisheries wealth. Mimeo. for *Law of the Sea Institute,* University of Rhode Island, June-July, 14 pp.

Christy, Francis T., Jr. (1968). Alternative régimes for the marine resources underlying the high seas. *Natural Resources Lawyer* **1**, 63-77.

Clark, Eugenie (1967). The need for conservation in the sea. *Oryx* **9**, 151-3.

Close, Frederick, J. (1968). *The Sleeping Giant. An Industrial Viewpoint on the Potential of Oceanography.* Mar. Tech. Soc., Washington, D. C. Reprinted by Alcoa, Pittsburgh, 12 pp.

Commission on Marine Science, Engineering and Resources (1969). *Our Nation and the Sea.* US Government Printing Office, Washington, D. C., xi + 305 pp.

Crutchfield, James A. (1968). The convention on fishing and living resources of the high seas. *Natural Resources Lawyer* **1**, 114-24.

Darling, F. Fraser (1967). A wider environment of ecology and conservation. *Daedalus* **96**, 1003-19.

Dasmann, Raymond F. (1968). *A Different Kind of Country.* Macmillan, New York, and Collier-Macmillan, London, viii + 276 pp., illustr.

Dozier, J. R. (1966). Offshore oil and gas operations present and future. Mimeo. for *Law of the Sea Institute,* University of Rhode Island, June-July, 11 pp.

Economic Associates, Inc. (1968). *The Economic Potential of the Mineral and Botanical Resources of the US Continental Shelf and Slope.* A Study Prepared for the National Council on Marine Resources and Engineering Development, Clearinghouse for Fed. Sci. & Tech. Information, Springfield, Virginia, 520 pp.

Ehrlich, Paul (1969). Eco-catastrophe. Reprinted from *Ramparts,* Int. Planned Parenthood Fed., New York, September, 5 pp.

Eichelberger, Clark M. (1968). A case for the administration of mineral resources underlying the high seas by the United Nations. *Natural Resources Lawyer* **1**, 85-94.

Elton, Charles S. (1958). *The Ecology of Invasions by Animals and Plants.* Methuen, London, and John Wiley, New York, 181 pp., illustr.

Ely, Northcutt (1967*a*). American policy options in the development of undersea mineral resources. Mimeo. for *90th Ann. Meeting Amer. Bar Assn,* Honolulu, August, 10 pp.

Ely, Northcutt (1967*b*). The administration of mineral resources underlying the high seas. Mimeo. for *Amer. Bar Assn National Institute on Marine Resources,* Long Beach, California, June, 12 pp.

Ely, Northcutt (1968). A case for the administration of mineral resources underlying the high seas by national interests. *Natural Resources Lawyer* **1**, 78-84.

Emery, K. O. (1966). Geological methods for locating mineral deposits on the ocean floor. Pp. 24-43 in *Exploiting the Ocean. Trans. Second Ann. Marine Tech. Soc. Conf. & Exhibit.,* Mar. Tech. Soc., Washington D. C.

Friedham, Robert L. (1966). Conflict over law: voting behavior at the United Nations Law of the Sea Conference. Mimeo. for *Law of the Sea Institute,* University of Rhode Island, June-July, 16 pp.

Frost, Justin (1969). Earth, air, water. *Environment* **11**, 14-33.

Griffin, William L. (1967). The emerging law of ocean space. *Int. Lawyer* **1**, 548-87.

Harlow, Bruce A. (1966). Territorial sea concept. Mimeo. for *Law of the Sea Institute,* University of Rhode Island, 1 p.

Hearn, Wilfred A. (1968). The role of the United States Navy in the formulation of federal policy regarding the sea. *Natural Resources Lawyer* **1**, 23-31.

Hedgpeth, Joel (in press). Atomic waste disposal in the sea: an ecological dilemma. In *The Careless Technology* (Ed. M. Taghi Farvar & John Milton). Natural History Press, Doubleday, New York.

Interagency Committee on Oceanography (1963). *Oceanography, the Ten Years*

*Ahead.* ICO Pamphlet No. 10, Federal Council for Science and Technology, Washington D. C., 54 pp.

Interagency Committee on Oceanography (1967). *National Oceanographic Program.* ICO Pamphlet No. 24, Federal Council on Science and Technology, iv + 107 pp.

Krueger, Robert B. (1968). The Convention on the Continental Shelf and the need for its revision and some comments regarding the régime for the lands beyond. *Natural Resources Lawyer* **1**, 1-18.

Luce, Charles F. (1968). The development of ocean minerals and law of the sea. *Natural Resources Lawyer* **1**, 29-35.

McDougal, Myers S. (1968). Revision on the Geneva Convention on the law of the sea (Comments). *Natural Resources Lawyer* **1**, 19-28.

Mero, John L. (1966). Review of mineral values on and under the ocean floor. Pp. 61-78 in *Exploiting the Ocean. Trans. Second Ann. Mar. Tech. Soc. Conf. & Exhibit.*, Mar. Tech. Soc., Washington, D. C.

Mero, John L. (1968). Mineral deposits in the sea. *Natural Resources Lawyer* **1**, 130-7.

National Academy of Sciences (1964). *Economic Benefits from Oceanographic Research.* NAS Publ. 1228, 50 pp.

National Academy of Sciences (1967). *Oceanography* 1966: *Achievements and Opportunities.* NAS Publ. 1492, 183 pp.

National Academy of Sciences (1969). *An Oceanic Quest: The International Decade of Ocean Exploration.* NAS Publ. 1709, 115 pp.

National Council on Marine Resources and Engineering Development (1967). *Marine Science Affairs–A Year of Transition.* US Govt. Printing Office, Washington, D. C., v + 157 pp.

National Council on Marine Resources and Engineering Development (1968*a*). *International Decade of Ocean Exploration.* US Govt. Printing Office, Washington, D. C., i + 7 pp.

National Council on Marine Resources and Engineering Development (1968*b*). *Marine Science Affairs–A Year of Plans and Progress.* US Govt. Printing Office, Washington, D. C., xiii + 228 pp.

Neblett, William R. (1966). A fishery view of recent law of the sea conferences. Mimeo. for *Law of the Sea Institute,* University of Rhode Island, June-July, 15 pp.

Nelson, T. W. and Burk, C. A. (1966). Petroleum resources of the continental margins of the United States. Pp. 116-33 in *Exploiting the Ocean. Trans. Second Ann. Mar. Tech. Soc. Conf. & Exhibit.*, Mar. Tech. Soc., Washington, D. C.

New York Times (1969). Seabed potential for arms studied, 8 Oct.

Ocean Science News (1969). 1970 federal ocean market. *Ocean Science News* **11**, 2-3.

Oda, Shigeru (1968). The Geneva Conventions on law of the sea: some suggestions for their revision. *Natural Resources Lawyer* **1**, 103-13.

Odum, Eugene P. (1959). *Fundamentals of Ecology,* second edn. W. B. Saunders, Philadelphia & London, xvii + 546 pp., illustr.

Osborn, Fairfield (1953). *The Limits of the Earth.* Little, Brown, Boston, x + 238 pp.

Panel on Oceanography, President's Science Advisory Committee (1966). *Effective Use of the Sea.* US Govt Printing Office, Washington, D. C., xv + 144 pp.

Polikarpov, G. G. (1966). *Radioecology of Aquatic Organisms.* Reinhold, New York, xxviii + 314 pp.

Program of Policy Studies in Science and Technology (1969). A critical review of the Marine Science Commission Report. The George Washington Univ. and the Mar. Tech. Soc. Law Committee, Washington, D. C., 114 pp.

Randall, John E. (1969). Conservation in the sea. *Oryx* **10**, 31-38.

Ray, Carleton (1961). Marine Preserves for ecological research. Pp. 323-8 in *Trans. 26th No. Amer. Wildlife & Nat. Res. Conf.,* Wildlife Man. Inst., Washington, D. C.

Ray, Carleton (1965). The scientific need for shallow-water marine sanctuaries. Pp. 83-98 in *Symp. on Sci. Use of Natural Areas,* XVI Int. Cong. Zool. Reprinted by *Field Research Projects, Natural Area Studies,* No. 2, Coconut Grove, Fla., x + 103 pp.

Ray, Carleton (1966). Inshore marine conservation. Pp. 77-87 in *First World Conference on National Parks.* US Govt Printing Office, Washington, D. C., xxxiv + 471 pp.

Ray, Carleton (1968). *Marine Parks for Tanzania.* Conservation Foundation, Washington, D. C., 47 pp., illustr.

Ripley, W. Dillon (1966). The future of environmental improvement. Reprinted by *The Graduate School Press,* from *Environmental Improvement: Air, Water and Soil,* US Dept Agriculture, Washington, D. C., pp. 85-93.

Ryther, John H. and Bardach, John E. (1968). *The Status and Potential of Aquaculture. Vol. 1: Particularly Invertebrates and Algal Culture.* Amer. Inst. Biol. Sci., Clearinghouse for Fed. Sci. & Tech. Infor., Springfield, Virginia, 261 pp.

Task Force on Environmental Health and Related Problems (1967). *A Strategy for a Liveable Environment.* Rept to the Sec. of Health, Education & Welfare, US Govt Printing Office, Washington, D. C., xxi + 90 pp.

Tubman, William C. (1966). The legal status of minerals located on or beneath the sea floor beyond the continental shelf. Pp. 379-404 in *Exploiting the Ocean. Trans. Second Ann. Mar. Tech. Soc. Conf. & Exhibit.,* Mar. Tech. Soc., Washington, D. C.

Walford, Lionel A. (1958). *Living Resources of the Sea.* Ronald Press, New York, xi + 321 pp.

Weber, Alban (1966). Our newest frontier: the sea bottom. Some legal aspects of the continental shelf status. Pp. 405-11 in *Exploiting the Ocean. Trans. Second Ann. Mar. Tech. Soc. Conf. & Exhibit.,* Mar. Tech. Soc., Washington, D. C.

Wilkey, Malcolm R. (1969). The role of private industry in the deep ocean. *Symp. on Private Industry Abroad.* Southwestern Legal Foundation, Dallas, Texas, June. Reprinted by Mathew Bender, Washington, D. C., 40 pp.

Young, Richard (1968). The legal régime of the deep sea floor. *Amer. Jour. Int. Law* **62**, 641-53.

# 41. Evolution of the Law of the Sea –Destruction of the Pristine Nature of Basic Oceanographic Research

GEORGE S. ROBINSON* 1973

The 1973 Law of the Sea Conference holds the most potential for destruction of the "majesty and rightness" of law since Hugo Grotius fabricated the myth in 1609 that the high seas are *res communis* to all maritime nations; and that freedom of the seas was premised upon some concept–of high and exalted origin–vaguely understood, but firmly grasped, as the "right of innocent passage." That courageous Dutch jurist took it upon himself to initiate the distant sire of a vast body of law built upon a mythical principle of unassailable social contract, i.e., the supranational right of all nations to use the high seas without interference.

Strangely, "freedom of the seas" seems to have evolved over the centuries into the catch-phrase for a mosaic of customary and formal law embodying the preservation of all that is good and unencumbered in relations among nations and individuals. "Freedom of the seas" has become accepted as a conglomerate principle of law ensuring the existence of certain vast bodies of water where all nations meet in their separate tasks on a parity with each other. However, it was not the equality, the equity of interest, the sense of uninhibited brotherhood, that moved Grotius to argue for *Mare Liberum.* To the contrary, the increasing colonial trade and exploration among the great sea powers at the time were directly responsible for the Grotius manifesto–national economics and domestic politics were responsible for its anonymous publication. Evolution of that manifesto has led to its propagandized status of the present day "44-40 or fight" battle joinder–"complete Freedom of the Seas, or nothing at all."

Although this slogan is most often uttered by the basic research scientists in oceanography and the apologists for unilateral establishment of jurisdiction over portions of the high seas and certain activities conducted therein, it is only a small minority voice–albeit an important one. To determine the majority view of nations regarding the present status of the law of the

* This article expresses the views and opinions of the author alone and does not necessarily represent the views of any government agency or institution with which he is associated.

Dr. George S. Robinson is Assistant General Counsel to the Smithsonian Institution. He is a member of the Washington, D.C., and Virginia Bars and author of over twenty articles, papers, and books.

From *Natural Resources Journal,* Vol. 13, No. 3, pp. 504-510, 1973. Reprinted with light editing and with permission of the author and *Natural Resources Journal* published by the University of New Mexico School of Law, Albuquerque, New Mexico 87131.

seas it is essential to review briefly the attitudes, politics, technology, and economics influencing use and potential use of the oceans. Of primary concern in this matrix of attitudes, technology, and uses is the fact that the law of the seas serves as the foundation of all spirit, if not legal substance, upon which international economic, political, etc., agreements and treaties rest.

## PRESENT ATTITUDES REFLECT SHAMBLES MADE OF OCEANS LAW BY POPULATION AND TECHNOLOGY

Grotius' concept of *Mare Liberum* prevailed for better than three centuries over John Selden's *Mare Clausum*, or closed seas concept. Although freedom of the seas might well have been a concept tarnished by compromise and growing questions of credibility during times of peace as well as war, it was a successful, and therefore acceptable, concept to the extent it served a majority of interests. However, today the concept is being subjected to an almost overwhelming attack–both frontal and on the flanks. The deep-rooted fundamental reasons are three: The incredible size of the world's population; increased accessibility of the high seas and substrate resources proportionate to the expanded state of basic sciences and new levels of technology; and the increasing geopolitical phenomenon of international racism and parochial interests manifest in ever-tightening, nationalistically oriented societies. Economics and some rather intricate and sophisticated views of national defense operations have combined, as a result of these three basic precipitants, to create dissension among nations, since World War II, as to what the width of the coastal State territorial sea should be, will be, could be, and from what geographic and jurisdictional reference points it will be measured.

Although there was almost unanimous accord before World War II that the seas extending beyond 12 nautical miles were "high seas" and "not subject to the territorial jurisdiction of any state," subsequent contentions between advocates of the 3 nautical miles and 12 nautical miles limits, and now the 200 nautical miles limit, has made international agreement on territorial limits seem impossible. On the other hand, both the extremity and adamancy of certain positions taken by several countries, regarding jurisdiction over territorial waters, combined with the politics of national and transnational economics and military planning requirements, may force early compromises leading to international accord–at the expense of less pressing issues, such as freedom of basic research in existing coastal waters, or what may become coastal waters through unilateral actions and multilateral compromise.

The 1958 and 1960 Law of the Sea Conferences amounted to relatively Herculean efforts to codify the law of the seas at the point of evolution it had reached. Regardless of the efforts, however, the Conferences were a culmination of little more than clarification fora regarding both the state of maritime law and non-law. The various jurisdictional issues, critical and sensitive at the same time, were not addressed. Since those Conferences, technological advances and the ever-growing number of unilateral claims to maritime jurisdiction–broad in scope and varied in objective–have generated conflicts between different users of the same ocean space. For example, as pointed out by John R. Stevenson, Legal Advisor of the U.S. Department of State,

> seabed drilling and mining may interfere with navigation and fishing, spills from tankers with recreation on beaches, and pollution control measures with maritime trade.[1]

In any event, an intricate and subtly shifting pattern of unilateral claims, to certain uses and jurisdictions over areas heretofore considered international waters, airspace, and substrate of the high seas, is evolving into a *de facto* patchwork of seemingly surrepti-

1. 6 Int'l Lawyer 468 (1972).

tious, or even blatant, expressions of parochial nationalisms.

For the most part, there is merit to both sides of the issue of whether unilateral claims to jurisdiction over portions of high seas is justified. The simple glaring fact is that the presently evolved body of law applicable to use of the high seas is totally inadequate to satisfy the economic standards and needs of the entire international community which have been shaped by the multitudinous facets of modern technology. There are many of the world's leading jurists who firmly believe that unless a rational, sophisticated, and organic reformation of the law of the seas is undertaken on a broad multilateral basis, the unilateral jurisdictional partition of the oceans–reasonable or not–will lead to fairly rapid disintegration of that body of law and inevitable wide-scale conflicts. In this context, it should be clearly understood that the "law of the sea lies at the heart of modern international law as it emerged in the 17th century." This body of law is, in fact, the foundation upon which rests the majority of the international community's innumerable unilateral and multilateral treaties, agreements, and "understandings" relating to matters ranging from economic accords, and commercial aircraft overflight rights, to political alliances for military and ideological objectives. If the law of the sea undergoes an undisciplined upheaval, it is rather easy to recognize the vast and substantive effects it will have on the legal stability of the entire international community. As observed by John Stevenson, in a statement before the House Subcommittee on International Organizations and Movements, April 1972, should the law of the sea

> collapse under the weight of conflicting unilateral actions based almost exclusively on immediate national interests, the result will be a severe blow to the prospects for the rule of law not only in the oceans, but in the international community generally.[2]

From the above sketch, it is fairly obvious that critical, expansive, and sophisticated interests are at issue presently, and will be the subject of intensive negotiation, compromise, and accord at the 1973, et seq., Law of the Sea Conference to be convened under the aegis of the United Nations. Of singular significance, also, is the fact that resolution of conflicting jurisdictional interests within a peaceful framework will be accomplished not by the so-called maritime super-powers, but by effective and often annoying participation of a multitude of nations often referred to in a diplomatically condescending manner as the Lesser Developed Countries. Without equivocation it can be said that one of the most, if not the principal, expendable items in the anticipated multilateral negotiations is the scientific research of the oceans. The reasons for such expendability lie in the views and relative influential posture of coastal States, impelling needs of the three or four major military countries, and the scientists themselves who are directly involved in investigation of the oceans.

## A DEFINITION OF SCIENTIFIC INVESTIGATION OF THE OCEANS–ATTITUDES OF NON-PARTICIPATING COASTAL STATES

Several countries have stated publicly their firm convictions that scientific research of oceans is of benefit to all mankind. For this reason alone, they feel that such research should be open to all and that there should be maximum freedom of scientific research in the oceans. However, certain of the coastal States have denied the efficacy and ultimate equity of this reasoning on the basis of their inability to (1) participate effectively in such research and utilize the resultant data in a beneficial way; (2) to protect national interest in resources in an area of recognizable jurisdiction; and (3) prevent

2. *Hearings on Law of the Sea and Peaceful Uses of the Seabeds Before the Subcomm. on International Organizations and Movements of the House Comm. on Foreign Affairs,* 92nd Cong., 2nd Sess., at 2 (1972).

environmental degradation of coastal waters and shorelines by mining, drilling, farming, etc., operations resulting from scientific research.

The general response to such national concerns is reflected in the observation of John Stevenson, that

> [a] new and more vigorous approach to the problems of training, participation, and technology sharing may provide the basis for an accommodation that protects freedom of scientific research and assures that it is of maximum benefit to all, including developing countries.[3]

To the developing country that happens to be a coastal State, the two basic interests in expanding and confirming their jurisdictional holds over territorial waters [as well as supra- and subjacent resources] are economic participation and/or leverage in international negotiations, and national defense interests. In the first instance, a coastal State with minimum or no ability to participate in oceanographic science or commercial exploitation of such research, arrogation of high seas jurisdiction can be used in direct or indirect negotiations of any nature with other countries capable of, and interested in, exploitation of resources located in such areas. This unilaterally assumed jurisdiction can be employed both as a quid-pro-quo in negotiations, or as an effective leverage to obtain action or compromise.

The coastal State need not be a world power to enforce its jurisdiction; all that is needed is a reasonably effective gunboat of fairly modern vintage. World politics and effective public condemnation of retaliation by "super powers" against annoying action of "lesser developed countries" involves minimal risk in the use of such gunboats. Further, covert unilateral accord between a coastal State attempting to extend its jurisdiction over high seas areas, and a State that continues to require free passage through such areas, permits maintenance by both parties of a public image that avoids confrontation and conflict. A coastal State can establish a *de jure* jurisdiction with the contesting State in fact obtaining its requirement of innocent passage—at the same time offering a minimum of face-saving remarks about the degradation of established international law and spirit of comity among nations.

In the second instance, expansion of jurisdiction or control can serve as a buffer, against foreign intelligence gathering, for developing countries which are unfortunate to have hostile neighbors, or which are the objects of extant colonial exploitation by other nations. Unpalatable as they may be, these are hard facts giving rise to national paranoia and xenophobia which will require more to dissipate than the virtuous orations of even basic research scientists.

The important aspect is that the principal issue is not the collection of data by foreign nationals in the waters of a coastal State; rather it is the use to which the research data is put, by nations having access to such data from the international science community, which may abuse or be hostile to the best economic, political, military, etc., interests of the coastal State concerned.

This is very much the same problem that the international community is struggling with regarding use of the present Earth Resources Technology Satellite, or the aeronautical and satellite remote resource sensing devices. Concisely, what is beneficial scientific data to one country, may be to another State a divulgence of vital economic or military intelligence to hostile or commercial adversaries. Again, palatable or not, these are realities that now must be dealt with by those involved in scientific research. They are facts which if not appreciated by the scientific community, certainly must be respected as legitimate concerns and accommodated in any new procedural and organizational restructuring of international law of the sea.

Scientific investigation of the high seas and territorial waters can best be defined,

3. 109 Cong. Rec. E 8934 (1972).

for present purposes, by the characteristics of types of investigation. Although scientific study and investigation very legitimately can be conducted in such a way as to obtain no more than systematized knowledge of a given subject or object, it more often than not must be related to the use to which it is put, or is capable of being put. In short, it must be evaluated within the context of existing political, economic, nationalistic, and technological realities.

## LEVEL OF AWARENESS OF THE SCIENTIFIC INVESTIGATOR

Although certain private institutions and advisory bodies, such as Scripps Institute of Oceanography and the National Academy of Sciences, have sounded the clarion to battle for freedom of the seas, the efforts seem to have been quite limited both in scope of evaluation and in terms of informing scientific investigators of the seriousness of the forthcoming Law of the Sea Conference regarding freedom of scientific research. There has been no real success in establishing a sophisticated position regarding scientific investigation of coastal waters, and the expansion of territorial waters jurisdiction. The response of many scientists seems to be "no compromise—freedom of the seas or nothing at all!!" Although this places a heavy burden on governmental officials, particularly in the United States, who are responsible for evolving positions to negotiate with other nations, it can simplify matters to the extent it already has, i.e., freedom of scientific research is easily and readily compromised for more important economic and military interests.

It appears that a working conference to educate scientists as to what is happening to the law of the sea and how the changes will affect oceanographic research is long overdue. Hopefully, detailed awareness of the situation may result in an effective influence of ocean scientists on the official positions negotiated by U.S. and other governments. Although freedom to conduct scientific research on the high seas always has been a myth, it certainly will not be detrimental to the interests of scientific investigators of the oceans if a rational approach to multilateral control of such investigations in coastal waters—regardless of ultimate seaward limits—is formulated by the user scientists and protected by the major maritime nations with advanced technology necessary for scientific research.

In any event, the controlling factor at this time should be recognition, by scientist and lawyer alike, that present accommodations for oceanographic research in foreign coastal waters and much of the area presently considered the high seas will not remain unchanged. Further, they will not become less complicated and easier to achieve. At best, if not traded cheaply through inattention of delegates to the 1973 Law of the Sea Conference, freedom of basic research of the oceans will become the object of a sophisticated legal framework and enervating controls sufficient to make scientists leave the subdisciplines of oceanographic research in frustration and disgust. Concisely, the time for rhetoric is long passed—the time for serious, realistic involvement of scientists is quite at hand.

# 42. Freedom for Science in the Oceans

GEORGE CADWALADER 1973

"Americans," wrote de Tocqueville in 1835, "judge that the diffusion of knowledge must necessarily be advantageous and the consequences of ignorance fatal" (*1*). No less true today, this characterization perhaps helps explain the astonishment with which most American oceanographers have reacted to the efforts of developing countries to curtail their freedom to conduct scientific research in the oceans. The response of our marine scientists has been to base their defense of this freedom largely on the intangible but deeply felt conviction that "the quest for knowledge about the oceans is a universal right not to be abridged by national restrictions" (*2*, p. 1). The comparatively few efforts that have been made to reply to the often well-articulated contrary views of the developing countries tend to stress the economic and social benefits that accrue from unrestricted basic research. This argument has proved less than convincing to countries whose mistrust of science is based on the belief that its benefits (which they do not question) are limited to the wealthy few possessing the technology to exploit its findings. For, not surprisingly, the growing tension that exists between the developed and developing countries has become a factor in the debate within the United Nations over freedom for science (*3*).

Since 1945, the area of the ocean known as the "high seas" has been steadily eroded by coastal states' expanding their claims of jurisdiction. More recently, the legal doctrine of freedom of the seas, which historically has applied beyond the limits of national jurisdiction, has come under increasing attack by states calling for the establishment of some form of international authority to regulate on behalf of the international community activities under and on the high seas. These pressures for change, exerted primarily by the developing countries, have led the U.N. General Assembly to call for a new Law of the Sea Conference to begin in 1973. A 90-nation "Committee on the Peaceful Uses of the Seabed and Ocean Floor Beyond the Limits of National Jurisdiction" (known simply as the Seabed Committee) is cur-

George Cadwalader is a retired Marine Corps officer and recently was an executive officer with the Marine Policy and Ocean Management Program, Woods Hole Oceanographic Institution, Woods Hole, Massachusetts.

From *Science*, Vol. 182, No. 4107, pp. 15-20, 1973. Reprinted with light editing and with permission of the author and the American Association for the Advancement of Science. Copyright 1973 by the American Association for the Advancement of Science.

rently engaged in negotiations preparatory to the conference.

Almost inevitably, the result of the 1973 conference will be that substantially more, if not all, of the ocean space will fall under some form of national or international jurisdiction. The extent of the jurisdiction exercised in the various areas of control that develop will be a matter for negotiation, and freedom for science will certainly be one of the more controversial bargaining points. If science is to continue with a minimum of regulation, the opponents of controls will have to approach these negotiations with more than impassioned pleas for total freedom. Their case will have to be built on a realistic assessment of what can be achieved in view of the prevailing political climate, and they will have to bring something to bargain with in terms of specific proposals aimed at meeting the objections of those who seek to restrict or prevent science in their areas of jurisdiction. Above all, they must be flexible enough to adapt their position to changes in the legal doctrines that justify actions within the ocean.

## FREEDOM VERSUS THE COMMON HERITAGE

The 17th-century doctrine of freedom of the seas provided the basis for all law of the sea for nearly 300 years. The preeminence of this doctrine was challenged in 1970, when the U.N. General Assembly declared the seabed and its resources beyond the limits of national jurisdiction, to be the "common heritage of all mankind" (*4*). To implement the concept of common heritage will require different legal arrangements than would prevail if the seabeds remained under traditional law. These differences are illustrated in Table 42-1.

## THE ATTACK ON FREEDOM

The dissatisfaction of developing countries with traditional law of the sea was evident at the 1958 Law of the Sea Conference (*5*). The acceptance of the common heritage concept 12 years later provided a basis for a legal system more compatible with their interests and has led to attacks of increasing

Table 42-1. Comparison of Freedom Doctrine and Common Heritage Concept.

| *Freedom* | *Common Heritage* |
|---|---|
| The seabed belongs to everyone (or to no one) and all have equal right of access to it. | The seabed is the common heritage of all mankind and the right of access to it is not necessarily equal for all purposes. |
| Everyone has an equal right to exploit the seabed for his personal gain and no one may deny this right to another. | Exploitation of the seabed is done on behalf of the international community. |
| Any usage of the seabed is permissible (unless specifically prohibited by treaty), providing only that it does not interfere "unreasonably" with other uses. | Uses of the seabed are allowed on the basis of their conformity to standards established under the concept of the common heritage. |
| If two users compete for the same part of the seabed or otherwise propose uses that are mutually exclusive, priority is established by who gets there first. | Priorities among competing uses are established by balancing the interests involved for the greatest net benefit of the world community. |
| Existing law of the sea requires no specific administering or enforcing agency. Claims of "unreasonable interference" are settled by persuasion or coercion. | Law devised to implement the common heritage concept may require an administering agency to determine priorities, collect revenues, issue licenses, and so forth. |

frequency on the doctrine of freedom of the seas.

Freedom of the seas evolved into accepted law during a period when the major European nations were beginning to develop sizable merchant fleets. The origin of this concept in 1609, as a counterclaim to the Pope's division of the ocean between Spain and Portugal, has not been lost on the developing countries, who correctly contend that international law is only valid as long as it reflects the interests of the majority of the international community. Freedom of the seas, they argue, met this test as long as the oceans were regarded primarily as avenues for commerce. The principle has become increasingly obsolete as traditional uses of the sea have been expanded and other uses have emerged. Moreover, some have contended that no principle can be held as binding on states that did not even exist during the period in which it became accepted international law.

The developing countries thus maintain that there exists today a need for new legal arrangements governing the uses of the sea—arrangements guaranteeing them access to the ocean resources, which are the common heritage, but which de facto are denied to all but the developed countries under the existing concept of freedom of the seas. This point was effectively presented to the U.N. International Law Commission by the Ecuadorian delegate, who argued that "the alleged equality of all states with respect to their rate of access to the high seas and their right to exploit its resources is somewhat illusory, because only the great maritime and shipping powers exercise this right on a really large scale. Thus, the exercise of this right depends on economic power, and equality before the law loses all reality in the face of the economic inequality of states" (*6*, p. 21).

The doctrine of common heritage meets this objection by providing that a state's right to share in seabed resources is not dependent on its economic power. The Seabed Committee has accordingly been charged with designing an International Seabed Authority (ISA) for the purpose of ensuring the equitable distribution of profits from seabed resources among the international community. A major problem in this effort has been the inability to agree on the limits of the geographical area in which the common heritage concept is to apply.

Developing countries have, by and large, argued with equal fervor for both the common heritage and the right to wide areas of national jurisdiction over ocean space. Their critics have been quick to point out that such national claims remove from the area of the common heritage most of the known seabed resources. This criticism has not yet moved the developing countries to reconsider their position, nor is it likely to, since it has yet to be shown that in the short term a coastal state will profit more from the international management of seabed resources than it would from outright ownership of its adjacent continental shelf. Thus, from the perspective of most poor countries, the most advantageous bargaining position is to claim ownership of their shelves and use the vehicle of common heritage to secure a share in whatever resources lie beyond.

This position portends ill for science. If it prevails, it promises: (i) the creation of a strong ISA with broad powers to regulate activities on and under the high seas and (ii) expanded national jurisdiction over ocean space now considered high seas.

## THE FUNCTIONS OF THE ISA

In general, the developing countries have maintained that the ISA should have broad powers to regulate activities (including scientific research) within the area of its jurisdiction (*7*). The developed countries argue that the ISA's functions should be limited to granting leases to mining rights on the sea floor and levying taxes on any resources recovered, with the proceeds being used to support projects of benefit to the international community. The traditional concept of freedom of the seas would remain applicable to all activities not specifically conceded to the ISA.

This apparently procedural dispute reflects the more fundamental disagreement over the legal basis for activities within the ocean. Underlying the position of the developing countries is the assumption that common heritage has replaced freedom as the basis for all law of the sea. The ISA, by virtue of its common heritage mandate, thus acquires at least potential jurisdiction over all activities formerly considered free.

The preference of developed countries for an ISA of strictly limited jurisdiction assumes that the two legal doctrines can coexist. The United States in particular reflects this attitude. The United States was among the first countries to endorse the concept of seabed resources as the common heritage of mankind and to call for the establishment of an international authority to oversee exploitation (*8*). At the same time, the United States has continued in its support of the principle of freedom of the seas, particularly as this freedom relates to navigation, overflight, and (with a much lower priority) science. By so doing, it perpetuates an ambiguity introduced originally in 1945, when President Truman claimed for the United States ownership of all seabed resources on its adjacent continental shelf out to a water depth of 200 meters. Then, as now, the United States held to a territorial sea of 3 (nautical) miles in the interest of maximum freedom for navigation. Thus the effect of the Truman Proclamation was to claim jurisdiction only out to 3 miles on the ocean surface, while at the same time claiming far more extensive jurisdiction on the ocean floor. How to exercise jurisdiction on the ocean floor without exerting some control over the water column above has never been made entirely clear.

This question ceases to be theoretical in the case of the proposed ISA. Any lease the ISA grants on the sea floor will inevitably result in some form of mining activities on the sea surface. Large-scale seabed mining, legal by virtue of the common heritage principle, may impede or prevent other, more traditional uses of the ocean still justified on the basis of freedom. When this does occur, no clear way exists to evaluate the relative merits of the two competing activities, since each claims rights arising from a different legal concept.

Priorities among mutually exclusive uses can only be established if some common standard for comparison applies. When, as is the case with traditional law of the sea, all peaceful uses are presumed free, no such standard is provided. The rather crude criterion of "unreasonable interference" developed because conflicts have occasionally occurred. But the concept of freedom, as its name implies, remains predicated on the assumption that such conflicts will be the exception and that they can be easily resolved in view of the vastness of the ocean and the limited number of activities it supports. However, as activities increase and the apparent size of the ocean decreases, there arises a need for more precise standards than those provided by "unreasonable interference" to establish the optimum balance among activities. The common heritage concept permits uses to be ranked by the degree to which they serve the common heritage, or, alternatively, by the degree to which they do not impede it. The latter is perhaps the better test, since there are many uses which benefit the user and neither help nor harm anyone else.

There obviously can be no universally applicable ranking of activities. Priorities will vary with circumstances, but priorities can always be established if there is a clear objective. Maximizing the common heritage is a vague objective in the abstract, but for any given situation it translates into the realistic and practical goal of balancing activities for the maximum benefit of the greatest number. This balance is not apt to occur naturally in a "free" environment, since often activities that compete for the same ocean space are not in direct economic competition with one another.

However, even if one agrees to the theoretical advantages of regulating activities for the maximum benefit, it is questionable whether, in practice, the ISA can effectively exercise this function. The difficulty here is not only organizational, it also involves achieving agreement on the limits of the ISA's authority. Even acceptance of the common heritage concept as the legal basis for all activities in the ocean should not empower the ISA with blanket jurisdiction. Its function is properly limited to regulating only those activities that are mutually exclusive, ecologically damaging, or economically and biologically wasteful. All other activities not included in these categories must, by definition, either serve the common heritage or not impede it, and thus the ISA has no legal claim to jurisdiction over them.

Be this as it may, positions at the forthcoming conference will be based on considerations of national and group interest rather than sound law. The developed countries have ignored the logical inconsistencies in their position simply because they cannot go on record as opposing common heritage in principle; at the same time, however, they are not willing to accept the possible curtailment of existing freedoms that its support implies. Their fears in this regard are not groundless, since the developing countries quite obviously support this concept largely as a means of exerting their collective influence in an area from which they are currently excluded by a combination of existing law and lack of technology. In view of the current international climate, it is unlikely that a strong ISA dominated by the developing countries would prove a particularly impartial judge of what activities constituted the common interest.

Regardless of how narrowly the role of the ISA is initially defined, the future will see continuing pressure exerted by the developing countries to broaden the ISA's functions within the area of its jurisdiction. Since science is one of the issues on which positions are divided most clearly along developed-developing lines, efforts to empower the ISA with control over research will continue, even if the attempt fails in 1973.

## LIMITS OF NATIONAL JURISDICTION

The seaward extension of national jurisdiction in the form of a territorial sea was an early exception to freedom of the seas. The right of a state to exercise sovereignty over the strip of ocean adjacent to its coast arose from the need to provide a measure of security against seaborne attack, and the initial seaward limit of jurisdiction of 3 miles was established for the very pragmatic reason that, in the 17th century, this was the maximum conceivable range of shore-based cannon. The original limit thus established a precedent for future adjustments as better cannon were invented or other new conditions arose. However, few states chose to avail themselves of this precedent until after the Truman Proclamation in 1945.

Although the proclamation was intended to claim jurisdiction only over the continental shelf beyond the territorial sea, the U.S. action has been invoked by other states to justify claims for more comprehensive jurisdiction. Iceland recently established an exclusive fisheries zone out to 50 miles from its coast. Chile claims a similar zone 200 miles wide, and Canada maintains the right to prosecute polluters in its Arctic waters. Brazil, Ecuador, and Peru have simply claimed a 200-mile territorial sea, although Ecuador and Peru refer euphemistically to this area as a "maritime zone." So the Truman Proclamation has come back to haunt the United States. The United States, along with the other great maritime powers, considers the major ocean "resource" to be freedom of navigation, and today it finds itself in the embarrassing position of having paved the way for claims that, if honored, will give its naval and research ships access to large parts of the ocean only upon the sufferance of coastal states, over 70 of which are classified as developing nations.

The limits of national jurisdiction have thus become one of the thorniest issues in the Seabed Committee negotiations. The alternatives currently being debated range from 12- to 200-mile limits, with the most likely compromise being a 12-mile territorial sea, with free transit guaranteed by treaty through all the straits that would otherwise come under national jurisdiction. Between 12 and 200 miles, in the area becoming known as the "resource zone," states will probably be given limited jurisdiction for specific purposes (conservation, resource and fisheries management, and so forth).

It is in these resource zones, where the relative jurisdictions of the state and the ISA remain to be defined, that positions on science have become polarized. Developing countries demand that research be one of the activities over which they retain jurisdiction. Developed countries are pushing (with varying degrees of emphasis) for minimum restrictions on science beyond a narrow territorial sea. The stakes involved are evident if one considers that the area between 12 and 200 miles seaward encompasses some 30 percent of the world ocean and is, by and large, the area of most interest scientifically and economically (*9*).

## COMMON HERITAGE AND ACCESS FOR SCIENCE

Access for scientists to all of the oceans beyond narrowly defined limits of national jurisdiction is one of the "freedoms" the developed countries hope to preserve at the forthcoming conference. Not unexpectedly, the attacks of developing countries on freedom for science have taken much the same form as those on the parent concept. Developing countries contend that science cannot be called a freedom when its exercise is limited only to the handful of nations who have a research capability, nor does it meet the test of being in the best interest of mankind when its results can provide military and economic advantage only to the few possessing the technological ability to exploit its findings.

These arguments are based on a quite different perception of basic research than exists among the developed countries. H. L. F. Von Helmholtz's famous statement that "whoever, in the pursuit of science, seeks after immediate practical utility may rest assured that he seeks in vain" has become such a truism for Western scientists that it appears in *Bartlett's Familiar Quotations* (*10*). In contrast is the developing country's view, as expressed by Brazilian diplomat Saraiva Guerreiro, that "in the last analysis, every particle of scientific knowledge can be translated into terms of economic gain or national security, and in the technological society, scientific knowledge means power" (*11*).

The frequent mention oceanographers make of the economic implications of their work contributes to this impression. Warren Wooster, a member of the National Academy of Sciences' Task Force on Freedom for Science, writes in an article demonstrating the "tenuous" connection between scientific research and economic payoff, that scientific geological investigations "will be less detailed and will otherwise differ from that of commercial petroleum or mineral prospectors" (*12*). Not long afterwards, K. O. Emery reported on his investigation of the Eastern Atlantic Continental Martin. He cited the mapping of two features that "may be potential sources of oil" (*13*). A great deal of additional work lies between the preliminary survey described and the actual drilling for oil in these areas. But developing countries have very few petroleum geologists, so they cannot be blamed if they see in the apparent contradiction between Wooster's statement and Emery's findings substantiation of their suspicion that "knowledge means power."

The actual relationship between basic research and power has been much debated. Suffice it to say here that, although this connection appears to be growing increasingly direct, it still remains impossible to predict what basic research will bear fruit in terms of social, military, or economic utility. The only certainly is that the more basic research is encouraged the better the chances for the kind of practical return from the oceans necessary to make the "common heritage" a meaningful concept.

Seen in this perspective, science can no longer be said to be the parochial concern of one group of men or one group of nations. If it can be organized to contribute to the common good, the entire international community will benefit from arrangements that most facilitate the conduct of research.

The question thus becomes one of whether the absence of regulations is the condition that produces the best basic research. Would it not be better to focus the collective attention of the limited number of research oceanographers on particular problems, perhaps by coordinating all research through the proposed ISA? Or, on a more local level, would not individual developing countries do better to stipulate the types of research they felt was needed off their coasts and only permit access to those willing to undertake it?

These might be feasible approaches if it were possible to predict what basic research will pay off in terms of tangible benefits. Research can be directed toward specific objectives, such as optimizing the return of food or minerals or minimizing the danger of hurricanes and pollution, but the potential of the ocean is so vast that further basic research will almost certainly lead to the discovery of other uses, and implications of existing uses, still undreamed of. Without knowing what these uses are, there is no way to mobilize scientific talent directly toward their achievement. The only alternative, as one laboratory director put it (*14*), is to "get good men and turn them loose," knowing from experience that even the most apparently esoteric investigation may lead to valuable results in solving the global problems of hunger, poverty, and pollution.

Another factor to consider in evaluating the implications of controlling basic research is the personality of the investigator himself. Very few scientists in basic research are much motivated by the possibility of their work leading to any practical results. More commonly, they are men driven mainly by a sense of curiosity developed sometimes to the point of eccentricity. While it is easy to make too much of the fact that scientists are somehow a breed apart, it is a fair generalization to say that, as a group, they are notoriously impatient with the petty intrusions of everyday life. Therefore, the environment in which they operate best is a fragile one, easily disrupted by the necessity to conform to bureaucratic regulations requiring lengthy advance notice of their investigations, detailed research plans, specific handling of data, and all the other requirements that follow with increased controls.

Both the proven but unpredictable return from basic research and the peculiar nature of the few men competent to conduct it suggest that restrictive regulations on science do in fact run counter to the common heritage concept. For if the ocean and its resources are the common heritage of mankind, it follows that states accepting this principle are obligated to subordinate, to some degree, their own interest in the area to the common interest of the international community. Scientific freedom can be justified on the grounds that, since research does yield knowledge of potential social utility, no state accepting the common heritage principle can properly erect barriers that restrict mankind from learning what he must know about the ocean in order to optimize its use for the benefit of all. The same logic condemns states that pay lip service to the common heritage concept, while at the same time claiming expansive areas of national jurisdiction. The concept is meaningless if the greater part of ocean resources is in the hands of individual states.

To maintain (as many will) that arguments such as these have little weight in the United Nations is to underestimate the amount of idealism underlying the concept of a common heritage. Although the developing countries have exploited this concept for the political leverage it affords, they and much of the rest of the world community are not blind to the hope that common heritage will provide the basis for a new world order based on cooperation rather than competition. Positions against regulation of science that are based on the idea of a common heritage will be difficult for any country to oppose, both politically and in principle.

## OPEN RESEARCH VERSUS LIMITED EXPLORATION

If science is governed by the common heritage concept, the test of scientific "legitimacy" (that is, whether or not a particular type of investigation is subject to regulation) becomes a question of whether the investigation is structured so that its results contribute to the common good or whether they contribute only to the advantage of the sponsor. The difficulty, of course, lies in making this distinction. "A proposed U.S. position on freedom for science in the oceans" (*2*), drafted by the National Academy of Sciences, attempts to do this by differentiating between open research, which is "intended for the benefit of all mankind and characterized by the prompt availability and full publication of results" and limited exploration, "intended for the economic benefit of a limited group" (*2*, p. 2). The proposal suggests that these definitions are "easily understood and subject to operational tests" and calls for no restrictions on open research in areas beyond the territorial sea.

The academy does not consider the issue of burden of proof. Does it suffice for the scientist to apply these "operational tests" to his own work, or must he convince someone else that his is really open research? Publication, after all, occurs after the fact. How can developing countries, with little scientific capability of their own, be assured that they are receiving all data collected, and of what use is it to them if they do receive it? Even if universally known, data are only useful to those with the technology to exploit them.

It would seem that even if the developing countries accept the academy's definition and agree that research should not be regulated in the resource zones and the deep sea, it is likely that they will insist on some form of neutral international machinery to verify the nature of research proposed in areas of concern. Granting this, it would certainly be good politics, as well as an indisputable gesture of good faith, if the developed countries themselves proposed specific machinery for verification and agreed to abide by its decisions as an arbitrator. In 1968, an informal proposal that the Intergovernmental Oceanographic Commission (IOC) act in this capacity, met with vehement opposition, particularly from some U.S. oceanographers who claimed that the IOC had neither the staff nor the scientific expertise to make judgments of this kind. The fear was also expressed that such a "clearinghouse" would cause interminable delays and frustrations to the researcher (*15*).

Arbitration procedures established by treaty for use on an ad hoc basis may prove less ponderous than an established agency. The procedures common to international arbitration, whereby the disputing parties select referees from a list of neutral experts, could certainly be employed in cases where the nature of a proposed investigation was in question. Regardless of the method, however, some delay and frustration are inevitable. The risk of the certifying procedures becoming a bureaucratic nightmare must be weighed against their advantages.

To date, the opponents of regulation have been on the defensive, fighting to retain as much of the status quo as possible in light of a changing international environment. A case for science, based on the common heritage concept, takes the initiative away from the advocates of control. The only part of their argument left intact, and the one they will certainly fall back on, is the contention that science is not in the common interest as long as it is used by the developed to exploit the developing. For the reasons given earlier, it is unlikely that the National Academy of Sciences' effort to differentiate between types of research will dissuade developing countries from this suspicion unless a mechanism that they can trust is created to assist in differentiating between open research and limited exploration. By proposing such a mechanism themselves, the advocates of scientific freedom eliminate the major remaining objection of their opponents with an alternative that, again, is difficult to oppose politically or in principle.

As matters now stand, the 1973 conference will very probably give states the right to regulate science within their resource zones. An effectively presented argument against regulations as being incompatible with the common heritage concept, combined with an offer to submit proposed investigations to the scrutiny of an impartial body, may not convince the developing countries to withdraw their demand that investigators request permission to work within their resource zones. A mechanism for third-party settlement could, however, provide an alternative to individual states' having the final authority over what science is done in the area between 12 and 200 miles off their coasts.

In areas where a 200-mile jurisdiction is now claimed, access for the purpose of doing research has been obtained by bilateral negotiations between the parties involved. This would certainly become the pattern if the 200-mile limit applied universally. Recourse to arbitration would be necessary only when bilateral negotiations broke down (a major objection to the IOC proposal was that the commission would act as an intermediary in *all* requests). The third party could be a neutral body to which a developing country without an oceanographic capability of its own could turn if it were uncertain of the implications of the research proposed. The third party could serve equally well as a court of appeals for those whose requests for access were summarily rejected, particularly if states agreed by treaty to abide by its decisions. The procedures established would also work in cases of disagreement between an investigator and the ISA over the nature of research, in the event that the ISA is given control over research in its area of jurisdiction.

The establishment by treaty of procedures for binding third-party settlement in cases where the ISA or the state withholds permission for research within their respective areas of control is the position most favorable to basic research that none of the competing interest groups at the 1973 conference can effectively oppose. Having claimed that a legitimate distinction exists between basic research and limited exploration, the developed countries cannot object to entrusting this determination, when contested, to a neutral body of experts. Nor can developing countries justify in the name of the common heritage claims to the right to bar from their resource zones research certified by an unbiased third party to be in the common interest.

Freedom for science is no longer a universal right. But access to the oceans for research "intended for the benefit of all mankind" is equally justified under the common heritage doctrine. It would be ironic if the new law of the sea that is being created to make this doctrine a reality were to contain provisions which would impede the understanding of the marine environment on which all nations, rich and poor alike, are going to depend increasingly in the years ahead.

## REFERENCES

1. A. de Tocqueville, *Democracy in America*, P. Bradley, Ed. (Knopf, New York, 1963), vol. 1, p. 393.

2. Ocean Affairs Board of the National Academy of Sciences, "A proposed U.S. position on freedom for science in the oceans" (unpublished, revised June 1972).

3. I make an obvious oversimplification in treating both the developed and the developing countries as unified blocs. The variety and complexity of the issues confronting the 1973 Law of the Sea Conference, sponsored

by the United Nations, assures that voting will not always be strictly along these lines. Science, however, is one of the issues in which the difference between developed and developing countries is most apparent.
4. U.N. General Assembly Resolution 2750 (17 December 1970), p. 2.
5. R. Friedheim, *World Polit.* **18**, 25 (1965).
6. As quoted by W. Marz, *Bull. At. Sci.* **24** (No. 9), 19 (1968).
7. Representative of the developing country's position in the debate over the ISA's jurisdiction is a statement by the Peruvian delegate to the July 1971 meeting of the Seabed Committee, who called for an authority empowered to carry out a wide range of activities, including the coordination of scientific research (see U.S. Department of State telegram from U.S. mission, Geneva, 241546Z, July 1971).
8. Statement by the President on U.S. Ocean Policy, Office of the White House Press Secretary, 23 May 1970.
9. P. M. Fye, "Ocean policy and scientific freedom," lecture given before the Marine Technology Society, Washington, D.C., 11 September 1972.
10. J. Bartlett, *Bartlett's Familiar Quotations,* E. Beck, Ed. (Little, Brown, Boston, 1968), p. 709.
11. U.N. General Assembly Document A/Ac 138/SR 54 (22 March 1971), p. 109; quoted by H. Franssen, in *Freedom of Oceanic Research,* W. S. Wooster, Ed. (Crane, Russak, New York, 1973), p. 158.
12. W. S. Wooster, "Costs and consequences of restrictions on research: Another view," discussion paper presented at Scripps Institution of Oceanography Center for Marine Affairs Workshop on Conditions for Freedom of Oceanic Research, 24-26 April 1972.
13. K. Emery, *Science* **178**, 298 (1972).
14. P. M. Fye, personal communication.
15. This proposal was made informally, and, although it generated considerable comment, it was apparently never mentioned in official records. I learned of it from A. E. Maxwell, provost of the Woods Hole Oceanographic Institution and a frequent delegate to the IOC.
16. This article would not have been possible without the help of Robertson P. Dinsmore, Richard L. Haedrich, Herman Franssen, Maureen Franssen, Paul M. Fye, Kaleroy L. Hatzikon, and, above all, P. Sreenivasa Rao, who spent many hours introducing me to the mysteries of international law. This article is Woods Hole Oceanographic Institution Contribution No. 3089.

# 8

# *SOME CONSERVATION ISSUES*

# 43. The Conservation of Marine Animals

K. RADWAY ALLEN 1975

The word "conservation" is currently used in such a diversity of ways that, in any discussion, it is essential to begin by defining the sense in which it will be used. The present article is based on the belief that it is not improper for us to regard most living organisms as resources which man may utilize to his best advantage. It is equally important, however, that even where a species has no practical value as a resource to be directly used by man, we should still do what we can to keep the species in being, and preserve at least a representative part of its population in a natural and healthy state. Acceptance of a species as a resource implies, of course, not only that it should be kept in being, but also that its population should be maintained at a substantial level. An extinct or very scarce animal can have no resource value. Conservation, as used here, therefore means (a) ensuring that resource species are preserved and utilized in a manner which will enable them to remain at a substantial population level and to provide the optimum yield of benefits to man, and (b) protecting and maintaining non-resource species at the highest practicable level.

## THE THREATS TO MARINE ANIMALS

We can probably distinguish four main kinds of threats to wild animals to-day. The first is by damage to their habitat, generally in the name of development for some other purposes, such as housing, mining, agriculture or forestry. The second is their direct destruction as an incidental result of some human activity directed to another purpose. The third is the deliberate destruction of animals because mankind or some segment of it considers that these animals are inimical to its interests. The fourth is, of course, the deliberate killing of animals so that they may be utilized as a resource. All these threats affect marine animals, but the last is by far the most widely significant and raises much the greatest variety of conservational problems.

The marine animals most affected by damage to their habitat are those which live along the coastal fringe, particularly in shal-

Dr. K. Radway Allen is the Chief of the Division of Fisheries and Oceanography in the Commonwealth Scientific and Industrial Research Organization, Cronulla, New South Wales, Australia. He is the author or co-author of over seventy-five articles, many of which are about marine mammals.

From *Search*, Vol. 6, No. 8, pp. 317-322, 1975, a publication of the Australian and New Zealand Association for the Advancement of Science. Reprinted with light editing and with permission of the author and ANZAAS.

low water and between tidemarks. Reclamation of shorelines and dredging of channels for harbor, industrial and residential development, all destroy the habitat and hence the chance of survival of the animals living in the affected areas. Oysters and prawns are particularly liable to suffer in this way. Offshore, the greatest dangers to the habitat probably arise from chemical pollution. This may be due to substances washing into the sea at many points after widespread use on land, or to more localized discharge or dumping of harmful wastes. The chlorinated hydrocarbons, such as DDT, which may now be detected almost throughout the world's oceans, constitute an excellent example of the former. Rectification can only be achieved if we ultimately cease to use such broadly lethal substances. Discharge of liquid wastes is being progressively controlled in most countries by legal action, while a recently negotiated international convention has gone far towards controlling the dumping of wastes in deep water. Australia has already taken significant steps to put the requirements of this convention into effect.

Accidental destruction of marine animals on a significant scale is probably rare, apart from that occurring in reclamation and dredging operations. One important example, however, is causing international concern at present. This is the incidental capture of porpoises in the American purse-seine fishery for tuna, particularly in the eastern tropical Pacific. It is believed that these deaths have amounted to about 250,000 annually in recent years. The United States Government has recently undertaken a vigorous research program on this problem and is now imposing restrictions on the fishery aimed at preventing this destruction.

Deliberate destruction of marine animals because they are considered harmful is also probably of minor significance. In some cases, for example, sharks on bathing beaches, the need to do this would be almost universally accepted. There can be more debate however about the destruction of seals and porpoises by fishermen who consider that they are interfering with fishing operations or damaging fishing gear.

By far the most important dangers to the population of marine animals are those arising from fishing and hunting. Unlike the situation on land, where the principal threat to many mammals and birds arises from recreational hunting, marine animals are mainly subject to commercial operations, and recreational fishing and hunting of marine animals probably constitute a threat to only a few species in restricted localities. Probably the animals most seriously threatened in this way are some of the mollusks and other slow-moving animals living between tide-marks on sandy beaches, or—with the recent growth in popularity of skin-diving—in the shallow waters of rocky shores. Thus it is commercial fishing and hunting which provide the greatest conservational problems connected with marine animals. This paper will be principally concerned with the nature of these problems and the means which are being adopted to overcome them.

One can distinguish four levels on which problems arise in conserving marine animals or in managing the fisheries. The first concerns the objective for which the fishery is being managed. In other words, what are the benefits which mankind desires to derive from the resource? The second concerns the biological characteristics of the resource and the conditions these impose on the means by which the benefit may be obtained. The third involves the technological problems of adjusting the methods of harvesting so as to meet the biological requirements. The fourth and last, but by no means least difficult, group of problems are the political ones—local, national and international—which arise in applying the desirable technological restraints on harvesting.

## THE GOALS OF FISHERY MANAGEMENT

The objectives for which a fishery may be pursued can be quite diverse, and vary at different levels within the industry (Crutchfield, 1972). At the basic level, the fisherman himself is usually primarily concerned with making a living. Like most of us, he wants to make as much money as possible, and therefore to catch as many fish as he can. It is probably true, however, that many fishermen pursue their calling because the relatively free open air life appeals to them, and that this is more important than the amount of money they can make. In the industrialized fisheries, the objectives at the next level—that of the managers—are almost entirely financial; they are to maximize the profits and obtain the greatest return on the capital investment. Finally, the objectives which a government may pursue in supporting or otherwise managing a nation's fisheries may be many and various, and probably they are not always clearly identified even in the minds of those directly concerned. They may include the maintenance of employment, either generally or in a particular area, provision of food for the nation, production of exportable products which will attract foreign currency, economic support for vessels which are desired for other purposes, such as defense, increase of the gross national product, or even national prestige.

These objectives may sometimes be incompatible. Thus, a government wishing to provide as much employment as possible will regulate in ways which reduce the efficiency of the fishing operation and so increase the number of men employed without permitting the stocks to be over-exploited. This will prevent the financial return to the industry or the nation being maximized. As another example, the maximum profit to the industry can only be obtained by taking a catch rather less than the maximum the stock would support (Scott, 1955). The decisions as to which objectives are to be pursued in the management of any particular fishery are clearly political and social ones.

Two basic biological principles underlie the management of a fishery. The first is that, at any level between the natural maximum and that at which the species is doomed to extinction, a natural population will, if disturbed, always tend to return to the level at which it is in equilibrium with its environment, i.e. to its natural maximum. At a level below the maximum it will therefore produce a surplus of increment over loss which will carry it a step back towards the maximum. If this surplus is removed as a harvest the population will remain at the same level. This is precisely what we attempt to do in managing a regulated fishery. We also try to stabilize the population at a level such that the particular objective, for example yield or profit, is maximized.

Commonly, this population-regulating mechanism works through the processes of reproduction and recruitment, and if we plot the number of offspring against the number of parents we get curves such as those shown in Figure 43-1 (Ricker, 1958). For some animals, particularly those which produce relatively small numbers of young or eggs, the curve is typically domed, as in Figure 43-1(a). Animals as diverse as salmon and whales generally behave in this way. In these cases the greatest harvest can be obtained by maintaining the population at the level at which the excess of offspring over parents is greatest. This is marked by the broken line in the figure.

The majority of marine fish and nearly all the commercially important marine invertebrates are, however, extremely fecund, and for these the parent/offspring curve has generally a shape more like that in Figure 43-1(b). In these the natural mortality among the eggs and young larvae is so great as to reduce the survivors to a more-or-less constant level, which is little affected by the initial number of breeding animals. Only when the parent population is extremely low does the number of eggs limit the number of recruits to the next generation.

Under these conditions, the second of the important principles applied in fisheries management comes into play. This is based on the fact that in most fisheries the aim is to catch the maximum weight, rather than

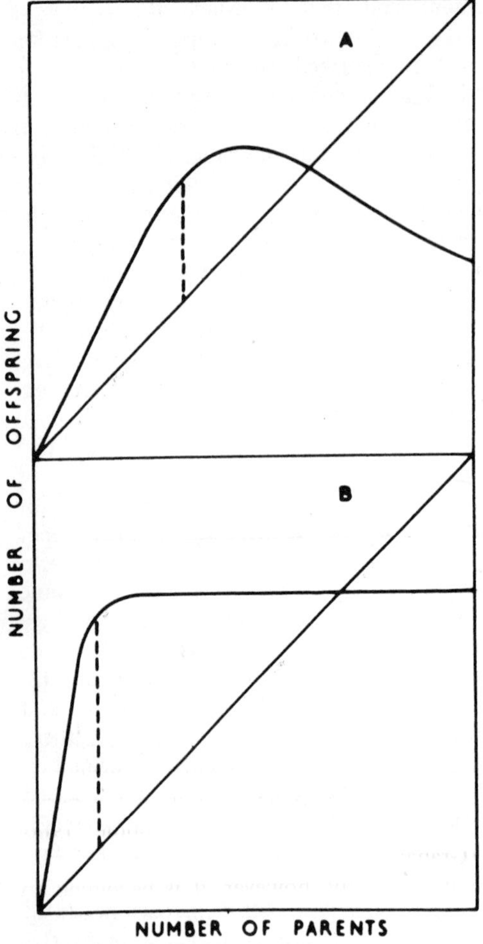


Figure 43-1. Typical relationships between the numbers of offspring and number of parents for—(a) a species of fairly low fertility (e.g. salmon); and (b) a highly fertile species (e.g. herring or lobster).

the maximum number, of animals. In each generation we start with a very large number of newly-hatched animals which are very small in size, so that their total weight is also small. Subsequently the numbers progressively diminish as the animals die, but the average weight of an animal increases. At first, the growth rate is faster than the death rate, so that the combined weight of the surviving animals increases. However as time goes on, the growth rate normally slows down, whereas the death rate stays relatively stable. As a result the death rate ultimately exceeds the growth rate and the weight of the survivors diminishes until the generation has finally disappeared. There is thus a point somewhere in middle life when the weight of the generation is at a maximum. Ignoring for the moment the necessity to provide some parents for the next generation, the greatest harvest from each generation would be obtained by catching it completely at the point when the weight of survivors is at a maximum. In practice this is hardly ever possible, both because of the need to leave some breeders and because of the inefficiency of most methods of fishing. However, the greatest achievable catch is still obtained by arranging for the midpoint of harvesting to be somewhere about the age of maximum surviving weight. The less efficient the harvesting, the longer the period over which it must spread and, therefore, the earlier the start needed to bring the midpoint to the right time.

The methods of population dynamics allow us to calculate fairly reliably the harvest which we can get for any combination of fishing intensity and age at the commencement of fishing. The results yield curves such as those in Figure 43-2, which is based on a typical stock of flatfish. The curves are contour lines of the weight of harvest which can be obtained for each recruit entering the exploited stock of fish. The fishing mortality rate is the instantaneous death rate due to fishing, that is, the ratio of the catch over one year to the original stock if the proportion being caught in each instant of time is kept constant.

It is apparent that to get the maximum catch the age of first harvesting must increase with the intensity of fishing, and that although a variety of combinations will yield harvests close to the maximum, any major departure from optimal combinations will cause great reductions in the sustainable catch.

Biological considerations, therefore, indicate that to obtain the maximum return from a fishery the factors which have to be

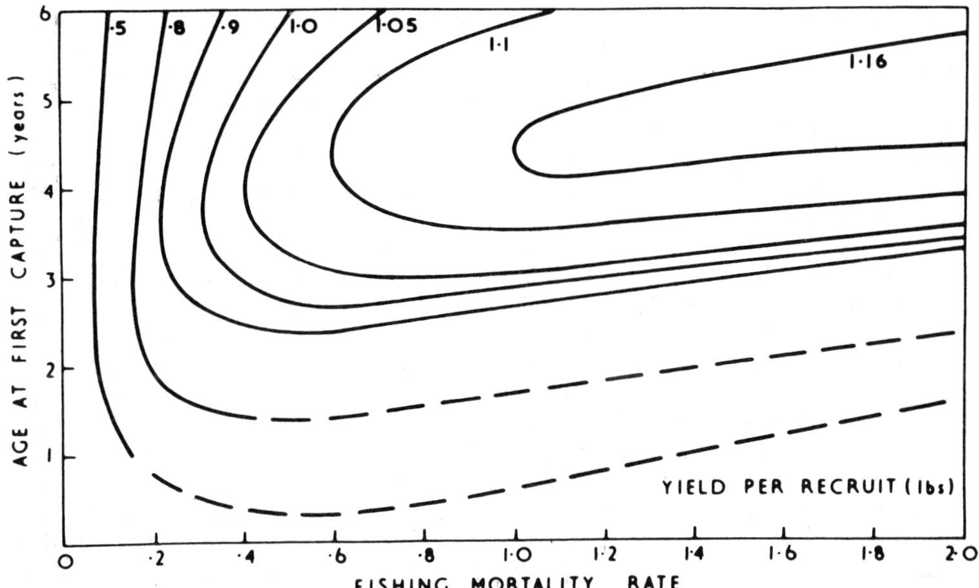


Figure 43-2. Contour diagram showing how the yield in pounds for each recruit entering the fishery varies with the fishing mortality rate and the age at first capture. The data are for a Canadian flounder fishery (Dickie and McCracken, 1955).

regulated are the size of the catch, the intensity of fishing and the size or age at which the animals are first caught. The possibility of manipulating each of these varies with the characteristics of the animals and of the fishery. Lobsters, for instance, cannot be effectively harvested until they have reached an age at which they will freely enter pots. Migratory fish like salmon or tuna are only available to the fisherman of certain areas during a particular phase of their lives. For example, southern bluefin tuna are generally present close to Australian coasts up only to about five years of age. Subsequently they move off into the high seas, where they are harvested by fishermen of other nations. The total world catch could be increased if no tuna were harvested until they were large but this could only be accomplished by the reduction of the Australian fishery. Fortunately for us there are at present no significant international pressures for this to be done.

The two concepts I have been discussing form the basis of classical fish management theory, which was largely developed and elaborated into the mathematical techniques of population dynamics during the period from the 1930s to the middle 1960s (Graham, 1943; Beverton and Holt, 1957). More recently, however, it is becoming apparent that, valuable though these approaches have been, they are essentially an over-simplification, and there are many complications which need to be taken into account in practice.

These complications arise in three ways: from the characteristics of the animals themselves, from their relations with their physical environment and from their interactions with other species. As an example of the effects of the animals' own characteristics, it is not always safe to assume, as in the calculation on which Figure 43-2 is based, that the rate at which an individual animal grows is independent of the population size. In practice fish will often grow much faster under conditions when the food supply is relatively abundant than when food is scarce, which means that as the population is reduced in numbers the rate at which the individual fish grow increases. Environmental influences often affect the numbers of young which survive each year to join the adult population. Fish vary greatly in this respect; some have relatively stable recruitment provided that there is an adequate number of spawners, others, like salmon, will show a range in number of recruits from year to year of about 5 to 1. In extreme cases, like the haddock in the Northern Hemisphere, fluctuations are so great that the population is virtually maintained by one good year-class every five years or so. Both these complications can be allowed for by modifications to the single species models of classical population dynamics. The greatest difficulty is in estimating the additional values which have to be inserted in the model. The third source of complications—interactions between species—adds a new dimension of complexity to the whole problem, however. What we do to one species may have considerable effects on the population of others, and if they also are commercially important then ideally we should be attempting to manage all of them simultaneously. Relatively little is yet known of the practical significance of these inter-specific effects, but with the increasing pressures to harvest as much as possible of the resources of the seas the need to consider them is increasing.

One example which is attracting some attention at present is the krill. These shrimp-like animals, which exist in enormous quantities in the Antarctic, form the main food of the whales. The reduction in the whale population to perhaps 20-30% of its original size might be expected to have left a substantial surplus of krill. Russian and Japanese fisheries scientists, in particular, are reported to have achieved considerable success in devising means of harvesting and utilizing these animals. The quantity which may be available is very great—it may approach 100 million tons annually, which is about 50% more than the existing world harvest from all fishery resources. This makes the project extremely attractive, but if large-scale harvesting of krill is undertaken, it may well have a serious effect on the ability of the whale stocks to recover in response to present and future protective measures.

Having seen that, biologically, the most useful measures for the management of a fishery are to regulate the catch, the intensity of fishing and the size at first capture, the next question to be faced is how this can be done in practice (Gulland and Carroz, 1968).

The *catch* can be regulated directly, and this is being done to an increasing extent. One way of doing this is to close the fishery when the catch has reached a predetermined total. To be effective this generally requires the fishery to be either highly organized or concentrated in time and space, so that the necessary monitoring and control can be carried out. Another way, applicable to highly organized fisheries with not too many units, is to allocate quotas to each unit individually.

*Intensity of fishing* can be regulated in two main ways. One is by limiting the number of units, such as boats, engaged in the fishery; the other is by limiting the effectiveness of each unit individually. Limitation of the number of units by licensing is a procedure which is now spreading widely in many countries, although in Australia we have at present marked differences among the States in this respect. Economically this system has the advantage that it does not require limitations on the efficiency of the operations—indeed, it can be so organized as to weed out the less efficient operators. Thus it helps to maximize the economic return from the fishery. On the other hand, if the objective is to provide employment, limitation of licenses is clearly unacceptable. The other alternative, limitation of the effectiveness of individual units, is also widely practiced. This is done by such means as limiting the length of the season, the number of lobster pots fishermen can use, or the size of the nets.

Control of the *minimum size* at which fish may be taken is one of the oldest forms of fisheries regulation, although in earlier times the motive was generally to ensure that fish were not caught before they could breed at least once. Regulation may be direct, by the imposition of minimal sizes at which fish may be killed or sold, or indirect by such means as minimum sizes of the mesh in net or by the provision of escape gaps in lobster pots.

## NATIONAL LAWS AND INTERNATIONAL AGREEMENTS

The final stage in the management of a fishery is of course the application in practice of the desirable measures. This calls for the making and enforcement of the necessary rules by the appropriate authority. In national waters, the problems are not intrinsically different from those involved in the application of any other measures of government. The two essential steps are the enactment of the necessary legislation and its enforcement when enacted. Legislation requires of course the degree of popular support appropriate to the government system of the country concerned. Its enforcement, like that of any other legislation, depends on the provision of an adequate system and staff for the purpose.

Outside national waters the problems of achieving adequate management and conservation of the fisheries are much more complex (Kasahara, 1972). Although important fisheries in international waters have existed for several centuries in a few places, such as the North Sea and the Newfoundland Grand Banks, their real development has only taken place in the last fifty years and particularly since the Second World War. This has been made possible by the great increase in the power of the fishing fleets—not so much in the number of vessels as in their size, range, technological equipment and ability to fish in deep water.

It has been further supported by the development of factory ships which can receive and process the catches on the fishing grounds, so that catchers do not have to return frequently to their home ports.

We now have reached the stage when the fishing fleets of several nations are roving virtually the whole world and fishing wherever worthwhile catches can be made. The result is that mankind now has the ability to deplete almost any of the marine resources unless positive steps can be taken to prevent it. Prevention requires a recognized authority with the power to regulate the fishery as necessary. General recognition of such an authority is difficult in international waters, but very considerable progress has been, and is being, made. Two lines of attack can be discerned (Gulland and Carroz, 1968). The first and oldest is by the provision of international consultation through special bodies established for the purpose. There are now more than a dozen of these bodies covering between them most of the major fisheries of the Northern Hemisphere and much of the tropics. They vary considerably in their composition and terms of reference. All are restricted to consideration of the fisheries in certain defined areas. Within the defined geographical limits some are open-ended as to the species they are concerned with, or the nations which may belong to them. Others are closely restricted in one or both respects. At one extreme, for example, the International Pacific Salmon Fisheries Commission is composed only of Canada and the United States and is concerned only with stocks of two species of salmon in the Fraser River system. At the other extreme, the International Commission for the North-West Atlantic Fisheries is concerned with all the fisheries in international waters in its area, and includes all nations concerned with these fisheries. The commissions also vary in their arrangements regarding Research. Some, such as the International Pacific Salmon Fisheries Commission and the International Pacific Halibut Commission, have their own research organizations. The majority, however, base their work on the scientific findings of research workers of the member nations and usually have some form of scientific advisory committee, which aims at coordinating the research programs and producing a consensus of advice.

These commissions generally exercise their regulatory functions through the national authorities of the member nations. In other words, the commission decides on certain management practices, and it is then the responsibility of the member nations to impose these in the appropriate way upon their fishermen. To reinforce the activities of the national authorities, the commissions are also increasingly setting up some form of international inspection. One limitation on the effectiveness of the commissions is due to the fact that no nation is likely to bind itself absolutely to accept the decisions of an international body which it considers may be adverse to its interests. The commissions therefore generally have some form of escape mechanism which will allow a country to opt out of applying a particular decision if it desires to do so. Despite these escape procedures, the moral force of a decision by the majority of nations in a commission is very considerable.

There are still substantial areas, particularly in the Southern Hemisphere, in which the international fisheries are not supervised by regulatory commissions of this kind. To some extent, this gap is being filled by consultative bodies established by FAO. The regions adjacent to Australia are, for example, covered by two such bodies, the Indian Ocean Fishery Commission and the Indo-Pacific Fisheries Council. These bodies have no regulatory functions but provide for discussion of problems of common interest. They deal not only with the problems of the international fisheries but also with the development of new national fisheries including those in fresh waters. They are concerned with such problems as the training and education of both fisheries managers and of fishermen, and with the establishment of statistical systems and research centers. It seems likely that they will lead in due course to the establishment of appropriate regulatory bodies.

The alternative to the commissions, as a means of managing international fisheries, has been developing rather more recently. This is through the extension of national rights and responsibilities to greater distances from shore. The basic concept here is that the coastal state should have the primary right to harvest and the responsibility for management of the fishery resources within this extended area. Linked to this is the view that, if the coastal state cannot fully harvest these resources, other nations may also exploit them. The responsibility for management would remain however with the coastal state, so that the other nations must accept its regulatory authority. These questions have been explored extensively during the various negotiations concerned with the Law of the Sea over the last seven or eight years. While no final decisions have yet been reached it seems likely that the current (April 1975) negotiations in Geneva will result in recommendations for the adoption of a two-zone system. Under this the coastal states will have absolute control of the fisheries of a territorial sea extending out to 12 miles. Outside this will be an economic zone, extending to 200 miles, where the coastal state will be responsible for management of the resources and will be able to exclude other nations so far as it fully utilizes the resources itself. Australia has announced its support for these principles.

In recent years there have been many unilateral actions by coastal states establishing fishing zones considerably wider than the traditional three miles. In general these countries seem to have been fairly successful in obtaining acceptance of such decisions. This, however, has not always been without friction, as the recent "Cod War" between Great Britain and Iceland over the extension of Icelandic limits to fifty miles witnesses. Some countries, such as Chile and Peru, have imposed two-hundred-mile limits for some considerable time, but generally limits are at present considerably less.

## AN EXAMPLE: THE STORY OF WHALING

The history and present situation of the whale stocks and the whaling industry illustrate many of the points involved in attempting to obtain international management of a marine resource (Gulland, 1972). In particular, they illustrate the disastrous effects which an entirely unregulated international fishery can have, the difficulties which face an international commission attempting to regulate such a fishery, and the successes which such a commission may achieve in the face of these difficulties.

Whaling falls into two main periods. The first extended from about the fourteenth century until 1870, during which time whales were almost invariably hunted with hand harpoons working from rowing or sailing boats. The catch was either towed to the nearest land or ice for cutting up, or else dealt with in the water alongside a larger vessel. Operations of this kind could deal successfully only with slow-moving whales which also floated when dead. They were therefore restricted almost entirely to two species, the right whale and the sperm whale. In spite of this limitation, they spread progressively from the Bay of Biscay to northern Norway and across the North Atlantic to the eastern Canadian Arctic. From there they spread south in the Atlantic to the sub-Antarctic, round into the Pacific and back north as far as the Bering Sea. The principal peoples concerned were the Basques, Norwegians, Dutch, British and Americans, more or less successively. In the tropics, hunting was mainly for sperm whales, but in cooler waters it was concentrated on right whales. The right whales in particular suffered extremely heavily in these operations, and, as the fleets moved on, they left only a shadow of the original schools behind. By the middle of the nineteenth century right whaling had virtually ended, except in the Bering Sea area, because it could no longer be profitably pursued. The catching of sperm whales also virtually ended about this time, but this was at least partly the result of a decline in the market for oil.

The second phase of whaling began in about 1870 with the invention of the harpoon gun firing an explosive harpoon. This, mounted on a steam-powered catcher, made the faster-swimming rorquals, such as the blue and fin whale, vulnerable to hunting. The new industry, starting from Norway, spread in a very similar pattern to that of the previous phase, but much more rapidly. The Antarctic was reached about the beginning of this century, and it was here that the great herds of blue, fin, humpback and sei whales were found.

Whaling in the Antarctic built up very rapidly between then and about 1930, by which time it accounted for 80% of the total world catch. In 1926 the first factory ship capable of processing whales on board was developed, and for the first time the modern whalers were free of the land. Within a very few years Antarctic whaling changed over virtually entirely to this type of operation. This is still the main form of whaling today, and the few remaining coastal operations account for only a small percentage of the total world catch. Since the War, the North Pacific Ocean has also become a major whaling area, although the stocks there are much smaller than those in the Antarctic. Still more recently, attention has swung back to sperm whales as the rorqual stocks have been reduced. They are being taken mainly in southern temperate and sub-tropical waters and they are also the mainstay of most of the coastal operations.

In both the Antarctic and the North Pacific the whalers have concentrated successively on a series of baleen whales, turning successively to a smaller and less valuable animal as the more valuable kinds could no longer be caught in sufficient numbers. In the Antarctic, for example, effort was concentrated on blue whales up to about 1936, from then to 1965 on fin whales, and since then on sei whales. In the last three seasons the still smaller minke whale has also been taken.

The effects of commercial whaling on the principal species of whales may thus be summarized as follows. By the mid-nineteenth century, it reduced the right whales to extremely low levels, from which they have hardly begun to recover in one hundred years of freedom from hunting. More recently, it has seriously reduced the stocks of blue and humpback whales, both in the Antarctic and elsewhere, to about 5 or 10% of the original population sizes. Following this it reduced the fin whale stocks, so that they are probably now at about 25% of original level in the Antarctic and in a similar state in the North Pacific. It has had much less effect on sei and sperm whales, which are generally at between 50 and 75% of original levels.

No serious attempt was made to conserve the whale stocks until the establishment of the International Whaling Commission in 1946. The Convention establishing this Commission recognizes the history of successive reduction of the most accessible and valuable whale stocks, and the need to prevent this occurring in the future, for the sake not only of the animals themselves, but also of the industry. The Commission almost immediately established a quota for the number of whales to be taken in the Antarctic. This, however, was set at levels which produced little effect, and as we have seen, the blue whales continued to decline in number, and the fin whales soon followed. It was not until 1960 that alarm about these events reached the point at which the Commission made a strong effort to obtain better scientific information on the state and future prospects of the stocks. The essential facts became clear by 1964, but it was several more years before the Commission fully accepted their implication. Complete protection was quickly imposed on blue and humpback whales, but it was about 1967 before quotas for other species in the Antarctic were reduced to a level which could prevent further depletion of the stocks. Since that time the Commission has been moving at an increasing rate in the direction of effective conservation of the whale stocks throughout the world (Gamble, 1974). Some of the main features of the present situation are:

- all the badly depleted species are fully protected by the Commission, i.e., right, blue, humpback and gray whales;
- fin whale quotas are at levels which will allow the stocks to rebuild, and the Commission has resolved that fin whaling in the Antarctic is to cease in 1976;
- sei and sperm whale stocks are generally now fairly close to their most productive levels, and quotas have been set which should maintain them in this condition. Quotas are being arranged on progressively smaller geographical units;
- a precautionary quota has been established for the minke whale in the Antarctic which will limit the rate at which the stock is reduced until more is known about its biology and population dynamics;
- the Commission has extended its interest from the large whales to the conservation of the smaller dolphins and porpoises;
- international inspection of whaling operations was begun in 1972;
- the Commission adopted in 1975 a set of rules under which all whales stocks are classified, on the scientific evidence, as either *protection stocks,* which are fully protected, or *sustained management stocks,* which must be maintained at optimum levels, or *initial management stocks,* which may be reduced to an optimum level under strict controls.

Although much remains to be done (Holt, 1974), the history of the conservation of whaling shows that, after an ineffective start, the International Whaling Commission has in recent years become an increasingly effective body in promoting and enforcing the wise conservation of the whale stocks. This progress could not have been made without the existence of a body of this kind, and it is interesting that the tendency for more effective conservation had become well developed before the recent popular interest in the protection of whales had become apparent.

## REFERENCES

Beverton, R. J. H. and S. J. Holt (1957). On the dynamics of exploited fish populations. *Fishery Invest., Lond.* (2) 10:553.

Crutchfield, J. A. (1972). Economic and political objectives in fisheries management *in World Fisheries Policy*, B. J. Rothschild ed., Univ. Washington Press, Seattle.

Dickie, L. M. and McCracken, F. D. (1955). Isopleth diagrams to predict equilibrium yields of a small flounder fishery. *J. Fish. Res. Bd. Can.* **12**(2): 187-209.

Gamble, R. (1974). The unendangered whale. *Nature* **250**:454-5.

Graham, M. (1943). *The fish gate.* Faber & Faber, London.

Gulland, J. A. and J. E. Carroz (1968). Management of fishery resources. *Adv. mar. Biol.* **6**: 1-171.

Gulland, J. A. (1972). The conservation of antarctic whales. *Biol. Conservation* **4** (5): 335-344.

Holt, S. J. (1974). Whales–conserving a resource. *Nature* **251**: 366-7.

Kasahara, H. (1972). International fishery disputes *in World Fisheries Policy,* B. J. Rothschild ed., Univ. Washington Press, Seattle.

Ricker, W. E. (1958). Stock and recruitment. *J. Fish. Res. Bd. Can.* **2**: 559-623.

Scott, A. (1955). *Natural resources: the economics of conservation.* Univ. of Toronto Press, Toronto.

Watt, K. E. F. (1968). *Ecology and resource management,* McGraw-Hill, New York.

# 44. Can Leviathan Long Endure So Wide a Chase?

SCOTT McVAY 1971

A hundred years ago, Herman Melville asked "whether Leviathan can long endure so wide a chase, and so remorseless a havoc?" Today, in more prosaic words, the question remains: What would be lost if the whales were gone from the sea? Of what possible use are whales to men? Esthetics aside, who cares if the whale goes the way of the dinosaur?

These words sound terrible and ominous to me; yet they represent the thinking of many people, including some of the men who set the whale-kill quotas every June. Few of these men have ever seen a whale. Few of them had ever heard a whale until biologist Roger Payne, of the New York Zoological Society and Rockefeller University, played a recording at the close of the final session of the International Whaling Commission meeting on June 26, 1970, in London.

It was 2:00 P.M., and the commissioners were hungry. The chairman, Mr. I. Fujita, noting at the outset of the final plenary session that business would have to be completed before lunch, pointed out brightly that "hunger will expedite our deliberations." But some delegates, notably the Japanese and Soviets, lingered to listen to sounds recorded at a depth of 250 fathoms—the song of the humpback whale. Spanning *six* octaves, it filled the conference room at River Walk House overlooking the Thames.

Henceforth, the commissioners' annual deliberations will take on a new dimension. These sounds have already made a profound impression on the thousands of Americans who recently heard them in New York's Philharmonic Hall, on television, and on radio. The unexpected fact revealed by this recording and many others, according to the analysis by Dr. Payne and me, is that the sounds often fall into true song forms that are predictable in broad outline.

The humpback songs have captured the

Scott McVay has led efforts by the Environmental Defense Fund to ban the importation of whale products into the United States and achieve a worldwide moratorium on whaling. He has served on the U. S. delegation to the International Whaling Commission, appeared before Congress, and written several articles on whales which have appeared in *Scientific American, Natural History, Bulletin of Atomic Scientists, Audubon,* and *The New York Times.* He has studied the communication of porpoises, co-authored the analysis of the "Songs of Humpback Whales" (*Science,* Vol. 173, 1971), and led an expedition to the Arctic to study the Bowhead whale.

From *Natural History,* Vol. 80, No. 1, pp. 36-40, 68, 70-72, 1971. Reprinted with light editing and by permission of the author and *Natural History* Magazine. Copyright by *Natural History* Magazine, 1971.

imagination of composers and musicians. In a musical ballad Pete Seeger wrote:

*If we can save*
*Our singers in the sea*
*Perhaps there's a chance*
*To save you and me.**

This thought cuts right to the heart of the matter. (See Figure 44-1.)

The decimation of the antarctic whale fishery is a grisly story. It has been catalogued since 1920, when the Bureau of International Whaling Statistics in Sandefjord, Norway, began recording every *reported* whale kill by species, length, sex, date, and place of death. During the 1960's, the yield in barrels of whale oil dropped fivefold, from more than 2 million barrels to less than 400,000 in the 1969-70 season. The whalers might have taken more than a million barrels year after year, indefinitely. But their insatiability in the past two decades has so ravished the stocks and so decimated the large species that the sustainable yield today is but a shadow of what it could be if the stocks had a chance to rebuild.

Last year, most of the world's whale catch was taken by two nations, the Soviet Union (43 per cent) and Japan (42 per cent). The remainder was taken by Peru (5.3 per cent), South Africa (2.8 per cent), Norway (2.5 per cent), Canada (1.7 per cent), Australia (1.4 per cent), Spain (0.8 per cent), and the United States (0.5 per cent).

The grim figures for the past season (1969-70) reflect the catch of smaller and smaller whales in the warm waters of lower and lower latitudes. Twelve years ago, 65 per cent of the catch was taken in antarctic waters south of 60° south latitude. Last season, 89 per cent of the catch was taken between 40° and 60° south latitude. In the heart of the antarctic fishery, once the most bountiful whaling ground on earth and a seemingly endless resource, the harvest has dropped in a dozen years from two-thirds of the total catch to one-tenth.

In the age of sail more than a century ago, when the whale hunt was directed principally at two species, the sperm and right whales, and the old-time methods were no match for the elusive and fast-swimming blue and fin whales, Melville could assert with dreamy eloquence: "The whale-bone whales can at last resort to their Polar citadels, and diving under the ultimate glassy barriers and walls there, come up among icy fields and floes; and in a charmed circle of everlasting December, bid defiance to all pursuit from man."

Melville could not have envisioned the rapacious efficiency of modern whaling, which has all but eliminated the rich Antarctic fishery. Today whales are hunted at both ends of their migratory cycle and, in the case of the sperm whale, on the way to the southern grounds.

Victor Scheffer deflates any notion of romance in the contemporary whale chase:

"In man's attempts to catch more whales more cheaply, he has tried to poison them with strychnine and cyanide and curare. He has tried to electrocute them. Spotters in airplanes and helicopters now search them out and report the position of the herds to whaling vessels below. The ships hunt them down by ASDIC, the system that can feel the whales in total darkness. A 'whale-scaring machine' frightens the beasts into flight with ultrasound and tires them so the hunter can overtake them. What will be next? Will the hunter cut a phonograph record of the mating call of the whale, or the cry of the calf for its mother, and play back the sounds beneath the bow of his ship? Will the orbiting satellite speak through space to tell the hunter where to find the last whale?"

In the past twenty-five years, 62,022 blue whales, at 85 feet and more the largest mammals on earth, and 15,025 humpbacks, perhaps the most playful of the great whales, have been taken in the Antarctic. Never very

* "The Song of the World's Last Whale," by Pete Seeger. © by Stormking Music, Inc., all rights reserved, used by permission.

abundant, both species have been pushed to the edge of life, but are now nominally protected. The finback is the next candidate for "commercial extinction," that is, when its numbers will have been so reduced that it will no longer be profitable to send expeditions to hunt them. The finback, a smaller cousin of the blue whale, was second only to the sperm whale in abundance. During the past quarter-century, 444,262 finbacks were taken in the Antarctic, more than half of them from 1954 to 1962 when more than 27,000 finbacks were taken each year. Their population is now estimated at 67,000 to 75,000, one-fourth of its original size. If the exploiters had shown restraint—if they had learned the lesson of the blue and humpback, had remembered the slaughter of the right and bowhead in the last century—then the Antarctic could have yielded 10,000 to 12,000 finbacks a year down the long hungry road of the future. Today the sustainable yield is estimated at less than 3,000 finbacks.

These numbers, combined with catch data, indicate the extreme pressure on the finbacks and are an indictment of the stewardship of the International Whaling Commission. The ravaged state of the whale stocks presents an essentially nonpolitical problem that could be eased enormously if the catch effort was radically reduced to

Figure 44-1. Breaching by the humpback whale is not uncommon during springtime near Bermuda, but its diminished numbers make this spectacle a rare event. (Photograph courtesy of John Dominis and Life Magazine © 1972, Time Inc.)

allow all whale populations to rebuild. The most desirable goal of all, a ten-year moratorium—for tagging, study, and population counts—seems beyond the capacities for cooperation and restraint of the nations present at the International Whaling Convention meeting: Argentina, Australia, Canada, England, France, Iceland, Japan, Norway, Panama, South Africa, the Soviet Union, and the United States.

With the stage set, we can better appreciate what happened at the 22nd meeting of the International Whaling Commission in London at River Walk House, overlooking the Thames, last June. The actions and inactions of the commission can be gauged by four items: (1) the whale quotas set, (2) the sperm whale, (3) the International Observer Scheme, and (4) the action by the U. S. Department of the Interior listing all great whale species as endangered.

As an observer to the meetings, I would like to point out that while the United States is involved in whaling only marginally (it operates one small land station in California), the constructive influence of the United States on the commission has been considerable. Dr. J. Laurence McHugh, the United States commissioner and vice-chairman of the commission, and Dr. Douglas G. Chapman of the Center for Quantitative Science at the University of Washington, have in recent years chaired the commission's two principal committees, the Technical (McHugh) and the Scientific (Chapman).

In addition, the United States is a major importer of whale oil and whale products, making up roughly one-fifth of the world market. Hopefully this market may be closed if the whales can be kept on the endangered species list published by the Department of the Interior. Whatever the use of whale products, whether for lipsticks or lubricants, a satisfactory substitute is available in every instance.

1. On the matter of quotas, the Scientific Committee annually recommends that the blue whale unit be eliminated. Under this curious and anachronistic arrangement one blue whale unit is equal to one blue whale or two finbacks or two and a half humpbacks or six sei whales. Because it did not specify which whales may be taken, the blue whale unit contributed to the collapse of the antarctic fishery. Again this year the commission stuck by the invidious blue whale unit in the Antarctic; in fact, the commissioners did not even raise the subject. The Scientific Committee (with the exception of the Japanese scientists) generally concurred that the sustainable yield for next season was 2,600 finbacks and 5,000 sei whales. The commission set a quota of 2,700 blue whale units, which works out to be 27 per cent more than that recommended by the Scientific Committee. Even recognizing that Norway will probably not take the 200 units assigned to her, the quota does not allow any margin for the stocks to recover and probably will cause further depletion.

In the North Pacific, the Scientific Committee's studies revealed that the sustainable yield is 1,300 finbacks and 3,100 sei whales. The commission set quotas of 1,308 for the finbacks and 4,710 for the seis. Worst of all, a fudge factor of 10 per cent—reminiscent of the blue whale unit—was built into these numbers, so that whatever the whalers fail to catch of one species they can take in the other.

2. Regarding the sperm whale, the collapse of the Antarctic fishery and the strain on the baleen whales in the North Pacific has meant that the damage inflicted on sperm whale stocks—so far without any quota whatsoever from the commission—has been intensified each year. For more than twenty years the number of sperm bulls caught in the Antarctic has ranged between 2,500 and 7,000 annually, with higher numbers killed earlier and lower numbers recently. For example, the peak was fifteen years ago when 6,974 sperm whales were reported taken, a catch that produced 342,000 barrels of sperm oil. During the 1969-70 season, 3,090 sperms were taken in the Antarctic for a production of 125,000 barrels of oil. The striking fact about these figures is that they

reflect a steady decline in the yield of barrels of oil per whale over the past fifteen years. The oil yield in the Antarctic has dropped alarmingly, from 49 barrels per sperm whale to 40 barrels. In a mere fifteen years the sperm whales are 18 per cent smaller. The pattern of predation seems intractable.

The ecology for male and female sperm whales differs markedly. While the males attain lengths of 50 to 55 feet and more, the females are mature at 35 to 40 feet; indeed, females shorter than 38 feet in length are "protected" from pelagic whaling, while those less than 35 feet are protected from land station whaling. The catch data piles up at these minimum legal lengths lending credence to the general belief that the infractions are many and blatant.

An analysis and estimate of the sustainable or potential yield of the sperm whale in the North Pacific has been made by three Japanese scientists. They estimate the present sustainable yield of male sperm whales in the North Pacific at 4,290. The catch the past two years has been 12,740 and 11,329. The Japanese scientists say that "this male sperm whale stock has . . . little or no further surplus." The population has been driven to a level of about one-half of its unexploited state. Privately, the North Pacific commissioners agreed to a catch 10 per cent below last year's. This catch limit–set provisionally behind closed doors outside of the formal business of the commission–is 240 per cent of the sustainable yield estimated by the Japanese scientists. The pattern of predation is familiar–as is the capacity of the International Whaling Commission to look the other way when the chips are down.

3. The most important single item on the agenda, the International Observer Scheme (IOS), was discussed at length. It was approved in principle seven years ago and has been piously reaffirmed annually. But no effective steps have been taken to implement it.

At the meeting, Dr. McHugh stated that the commission's inability to implement an observer scheme weakens it as a conservation organization because it seems to lack the ability to enforce its regulations and quotas. The Japanese commissioner, Mr. Fujita, said that his country would support the implementation of the observer scheme for the next Antarctic season and felt that the plan should extend to land stations as well.

The Soviet commissioner, Mr. M. N. Sukhoruchenko, said that the IOS could be used at present with some small changes. He urged that two persistent problems be settled: every country has an obligation to send observers as well as receive them; the IOS will be effective only if implemented both for land stations and pelagic operations. He recommended that the commissioners meet on and settle this matter prior to the 23rd meeting in June, 1971, in Washington.

Mr. Fujita said that there was no basic disagreement on implementation, but that the commission did not have time to pursue the matter further.

All these words sound reassuring, but the IOS is still not implemented. A possibility exists that the United States and Japan may work out some modest form of exchange for their land stations that could serve as a model for other countries next year.

A beginning may yet be made. It is crucial to know when a protected species is taken and labeled something else; as, for example, when an immature blue whale, unmistakable because of its splotchy exterior, is harpooned and listed in the day's log as a finback.

Another example of the most egregious sort of violation of the regulations took place in the 1962-63 season when a factory ship and its catchers swept in on a small colony of "protected" right whales near the island of Tristan da Cunha in the South Atlantic. The few dozen rights, one of the largest grouping to be seen in any ocean in years, was completely wiped out. This well-known incident has never been aired at the International Whaling Commission meetings nor has it appeared in print, but it is a tragic example of what happens in the absence of an International Observer Scheme. And there are many other unreported tragedies. Just talk to the whalers.

4. The meeting of the International Whaling Commission barely touched on the U.S. Department of the Interior's bold action in placing all the great whale species on the endangered species list of June 2, 1970, implementing the Endangered Species Conservation Act of 1969. According to the provisions of the act, no species that is demonstrated to be threatened with extinction may be imported, alive or dead, whole or in part, into this country. By placing baleen whales, as well as the sperm whale, on the list the Department of the Interior went beyond the mere protection of species already struggling for survival. With the threat of economic boycott, perhaps the member nations of the International Whaling Commission will be spurred to take their task more seriously.

Until last November, a big question remained as to the chances of all these species remaining on the list. The sperm whale was especially vulnerable. Interior Secretary Walter J. Hickel was under great pressure from whale oil importers, from other departments within the government, and from overseas to drop the sperm whale from the list. On November 24, 1970, after six months' intensive review, Secretary Hickel affirmed that all eight threatened species of great whales will be kept on the list and banned from importation to "prevent conditions that lead to extinction."

Explaining why the department kept the fin, sei, and sperm whales on the list, Hickel said it is "clear that if the present rate of commercial exploitation continues unchecked, these three species will become as rare as the other five." He also called for a conference, jointly sponsored by the Department of the Interior and the Smithsonian Institution, to be held early in 1971 to review what can be done to restore whale populations in the oceans of the world.

The Secretary omitted mention of one aspect crucial to any effort to save whales: funding. Scientific programs to monitor the size of the whale herds and the United States share of an observer scheme both need financial support.

This break for the threatened whales was accompanied by some good news from Japan. Last August I went there on behalf of the Environmental Defense Fund and the New York Zoological Society, to discuss with Japanese scientists the initiation of a campaign to save whales. The scientists have formed a Committee for the Protection of Whales, chaired by Dr. Seiji Kaya. Along with writers Kenzaburo Oe and Sakyo Komatsu, they have taken the whale problem to the public for the first time. They are urging the Japanese government to curb the whaling industry and to strengthen the powers of the International Whaling Commission.

The big question remaining is the Soviet Union, but we have prospects of positive developments there, too. The problem of the survival and continuity of the great whales would be eased if the Soviets extended to large whales the attitude they take toward the smaller dolphins and porpoises. In March, 1966, the Soviet government banned the catching and killing of dolphins. This decision was taken, according to Alexander Ishkov, Soviet Minister of Fisheries, because research has shown that dolphins have brains "strikingly close to our own." Dr. Ishkov, therefore, regards the dolphin as the "marine brother of man," noting, "I think that it will be possible to preserve dolphins for the sake of science. Their catch should be discontinued in all seas and oceans of the world."

May the song of the humpback whale soon sound in the Bolshoi Opera House.

We know very little about whales. Until a few months ago, for instance, we did not know that some whales sing, and that these songs make a profound impression on the human listener.

What we have seen closely of whales to date—and watched with strange fascination—are "death flurries," the tragic scene that has played to an inert, bloated conclusion

60,000 times a year for eight years (1958 to 1965) and now occurs 40,000 times a year. Today, a whale is harpooned every 12 minutes on the average. The "life flurries" remain essentially unknown because no man has stayed with a whale pod hour after hour, day and night, week after week.

Melville concluded:

"Dissect him how I may, then, I but go skin deep; I know him not, and never will. But if I know not even the tail of this whale, how understand his head? much more, how comprehend his face, when face he has none? Thou shalt see my back parts, my tail, he seems to say, but my face shall not be seen. But I cannot completely make out his back parts; and hint what he will about his face, I say again he has no face."

As a species, man is at a point in his own evolution where he cannot yet create a flea but is wholly capable of destroying the whale. The job is three-quarters completed when measured by the great whale species that are threatened with extinction.

Our survival is curiously intertwined with that of the whale. Just as all human life is interconnected (in the Monkey-Rope situation in *Moby Dick,* Ishmael declares, "I saw that this situation of mine was the precise situation of every mortal that breathes; only, in most cases, he, one way or other, has this Siamese connexion with a plurality of other mortals. . . ."), so have we finally begun to perceive the connections between all living things. The form of our survival, indeed our survival itself, is affected as the variety and abundance of life is diminished. To leave the oceans, which girdle seven-tenths of the world, barren of whales is as unthinkable as taking all music away and everything associated with music—composers and their works, musicians and their instruments—leaving man to stumble on with only the dryness of his own mutterings to mark his way.

# 45. The Survival Situation of the Hawksbill Sea-Turtle in Madagascar

GEORGE R. HUGHES 1973

Of the five species of sea-turtles still extant around the shores of Madagascar, none is regarded as more typical than the Hawksbill, *Eretmochelys imbricata* Linnaeus (see Figure 45-1), which made Madagascar famous as a source of tortoiseshell.

Although numerically inferior to the Green Turtle (*Chelonia mydas*), Hawksbills or their products are found everywhere in the island and are so characteristic of Madagascar that some special measures should be taken to prevent any further decline in their already much-reduced population.

The data presented below were gathered during two lengthy visits to Madagascar as part of a survey of the status of sea-turtles in South East Africa (World Wildlife Fund Project No. 648 [originally]; cf. Hughes, 1972).

## PAST STATUS

Few, if any, quantitative records exist concerning the past status of the Hawksbill Sea-turtle around Madagascar, but, from as early as 1613, tortoiseshell was remarked upon as an important export (Decary, 1950). Further, this export importance was maintained throughout the 19th century, with figures reaching 4,000 kg. in the mid-1800s.

At the turn of the century this figure was still being maintained, more or less; but soon after the end of World War I, the first signs of a significant and drastic decline were recorded (Petit, 1930).

As indicated in our Figure 45-2, the decline has continued steadily, with exports reaching barely 1,000 kg annually at mid-century, while at present the trade has virtually no export importance (*see* below).

The decline cannot be attributed to any factor other than overexploitation, for the drop in exports came long before the advent of plastics which have, to a very limited extent, replaced tortoiseshell for certain commodities. Further, it has not resulted from a lack of demand, as prices on the open market can reach 14,000 FMG/kg (Rands 40).

If one considers that some 2.5 kg of tortoiseshell may be obtained from one adult Hawksbill, then at least 1,600 adult turtles must have been slaughtered annually for a period certainly exceeding 100 years. It is therefore surprising to report that there are still considerable numbers of Hawksbills in Madagascar's coastal waters.

George R. Hughes is with the Oceanographic Research Institute, Durban, Natal, South Africa.

From *Biological Conservation,* Vol. 5, No. 2, pp. 114-118, 1973. Reprinted with light editing and with permission of the author and Applied Science Publishers, Ltd., Great Britain.

Figure 45-1. Hawksbill sea-turtle.

## PRESENT DISTRIBUTION

Although Hawksbill Sea-turtles are found in all coastal parts of Madagascar, they appear to be most common around the northern third of the island, which also constitutes the major nesting-ground (Figure 45-3).

The east coast from Tamatave southwards is the region of least occurrence, probably owing to the lack of suitable feeding grounds

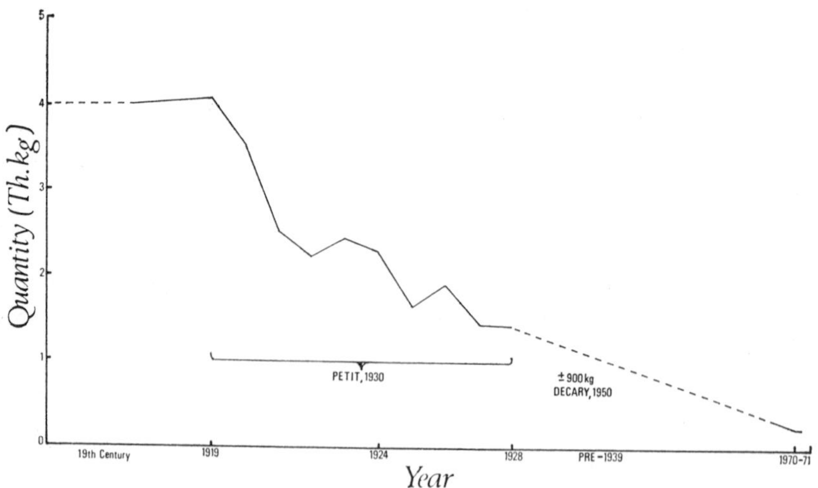


Figure 45-2. Graph reflecting drastic decline in tortoiseshell exports from Madagascar. The amounts are in thousands of kilograms (*i.e.* tonnes).

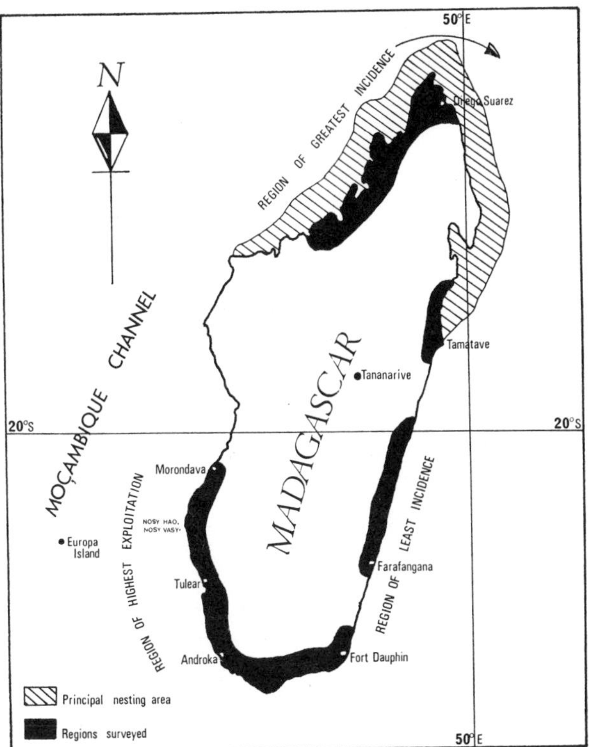


Figure 45-3. Sketch-map of Madagascar showing area surveyed and variations in Hawksbill distribution and nesting activity. This huge island is some 1,700 km long and has a maximum width of 576 km.

and the presence of heavy and continual surf. South of Morondava along the west and south coasts the Hawksbill population is high, and this probably constitutes the area of most intense exploitation as a result of the numbers of fishermen operating on the coastal reefs. The Vezo people, in particular, hunt extensively for sea-turtles and do not discriminate between species when it comes to capturing or killing them (Hughes, 1971). Apart from the northern third of Madagascar, Hawksbills are reputed to nest also on Nosy Hao and Nosy Vasy; these are small islands off the south-west coast (Figure 45-3).

The Malagasy people refer to all sea-turtles as *'Fano'*, but the Hawksbill has specific names in certain regions, namely *Fanohara* (Northern Sakalava tribe, Vezo tribe), *Fanojaty* (South Sakalava tribe), and *Fanotanga* (Antonosy tribe). The French refer to the Hawksbill as *'le Caret'* or *'la Tortue d'Ecaille'*.

## EXPLOITATION

### Catch Size and Numbers

When dealing with a country the size of Madagascar it would be presumptuous to claim full accuracy for the figures presented in Table 45-1. Yet the figures reflect, albeit roughly, the extent of exploitation that is being carried out today.

The figures included above were derived from direct specific information and, in the case of adults, from annual weights of tortoiseshell handled or exported (2.5 kg = 1 adult).

The number of juvenile Hawksbills pre-

Table 45-1. The Estimated Numbers of Hawksbill Sea-turtles Killed Annually in the Coastal Waters of Madagascar, with Percentage Make-up of Different Size-groups.

| *Region* | *Juveniles (carapace <40 cm)* | *Sub-adults (carapace 40-60 cm)* | *Adults (carapace >60 cm)* |
|---|---|---|---|
| SW Region (Morondava-Androka) | 1,200 | 400+ | 400 |
| Diego Suarez | 400+ | ? | 40 |
| NE Coast (including Narinda Bay) | ? | ? | 130 |
| Tamatave | 40 | ? | ? |
| TOTALS | 1,600+ (62.3%) | 400+ (15.6%) | 570 (22.1%) |
| GRAND TOTAL: 2,500+ turtles | | | |

pared for sale in Madagascar is remarkable, for they are displayed in virtually every shop, stall, and marketplace, in the coastal region and in Tananarive. In Diego Suarez not less than 50 were counted in one single workshop.

Tortoiseshell jewellery and bric-à-brac are found in every jewellery or tourist shop, and quantities are difficult to assess (*see* below).

## Hunting Methods

(a) 'Turning' nesting females on beaches is common on the north-east coast. (Turning is a term that is commonly used by turtle people and is derived from the habit of rolling the females onto their backs prior to slaughtering them: one man can 'turn' many turtles, which are then helpless, and he may return hours later to kill them at leisure.)

(b) Harpoons are used widely in the southwestern area, particularly by the Vezo tribe who use a special turtle harpoon known as the Teza, or Samona, harpoon (Figure 45-4).

(c) In the north-east region, nets are set parallel to the edge of the reefs and these catch the turtles as they try to regain deeper water during the falling tide.

(d) Fishermen in the north-east also use a method involving many small grapnels attached to strong cords. The grapnels are thrown over a feeding or sleeping turtle and jerked upwards, so that the tines become embedded in the plastron.

(e) Remora fishing was once widespread in the north but is not employed widely today. It involves catching turtles by means of suckerfish of the genus *Remora* which are released near a basking turtle. A cord from the boat is attached to the fish by means of a brass ring around the caudal constriction. When the fish has attached itself to the turtle, the fishermen pull the fish and turtle to the boat.

## Value

There appears to be considerable disparity between prices paid to the fishermen collecting tortoiseshell and the final sales figure. Fishermen are paid 500 FMG (R1.50 = US$2) per kg of shell, irrespective of quality. The same shell is, in turn, sold for 1,000 FMG/kg to buyers in the capital.

Shell exported to Italy and France obtains prices varying from 5,000 to 14,000 FMG/kg. However, only some 250 kg is exported annually as unworked shell. Worked shell fetches much higher prices, but as it is sold as definable objects and not by weight it is difficult to allocate a bulk value. For example, a necklace of polished tortoiseshell fragments weighing less than 100 grams retails at 2,000 FMG (R6, US$8), so 1 kg of worked shell is worth at least 20,000 FMG;

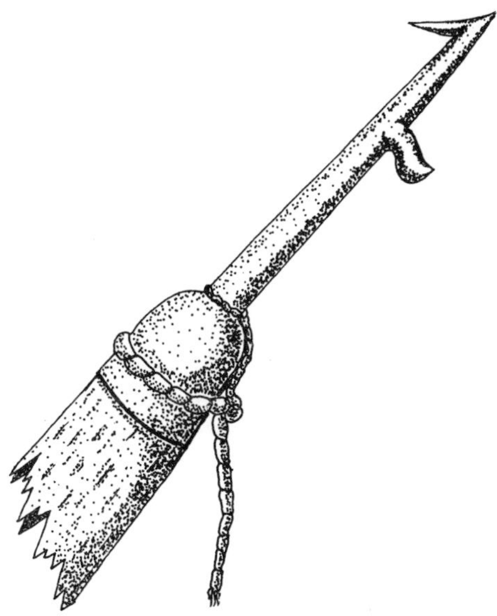

Figure 45-4. Teza or Samona harpoon as used by the Vezo tribesmen of the SW Coast of Madagascar.

allowing for 20 per cent wastage, the mean worked shell value can be taken at 16,000 FMG.

In contrast to all other sea-turtles in Madagascar, the Hawksbill has no value as food. Hawksbill meat is generally discarded, although some Malgache living in penury will consume it.

No documented incidents involving poisoning as a result of eating Hawksbill meat have been found in Madagascar, although the possibility of such cases occurring may be the reason for the lack of interest. It is illegal in Mauritius to sell Hawksbill meat on the market (Jones, 1956). This law was first passed in 1884 as a result of numerous poisonings on the island. Considering the relatively close proximity of Mauritius to Madagascar, it is probable that an occasional poisoning has occurred in Madagascar.

Table 45-2. Estimated Annual Value of Hawksbill Sea-turtle Products during 1971.

| | *Quantity (Kg)* | *Sale value* | | |
|---|---|---|---|---|
| | | *FMG* | *Rands* | *US dollars* |
| (i) Raw tortoiseshell exports at 7,000 FMG/kg | 250 | 1,750,000 | 5,239 | 7,479 |
| (ii) Worked tortoiseshell at 16,000 FMG/kg | 1,175 | 18,800,000 | 55,294 | 73,438 |
| (iii) Stuffed and polished juveniles at 6,000 FMG each | 1,000 approx. | 6,000,000 | 17,964 | 25,641 |
| | *Total value:* | 26,550,000 | 78,497 | 106,558 |

## DISCUSSION AND CONCLUSION

If the 1971 figures reflected in Table 45-2 are approximately correct, the annual exploitation of adults is roughly the same as it was in 1950; for although the export figures were lower in 1971 than in 1950, the local trade (sales to tourists, etc.) has probably increased. This would suggest that either the rate of exploitation is identical and there is a balance between exploitation and recruitment, or that more people are working harder to collect the same quantity of shell—which means that the Hawksbill populations are dwindling even further.

From the survey that was carried out, this latter possibility would not appear to be the case, and some fishermen, interviewed in the north-west, claimed that Hawksbill populations were actually increasing. The Northern Sakalava people are completely disinterested in sea-turtles and neither hunt nor kill them deliberately. Incidental catches of Hawksbills may be sold, but among these people, there is a distinct social stigma attached to the killing of sea-turtles. Unfortunately, other clan areas of Madagascar, *e.g.* the Antakarana and Vezo people, have no such stigma attached to their killing.

It is thus concluded that, in its Hawksbill Sea-turtle populations, Madagascar once had a very valuable resource which has been badly misused; this has led to its serious decline. The general situation must be regarded as in poor condition but far from being irrecoverable. Given sound enforcement of the perfectly adequate laws governing the exploitation of sea-turtles in Madagascar, an increase in turtle populations could be expected, followed by an increasing source of revenue and the re-creation of one of the greatest Hawksbill Sea-turtle concentrations in the world.

## RECOMMENDATIONS

(i) Considering the data presented in this report, it is recommended that a strong effort be made to stop the killing of nesting Hawksbill females on the north-east coast of Madagascar.

(ii) Any killing of Hawksbill Sea-turtles should be done under license from the Government, which, at present, has no income at all from the exploitation of animals on which it expends some revenue for protection.

(iii) Only a very limited number of such licenses should be issued. By operating under the license system, greater control would be possible and a much clearer picture of Hawksbill exploitation would result.

## ACKNOWLEDGEMENTS

My grateful thanks are extended to the coastal peoples of Madagascar without whose assistance this report would never have been possible. Acknowledgement is also made of the unstinting assistance and cooperation afforded to me by the Departement de Pêche Maritime. In this, especial thanks are due to Dr E. Rakotovahiny, Chef de la Service des Pêche Maritime. The Unicorn Shipping Line is gratefully acknowledged for providing an assisted passage to Madagascar. Finally, my sincere thanks are due to the Southern African Wildlife Foundation and the Oceanographic Research Institute, Durban, for their generous financial support.

## REFERENCES

Decary, R. (1950). *La Faune Malgache.* Payot, Paris: 236 pp., 22 figs.

Hughes, G. R. (1971). Preliminary report to the Southern Africa Wildlife Foundation (World Wildlife Fund) on the status of sea-turtles in south-east Africa. Section 2: Madagascar and the Mascarenes. *Oceanographic Research Inst. Int. Rep.,* 47 pp. (mimeographed), 2 maps, 16 figs, 2 tables.

Hughes, G. R. (1972). The Olive Ridley Sea-turtle (*Lepidochelys olivacea*) in Southeast Africa. *Biological Conservation,* 4(2), pp. 128-34, 4 figs.

Jones, J. D. (1956). Observations on fish poisoning in Mauritius. *Proc. Roy. Soc. Arts and Sci. Maur.,* **1**(4), pp. 367-85.

Petit, G. (1930). *L'Industrie des pêche à Madagascar.* Societé d'Edit. Géog. Marit. et Colon., Paris: vii + 392 pp., 24 pls, 21 figs.

# 46. The Great Barrier Reef Conservation Issue – A Case History

D. W. CONNELL 1971

## INTRODUCTION

In 1770, Captain Cook's *Endeavour* almost met disaster on the crags and peaks of coral of the Great Barrier Reef. Those first Europeans to discover the Reef saw it as little more than a vast navigational hazard. Geographical names such as Cape Tribulation, Weary Bay, and Hope Island, are a permanent reminder of this early encounter. Settlement of Australia led to further voyages of discovery. Even Matthew Flinders, perhaps the most prominent of navigators in Australian waters, was wrecked in the *Porpoise* on the coral patches now known as Wreck Reef.

To most Australians a dawning awareness of the Reef as a biological marvel probably began late in the 19th century with the publication of a classic book by Saville-Kent (1893). Since then an avalanche of richly illustrated books has poured forth, revealing the true character and beauty of the reef. Thousands of Australians and overseas tourists now visit the Reef each year. There would be few, if any, Australians who do not know of the Reef. Whether there is legal justification or not, the Reef is known throughout the world as *Australia's* Great Barrier Reef (Figure 46-1).

For many years the Reef's vast size permitted Australians to feel complacent, satisfied that nothing could cause significant damage to it. This attitude still persists and remains perhaps the most important single obstacle to conservation efforts. However, in the last five years problems of critical importance for the future of the Reef have emerged. The Crown-of-thorns starfish (*Acanthaster planci*) outbreak first became apparent in 1960 (Anon., 1970*a*). The subsequent destruction of coral necessitated remedial action in 1965 (Pearson, 1970), and a short time later there were proposals for oil drilling and mining.

## ELLISON REEF MINING

The controversy on Reef exploitation began in a small way in 1967 (Anon., 1969*a*).

Dr. D. W. Connell is an organic chemist and senior research scientist with an Australian research institution. He is a member of the Council of the Australian Conservation Foundation and vice president and former president of the Queensland Littoral Society. His research interests include the chemical aspects of pollution of the sea by petroleum products.

From *Biological Conservation*, Vol. 3, No. 4, pp. 249-254, 1971. Reprinted with light editing and by permission of the author and *Biological Conservation*, Elsevier Publishing Company, Ltd., England.

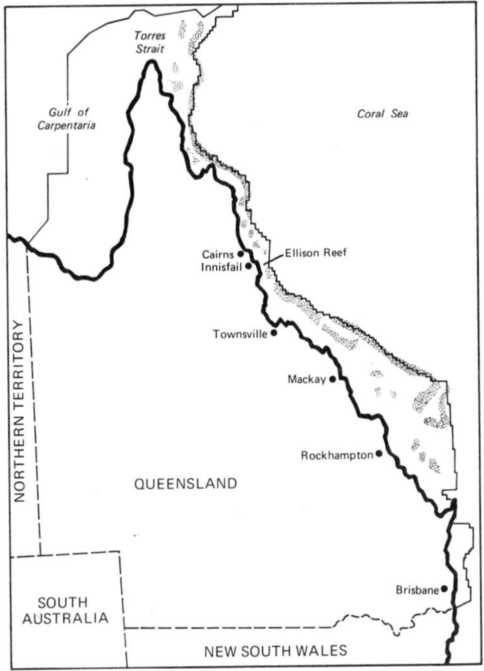


Figure 46-1. Sketch-map of the Queensland coastline (thick line) showing the outer boundary of the off-shore oil exploration lease areas (thin line) and the general location of coral-reef areas within the Great Barrier Reef (dotted areas). (Adapted from a "titles" map released by the Queensland Department of Mines on 18 August 1970.)

Notice was served that an application to mine Ellison Reef (Figure 46-1) in the central area of the Great Barrier Reef had been received by the Queensland Department of Mines, and that hearing of objections would be held in the Innisfail Mining Warden's Court. The Wildlife Preservation Society of Queensland (Innisfail Branch) in North Queensland saw this as an event of great significance. They claimed that the granting of the lease would establish a dangerous legal precedent which could allow complete commercial exploitation of the Reef.

The North Queenslanders began their campaign by enlisting the support of the Wildlife Preservation Society of Queensland in Brisbane. As well as publicity, facts were needed to face this challenge effectively. The Queensland Littoral Society sent a team of skin-divers to examine Ellison Reef. Their evidence, which was presented in the Mining Warden's Court, indicated that the reef was not *dead* in the manner that had been claimed by the mining applicants. Although there was a high proportion of coral rubble and sand, a rich faunal population was present. Dr. D. F. McMichael, Director of the Australian Conservation Foundation at that time, presented biological evidence resulting from personal experience on Ellison Reef. Many others also presented evidence, and finally the application was rejected.

This case did not generate the high level of public interest which occurred with later issues (see Figure 46-2), but was important as the initial stage of a snowballing build-up in public interest.* The case taught conservationists in Queensland that at least two requirements are usually necessary to present a case for conservation; these are, firstly, sound logical evidence, and, secondly, widespread publicity of the issues.

## A CRISIS POINT

Up until mid-1968, neither the Queensland Government nor large commercial interests had become publicly involved in the growing controversy surrounding potential mining or oil exploitation activities on the Reef. In response to accelerating public interest, and

* In a matter such as this it is important to be able to assess public interest in some meaningful way. An approximate estimate can probably be obtained by measuring the actual amount of newspaper space devoted to a particular issue, and so getting a newspaper coverage rating. This operation was carried out with three newspapers: the Australian national newspaper (*The Australian*), the Queensland daily newspaper (*The Courier Mail*), and the Queensland weekly newspaper (*The Sunday Mail*). Front-page areas were multiplied by ten, second- and third-page areas by five, and the remainder by two, and then totalled on a monthly basis for each subject of interest to give the results plotted in Figure 46-2.

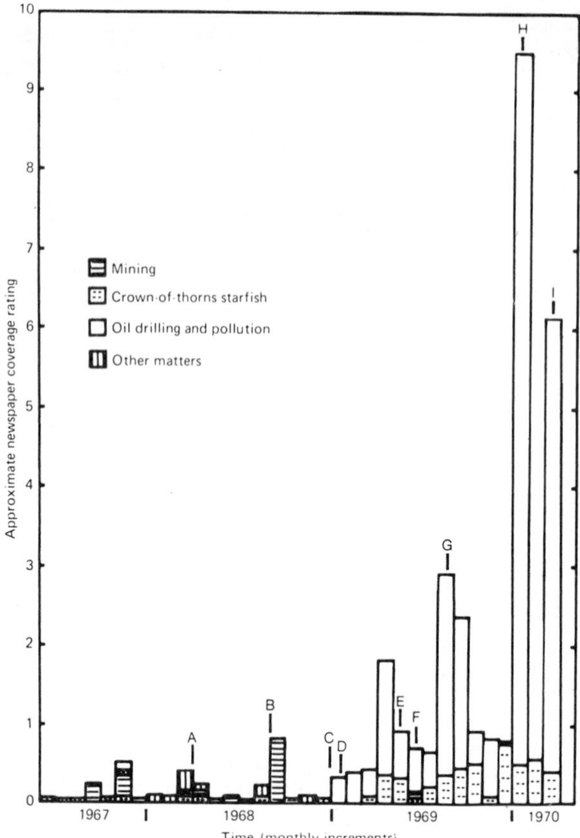


Figure 46-2. Plotting of the approximate newspaper-coverage rating of Great Barrier Reef conservation matters against time.
A. Ellison Reef mining finally rejected.
B. Recommendations of the Ladd report released.
C. Tenders for oil exploration leases called.
D. Santa Barbara oil blow-out.
E. Planned Japex exploratory drilling announced.
G. Japex well approved.
H. Trade union "black" ban on supplies to the Japex well announced.
I. Australian Academy of Science report of the Crown-of-thorns starfish problem and a spill from the tanker *Oceanic Grandeur* in Torres Strait.

to clarify the Reef exploitation position, the Queensland Government introduced Dr. Harry S. Ladd from the United States Geological Survey to survey the Reef and advise on possible exploitation. After a one-month survey, Ladd (1968) pointed out that the Reef should be protected from possible damage, and that exploitation should be controlled. In addition he said, "Petroleum is potentially the Reef's most valuable resource but if not properly controlled it could present the greatest of all dangers. If oil is discovered I believe it would be possible to prevent damaging pollution." In commenting on mining he said, "Dead parts of the coral could be developed for agricultural lime and cement."

Thus in general terms a blueprint and go-ahead for widespread exploitation was provided.

At this time Dr. F. Grassle, an American Fulbright Scholar, was studying reef ecology at the University of Queensland. He issued a serious and widely publicized challenge to the Ladd report by pointing out the *meager scientific evidence* on which it was based. The dead coral myth was largely dispelled when Grassle (1968) commented that "During the past year, I have found that dead pieces of coral contain the greatest diversity of species yet reported in any marine environment."

The Queensland Premier, Mr. Bjelke-Petersen (1968), replied "No mining industry based on harvesting dead coral was permitted on the Reef. This would not be changed unless overwhelming evidence was produced to suggest that limited exploitation would not adversely affect the Reef in any way." Thus, by the application of specialized knowledge and publicity, public and governmental opinion had been favorably influenced.

It is noteworthy that on the same day that the Ladd Report was released, a petition organized by the Queensland Littoral Society, containing over 10,000 signatures, was presented to the Queensland Parliament. The petition called for a moratorium on drilling and mining activities and for the establishment of a National Authority to manage the Reef. This drew no official comment whatsoever and would appear to have been largely ineffectual.

## AN OIL INDUSTRY ON THE REEF?

Toward the end of 1967, the Queensland Parliament passed joint legislation with the Australian Commonwealth Parliament on offshore petroleum exploration and extraction [*Petroleum* (*Submerged Lands*) *Act* of 1967]. Tenders were called under this legislation in early 1969. By 14 January 1969, forty groups of oil-search companies, some backed by giant international corporations, had applied for leases.

Conservationists and the general public were aware of the biological effects of oil and detergents used for clean-up since these matters were dramatically publicized during the *Torrey Canyon* incident in Britain. The problems of oil-well blow-outs were emphasized by a gas blow-out in Bass Strait, between mainland Australia and Tasmania, which took some weeks to cap. However, on 30 January 1969, the Santa Barbara oil blow-out occurred. This incident produced a turning point in Barrier Reef conservation, and moreover, throughout the reef oil-drilling controversy, the incidence of dramatic and repeated spillages within the oil industry itself influenced public opinion more than any of the efforts of conservationists.

At this time, the Senate Select Committee on Off-Shore Petroleum Resources was holding hearings in Queensland. These provided an excellent forum for comments on oil exploration on the Reef by conservationists and their opponents. Well-publicized submissions were made by university personnel, fishing organizations, and trade unions, as well as by conservation groups, calling for a halt to proposed oil exploration activities. Submissions by mining engineers claimed that it was problematical whether escaping oil would kill polyps: it would affect the air-oil-sea interface but not the coral beneath. In addition it was stated that oil and gas blow-outs at Santa Barbara and elsewhere had not affected marine life. In the event of any blow-out, dispersal detergents which were non-toxic, and would affect neither reef nor marine life, could be air-sprayed over the affected area within 24 hours. These statements were strongly attacked in the press by conservationists who were able to cite examples of oil damage to coral and other marine animals. Nevertheless the battle continued to rage with almost unabated publicity as statements and counter statements were issued by the various protagonists (see Figure 46-2).

## POLITICAL SITUATION AND LEASES

The Queensland State Parliamentary Opoosition had expressed grave doubts about oil drilling on the Great Barrier Reef in 1967 when the Petroleum (Submerged Lands) Act was first debated in the Queensland Parliament. It publicly stated a policy of opposition to Reef oil exploration in March 1969, before the State elections were held that year. Nevertheless the incumbent government was returned to office. Within a short time it was announced that oil drilling on the Great Barrier Reef area was planned by Japex, a Japanese oil exploration company, under a farm-out agreement with an Australian company, Ampol Pty. Ltd. Final approval was given to the Japex operation in August 1969, when it was stated that safety precautions would be required that would be more stringent than those applied to drilling on land.

At this time another important political factor entered the controversy. The Australian Prime Minster, Mr. Gorton, on a visit to Queensland, said that despite his avowed intention of preserving the Barrier Reef as a national heritage, he could do nothing to prevent the Japex well from spudding in.

The sketch-map (Figure 46-1) is based on the map which was released by the Queensland Department of Mines in August 1970. A similar map, which did not indicate leases in the Gulf of Carpentaria or some Great Barrier Reef areas, had been released in September 1969 (Anon., 1969*b*). Nevertheless, this earlier map showed quite clearly that the leases covered most of the Great Barrier Reef region. Allen and Hogetoorn (1970) have described the hydrocarbon potential of off-shore basins in the Great Barrier Reef area as ranging from poor to fair.

## THE CONSERVATION CAMPAIGN

The conservation campaign for the Great Barrier Reef has been large and complex. Many individuals and organizations have participated and presented a variety of points of view. From the very outset the campaign has involved a comparatively large body of the public and has in no way been confined to the organized conservation groups. It is probably because of this public involvement that the campaign has achieved some successes.

In September 1969, a group of concerned individuals in Brisbane formed the Save the Barrier Reef Campaign Committee to promote Reef conservation specifically. It is most significant that the large majority of these people were not already members of conservation organizations. Many of them were disillusioned members of government political parties, disturbed at the governmental attitude on Reef conservation. Others were simply members of the public or were associated in some way with the tourist industry.

In general the conservation groups have based their case on two basic principles: firstly, the acquisition of sound knowledge of matters affecting the Reef; and secondly, as wide publicity of this information as possible, the major objective being to create a favorable social and political climate for the introduction of measures for Reef conservation.

Fortunately, many biologists and other scientists have been involved in gathering the pertinent information. Much of this information has come from overseas sources, but the Queensland Littoral Society has embarked on its own research program. This has involved an investigation of the effects of oil dispersants on Reef animals, and a study of oil clean-up measures used during a recent tanker spillage in Torres Strait. Almost all of this information has been assembled into reports in non-specialist language and has been reproduced and distributed to the public in fairly large numbers.

The Australian Conservation Foundation held a symposium called *The Future of the Great Barrier Reef* in Sydney in May 1969. Papers were presented by authoritative speakers on all aspects of Reef conservation. A great deal of useful information was brought forward, and the subsequent publication and distribution of the symposium proceedings has done much to bring to the fore the facts of the various issues.

During the campaign, much of the information available was issued in the form of press, radio, and television statements. As an example, the Queensland Littoral Society issued over fifty statements to the various media in 1969, and numerous other statements and appearances were made by members of the Wildlife Preservation Society of Queensland and members of the Save the Barrier Reef Campaign Committee (*see* above).

Apart from the more common publicity methods which have been mentioned previously, two specific activities have been undertaken which have played an important, perhaps decisive, role in the Reef issue. The first was the production and sale of *Save the Barrier Reef* car-bumper stickers. Over thirty thousand of these were sold, in addition to over one hundred thousand similar *mini-stickers* which were used on letters and other articles.

The second activity was a public opinion poll organized by the Save the Barrier Reef Campaign Committee and the Wildlife Preservation Society of Queensland. The poll was a random one conducted by nonprofessional interviewers, and as such would not be as accurate as a professional conducted poll. However, the Department of Mathematics of the University of Queensland advised that the expected error was considerably reduced because of the large size of the sample (1,000 people). Over 91 per cent of the people who expressed an opinion were against the establishment of an oil industry on the Reef. This result was well publicized; it was a morale-booster for conservationists and probably influenced many politicians.

## THE CROWN-OF-THORNS STARFISH PROBLEM

Most of the previous discussion has centered on the mining and oil-industry controversies, but concurrently with these issues the Crown-of-thorns starfish (Figure 46-3) outbreak has also become a major public issue. Although each of these problems has been discussed as an almost entirely divorced activity, the newspaper coverage ratings illustrated in Figure 46-2 indicate that both issues have generated a rise in public interest during the same period. This would suggest that each may have helped to stimulate public interest in the other.

The tourist industry has played an active role in many aspects of the Crown-of-thorns starfish problem. The outbreak first became apparent at Green Island, a popular Barrier Reef resort off Cairns in North Queensland. The management employed a skin-diver to collect the starfish and in fifteen months from early 1965 he collected 27,000 specimens. In early 1966 the resort appealed to the Queensland State Government for assistance, and a biologist was assigned to work on the problem under the supervision of Dr. Robert Endean of the University of Queensland.

Dr. Endean submitted a report on the problem to the Queensland Government in December 1968. Months later the Government had not taken any action or released any of the report's findings. In addition to commenting adversely on this, Dr. Endean mounted a campaign to publicize the problem and initiate some decisive action.

The Premier of Queensland, Mr. Bjelke-Petersen (1969), reacted to the situation by stating, "Expert advice is that there is no great plague of the Crown-of-thorns starfish. Recent publicity has presented an unduly alarming picture of the situation. Dr. Endean obviously is sincere but many men with expert local knowledge disagree with him."

Undeterred, Dr. Endean continued to publicize the problem, bringing forward further evidence as to the spread of the starfish. Unfortunately, conservation organizations have been at a disadvantage in deciding on an effective course of action with regard to this problem, as most of the information has

Figure 46-3. A juvenile Crown-of-thorns starfish (*Acanthaster planci*) on dead coral. Photo: O. E. S. Kelly.

been in hands either of the State Government or of Dr. Endean.

Later, Pearson (1970), of the Queensland Department of Primary Industries, reported that 8.1 per cent of reefs in the total Great Barrier Reef area had suffered extensive damage. Also, the Australian Academy of Science reported that Crown-of-thorns starfish destruction of the Great Barrier Reef was impossible to control except in a few selected tourist areas. To clarify the situation, the Queensland State and Commonwealth Governments have instituted an inquiry into all aspects of this problem.

## DECISIVE EVENTS

The first day of 1970 opened on a grim note for conservationists. The *Brisbane Courier Mail* announced "the 330-ft long, self-propelled oil-rig, *Navigator,* is expected to enter Queensland waters in a few weeks to prepare for oil drilling off the North Queensland coast." After many months of controversy, *The Australian* of 24 December 1969 summed up the situation as follows: "The Great Barrier Reef has been the object of a shameful exercise in buck-passing throughout this year. . . . The political dereliction has taken place despite the most sustained public campaign in memory on a conservation issue." At this time the conservation camp was reduced to considering a challenge to the legality of the State Government's authority to issue prospecting licenses.

The Trade Union movement now took what was to be decisive action. Key unions such as Transport Workers, Waterside, Storemen, and Packers, etc., threatened a total ban on all goods and services for the Japex oil-rig (January 6, 1970). Within a few days Ampol Pty. Ltd. announced suspension of the drilling operation and asked that an inquiry be instituted.

This offer was welcomed by the federal Prime Minister, Mr. Gorton, but the Queensland Premier, Mr. Bjelke-Petersen (1970), insisted that the drilling proceed, saying "There could be no useful purpose to a further investigation. An expert survey has been completed in a most competent way." Nevertheless the Prime Minister (Gorton, 1970) continued to press for the institution of an inquiry, explaining that "In my view the slightest danger is too much danger." Finally there was joint agreement to a Committee of Inquiry into Oil Drilling on the Great Barrier Reef which was later up-graded to Royal Commission status (Connell, 1970*a*).

This outcome, although a great step forward, was not altogether satisfactory for conservationists. Insufficient funds would entirely preclude representation for the conservation case at the Royal Commission which was likely to continue for many months.

At this time, once again events within the oil industry itself served to emphasize spillage dangers. The oil tanker *Oceanic Grandeur* was holed in Torres Strait and, probably only due to favorable weather, was saved from disaster with the release of relatively small quantities of oil. Also, an extensive oil-slick was released from an oil-well in the Gulf of Mexico.

Perhaps stimulated by this, a concerned group of solicitors and barristers offered legal assistance on a part-time basis. They pointed out that, while this makeshift effort would at least provide representation, it could not be regarded as a satisfactory solution to the problem.

Finally, after a number of requests to the Australian Prime Minster, the Commonwealth Government generously offered to pay all reasonable expenses for the legal representation of a number of conservation organizations. The proceedings of the Royal Commission are expected to continue for some time, and a final report cannot be expected until late in 1971.

## CONCLUSIONS

The Great Barrier Reef issue has a number of important lessons for conservationists. Most importantly, every effort must be made to influence the whole community in order to introduce conservation measures. Such support can win favorable political, industrial, and commercial, decisions.

Conservationists have emphasized the community value of the controlled development of the tourist and fishing industries (Anon., 1970*b*). In addition, positive action leading to the formation of a Great Barrier Reef Authority has been requested, so that the Reef can be managed in a rational way that is consistent with its continued existence (Connell, 1970*b*).

However, with the Great Barrier Reef, the community had made a favorable value-assessment before conservation issues arose. Few would advocate the destruction of the Reef for industrial purposes. The magnitude of the various threats has been the heart of the matter.

It is quite clear that sound and detailed knowledge of the problems and surrounding circumstances was a first essential requirement. This information then needs to be disseminated to the community by means of publications, public meetings, addresses to private organizations, and all the forms of mass media that can be utilized. Even after all of these actions have been taken, results cannot be achieved overnight, and both patience and perseverance are required.

## ACKNOWLEDGMENT

The substance of this paper was presented on 27 June 1970 at a symposium entitled *The Process and Problems of Seeking Conservation,* organized by, and held at, the

Centre for Continuing Education, Australian National University, Canberra.

## REFERENCES


Allen, R. J. and Hogetoorn, D. J. (1970). *Petroleum Resources of Queensland,* Queensland Department of Mines, 42 pp., 7 maps.

Anon. (1969*a*). Conservation of the Great Barrier Reef of Australia. *Biol. Conserv.* **1**(3), 249-50.

Anon. (1969*b*). Press Report. *Brisbane Courier Mail,* 4 September, p. 3.

Anon. (1970*a*). Population explosion of the Crown-of-thorns Starfish, *Acanthaster planci. Biol. Conserv.* **2**(2), 96.

Anon. (1970*b*). Statement on the Great Barrier Reef. *Wildlife in Australia* **7**, 1.

Bjelke-Petersen, J. (1968). Press Report. *Brisbane Courier Mail,* 13 September, p. 3.

Bjelke-Petersen, J. (1969). Press Report. *Brisbane Courier Mail,* 9 September, p. 3.

Bjelke-Petersen, J. (1970). Press Report. *Brisbane Courier Mail,* 11 January, p. 1.

Connell, D. W. (1970*a*). Inquiry into advisability of oil-drilling in the Great Barrier Reef, Australia. *Biol. Conserv.* **3**(1), 60-1.

Connell, D. W. (1970*b*). The conservation viewpoint on Great Barrier Reef oil drilling. *Living Earth, Australia* **14**, 39-40.

Gorton, J. (1970). Press Report. *The Australian,* 19 January, p. 3.

Grassle, F. (1968). Press Report. *Brisbane Courier Mail,* 11 September, p. 3.

Ladd, H. S. (1968). *Preliminary Report on Conservation and Controlled Exploitation of the Great Barrier Reef.* Queensland State Government, Brisbane, 51 pp., illustr.

Pearson, R. (1970). Studies of the Crown-of-thorns Starfish on the Great Barrier Reef. *Newsletter, Qd Littoral Soc.,* No. 36, pp. 1-10.

Saville-Kent, W. (1893). *The Great Barrier Reef of Australia.* W. H. Allen, London, xvii + 387 pp., illustr.